NEVADA CIVIL WAR CLAIMS

Legislative Reports

1888-1900

Diane E. Greene, A.G.

HERITAGE BOOKS
2008

HERITAGE BOOKS
AN IMPRINT OF HERITAGE BOOKS, INC.

Books, CDs, and more—Worldwide

For our listing of thousands of titles see our website
at
www.HeritageBooks.com

Published 2008 by
HERITAGE BOOKS, INC.
Publishing Division
100 Railroad Ave. #104
Westminster, Maryland 21157

Other books by the author:

*Boulder City Cemetery, Boulder City, Clark County, Nevada, 1942 to June 2000
Volumes 1–3*

Mary Eliza Easton Diary, Loudon, Franklin County, Pennsylvania

*The Civil War Diary of Lieutenant Robert Molford Addison, Co. E,
23rd Wisconsin Volunteer Infantry, December 24, 1863–December 29, 1864*

International Standard Book Number: 978-1-58549-956-4

Contents

IN THE SENATE OF THE UNITED STATES.

APRIL 16, 1888.—Ordered to be printed.

Mr. STEWART, from the Committee on Claims, submitted the following

REPORT:

[To accompany bill S. 2542.]

The Committee on Claims, to whom was referred the bill (S. 2542) to reimburse certain persons who expended moneys and furnished services and supplies in repelling invasions and suppressing Indian hostilities within the Territorial limits of the present State of Nevada, submit the following report:

The claims to be paid under the provisions of this bill are fifty-three in number, and aggregate in amount to $29,144. The persons named in the bill furnished money, supplies, and services in the Indian war in 1860 in what was then western Utah, now Nevada.

The Comstock lode was discovered in 1859. During the winter of 1859-'60 a large number of miners crossed the Sierra Nevada Mountains from California, attracted by the new mineral discoveries. The country previous to that time was very sparsely settled by farmers and stock-raisers. The Pah-Ute (or Piute) Indians, who occupied this region, were numerous and warlike. In the latter part of April, 1860, these Indians commenced hostilities against the whites by an attack on a neighborhood of settlers and stockmen residing on the Carson River, about 30 miles east of Virginia City, Nev. They killed several persons and drove off a large amount of stock.

Previous to the outbreak threats had been made by the Indians to massacre all the whites on the east side of the Sierra Nevada Mountains. At the time of the outbreak the snow on the mountains was very deep, averaging from 10 to 20 feet, and at that season of the year was soft and impassable for teams. To protect the inhabitants and repel these Indians a company was organized in Carson City, consisting of 125 men, under the command of Maj. William Ormsby. They were joined by a small company from the neighboring town of Genoa, and another from Virginia City. They proceeded to the place of the massacre, known as Williams' Ranch, and from there pursued the Indians to Truckee River, near Pyramid Lake, where a battle ensued, in which about sixty of the whites were killed, among whom were Major Ormsby, Henry Meredith, the law-partner of the writer of this report, and other prominent citizens. Others were wounded, and those that escaped with their lives returned to the settlements destitute of horses, and in a pitiable condition.

Immediately after this event home guards were formed and a regular force of volunteers were enrolled and placed under the command of Col. John C. Hays. These volunteers were composed of soldiers, who enlisted

2   PERSONS REIMBURSED FOR MONEYS EXPENDED.

in Nevada and several volunteer companies who crossed the mountains from California. A small company of United States soldiers, under command of Captain Stewart, of the regular Army, also crossed the mountains and co-operated with the forces under Colonel Hays. The combined force consisted of several hundred men, who were supplied with horses, provisions, etc., by the inhabitants of Nevada, assisted by contributions from California. This force moved against the Indians, but the Indians refused to give regular battle against so formidable an army; but after considerable irregular fighting and skirmishing for several days, in which a number of white men and a few Indians were killed, the Indians sued for peace, which was granted and has ever since been observed. The whites have had no trouble with these particular Indians since that time, but they have lived in peace together.

During the second expedition above mentioned Captain Storey, a gentleman of great courage and popularity, was killed, and the county of Storey, in which Virginia City is situated, was given his name to commemorate his services, and the county of Ormsby, in which Carson City, the capital of the State, is located, was named after Major Ormsby.

A large amount of money and supplies were necessary for these expeditions. All the horses and mules in the country were freely surrendered for the use of the soldiers, and every citizen contributed money, food, or clothing to the extent of their means, or whatever else would be serviceable to the forces in the field. Contributions were also liberally made from California.

On December 19, 1862, the legislative assembly of Nevada Territory passed the following memorial to Congress in relation to depredations committed by Indians in the Territory, and expenses incurred in the protection of settlements:

To the honorable the Senate and House of Representatives of the United States in Congress assembled:

Your memorialists, the governor and legislative assembly of the Territory of Nevada, respectfully represent that during the winter and spring of 1860 the Indians inhabiting what was at that time the western portion of Utah Territory, now organized as Nevada Territory, became hostile towards the white settlers, and that in consequence of the massacres being committed it became necessary, in order to save the settlements from annihilation, to employ not only the few United States troops within reach, but to call for aid from the neighboring State of California, and to accept the services of considerable numbers of volunteers from that State, who generously came to the rescue; that this occurred at a time when the transportation of forage and provisions over the snows of the Sierra Nevadas was almost impossible. Supplies for the necessities of volunteers and others became exceedingly scarce, and rose to extraordinary prices. Persons who had transported provisions at a great toil and expense ministered most generously to the wants of the troops; and others, under that "necessity which knows no law," submitted to forced contributions. Many horses and other animals were taken for the use of the expedition, for which no recompense has ever been made. Much of these supplies were accredited at the time, or soon after, by certificates from the officers of the expedition, or other evidences of indebtedness, the most regular and authentic that could be made under the circumstances existing at the time, but we believe as yet no provision has been made for the payment thereof, and the losses thus incurred fall with crushing weight on many worthy individuals, who were deprived of almost their entire substance. We would further represent that numerous depredations were committed by the savages on the stock and other property of the settlers, in some instances almost entire herds being driven off. We know of no legal means of liquidating this indebtedness by our Territorial government, or indemnifying parties for losses thus sustained, and we would most earnestly petition your honorable body to appoint commissioners to examine claims and adjust the same.

On March 10, 1868, the writer of this report presented a report of a commission appointed by the State of Nevada to examine certain claims for Indian depredations, which was referred to the Committee on Claims of the Senate, but no action was taken thereon, and papers accompanying the report were lost or mislaid—at all events they can not now be found. On May 29, 1868, the writer of this introduced a joint resolution (S. 138) to appoint a board of examiners for claims against the United States in the State of Nevada, which was also referred to the Committee on Claims, and on June 18 of the same year an order was made, at the request of one of the members of the committee, discharging it from further consideration of the resolution.

On December 13, 1883, first session Forty-eighth Congress, the following bill was introduced for the payment of the claims now under consideration, and referred to the Committee on Military Affairs:

[S. 657, Forty-eighth Congress, first session.]

A bill to authorize the Secretary of the Treasury to adjust and settle the expenses of Indian wars in Nevada.

Be it enacted by the Senate and House of Representatives of the United States of America in Congress assembled, That the Secretary of the Treasury be, and he is hereby, authorized and directed to adjust and settle, on just and equitable principles, all claims for services rendered or supplies furnished in any of the Indian wars in the Territory or in the State of Nevada by the people thereof, not heretofore provided for by law, including subsistence, forage, medical stores, clothing, transportation, and services of and losses of horses used therein, as well as for any other necessary and proper supplies furnished and expenditures made for the prosecution of said wars; and that on such adjustment the same shall be paid out of any money in the Treasury not otherwise appropriated.

It appears that the foregoing bill was referred by the committee to the Secretary of War, upon which he made a report stating that all the claims provided for in the bill could be adjusted and paid under existing laws, whereupon the Committee on Military Affairs made the following report:

[Senate Report No. 406, Forty-eighth Congress, first session.]

The Committee on Military Affairs, to which was referred the bill (S. 657) to authorize the Secretary of the Treasury to adjust and settle the expenses of Indian wars in Nevada, respectfully submits the following report:

Attention is directed to the letter of the Secretary of War, dated January 26, 1884, as follows:

WAR DEPARTMENT,
Washington City, January 26, 1884.

SIR: In response to so much of your communication of the 22d ultimo as requests information concerning Senate bill 657, "to authorize the Secretary of the Treasury to adjust and settle the expenses of Indian wars in Nevada," I have the honor to invite your attention to the following report of the Third Auditor of the Treasury, to whom your request was duly referred:

"The State of Nevada has filed in the office abstracts and vouchers for expenses incurred on account of raising volunteers for the United States to aid in suppressing the late rebellion amounting to $349,697.49, and for expenses on account of her militia in the 'White Pine Indian war' of 1875, $17,650.95. Also, expenses of her militia in the 'Elks Indian war' of 1878, amounting to $4,654.64, presented under act of Congress approved June 27, 1882 (22 Statutes 111, 112).

"These abstracts and vouchers will be sent to your Department for examination and report as soon as they can be stamped, as that statute requires a report from the Secretary of War as to the necessity and reasonableness of the expenses incurred. This statute is deemed sufficiently broad enough to embrace all proper claims of said State and Territory of Nevada.

Very respectfully, your obedient servant,

ROBERT T. LINCOLN,
Secretary of War.

Hon. S. B. MAXEY,
Of Committee on Military Affairs, United States Senate.

The copy of Senate bill No. 657 is herewith returned, as requested by you.

4   PERSONS REIMBURSED FOR MONEYS EXPENDED.

It will be observed that it is deemed by the Department that the act approved June 27, 1882, is sufficiently broad to embrace all proper claims of Nevada, whether a State or Territory.

For convenience of reference the above act accompanies this report, and an examination thereof and of the construction thereon, satisfies the committee that no additional legislation is necessary.

Wherefore, for this reason, the committee reports back said Senate bill 657, and recommend that it be indefinitely postponed.

The committee evidently understood that the Secretary of War regarded the existing law sufficient for the payment of the claims in question, and that it was as comprehensive as the bill which was introduced by Senator Jones and referred to the Secretary of War, which contained provisions amply sufficient to pay for services rendered, supplies furnished, and everything which was done to aid in prosecuting the Indian war of 1860. This construction of existing laws was accepted by the legislature of the State of Nevada as an assurance that the Indian war claims of the State and Territory, and the people thereof, when ascertained and established, would be paid. The legislature of Nevada at its next session passed the following act:

AN ACT relative to the proving of Indian war claims (approved February 27, 1885.)

The people of the State of Nevada, represented in senate and assembly, do enact as follows: SECTION 1. The State board of examiners are hereby authorized and directed to examine into all claims for services rendered, moneys expended, indebtedness incurred, and supplies and necessaries furnished between the first day of January, anno Domini one thousand eight hundred and sixty, and the date of the approval of this act, in repelling invasions and suppressing Indian outbreaks and hostilities within the territorial limits of the present State of Nevada. Said board shall also examine into all claims for horses, equipments, and wagons actually lost by those engaged as aforesaid, while in the line of duty in active service.

SEC. 2. That immediately after the approval of this act the board shall give notice, by publication in some daily newspaper published at the State capital, to all persons having such claims to present them by petition, showing the items and amounts thereof to the board within sixty days from the first publication of the notice, which notice shall be published in each issue of such newspaper for a period of at least thirty days: *Provided,* That if no daily newspaper be published at the State capital, then the notice may be published in such other daily newspaper as shall be designated by the board. Any and all claims presented in accordance with the requirements of said notice shall be examined, and final action thereon taken by the board, as soon as practicable thereafter.

SEC. 3. That all persons having such claims shall be permitted to appear personally before the board and produce such evidence as they may have in support of their respective demands; and all the provisions of sections eight, nine, ten, eleven, and twelve of an act entitled "An act relating to the board of examiners, to define their duties and powers, and to impose certain duties upon the controller and treasurer," approved February seventh, one thousand eight hundred and sixty-five, are hereby made applicable to the examination of claims presented under this act.

SEC. 4. That the evidence presented to the board in support of any such claim shall be reduced to writing, and immediately after the approval or disapproval of the claim, the petition and evidence shall be filed in the office of the governor of the State. If the claim be entirely disapproved the board shall indorse their disapproval upon the petition, and such claim shall not be reconsidered, unless upon presentation by the claimant, within thirty days thereafter, of new and material testimony in its support. If the claim be approved, either in whole or in part, the board shall indorse such approval upon the petition, which indorsement shall show the items and amounts for which the claim is approved, and a certificate of like tenor and effect shall also be given to the claimant whose claim shall have been so approved.

SEC. 5. That as soon as all the claims presented under the provisions of this act shall have been finally acted upon by the board, it shall be the duty of the governor to transmit the claims that have been approved for any amount, together with the evidence in support of them, to the Secretary of the Treasury of the United States, or other proper officer, and to urge the payment thereof by the United States Government at the earliest practicable day.

SEC. 6. Nothing herein contained shall be so construed as to make the State of Nevada liable for the amount of any approved claim, or any amount of money whatever, except as the same may be received from the Treasury of the United States for the payment of such claims, and then only for the particular claims allowed by the United States Government, and to the extent of such allowance (Stats. Nev. 1885, p. 47).

Under this act many of the claims for the Piute Indian war of 1860 were presented and laboriously and carefully examined by the board of examiners of the State of Nevada. This board of examiners is a permanent board which passes upon all claims against the State of Nevada before the same can be paid, and was not a special board organized for the purpose of examining these claims. It is composed of the governor, secretary of state, and attorney-general, and has served a most beneficial purpose in protecting the treasury of the State from the payment of unjust demands. A notice was published, as provided in the act above quoted, and all claims presented within the time provided in the notice were examined; and only such claims were allowed as were established by evidence. Many claims were rejected altogether, and most of the claims presented were reduced in amount. All the allowances made and provided for in the bill under consideration are established by the evidence reported by the board and referred to your committee. The investigation made by the board was much more careful and accurate than a committee of Congress could make on the *ex-parte* evidence usually presented for the adjustment of claims of this character. The committee, however, have not relied on the findings of the board, but have examined the evidence in each case upon which the findings were made, and have arrived at the same conclusions which the board of examiners reached in its investigation, with the exceptions hereinafter stated.

The following is a synopsis of the result of the examination made by the board, taken from the biennial report of the secretary of state of Nevada for 1885–'86:

INDIAN WAR CLAIMS.

At the last session of the legislature an act was passed directing the board of examiners to inquire into and pass upon all claims for services rendered, moneys expended, indebtedness incurred, and necessaries furnished between January 1, 1860, and February 27, 1885, in repelling invasions and suppressing Indian outbreaks and hostilities within the territorial limits of the present State of Nevada. By virtue of this act the board of examiners devoted much time and care to the taking of testimony and to the faithful performance of the arduous duties imposed upon them by the legislature in this connection. It required several months of industrious application on the part of the board, involving a mass of correspondence that reached to nearly every portion of the United States. The amounts allowed the several claimants are given below:

Claimant.	Principal.	Interest.	Total.
Mrs. Kate Miot	$150.00	$225.00	$375.00
Mrs. Ellen E. Adams	740.00	1,110.00	1,850.00
William H. Naleigh	385.00	577.50	962.50
John T. Little	219.00	328.50	547.50
A. G. Turner	979.00	1,468.50	2,447.50
Oscar C. Steele	326.00	489.00	815.00
Estate of Samuel Turner	307.00	460.50	787.50
J. H. Mathewson	350.00	525.00	875.00
Charles Shad	327.00	490.50	817.50
Theodore Winters	1,549.00	2,323.50	3,872.50
J. F. Holliday	95.00	142.50	237.50
Franklin Bricker	152.00	228.00	380.00
George Seitz	120.00	180.00	300.00
B. F. Small	110.00	165.00	275.00
Purd Henry	157.00	258.00	430.00
Andrew Lawson	266.00	399.00	665.00
Louis B. Epstein	269.00	403.50	672.50
John Q. A. Moore	530.00	225.00	805.00
Lucy Ann Hetrick	405.00	607.50	1,012.50
Charles C. Brooks	152.00	228.00	380.00
Lizzie J. Donnell, heir of Major Ormsby	1,825.00	2,737.50	4,562.50
J. M. Gatewood	894.00	1,341.00	2,235.00
J. M. Gatewood, supplemental claim	150.00	225.00	375.00
Seymour Pixley	305.00	457.50	762.50

Claimant.	Principal.	Interest.	Total.
J. D. Roberts	3,231.00	4,846.50	8,077.50
H. P. Phillips	269.00	403.50	672.50
J. M. Horton	95.00	132.50	227.50
George Hickox Cady	168.00	252.00	420.00
James H. Sturtevant	513.00	769.50	1,282.50
Gould and Curry Mining Company	1,000.00	1,500.00	2,500.00
John H. Tilton	519.00	778.50	1,297.50
R. G. Watkins	290.00	435.00	725.00
Estate of J. L. Blackburn	763.00	1,144.50	1,9...50
John O. Earl	750.00	1,125.00	1,875.00
L. M. Pearlman	3,130.00	5,445.00	8,575.00
Robert Lyon	1,694.00	2,541.00	4,235.00
Thomas Marsh	150.00	225.00	375.00
Abraham Jones	310.00	465.00	775.00
A. McDonald	750.00	1,125.00	1,875.00
G. H. Berry	130.00	195.00	325.00
Robert M. Baker	171.00	256.50	427.50
P. S. Corbett	95.00	132.50	227.50
John S. Child	505.00	757.50	1,262.50
Benjamin F. Green	225.00	337.50	562.50
Alex. Crow	95.00	132.50	227.50
Mary Curry, widow of Abe Curry	500.00	750.00	1,250.00
Warren Wasson	499.00	748.50	1,247.50
Michael Tierney	145.00	217.50	362.50
Samuel T. Curtis	590.00	885.00	1,475.00
J. Harvey Cole	202.00	303.00	505.00
Isaac P. Lobo	334.00	508.00	835.00
E. Penrod	664.00	996.00	1,660.00
J. B. Preusch	95.00	132.50	227.50
Wellington Stewart	400.00	600.00	1,000.00

The action of the board of examiners upon each claim in the foregoing list, together with the evidence upon which it was based, was transmitted to the Secretary of the Treasury, in accordance with the act of the State of Nevada above quoted, accompanied with the following letter:

EXECUTIVE DEPARTMENT, GOVERNOR'S OFFICE,
Carson City, Nev., February 13, 1886.

SIR: In compliance with the provisions of section 5 of an act of the legislature of this State, entitled "An act relative to the proving of Indian war claims," approved February 27, 1885, I have the honor to transmit herewith the claim of —— —— for the sum of $——, and respectfully urge the payment thereof at the earliest practicable day.

I have the honor to remain, your obedient servant,

CHAS. E. LAUGHTON,
Lieutenant and Acting Governor.

Hon. DANIEL MANNING,
Secretary of the Treasury, Washington, D. C.

On receipt of the papers in these cases by the Secretary of the Treasury they were duly referred to the Third Auditor of the Treasury for report, who, on March 2, 1886, replied as follows:

TREASURY DEPARTMENT, THIRD AUDITOR'S OFFICE,
Washington, D. C., March 2, 1886.

SIR: I have the honor to return claims of Ellen E. Adams and fifty-four others, being those which were transmitted to you by the letter of the acting governor of Nevada, dated February 13, 1866.

An act of the legislature of Nevada, approved February 27, 1885, provided that certain claims might be presented to the State board of examiners, consisting of governor, secretary of state, and attorney-general; and that the governor should transmit to the Secretary of the Treasury of the United States, or other proper officer, such of the claims as should be approved in any sum by said board, and urge their payment by the United States.

The claim of Mary M. Stiles (formerly McDowell), will be specially mentioned below.

The claims of the fifty-four others are for compensation for military service in, or supplies, etc., furnished to, militia of the State engaged in suppressing Indian hostilities in 1860. I do not find that provision has been made by any law of the United States for the adjudication of such claims. For two reasons at least they do not come within the provisions of the act of Congress of June 27, 1882 (18 Stat., 111):

First. The act was confined to expenses, etc., in organizing, etc., forces called into active service by the authorities of a State or Territory between April 15, 1861, and June 27, 1882, whereas all these claims are alleged to have occurred in 1860.

Second. The act did not authorize the adjudication of any claims of individuals, but only claims of States or Territories, and only for expenses incurred or *indebtedness assumed* by the *States* or *Territories*. Nevada has *not* assumed to pay any part of the indebtedness alleged in the fifty-four claims, on the contrary the sixth section of the State act above referred to is in these words: "Nothing herein contained shall be construed as to make the State of Nevada liable for the amount of any approved claim, or any amount of money whatever, except as the same may be received from the Treasury of the United States for the payment of such claims allowed by the United States Government, and to the extent of such allowance."

The board did not consider the claim of Mary M. Stiles (formerly McDowell), holding that it was not of the class of claims which the State act of February 27, 1885, authorized it to pass upon ; but, by oversight, probably, it has been forwarded to you with the others. Her claim is for boarding and lodging officers and soldiers of the United States at her hotel April 1, 1863, to about May 1, 1864, $3,450. In its present form it is not entitled to any adjudication, there being no attempt to set out any account, and the amount demanded being the product of mere guess-work. The United States is not liable for hotel bills of its officers ; and if she furnished board or lodging to United States soldiers under any proper authority she could readily have collected at the time all which was due her. The presumption is that she would not have deferred a demand for twenty-two years.

I recommend that the papers in her case be transmitted to the Secretary of War, with suggestion that they be placed on file, for use in the event of the presentation of a claim by her.

I recommend that the fifty-four other claims be returned to the governor of Nevada, this Department having no authority to entertain them.

Very respectfully

JNO. S. WILLIAMS,
Auditor.

Hon. DANIEL MANNING,
Secretary of the Treasury.

On the receipt of the foregoing report from Third Auditor, the Secretary of the Treasury returned all the papers to the governor of Nevada, with the following letter:

TREASURY DEPARTMENT,
March 5, 1886.

The honorable GOVERNOR OF NEVADA :

SIR : I have the honor to acknowledge the receipt of your communication of the 13th ultimo, transmitting to this Department, in compliance with an act of the legislature of Nevada, February 27, 1885, fifty-five claims for compensation for military service in, or supplies, etc., furnished to militia of the State engaged in suppressing Indian hostilities in 1860, with the exception of the claim of Mary M. Stiles (formerly McDowall), which is for boarding and lodging officers and soldiers of the United States in 1863 and 1864.

In reply thereto, I have to state that no provision has been made by Congress for the adjudication of these claims. They do not come within the terms of the act of June 27, 1882 (22 Stat., 111), being "An act to authorize the Secretary of the Treasury to examine and report to Congress the amount of all claims of the States of * * * and Nevada * * * for money expended and indebtedness assumed by said State * * * in repelling invasions and suppressing Indian hostilities, and for other purposes," and are returned herewith as a class of claims which can not be entertained without legislation by Congress.

A copy of the Third Auditor's report in the matter is inclosed for your information, and the papers of the case of Mrs. Stiles have been forwarded to the Secretary of War, as recommended by the Auditor.

Respectfully, yours,

D. MANNING,
Secretary.

It will be observed by the foregoing that the Treasury Department differed from the conclusions of the Committee on Military Affairs (which were based on the letter of the War Department), in holding that the claims could not be paid without further legislation by Congress.

More than one-half of the allowances made by the board of examiners of Nevada was for interest. This your committee disallow. There are several items allowed by the board for services during the first expedition under Major Ormsby before the arrival of the United States troops. These items your committee have also rejected, and confined the allowances for services in the expedition in which the volunteer troops under Colonel Hays acted in conjunction with the United States forces under Captain Stewart.

There is no question about the justice of the claims allowed by your committee. It is true many years have elapsed since these claims arose, but the claimants can hardly be charged with negligence, having prepared their claims within a reasonable time and presented them to Congress, with the evidence upon which they are based. The claims are all small, averaging a little over $500 each, and the claimants are generally poor and unable to come to Washington to prosecute their individual claims. The amount involved is probably less than one-tenth of the money, supplies, and services contributed by citizens during the Pi-Ute war.

Congress has already recognized the obligation of the United States to pay these claims. On June 17, 1874, an act was passed directing the Secretary of the Treasury to pay the sum of $19,473.50 to John M. McPike, in full settlement for beef and supplies furnished the troops by Jordan & McPike in quelling the Indian disturbances in the Territory of Utah, now the State of Nevada, in 1860. (See U. S. Stat., p. 40 of private acts, chap. 296.)

On March 3, 1885, an act was passed directing the payment to John M. Dorsey of $9,021.33, and to William F. Shepard $3,746.66, in full settlement for beef and supplies furnished the troops by Wallace, Dorsey & Shepard, and S. B. Wallace, in quelling the Indian disturbances in the Territory of Utah, now the State of Nevada, in the year 1860. (See U. S. Stats., vol. 23, p. 674.)

These claims were sufficiently large to enable the claimants to prosecute them in Washington, but they were no more meritorious than the small individual claims provided for in the bill under consideration, which arose out of the same war and under the same circumstances as the claims already paid by Congress. Several reports were made in both Houses upon the claims of Dorsey & Shephard and Jordan & McPike. The first of these reports was made by Mr. Willey from the Senate Committee on Claims during the third session of the Forty-first Congress, from which we make the following extracts:

In the spring of 1860 great alarm was excited among the inhabitants of Virginia City and its vicinity, then in Utah Territory, by the depredations of the Pi-Ute Indians. An irregular force of about one hundred persons, consisting of many of the best citizens, was organized, armed with such weapons as they could procure, and went out from Virginia City to chastise the Indians. The expedition was unfortunate, falling into ambush, where some sixty of said citizens were killed by the Indians and the others dispersed. This greatly increased the alarm, and there was good reason to fear that the settlements around Virginia City, if not the town itself, would be attacked by the Indians in large force. There were no troops or arms of Government nearer than Salt Lake, five or six hundred miles distant. Under these circumstances the governor of California and the United States officer in command of the Department of the Pacific sent forward to Virginia City arms and ammunition, in charge of proper officers. Two or three hundred volunteers also came along with the United States troops. The citizens of Virginia City and vicinity, together with the

United States troops and volunteers from California, organized a regiment and selected Col. Jack Hays, who happened to be there at the time, to take command thereof. Thus organized and thus commanded, this improvised regiment marched against the Indians, and, after a hard-fought battle, whipped them severely and secured peace and safety.   *   *   *

The evidence shows that this expedition against the Indians was necessary for the preservation of the lives and property of the people of Virginia City and vicinity, and that its organization and success perhaps preserved the people there from destruction. The Government had no troops there ; the danger was instant; there were no means of preventing destruction excepting those adopted.   The people themselves did what the Government should, perhaps, have been prepared to do.   Under these circumstances the committee think there is a moral and equitable obligation resting on the Government to pay the necessary expenses of the expedition.

The prices charged for the supplies seem to be high, but the testimony is all to the effect that, under the adverse circumstances of the case, they could not have been furnished for less.   *   *   *

STATEMENT OF WILLIAM M. STEWART.

UNITED STATES SENATE, *April* 14, 1888.

William M. Stewart states that he was in Virginia City during the war of 1860; that he aided in fitting out both expeditions against the Indians and contributed for that purpose $1,000, for which he never has and never will present a claim ; that many citizens of both California and Nevada contributed considerable sums of money who will never make claims for the same ; that he knows most of the persons for whose relief this bill is presented, and knew them at the time of the war; that he is unable to state what amount any particular individual contributed, but does know that nearly every person in the Territory of Nevada contributed freely to the full extent of their means, and that from his general knowledge of the subject he believes the claims presented are just and reasonable.

WM. M. STEWART,
Nevada.

Congress has in numerous instances paid claims of the same character of those provided in the bill under consideration, among which the following are cited as precedents :

By act approved March 3, 1797, entitled "An act making appropriations for the military and naval establishments for the year 1797," appropriations were made, to satisfy and discharge claims for militia service on the frontiers of Georgia, the sum of $70,496.35; for militia service on the frontiers of Kentucky, $3,836.76; and for militia service on the frontiers of South Carolina, the sum of $8,400.25.

By an act approved May 13, 1800, the accounting officers of the Treasury were authorized to settle the accounts of the militia who served on an expedition commanded by Maj. Thomas Johnson against the Indians in the year 1794, the same to be paid out of any moneys in the Treasury not otherwise appropriated.

By section 3 of an act of Congress approved March 14, 1804, making appropriations for the support of Government for the year 1804, it was provided " that the sum which shall be found due on a settlement of the accounts of the militia who served on an expedition commanded by Maj. Thomas Johnson against the Indians in the year 1794, be paid out of any moneys in the Treasury not otherwise appropriated, the appropriation made by the act of the 13th of May, 1800, having been carried to the credit of the surplus fund."

By the second section of an act approved March 2, 1829 (Army appropriation bill), an appropriation was made of $856.55 to pay a company of Illinois militia commanded by Captain Morgan, called into service on the northwestern frontier in 1827, to be settled by the Secretary of War agreeably to the third section of the Army appropriation bill, approved March 21, 1828.

By an act approved July 2, 1836, the Secretary of War was directed to ascertain the sums severally due to persons who performed duty in the companies commanded by Captains Crawford, Wallis, and Long, of the militia of Missouri, and in the companies of Captain Siglor, of the militia of Indiana, for the protection of the frontiers of those States against the Indians, and to cause them to be paid for the time they were actually engaged in said service in the year 1832, at the rate and according to the principles established for the payment of similar services rendered the United States.

By the third section of an act approved March 1, 1837, the Secretary of War was directed to cause to be paid to the volunteers and militia of Kentucky, Tennessee, Alabama, and Mississippi, including the companies in Mississippi mustered into the service, who were duly called into service, and whose service was accepted by the executives of the States, respectively, during the summer of the year 1836, under requisitions from the Secretary of War, or from generals commanding the troops of the United States, and who were discharged before marching, the amount of one month's pay, with all the allowances to which they would have been entitled if they had been in actual service during the period of one month; and by the fourth section of said act an appropriation was made for paying the Rifle Rangers, Coosada Volunteers, and Independence Blues, under the command of Major Holt; and for the payment of Major Holt and battalion staff, to be paid on presentation of the rolls of said companies and battalion staff to the Paymaster-General, with evidence of the time they were in the service against the Creek Indians in the months of May and June, 1836.

By an act approved February 4, 1843, the Secretary of War was authorized to cause to be paid to the companies of Captains Johnson, Henderson, Knight, Jones, and North, for services rendered in the year 1840, according to the muster-rolls of said companies, and also the companies of Captains Jernigan and Sweat, for services rendered in the year 1841, according to the muster-rolls of said companies, such payment to be governed by the laws and regulations applicable to the payment of volunteers and militia of the United States.

By act approved March 3, 1843, the accounting officers of the Treasury were authorized and required to settle the claims for supplies furnished the Florida militia, the payment of which was provided for by act of August 23, 1842, upon principles of equity and justice, under the directions of the Secretary of War.

By act approved August 7, 1848, the Secretary of the Treasury was directed to pay to the mounted Tennessee volunteers who served in the companies of Captains Gillespie, Peake, Vernon, and Rogers in 1836, to each the sum of 40 cents per day for the use and risk of his arms, and the sum of 15 cents per day for forage from the 1st of November, 1836, until they were finally discharged.

By act approved March 2, 1835, the Secretary of the Treasury was directed out of the appropriation mentioned in the act to "settle and adjust the expenses of the defense of the people of Oregon from the attacks and hostilities of the Cayuse Indians, in the years of 1847 and 1848, approved February 14, 1851," the sums found due and allowed by Commissioners Wait and Rice and by the governor of Oregon.

By act approved March 3, 1853, supplying deficiencies in the appropriations for the year ending June 30, 1853, the sum of $10,569.06 was appropriated for Mexican hostilties.

By the same act the sum of $18,060.49 was appropriated for pay of Louisiana and Texas volunteers.

By an act approved March 3, 1855, making appropriations for the civil and diplomatic expenses of Government for the year ending June 30, 1856, it was provided that the sum of $25,000 be appropriated to pay the necessary expenses of six companies of volunteers called into the service of the United States by Brigadier-General Smith, in the State of Texas, to be paid under the direction of the Secretary of War.

By an act making appropriations for the support of the Army for the year ending the 30th of June, 1856, and for other purposes, approved March 3, 1855, an appropriation of $137,755.38 was made for pay, supplies, and traveling expenses of six companies of Texas volunteers called into the service by the governor of Texas and mustered into the service of the United States.

By act of March 2, 1861, $400,000 was appropriated for pay of volunteers in Oregon and Washington in suppression of Indian hostilities in 1855-'56.

AN ACT making appropriations for the payment of the awards made by the commissioners appointed under and by virtue of an act of Congress entitled "An act for the relief of persons for damages sustained by reason of the depredations and injuries by certain bands of Sioux Indians." Approved February 16, 1863.

Be it enacted by the Senate and House of Representatives of the United States of America in Congress assembled, That the sum of nine hundred and twenty-eight thousand four hundred and eleven dollars, or so much thereof as may be necessary, be, and the same is hereby, appropriated, out of any money in the Treasury not otherwise appropriated, for the payment of the several amounts awarded by the commission appointed under and by virtue of an act of Congress entitled "An act for the relief of persons for damages sustained by reason of the depredations and injuries by certain bands of Sioux Indians," approved February 16, 1863, to the several persons, firms, estates, and corporations, respectively, to whom such amounts were awarded by said commissioners. * * * (13 Stats. at Large, p. 92.)

By act approved March 3, 1875, making appropriations for sundry civil expenses of the Government for the year ending June 30, 1876, the sum of $25,000 was reappropriated for the payment of volunteers of Washington and Oregon Territories, who were engaged in the suppression of Indian hostilities therein in the years 1855 and 1856, and for the payment of claims for services, supplies, and transportation incurred in the maintenance of said volunteers, and for horses and other property lost or destroyed in said service, as provided for by the act of Congress approved March 2, 1861.

AN ACT for the relief of citizens of Montana who served with the United States troops in the war
with the Nez Perces and for the relief of the heirs of such as were killed in such service.

*Be it enacted by the Senate and House of Representatives of the United States of America
in Congress assembled,* That each volunteer who joined the forces of the United States,
in the Territory of Montana, during the war with the Nez Perce Indians, shall be
paid one dollar per day during the term of such service, from the time that he left
his home until he was returned thereto, including all time spent in hospital under
treatment by such as received wounds or other injuries in such service.

SEC. 2. That all persons who were wounded or disabled in such service, and
the heirs of all who were killed in such service, shall be entitled to all the benefits
of the pension laws, in such manner and to the same extent as if they had been duly
mustered into the regular or volunteer forces of the United States.

SEC. 3. That all horses and arms lost in such service shall be paid for at their actual
value, to be duly ascertained by the commanding officer of the district of Montana:
Provided, That no payment shall be made for such losses except upon the statement of
the commanding officer of the United States troops or such other officer of the regular Army as might be in control of the volunteers at the time of such loss, and such
other proofs as may be required by the commanding officer and the United States
quartermaster for the district of Montana, to establish the fact that such losses were
made in the service of the United States.

Approved, March 3, 1881.   (U. S. Stat. at Large, vol. 21, p. 641.)

And by the second section of an act approved January 6, 1883, the
Secretary of the Treasury was directed to pay to the State of California and to the citizens thereof, their heirs, representatives, or assigns,
the sum of $4,441.33 for arms, ammunition, supplies, transportation,
and services of volunteer forces in suppressing Indian hostilities in
said State during the said years of 1872–'73, as the same were specifically reported to Congress by the Secretary of War December 15,
1874.

The committee report back a substitute for the bill (S. 2542), and recommend its passage.

IN THE SENATE OF THE UNITED STATES.

MAY 14, 1888.—Ordered to be printed.

Mr. STEWART, from the Committee on Military Affairs, submitted the
following

REPORT:

[To accompany bill S. 2918.]

The majority of the Committee on Military Affairs make the following report in support of the bill offered herewith:

OBJECT OF THIS BILL.

The object of this bill is to re-imburse the State of Nevada for moneys paid and contracted to be paid by the Territory of Nevada and afterwards assumed and paid by that State, and also for moneys actually expended by Nevada after becoming a State for the general defense and in furnishing troops to the United States during the suppression of the war of the rebellion, and for guarding the overland mail and emigrant route between the Missouri River and California, and for suppressing Indian hostilities under circumstances hereinafter set forth.

APPEAL OF PRESIDENT LINCOLN, THROUGH SECRETARY SEWARD, TO THE NATION FOR AID.

On October 14, 1861, Mr. Seward, Secretary of State, addressed a circular letter to the governors of the loyal States and Territories, calling for assistance for the General Government in suppressing hostilities in the so-called Confederate States, and for the improvement and perfection of the defenses of the loyal States respectively. A copy of this letter is printed in the appendix hereto, marked Exhibit No. 1, page 23.

ACTION TAKEN BY NEVADA IN RESPONSE TO THE FOREGOING APPEAL OF SECRETARY SEWARD.

Upon the receipt of this letter the legislative assembly of Nevada Territory at its first session passed appropriate resolutions pledging the support of the people of that Territory to the Union cause to the extent of their means, which resolutions are printed in the appendix, marked Exhibit No. 2, page 24.

On the 28th day of November, 1861, three days after the passage of the resolutions above mentioned, the legislative assembly of Nevada also passed an elaborate law for the enrollment and organization of a militia force to aid the United States when called upon in the suppression of the rebellion, and to carry out the spirit and intent of the aforesaid circular letter of Secretary Seward. This law will be found on

pages 106 to 125 of the Laws of Nevada Territory, 1861. This act provided that the militia of the Territory organized under its provisions should be subject to be called into the service of the United States by the President, or any officer of the United States Army commanding a division or a department. A militia force was immediately organized under its provisions. II. P. Russell was appointed adjutant-general, and was succeeded by Col. John Cradlebaugh, who is mentioned in the resolutions above referred to and printed in the appendix as Exhibit No. 2, page 24.

It will thus be seen that Nevada made the necessary preparations, organized her militia, and was ready to answer any call that might be thereafter made upon her by the General Government, and also to protect the Territory against a large portion of its inhabitants who desired to join the Confederacy.

CONDITION OF AFFAIRS THAT RENDERED A CALL FOR NEVADA VOLUNTEERS NECESSARY.

The Territory of Nevada was organized by Congress on March 2, 1861 (12 U. S. Stats., 209). At the breaking out of the rebellion it became a serious question what attitude Nevada would occupy, and home guards were immediately organized. These guards afterwards formed a portion of the militia of the Territory as provided for in the aforesaid militia law, and protected the inhabitants from violence, without any expense to the Government.

In the early part of April, 1863, the overland mail and emigrant route was attacked by Indians, and communication was closed between the Atlantic States and the Pacific coast. This route extended from the Missouri River to California via the Platte River, Salt Lake City, through Nevada to Sacramento, in California, and was the only means at that date of direct overland communication between the Missouri River and California. At this time the gold discoveries in California continued to invite a large immigration, the interest in which was more or less intensified by the continued extensive silver discoveries in Nevada Territory, and principally on the Comstock lode in the western part of the Territory. The routes via Cape Horn, and especially that via the Isthmus of Panama, were rendered extremely doubtful, dangerous, and expensive, on account of Confederate privateer cruisers hovering around the West India Islands and along both these sea routes, and in anticipation of other Confederate cruisers infesting the waters of the Pacific (which soon thereafter became the theater of the operations and extensive depredations of the Confederate privateer cruiser *Shenandoah*) the overland route, therefore, although in itself both dangerous and difficult, was yet considered the better and preferable route by which to reach the Pacific.

On account of a general uprising of the Indians along the entire overland route, and especially that portion between Salt Lake City, in the Territory of Utah, and the Sierra Nevada Mountains, and because of the doubts as to the loyalty of the Mormons to the Government of the United States, the maintenance and protection of the mail and emigrant route through that section of the country and along the aforesaid line was regarded by the Government as a military necessity. Apparently in anticipation of no immediate danger of attack on the Pacific coast, nearly all the troops of the regular Army at this time had been withdrawn from service throughout this entire region of country and transferred to other fields of military operations. This left the entire coun-

try between Salt Lake City and the Sierra Nevada Mountains without adequate and efficient military protection. The Government thus having but few troops of its regular Army in that region, was therefore compelled to call upon the inhabitants of Nevada Territory to raise and organize volunteer military companies to suppress Indian disturbances which threatened the entire suspension of all mail facilities and emigration from the East, as will be hereafter shown.

At the time of the calls upon Nevada for troops the prices of labor and supplies of all descriptions in Nevada were extremely high. There were then no railroads, and the snow on the Sierra Nevada Mountains formed an almost impassable barrier against teams from about the 1st of December until about June. The average cost of freight from San Francisco, the main source of supply for western Nevada, was about $80 a ton, and it was necessary to lay in supplies during the summer and fall for the remainder of the year. A great mining excitement prevailed at this time, occasioned by the marvelous development of the great Comstock lode, and wages were from $4 to $10 a day in gold. The people who had emigrated to the new gold and silver fields went there for the purpose of mining and prospecting for mines, and were generally reluctant to enter the irregular military service of guarding the overland mail and emigrant route. Besides, on account of the extraordinary high price of supplies of every description, and also of wages and services of every kind, it was impossible for them to maintain themselves and families without involving much more expense than any compensation which could be paid them as volunteer troops under the laws of the United States, and, as will be seen by the letters of General Wright, hereafter quoted, they were expected, as volunteer troops, to furnish themselves with horses and equipments, in addition to what could be furnished by the Government.

The military authorities of the United States well knew at that time the exact condition of the country and of the roads across the mountains leading thereto and of the cost of transportation and of the prices of labor and of supplies and of their own inability to furnish either horses or equipments for a military service that required mounted troops.

FIRST CALL BY THE UNITED STATES FOR NEVADA VOLUNTEERS.

In view of the necessities of the situation, and with all the facts fully known to the military authorities of the United States, General Wright, commanding the Department of the Pacific, was authorized by the War Department to raise volunteer military companies in Nevada Territory for the protection of said overland mail and emigrant route, and on April 2, 1863, he addressed the following requisition for troops to the governor of the Territory:

HEADQUARTERS DEPARTMENT OF THE PACIFIC,
San Francisco, Cal., April 2, 1863.

His Excellency O. CLEMENS,
Governor of Nevada Territory, Carson City, Nev.:

SIR: I have been authorized by the War Department to raise volunteer companies in Nevada Territory for the purpose of moving east on the overland mail route in the direction of Great Salt Lake City. If it is possible to raise three or four companies in the Territory for this service I have to request your excellency may be pleased to have them organized. I should be glad to get two companies of cavalry and two of infantry. The mounted troops to furnish their own horses and equipments. Arms, ammunition, etc., will be furnished by the United States. Should your excellency consider it improbable that this volunteer force can be raised, even one company will be

accepted. I will send you a plan of organization, and an officer with the necessary instructions for mustering them into the service.

With great respect, I have the honor to be, your most obedient servant,

G. WRIGHT,
Brigadier-General, U. S. Army, Commanding.

Official copy.

J. C. KELTON,
Colonel, A. A. G.

While correspondence was being conducted between the governor of Nevada and General Wright as to the method of organizing Nevada's troops, the following telegram was dispatched by General H. W. Halleck, general-in-chief of the U. S. Army, to General Wright:

HEADQUARTERS OF THE ARMY,
Washington, D. C., April 15, 1863.

Brig. Gen. G. WRIGHT,
San Francisco, Cal.:

The Secretary of War authorizes you to raise additional regiments in California and Nevada to re-enforce General Connor and protect overland route. Can not companies be raised in Nevada and pushed forward immediately? General Connor may be able to raise some companies in Utah or out of emigrant trains.

H. W. HALLECK,
General-in-Chief.

————

Whereupon General Wright addressed the governor of Nevada Territory the following communication:

HEADQUARTERS DEPARTMENT OF THE PACIFIC,
San Francisco, Cal., April 16, 1863.

His Excellency ORION CLEMENS,
Governor of Nevada Territory, Carson City, Nev.:

SIR: I have the honor to acknowledge the receipt of your excellency's communication of the 9th instant.

The Indian disturbances along the line of the overland mail route, east of Carson City, threaten the entire suspension of our mail facilities, as well as preventing any portion of the vast immigration approaching from the east reaching Nevada. The interest and prosperity of your Territory depend much upon maintaining free and safe access to it from all directions. My force immediately available for operation on that line is small. A company of cavalry stationed at Fort Churchill, and under orders to move towards Ruby Valley, I was compelled to divert for temporary service to assist in quelling an Indian outbreak in the Owen's Lake district. As soon as the services of this company can be dispensed with there, it will operate on the mail and emigrant line. Some infantry companies will also be thrown forward from this side of the mountains as soon as transportation can be prepared and the roads are in order. In the mean time it is of such importance to keep the mail and emigrant route east of you open, that I would earnestly recommend that one or two companies of cavalry be promptly organized and prepared for muster into the service of the United States. It is impossible for us at this moment to purchase horses and equipments. Each man would have to furnish his own.

I can furnish arms, ammunition, forage, clothing, provisions, etc.; in fact, everything except horses and equipments.

The organization of a company or troop of cavalry is: one captain, one first lieutenant, one second lieutenant, one first sergeant, one quartermaster-sergeant, one commissary sergeant, five sergeants, eight corporals, two teamsters, two farriers or blacksmiths, one saddler, one wagoner, and seventy-eight privates.

This is the first appeal that has been made to Nevada Territory, a Territory soon to add another star to that glorious galaxy which adorns our beautiful banner, and I doubt not this call will be nobly responded to by the loyal and patriotic citizens of the Territory.

With great respect, your excellency's most obedient servant,

G. WRIGHT,
Brigadier-General U. S. Army, Commanding.

Official copy.

J. C. KELTON,
Colonel, A. A. G.

NEVADA'S RESPONSE TO THE FOREGOING CALL FOR TROOPS BY THE UNITED STATES.

Immediately upon the receipt of the foregoing requisition for troops the governor of Nevada issued the following proclamation:

PROCLAMATION.

EXECUTIVE DEPARTMENT,
Carson City, April 24, 1863.

Whereas Brigadier-General George Wright, United States Army, commanding officer of the Department of the Pacific, has, by authority of the War Department called upon me for two companies of infantry and two companies of cavalry to serve three years, or during the war:

Now, therefore, I, Orion Clemens, governor of the Territory of Nevada and commander-in-chief of the militia thereof, do hereby authorize and call upon the citizens of the Territory, as many as shall be necessary to fill up the preceding requisition, to immediately organize themselves into companies as required hereby.

In witness whereof I have hereunto set my hand and affixed the great seal of the Territory.

Done at Carson City, Territory of Nevada, this 24th day of April, in the year of our Lord one thousand eight hundred and sixty-three.

ORION CLEMENS,
Secretary and Acting Governor.

In answer to these calls and requisitions of General Wright and said proclamation of the governor of Nevada four companies of cavalry were completely organized, two of which were sent to Camp Douglas, Utah Territory, for military service, and the remaining two were sent to station Fort Churchill, Nev.

SECOND CALL AND REQUISITION OF THE UNITED STATES FOR NEVADA VOLUNTEERS.

Thereafter General Wright made a further requisition upon the governor of Nevada for two additional companies of cavalry and a regiment of infantry, as will appear from the following:

HEADQUARTERS DEPARTMENT OF THE PACIFIC,
San Francisco, December 22, 1863.

SIR: The four companies of cavalry called for from the Territory of Nevada have completed their organization; two of the companies have reached Camp Douglas, Utah, and the remaining two are at Fort Churchill, Nev. On the representations of Governor Nye that additional troops can be raised in Nevada, I have, under the authority conferred upon me by the War Department, called upon the governor for a regiment of infantry and two more companies of cavalry.

Very respectfully, your obedient servant,

G. WRIGHT,
Brig. Gen., U. S. Army, Commanding.

ADJUTANT-GENERAL, U. S. ARMY,
Washington, D. C.

WHAT WAS DONE BY NEVADA UNDER THE SECOND CALL AND REQUISITION BY THE UNITED STATES FOR NEVADA VOLUNTEERS.

In response to General Wright's second requisition for troops made in the latter part of November, 1863, the governor of Nevada issued the following proclamation:

PROCLAMATION.

Whereas a requisition having been made upon me by Brig. Gen. George Wright, U. S. Army, commanding the Department of the Pacific, for one regiment of volunteer infantry and two companies of cavalry, for service in the employ of the General Government of the United States;

Now, therefore, I, James W. Nye, governor of the Territory of Nevada and com-

mander-in-chief of the militia thereof, by virtue of the authority in me vested, do issue this my proclamation, calling upon the people of this Territory to forthwith proceed to organize a regiment of infantry, consisting of ten companies, and two companies of cavalry, in full compliance of said requisition.

All applicants for line officers will present themselves before the Army examining board for examination, and report to me with certificate of such examination as soon as practicable.

Given under my hand and seal at Carson, Nev., this 4th day of December, A. D. 1863.

JAMES W. NYE,
Governor of the Territory of Nevada.

Attest:
   ORION CLEMENS,
      Secretary of the Territory.

Under this last requisition of General Wright and last proclamation of the governor of Nevada two additional cavalry companies and the First Battalion Nevada Infantry Volunteers, composed of four companies, were raised and assigned to duty to such fields of military service in Utah and Nevada as were determined upon by General Wright, as will appear from the correspondence printed in the appendix, marked "Exhibit 3, pages 24 to 29.

It will thus be seen that the people of the Territory of Nevada responded promptly to and complied fully with the appeals of the United States Government for troops and in accordance with the requisitions and calls of the War Department. The action of the people of Nevada was reported to Mr. Seward, Secretary of State, by the governor of Nevada on March 25, 1864. He wrote to Mr. Seward the condition of affairs in the Territory, which letter was transmitted to the Senate by President Lincoln on April 29, 1864 (see Senate Ex. Doc. No. 41, 38th Cong., 1st sess.). In his report Governor Nye said:

We have raised in the Territory within the last two years one company of infantry, now attached to a California regiment, a battalion of cavalry, consisting of six companies, four of which are in the field; the remaining two will be there also as soon as they can be mounted. In addition we are raising a regiment of infantry, now in a good state of forwardness, and we can raise a brigade easily if necessary.

SOME OF THE DUTIES OF THE TROOPS CALLED TO AID THE UNITED STATES AT THIS TIME.

The first duty of these troops was to open and guard the overland mail and emigrant route from the Sierra Nevada Mountains to Utah. The campaign in which this was accomplished was under the command of General Conner. The volunteer troops under this gallant officer had already conducted a most successful campaign against the Indians of eastern Nevada, Utah, and Idaho, in the region where the Mormon influence was most potential, conquered many Indian tribes, and secured lasting peace.

The Secretary of War, in reporting to Congress the condition of things in that region of country, then under the military command of General Conner, said as follows, to wit:

DEPARTMENT OF THE PACIFIC.

This department has been most signally exempt from the evils of civil war, and consequently has enjoyed unexampled prosperity. Some thefts and robberies having been committed by roving bands of Indians on the overland stage route in January last, General Conner marched with a small force to Bear River, Idaho, where, on the 26th, he overtook and completely defeated them in a severe battle, in which he killed 224 of the 300 and captured 175 of their horses. His own loss in killed and wounded was 63 out of 200. Many of his men were severely injured by the frost. Since this severe punishment the Indians in that quarter have ceased to commit depredations on the whites. (Secretary of War's report, first session Thirty-eighth Congress.)

ADDITIONAL CAUSES THAT LED TO A THIRD CALL AND REQUISITION BY THE UNITED STATES FOR NEVADA VOLUNTEERS.

Congress having on July 1, 1862, chartered the Union Pacific Railroad Company, to which, and also to the Central Pacific Railroad Company, aid was given to build one continuous line of railroad from the Missouri River to the Pacific Ocean through this region of country, did, on July 2, 1864, still further foster these enterprises by additional grants. These two companies thereupon placed in the field numerous corps of surveyors, civil engineers, and employés to explore said country in the effort to discover the most practicable and economical railroad route from the Missouri River to the Pacific, and to run trial lines and definitely locate the lines of the two subdivisions of said railroad route. In regard to these roads the Secretary of War, in his annual report for 1864-'65, page 144, said:

It is, in a military sense, of the utmost importance that the Pacific Railroad should be pressed to the earliest possible completion.

The exploration and location for a Pacific railroad through that region of country then mostly uninhabited except by large tribes and roving bands of hostile Indians, called for additional military protection and rendered it necessary for the United States to again call upon Nevada to raise additional troops. Accordingly General McDowell, commanding the Department of the Pacific, made the following call on October 13, 1864, upon the Governor of Nevada Territory:

HEADQUARTERS DEPARTMENT OF THE PACIFIC,
Virginia City, October 13, 1864.

SIR: I have the honor to acquaint you that I have received authority from the War Department to call on you, from time to time, as the circumstances of the service may require, for not to exceed in all, at any one time, one regiment of volunteer infantry and one regiment of volunteer cavalry, to be mustered into service of the United States as other volunteer regiments, under existing laws and regulations.

Under this authority I have to request you will please raise, as soon as possible, enough companies of infantry to complete, with those already in service from Nevada, a full regiment of infantry.

Brigadier-General Wason will confer with you and give all the information necessary to details for this service.

I have the honor to be, governor, very respectfully, your most obedient servant,
IRWIN McDOWELL,
Major-General, Commanding Department.

His Excellency JAMES W. NYE,
Governor of Nevada Territory.

WHAT WAS DONE BY NEVADA IN RESPONSE TO THIS CALL.

The governor of Nevada responded to this call by issuing the following proclamation:

PROCLAMATION.

TERRITORY OF NEVADA, EXECUTIVE DEPARTMENT,
Carson City, October 19, 1864.

Whereas I have received a requisition from Maj. Gen. Irwin McDowell, commanding Department of the Pacific, the same having been made under authority from the War Department, to raise, as soon as possible, enough companies of infantry to complete, with those already in service from Nevada, a full regiment of infantry:

Now, therefore, I, James W. Nye, governor of the Territory of Nevada, and commander-in-chief of the militia thereof, do hereby call upon the citizens of this Territory to organize themselves into seven companies, sufficient to fill the battalion of infantry now in service from this Territory, and the requirements of said requisition.

In witness whereof I have hereunto set my hand and caused the great seal of the

Territory of Nevada to be affixed. Done at Carson City this 19th day of October, 1864.

JAMES W. NYE,
Governor and Commander-in-Chief of the Territory of Nevada.

Attest:
ORION CLEMENS,
Secretary of the Territory.

Afterward the Indians became troublesome between Utah and the Missouri River. During the years 1865–'66 the Nevada cavalry were actively engaged in Colorado, Wyoming, Kansas, and Nebraska in the Indian wars in that region. The writer of this report crossed the continent in the summer of 1865, and met several small detachments of Nevada cavalry in active service against the Indians, and was much gratified to learn that they were quite celebrated for their gallantry and faithful services in that kind of warfare, which subjects the soldier to the severest test of endurance, and requires individual exertion and watchfulness unknown in civilized war.

METHOD RECOGNIZED BY NEVADA FOR THE ENROLLMENT OF HER TROOPS CALLED INTO THE MILITARY SERVICE OF THE UNITED STATES AND HER MODE OF DEFRAYING THE EXPENSES OF SUCH ENROLLMENT FOR SUCH SERVICE.

The citizens of Nevada were never drafted, nor did they ever hire substitutes, but were organized into military companies by commanding officers, most of whom had undergone an examination for commission before military boards instituted for that purpose and satisfactory to the general of the United States Army commanding the military Department of the Pacific.

As a compensation to and a re-imbursement for all the costs by them for raising and organizing said volunteer military companies, and in lieu of all other kinds of expenses necessarily incident to enrolling and enlisting the members of said companies for the military service of the United States, the legislature of Nevada passed an act providing for the payment to the commanding officers of said companies of $10 per capita for each volunteer soldier by them for said purposes enrolled and enlisted, aggregating the sum of $11,840. This provision in said statute was improperly called a "bounty;" but this expenditure was not in any sense whatsoever a "bounty," but, on the contrary, it was an actual disbursement by Nevada to cover all the legitimate expenses of every kind incident to enrolling and enlisting Nevada's troops to perform military service for the United States.

The history of this expenditure and of this mode of enrollment of troops by the Territory of Nevada, and the economy and reasons therefor, are all fully set forth in a memorial to Congress signed by all the State officers of Nevada, which is printed in the appendix, marked Exhibit No. 4, page 29.

METHOD ADOPTED BY NEVADA TO PAY THE TROOPS CALLED INTO THE MILITARY SERVICE OF THE UNITED STATES BY THE TERRITORY OF NEVADA, AND THE EXTENT TO WHICH THE STATE OF NEVADA PLEDGED HER FAITH TO PAY THE OBLIGATIONS CONTRACTED BY THE TERRITORY OF NEVADA TO AID THE UNITED STATES.

This same act of the legislature of Nevada, among other things, provided that each citizen of Nevada so volunteering and enlisting as a private soldier for the military service of the United States, not being

drafted or acting as a substitute for another, should, during each and every month while honorably serving the United States, be paid out of the treasury of Nevada the sum of $5 per month, gold coin. It further provided that, in the case of an enlisted married man, an allotment of the whole or a portion of the extra monthly pay could be drawn by his family dependent upon him for support (see Laws of Nevada Territory, 1864, page 81, or appendix, Exhibit No. 5, page 31).

On March 11, 1865, after Nevada became a State, an act similar to this Territorial act, but more liberal in its provisions, was passed, to take the place of the Territorial law. The State legislature having deemed the situation so important to maintain the good faith of the Territory, that had been pledged to aid the United States, it passed this act *over the veto of Governor Blasdel*, who alleged in his veto message his fear that the expense might exceed the constitutional limit, etc.

This act provided for the assumption and payment by the State of Nevada of all obligations of every kind that had been incurred and contracted to be paid by the Territory for the enlistments, enrollments, bounties, extra pay, etc., of volunteer soldiers that had been theretofore called into the military service of the United States. The bonds now outstanding and still due by Nevada, though at a smaller rate of interest than that named in the original issue and still drawing interest, were issued under the provisions of this latter act (see Statutes, Nevada, 1864-'65, page 389, or appendix, Exhibit No. 6, page 34).

RESULTS OF THE FOREGOING LEGISLATION BY NEVADA.

By these legislative enactments of Nevada substantial and effectual aid was given and guaranteed by Nevada, both as a Territory and State, to the Government of the United States in guarding its overland mail and emigrant route and the line of the proposed transcontinental railroad in furnishing troops during the war of the rebellion and for suppressing Indian hostilities and maintaining peace in the country inhabited by the Mormons, and for the general defense as contemplated in said circular letter of Secretary Seward along an exposed, difficult, and hostile Indian frontier, and then but sparsely populated. These enactments were fully known to the authorities of the United States and to Congress; they have ever been acquiesced in and met with the sanction and practical indorsement of the United States, in whose interest and for whose benefit they were made. As a partial compensation to these volunteers for this irregular, hazardous, and exposed service in the mountains and on the desert plains, and to aid them to a small extent to maintain families dependent upon them for support, first the Territory and afterwards the State of Nevada offered and paid this small stipend, never suspecting that the United States would not promptly and willingly respond when asked to re-imburse the same. These citizens of Nevada who volunteered and enlisted and did military service for the United States were compelled in many cases to abandon their employments, in which their wages were always lucrative and service continuous, so that nothing less than the individual patriotism of these volunteers enabled the Territory and State of Nevada to cheerfully and promptly respond to every call and requisition made upon them for troops by the United States.

The records of the War Department, in addition to what is already quoted and referred to in substantiation of the facts herein stated, are printed in the appendix, marked Exhibit No. 3, pages 24 to 29.

THE BASIS AND AUTHORITY OF NEVADA'S CLAIM AGAINST THE UNITED
STATES AND THE PRECEDENTS IN SUPPORT THEREOF.

These enactments of Nevada both as a Territory and a State, and
various acts done under them in and execution thereof, when complying
according to her own methods with the various calls and requisitions of
the United States for troops, have resulted in the expenditure of a large
sum of money which constitutes the present claim of Nevada against
the United States. The authority upon which this claim rests is found
in the fourth section of the fourth article of the Constitution of the
United States, which provides that—

The United States shall guaranty to every State in the Union a republican form of
government, and shall protect each of them against invasion; and, on application of
the legislature, or of the executive (when the legislature can not be convened),
against domestic violence.

And upon the latter part of the tenth section of the first article of
the Constitution; which is as follows:

No State shall, without the consent of Congress, lay any duty on tonnage, keep
troops or ships of war in time of peace, enter into any agreement or compact with
another State, or with a foreign power, or engage in war, unless actually invaded or
in such imminent danger as will not admit of delay.

And also upon the act of July 28, 1795, chapter 36, section 1, page
424, now section No. 1642, U. S. Revised Statutes, which provides
that—

Whenever the United States are invaded or are in imminent danger of invasion
from any foreign nation or Indian tribe, or of rebellion against the authority of the
Government of the United States, it shall be lawful for the President to call forth such
number of the militia of the State or States most convenient to the place of danger
or scene of action, as he may deem necessary to repel such invasion or to suppress such
rebellion, and to issue his orders for that purpose to such officer of the militia as he
may think proper."

In reference to the foregoing the courts have held that—

When a particular authority is confided to a public officer, to be exercised by him
in his discretion, upon an examination of the facts of which he is made the appropriate judge, his decision upon the facts in the absence of any controlling provision,
is absolutely conclusive as to the existence of those facts (Allen vs. Blunt, 3 Story,
U. S. Circuit Court Reports, 745)."

And again the supreme court of the State of New York (Hon. Chancellor Kent presiding as chief justice) held in the case of Vanderheyden
vs. Young, 11 Johnson's New York Reports, 157, that—

It is a general and sound principle that when the law vests any person with a
power to do an act, and constitutes him a judge of the evidence on which that act
may be done, and at the same time contemplates that the act is to be carried into
effect through the instrumentality of agents, the person thus clothed with power is
invested with discretion and is quoad hoc a judge.

His mandates to his legal agents on his declaring the event to have happened will
be a protection to those agents, and it is not their duty or business to investigate the
facts thus referred to their superior, and to rejudge his determination."

The United States Supreme Court in Martin vs. Mott, 12 Wheaton,
19, unanimously held—

That the authority to decide upon what occasions and upon what emergencies Federal calls should be made and Federal assistance given, "belongs exclusively to the
President, and that his decision is conclusive upon all other persons."*

And Chief Justice Taney, in Luther vs. Borden, 7 Howard, referred
approvingly to the opinion of the United States Supreme Court in Martin vs. Mott, as expressed in these words:

That whenever a statute gives a discretionary power to any person to be exercised
by him upon his own opinion of certain facts, it is a sound rule of construction that
the statute constitutes him the sole and exclusive judge of the existence of those facts."

---

* NOTE.—The acts of heads of Departments of the Government are in law the acts
of the President (Wilcox vs. Jackson, 13 Peters., 498).

The obligations arising under these provisions of the Constitution and laws and decisions have been recognized by the Government from its foundation, as will fully appear from the authorities cited by Senator Dolph in a report made by him from the Senate Committee on Claims on February 25, 1885 (Forty-eighth Congress, second session), Report No. 1438. These authorities are printed in the appendix, marked Exhibit No. 7, page 37 et sequiter.

NEVADA'S DILIGENCE IN THESE PREMISES.

The State of Nevada has not slept upon her rights in any of these premises nor been guilty of any laches; on the contrary, at all proper times she has respectfully brought the same to the attention of Congress by memorials of her legislature and of her State authorities, and through her representatives in Congress. On March 29, 1867, her legislature first asked for the payment of the claims of the State by a joint resolution, which is printed in the appendix, marked Exhibit No. 8, page 64. And again, on February 1, 1869, the legislature of Nevada passed a memorial and joint resolution renewing her prayer in these premises, which is also so printed in the appendix, marked Exhibit No. 9, page 65.

The Journals of the United States Senate show that on March 10, 1868, the writer of this report presented the first-mentioned memorial and resolution to the Senate, accompanied with an official statement of the amount of the claims of the State referred to therein. These papers were referred to the Committee on Claims, but the records fail to show that any action was ever taken upon them. On May 29 of the same year the writer of this report introduced a joint resolution (S. 138) providing for the appointment of a board of examiners to examine the claims of the State of Nevada against the United States, and on June 18 of the same year the Committee on Claims, to whom this joint resolution was referred, was discharged from its further consideration. The official statement of the moneys expended by the State of Nevada on account of the United States, and presented to the Senate on March 10, 1868, can not now be found on the files of the Senate.

On February 11, 1885, and January 26, 1887, the legislature of Nevada, renewing its prayer for a re-imbursement of the money by her expended for the use and benefit of the United States, further memorialized Congress, asking for the settlement of her claims, which are printed in the appendix and marked Exhibits Nos. 10 and 11, pages 65 and 66.

PROCEEDINGS IN CONGRESS TO REDEEM THE OBLIGATIONS OF THE UNITED STATES DUE TO NEVADA IN THIS CASE.

The circumstances under which these expenditures were made by the Territory and State of Nevada being exceptional, and their re-imbursement not being provided for by any existing law, general or special, Senator Fair, of Nevada, on December 13, 1881, introduced a joint resolution in the Senate providing for the equitable adjustment of these claims of Nevada now under consideration, which was referred to the Committee on Military Affairs. A copy of said resolution will be found in the appendix, marked Exhibit 12, page 67.

This committee, instead of reporting back this joint resolution, reported back a substitute in the form of a bill providing for the payment of the claims of several States and Territories, including the State of Nevada, and which bill finally resulted in the act of June 27, 1882. This bill was reported on May 12, 1882, by Hon. L. F. Grover, and

Nevada believed then and believes now that it was then the intention of Congress to equitably and explicitly provide for the re-imbursement to her of the amount of money which she had actually and in good faith expended in these premises. This bill was accompanied by a report in which the following statement is made in relation to the claims of the State of Nevada:

NEVADA.

It appears by the report of the Adjutant-General U. S. Army, of February 25, 1882, that one regiment of cavalry and one battalion of infantry were raised in the late Territory of Nevada during the late war of the rebellion, and that the expenses of raising, organizing, and placing in the field said forces were never paid by said Territory, but were assumed and paid by the State of Nevada, and that none of said expenses so incurred by said Territory, and assumed and paid by said State, have ever been re-imbursed the State of Nevada by the United States, and that no claims therefor have ever been heretofore presented by either said Territory or said State for audit and payment by the United States. Under section 3480 of the Revised Statutes, hereinbefore referred to, the payment of these claims is barred by limitation.

These forces were raised to guard the overland mail route and emigrant road to California, east of Carson City, and to do other military service in Nevada, and were called out by the governor of the late Territory of Nevada upon requisitions therefor by the commanding general of the Department of the Pacific, and under authority of the War Department, as appears by copies of official correspondence furnished to your committee by the Secretary of War and the general commanding the Division of the Pacific. * * *

PRESENTATION BY NEVADA TO THE UNITED STATES OF HER CLAIM.

This bill reported from this committee having become a law in an amended form on June 27, 1882, thereupon the governor and controller of the State of Nevada transmitted to the Secretary of the Treasury and Secretary of War a detailed account of the moneys actually expended and actual indebtedness assumed and paid by the State of Nevada on account of the volunteer military forces enrolled by the Territory and State of Nevada, as shown by the books of the State controller.

This statement of the claim of Nevada against the United States was prepared with great care by the proper officers of the State of Nevada, being first submitted by them to the legislature thereof in printed form at the expense of the State, and thereafter transmitted, as above stated, with proper original vouchers and evidence of every kind then in her possession, to the authorities of the Government of the United States and as provided for in said act of June 27, 1882. This statement is printed in the appendix, marked Exhibit No. 13, page 67.

DELAY OF THE UNITED STATES IN THE EXAMINATION OF NEVADA'S CLAIM AND THE CAUSES THEREOF.

This claim, with said vouchers and evidence, was first presented to the Secretary of the Treasury in 1883, where, being properly stamped, it was duly transmitted to the Secretary of War for examination and action thereon. It remained of record in the War Department unacted on up to and after August 4, 1886, because, as was stated to Congress by Hon. Robert T. Lincoln, Secretary of War, he required the aid of a board of at least three army officers to assist his Department in such examination, and he requested Congress to make an appropriation of $25,000 to defray expenses of the examination of the different State and Territorial claims presented under the act of June 27, 1882. Congress delayed action upon these requests of the Secretary of War until August 4, 1886, on which date acts were passed providing for said board of

army officers, as asked for, and also appropriated $10,000 to defray the expenses of said examinations (see vol. 24, Stats. at Large, pages 217 and 249.)

SECRETARY LINCOLN'S CONSTRUCTION OF THIS ACT OF JUNE 27, 1882, FOR THE RELIEF OF NEVADA, ETC.

Prior to any action by the War Department on this claim of the State of Nevada, and prior to any action by Congress on the request of the Secretary of War for a board of Army officers to examine said claim, a bill was introduced in Congress by Senator Jones, of Nevada, and referred to the Secretary of War for report, providing for the payment of certain individual claims of citizens of Nevada on account of Indian hostilities in Nevada in 1860, upon which the Secretary of War reported as follows:

WAR DEPARTMENT,
Washington City, January 26, 1884.

SIR: In response to so much of your communication of the 22d ultimo as requests information concerning Senate bill 657, " to authorize the Secretary of the Treasury to adjust and settle the expenses of Indian wars in Nevada," I have the honor to invite your attention to the following report of the Third Auditor of the Treasury, to whom your request was duly referred :

"The State of Nevada has filed in the office abstracts and vouchers for expenses incurred on account of raising volunteers for the United States to aid in suppressing the late rebellion amounting to $349,697.49, and for expenses on account of her militia in the 'White Pine Indian war' of 1875, $17,650.98. Also, expenses of her militia in the 'Elko Indian war' of 1878, amounting to $4,654.64, presented under act of Congress approved June 27, 1882 (22 Statutes, 111, 112).

"These abstracts and vouchers will be sent to your Department for examination and report as soon as they can be stamped, as that statute requires a report from the Secretary of War as to the necessity and reasonableness of the expenses incurred. This statute is deemed sufficiently broad enough to embrace all proper claims of said State and Territory of Nevada."

Very respectfully, your obedient servant,

ROBERT T. LINCOLN,
Secretary of War.

Hon. S. B. MAXEY,
Of Committee on Military Affairs, United States Senate.

In accordance with this letter the Committee on Military Affairs reported back the bill referred to (S. 657), and asked that it be indefinitely postponed, and because of the explanation made by said committee, as follows, to wit :

It will be observed that it is deemed by the Department that the act approved June 27, 1882, is sufficiently broad to embrace all proper claims of Nevada, whether as State or Territory.

For convenience of reference the above act accompanies this report, and an examination thereof, and of the construction thereon, satisfies the committee that no additional legislation is necessary.

The State of Kansas presented her claim to Secretary Lincoln under this act, which claim was by him examined, audited, and allowed for almost exactly the sum that Kansas had actually expended for the use and benefit of the United States, and all of which allowance has since been paid to Kansas by the United States, and aggregating the sum of $332,308.13 (23 U. S. Stats., 474).

AFTER OVER FOUR YEARS DELAY, SUBSEQUENT TO THE PASSAGE OF THE ACT OF JUNE 27, 1882, THE UNITED STATES TAKES UP NEVADA'S CLAIM FOR EXAMINATION, WHEN THE VERY FIRST QUESTION RAISED IS ONE OF JURISDICTION, AND WHICH IS DECIDED AGAINST NEVADA.

After the passage of said act of August 4, 1886, the War Department detailed a board of three Army officers under Special Orders No. 232,

dated October 6, 1886, to proceed to examine the claims arising under the act of June 27, 1882, and in the manner contemplated and as provided for in said acts. The claim of the State of Nevada was the first claim submitted to and examined by said board. This board being in doubt whether, under the terms of said act of June 27, 1882, they could allow a re-imbursement to Nevada of the amount by her expended for interest and extra pay to her troops while in the military service of the United States, referred these two questions to the Secretary of War for his decision. On February 8, 1887, after argument was submitted to him in support of these two elements of Nevada's claim against the United States, the Secretary of War decided "that after a careful consideration of the subject" he was "of opinion that neither the extra pay nor the interest can, under the provisions of the act, be allowed," meaning the act of June 27, 1882, and refused the same (see appendix, Exhibit No. 14, page 83).

TWO SEPARATE REPORTS (A MAJORITY AND MINORITY) MADE BY THE ARMY BOARD OF WAR CLAIMS EXAMINERS, THE MINORITY REPORT ALLOWING ONLY ABOUT 2½ PER CENT. OF THE AMOUNT ACTUALLY EX-PENDED BY NEVADA, AND WHICH MINORITY REPORT IS APPROVED BY THE SECRETARY OF WAR.

It will be borne in mind that on January 26, 1884, Secretary Lincoln was of opinion that the act of June 27, 1882, was sufficiently broad to embrace all proper claims of the State of Nevada, and the Committee on Military Affairs, in consequence thereof, reported to the Senate that that committee was satisfied that no additional legislation was necessary in regard thereto, while Secretary Endicott, on February 8, 1887, decided that the claims for expenditure for interest and extra pay to said troops while in the service of the United States could not be allowed by him under said act, and further, by approving the award made by the minority examiner, and, as will hereinafter be more particularly referred to, also disallowed the amount expended by Nevada and by her paid as her costs for the enrollment of those very troops so called into the service of the United States.

The day following the decision of the Secretary of War, to wit, February 9, 1887, and contrary to a practice usual in similar cases, said board of Army officers, instead of submitting one report to the Secretary of War, submitted two separate and independent reports, one signed by the majority of said board and the other in the nature of a minority report. These two reports are submitted herewith, and printed in the Appendix, marked Exhibits Nos. 15, 16, and 17, pages 89 to 90.

The total of this particular claim of the State of Nevada so presented to said board amounted to $349,697.49. The amount thereof that was allowed in said minority report was only $8,559.61. This minority report was approved by the Secretary of War, thereby disallowing or suspending all of Nevada's claim except the paltry sum of about 2½ per cent. of the money actually expended by Nevada for troops called into the service of the United States and at the urgent solicitation of the Government of the United States in its hour of need, while this same board allowed nearly $1,000,000 of the claim of Texas, to wit, $927,242.30, being about 50 per cent. of the claim of that State of $1,867,259.13, as presented for re-imbursement for the expenses of her Indian wars, which occurred since the rebellion, and prosecuted chiefly, if not solely, for the protection of the inhabitants of the State of Texas. It is worthy of remark that no minority report was submitted in the case of Texas.

It will be observed by a perusal of the reports of the board of war claims examiners that the great mass of this claim of the State of Nevada for re-imbursement for moneys, expended under very extraordinary circumstances, was rejected by the board of examiners on either purely technical grounds or for an alleged want of jurisdiction to make an award under what has since been admitted and found to be the most restrictive act that was ever drawn since 1789 intended as an "act of relief."

Only $8,559.61 was finally awarded to Nevada by the Secretary of War.

The want of specific information on the part of the officer making the minority report which reduced the amount of the claim to the sum named may be shown in part by the mistakes made in reference to the statutes of Nevada, which are in several public libraries here, and could have been easily examined. For example, he seems to have inferred that the act of the Nevada legislature of March 4, 1865, was the first act of the Territory providing for the organization of its militia, whereas, as we have already shown, there was an elaborate act for that purpose passed by the Territorial legislature as early as November 28, 1861, and apparently on the assumption that there was no law creating the office of adjutant-general prior to 1865, and upon the fact that no evidence was furnished that Nevada previous to April 2, 1863, had soldiers, that therefore the salary of that officer ought not to commence prior to the time when the volunteers were actually called for service into the Army. But it will be observed that he was mistaken as to the time the law was passed creating the office of adjutant-general. The second section of the act of November 28, 1861, provides that—

The adjutant-general shall be appointed by the commander-in-chief, and shall hold his office for the term of two years. He shall be *ex officio* chief of staff, quartermaster-general, commissary-general, inspector-general, and chief of ordnance. He shall receive a salary of $1,000 annually, to be paid out of moneys appropriated for that purpose. He shall reside at the seat of government, and shall keep his office open for the transaction of business every day (Sundays excepted) from 10 o'clock a. m. to 3 o'clock p. m.

The minority examiner is again mistaken if he assumed that the secretary of state of Nevada became *ex officio* adjutant-general on March 3, 1866. It is true that an act devolving the duties of adjutant-general upon the secretary of state was passed on that date, but the second section of said act provides that—

This act shall take effect and be in force from and after the first day of January, 1867 (Stats. Nev., 1866, p. 206).

Thus it appears that the secretary of state did not in fact or in law become *ex officio* adjutant-general until January 1, 1867. The original section of the militia law of 1861 in regard to the office of adjutant-general was afterward amended, changing the length of time that officer was to hold office and increasing his salary to $2,000 per annum, but the abolishment of the office did not take effect until January, 1867.

PROBABLY CONFOUNDING THE ACT OF JUNE 27, 1882, WITH THE ACT OF JULY 27, 1861.

The minority examiner in terminating the salary of adjutant-general on August 20, 1866, undoubtedly had in mind the act of July 27, 1861, and not the act of June 27, 1882, under which last act alone said board was authorized to make an examination and award; otherwise he would not have limited the salary to August 20, 1866, the end of the war of the rebellion, as heretofore officially declared, but would have certainly al-

lowed Nevada a re-imbursement for the money actually paid by her as salary to that officer until his services terminated, and the Indian wars on the plains were actually suppressed and the office of adjutant-general abolished, which was done on December 31, 1866, since which time either the secretary of state or lieutenant-governor has acted as *ex officio* adjutant-general.

Attention is called to these discrepancies simply to show that the minority examiner apparently fell into error, unintentionally, of course, in his examination of the statutes of Nevada, or failed to consider all the circumstances under which this claim of the State arose. The majority of the board who made the same award and allowance as the minority, with the exception of $1,233.50 for salary of adjutant-general prior to the time when the troops were mustered in the service, made a very thorough examination of all the vouchers showing each item of expenditure made by the State, and this examination may be assumed as correct and as establishing the fact that the State expended all the moneys for which this claim is made, leaving the question as to the liability of the Government to re-imburse the State to the discretion of Congress. There is but one item stated in the account by the board of examiners which appears to have been charged by mistake. It was undoubtedly paid by the State, but if the board are correct, it was such a palpable mistake of the State officers that the State ought to lose it. It was a double charge for rent, amounting to $38.33. This amount, together with the $8,559.61 allowed by the minority of the board of examiners, and already paid to the State, making a total of $8,597.94, should be deducted from the claim now presented by the State. The State, however, should have the benefit of the fact that no other error in the accounts was discovered. All the other disallowed claims were rejected, not because the State did not pay the money, but because the board of examiners thought they were not authorized to allow the same under the act of June 27, 1882. We print in the appendix, Exhibit No. 17, page 92, the table accompanying report of the majority of the board of war claims examiners showing the amounts allowed and disallowed, together with the reasons therefor.

The question is now presented in this case whether it is the duty of the Government to re-imburse the State for moneys honestly expended, at the request of the United States, under circumstances which rendered it impossible for the Territory and State of Nevada to comply with such request without making the expenditures in question. It must be conceded that if the State or Territory made larger expenditures than would have been required to secure like services in any other section of the country, the services secured by these expenditures at the time, place, and under the circumstances were a necessity and could not have been furnished by the State on more favorable terms, and it seems that the State and Territory did not make any expenditure that appeared at the time unnecessary.

WHAT NEVADA THOUGHT WAS INTENDED BY CONGRESS TO BE AN ACT FOR HER RELIEF AND BENEFIT IS NOW FOUND TO BE AN ACT "SO WELL AND CAREFULLY AND CLOSELY GUARDED" BY RESTRICTIONS THAT WHEN CONSTRUED BY THOSE CALLED UPON TO EXECUTE IT, IS FOUND TO BE INOPERATIVE AS A RELIEF MEASURE, AND A PRACTICAL DENIAL OF JUSTICE.

We fully concur with the officer who made the minority report, that "the restrictions imposed in the second section of the act of June 27,

1882, have been complied with as far as was possible," whatever question there may be as to his complying with the provisions of the act itself. The argument that the Government might have bought supplies cheaper under its contract system than were furnished in Nevada is one which your committee are unwilling to urge under the circumstances. The Government was not situated so as to obtain troops or supplies by contract or otherwise, but was compelled to call upon the Territory to furnish both troops and supplies. All prices of all supplies, and also of all services, at that time in Nevada were on a gold basis, and coin was the only circulating medium. The roads over the mountains were blocked by snow and no considerable amount of supplies could be transported over them. The supplies in the Territory had been carried there during the previous summer for the use of the inhabitants, and the troops had to be furnished from the limited stock of individuals found in the Territory, and at a moment's notice. The Government could not wait to advertise. The overland mail route was closed and immediate action was required. The cheapest, most effective, and in fact the only immediate relief that could be had was furnished by the militia and volunteer troops of Nevada, who, leaving their workshops and employments of every character, and the high wages for their services, were organized and marched immediately in the direction of Salt Lake City to open the mail and emigrant route. They subsequently joined General Conner's forces from California, subdued the Indians, fortified Camp Douglas, overlooking Salt Lake City, and were in the field, subject to call, to go wherever ordered or needed.

PAYMENT BY THE UNITED STATES OF ABOUT 2½ PER CENT. OF THIS CLAIM ON ACCOUNT IS NOT A VALID BASIS FOR THE UNITED STATES TO REPUDIATE THE BALANCE THEREOF, OR TO REFUSE TO PAY THE SAME, AND SHOULD NOT, IN GOOD CONSCIENCE, BE EVER PLEADED BY AN HONEST DEBTOR, FOR WHOSE RELIEF AND AT WHOSE URGENT SOLICITATION SUCH DEBT WAS INCURRED.

The fact that a small fraction only of this claim has been allowed and paid on account, to wit, about 2½ per cent., and the great bulk thereof rejected for want of jurisdiction only, is no valid objection to an authorization by Congress for the payment of what is honestly due the State of Nevada, and for this there are numerous precedents, some of which are cited in the appendix in Exhibit No. 18, pages 96 to 98.

"INTEREST" PAID IN THIS CASE BY NEVADA IS IN REALITY, IN JUSTICE, IN REASON, AND IN LAW A PROPER PART OF THE DEBT DUE NEVADA BY THE UNITED STATES, THE PAYMENT OF WHICH, TOGETHER WITH THAT OF THE PRINCIPAL IS NECESSARY TO A COMPLETE INDEMNITY.

The embarrassments under which Nevada paid the principal of the money involved in this claim is shown by the enormous rates of interest which the Territory and State were compelled to pay in order to raise money to fully comply with these calls and requisitions made for troops and as hereinbefore recited. The rates of interest which were actually paid by Nevada are shown by the official statement of her controller and as furnished to the Secretary of the Treasury and the Secretary of War, as before stated, as follows:

S. Rep. 1286——2

ABSTRACT G.—*Showing the amount actually paid by the State of Nevada and as successor to the Territory of Nevada on account of interest money on disbursements and liabilities for Nevada volunteers in the service of the United States, and employed in the defense of the United States during the war of the rebellion.*

	Amount.
First –Interest paid on $46,950.12 from February 10, 1865, to March 3, 1866, at 2 per cent. per month .... [See acts legislature of Nevada for 1864-'65, page 82, act January 4, 1865.]	$11,925.33
Second—Interest paid on $46,950.12 from March 3, 1866, to May 30, 1867, at 15 per cent. per annum .... [See acts legislature of Nevada for 1866, page 47, act January 19, 1866.]	8,744.46
Third—Interest paid on $119,800.12 from May 30, 1867, to March 28, 1872, at 15 per cent. per annum .... [See acts legislature of Nevada for 1867, pages 50 and 65, act February 6, 1867.]	86,755.25
Fourth—Interest paid on $119,800.12 from March 28, 1872, to January 1, 1883, at 9½ per cent. per annum .... [See acts legislature of Nevada for 1871, page 84, act February 27, 1871.]	122,472.33
	229,897.37

Your committee, however, deem it unwise to establish a precedent under any circumstances, however extraordinary, and they admit that the recitals in support of this claim render it one extraordinary in character, of refunding interest to the full extent as paid by the Territory and State of Nevada, and as shown by the foregoing statement. The legal rate of interest of the Territory and State of Nevada was, at all the times herein stated, 10 per cent. per annum where no different rate was fixed by contract.

Your committee therefore do not feel warranted in recommending re imbursing the State of Nevada for a higher rate of interest than the legal rate fixed by her own statutes during the period of time in which these disbursements were made, and including the period up to the date of the re-imbursement of the principal by the United States, and for that reason they have incorporated in this bill, herewith reported, a provision that the aggregate of interest accruing to Nevada between the date of the expenditure by her of the principal and of the date of the re imbursement of such principal by the United States shall not exceed the actual amount of interest paid by the State and Territory, nor the amount of interest which would accrue to her on said principal if interest thereon were calculated during said period at the legal rate as established by the statutes of the Territory and State of Nevada. In support of the proposition that interest and principal are simply but two elements of one and the same unit and constituting a complete indemnity, your committee cite Senate Report 1069, made by Senator Spooner during the first session of the Forty-ninth Congress from the Committee on Claims (see appendix, Exhibit No. 19, pages 98 to 109.)

PRECEDENTS FOR THE PAYMENT TO STATES OF INTEREST ON THE PRINCIPAL BY THEM EXPENDED FOR THE USE AND BENEFIT OF THE UNITED STATES UNDER SIMILAR CIRCUMSTANCES.

The United States has in all cases, where the question has been properly presented, re imbursed States for interest paid by such States on moneys by them borrowed and expended for the purpose of either enrolling, subsisting, clothing, supplying, arming, equipping, paying, furnishing, or transporting volunteer and militia forces called into the service of the United States. If it be suggested that the bill under consideration providing for the payment of both principal and interest is against precedent, we answer that, in the opinion of your committee, it is the better practice to deal with a case in its entirety in a single act, and your committee state that there are abundant precedents for this practice, some of which your committee cite in the appendix,. Exhibit 20 on page 109.

We call particular attention to the precedents collected in the appendix, authorizing the payment of claims of States for interest on moneys by them expended for the use and benefit of the United States (see appendix, Exhibits Nos. 18, 19, 20, and 21, pages 96 to 149).

In addition to the authorities cited in the appendix in support of Nevada's claim for interest, your committee also refer to the case before the Second Comptroller of the Treasury in 1869, in which that officer made the following decision :

Interest can in no case be allowed by the accounting officer upon claims against the Government either in favor of a State or an individual. But in cases where the claimant has been compelled to pay interest for the benefit of the Government, it then becomes a part of the principal of his claim, and as such is allowable. Such is the case of a State which has been obliged to raise money upon interest for the suppression of hostilities against which the United States should protect her. In such cases the amount of interest actually and necessarily paid will be allowed, without reference to the rate of it (section 997, Dec. 2, Comp. Ed. 1869), p. 137).

This ruling is in harmony with a long line of precedents established by Congress, beginning in 1812, and printed in the appendix hereto attached and marked Exhibit Nos. 18 to 21, inclusive, pages 96 to 145.

In addition to the foregoing, your committee cite in support of Nevada's claim for interest the following, to wit:

1. Forty-eighth Congress, first session, House Report No. 1670, from Committee on Judiciary (see appendix, Exhibit 21, page 112).

2. Forty-eighth Congress, second session, House Report No. 1102, from Committee on War Claims (published in Exhibit No. 14, page 86).

3. Forty-ninth Congress, first session, Senate Report No. 183, from the Committee on Military Affairs (see appendix, Exhibit 21, page 135).

4. Forty-ninth Congress, first session, Senate Report No. 2, from the Committee on Claims (published in Exhibit No. 14, page 85).

5. Forty-ninth Congress, first session, House Report No. 303, from Committee on Claims (see appendix, Exhibit 21, page 119).

6. Forty-ninth Congress, first session, House Report No. 3126, from Committee on Claims (see appendix, Exhibit 21, page 120).

7. Fiftieth Congress, first session, Senate Report No. 518, from the Committee on Military Affairs (see appendix, Exhibit 21, page 138).

8. Fiftieth Congress, first session, House Report No. 309, from the Committee on War Claims (see appendix, Exhibit 21, page 137).

9. Fiftieth Congress, first session, House Report No. 1179, from the Committee on Claims (see appendix, Exhibit 21, page 145).

10. Fiftieth Congress, first session, House Report No. 2198, from the Committee on War Claims (see appendix, Exhibit 21 page 144).

The precedents cited or referred to in the appendix herewith abundantly establish the fact that the United States has paid the claims of States incurred under circumstances such as those in which Nevada ex-

pended her money for the benefit of the United States, and that in all
cases properly presented to Congress, where the States were compelled
to borrow money and pay interest thereon and expended the same for
the use and benefit of the United States, that either at the time of providing payment for the principal or subsequently the United States has
invariably assumed and paid such interest.

As before stated, the claim of the State of Nevada, provided for in
this bill, has been thoroughly examined by a board of Army officers
appointed for that purpose. The evidence upon which this claim was
founded was submitted to said board, and the evidences of payment
found by them to be correct; but said board of war-claims examiners,
while finding these facts, did not, under the very restrictive and prohibitory provisions and conditions of the acts of June 27, 1882, and
August 4, 1886, recommend an award to Nevada of the amount of money
which they found that Nevada had actually expended for the use and
benefit of the United States and in the manner as set forth in the claim
as presented by Nevada for the examination of and allowance by the
Treasury and War Departments; and under the terms of these acts,
as construed and declared by the Secretary of War, the proper accounting officers of the Treasury could not allow Nevada any sum,
either as principal or interest, not allowed by the War Department as
assisted by said Army board of war-claims examiners.

COST OF TRANSPORTATION OF ARMY SUPPLIES FROM FORT LEAVEN-WORTH WESTWARD IN 1864-'66.

It is evident that the supplies and services furnished could not at the
times and places have been obtained on more reasonable terms. And
in support of this statement your committee refer to the report of the
Secretary of War made during that period, and in reference to a region
of country much more favorably situated than was even Nevada at
that time, to wit:

The troops operating on the great western plains and in the mountain regions of
New Mexico, Colorado, Utah, and Idaho are supplied principally by the trains of the
Quartermaster's Department from depots established on the great routes of overland
travel, to which depots supplies are conveyed by contract. * * *

Travelers by the stage from Denver to Fort Leavenworth, a distance of 683 miles,
in the month of July, 1865, were never out of sight of wagons trains belonging either
to emigrants or to the merchants who transport supplies for the War Department,
for the Indian Department, and for the miners and settlers of the central Territories.

The cost of transportation of a *pound* of corn, hay, clothing, subsistence, lumber,
or any other necessary from Fort Leavenworth—

To Fort Riley is	$0.0244
To Fort Union, the depot for New Mexico	.1425
To Santa Fé, N. Mex	.1685
To Fort Kearny	.0644
To Fort Laramie	.1410
To Denver City, Colo	.1542
To Salt Lake City, Utah	.2784

The cost of a bushel of corn purchased at Fort Leavenworth and delivered at each
of these points was as follows:

Fort Riley	$2.79
Fort Union	9.44
Santa Fé	10.84
Fort Kearny	5.03
Fort Laramie	9.26
Denver City	10.05
Great Salt Lake City	17.00

(Secretary of War's report, 1865-'66, part 1, pages 23 and 112; also see General
Halleck to Adjutant-General, and General McDowell to Adjutant-General U. S. Army,
report of Secretary of War, October 18, 1866, pages 31 and 32.)

This table is cited to show the costs of maintaining troops in that section of the country, and also to show the comparative costs of furnishing troops and supplies in Nevada and the points immediately east thereof during the periods of time involved herein.

The details concerning the peculiar and difficult and expensive service on the plains and mountains by the troops doing military service, similar in all respects to those performed by these Nevada volunteers, are fully set forth in the report of the Secretary of War respecting the protection of the overland mail and emigrant route to the Pacific from the molestations and depredations by hostile Indians, and set forth in Ex. Docs. Nos. 9 to 24, second session Thirty-ninth Congress, 1866–'67.

CONCLUSIONS AND RECOMMENDATIONS.

Nevada has not demanded a bounty, nor presented a claim against the United States for re-imbursement of any expenditure she did not in good faith actually make for the use and b. nefit of the United States, and made, too, only subsequent to the date of the aforesaid appeal of Secretary Seward to the nation, and made, too, in consequence of said appeal and of the subsequent calls and requisitions made upon her then scanty resources and sparse population, and wherein the good faith of the United States was to be relied upon to make to her ungrudgingly a just re-imbursement whenever the United States found itself in a condition to redeem all its obligations.

Nevada has been diligent in making her claim known to Congress, but she has not with an indecorous speed demanded her pound of flesh, but has waited long and patiently, believing upon the principle that the higher obligations between States, like those among men, are not always "set down in writing, signed and sealed in the form of a bond, but reside rather in honor," and that the obligation of the United States due her in this case was as sacred as if it had originally been in the form of a 4 per cent. United States bond, now being redeemed by the United States at $1.27 upon each $1 of this particular form of its unpaid obligations.

Nevada has not solicited any charity in this case, but, on the contrary, by numerous petitions and memorials she has respectfully represented to Congress why the taxes heretofore levied upon her people and paid out of her own treasury to her volunteer troops in gold and silver coin to aid the United States at its own solicitation to protect itself and maintain the general welfare should be now returned to her by the General Government.

Congress should not forget that during the long period of the nation's peril the citizens of Nevada, like those of California (when not engaged in the military or naval service of the United States) not only guarded the principal gold and silver mines of the country then discovered, and prevented them from falling into the hands of the public enemy, but also worked them so profitably for the general welfare as to enable the United States to make it possible to resume specie payment, and to redeem its bonds at 27 per cent. above par, and to repay all its money-lenders at a high rate of interest, and that, too, not in the depreciated currency with which it paid Nevada's volunteer troops, but in gold coin of standard value.

As these expenditures were honestly made by the Territory and State of Nevada, your committee do not think that, under all the peculiar and exceptional circumstances of this case, the action of the Territory and State of Nevada should be hewn too nicely or too hypercritically by the United States at this late date. These expenditures were

all made in perfect good faith and for patriotic purposes, and secured effectual aid to the United States which otherwise could not have been obtained without a much larger expenditure. The State of Nevada in good faith assumed and paid all the obligations of the Territory of Nevada to aid the United States, and issued and sold its own bonds for their payment, upon which bonds it has paid interest until the present time. The only question now for consideration is, shall the United States in equal good faith and under all the circumstances herein recited relieve the State of Nevada from this obligation, or shall the United States insist and require it to be paid by the people of that State alone?

The majority of the committee therefore recommend the passage of the bill herewith reported.

APPENDIX.

EXHIBIT No. 1.

CIRCULAR LETTER OF WILLIAM H. SEWARD, SECRETARY OF STATE, ADDRESSED TO AND CALLING ON ALL THE LOYAL STATES AND TERRITORIES TO AID IN SUPPRESSING REBELLION.

DEPARTMENT OF STATE,
Washington, October 14, 1861.

His Excellency —— ——,
Governor of the State of ——:

SIR: The present insurrection had not even revealed itself in arms when disloyal citizens hastened to foreign countries to invoke their intervention for the overthrow of the Government and the destruction of the Federal Union. These agents are known to have made their appeals to some of the more important states without success. It is not likely, however, that they will remain content with such refusals. Indeed, it is understood that they are industriously endeavoring to accomplish their disloyal purposes by degrees and by indirection. Taking advantage of the embarrassments of agriculture, manufacture, and commerce in foreign countries, resulting from the insurrection they have inaugurated at home, they seek to involve our common country in controversies with states with which every public interest and every interest of mankind require that it shall remain in relations of peace, amity, and friendship. I am able to state, for your satisfaction, that the prospect of any such disturbance is now less serious than it has been at any previous period during the course of the insurrection.

It is nevertheless necessary now, as it has hitherto been, to take every precaution that is possible to avert the evils of foreign war to be superinduced upon those of civil commotion, which we are endeavoring to cure. One of the most obvious of such precautions is that our ports and harbors on the seas and lakes should be put in a condition of complete defense, for any nation may be said to voluntarily incur danger in tempestuous seasons when it fails to show that it has sheltered itself on every side from which the storm might possibly come.

The measures which the Executive can adopt in this emergency are such only as Congress has sanctioned and for which it has provided. The President is putting forth the most diligent efforts to execute these measures, and we have the great satisfaction of seeing that these efforts, seconded by the favor, aid, and support of a loyal, patriotic, and self-sacrificing people, are rapidly bringing the military and naval forces of the United States into the highest state of efficiency.

But Congress was chiefly absorbed during its recent extra session with these measures and did not provide as amply as could be wished for the fortification of our sea and lake coasts.

In previous wars, loyal States have applied themselves by independent and separate activity to support and aid the Federal Government in its arduous responsibilities. The same disposition has been manifested in a degree eminently honorable by all the loyal States during the present insurrection.

In view of this fact, and relying upon the increase and continuance of the same disposition on the part of the loyal States, the President has directed me to invite your consideration to the subject of the improvement and perfection of the defenses of the State over which you preside, and to ask you to submit the subject to the consideration of the legislature, when it shall have assembled.

Such proceedings by the State would require only a temporary use of its means. The expenditures ought to be made the subject of conference with the Federal authorities.

Being thus made, with the concurrence of the Government for general defense, there is every reason to believe that Congress would sanction what the State should do, and would provide for its re-imbursement. Should these suggestions be accepted, the President will direct proper agents of the Federal Government to confer with you and to superintend, direct, and conduct the prosecution of the system of defense of your State.

I have the honor to be, sir, your obedient servant,

WILLIAM H. SEWARD.

23

EXHIBIT No. 2.

RESOLUTIONS OF THE LEGISLATIVE ASSEMBLY OF NEVADA TERRITORY PLEDGING FULL SUPPORT TO THE GOVERNMENT IN THE UNION CAUSE.

Be it resolved by the governor and legislative assembly of the Territory of Nevada, as follows : That whereas the peace and harmony of our beloved Union, after years of prosperity unprecedented in the annals of national history, have been suddenly disturbed, and revolutionary theories destructive of all constitutional liberty, heretofore unthought of, are now unblushingly announced and advocated; and whereas the first legislative assembly ever convened within this Territory, which owes so much to the fostering care of our maternal Government, is now in session: Therefore,

Resolved, That the legislative assembly fully concur in the just and patriotic sentiments so eloquently expressed by the governor in his message, and that we earnestly sympathize with and cordially and heartily approve the national administration in its efforts to maintain the integrity of the Government and the perpetuity of the Union.

Resolved, That we deem a full, fair, and candid expression of our sentiments as not only highly proper, but also demanded by the exigencies of the times.

Resolved, That the people of the United States owe paramount allegiance to the national, and a subordinate allegiance to their State governments.

Resolved, That the present efforts of traitors and rebels to demolish the Government and to sever the union of the States is a lamentable illustration of the fruits of reckless ambition and the insane folly that would carry us back to barbarism for the sake of retaining in rebel hands the spoils of office and the brief prerogatives of power.

Resolved, That the doctrine that a majority should rule is the only one upon which a revolution can be avoided after the recurrence of each election, and that it is safer to trust to the intelligence of an educated community of voters than to force of arms.

Resolved, That this Government was formed for the purpose of a more perfect union, and declared to be so formed by the people of the United States, and, therefore, that the doctrine that a State may secede from the same is not only vitally at war with the principles upon which it was founded, but also a dangerous heresy.

Resolved, That the formidable rebellion which now seeks to destroy the best political system on earth has no terrors for the loyal and true citizen ; that the Government whose infancy has been nursed in the tempest and rocked by the whirlwinds of national strife, and whose young vigor and mature strength has thus far been more than a match for its enemies at home and abroad, is not destined to expire ingloriously at the hands of rebels and traitors.

Resolved, That the readiness with which the people have everywhere responded to the call of the Government, and the alacrity with which men and money have been furnished for the impending struggle, give cheering promise of future victory and final triumph.

Resolved, That the Territory of Nevada sends greeting to her sister Territories and the whole family of States, and pledges the strength of her mountains, the wealth of her mines, the unswerving loyalty of the popular heart, and the intense energy of her people to the service of our common country in its present hour of trial.

Resolved, That our Delegate to Congress, Hon. John Cradlebaugh, is hereby requested to present the foregoing resolutions to the President, and that he have full authority at all times to pledge Nevada Territory for her full share in the existing struggle for the perpetuity of the Union and the integrity of the Government.

(Adopted November 25, 1861. See Laws Nevada Territory, 1861, p. 616.)

EXHIBIT No. 3.

MISCELLANEOUS CORRESPONDENCE AS TO MILITARY OPERATIONS IN NEVADA.

HEADQUARTERS DEPARTMENT OF THE PACIFIC,
San Francisco, Cal., May 4, 1863.

His Excellency O. CLEMENS,
  Governor of Nevada Territory, Carson City, Nev. :

SIR: The examination of David McGowan, E. B. Zabriskie, John H. Dalton, Almond B. Wells, and William H. Dodds, before the board instituted for that purpose, is satisfactory to the general commanding the department.

The general desires you to report by telegraph as soon as the companies are in readiness to be mustered in, when an officer will be sent to Fort Churchill for that purpose. Inclosed you will receive the order prescribing the organization of cavalry and infantry, which you will see differs from that stated in your proclamation.

Very respectfully, your obedient servant,

R. C. DRUM,
Assistant Adjutant-General.

Official copy :

J. C. KELTON,
Colonel, Assistant Adjutant-General.

HEADQUARTERS DEPARTMENT OF THE PACIFIC,
San Francisco, Cal., May 15, 1863.

GOVERNOR OF NEVADA TERRITORY,
(Through Commanding Officer Fort Churchill, Nev.) :

SIR : The examination of Noyes Baldwin and Joseph A. Mathewson for commission in Nevada Territory contingent, is satisfactory to the general commanding.

Very respectfully, your obedient servant,

R. C. DRUM,
Assistant Adjutant-General.

Official copy :

J. C. KELTON,
Colonel, Assistant Adjutant-General.

WAR DEPARTMENT,
Washington City, March 11, 1882.

SIR : I have the honor to acknowledge the receipt of your letter of the 16th of January last, inclosing S. R. 13, Forty-seventh Congress, first session, a " joint resolution to authorize the Secretary of War to ascertain and report to Congress the amount of money expended and indebtedness assumed by the State of Nevada in repelling invasions, suppressing insurrection and Indian hostilities, enforcing the laws, and protecting the public property," and requesting full information concerning the matters mentioned in said resolution.

In reply, I beg to invite your attention to the inclosed report on the subject, dated the 25th ultimo, from the Adjutant-General, and accompanying copies of all correspondence of record in this Department relating to matters referred to in the resolution.

Very respectfully, your obedient servant,

ROBERT T. LINCOLN,
Secretary of War.

Hon. L. F. GROVER,
Subcommittee of the Committee on Military Affairs,
United States Senate.

WAR DEPARTMENT, ADJUTANT-GENERAL'S OFFICE,
Washington, D. C., February 25, 1882.

SIR : I have the honor to return herewith a letter of the Hon. L. F. Grover, of Senate Committee on Military Affairs, of the 16th ultimo, inclosing a copy of a joint resolution (S. R. 13, Forty-seventh Congress, first session) " to authorize the Secretary of War to ascertain and report to Congress the amount of money expended and indebtedness assumed by the State of Nevada in repelling invasions, suppressing insurrection and Indian hostilities, enforcing the laws, and protecting the public property," and to report the following concerning the matters referred to in the resolution :

It appears from the records of this office that one regiment of cavalry and one battalion of infantry were raised in the Territory of Nevada, under authority granted by the Secretary of War in the early part of 1863.

The following statement shows the dates of musters in and out and the strength of the companies of the organizations referred to :

First Regiment Nevada Cavalry Volunteers, composed of six companies.

Company.	When mustered in.	Strength.		When mustered out.
		Commis-sioned.	Enlisted.	
A	August 9, 1863	2	82	July 12, 1866.
B	June 22, 1863	3	82	July 12, 1866.
C	December 24, 1863	2	61	July 12, 1866.
D	September 25, 1863	3	84	Nov. 18, 1865.
E	April 7, 1864	3	83	Nov. 18, 1865.
F	April 4, 1864	3	79	July 21, 1866.
	Field and staff	4	· 3	
	Recruits enlisted subsequent to muster-in of companies		307	

First Battalion Nevada Infantry Volunteers, composed of four companies.

Company.	When mustered in.	Strength.		When mustered out.
		Commis-sioned.	Enlisted.	
A	June 30, 1864	3	86	Dec. 22, 1865
B	......do	3	91	Dec. 15, 1865
C	......do	3	89	Dec. 23, 1865
D*	Recruits enlisted subsequent to muster-in of companies.		100	

* Company D was not organized; the men recruited for it were transferred to the other three companies in July or August, 1865.

The Territory of Nevada is credited on the records of the late Provost-Marshal-General's office with having furnished 1,180 three years' volunteers during the late war.

The records of this office fail to show that any troops, volunteer or militia, other than the cavalry regiment and infantry battalion before referred to, were raised in either the Territory or State of Nevada during the late war of the rebellion or since, or that any Nevada troops excepting those named performed military service of any kind for the United States in said Territory or State.

Neither does it appear that any payment has been made by the United States to the Territory or State of Nevada, nor that any demand for such payment has been made on account of money expended or indebtedness assumed by the State in repelling invasions, suppressing insurrection and Indian hostilities, etc.

Some individual claims were made for expenses incurred in recruiting Nevada volunteers—that is, claims for re-imbursement for subsistence and transportation furnished and for rent of rendezvous, etc.— a few which have been allowed, and paid out of the appropriation for "collecting, drilling, and organizing volunteers."

Copies of all correspondence of record in this office relating to the matters named in the resolution are hereto appended.

I am, sir, very respectfully, your obedient servant,

R. C. DRUM,
Adjutant-General.

The SECRETARY OF WAR.

[Office acting assistant provost-marshal-general of California and Nevada Territory.]

SAN FRANCISCO, CAL., *April 11, 1864.*

Col. JAMES B. FRY,
  Provost-Marshal-General, Washington, D. C.

[Extract.]

*   *   *   *   *   *   *

Whilst on this subject, I would state that there is a regiment of infantry authorized for Nevada. Six companies of cavalry have been raised. I would suggest that four more companies of cavalry be authorized; that the recruits now belonging to the infantry regiment be transferred to them, and that the infantry regiment be disbanded. I do not believe it can ever be raised, and it is creating enormous expenses.

* * * * * * *

Your obedient servant,

JNO. S. MASON,
Brig. Gen. Vols., Supt. Vol. Rec'l'g Service.

Respectfully submitted to General Halleck, chief of staff, for his views as to the propriety of adopting the suggestions of General Mason.

I have no doubt General Mason is right as to the expense of this long-continued effort to raise an infantry regiment, but I do not know the number or kind of troops equired there.

JAMES B. FRY,
Provost-Marshal-General.

MAY 13, 1864.

I do not understand how converting infantry into cavalry *saves* expenses, but quite the contrary. Why not consolidate the infantry already raised into a small battalion for immediate service? This would be more economical than increasing the cavalry force.

H. W. HALLECK,
Major-General, Chief of Staff.

MAY 17, 1864.

————

SPECIAL ORDERS, }   WAR DEPARTMENT, ADJUTANT-GENERAL'S OFFICE,
No. 181.   *Washington, May 19, 1864.*

[Extract.]

* * * * * * *

23. The recruitment of regiment of volunteer infantry authorized to be raised in the Territory of Nevada will be discontinued upon the receipt of this order, and that portion of the regiment which at that date may be recruited will be consolidated into as many companies of maximum strength as the number enlisted will permit, and the battalion thus formed will be reported for immediate service.

The superintendent of recruiting service is charged with the immediate execution of this order.

* * * * * * *

By order of the Secretary of War.

E. D. TOWNSEND,
Assistant Adjutant-General.

————

HEADQUARTERS DEPARTMENT OF THE PACIFIC,
San Francisco, April 30, 1864.

ADJUTANT-GENERAL, U. S. ARMY,
Washington, D. C.:

SIR: I have six companies of cavalry, Nevada Territory Volunteers, mustered into service. Two of these companies I sent to Camp Douglas, Utah Territory, last October; the remaining four are at Fort Churchill. Only one of the companies at Churchill has been mounted. My design was to send all the Nevada cavalry to Utah; but the threatening aspect of our foreign relations, indicating the propriety of my holding all my available force well in hand and prepare for concentration on the Pacific coast, has caused me to hesitate until the policy of my Government is known. In consequence of the enormous cost of forage at Fort Churchill, I have suspended the purchase of horses for mounting the three cavalry companies now there until their destination is determined on. •

Under the call I made on the governor of Nevada Territory for a regiment of infantry, two hundred men have been enrolled; they are at Fort Churchill. The governor is quite confident of his ability to complete the organization of the regiment.

During the quiet and peaceful times on this coast we can not expect to raise many volunteers; but if we should have foreign war, there will be no lack of men.

Very respectfully, your obedient servant,

G. WRIGHT,
Brigadier-General, U. S. Army, Commanding.

WAR DEPARTMENT, *Washington City, March 24, 1888.*

SIR: In response to your letter of the 21st ultimo, requesting such information of record in the Department as relates to the soldiers enrolled and paid by either the Territory or State of Nevada during the war of the rebellion, I have the honor to invite attention to the inclosed report of the 22d instant, and its accompanying paper, from the Adjutant-General's Office, which, it is believed, afford the information desired.

Very respectfully, your obedient servant,

WILLIAM C. ENDICOTT,
Secretary of War.

Hon. WM. M. STEWART,
United States Senate.

WAR DEPARTMENT, ADJUTANT-GENERAL'S OFFICE,
Washington, March 22, 1888.

SIR: I have the honor to return herewith a letter of Hon. William M. Stewart, United States Senate, dated the 21st ultimo, requesting to be furnished with such information as the records of the Department afford relative to soldiers enrolled and paid by either the Territory or State of Nevada during the war of the rebellion, and to report as follows:

The records of this office show that one battalion of cavalry, composed of six companies, and one battalion of infantry, composed of four companies, were raised in the Territory of Nevada under authority granted by the Secretary of War. The cavalry battalion was mustered into the military service of the United States, by companies, from August 9, 1863, to April 7, 1864, to serve three years, and the infantry battalion was mustered into the same service on June 30, 1864, for the same period.

Herewith are copies of letters of Lieut. Col. Milo George, First Battalion Nevada Cavalry, addressed to the adjutant-general of the State of Nevada, dated April 3, and May 3, 1865, referring, respectively, to an appropriation made by the legislature of Nevada Territory in 1863, of $5 per month to each enlisted man of Nevada volunteers, and to an act of the legislature of the State of Nevada, approved March 11, 1865, to encourage enlistments and provide bounties and extra pay for volunteer troops called into the United States service from Nevada.

Nothing further is found of record in regard to soldiers enrolled and paid by either that Territory or State during the war of the rebellion.

I am, sir, very respectfully, your obedient servant,

J. C. KELTON,
Assistant Adjutant-General.

The SECRETARY OF WAR.

HEADQUARTERS FIRST BATTALION NEVADA VOLUNTEER CAVALRY,
Camp Douglas, Utah, April 3, 1865.

GENERAL: Being desirous of obtaining some information with regard to the appropriation made by the legislature of Nevada Territory in 1863, of $5 per month to each enlisted man of the Nevada volunteers, I take this opportunity to address you on the subject.

I have been laboring under the impression that this appropriation was to be divided among the troops at the end of the year 1864, but as I am not positive with regard to the matter, you would confer a favor upon this battalion by giving the necessary information.

I am informed that certain companies of my battalion have not reported to the adjutant-general the number of their command, in accordance with the law making the appropriation of $5 per month, from the fact that the adjutant-general did not notify them of the necessity of so doing.

I am, very respectfully, your obedient servant,

MILO GEORGE,
Lieutenant-Colonel, First Battalion Nevada Volunteer Cavalry.

To Brig. Gen. J. G. CRADLEBAUGH,
Adjutant-General State of Nevada, Carson City, Nev.

HEADQUARTERS FIRST BATTALION NEVADA VOLUNTEER CAVALRY,
Camp Douglas, Utah, May 3, 1865.

GENERAL: I have just read an act passed by the legislature of Nevada and approved March 11, 1865, "to encourage enlistments and provide bounties and extra pay for our volunteer soldiers called into the service of the United States," and as part of section 2 of said act provided "that no such allowance or monthly pay as hereinbefore provided for shall be made for any service in the Army of the United States rendered prior to the 20th day of February, 1864," as I construe it, cuts off all company commanders whose companies were organized previous to that time from receiving the benefit ($10 premium) for procuring recruits.

You will see by roster forwarded to-day that Companies A, B, C, and D were organized previous to February 20, 1864; consequently, as I interpret this law, are not entitled to the benefit of this act as far as the $10 premium is concerned, but as I feel satisfied this law was made for the benefit of all Nevada volunteers, I wish to lay this matter before you, hoping that your decision or interpretation may be such as to include, in this respect, my whole command.

I do not think that the Nevada legislature intended to do injustice to any officer or enlisted man who was patriotic enough to volunteer to serve in the "Sage Brush" as they all have done who entered the service from that State, but think there must be some mistake in printing this law, as it really cuts off the most deserving ones from receiving the benefit which is justly due them.

Organizations started since February 20, 1864, have really not expended one-fourth the amount in filling their commands up to maximum strength that those did who commenced previous to that time, from the fact that, since that time, times have been very dull, and consequently recruits were easily procured; again, they have had the benefit of the provost-marshal's assistance, which has lessened expenses nearly one-half.

By giving me the proper interpretation of this law you will confer a favor upon my command which will be duly appreciated.

I am, very respectfully, your obedient servant,

MILO GEORGE,
Lieut. Col., First Batt. Nevada Vol. Cav. Commanding.

Brig. Gen. J. G. CRADLEBAUGH,
Adjutant-General State of Nevada, Carson City, Nev.

EXHIBIT No. 4.

MEMORIAL OF THE STATE OFFICERS OF NEVADA SHOWING THE MODE OF AND THE MANNER OF THE PAYMENT FOR THE ENROLLMENT OF TROOPS BY NEVADA.

To the Senate and House of Representatives
of the United States of America in Congress assembled :

Your memorialists, now the State executive officers of the State of Nevada (the legislature of Nevada not being now in session), most respectfully represent to your honorable bodies that the State of Nevada has heretofore presented a claim to the United States for expenses by her incurred and by her paid as "costs, charges, and expenses properly incurred for enrolling" her military forces during the war of the rebellion, in response to and under requisitions made by the officer commanding the Military Department of the Pacific, and which "costs, charges, and expenses" so incurred and paid by Nevada aggregate the sum of $11,840 for enrolling 1,184 men, preliminary to their being mustered into the military service of the United States.

A claim for re-imbursement by the United States for the aforesaid expenditure has been presented by the State of Nevada to the United States, and payment thereof has been refused, and because its examining and accounting and auditing officers seem to have regarded this expenditure simply as a bounty or gratuity paid by Nevada to the officers of her military forces who enrolled said 1,184 men.

Nevada selected as her enrolling agents those officers of her military forces who were to be the commanding officers of the men who might be thereafter enrolled; and there can not be any valid question as to the wisdom or economy of such a course as adopted and uniformly pursued by Nevada, and especially when we consider the importance of each commanding officer being perfectly familiar with the qualifications of those he was to command in the field both as to their mental and physical fitness.

This method of enrollment as adopted by Nevada, and seeming no doubt to her, at the time, as the most ready and economical one for putting her troops in the field for the United States military service, in obedience to requisitions made upon her, was the one followed in all cases; and this claim for re-imbursement by the United States for the "costs, charges, and expenses" so incurred was in lieu of all other "costs, charges, and expenses" that would have to be incurred and as incident to said enrollment—such, for instance, as rent, fuel, furniture, salaries of enrolling officers, subsistence, and all the other detailed and expensive paraphernalia which pertain to the regular military recruiting or enrolling office of a State or of the United States, and such as the United States would herself have been compelled to incur if she had invoked or exercised her own Federal military machinery for the same purpose in the State of Nevada.

No express method of enrolling having been designated to Nevada by the United States, she was left to adopt that method of organizing, collecting, and enrolling her military forces to meet the requisitions so made upon her at the time, and such as appeared to her to be the wisest and the most practicable.

To provide for and to pay the "costs, charges, and expenses" so incurred and to be incurred by Nevada on account of said enrollment, the legislature of Nevada passed a law on March 11, 1865, which provided substantially that each enrolling or recruiting agent of her army intended by her for the military service of the United States should be allowed for all expenses of said enrollment $10 per capita. The law is as follows, to-wit:

"*The people of the State of Nevada, represented in senate and assembly, do enact as follows:*

"SECTION 1. A sum not exceeding $100,000 is hereby appropriated and set aside, to constitute a separate fund to be known as the 'soldiers' fund,' for the purpose of paying a compensation to the soldiers of the companies of Nevada volunteers already raised in the Territory and in the State of Nevada, and to be raised in this State, for the service of the United States, to aid in repelling invasion, suppressing insurrections, enforcing the laws, and protecting the public property, in addition to the pay allowed them by the United States.

"SEC. 2. There shall be paid out of the fund created and set apart by the first section of this act *   *   * a bounty of $10, to be paid to the captain or commanding officer of any company for every recruit by him enlisted and subsequently mustered into the service of the United States: *Provided,* That the provisions of this section shall not be deemed applicable to any soldier who may be drafted, or enlisted as a substitute, or any person drafted into the Army of the United States. *   *   *

"SEC. 3. The captains or commanding officers of companies of Nevada volunteers, raised, or to be raised, for service in the Army of the United States, shall, before such officers, as recruiting agents of the Army, can be entitled to secure the benefits of this act, file in the office of the adjutant-general their affidavit, setting forth the number and names of recruits enlisted by them, and accepted by the proper medical examiners (who shall in each case be named), and sworn into the service; and further setting forth that no affidavit of the same character, for the same enlisted men has heretofore been made or filed. The adjutant-general of the State is hereby authorized and directed to certify to the controller of State the number of men enlisted by each captain or commanding officer of a company, whenever the affidavit herein required is filed in his office, indorsed by the provost-marshal of this State or the commanding officer of the post where the enlisted men referred to and enumerated in the affidavit may have been rendezvoused on enlistment. Upon the filing of the adjutant-general's certificate, above required, in the office of the controller of State, the controller shall make out a copy of said certificate, and forward the same to the State board of examiners, and if the State board of examiners shall indorse the certificate as 'approved,' then the controller shall draw his warrant upon the fund herein constituted for the sum set forth in the certificate of the adjutant general in favor of the officers, or their legal assignees, named in the certificate, for the sums respectively set forth to be due them.

"SEC. 6. For the purpose of carrying into effect the provisions of this act and providing for the fund created by section 1 of this act, the treasurer of the State of Nevada shall cause to be prepared bonds of the State to the amount of $100,000, in sums of $500 each, redeemable at the office of the treasurer of the State on the 1st day of July, 1870. The said bonds shall bear interest, payable semi-annually, at the rate of 10 per cent. per annum from the date of their issuance, which interest shall be due and payable at the office of the treasurer of this State on the 1st day of January and July of each year: *Providing,* That the first payment of interest shall not be made sooner than the 1st day of January, in the year of our Lord 1866. These said bonds shall be signed by the governor and countersigned by the controller and indorsed by the treasurer of State, and shall have the seal of the State affixed thereto. Such bonds shall be issued from time to time as they may be required for use. The expense of preparing such bonds and disposing of the same shall be audited as a claim against the soldiers' fund created by this act.

"SEC. 10. For the payment of the principal and interest of the bonds issued under this act there shall be levied and collected annually, until the final payment and redemption of the same and in the same manner as other State revenue is or may be directed by law to be levied and collected annually, a tax of 25 cents in gold and silver coin of the United States, on each $100 of taxable property in the State, in addition to the other taxes for State purposes, and the fund derived from this tax shall be set apart and applied to the payment of interest accruing on the bonds herein provided for and the final redemption of the principal of said bonds; and the public faith of the State of Nevada is hereby pledged for the payment of the bonds issued by virtue of this act and the interest thereon, and, if necessary, to provide other and ample means for the payment thereof." (Statutes of Nevada, March 11, 1865, pages 389–393.)

This small sum of $10 per capita, when the peculiar condition of Nevada at that time is considered, in connection with her then limited and expensive means of travel, which was then exclusively by wagon or horseback, and before any railroads were built in this State, will be considered to be not exorbitant, but, as your memorialists now submit, the same was and is very reasonable.

True, the act of the legislature termed this $10 per capita for enrollment a "bounty" to the captains or commanding officers who might organize a company to be thereafter mustered into the service of the United States, yet as a matter of fact it was not a bounty in the sense of a gratuity and as is frequently used by the United States as meaning money in addition to the pay and allowances as set forth in the agreement with her commanding officers and enlisted men about to enter her military service; on the contrary, it was a lump compensation paid or to be paid by the State to her recruiting or enrolling officers in lieu of all other expenses or compensation for organizing its military forces and such as have been hereinbefore recited, and covered and was intended to cover all expense of travel, subsistence, lodging, and other incidental expenses, and such as United States recruiting and enrolling officers might properly incur in getting together and preparing men for the military service of the State and of the United States.

Your memorialists call attention to the fact that on March 11, 1865, Nevada did not even have in her treasury the money with which to pay this disbursement, but in section 6 of said act she was compelled to issue and to sell her own State bonds with which to raise money to pay this and other expenses of a military character in order to aid in defraying the State expenses in a time of war.

Not only this, but in section 10 of said act Nevada levied a tax in gold or silver coin of the United States upon every $100 taxable property in the State of Nevada, in addition to other taxes for State purposes, to create a fund with which to pay said expenses, and which tax was to continue until all of said bonds were wholly paid and fully redeemed; and in addition thereto the public faith of Nevada was pledged to pay said bonds and interest thereon, and, if necessary, to provide other and ample means for the payment thereof.

The public faith of Nevada was therefore pledged for the benefit of the United States, and at a time when the public credit of the United States was itself put to the test and its paper largely depreciated in parts of the country outside the limits of Nevada.

Wherefore, your memorialists (the legislature not now being in session) believing that if the attention of Congress were respectfully and properly invited to this matter it would not permit this expenditure to be repudiated by being disallowed or payment refused, now, therefore, petition your honorable bodies to re-imburse Nevada in the sum of $11,840 so by her expended and paid as "costs, charges, and expenses," and by her incurred for enrolling 1,184 men for the military service of the United States, and who did perform active United States military service during the war of the rebellion wherever their military services were needed.

Respectfully,

C. C. STEVENSON, *Governor.*
H. C. DAVIS, *Lieutenant-Governor and Adjutant-General.*
JOHN M. DORMER, *Secretary of State.*
J. F. HALLOCK, *State Controller.*
GEORGE TUFLY, *State Treasurer.*
JOHN F. ALEXANDER, *Attorney-General.*
JOHN E. JONES, *Surveyor-General.*
W. C. DOVEY, *Superintendent Public Instruction.*
J. C. HARLOW, *Superintendent State Printing.*

EXHIBIT No. 5.

ACT OF THE LEGISLATIVE ASSEMBLY OF NEVADA TERRITORY PROVIDING FOR COMPENSATION TO COMMANDING OFFICERS FOR THEIR COSTS FOR THE ENROLLING VOLUNTEERS AND EXTRA PAY TO VOLUNTEERS, ETC.

AN ACT to encourage enlistments and give bounties and extra pay to our volunteer soldiers.

Be it enacted by the governor and legislative assembly of the Territory of Nevada, as follows:

SECTION 1. A sum not exceeding one hundred thousand dollars is hereby appropriated and set aside to constitute a separate fund, to be known as the soldiers' fund, for the purpose of paying a compensation to the soldiers of the companies of Nevada volunteers already raised and to be raised in this Territory for the service of the United States to aid in repelling invasion, suppressing insurrections, enforcing the laws, and protecting the public property, in addition to the pay allowed them by the United States. All liabilities created by this act shall be paid out of this fund.

Sec. 2. There shall be paid out of the fund created and set apart by the first section of this act, to each and every enlisted soldier of the companies of the Nevada volunteers raised or hereafter to be raised in this Territory under the requisition made on the governor thereof by the officer commanding the Department of the Pacific, for one regiment of volunteer infantry and two companies of cavalry, and the proclamation of the said governor calling for the raising of the same, issued on the fourth day of December, anno Domini eighteen hundred and sixty-three, for the service of the United States, to aid in repelling invasion, suppressing insurrection, enforcing the laws, and preserving and protecting the public property, the sum of five dollars per month, and a bounty of ten dollars to the captain or commanding officer of any company for every recruit by him or his authority enlisted.

Sec. 3. The captain or commanding officers of companies of Nevada volunteers, raised or to be raised under the requisition and proclamation noted in section two of this act, shall, before said enlisted men or officers shall be entitled to receive the benefit of this act, file a certificate, signed by the adjutant and commanding officer at the post at Fort Churchill, addressed to the adjutant-general of the Territory, to the effect that the number of men mentioned therein have been enlisted by the captain or commanding officer therein mentioned, or by his authority; that they have passed due medical examination, and been sworn into the service, and that no certificate of the kind has been issued for the men mentioned therein. Upon the filing of the before-mentioned certificate in the office of the adjutant-general of this Territory, the adjutant-general shall make a requisition upon the Territorial auditor, who shall draw his warrant upon the Territorial treasurer, in favor of the adjutant-general, for a sum sufficient to cover the whole amount of money due said officers for bounty, viz, ten dollars for each enlisted soldier of the Nevada volunteers for the number of men mentioned in said certificate, which sum the adjutant general shall pay, or cause to be paid, to the officer in whose favor the certificate is drawn.

Sec. 4. In addition to the bounty herein provided for, there shall be paid out of the fund created and set apart by the first section of this act, to each and every enlisted soldier of the companies of Nevada volunteers heretofore raised in this Territory, other than those raised or to be raised under the requisition and proclamation mentioned in section two of this act, from the time of the passage of this act, and to each and every enlisted soldier of the companies of Nevada volunteers raised or to be raised under the requisition and proclamation aforesaid, from the time of his enlistment, the sum of five dollars per month for one year: Provided, That this provision shall not apply to any soldier who may be drafted or enlisted as a substitute for any person drafted into the service of the United States.

Sec. 5. No money shall be drawn out of the soldiers' fund herein provided for, except as provided in sections three and six of this act.

Sec. 6. The captains or commanding officers of companies of Nevada Volunteers wishing to avail themselves of the provisions of section four of this act shall, after each and every muster, file in the office of the adjutant-general of this Territory a complete muster-roll (duly certified) of their companies from the date of the passage of this act, or of their enlistment, noting desertions, deaths, discharges, and dismissals, and stating the causes of such discharges, deaths, and dismissals from the service. No officer or private shall be entitled to the benefit of this act, in the matter of extra monthly pay mentioned in this act, until the expiration of one year from the passage of this act, or unless he shall sooner receive an honorable discharge or die in the service, except as herein otherwise provided, and no money shall be drawn for extra pay from the fund hereby authorized and set apart until he has been honorably discharged from or die in the service, or until the expiration of one year from the passage of this act: Provided, however, That the monthly amount hereby appropriated may be drawn by such enlisted married men as have families depending upon them for support, who shall have the power to allot the whole or a portion of the same for the support of their families. The amount of pay thus allotted shall be paid to the person to whom the same shall be legally allotted upon the following certificate of the adjutant-general of this Territory, with seal of office attached, if said officer have a seal, being indorsed thereon, namely: " I hereby certify that ——— is a ——— in ——— company, ——— regiment, Nevada Volunteers, and that he is entitled to the benefit of an act entitled an act to encourage enlistments and give bounties and extra pay to our volunteer soldiers, approved February twentieth, A. D. eighteen hundred and sixty-four, and that this allotment is made according to law." After the term of enlistment shall have been served or an honorable discharge granted to, or on the death of, any enlisted man, a certified copy of his final statement shall be transmitted to the adjutant-general of this Territory, who shall certify on the back of the same the amount due under this act to the person discharged or deceased, and the auditor shall draw his warrant upon the treasurer of the Territory for the amount so certified, payable out of the fund hereby created : *Provided*, That if a volunteer be discharged for disability that existed at the time of his enlistment, he shall not be entitled to the benefits of this act.

SEC. 7. For the purpose of carrying into effect the provisions of this act, and providing for the fund created by section one of this act, the treasurer of the Territory of Nevada shall cause to be prepared bonds of the Territory to the amount of one hundred thousand dollars each, redeemable at the office of the treasury of the Territory on the first day of July, one thousand eight hundred and sixty-seven. The said bonds shall bear interest, payable semi-annually, at the rate of ten per cent. per annum from the date of their issue, which interest shall be due and payable in the city of San Francisco, California, on the first day of January and July of each year, providing that the first payment of interest shall not be made sooner than the first day of January, A. D. one thousand eight hundred and sixty-five. The said bonds shall be signed by the governor and countersigned by the auditor, and indorsed by the treasurer of the Territory, and shall have the seal of the Territory affixed thereto. Such bonds shall be issued, from time to time, as they may be required for use. The expense of preparing such bonds and disposing of the same shall be audited as a claim against the soldiers' fund created by this act.

SEC. 8. Coupons for the interest shall be attached to each bond, consecutively numbered, and signed by the treasurer of the Territory, and it shall be the duty of the auditor and treasurer of the Territory each to keep a separate record of all such bonds as may be issued, showing the number, date, and amount of each bond, and to whom the same was issued.

SEC. 9. All demands against the soldiers' fund shall be audited by a board of examiners, to consist of the governor secretary, and auditor of the Territory.

SEC. 10. The treasurer of the Territory shall sell and dispose of said bonds for gold and silver coin of the United States, from time to time, as may be necessary to provide for the payment of liabilities against the said soldier's fund. Said bonds may be disposed of either at private or public sale, providing that the fractional part of no bond shall be disposed of by sale; and provided further, that said bonds shall not be sold or negotiated by the treasurer at a greater discount than fifteen cents on the dollar of the par value thereof. On the receipt of the purchase money of said bonds, the treasurer shall deliver the same to the purchaser. All moneys received by the treasurer from the sale of bonds as herein provided shall be by him placed to the credit of the said soldier's fund.

SEC. 11. For the payment of the principal and interest of the bonds issued under this act, there shall be levied and collected annually, until the final payment or redemption of the same, and in the same manner as other Territorial revenue is or may be directed by law to be levied and collected annually, a tax of twenty cents on each one hundred dollars of taxable property in the Territory, in addition to the taxes for Territorial purposes; and the fund derived from this tax shall be set apart and applied to the payment of interest accruing on the bonds herein provided for, and the final redemption of the principal of said bonds; and the public faith of the Territory of Nevada is hereby pledged for the payment of the bonds issued by virtue of this act, and the interest thereon, and, if necessary, to provide other and ample means for the payment thereof.

SEC. 12. Whenever, on the first day of January or July, anno Domini eighteen hundred and sixty-five, or upon the first day of January or July in any subsequent year, there shall remain a surplus after the payment of the interest as hereinbefore provided, of five thousand dollars or more, in the funds created by the twelfth section of this act, it shall be the duty of the treasurer to advertise in two daily newspapers published in English in the Territory of Nevada and two published in the State of California, for sealed proposals for the surrender of bonds issued under the provisions of this act. He shall state in such advertisement the amount of money on hand applicable to the redemption of said bonds, and he shall accept such proposals at rates not exceeding par value, as will redeem the greatest number of bonds, until the amount of cash on hand for redemption is exhausted.

SEC. 13. Full and particular account and record shall be kept by the treasurer of the condition of the funds collected in accordance with the provisions of this act, open at all times to the inspection of the governor and auditor, and of any committee appointed by the legislature, or either branch thereof.

SEC. 14. It shall be the duty of the treasurer of the Territory to make arrangements for the payment of interest of said bonds when the same becomes due, and in the event that the said interest fund shall be insufficient, the said treasurer shall make up the deficiency from the general fund; and in the event of the insufficiency of the general fund, the said treasurer is authorized and required to make such contracts and arrangements as may be necessary for the payment of said interest and the protection of the credit of the Territory; and in case there should be at any time in the fund created by this act for the payment of said interest and the redemption of said bonds any surplus moneys not needed for the payment of said interest or the redemption of any bonds, it shall be the duty of the treasurer of the Territory to transfer such surplus moneys to the general fund of the Territory. Said bonds shall be redeemed and the interest paid in gold and silver coin of the United States.

SEC. 15. Before the issue or sale of any bonds, as provided in this act, the Territorial treasurer shall execute to the people of the United States, in the Territory of Nevada, a special bond, additional to his other bonds required by law, in the sum of twenty-five thousand dollars, with good and sufficient sureties, to be approved by the governor, conditioned to pay over all moneys belonging to the soldiers' fund at such times and in the manner provided in this act, and also for the faithful performance of all the duties required of him by this act. Said bonds shall be filed in the office of the secretary of the Territory.

SEC. 16. The adjutant-general of the Territory shall, before receiving or paying out of the soldiers' fund any moneys as provided by this act, execute to the people of the United States in the Territory of Nevada a special bond, additional to his other bonds required by law, in the sum of five thousand dollars, with good and sufficient sureties, to be approved by the governor, conditioned to pay over all moneys that may be received by him belonging to the soldiers' fund, in the manner provided in this act, and also for the faithful performance of all the duties required of him by this act. Said bond shall be filed in the office of the secretary of the Territory.

SEC. 17. In case of the refusal or neglect of the treasurer or adjutant-general of the Territory to execute and file the bonds mentioned in the two preceding sections, in the manner therein provided, it shall be the duty of the governor to declare his office vacant, which vacancy shall be filled by the governor appointing some competent person who will comply with the provisions of this act.

SEC. 18. This act shall take effect from and after its passage.

(See laws Nevada Territory, 1864, page 51.)

EXHIBIT No. 6.

ACT OF THE LEGISLATURE OF THE STATE OF NEVADA PROVIDING FOR THE ASSUMPTION AND PAYMENT OF ALL OBLIGATIONS INCURRED BY THE TERRITORY OF NEVADA FOR ENLISTMENTS, ENROLLMENTS, EXTRA PAY, ETC., OF VOLUNTEER SOLDIERS, ETC., FOR THE MILITARY SERVICE OF THE UNITED STATES.

AN ACT to encourage enlistments and provide bounties and extra pay for our volunteer soldiers called into the service of the United States.

The people of the State of Nevada, represented in senate and assembly, do enact as follows:

SECTION 1. A sum not exceeding one hundred thousand dollars is hereby appropriated and set aside to constitute a separate fund, to be known as the "soldiers' fund," for the purpose of paying a compensation to the soldiers of the companies of Nevada volunteers already raised in the Territory and in the State of Nevada, and to be raised in this State for the service of the United States, to aid in repelling invasion, suppressing insurrections, enforcing the laws, and protecting the public property, in addition to the pay allowed them by the United States.

SEC. 2. There shall be paid out of the fund created and set apart by the first section of this act: To each first and second lieutenant, the sum of twenty-five dollars per month; to each captain, the sum of thirty-five dollars per month; to each major, the sum of forty dollars per month; to each lieutenant-colonel, the sum of forty-five dollars per month; to each colonel the sum of fifty dollars per month; and to each and every enlisted soldier of the companies of the Nevada volunteers, raised for the United States Government, in the Territory or State of Nevada, or hereafter to be raised in this State, under the requisition made on the governor of the Territory of Nevada by the officer commanding the Department of the Pacific, to aid in repelling invasion, suppressing insurrection, and defending the State in a time of war, the sum of five dollars per month; and a bounty of ten dollars, to be paid to the captain or commanding officer of any company for every recruit by him enlisted and subsequently mustered into the service of the United States: *Provided*, That the provisions of this section shall not be deemed applicable to any soldier who may be drafted or enlisted as a substitute, or any person drafted into the Army of the United States: *And furthermore provided*, That no such allowance or monthly payment as is hereinbefore provided for shall be made for any service in the Army of the United States rendered prior to the twentieth of February, eighteen hundred and sixty-four.

Sec. 3. The captains or commanding officers of companies of Nevada volunteers, raised or to be raised, for service in the Army of the United States, shall, before such officers, as recruiting agents of the Army, can be entitled to secure the benefits of this act, file in the office of the adjutant-general their affidavit, setting forth the number and names of recruits enlisted by them and accepted by the proper medical examiners (who shall in each case be named), and sworn into the service; and further setting forth that no affidavit of the same character, for the same enlisted men, has heretofore been made or filed. The adjutant-general of the State is hereby authorized and directed to certify to the controller of the State the number of men enlisted by each captain or commanding officer of a company, whenever the affidavit herein required is filed in his office, indorsed by the provost-marshal of this State, or the commanding officer of the post where the enlisted men referred to and enumerated in the affidavit may have been rendezvoused on enlistment. Upon the filing of the adjutant-general's certificate, above required, in the office of the controller of State, the controller shall make out a copy of said certificate, and forward the same to the State board of examiners; and if the State board of examiners shall indorse the certificate as "approved," then the controller shall draw his warrant upon the fund herein constituted for the sum set forth in the certificate of the adjutant-general in favor of the officers, or their legal assignees, named in the certificate, for the sums respectively set forth to be due them.

Sec. 4. The captains or commanding officers of companies of Nevada volunteers, in order to secure the soldiers of the Nevada volunteers the benefits of the provisions of section 3 of this act, shall, after each and every muster, file in the office of the adjutant-general of this State a complete muster-roll (duly certified) of their companies, showing the date of their enlistment, noting desertions, deaths, discharges, and dismissals, and stating the cause of such discharges, deaths, and dismissals from the service. The amount of pay herein provided for shall be specially named in the following form of certificate of the adjutant-general of this State, with seal of office attached, if said officer have a seal, being indorsed thereon, namely: "I hereby certify that ——— is a ——— in ——— Company, ——— Regiment, Nevada Volunteers, and that he is entitled to the benefit of an act entitled "An act to encourage enlistments and provide bounties and extra pay for our volunteer soldiers called into the service of the United States, and that this allotment is made according to law." After the term of enlistment shall have been served, or an honorable discharge granted to, or on the death of, any enlisted man, a certified copy of his final statement shall be transmitted to the adjutant-general of this State, who shall certify on the back of the same the amount due under this act to the person discharged or deceased, and the controller shall draw his warrant upon the State treasurer for the amount so certified, payable out of the fund hereby created: Provided, That if a volunteer be discharged for disability that existed at the time of his enlistment, he shall not be entitled to the benefits of this act.

Sec. 5. The officers of the Nevada volunteers mustered into the service of the United States shall, on the certificate of their actual service, given by the adjutant-general, and its approval and indorsement by the State board of examiners, be entitled to receive their extra pay, as provided for them in section two of this act; and the controller of State is hereby authorized and directed to draw his warrants in favor of such officers, in the sums audited and allowed, as herein provided. These certificates shall be issued every two months on the request of the officers entitled to the same.

Sec. 6. For the purpose of carrying into effect the provisions of this act, and providing for the fund created by section one of this act, the treasurer of the State of Nevada shall cause to be prepared bonds of the State to the amount of one hundred thousand dollars, in sums of five hundred dollars each, redeemable at the office of the treasurer of the State on the first day of July, one thousand eight hundred and seventy. The said bonds shall bear interest, payable semi-annually, at the rate of ten per centum per annum from the date of their issue, which interest shall be due and payable at the office of the treasurer of this State on the first day of January and July of each year; providing, that the first payment of interest shall not be made sooner than the first day of January, in the year of our Lord one thousand eight hundred and sixty-six. The said bonds shall be signed by the governor and countersigned by the controller and indorsed by the treasurer of state, and shall have the seal of the State affixed thereto. Such bonds shall be issued from time to time as they may be required for use. The expense of preparing such bonds and disposing of the same shall be audited as a claim against the soldiers' fund created by this act.

Sec. 7. Coupons for the interest shall be attached to each bond, consecutively numbered and signed by the treasurer of state, and it shall be the duty of the controller and treasurer of state each to keep a separate record, showing the number, date, and amount of each bond, and to whom the same was issued.

SEC. 8. All demands against the soldiers' fund shall be audited by the State board of examiners.

SEC. 9. The State treasurer and secretary of state shall sell and dispose of said bonds, for gold and silver coin of the United States, from time to time, as may be necessary, to provide for the payment of liabilities against the said soldiers' fund. Said bonds may be disposed of either at private or public sale, providing that the fractional part of no bond shall be disposed of by sale, and provided further that said bonds shall not be sold or negotiated by the treasurer and secretary of state at a greater discount than twenty cents on the dollar of the par value thereof. On the receipt of the purchase-money of said bonds the treasurer and secretary of state shall deliver the same to the purchaser. All moneys received by the treasurer and secretary from the sale of bonds, as herein provided, shall be by them placed to the credit of said soldiers' fund.

SEC. 10. For the payment of the principal and interest of the bonds issued under this act there shall be levied and collected annually, until the final payment or redemption of the same, and in the same manner as other State revenue is, or may be directed by law to be levied and collected annually, a tax of twenty-five cents, in gold and silver coin of the United States, on each one hundred dollars of taxable property in the State, in addition to the other taxes for State purposes; and the fund derived from this tax shall be set apart and applied to the payment of interest accruing on the bonds herein provided for and the final redemption of the principal of said bonds; and the public faith of the State of Nevada is hereby pledged for the payment of the bonds issued by virtue of this act, and the interest thereon, and if necessary to provide other and ample means for the payment thereof.

SEC. 11. Whenever, on the first day of January or July, in the year of our Lord one thousand eight hundred and sixty-six, or upon the first day of January and July in any subsequent year, there shall remain a surplus, after the payment of the interest as hereinbefore provided, of five thousand dollars or more in the fund created by the tenth section of this act, it shall be the duty of the treasurer to advertise in two daily newspapers published in English in the State of Nevada, and one published in the city of San Francisco, State of California, for sealed proposals for surrender of bonds issued under the provisions of this act. He shall state in such advertisement the amount of money on hand applicable to the redemption of said bonds, and he shall accept such proposals, at rates not exceeding par value, as will redeem the greatest number of bonds, until the amount of cash on hand for redemption is exhausted.

SEC. 12. It shall be the duty of the State treasurer to make arrangements for the payment of interest on said bonds when the same becomes due, and in the event that the said interest fund shall be insufficient, the said treasurer shall make up the deficiency from the general fund; and in the event of the insufficiency of the general fund, the said treasurer is authorized and required to make such contracts and arrangements as may be necessary for the payment of said interest and the redemption of said bonds. Said bonds shall be redeemed and the interest paid in gold and silver coin of the United States.

SEC. 13. Before the issue or sale of any bonds as provided in this act the State treasurer and secretary of state shall execute to the State of Nevada a special bond, additional to their other bonds required by law, in the sum of twenty-five thousand dollars, with good and sufficient sureties, to be approved by the governor, conditional to pay over all moneys belonging to the soldiers' fund at such times and in the manner provided in this act, and also for the faithful performance of all the duties required by them by this act. Said bond shall be filed in the office of the controller of State.

SEC. 14. All moneys which have been received into the Territorial and State treasuries from the tax levied in and by an act of the Territory of Nevada approved February twentieth, one thousand eight hundred and sixty-four, entitled "An act to encourage enlistments and give bounties and extra pay to our volunteer soldiers," are hereby ordered to be transferred to and made a part of the soldiers' fund named and provided for in section ten of this act.

SEC. 15. All Territorial warrants and all certificates by the adjutant-general of the Territory of Nevada, issued in accordance with an act approved February twentieth, one thousand eight hundred and sixty-four, entitled "An act to encourage enlistments, and give bounties and extra pay to our volunteer soldiers," shall, on their indorsement as approved by the State board of examiners, be received by the controller and cancelled; and warrants of the State of Nevada on the soldiers' fund shall be issued, in like sums, in lieu thereof, to the parties lawfully holding the same: *Provided*, That the same form of proof shall be required by the State board of examiners in this as in any other case of claims on the soldiers' fund.

SEC. 16. An act passed by the legislature of the Territory of Nevada, and approved February twentieth, one thousand eight hundred and sixty-four, entitled "An act to encourage enlistments and give bounties and extra pay to our volunteer soldiers," is hereby repealed, and all warrants of the Territory of Nevada, duly issued under the provisions of said act, shall be audited, exchanged, and liquidated, and canceled, as provided in the next preceding section of this act. (Statutes of Nevada, 1864–'65, p. 389.)

EXHIBIT No. 7.

PRECEDENTS OF CASES AUTHORIZING PAYMENT OF CLAIMS OF STATES AND TERRITORIES AND TO STATE AND TERRITORIAL TROOPS FOR MONEYS BY THEM EXPENDED FOR TROOPS AND ARISING OUT OF INVASION AND INDIAN HOSTILITIES WHEN DOING MILITARY SERVICE FOR THE UNITED STATES.

1. By act approved March 3, 1797, entitled "An act making appropriations for the military and naval establishments for the year 1797," appropriations were made to satisfy and discharge claims for militia service on the frontiers of Georgia, the sum of $70,496.35; for militia service on the frontiers of Kentucky, $3,836.76; and for militia service on the frontiers of South Carolina, the sum of $8,400.25.

2. By an act approved May 13, 1800, the accounting officers of the Treasury were authorized to settle the accounts of the militia who served on an expedition commanded by Maj. Thomas Johnson against the Indians, in the year 1794, the same to be paid out of any moneys in the Treasury not otherwise appropriated.

3. By section 3 of an act of Congress approved March 14, 1804, making appropriations for the support of Government for the year 1804, it was provided "that the sum which shall be found due on a settlement of the accounts of the militia who served on an expedition commanded by Maj. Thomas Johnson against the Indians in the year 1794, be paid out of any moneys in the Treasury not otherwise appropriated, the appropriation made by the act of the 13th of May, 1800, having been carried to the credit of the surplus fund."

4. By an act approved February 21, 1812, making appropriations for the support of the military establishment of the United States for the year 1812, the sum of $32,800 was appropriated for the expenses of calling into actual service in the years 1809, 1810, and 1811 the militia of the Louisiana and Indiana Territories and State of Kentucky.

5. By an act approved March 3, 1817, entitled "An act making additional appropriations to defray the expenses of the army and militia during the late war with Great Britain," provision was made for the payment of balances due certain States on account of disbursements for militia employed in the service of the United States during the war of 1812, and under the provisions of which were adjusted and paid the war claims of the States of Rhode Island, Virginia, North Carolina, South Carolina, Mississippi, Vermont, New Hampshire, New York, Maryland, Pennsylvania, Connecticut and Delaware.

6. By an act entitled "An act making appropriations for the military service of the United States for the year 1827," approved March 2, 1827, an appropriation of $129,375.66, to be paid under the direction of the Secretary of War, was made for the settlement of the claims of the militia of Georgia for services rendered during the years 1793 and 1794, agreeably to the estimates of Constant Freeman.

7. By act approved March 21, 1828, the Secretary of War was required to pay the claims of the militia of the State of Illinois and the Territory of Michigan, called out by any competent authority, on the occasion of the then recent Indian disturbances, and that the expenses incident to the expedition should be settled according to the justice of the claims (see Laws of the United States, vol. 4, p. 258).

8. By the second section of an act approved March 2, 1829 (Army appropriation bill), an appropriation was made of $856.55 to pay a company of Illinois militia, commanded by Captain Morgan, called out for service on the northwestern frontier in 1827, to be settled by the Secretary of War agreeably to the third section of the Army appropriation bill, approved March 21, 1828.

9. By an act approved February 11, 1830, the Secretary of the Treasury was directed to cause to be paid to the proper officer of the Commonwealth of Pennsylvania the sum of $13,795.54, standing on the books of the Treasury Department to the credit of the agent of Pennsylvania, for paying the militia of that State in the year 1794.

10. By an act approved March 2, 1831 (Army appropriation bill), an appropriation of $9,085.54 was made for the payment of the claim of the State of Missouri against the United States for the service of her militia against the Indians in the year 1829, provided that the Secretary of War should, upon a full investigation, be satisfied that the United States was liable for the payment of the said militia, under the second paragraph of the tenth section of the first article of the Constitution of the United States.

11. By the second section of an act approved April 5, 1832 (Army appropriation bill), the Secretary of War was required to adjust and pay claims of the militia called out by competent authority and received into the service of the United States by general officers of the United States Army in the year 1831, and all charges and expenses incident to the service of said troops agreeably to the provisions of the third section of an act making appropriations for the military service of the United States, approved March 21, 1828, which provides for the payment of like expenses of troops called out in 1827; and by an act approved January 14, 1836, the sum of $120,000 was appropriated to defray the expenses attending the suppression of hostilities with the Seminole Indians of Florida, to be expended under the direction of the Secretary of War, conformably to the provisions of the above act of April 5, 1832.

12. By the third section of an act approved June 15, 1832, entitled "An act for the re-appropriation of certain unexpended balances of former appropriations, and for other purposes," an appropriation of $300,000, or so much thereof as might be necessary, was made for the purpose of paying the militia of the State of Illinois, called into the service of the United States by competent authority, and for paying the expenses incurred in defending the frontier from invasion by several bands of hostile Indians, including the pay of the militia legally called out for the same purpose in the neighboring States and Territories, to be paid under the authority of the Secretary of War, agreeably to the second section of an act making appropriations for the support of the Army for the year 1832; and by an act approved July 14, 1832, an additional appropriation of $100,000 was made for the same purpose.

13. By an act approved May 14, 1834 (Army appropriation bill), appropriations were made for the payment of the general and staff officers and six companies of Missouri militia ordered into the service by the governor of that State in 1832; for paying any balance which might be found due for militia service in the Territory of Michigan in the late war against Black Hawk and his followers; and for the payment of Captain McGeorge's company of Indian militia for services prior to the year 1832, provided the Secretary of War should be satisfied that the said company was entitled thereto.

14. By an act approved May 28, 1836, the Secretary of War was directed to cause to be paid the expenses that had been incurred and the supplies that had been furnished in the States of South Carolina, Georgia, Alabama, Louisiana, and the Territory of Florida, on account of the militia or volunteers received into the service of the United States for the defense of Florida, provided that the accounts for such claims should be examined and audited at the Treasury, as in other cases.

15. By the second section of said act the Secretary of War was authorized to cause the militia called out to defend east Florida by Clinch and Hernandez, by the governor, in middle and west Florida, and such other militia and volunteers as had been received and mustered into the service of the United States and regularly discharged, to be paid in like manner with the volunteers and militia ordered into service under orders from the War Department.

16. By an act approved July 2, 1836, the Secretary of War was directed to ascertain the sums severally due to persons who performed duty in the companies commanded by Captains Crawford, Wallis, and Long, of the militia of Missouri, and in the companies of Captain Siglor, of the militia of Indiana, for the protection of the frontiers of those States against the Indians, and to cause them to be paid for the time they were actually engaged in said service in the year 1832, at the rate and according to the principles established for the payment of similar services rendered the United States.

17. By act approved March 1, 1837, an appropriation was made for the payment of the Tennessee volunteers, called out by the proclamation of Governor Cannon, on the 28th of April, 1836, to suppress Indian hostilities; and an appropriation was also made to re-imburse Governor Cannon for moneys expended on account of such volunteers (see Laws of United States, vol. 5, p. 150).

18. By the second section of an act approved March 1, 1837, an appropriation was made for pay, traveling, and clothing for six months and other legal expenses of the Tennessee volunteers mustered into the service of the United States, under the requisition of Governor Gaines, under date April 8, 1836, and the proclamation of Governor Cannon of 28th of same month, and approved by the Secretary of War, May 9, by direction of the President; and also for pay, traveling, and clothing and other legal expenses of Tennessee volunteers mustered into the service of the United States, under the order of the Secretary of War, May 25, and of Governor Cannon's proclamation of June 6, 1836; also for pay, traveling, and clothing and other legal expenses of Tennessee volunteers, mustered into the service of the United States, under General Gaines's requisition, under date June 28, and Governor Cannon's proclamation of June 20, 1836; also for payment of liabilities incurred by Governor Cannon in raising money, so far as said money was properly expended in the service of the United States, on account of the aforesaid volunteers; also for the payment of the executive staff of the governor of Tennessee while actually engaged in obtaining, organizing, mustering,

or marching volunteers, during the year 1836, to place of their rendezvous, or making returns of said volunteers.

19. By the third section of said act the Secretary of War was directed to cause to be paid to the volunteers and militia of Kentucky, Tennessee, Alabama, and Mississippi, including the companies in Mississippi mustered into the service, who were duly called into service, and whose service was accepted by the executives of the States, respectively, during the summer of the year 1836, under requisitions from the Secretary of War, or from generals commanding the troops of the United States, and who were discharged before marching, the amount of one month's pay, with all the allowances to which they would have been entitled if they had been in actual service during the period of one month; and by the fourth section of said act an appropriation was made for paying the Rifle Rangers, Coosada Volunteers, and Independence Blues, under the command of Major Holt; and for the payment of Major Holt and battalion staff, to be paid on presentation of the rolls of said companies and battalion staff to the Paymaster-General, with evidence of the time they were in the service against the Creek Indians in the months of May and June, 1836.

20. By act approved July 7, 1838, an appropriation was made of such amount as should be found due by the Secretary of War and the accounting officers of the Treasury, out of the appropriation for the prevention of hostilities on the northern frontier, to re-imburse the State of New York for expenses incurred in the protection of the frontier in the pay of volunteers and militia called into service by the governor (see 5 U. S. Stats., p. 268).

21. By act approved March 3, 1841, a direct appropriation was made to the city of Mobile for advances of money and expenses incurred in equipping, mounting, and sending to the place of rendezvous two full companies of mounted men, under a call from the governor of Alabama at the beginning of the hostilities of the Creek Indians (see Laws, vol. 5, p. 435).

22. By an act approved September 9, 1841, $19,388.02 was appropriated for the payment of the balance required in addition to the sum applicable out of the amount appropriated at the previous Congress for arrearages of pay of Florida militia called into the service by the governor of the Territory in 1840, and $297,213.92 was appropriated for arrearages of pay due Florida militia commanded by Brigadier-General Read for six months' service, commencing November, 1840.

23. By the same act, $78,495.92 was appropriated for arrearages of pay due to a battalion of Georgia militia for service on the frontiers of Georgia and Florida in 1840 and 1841.

24. By an act approved June 13, 1842, the State of Maine was re-imbursed for the expenses of the militia called into service by the governor for the protection of the northeastern frontier (see 5 U. S. Stats., p. 490).

25. By act of August 11, 1842, $175,000 was appropriated as a balance for the payment and indemnity of the State of Georgia for any moneys actually paid by said State on account of expenses in calling out her militia during the Seminole, Cherokee, and Creek campaigns, or for the suppression of Indian hostilities in Florida and Alabama (see Laws, vol. 5, p. 504). By act approved August 29, 1842, a similar appropriation was made to the State of Louisiana (see Laws, October 5, p. 542).

26. By an act approved August 16, 1842, the Secretary of War was directed to audit and adjust the claims of the State of Alabama under such laws and regulations as had theretofore governed the Department in auditing and allowing the claims of the States upon the United States for moneys paid by said States for subsistence, supplies, and services of local troops called into the service by the authorities of said State, but not mustered into the service of the United States, and for provisions and forage furnished friendly Indians during the Creek and Seminole hostilities in the years 1836 and 1837, in all cases in which payment was for subsistence, supplies, and service, provisions, and forage which would have been paid for under existing laws and regulations if such troops had been mustered into the service of the United States and the provisions and forage had been furnished by an agent of the United States.

27. By act approved August 23, 1842, the proper accounting officers of the War Department were directed to examine and adjust the claims for pay of Lieutenant-Colonel Bailey and staff, Major Bailey and staff, the officers of the quartermaster's department, and the companies of Captains Grigsby, Hogan, McIvers, Langford, Hall, Burney, and Bailey, all of the Florida militia called into the service in 1839 and 1840, as if they had been regularly called out and mustered; and by an act approved August 31, 1842, the appropriations made for subsistence by the above act were made applicable to the settlement of any claims for subsistence furnished to the Florida militia in 1839 and 1840, not theretofore settled.

28. By an act approved August 29, 1842, the sum of $61,378.15 was appropriated to pay the balance due the State of Louisiana for expenditures incurred in raising, equipping, and paying off a regiment of volunteer militia employed in the service of the United States in the Seminole war.

29. By an act approved February 4, 1843, the Secretary of War was authorized to cause to be paid to the companies of Captains Johnson, Henderson, Knight, Jones, and North, for services rendered in the year 1840, according to the muster rolls of said companies, and also the companies of Captains Jernigan and Sweat, for services rendered in the year 1841, according to the muster rolls of said companies, such payment to be governed by the laws and regulations applicable to the payment of volunteers and militia of the United States.

30. By an act approved February 24, 1843, the proper accounting officers of the Treasury were required to settle the accounts of four companies of the militia of the State of Michigan, ordered into service by the governor of the State, on the requisition of the United States marshal, for the maintenance of neutral obligations and laws of the United States, and also to audit and settle the claims of the Brady Guards and volunteer company of the city of Detroit, for like services during the disturbances in the year 1838 on the frontiers of Canada.

31. By act approved March 3, 1843, the accounting officers of the Treasury were authorized and required to settle the claims for supplies furnished the Florida militia, the payment of which was provided for by act of August 23, 1842, upon principles of equity and justice, under the directions of the Secretary of War.

32. By an act approved August 10, 1846, there was directed to be paid to the State of Alabama the sum of $13,455.32 for moneys paid by said State for subsistence and supplies furnished the friendly Indians during the Creek and Seminole hostilities in the years 1836 and 1837.

33. By act approved August 7, 1848, the Secretary of the Treasury was directed to pay to the mounted Tennessee volunteers who served in the companies of Captains Gillespie, Peake, Vernon, and Rogers, in 1836, to each the sum of 40 cents per day for the use and risk of his arms, and the sum of 15 cents per day for forage from the 1st of November, 1836, until they were finally discharged.

34. By the second section of the act approved September 30, 1850, making appropriations for the expenses of the Indian Department, the accounting officers of the Treasury were directed to settle the accounts of the companies of Texas mounted rangers commanded by Captains Hill, Smith, Roberts, Sutton, Ross, McCulloch, Johnson, and Blackwell, who were retained or called into service by the governor of said State.

35. By an act approved February 14, 1851, the Secretary of the Treasury was directed to settle the actual and necessary expenses incurred by the provisional government of Oregon in defending the people of said Territory from the attacks and hostilities of the Cayuse Indians in 1847 and 1848, upon the presentation by the governor of said Territory to the Secretary of the Treasury of a full, accurate, and detailed statement of the actual and necessary expenses of said defense from said hostilities, accompanied by proper vouchers and satisfactory proof of the correctness thereof, authenticated in conformity with the usages of the Department.

36. By act approved March 2, 1853, the Secretary of the Treasury was directed, out of the appropriation mentioned in the act to "settle and adjust the expenses of the defense of the people of Oregon from the attacks and hostilities of the Cayuse Indians in the years of 1847 and 1848, approved February 14, 1851," the sums found due and allowed by Commissioners Wait and Rice and by the governor of Oregon.

37. By act approved May 31, 1854, to supply deficiencies in the appropriations for the year ending June 30, 1854, the sum of $1,000 was appropriated to pay arrearages of pay for services of volunteers in the Kentucky regiment called into service in 1836.

38. By act approved March 3, 1855, supplying deficiencies in the appropriations for the year ending June 30, 1853, the sum of $10,569.06 was appropriated for Mexican hostilities.

39. By the same act the sum of $18,060.49 was appropriated for pay of Louisiana and Texas volunteers.

40. By the same act the unexpended balance of the appropriation by the act of June 19, 1834 (see vol. 5, p. 680, Stats. at Large), "for payment of the Georgia militia," etc., which had passed by subsequent acts into the surplus fund, was re-appropriated.

41. By the same act $7,241.93 was appropriated for arrearages of pay due Florida militia under General Read.

42. By an act approved March 3, 1855, making appropriations for the civil and diplomatic expenses of Government for the year ending June 30, 1856, it was provided that the sum of $25,000 be appropriated to pay the necessary expenses of six companies of volunteers called into the service of the United States by Brigadier-General Smith, in the State of Texas, to be paid under the direction of the Secretary of War.

43. By an act making appropriations for the support of the Army for the year ending the 30th of June, 1856, and for other purposes, approved March 3, 1855, an appropriation of $137,755.38 was made for pay, supplies, and traveling expenses of six companies of Texas volunteers called into the service by the governor of Texas and mustered into the service of the United States.

44. By act approved March 3, 1857 (section 9), the Secretary of War was authorized and required to pay to the State of Arkansas such sums of money as were paid by said State, under act of legislature of that State approved January 5, 1849, to the Benton County militia, called into service to resist incursions of the Cherokee Indians in July, 1846, not to exceed $1,212.

45. By the eleventh section of an act approved March 3, 1857, making appropriations for the support of the Army for the year ending June 30, 1858, the Secretary of War was required to cause to be audited and settled the accounts of the State of Florida against the United States for money advanced by that State in payment of volunteers called into service for the supression of Indian hostilities in 1849 and 1852, provided it should be satisfactorily shown that said claims had been actually allowed and paid by the State; and by the twelfth section of the same act the Secretary of War was directed to settle the actual and necessary expenses incurred by the militia called into the service in the Territory of New Mexico, by acting Governor Messervey, in the year 1854, to suppress Indian hostilities in said Territory, provided the Secretary should be first satisfied that the calling out of said militia was necessary and proper for the defense of the Territory.

46. By a clause of the same act (for the support of the Army for the year ending June 30, 1860) provision was made for the payment to Minnesota for expenses incurred by Capt. James Starkey's company of Minnesota Volunteers, called out by the governor of the State in 1857, to protect the settlers of the valley of Sunrise River against the Chippewa Indians.

47. By section 2 of the same act the Secretary of War was authorized to repay to the State of Texas moneys advanced by that State for the payment of six companies of mounted volunteers called into service by General Persifor F. Smith, November 1, 1854, for three months, provided that no greater pay or allowances be given these troops than was given to similar troops in the service of the United States.

48. By section 2 of an act approved June 21, 1860, the provisions of the act of March 3, 1859, were extended so as to include all the moneys advanced by the State of Texas in payment of volunteers called out in defense of the frontier of that State since February 28, 1855, provided the Secretary of War should be satisfied that there was necessity for calling out these troops, that they were called out by competent authority, and that the amount so claimed was actually paid by the State. The amount was limited to $123,544.51, and the troops to be paid only for time in active service.

49. By the seventh section of same act (June 21, 1860) the twelfth section of act of March 3, 1857, was extended so as to embrace the pay proper and allowances of the militia of New Mexico therein named, the amount being limited to $74,009; and the troops to be paid only for time in active service, at no greater rate than those in United States service.

50. By the fifth section of same act the Secretary of War was authorized to pay to the State of Iowa moneys paid by that State to troops called out by the governor of that State in 1857-'58-'59, to protect the frontier from Indian incursions, provided there was necessity for such calling out of troops and the moneys had been actually paid out by the State, with the usual provisos as to necessity, rate of pay, and limitation as to amount, which was $18,988.84.

51. By the act approved June 21, 1860 (it being an Army appropriation bill), the sum of $18,988 was appropriated to re-imburse the State of Iowa for the expenses of militia called out by the governor "to protect the frontier from Indian incursions" (see 12 U. S. Stats., p. 68).

52. By the same act the sum of $123,544.51 was appropriated to the State of Texas for the "payment of volunteers called out in the defense of the frontier of the State since the 28th of February, 1855." By the "act making appropriations for the sundry civil expenses of the Government for the year ending June 30, 1864, and for other purposes," an appropriation was made to "pay the governor of the State of Minnesota, or his duly authorized agent, the costs, charges, and expenses properly incurred by said State in suppressing Indian hostilities within said State and upon its borders, in the year 1862, not exceeding $250,000, to be settled upon proper vouchers to be filed and passed upon by the proper accounting officers of the Treasury (see 12 U. S. Stats., p. 754).

53. By act approved February 2, 1861, there was appropriated to re-imburse the Territory of Utah "for expenses incurred in suppressing Indian hostilities in said Territory in the year 1853," the sum of $53,512 (see 12 U. S. Stats., p. 15).

54. By act approved March 2, 1861, the State of California had appropriated to her $400,000 to defray the expenses incurred by the State in suppressing Indian hostilities for the years 1854, 1855, 1856, 1858, and 1859 (see 12 U. S. Stats., p. 199).

55. By another act of March 2, 1861, $400,000 was appropriated for pay of volunteers in Oregon and Washington in suppression of Indian hostilities in 1855-'56.

56. In the sundry civil bill passed July 2, 1864, an appropriation of the sum of $117,000 was made "to supply a deficiency in the appropriation for the costs, charges, and expenses properly incurred by the State of Minnesota in suppressing Indian hostilities in the year 1862" (see 13 U. S. Stats., pp. 350, 351).

57. By act approved May 28, 1864, the sum of $928,411 was appropriated for the payment of damages sustained by citizens of Minnesota " by reason of the depredations and injuries by certain bands of Sioux Indians" (see 13 U. S. Stats., p. 92).

58. By act approved March 3, 1873 (sundry civil bill for the year ending June 30, 1874), $10,000 was appropriated to re-imburse the State of Nebraska for expenses incurred in the suppression of Indian hostilities in 1864, to be paid by warrant in favor of the treasurer of said State.

59. By act approved March 3, 1875, making appropriations for sundry civil expense of the Government for the year ending June 30, 1876, the sum of $25,000 was re-appropriated for the payment of volunteers of Washington and Oregon Territories who were engaged in the suppression of Indian hostilities therein in the years 1855 and 1856, and for the payment of claims for services, supplies, and transportation incurred in the maintenance of said volunteers, and for horses and other property lost or destroyed in said service, as provided for by the act of Congress approved March 2, 1861.

60. By the first section of an act of Congress approved June 27, 1882, the Secretary of the Treasury was authorized and directed, with the aid and assistance of the Secretary of War, to cause to be examined and investigated all the claims of the States of Texas, Colorado, Oregon, Nebraska, California, Kansas, and Nevada, and the Territories of Washington and Idaho against the United States for money alleged to have been expended and for indebtedness alleged to have been assumed by said States and Territories in organizing, arming, equipping, supplying clothing, subsistence, transporting, and paying the volunteer and military forces of said States and Territories called into active service by the proper authorities thereof between the 15th day of April, 1861, and the date of said act, to repel invasion and Indian hostilities in said States and Territories and upon their borders, including all proper expenses necessarily incurred by said States and Territories on account of said forces having been so called into active service, and all proper claims paid or assumed by said States and Territories for horses and equipments actually lost by said forces in the line of duty in active service, excepting the claim of the State of Oregon for expenditures in suppressing the Modoc Indian hostilities.

61. By the second section of said act it was provided that no higher rate for supplies, transportation, and other proper expenses than was allowed and paid by the United States for similar services in the same grade and for the same time in the U. S. Army serving in said States and Territories, and for similar supplies, transportation, and other proper expenses during the same time furnished the U. S. Army in the same country, and that no allowance should be made for the services of such forces except for the time during which they were engaged in active service in the field, or for expenditures for which the Secretary of War should decide there was no necessity at the time and under the circumstances.

62. By an act approved January 6, 1883, to re-imburse the State of Oregon, the Secretary of the Treasury was authorized and directed to pay to the State of Oregon the sum of $70,268.05 in full for moneys paid by said State in suppressing Modoc Indian hostilities during the Modoc war, and in defending the State from invasion by said Indians during the years 1872 and 1873.

63. And by the second section of said act the Secretary of the Treasury was directed to pay to the State of California and to the citizens thereof, their heirs, representatives, or assigns the sum of $4,441.33 for arms, ammunition, supplies, transportation, and services of volunteer forces in suppressing Indian hostilities in said State during the said years of 1872–'73, as the same were specifically reported to Congress by the Secretary of War December 15, 1874.

64. By an act entitled "An act to refund to the State of Georgia certain money expended by said State for the common defense in 1777," approved March 3, 1883, the Secretary of the Treasury was required to pay to the State of Georgia the sum of $35,555.42 for money paid by said State for supplies for the troops in 1777 under the command of General Jackson engaged in local defense.

' There can be no doubt, we think, that it is the duty of a National Government to assume the payment of expenses incurred in the general military defense.

PRECEDENTS OF CASES FOR THE PAYMENT OF CLAIMS TO STATES FOR MONEYS BY THEM EXPENDED FOR TROOPS DOING MILITARY SERVICE FOR THE UNITED STATES AND ARISING OUT OF THE REVOLUTIONARY WAR.

1. In the year 1787, Congress by ordinance provided for the creation of a commission to audit the claims of the several States against the United States on account of payments made for the common defense during the war of the Revolution, and in 1790 the first Congress passed an act recognizing such commission and providing for the payment of all claims which had been prior to September 24, 1788, allowed by the States. Afterwards the act was amended and the commission extended.

---

* NOTE.—For payment to citizens of Montana on account of Indian war claims, see 18 U. S. Stats, 410.

2. By an act approved July 5, 1832, to provide for liquidating and paying certain claims of the State of Virginia, the accounts of Virginia for payments to officers of the Virginia line in the Revolutionary war, etc., were authorized to be paid, $139,543.66 being appropriated ; and the Secretary of the Treasury was directed to pay Virginia the amount of judgments rendered against her in favor of certain Revolutionary officers ; amount appropriated, $241,345.

3. By act approved February 27, 1851 (deficiency appropriation bill), there was appropriated $36,934.34 for the pay and expenses of three companies of Texan volunteers called into the service by requisition of Brevet Major-General Brooke, and it was provided that such pay and allowance should conform to the pay and allowance of similar troops employed during the war with Mexico ; and for re-imbursing the State of Florida under such rules and regulations as had theretofore governed similar claims of the several States against the United States for moneys advanced and paid for expenses incurred and obligations contracted by said States for subsistence, supplies, and services of local troops called into service during 1849 by and under the authorities of said States $75,000 was appropriated ; and for pay and expenses of four companies of volunteers called into the service of the United States by Brevet Lieutenant-Colonel Washington, of New Mexico, in the year 1849, $135,530 was appropriated.

4. By an act approved August 3, 1852, making appropriations for the support of the Army for the year ending June 30, 1853, appropriations were made to refund to the State of North Carolina the amount of money advanced and transportation furnished to volunteers from that State during the war with Mexico ; and for refunding to the State of Michigan the amount advanced by that State in organizing, subsisting, and transporting volunteers previous to their being mustered into the service of the United States during the war with Mexico.

5. By the same act the Secretary of War was directed to allow and pay to the State of Virginia all such sums as had been advanced by that State to officers and men of her regiment engaged to serve for and during the war then existing between the United States and Mexico for pay for their services from the day of their enrollment until they were mustered into the service of the United States.

6. By said act also the proper accounting officers of the Treasury were authorized to settle the claims of Florida for the service of her troops under the act of February 27, 1851, by the provisions stated in said act for the settlement of the claim of Virginia for like service.

7. By an act approved June 29, 1854, entitled "An act to re-imburse the common council of New York City for expenditures made for the First Regiment of New York Volunteers," the Secretary of War was authorized and required in the settlement and adjustment (under act of Congress June 2, 1848) of the claims of the common council of New York for expenditures made in organizing, transporting, clothing, and subsisting the First Regiment of New York Volunteers, commanded by Col. Ward B. Burnett, prior to the mustering of the said regiment into the service of the United States, to allow such of those claims as might be supported by satisfactory vouchers showing that such expenditures had been fairly made and were necessary and proper for the service, notwithstanding such vouchers might be informal and defective for want of particularity, provided that the amount allowed should not exceed $3,672.90.

8. By an act approved February 9, 1859, the accounts of Maine for expenses incurred by that State in organizing a regiment of volunteers for the Mexican war in 1846 were required to be audited and settled by the officers of the Treasury pursuant to act June 2, 1848.

PRECEDENTS OF CASES AUTHORIZING RE-IMBURSEMENTS TO STATES AND TERRITORIES FOR EXPENSES BY THEM INCURRED ON ACCOUNT OF THE TROOPS BY THEM RAISED OR DOING SERVICE FOR THE UNITED STATES DURING THE WAR OF THE REBELLION.

1. By act of Congress approved July 27, 1861, it was provided that the Secretary of the Treasury was directed to pay, out of any moneys in the Treasury not otherwise appropriated, to the governor of any State, or his duly authorized agents, the costs, charges, and expenses properly incurred by such State for enrolling, subsisting, clothing, supplying, arming, equipping, paying, and transporting its troops employed in aiding to suppress the rebellion.

2. By act approved April 12, 1866, entitled an "Act to re-imburse the State of Pennsylvania for moneys advanced Government for war purposes," $800,000 was appropriated to supply a deficiency in paying the Army under the act of March 14, 1864, and to re-imburse the State of Pennsylvania for money expended for payment of militia in the service of the United States.

3. The act approved June 20, 1878, "making appropriations for sundry civil expenses of the Government for the year ending June 30, 1879, and for other purposes," contains the following clause :

"Refunding to States expenses incurred in raising volunteers: To indemnify the States for expenses incurred by them in enrolling, equipping, and transporting troops for the defense of the United States during the late insurrection, to wit: For the State of New York, $82,736.78; for the State of Pennsylvania, $29,527.23 ; in all, $112,264.01."

4. By act approved April 17, 1866, the President was authorized, by and with the advice and consent of the Senate, to appoint three commissioners to ascertain, the amount of moneys expended by the State of Missouri in enrolling, equipping, subsisting, and paying such State forces as had been called into the service in said State since 24th of August, 1861, to act in concert with the United States forces in suppressing the rebellion. Said commissioners were required to proceed, subject to regulations to be prescribed by the Secretary of War, at once to examine all items of expense made by said State for the purpose, subject to certain conditions and limitations mentioned, but no allowance was authorized to be made for any troops which did not perform actual military service in full concert and co-operation with the authorities of the United States, and subject to their orders.

5. By act approved June 8, 1872, the Secretary of the Treasury was directed to cause to be examined, settled, and paid any proper claims of the State of Kentucky for money expended in enrolling, equipping, subsisting, and paying State forces of Kentucky, called into service in said State after August 24, 1861, to act in concert with the United States forces in suppressing the rebellion, settlement to be made upon the principles and conditions and under the limitations provided in the act of Congress approved April 17, 1866, to re-imburse the State of Missouri for moneys expended for like purposes.

6. By act of June 16, 1880, payment of bounty to enlisted men of the Fifteenth and Sixteenth Missouri Cavalry was authorized.

Under these acts large sums have been paid to the several States and Territories, a statement of which will be found in a letter from the Third Auditor of the Treasury, subjoined hereto.

Payments made to the States and Territories for expenditures made by them in the suppression of Indian hostilities, as shown by the books of the Third Auditor of the Treasury.

Year of payment.	For what paid.	Paid through Third Auditor's Office.	Amount paid by Second Auditor, as per books of this office.	Total.
1859	Payment to the State of Arkansas for expenses in resisting incursions of the Cherokee Indians (act March 3, 1857)	$1,212.00	....	$1,212.00
1850 } 1852 } 1852	Claims of the State of New Hampshire for services of her militia from 1835 to 1837 (act March 2, 1849)	....	$5,487.56	5,487.56
1852	Payment of interest on expenditures of the State of New Hampshire in Indian war of 1835, 1836, and 1837 (act January 27, 1852)	....	4,390.86	4,390.86
1853	Refunding expenses incurred by the State of North Carolina in the Florida war in 1836, 1837, and 1838 (act August 31, 1852)	9,382.48	....	9,382.48
1854 } 1855 } 1857	Payment of claims of the State of South Carolina relating to Florida war of 1836 (act August 31, 1852)	19,369.05	....	19,369.05
1858 } 1859 } 1860 } 1861	Refunding to the State of California expenses incurred in suppressing Indian hostilities prior to January 1, 1854 (acts of August 5, 1854, and August 18, 1856, sec. 8)	914,077.02	....	914,077.02
1863 } 1872 }	Refunding to the State of California expenses incurred in suppressing Indian hostilities in 1854, 1855, 1856, 1857, 1858, and 1859 (acts March 2, 1861, and July 25, 1868)	231,067.87	....	231,067.87
1883 } 1884 }	Re-imbursing State and citizens of California for expenses in suppressing Modoc Indian hostilities (act January 6, 1883)	4,142.82	....	4,142.82
1883	Re-imbursing State of Oregon for expenses in suppressing Modoc Indian hostilities (act January 6, 1883)	70,263.08	....	70,268.08
1843 } 1845 } 1846 } 1851 } 1852 } 1853 }	Claim of the State of Maine for services of her militia in defense of the Northeastern frontier in 1839 (act June 13, 1842)	73,343.96	120,557.57	193,901.53
1851 } 1852 } 1853 } 1854 }	Allowance of interest to the State of Maine on expenditures in defense of the Northeastern frontier in 1839, 1840, and 1841 (acts March 3, 1851, and August 31, 1852)	33,822.12	40,336.83	74,158.95

Payments made to the States and Territories for expenditures made by them, etc.—Cont'd.

Year of payment.	For what paid.	Paid through Third Auditor's Office.	Amount paid by Second Auditor as per books of this office.	Total.
1851 } 1852 } 1853 }	To reimburse the State of Florida for expenses incurred in 1849 and 1852 (act February 27, 1851)	$30,812.11	$41,142.08	$71,954.19
	NOTE.—The sum of $92,788.10 is reported in " receipts and expenditures" as paid to State of Florida in 1857, on account expenses incurred in 1849-'52 (act March 3, 1857), and is presumed to have been paid through the Second Auditor's Office.			
1868	Payment to the State of Iowa for advances to troops in 1857, 1858, and 1859 (act June 21, 1860).....	18,088.84	....	18,088.84
1856 } 1857 } 1867 }	Refunding to the Territory of Utah expenses incurred in suppressing Indian hostilities (act July 17, 1854)........	7,222.05	12,468.00	19,690.05
1871 } 1872 } 1882 } 1863 }	Re-imbursing Nebraska for expenses incurred in suppressing Indian hostilities in 1864 (act July 27, 1866)	38,287.15	....	38,287.15
1865 } 1868 } 1860 } 1870 }	Payment of the State of Minnesota for expenses incurred in suppressing Indian hostilities in the year 1862. (Acts March 3, 1863, and July 2, 1864).........................	359,570.81	....	359,570.81
1861 } 1862 } 1846 }	Payment of the State of Minnesota for expenses incurred by Capt. James Starkey's company of Minnesota Volunteers. (Act March 3, 1859).........................	1,247.37	....	1,247.37
1848 } 1852 } 1853 }	Claims of the State of Alabama for militia services in 1836 and 1837. (Act August 16, 1842)	71,112.29	40,101.84	111,214.13
1849 } 1851 }	Payment of interest on advances made by the State of Alabama. (Act January 20, 1840)	51,162.79	17,975.20	69,137.99
1847 } 1848 }	An act to authorize the payment of certain claims of the State of Alabama. (Approved August 10, 1846)	13,455.32	....	13,455.32
1827 } 1832 }	Payment of Georgia claims for services of her militia in 1792-'93-'94. (Act March 2, 1827)	91,676.19	....	91,676.19
1842 } 1859 } 1853 }	Claims of the State of Georgia for services of her militia from 1835 to 1838. (Act August 11, 1842)..............	128,266.85	46,733.15	175,000.00
1854 } 1855 } 1857 }	Payment to State of Georgia for services of her militia from 1835 (section 8, act March 3, 1853)..................	83,947.54	55,060.92	139,008.46
1851 } 1852 } 1853 }	Allowance of interest to the State of Georgia (act March 3, 1851)..	21,857.55	13,101.10	34,958.65
1836	For amount advanced to the State of Georgia on account of expenses incurred in calling out her militia in 1836, as per Second Comptroller's letter, No. 1160, January 10, 1846..	40,725.36	....	40,725.36
1879	Refunding to State of Georgia expenses of Indian wars from 1835 to 1838 (act March 3, 1879)	72,206.94	....	72,206.94
	NOTE.—Amount passed to the credit of the State of Kansas on Second Comptroller's letter, No. 4756, dated November 13, 1884, under Act June 27, 1882, for expenses incurred in suppressing Indian hostilities; and the same has been reported to Congress for appropriation, $332,308.13.			

Payments to States by the United States for expenditures made by them on account of pay, supplies, and equipments of their militia, for the war of 1812, as shown by books of the Third Auditor of the Treasury.

VIRGINIA.

Warrants and requisitions after July 1, 1822.		Pay of the militia.	Subsistence, quartermaster's supplies, and contingencies.	Payment of balances due certain States (act March 3, 1817).	Payment of interest due the State (act March 3, 1825).	Total.
Date.	Number.					
October 4, 1814	War. 1504	....	$100,000.00	....	....	$100,000.00
July 23, 1815	War. 2612	....	15,300.00	....	....	15,300.00
March 23, 1816	War. 2571	$200,000.00	....	....	....	200,000.00
October 18, 1816	War. 359	350,000.00	....	....	....	350,000.00
January 27, 1816	War. 3694	400,000.00	....	....	....	400,000.00
April 21, 1817	War. 252	....	....	$250,000.00	....	250,000.00
November 14, 1817	War. 1263	....	....	200,000.00	....	200,000.00
June 26, 1818	War. 2237	....	....	150,000.00	....	150,000.00
May 4, 1819	War. 3892	....	....	48,991.19	....	48,991.19
March 7, 1820	War. 5286	....	....	40,628.33	....	40,628.33
May 11, 1821	War. 8047	....	....	30,000.00	....	30,000.00
April 25, 1822	War. 9031	....	....	5,868.99	....	5,868.99
January 17, 1823	Req. 643	....	....	6,841.50	....	6,841.50
April 19, 1825	Req. 3288	....	....	....	$50,000.00	50,000.00
July 11, 1825	Req. 3513	....	....	....	128,480.11	128,480.11
January 5, 1828	Req. 1080	....	....	7,591.20	....	7,591.20
July 14, 1829	Req. 2872	....	....	2,216.85	....	2,216.85
Total		950,000.00	115,300.00	742,138.06	178,480.11	1,985,918.17

NORTH CAROLINA.

Warrants and requisitions after July 1, 1822.		Pay of the militia.	Payment of balances due certain States (act March 3, 1817).	Claims of the State of North Carolina (act March 1, 1837).	Total.
Date.	Number.				
September 17, 1816	War. 286	$30,000.00	....	....	$30,000.00
November 20, 1817	War. 1284	....	$17,000.00	....	17,000.00
June 10, 1837	Req. 6948	....	....	$30,000.00	30,000.00
Total					77,00^ 00

MISSISSIPPI.

Warrants and requisitions after July 1, 1822.		Payment of balances due certain States (act March 3, 1817).	Total.
Date.	Number.		
March 6, 1819	War. 3590	$4,585.64	$4,585.64

Payments to States by the United States for expenditures made by them, etc.--Continued.

SOUTH CAROLINA.

Warrants and requisitions after July 1, 1822.		Payment of balances due certain States (act March 3, 1817).	An act for the adjustment and settlement of the claims of South Carolina (approved March 22, 1852).	Total.
Date.	Number.			
October 24, 1821	War. 8552	$114,000.00	....	$114,000.00
October 31, 1821	War. 8580	15,000.00	....	15,000.00
June 15, 1822	War. 9450	26,000.00	....	26,000.00
June 16, 1832	Req. 1754	....	$3,000.00	3,000.00
July 19, 1832	Req. 1911	....	154,259.16	154,259.16
Total		155,000.00	157,259.16	312,259 16

VERMONT.

Warrants and requisitions after July 1, 1822.		Payment of balances due certain States (act March 3, 1817).	Total.
Date.	Number.		
March 30, 1820	War. 5388	$4,421.18	$4,421.18

RHODE ISLAND.

Warrants and requisitions after July 1, 1822.		Pay of the militia.	Subsistence, quartermaster's supplies, and contingencies.	Payment of balances due certain States (act March 3, 1817).	Total.
Date.	Number.				
April 27, 1816	War. 2706	$18,500.00	$3,417.62	....	$21,917.62
May 15, 1820	War. 5796	....	....	$15,000.00	15,000.00
June 19, 1821	....	....	....	1,890.62	1,890.62
June 30, 1821	War. 8209	....	....	3,614.33	3,614.33
Total		....	....	20,504.95	42,422.57

MASSACHUSETTS.

Warrants and requisitions after July 1, 1822.		Payment of the claim of the State of Massachusetts (act May 31,1830).	Subsistence, quartermaster's supplies, and contingencies.	Payment to the State of Massachusetts (section 3, act March 1, 1859).	Total.
Date.	Number.				
March 22, 1817	War. 85	....	$11,000.00	....	$11,000.00
March 3, 1831	Req. 159	$419,748.26	....	....	419,748.26
May 19, 1859	Req. 1859	....	....	$227,176.48	227,176.48
Total		....	....	....	657,924.74

Payments to States by the United States for expenditures made by them, etc.--Continued.

PENNSYLVANIA.

Warrants and requisitions after July 1, 1822.		Balances due certain States (act March 3, 1817).	Subsistence, quartermaster's supplies, and contingencies.	Interest on loan to United States in 1815 (contingencies).	Payment of interest to the State of Pennsylvania (act March 3, 1827).	Total.
Date.	Number.					
April 26, 1815	War. 4255		$75,000.00			$75,000.00
June 26, 1816	War. 99	$100,000.00				100,000.00
May 8, 1817	War. 362	75,000.00				75,000.00
November 21, 1817	War. 1296	30,000.00				30,000.00
April 22, 1817	War. 263			$33,670.97		33,670.97
August 13, 1824	Req. 2493	5,510.27				4,510.27
November 18, 1825	Req. 3883	6,610.56				6,610.56
July 5, 1827	Req. 610				$17,577.60	17,577.60
Total		217,120.83				343,369.40

CONNECTICUT.

Warrants and requisitions after July 1, 1822.		Balances due certain States (act March 3, 1817).	Pay of the militia.	Claims of the State of Connecticut (act March 1, 1827).	Total.
Date.	Number.				
September 20, 1813	War. 1407		$3,000.00		$3,000.00
March 11, 1817	War. 5	$50,000.00			50,000.00
July 19, 1838	Req. 9264			$55,923.70	55,923.70
December 20, 1838	Req. 670			9,145.50	9,145.50
Total				65,069.20	118,069.20

NEW HAMPSHIRE.

Warrants and requisitions after July 1, 1822.		Balances due certain States (act March 3, 1817).	Pay of the militia.	Total.
Date.	Number.			
July 22, 1816	War. 150		$40,000.00	$40,000.00
March 22, 1817	War. 84	$12,000.00		12,000.00
April 14, 1818	War. 1913	6,000.00		6,000.00
Total		18,000.00		58,000.00

Payments to States by the United States for expenditures made by them, etc.—**Continued.**

NEW YORK.

Warrants and requisitions after July 1, 1822. Date.	Number.	Balances due certain States (act March 3, 1817).	For balances of property account between the United States and State of New York, for military stores in war of 1812 (act August 5, 1854).	Payment of interest due the State of New York (act May 22, 1826).	Total.
February 3, 1819	War. 3270	$80,000.00			$80,000.00
May 6, 1819	War. 3908	20,000.00			20,000.00
March 24, 1821	War. 7904	23,561.36			23,561.36
April 25, 1822	War. 9030	2,948.24			2,948.24
December 28, 1822	Req. 599	6,000.00			6,000.00
March 27, 1826	Req. 4259	6,615.02			6,615.02
October 25, 1826	Req. 4927			$40,264.86	40,264.86
January 2, 1855	Req. 4317		$11,929.45		11,929.45
Total		139,124.62			191,318.93

MARYLAND.

Warrants and requisitions after July 1, 1822. Date.	Number.	Balances due certain States (act March 3, 1817).	Payment of interest due the State of Maryland (act May 13, 1826).	Payment of money expended by the city of Baltimore in her own defense, and interest on same (acts May 20, 1826, and April 8, 1830).	Act for settlement of account between the United States and State of Maryland (approved March 3, 1857).	Total.
September 28, 1818	War. 2608	$40,000.00				$40,000.00
January 27, 1819	War. 3239	40,000.00				40,000.00
December 1, 1819	War. 4840	100,000.00				100,000.00
January 3, 1821	War. 7478	94,710.21				94,710.21
November 30, 1821	War. 8653	4,916.33				4,916.33
January 10, 1822	War. 8760	2,070.00				2,070.00
July 6, 1822	Req. 20	527.00				527.00
June 27, 1826	Req. 4591		$30,000.00			30,000.00
September 18, 1826	Req. 4827		31,582.63			31,582.63
November 10, 1826	Req. 4959	10,424.49				10,424.49
December 2, 1826	Req. 4995		4,980.59			4,980.59
August 29, 1857	Req. 9178				$275,770.23	275,770.23
1813			527.00			527.00
1822			527.00			527.00
City of Baltimore.						
August 15, 1826	Req. 4717			$21,710.25		21,710.25
April 14, 1857	Req. 345			14,844.71		14,844.71
Total		292,648.03	67,617.22	36,554.96	275,770.23	672,590.44

Payments to States by the United States for expenditures made by them, etc.—Continued.

DELAWARE.

Warrants and requisitions, act July 1, 1822.		Balances due certain States (act March 3, 1817).	Interest due the State (act May 20, 1826).	Total.
Date.	Number.			
October 13, 1818...............................	War. 2721	$25,000.00	....	$25,000.00
December 7, 1822...............................	Req. 529	9,545.72	....	9,545.72
December 12, 1826..............................	Req. 5017	....	$6,530.00	6,530.00
Total		34,545.72	6,530.00	41,075.72

RECAPITULATION.

Virginia..	$1,985,918.17
North Carolina...	77,000.00
Mississippi..	4,585.61
South Carolina...	512,259.16
Vermont..	4,421.18
Rhode Island...	42,422.57
Massachusetts..	657,924.74
Pennsylvania...	343,369.40
Connecticut..	119,069.20
New Hampshire..	58,000.00
New York...	191,318.93
Maryland...	672,590.44
Delaware...	41,075.72

MEXICAN WAR.

Payments to the States by the United States on account of money expended by them in the prosecution of the war, as shown on the books of the Third Auditor.

[NOTE.—Payments were made on this account through Second Auditor, and are not in this report.]

State and period of payments.	Appropriations.			Total.
	Mexican hostilities.	Refunding expenses incurred for use of volunteers before being mustered into United States service (act June 2, 1848).	Army transportation, etc.	
Tennessee:				
1846 and 1847	$21,598.21	....	....	$21,598.21
1849 and 1850	....	$1,343.00	....	1,343.00
1848...	....	....	$306.00	306.00
Total				23,247.21
Louisiana:				
1846 and 1847	23,551.72	....	....	23,551.72
1848 to 1853	....	8,999.07	....	8,999.07
1847...	....	....	*138.00	138.00
Total				32,688.79
Mississippi:				
1848...	....	594.07	....	594.07
1848...	....	....	†1,105.19	1,105.19
Total				1,699.26

* Transportation supplies, etc., Quartermaster's Department.   † Subsistence.

Payments to the States by the United States on account of money expended, etc.—Cont'd.

State and period of payments.	Appropriations.			Total.
	Mexican hostilities.	Refunding expenses incurred for use of volunteers before being mustered into United States service (act June 2, 1848).	Army transportation, etc.	
Texas:				
1817............................	....	....	*$9,171.76	$9,171.76
Alabama:				
1848...........................	$236.66	....	....	236.66
1848 to 1852	....	$9,714.78	....	9,714.78
Total	....	....	....	9,951.44
South Carolina:				
1848 to 1851	....	5,936.64	....	5,936.64
Virginia:				
1817...........................	6,218.73	....	....	6,218.73
1850 to 1853...................	....	5,383.14	....	5,383.14
Total	....	....	....	11,601.87
North Carolina:				
1853...........................	....	3,084.84	....	3,084.84
Pennsylvania:				
1853...........................	....	1,569.39	....	1,569.39
Ohio:				
1846 to 1848..................	14,623.54	....	....	14,623.54
Illinois:				
1840...........................	....	299.00	....	299.00
Indiana:				
1852 and 1853.................	....	8,287.46	....	8,287.46
Michigan:				
1852 and 1853.................	....	1,070.18	....	1,070.18
1852...........................	....	....	†18,568.81	18,568.81
Total	....	....	....	19,638.99
Maine:				
1860...........................	....	....	‡10,308.28	10,308.28

* For payment of four companies of Texas volunteers (act May 8, 1846).
† To refund expenses incurred by State (act August 31, 1852).
‡ Claim of the State of Maine for advances (act February 9, 1859).

RECAPITULATION.

Tennessee	$23,247.21
Louisiana	32,688.79
Mississippi	1,699.26
Texas	9,171.76
Alabama...	9,951.44
South Carolina..	5,936.64
Virginia	11,601.87
North Carolina..	3,084.84
Pennsylvania..	1,569.39
Ohio	14,623.54
Illinois..	299.00
Indiana..	8,287.46
Michigan	19,638.99
Maine..	10,308.28
Total	152,108.47

*Statement of amounts and dates of payments made by the United States to the States, for
expenses incurred by them in suppressing the rebellion; as shown by the books of the Third
Auditor of the Treasury.*

[NOTE.—Act approved July 27, 1861, was general in application as relating to this class of claims, furnishing to the accounting officers of the Treasury authority for their settlement.]

CONNECTICUT.

Requisitions.		Refunding to States expenses incurred in raising volunteers (acts July 17, 1861, February 25, 1862, etc.).
Date.	Number.	
March 18, 1862	6890	$600,000.00
December 31, 1863	3553	612,785.71
March 14, 1866	9178	171,405.70
April 16, 1866	9320	154,915.75
April 26, 1866	9382	102,189.05
February 1, 1867	1853	6,750.20
May 1, 1867	3123	21,902.14
March 11, 1870	3435	23,447.01
April 22, 1871	6500	10,135.12
May 2, 1871	6551	133,195.96
June 30, 1871	7155	154,273.84
July 23, 1872	344	10,824.69
December 5, 1872	2022	16,591.21
April 24, 1873	3682	16,675.00
December 3, 1873	6796	850.87
May 15, 1876	8146	9,323.75
July 22, 1876	9709	9,808.57
June 27, 1876	6884	1,127.67
June 21, 1880	6520	8,513.06
March 15, 1881	237	1,703.88
August 9, 1882	6379	15,257.20
Total		2,096,950.46

MASSACHUSETTS.

Requisitions.		Refunding to States expenses incurred in raising volunteers (acts July 17, 1861, February 25, 1862, etc.).	Subsistence for three years' volunteers.	Total.
Date.	Number.			
September 11, 1861	4995	$775,000.00		$775,000.00
April 27, 1865	7374	309,088.95		309,088.95
March 5, 1866	9160	700,894.14		700,894.14
Do	9161	621,435.53		621,435.53
February 14, 1868	6091	370,509.67		370,509.67
April 7, 1868	6342	300,000.00		300,000.00
October 20, 1868	8414	205,999.14		205,999.14
February 3, 1869	9613	28,700.97		28,700.97
August 12, 1869	1717	55,604.96		55,604.96
March 24, 1870	3753	132,990.32		132,990.32
June 5, 1872	2721	79,375.41		79,375.41
March 13, 1883	411	11,754.12		11,754.12
July 11, 1884	5903	28,610.33		28,610.33
October 18, 1861	5368		$18,668.41	18,668.41
Do	5369		6,763.27	6,763.27
Do	5370		14,988.85	14,988.85
Total		3,620,062.54	40,420.53	3,660,483.07

Amounts and dates of payments made by the United States to the States, etc.—Continued.

RHODE ISLAND.

Requisitions.		Refunding to States expenses incurred in raising volunteers (acts July 17, 1861, February 25, 1862, etc.).	Subsistence for three-years volunteers.	Total.
Requisitions.	Number.			
October 18, 1861	5356	$231, 478. 51	....	$231, 478. 51
January 5, 1867	1616	208, 087. 54	....	208, 087. 54
Do	1617	99, 419. 11	....	99, 419. 11
June 22, 1867	3778	119, 532. 24	....	119, 532. 24
November 6, 1867	5326	35, 634. 89	....	35, 634. 89
Do	5327	5, 385. 00	....	5, 385. 00
December 19, 1867	5832	6, 896. 72	....	6, 986. 72
January 17, 1868	6031	9, 277. 32	....	9, 277. 32
January 20, 1869	9582	6, 012. 53	....	6, 012. 53
March 3, 1864	4145	....	$1, 206. 29	1, 206. 29
Total	....	722, 323. 86	1, 206. 29	723, 530. 15

MAINE.

Requisitions.		Refunding to States expenses incurred in raising volunteers (acts July 17, 1861, February 25, 1862, etc.).
Date.	Number.	
September 2, 1861	4011	$200, 000, 00
January 14, 1862	6354	120, 000. 00
March 2, 1867	2236	198, 462. 12
Do	2237	357, 702. 10
November 22, 1867	5545	10, 682. 23
September 5, 1868	7708	127, 473. 34
October 16, 1868	8361	6, 728. 96
June 27, 1871	7140	3, 938. 93
March 13, 1883	410	2, 197. 32
Total	....	1, 027, 185. 00

NEW HAMPSHIRE.

Requisitions.		Refunding to States expenses incurred in raising volunteers (acts July 17, 1861, February 25, 1862, etc.).	Subsistence for three-years volunteers.	Total.
Date.	Number.			
October 7, 1861	5211	$200, 000. 00	....	$200, 000. 00
September 19, 1863	2365	224, 000. 00	....	224, 000. 00
January 13, 1864	3654	47, 134. 19	....	47, 134. 19
Do	3653	185, 645. 67	....	185, 645. 67
December 19, 1864	6518	200, 000. 00	....	200, 000. 00
April 17, 1866	9324	44, 218. 79	....	44, 218. 79
May 1, 1867	3129	7, 523. 86	....	7, 523. 86
June 5, 1867	3370	8, 298. 02	....	8, 298. 02
November 14, 1867	5433	2, 700. 32	....	2, 700. 32
January 16, 1869	9534	20, 175. 00	....	20, 175. 00
Do	9535	21, 983. 21	....	21, 983. 21
June 10, 1869	1039	901. 10	....	906. 10
December 13, 1869	2757	2, 326. 06	....	2, 326. 06
January 13, 1870	3006	2, 961. 28	....	2, 961. 28
June 6, 1873	4322	1, 363. 44	....	1, 363. 44
December 11, 1873	6939	2, 639. 58	....	2, 639. 58
October 18, 1861	5367	....	$4, 206. 40	4, 206. 40
Total	....	971, 875. 52	4, 206. 40	976, 081. 92

Amounts and dates of payments made by the United States to the States, etc.—Continued.

VERMONT.

Requisitions.		Refunding to States expenses incurred in raising volunteers (acts July 17, 1861, February 25, 1862, etc.).	Payment of the State of Vermont for expenses in protection against invasion from Canada in 1864 (act June 23, 1866).	Total.
Date.	Number.			
September 7, 1861................................	4972	$123,000.00	....	$123,000.00
May 5, 1862	7383	152,000.00	....	152,000.00
May 25, 1863	994	179,407.80	....	179,407.80
Do...	995	152,895.31	....	152,985.31
September 4, 1867	4484	41,173.90	....	41,173.90
June 17, 1869....................................	1136	49,691.90	....	49,691.90
August 4, 1869	1591	58,364.41	....	58,364.41
May 28, 1872	2640	56,502.18	....	56,502.18
September 10, 1877	4623	1,252.13	....	1,252.13
February 7, 1878	5258	835.75	....	835.75
May 11, 1878.....................................	6152	970.21	....	970.21
September 4, 1867	4484	....	$16,463.81	16,463.81
Total	....	816,093.59	16,463.81	832,557.40

NEW YORK.

Requisitions.		Refunding to States expenses incurred in raising volunteers (acts July 17, 1861, February 25, 1862, etc.).
Date.	Number.	
December 17, 1861................................	6089	$1,113,000.00
September 26, 1865...............................	8356	262,763.17
June 14, 1867....................................	3595	879,058.22
September 23, 1870...............................	5026	41,220.83
Do...	5027	702.90
Do...	5028	37,260.72
May 25, 1871.....................................	6836	194,799.15
June 27, 1871....................................	7141	348,295.50
December 10, 1871...............................	2061	272,087.02
December 30, 1872...............................	2170	192,650.31
March 17, 1873..................................	3039	107,498.08
December 30, 1875	7262	81,230.25
November 18, 1876..............................	1771	57,047.80
Do...	1772	24,936.80
June 23, 1877....................................	4475	41,138.50
July 5, 1878.....................................	7274	82,730.78
July 1, 1880.....................................	6761	61,858.95
March 15, 1881..................................	236	21,421.13
August 9, 1882..................................	6380	83,344.35
July 11, 1884....................................	5905	54,946.52
Total	....	3,957,996.08

Amounts and dates of payments made by the United States to the States, etc.—Continued.

NEW JERSEY.

Requisitions.		Refunding to States expenses incurred in raising volunteers (acts July 17, 1801, February 25, 1862, etc.).	Expenses incurred in raising 100 days volunteers (act May 6, 1864).	Expenses incurred by the State of New Jersey in the erection of barracks, etc., for nine months men in 1862. Paid out of appropriation for barracks and quarters.	Total.
Date.	Number.				
August 31, 1801	4909	$74,000.00			$74,000.00
August 1, 1807	3006	100,000.00			100,000.00
December 7, 1867	5674	551,617.48			551,617.48
Do	5675	382,613.90			382,613.90
June 5, 1868	6509	60,830.79			60,830.79
July 9, 1868	7177	27,978.20			27,978.20
October 19, 1868	8403	40,409.62			40,409.62
January 13, 1809	9490	1,037.90			1,037.90
June 10, 1869	1022	14,613.21			14,613.21
November 6, 1869	2458	11,898.34			11,898.34
May 25, 1870	4315	17,005.98			17,005.98
August 9, 1870	4846	8,024.44			8,024.44
December 24, 1870	5714	20,669.87			20,669.87
June 23, 1871	7122	11,404.60			11,404.60
June 20, 1871	7153	56,264.05			56,264.05
August 6, 1875	6190	10,889.20			10,889.20
December 24, 1870	5714		$6,883.08		6,883.08
March 10, 1865	7041			$24,025.79	24,025.79
Total		1,389,257.58			1,420,167.35

PENNSYLVANIA.

Requisitions.		Refunding to States expenses incurred in raising volunteers (acts July 17, 1861, February 25, 1862, etc.).	Total.
Date.	Number.		
September 10, 1861	5069	$606,000.00	$606,003.00
May 1, 1867	3124	1,304,711.43	1,304,711.43
Do	3125	78,516.89	78,516.89
October 27, 1868	8511	105,651.46	105,651.46
August 26, 1870	4884	136,846.09	138,846.09
April 11, 1871	6408	137,822.59	137,832.59
May 15, 1871	6689	242,167.57	242,167.57
June 23, 1871	7123	298,753.08	298,753.08
August 10, 1875	6215	2,865.61	2,865.61
October 20, 1877	4742	58,490.41	58,490.41
March 4, 1878,	5342	22,557.75	22,557.75
July 5, 1878	7275	29,527.23	29,527.23
March 10, 1879	716	8,236.56	8,236.56
July 1, 1880	6702	39,005.78	39,005.78
March 15, 1881	238	5,156.06	5,156.06
August 9, 1882	6382	94,561.15	94,561.15
March 13, 1883	413	33,766.58	33,766.58
Total		3,204,636.24	3,204,636.24

Amounts and dates of payments made by the United States to the States, etc.—Continued.

OHIO.

Requisitions.		Refunding to States expenses incurred in raising volunteers (acts July 17, 1861, February 25, 1862, etc.).	Quartermaster's Department.	To refund to the State expenses incurred in raising 100 days troops (acts May 6, 1866).	To reimburse the State for expenses in enrolling, etc., militia in the United States service (act March 29, 1867).	Total.
Date.	Number.					
November 13, 1861	5635	$177,600.00	....	....	....	$177,600.00
August 8, 1861	4739	900,000.00	....	....	....	900,000.00
December 24, 1864	6573	766,896.04	....	....	....	766,896.94
February 7, 1867	2075	1,880.34	$200.00	....	....	2,080.34
Do	2076	185,128.99	....	....	....	185,128.99
August 22, 1867	4444	56,623.70	....	$102,403.52	....	159,027.22
December 30, 1867	5857	60,900.80	....	59,428.98	....	120,329.78
December 10, 1868	9140	2,963.48	....	....	$258,767.66	261,731.14
August 13, 1869	1762	23,372.29	....	....	....	23,372.29
June 21, 1870	4513	73,639.26	....	158.04	7,515.12	80,313.32
April 3, 1871	6376	143,436.32	....	....	....	143,436.32
May 13, 1871	6587	1,808.28	....	....	....	1,808.28
March 11, 1873	2952	80,557.09	....	....	....	80,557.09
August 13, 1873	5374	4,617.41	....	....	....	4,617.41
May 26, 1874	9396	22,021.48	....	....	....	22,021.48
September 10, 1874	1059	13,760.52	....	....	....	13,760.52
December 17, 1875	7158	5,578.27	....	....	....	5,578.27
August 9, 1882	6378	67,674.98	....	....	....	67,674.98
March 13, 1883	409	70,943.96	....	....	....	70,943.96
July 11, 1884	5906	90,246.92	....	....	....	90,246.92
September 21, 1867	4858	....	....	....	680.31	680.31
Do	4859	....	....	....	435.19	435.19
September 26, 1867	4954	....	....	....	141.56	141.56
October 8, 1867	5019	....	....	....	50.00	50.00
Do	5020	....	....	....	19.50	19.50
November 18, 1867	5466	....	....	....	34.50	34.50
November 26, 1867	5586	....	....	....	4.50	4.50
April 21, 1866	9370	....	*57,368.77	....	....	....
Total	....	2,758,111.03	57,568.77	161,991.44	267,648.34	3,245,319.58

*Paid the State out of appropriation for payment of expenses of minute men and volunteers in Ohio, Kentucky, and Pennsylvania.

WISCONSIN.

Requisitions.		Refunding to States expenses incurred in raising volunteers (acts July 17, 1861, February 25, 1862, etc.).
Date.	Number.	
September 2, 1861	4910	$205,000.00
July 18, 1862	8005	110,000.00
September 30, 1862	8507	147,163.83
May 19, 1865	7776	300,238.26
January 25, 1870	3092	219,742.06
March 17, 1873	3049	42,567.49
November 1, 1875	6772	10,347.53
Total	....	1,035,059.17

Amounts and dates of payments made by the United States to the States, etc.—Continued.

IOWA.

Requisitions.		Refunding to States expenses incurred in raising volunteers (acts July 17, 1861, February 25, 1862, etc.).	To reimburse the State for expenses incurred during the rebellion (act March 3, 1869).	Total.
Date.	Number.			
September 25, 1861	5112	$80,000.00		$80,000.00
September 7, 1862	7111	20,000.00		20,000.00
July 8, 1868	5917	135,442.44		135,442.44
Do	5918	384,274.80		384,274.80
June 17, 1869	1137		$229,827.39	229,827.39
January 25, 1870	3093	85,079.64		85,079.64
June 4, 1872	2079	101,376.02		101,376.02
March 7, 1874	8905	3,496.99		3,496.99
May 26, 1874	9395	262.17		262.17
Total		809,932.06		1,039,759.45

ILLINOIS.

Requisitions.		Refunding to States expenses incurred in raising volunteers (acts July 17, 1861, February 25, 1862, etc.).	Clothing, etc.	Total.
Date.	Number.			
August 6, 1861	4716	$400,000.00		$400,000.00
June 23, 1862	7804		$124,234.23	124,234.23
June 25, 1862	7879	357,747.48		357,747.48
October 28, 1862	8789	974,568.63		974,568.63
Do	8790	110,028.44		110,028.44
April 17, 1863	627	320,000.00		320,000.00
August 8, 1864	5164	30,000.00		30,000.00
February 7, 1865	6810	438,285.98		438,285.98
June 7, 1867	3403	25,080.68		25,080.68
December 12, 1867	5791	71,620.04		71,620.04
December 23, 1868	9256	130,345.81		130,345.81
Do	9257	0.00		0.00
December 28, 1869	2902	52,397.69		52,397.69
July 14, 1870	4689	39,023.78		39,023.78
April 12, 1871	6426	514.75		514.75
Total		2,950,208.28		3,080,442.51

Amounts and dates of payments made by the United States to the States, etc.--Continued.

INDIANA.

Requisitions.		Refunding to States expenses incurred in raising volunteers (acts July 17, 1861, February 25, 1862, etc.).	Collecting, organizing, and drilling volunteers (act August 5, 1861).	To re-imburse the State for expenses in enrolling, etc., her militia (act March 29, 1867).	To refund to State expenses in curred in raising 100 days' troops (act May 8, 1864).	Total.
Date.	Number.					
July 30, 1861	4084	$450, 000. 00				$450, 000. 00
August 20, 1861	4813		$100, 000. 00			100, 000. 00
October 24, 1865	8666	133, 302. 91				133, 302. 91
November 24, 1868	8917	415, 655. 39				415, 655. 39
Do	8918	700, 442. 43				700, 442. 43
Do	8919	198, 128. 14				198, 128. 14
April 19, 1869	417			$243. 54		243. 54
Do	418			325. 39		325. 39
May 27, 1869	871			289. 17		289. 17
June 4, 1869	955			545. 00		545. 00
Do	956			289. 17		289. 17
June 17, 1869	1130			298. 07		298. 07
Do	1131			298. 07		298. 07
Do	1132			298. 07		298. 07
July 28, 1869	1515			118. 17		118. 17
Do	1516			289. 17		289. 17
Do	1517			90. 59		90. 59
Do	1518			289. 17		289. 17
July 30, 1869	1529			289. 17		289. 17
August 14, 1869	1777			298. 67		298. 67
Do	1778			298. 67		298. 67
Do	1779			298. 67		298. 67
Do	1780			362. 10		362. 10
October 16, 1869	2291			722. 07		722. 67
December 2, 1869	2654			240. 13		240. 13
Do	2655			647. 77		647. 77
Do	2656			667. 36		667. 36
December 22, 1869	2885			104. 00		104. 00
June 22, 1870	4574			464, 923. 24		464, 923. 24
December 4, 1869	2680	40, 523. 55			$888. 60	41, 412. 15
January 25, 1870	3085			122. 00		122. 00
September 12, 1870	4956	23, 255. 00				23, 255. 00
January 9, 1871	5765			100. 00		100. 00
November 10, 1871	951			22. 60		22. 60
Do	952			13. 40		13. 40
September 9, 1874	1030			11, 218. 96		11, 218. 96
October 30, 1874	1505	112, 267. 56				112, 267. 56
February 10, 1875	2294	10, 362. 01				10, 362. 01
Total		2, 083, 036. 99		483, 704. 19		2, 668, 529. 78

MINNESOTA.

Requisitions.		Refunding to States expenses incurred in raising volunteers (acts July 17, 1861, etc.).	Total
Date.	Number.		
November 12, 1868	8684	$15, 137. 74	$15, 137. 74
November 12, 1868	8685	45, 215. 23	45, 215. 23
November 28, 1868	8968	10, 445. 48	10, 445. 48
Total		70, 798. 45	70, 798. 45

Amounts and dates of payments made by the United States to the States, etc.—Continued.

KANSAS.

Requisitions.		Refunding to States expenses incurred in raising volunteers (acts July 17, 1861, etc.].	Reimbursing the State for expenses in suppressing the rebellion (acts February 2, 1871, and June 8, 1872).	Total.
Date.	Number.			
March 19, 1870	3734	$9, 360. 82	....	$9, 360. 82
April 18, 1871	6473	....	$110. 00	110. 00
Do	6474	....	110. 00	110. 00
Do	6475	....	110. 00	110. 00
August 14, 1872	827	....	336, 817. 37	336, 817. 37
February 4, 1878	5245	2, 073. 34	....	2, 073. 34
June 14, 1881	2651	26, 604. 05	....	26, 604. 05
August 9, 1882	6383	8, 952. 57	....	8, 952. 57
Total	....	46, 990. 78	337, 147. 37	384, 138. 15

NEBRASKA.

Requisitions.		Refunding to States expenses incurred in raising volunteers (acts July 17, 1861, etc.).	Total.
Date.	Number.		
July 12, 1884	6018	$485. 00	$485. 00

COLORADO TERRITORY.

Requisitions.		Payment for services of militia in 1864 (act July 25, 1868).	Total.
Date	Number.		
January 23, 1869	9568	$55, 238. 84	$55. 238. 84

MISSOURI.

Requisitions.		Refunding to States expenses incurred in raising volunteers (acts July 17, 1861, etc.).	Supplying and transporting arms, etc., to loyal citizens of revolting States (act July 31, 1861).	Reimbursing State for militia expenses during the rebellion (act April 17, 1866).	Act to authorize the Secretary of the Treasury to examine and report upon claims for payments made by the State to her militia since April 17, 1866 (approved January 27, 1879).	Total.
Date.	Number.					
October 6, 1862	8606	....	$125, 000. 00	....	....	$125, 000. 00
April 24, 1867	3042	....	....	$3, 023. 79	....	3, 023. 79
Do	3043	....	....	645, 331. 08	....	645, 331. 08
July 17, 1867	3944	....	....	1, 696, 391. 46	....	1, 696, 391. 46
August 22, 1867	4443	....	....	1, 000, 000. 00	....	1, 000, 000. 00
September 4, 1867	4500	....	....	1, 817, 864. 66	....	1, 817, 864. 66
September 27, 1867	4982	....	....	1, 128, 807. 25	....	1, 128, 807. 25
September 9, 1867	4605	$646, 958. 23	....	....	....	646, 958. 23
October 24, 1867	5280	....	....	78, 044. 60	....	78, 044. 60
Do	5281	....	....	171, 960. 86	....	171, 960. 86
August 12, 1868	7587	....	....	32, 445. 40	....	32, 445. 40
August 9, 1882	6376	....	....	....	$234, 407. 10	234, 407. 10
Do	6377	....	....	....	187. 00	187. 00
Total	....	....	....	6, 573, 869. 10	234, 594. 10	7, 580, 421. 43

Amounts and dates of payments made by the United States to the States, etc.—Continued.

MICHIGAN.

Requisitions.		Refunding to States expenses incurred in raising volunteers (acts July 17, 1861, etc.).
Date.	Number.	
August 27, 1861	4848	$92,000.00
June 14, 1867	3594	254,400.59
June 10, 1868	6672	171,598.44
Do	6673	172,008.24
October 22, 1868	8444	17,302.41
January 5, 1870	2928	19,035.55
June 15, 1872	2695	58,802.00
May 4, 1876	8115	14,224.15
December 7, 1876	2064	555.10
May 11, 1877	4154	1,088.80
February 7, 1878	5259	373.70
July 1, 1880	6760	347.60
July 11, 1884	5904	42,345.95
Total		844,262.53

DELAWARE.

Requisitions.		Refunding to States expenses incurred in raising volunteers (acts July 17, 1861, etc.).	Subsistence.	Total.
Date.	Number.			
June 12, 1877	4378	$6,511.41		$6,511.41
June 25, 1877	4476	15,072.09		15,072.09
August 24, 1877	4605	4,558.26		4,558.26
September 25, 1877	4653	2,828.00		2,828.00
October 20, 1864	5963		$3,019.20	3,019.20
Total		28,969.76	3,019.20	31,988.96

MARYLAND.

Requisitions.		Refunding to States expenses incurred in raising volunteers (acts July 17, 1861, etc.).
Date.	Number.	
July 9, 1868	7181	$7,101.52
July 13, 1872	208	3,550.28
January 25, 1873	2467	4,141.71
November 3, 1875	6791	60,063.14
January 11, 1876	7350	16,861.70
January 25, 1877	2393	32,893.92
March 29, 1877	3194	13,759.88
July 28, 1877	4546	4,708.84
Total		133,140.99

Amounts and dates of payments made by the United States to the States, etc.—Continued.

VIRGINIA.

Requisitions.		Refunding to States expenses incurred in raising volunteers (acts July 17, 1861, etc.).
Date.	Number.	
November 22, 1861	5780	$12,000.00
July 26, 1862	8128	14,319.24
July 24, 1868	7407	6,128.62
January 18, 1869	9536	16,022.11
Total		48,469.97

WEST VIRGINIA.

Requisitions.		Refunding to States expenses incurred in raising volunteers (acts July 17, 1861, etc.).	Reimbursing the State for expenses incurred (act June 21, 1866).	Total.
Date.	Number.			
March 27, 1867	2434		$1,068.38	$1,068.38
Do	2485		420.08	420.08
March 29, 1867	2486		1,086.63	1,086.63
April 4, 1867	2594		391.67	391.67
Do	2595		407.17	407.17
Do	2596		391.67	391.67
May 20, 1867	3342		382.17	382.17
Do	3343		385.17	385.17
Do	3344		291.00	291.00
Do	3345		119.00	119.00
Do	3346		366.17	366.17
July 8, 1867	3842		376.17	376.17
July 9, 1867	3843		376.17	376.17
Do	3844		298.67	298.67
August 5, 1867	4029		364.17	364.17
Do	4030		289.17	289.17
Do	4031		364.17	364.17
August 19, 1867	4431		376.17	376.17
Do	4432		298.67	298.67
Do	4434		376.17	376.17
September 13, 1867	4673		298.67	298.67
Do	4674		376.17	376.17
Do	4675		376.17	376.17
October 10, 1867	5108		364.17	364.17
Do	5109		289.17	289.17
Do	5110		364.17	364.17
November 22, 1867	5559		376.17	376.17
Do	5560		376.17	376.17
January 22, 1868	6069		216.00	216.00
Do	6070		1,012.19	1,012.19
Do	6071		983.33	983.33
Do	6072		944.89	944.89
June 12, 1868	6744		302,679.28	302,679.28
Do	6745	$153,978.75		153,978.75
Total		153,978.75	317,085.19	471,063.94

Amounts and dates of payments made by the United States to the States, etc.—Continued.

KENTUCKY.

Requisitions.		Refunding to States expenses incurred in raising volunteers (acts July 17, 1861, etc.).	Reimbursing the State for expenses in suppressing the rebellion (act June 8, 1872, etc.).	Army transportation, 1871 and prior years, act March 3, 1877 (deficiencies).	Total.
Date.	Number.				
May 26, 1862	7604	$315,000.00			$315,000.00
June 27, 1862	9901	436,000,00			436,000.00
June 3, 1863	1056	100,000.00			100,000.00
March 8, 1864	4172	200,000.00			200,000.00
February 8, 1867	2086	155,115.09			155,115.09
Do	2087	606,641.03			606,641.03
April 24, 1867	3044	40,398.30			40,398.30
June 5, 1867	3369	79,674.75			79,674.75
August 26, 1867	4445	40,623.39			40,623.39
October 15, 1867	5183	83,412.64			83,412.64
March 9, 1868	6261	34,341.78			34,341.78
June 11, 1868	6693	40,823.56			40,823.56
August 25, 1868	7691	31,812.53			31,812.53
August 5, 1869	1607	14,308.48			14,308.48
April 27, 1870	4062	28,174.51			28,174.51
October 22, 1870	5236	145,710.00			145,710.00
May 29, 1871	6868	50,119.75			50,119.75
June 17, 1871	7081	130,543.60			130,543.60
August 20, 1872	966		$525,258.72		525,258.72
March 16, 1874	8136	30,588.53	58,199.32		88,787.85
April 18, 1874	8730		6,728.25		6,728.25
November 2, 1874	1535	3,568.23	35,490.65		39,058.88
July 13, 1875	5981	24,817.23	33,739.93		58,557.16
December 17, 1875	7157	4,538.85	8,411.33		12,950.18
June 13, 1876	9080	25,531.94	7,046.38		32,578.32
November 25, 1876	1982	4,967.08	390.27		5,357.35
May 9, 1877	4136			$101,121.05	101,121.05
June 1, 1877	4270	10,452.27	4,114.53		14,566.80
March 10, 1879	717	6,091.85			6,091.85
July 1, 1880	6763		15,000.00		15,000.00
August 9, 1882	6381	36,211.81			36,211.81
March 13, 1883	412	29,498.94			29,498.94
Total		2,708,960.14	694,379.38	101,121.05	3,504,460.57

APPENDIX A.—*Statement of amounts refunded to States for expenses incurred in raising volunteers for war of the rebellion, paid through the office of the Second Auditor.*

State.	Date of payment.	No. of warrant.	Amount paid to States.	Total.
New Hampshire	June 15, 1863	8430	$450.00	$450.00
Massachusetts	Apr. 18, 1862	8565	7,608.88	7,608.88
New York	Apr. 13, 1863	6750	191,288.46	198,938.52
	Apr. 19, 1864	5760	5,787.65	
	July 16, 1864	7155	1,862.41	
New Jersey	Dec. 18, 1883	2589	46,042.93	96,859.44
	Jan. 19, 1865	1342	50,816.51	
Pennsylvania	June 18, 1866	8447	667,074.35	667,074.35
Indiana	Apr. 17, 1862	8477	68,701.60	1,073,208.51
	July 14, 1862	838	74,508.95	
	Nov. 7, 1862	2795	61,439.45	
	Nov. 7, 1862	2796	2,707.91	
	Dec. 8, 1862	3408	72,445.80	
	Jan. 8, 1863	4017	237,269.30	
	Apr. 1, 1863	6443	23,207.64	
	Apr. 1, 1863	6444	49,122.20	
	May 2, 1863	7208	17,928.98	
	July 8, 1863	8970	47,594.30	
	Aug. 5, 1863	9569	38,548.76	
	Sept. 27, 1863	527	53,971.55	
	Nov. 7, 1863	1932	41,361.88	
	Apr. 13, 1864	5625	50,217.17	
	Apr. 23, 1864	5015	16,933.39	
	Apr. 15, 1864	5654	47,355.62	
	Apr. 19, 1864	5786	27,404.56	
	June 20, 1864	6685	64,352.26	
	Jan. 22, 1864	3466	32,000.00	
	June 20, 1864	6686	13,273.82	
	July 23, 1864	7317	3,026.79	
	Feb. 14, 1866	7352	5,902.55	
	Apr. 9, 1866	7813	74.75	
	Dec. 18, 1868	5168	23,859.28	
Minnesota	Dec. 16, 1863	2577	276.75	276.75
Total				2,044,416.45

RECAPITULATION.

States.	Amount.	States.	Amount.
Connecticut	$2,096,050.46	Kansas	$384,138.15
Massachusetts	3,660,483.07	Nebraska	485.00
Rhode Island	723,530.15	Colorado Territory	55,233.84
Maine	1,027,185.00	Missouri	7,580,421.43
New Hampshire	976,081.92	Michigan	844,262.53
Vermont	832,557.40	Delaware	31,088.96
New York	3,957,996.98	Maryland	133,140.99
New Jersey	1,420,167.35	Virginia	48,469.97
Pennsylvania	3,204,636.24	West Virginia	471,063.94
Ohio	3,245,319.58	Kentucky	3,504,466.57
Wisconsin	1,035,059.17		
Iowa	1,039,759.45		42,093,173.89
Illinois	3,080,442.51	Appendix A	2,044,416.45
Indiana	2,668,529.78		
Minnesota	70,798.45	Total	44,137,590.34

Statement of appropriations, under general act approved July 27, 1861, on account of refunding to States expenses incurred in raising volunteers for the suppression of the rebellion, and of amount carried to the surplus fund, showing total amount of advances to the States on this account.

Date of acts making appropriations.	No. of warrant.	Date of warrant.	Amount of appropriations.
July 17, 1861	2	July 22, 1861	$10,000,000.00
February 25, 1862	7	Mar. 18, 1862	15,000,000.00
"Indefinite act"	80	June 30, 1869	1,144,815.04
Do	95	June 30, 1870	814,027.25
Do	115	June 30, 1871	2,379,246.72
May 18, 1872	124	May 20, 1872	1,000,000.00
June 10, 1872	135	July 1, 1872	500,000.00
March 3, 1873	153	July 1, 1873	300,000.00
June 23, 1874	171	July 1, 1874	250,000.00
March 3, 1875	196	July 1, 1875	250,000.00
June 20, 1878	273	July 1, 1878	112,264.01
March 3, 1879	282	Mar. 7, 1879	14,328.41
June 16, 1880	308	June 21, 1880	109,725.39
March 3, 1881	330	Mar. 11, 1881	54,975.12
August 5, 1882	377	Aug. 8, 1882	306,002.15
March 3, 1883	386	Mar. 10, 1883	148,160.92
July 7, 1884	426	July 8, 1884	216,643.72
Total			32,600,188.73
Deduct amount carried to surplus fund			467,538.83
Total advanced to the States			32,132,649.90

Surplus fund, warrants, number, date, and amount.

193.	June 30, 1875	$441,126.67
247.	June 30, 1877	18,863.61
267.	June 29, 1878	7,548.55
	Total to surplus fund	467,538.83

EXHIBIT No. 8.

JOINT RESOLUTION OF THE LEGISLATURE OF NEVADA, DATED MARCH 29, 1867, PROVIDING FOR ASCERTAINMENT AND ASKING PAYMENT OF INDEBTEDNESS INCURRED BY TERRITORY OF NEVADA IN SUPPRESSING INDIAN HOSTILITIES, ENROLLING VOLUNTEERS, ETC.

Whereas the national Government has invariably paid all proper expenses incurred in carrying on the Territorial governments inaugurated by Congress; and

Whereas, on account of our peculiar locality and situation, the amount appropriated by Congress to carry on our late Territorial government was wholly inadequate to meet the necessary expenses of the Territorial government; and

Whereas a large amount of equitable indebtedness, created prior to the organization of the Territory of Nevada, while we were yet a part of Utah, had accrued, which the Territory deemed to be resting upon the community as a just obligation, and which was assumed and paid by the Territory and State of Nevada; and

Whereas other moneys have been expended by the State and Territory in suppressing Indian hostilities, and also in payment of our volunteers in the service of the United States: Therefore, be it

Resolved by the senate, the assembly concurring, That the governor of the State of Nevada be, and he is hereby, authorized to cause to be made up a true and correct statement of the amount of Territorial indebtedness of the late Territory of Nevada assumed by the State of Nevada, including therein the entire amount paid by the State to the Nevada soldiers in the service of the National Government, the amount paid on old Carson County indebtedness, and the amount expended by the State for the suppression of Indian disturbances, and forward the same to our Senators and Representative in Congress for adjustment (Stats. Nev., 1867, p. 183).

EXHIBIT No. 9.

MEMORIAL OF THE LEGISLATURE OF THE STATE OF NEVADA, DATED FEBRUARY 1, 1869, RENEWING PRAYER FOR PAYMENT OF INDEBTEDNESS INCURRED BY TERRITORY OF NEVADA IN FURNISHING TROOPS FOR THE SUPPRESSION OF THE REBELLION AND INDIAN HOSTILITIES.

To the honorable the Senate and House of Representatives of the United States in Congress assembled:

Your memorialists, the legislature of the State of Nevada, would respectfully represent that the National Government has invariably paid all proper expense incurred in carrying on the Territorial governments inaugurated by Congress; and

Whereas the present State of Nevada, on account of its peculiar situation and locality, has found the amount appropriated by Congress to carry on its late Territorial government was wholly inadequate to meet the necessary expenses of the said Territorial government; and

Whereas a large amount of equitable indebtedness, created prior to the organization of the Territory of Nevada, while we yet were a part of Utah, had accrued, which the Territory deemed to be resting upon the community as a just obligation, and which was assumed and paid by the Territory and State of Nevada; and

Whereas other moneys have been expended by the State and Territory in suppressing Indian hostilities, and also in payment of our volunteers in the service of the National Government; and

Whereas the legislature of the State of Nevada, in special session, passed on the 29th day of March, A. D. 1867, a joint resolution authorizing the governor to cause to be prepared a correct statement of the amount of such indebtedness assumed by the State, including the amount paid by the State of Nevada to the soldiers of that State in the service of the National Government, the amount paid on old Carson County (then a part of Utah) indebtedness, and the amount expended by the State for the suppression of Indian disturbances, and to forward the same to our Senators and Representative in Congress for adjustment; and

Whereas his excellency the governor, in his second biennial message to the legislature of the State of Nevada, informed that honorable body that in conformity with such a request he caused such statement to be made and forwarded, and that he received due notice of its arrival at the national capital in the month of February last, and its presentment before the Committee on Claims of the Senate; and

Whereas the said message informs this legislature that he has not been informed of any further action thereon: Therefore, be it

Resolved by the assembly, the senate concurring, That the governor of the State of Nevada be, and he is hereby, authorized to cause to be made up a copy of the statement already sent for adjustment to the national authorities touching such claim and indebtedness, and forward the same to our Senators and Representative in Congress, urging its payment at an early day, as an act of justice no less due to Nevada than to other States of the National Union in similar cases (Stats. Nev., 1869, p. 293).

EXHIBIT No. 10.

MEMORIAL OF LEGISLATURE OF NEVADA, DATED FEBRUARY 11, 1885, SIMILAR TO "EXHIBIT No. 9," ASKING FOR RE-IMBURSEMENT ON ACCOUNT OF EXPENSES INCURRED IN FURNISHHING TROOPS FOR THE SUPPRESSION OF THE REBELLION AND INDIAN HOSTILITIES.

Whereas the law of July 27, 1861, and the joint and declaratory resolutions of March 8, 1862, provided for the re-imbursement to the States of all sums by them expended in defense of the United States; and

Whereas under the interpretation of said original act of 1861, made two days after its passage by the Secretary of the Treasury, the States were led to believe that if they, respectively, borrowed money on their own account, and advanced it to the United States under the conditions mentioned in said law, that said sums, together with the interest paid thereon, would be refunded to them, that having been the practice of the United States in such cases for more than sixty years; and

S. Rep. 1286——5

Whereas acting under this impression and belief, many of the States did borrow moneys and advance them to the United States, and paid interest thereon from their own resources; and

Whereas the principal has in a great measure been refunded by the United States to the States advancing said moneys, still the interest paid by such States as aforesaid has not been refunded; and

Whereas it is held by the Treasury Department, through which such re-imbursement settlements are made, that specific legislation will be required to justify the payment of such interest; and

Whereas Congress has always heretofore provided specifically for the payment of interest on such advances made in any war, either foreign or Indian, beginning with the act of March 3, 1825, to re-imburse Virginia for interest on advances made during the war of 1812, to that of March 3, 1881, to re-imburse California on account of similar expenditures made in one of its Indian wars; and

Whereas during the late war, and under the authority of said re-imbursement acts of 1861 and 1862, the State of Nevada advanced to the United States money which it borrowed, and on which it paid interest, and which interest has in no part been refunded by the United States, but is now justly due the State; and

Whereas there are now pending in both branches of the present Congress measures designed to authorize the settlement of the claims of the several States for such interest (being bills S. 2000 and H. R. 2463), and which said measures have been reported on by the committees to which they were referred, in both houses, in unanimously favorable reports: Therefore, be it

Resolved by the senate, the assembly concurring, That our Senators and Representative in Congress be, and they are hereby, requested to give their active support to said bills, or to others having the same object in view, and to use their best endeavors in co-operation with the agent of this State, and in support of his efforts, to thus secure to the State the amounts by her expended, as aforesaid.

Be it further resolved, That a copy of the above preamble and resolution be sent by the governor of this State to our Senators and Representative in Congress and to our State agent. (Stats. Nev., 1885, p. 145.)

EXHIBIT No. 11.

MEMORIAL OF LEGISLATURE OF NEVADA, DATED JANUARY 26, 1887, SIMILAR TO "EXHIBIT NO. 9," ASKING FOR RE-IMBURSEMENT FOR EXPENSES INCURRED IN FURNISHING TROOPS FOR THE SUPPRESSION OF THE REBELLION AND INDIAN HOSTILITIES.

Whereas claims of the State of Nevada against the United States, growing out of the late war of the rebellion, have been properly made out, authenticated, and forwarded to the proper authorities of the Government for allowance and payment; and

Whereas it appears from correspondence between the agent of this State at Washington City and the State comptroller that there is danger of great delay in respect to final action upon said claims, if not of their ultimate rejection and non-payment in part, if not wholly; and

Whereas it has been established that said claims are most just and equitable, and ought to be paid without further delay, therefore the senate and assembly of the State of Nevada hereby jointly memorialize our Senators and Representative in Congress, and do most respectfully and urgently request them and each of them, to use all proper means and efforts before the honorable Secretary of War, before Congress, or any other Department, body, or officer, so far as necessary, to secure the earliest possible allowance and payment of our said war claims against the United States; and be it

Resolved by the senate and assembly, jointly, That his excellency the governor be, and hereby is, respectfully requested to forward by mail a certified copy of the foregoing (to be accompanied by a printed copy of the recent argument of Capt. John Mullan before the honorable Secretary of War upon the allowance of said claims) to each of our Senators and Representative in Congress, at the earliest practicable date; and that he and Hon. J. F. Hallock immediately telegraph to Capt. John Mullan that said memorial and argument will be so forwarded without delay. (Stats. Nev., 1887, p. 149.)

EXHIBIT No. 12.

JOINT RESOLUTION INTRODUCED BY SENATOR FAIR PROVIDING FOR AS-CERTAINMENT BY SECRETARY OF WAR OF CLAIM OF THE STATE OF NEVADA, ON ACCOUNT OF THE WAR OF THE REBELLION, ETC.

[S. R. 13, Forty-seventh Congress, first session.]

IN THE SENATE OF THE UNITED STATES.

DECEMBER 13, 1881.—Mr. FAIR asked and, by unanimous consent, obtained leave to bring in the follow-ing joint resolution; which was read twice and referred to the Committee on Military Affairs.

Joint resolution to authorize the Secretary of War to ascertain and report to Congress the amount of money expended and indebtedness assumed by the State of Nevada in repelling invasions, suppressing insurrection and Indian hostilities, enforcing the laws, and protecting the public property.

Resolved by the Senate and House of Representatives of the United States of America in Congress assembled, That the Secretary of War be, and he is hereby, authorized and directed to cause to be examined and adjusted all the accounts of the State of Nevada against the United States for money expended and indebtedness assumed in organiz-ing, arming, equipping, supplying, clothing, subsisting, transporting, and paying either the volunteers or militia, or both, of the late Territory of Nevada and of the State of Nevada, called into active service by the governor of either thereof after the fifteenth day of April, eighteen hundred and sixty-one, to aid in repelling invasions, suppressing insurrections and Indian hostilities, enforcing the laws, and protecting the public property in said Territory and said State, and upon the borders of same.

SEC. 2. That the Secretary of War shall also examine and adjust the accounts of the late Territory of Nevada and of the State of Nevada for all other expenses neces-sarily incurred on account of said forces having been called into active service as herein mentioned, including the claims assumed or paid by said Territory and said State to encourage enlistments, and for horses and other property lost or destroyed while in the line of duty of said forces: *Provided,* That in order to enable the Secre-tary of War to fully comply with the provisions of this act there shall be filed in the War Department by the governor of Nevada, or a duly-authorized agent, an abstract, accompanied with proper certified copies of vouchers or such other proof as may be required by said Secretary, showing the amount of all such expenditures and in-debtedness, and the purposes for which the same were made.

SEC. 3. That the Secretary of War shall report in writing to Congress, at the ear-liest practicable date, for final action, the results of such examination and adjust-ment, together with the amounts which he may find to have been properly expended for the purposes aforesaid.

EXHIBIT No. 13.

STATEMENT OF CONTROLLER OF NEVADA, SHOWING AMOUNTS PAID AND ASSUMED BY THE TERRITORY AND SUBSEQUENTLY ASSUMED AND PAID BY THE STATE OF NEVADA ON ACCOUNT OF THE WAR OF THE RE-BELLION.

WAR CLAIMS.

OFFICE OF THE STATE CONTROLLER,
Carson City, Nev., November 1, 1882.

To His Excellency JOHN H. KINKEAD,
Governor of Nevada :

SIR: In conformity with a law of Congress providing for the adjustment of the claims of this State against the United States, I have the honor to report that the following abstracts show the amounts paid and assumed by the Territory and State of Nevada on account of the war of the rebellion, * * * as appears by the records of this office.

Respectfully submitted.

J. F. HALLOCK,
State Controller.

ABSTRACT A.—*Showing disbursements by the State of Nevada, and as successor to the Territory of Nevada, on account of costs, charges, and expenses for recruiting, organizing and enrolling the volunteers and military forces in the Territory and State of Nevada, in the service of the United States, and employed in the defense of the United States during the war of the rebellion.*

Date.	No. of warrant.	To whom issued.	Remarks.	Amount.
1865.				
May 1	1174	N. P. Sheldon	65 men, at $10 per capita	$650.00
1	1175	A. B. Wells	32 men, at $10 per capita	320.00
1	1176	A. Koneman	20 men, at $10 per capita	200.00
1	1177	Steiner & Koneman	15 men, at $10 per capita	150.00
1	1178	A. Koneman	38 men, at $10 per capita	380.00
1	1179	Noyes Baldwin	90 men, at $10 per capita	900.00
May 29	1234	L. O. McKeeley	10 men, at $10 per capita	100.00
31	1238	A. B. Wells	5 men, at $10 per capita	50.00
31	1239	Milo George	93 men, at $10 per capita	930.00
June 6	1266	William Kline	30 men, at $10 per capita	300.00
Aug. 22	1414	Jos. W. Calder	7 men, at $10 per capita	70.00
4	1421	Jos. W. Calder	50 men, at $10 per capita	500.00
31	1905	J. Neeley Johnson	90 men, at $10 per capita	900.00
Sept. 2	1976	C. C. Warner	46 men, at $10 per capita	460.00
Nov. 10	2070	George A Thurston	35 men, at $10 per capita	350.00
Dec. 8	2208	Noyes Baldwin	39 men, at $10 per capita	390.00
19	2292	E. B. Zabriskie	126 men, at $10 per capita	1,260.00
May 1	1167	M. P. Sheldon	66 men, at $10 per capita	660.00
1	1168	M. P. Sheldon	50 men, at $10 per capita	500.00
1	1169	M. P. Sheldon	45 men, at $10 per capita	450.00
1	1170	M. P. Sheldon	25 men, at $10 per capita	250.00
1	1171	M. P. Sheldon	119 men, at $10 per capita	1,190.00
1	1172	M. P. Sheldon	60 men, at $10 per capita	600.00
1	1173	M. P. Sheldon	13 men, at $10 per capita	130.00
1863.				
Oct. 1	417	John Church & Co	Publishing governor's proclamation for volunteers.	30.00
Jan. 18	492	John Church & Co	......do	25.00
1865.				
Feb. 18	....	Daily Evening Post	......do	18.00
1863.				
Dec. 7 / Oct. 20	*222	{Gold Hill Daily News / Gold Hill Daily News	......do / ......do	21.00 / 13.30
1864.				
Oct. 29	*261	E. B. Wilson	......do	13.75
1863.				
Dec. 3 {	*217 / *218	}Daily Independent	......do	20.00
1864.				
Oct. —	....	Lyon County Sentinel	......do	5.00
				11,986.05

* Bonds.

ABSTRACT B.—*Showing disbursements of the State of Nevada and as successor to the Territory of Nevada, on account of costs, charges, and expenses for supplying the volunteers and military forces in the Territory and State of Nevada, in the service of the United States and employed in defense of the United States, during the war of the rebellion.*

Date.	No of warrant.	To whom issued.	Character of supplies.	Amount.
1865.				
Apr. 6	1097	Gillig, Mott & Co	Furniture for adjutant-general's office	$37.00
29	1154	W. E. Sheen	Repairing and putting down carpet, etc.	6.00
29	1155	E. Barber	Seal for adjutant-general's office	26.00
29	1156	Cowing & Co	Sign for adjutant-general's office	18.00
29	1157	John G. Fox	Stationery for adjutant-general's office	43.00
29	1158	E. F. Small, postmaster	Postage, etc., for adjutant-general's office.	21.00
May 12	1210	P. Cavanaugh	Rent for adjutant-general's office	83.33
12	1211	Silas Caulkins	Clerk for adjutant-general's office	125.00
12	1213	Silas Caulkins	Traveling expenses for adjutant-general's office.	50.00
29	1227	John G. Fox	Stationery for adjutant-general's office	41.00
29	1232	Daily Morning Post	Printing for adjutant-general's office	10.00
June 6	1261	Silas Caulkins	Clerk for adjutant-general's office	125.00
July 1	1334	Silas Caulkins	Clerk for adjutant-general's office	125.00

ABSTRACT B.—*Showing disbursements of the State of Nevada, etc.*—Continued.

Date.	No. of warrant.	To whom issued.	Character of supplies.	Amount.
1865.				
July 3	1331-2	John Church.............	Printing for adjutant-general's office.....	$35.00
Aug. 4	1481	Silas Caulkins.............	Clerk for adjutant-general's office	50.00
4	1484	F. Foster	Stationery for adjutant-general's office....	85.00
4	1485	Edwards & Co.............	Stationery for adjutant-general's office ...	448.75
31	1970	C. Tillon	Rent for adjutant-general's office	120.00
Sept. 2	1972	Silas Caulkins.............	Clerk for adjutant-general's office........	50.00
Nov. 21	2118	Silas Caulkins.............	Rollers for adjutant-general's office.......	5.00
Dec. 19	2253	Silas Caulkins.............	Clerk for adjutant-general's office........	200.00
19	2257	Mason, Huff & Co.........	Oil for adjutant-general's office...........	10.00
19	2262	E. B. Rall...................	Hardware for adjutant-general's office...	38.87
19	2267	John G. Fox..............	Stationery for adjutant-general's office ...	27.75
19	2275	John Cradlebaugh	Rent for adjutant-general's office........	105.00
19	2277	Chas. S. Hammer	Oil and glass for adjutant-general's office..	11.00
19	2281	R. C. Crandall	Wood for adjutant-general's office.......	52.50
19	2282	B. F. Small, P. M...........	Postage for adjutant-general's office......	23.25
1866.				
Mar. 7	3426	Mason, Huff & Co	Oil, etc	10.50
21	3503	E. B. Rall..............	Spittoons	9.50
Apr. 23	3551	John G. Fox.............	Stationery	3.00
23	3553	Carson Appeal	Printing............................	14.00
23	3558	John G. Fox.............	Stationery	3.50
May 1	3572	B. F. Small, P. M...........	Postage, etc	35.10
23	3609	John Church	Printing	52.00
July 6	3734	Mason, Huff & Co	Oil, etc.............................	11.81
23	4367	B. F. Small, P. M..........	Box rent............................	8.70
Dec. 24	4475	B. F. Small, P. M..........	Box rent............................	8.40
28	4494	E. B. Rall.................	Lamps	2.50
1867.				
Mar. 29	312	J. Cradlebaugh	Rent..............................	270.00
	313	J. Cradlebaugh	Rent	90.00
Apr. 23	678	C. N. Noteware	Cartage............................	5.00
Dec. 31	....	Premium on gold............	To pay soldiers' warrants...............	42.92
1863.				
Oct. 31	450	Daily Independent	Printing military commissions note.......	30.00
1864.				
Jan. 5	489	H. P. Russell...............	Office desk, $35; stationery, $10...........	45.00
1865.				
May 1	Bond 157	H. P. Russell	Rent of adjutant-general's office, and stationery.	500.00
				3,114.38

ABSTRACT C.—*Showing disbursements by the State of Nevada, and as successor to the Territory of Nevada, on account of costs, charges, and expenses for monthly pay of volunteer and military forces in the Territory and State of Nevada in the service of the United States, and employed in defense of the United States during the war of the rebellion.*

Date.	Warrant.	To whom issued.	Amount.	Date.	Warrant.	To whom issued.	Amount.
1865.				**1865.**			
May 12	1212	W. H. Clark	$306.66	June 28	1306	P. Peterson...........	$25.50
23	1218	Charles Brainerd	637.62	28	1307	John G. Kelly	70.00
24	1222	Charles Brainerd	61.33	28	1308	W. W. Farries.......	29.16
29	1234	L. C. McKeeley	351.00	28	1309	W. J. Douglas	43.66
29	1235	J. E. Garrett........	807.33	28	1310	William Lawrence ..	47.66
29	1236	Sol Lewis.............	1,471.11	28	1311	John Turnbull	52.16
29	1237	W. B. Hickok.........	1,556.42	28	1313	William K. Desmond .	61.33
31	1238	A. B. Wells	478.33	28	1314	Dayton Field........	61.33
June 2	1240	C. H. Kibbee.........	59.00	July 3	1363	John Littlefield......	327.71
6	1265	H. A. Rhodes	491.78	3	1364	John Wolverton	272.64
6	1266	William Kline........	2,458.77	3	1365	Alex. Thompson......	33.66
6	1267	Sol Lewis............	4,688.55	31	1380	William B. Mann.....	61.33
8	1275	William Cline	122.66	31	1381	Jos. D. Budd	61.33
9	1276	Charles Brainerd	355.64	31	1382	Dudley Phelps........	61.33
13	1278	William Cline........	2,838.84	31	1383	H. F. Barlow........	61.33
13	1279	William Cline	1,454.09	31	1384	Frank Marrion........	60.00
28	1297	William Cline........	183.99	31	1385	William Rafferty.....	55.50
28	1298	R. Armstrong	61.33	31	1386	Charles R. Judd.....	56.16
28	1299	F. Alderson	65.83	31	1387	William M. Wilson ...	56.33
28	1300	J. W. Worfield.......	61.33	31	1388	J. Van Valkenburg ...	56.00
28	1301	Abe Skinkel........	46.33	31	1389	Henry E. Scott	47.50
28	1302	M. McCoy	48.33	31	1390	Thomas McBryde	55.16
28	1303	L. Duncan	61.33	31	1391	George T. Austin......	61.33
28	1304	P. Kavana	34.00	31	1392	William S. Alexander.	46.00
28	1305	Ed. Morgan...........	61.33	31	1393	Charles M. Beard.....	61.33

ABSTRACT C.—*Showing disbursements by the State of Nevada, etc.*—Continued.

Date.	War-rant.	To whom Issued.	Amount.	Date.	War-rant.	To whom issued.	Amount.
1865.				1865.			
Aug. 22	1394	A. Opeleslio	$61.33	Aug. 7	1519	Charles P. Frost	$61.33
July 31	1395	Edwin Billings	50.50	7	1520	John D. Arnold	61.33
31	1396	H. M. Barnes	28.00	7	1521	James P. Fagan	61.33
31	1397	Martin Chandler	55.83	7	1522	Thomas Fitzpatrick	61.33
31	1398	Joseph Cullen	56.00	7	1523	Richard Grace	61.33
31	1399	Michael Denn	61.33	7	1524	Isam Groyun	15.00
31	1400	Thomas Delay	55.60	7	1525	William F. Huftill	61.33
Aug. 4	1401	John Carey	61.33	7	1526	F. J. Haight	61.33
4	1403	William Huston	53.33	7	1527	M. J. Hay	61.33
July 31	1404	F. R. Fish	32.00	7	1528	M. Handlin	61.33
31	1405	L. W. Flye	31.50	7	1529	M. B. Hoyt	61.33
31	1406	S. Gibbens	20.00	7	1530	George P. Hellerman	43.16
31	1407	A. F. Gordon	30.83	7	1531	A. Hanson	14.16
31	1408	W. M. Grant	33.83	7	1532	Jessie Jenery	61.33
31	1409	Chas. Gersbach	40.00	7	1533	J. J. Jackson	61.33
Aug. 4	1410	James Richmond	59.66	7	1534	M. Jernegan	61.33
July 31	1411	George E. Gray	61.33	7	1535	S. J. Keeler	61.33
31	1412	N. Hazel	61.33	7	1536	George R. Kellogg	61.33
31	1413	Thomas Hall	61.33	7	1537	George F. Kibling	61.33
Aug. 22	1415	D. K. Hegarty	39.33	7	1538	John Kyle	61.33
22	1416	H. Henning	33.83	7	1539	Andrew Koontz	61.33
22	1417	H. Kriester	18.50	7	1540	B. F. Logan	11.16
22	1418	Joseph Lindsay	61.33	7	1541	A. C. Leach	61.33
22	1419	John C. Lum	61.33	7	1542	B. J. Lee	61.33
22	1420	Gilbert Liddle	56.16	7	1543	William Minor	25.00
July 31	1422	Henry Melcher	61.33	7	1544	M. McCafferey	61.33
1885				7	1545	H. McQuaid	61.33
July 31	1423	George A. Miller	61.33	7	1546	St. L. McNaghton	61.33
31	1424	Henry McOnie	61.33	7	1547	L. A. Myers	14.50
31	1425	William Manson	61.33	7	1548	James Mullett	61.33
31	1426	John McConnell	61.33	7	1549	James Monroe	3.16
31	1427	John Morris	33.83	7	1550	George W. Norton	61.33
Aug. 4	1428	Fred Smith	61.33	7	1551	F. W. Norval	13.16
July 31	1429	Henry Noyes	57.66	7	1552	C. Ottman	61.33
31	1430	C. O. Laughlin	55.50	7	1553	J. F. Pennoyer	61.33
31	1431	George Peabody	55.00	7	1554	George Peterson	61.33
31	1432	G. W. Patterson	30.16	7	1555	Thomas Ryan	61.33
31	1433	Levi L. Reese	33.83	7	1556	John Rush	61.33
Aug. 4	1434	James R. Robinson	61.33	7	1557	John Reed	12.50
July 31	1435	Samuel Randle	61.33	7	1558	John Rogers	19.16
31	1436	John Roohan	57.83	7	1559	George M. Smith	61.33
31	1437	John Smith	56.00	7	1560	S. P. Stamper	61.33
31	1438	L. Sawyer	50.50	7	1561	John A. Silvers	10.33
31	1439	Joseph S. Small	26.66	7	1562	Z. Stokes	14.50
31	1440	N. R. Scovell	31.16	7	1563	L. Singleton	13.16
31	1442	Joseph Traverse	61.33	7	1564	John Spencer	13.16
31	1443	Charles L. Teal	54.16	7	1565	James A. Stewart	12.66
31	1444	James Tuckey	43.83	7	1566	G. D. Shell	11.66
31	1445	J. M. Vance	55.66	7	1567	E. P. Thomas	61.33
31	1446	Rufus Williams	58.83	7	1568	J. Thoroughman	61.33
31	1447	A. Wapelhorst	33.83	7	1569	F. M. White	61.33
31	1448	George W. Langley	61.33	7	1570	R. C. White	61.33
Aug. 7	1489	S. M. Taylor	61.33	7	1572	Thomas Watson	59.00
7	1490	S. C. Connell	61.33	7	1573	F. M. Mountz	61.33
7	1491	J. H. Marshall	61.33	7	1574	William H. Chipman	61.33
7	1492	E. J. Soulsby	61.33	7	1575	Wm. H. Shoemaker	61.33
7	1493	Charles Pickard	61.33	7	1576	J. B. Robinson	61.33
7	1494	William McCormick	61.33	7	1577	Thomas P. Hess	61.33
7	1495	George J. Jones	61.83	7	1578	James T. Byrnes	61.33
7	1496	Charles Petry	61.33	7	1579	Joseph P. Westwood	61.33
7	1497	Paul Sherman	61.33	7	1580	Pat Walsh	61.33
7	1498	E. C. Dunning	61.33	7	1581	John McDonald	61.33
7	1499	S. McCall	61.33	7	1582	John L. Nelson	61.33
7	1500	George Stoll	61.33	7	1583	William C. Matlock	61.33
7	1501	J. C. Quaile	61.33	7	1584	Pat McNicklo	61.33
7	1502	J. C. McQuire	61.33	7	1585	William H. Bennett	61.33
7	1503	J. J. Anderson	61.33	7	1586	I. Sanderson	61.33
7	1504	James Byrne	18.00	7	1587	E. Carters	61.33
7	1505	James Blasha	61.33	7	1588	Fred Iseman	61.33
7	1506	P. Bonham	61.33	7	1589	Pat. Mooney	61.33
7	1507	A. Belfast	61.33	7	1591	William A. Reid	8.33
7	1508	F. P. Blowers	61.33	7	1592	John Androws	61.33
7	1509	J. T. Barnett	61.33	7	1593	S. Stewart	61.33
7	1510	William Brunson	61.33	7	1594	J. C. Logan	61.33
7	1511	L. C. Bechtel	14.66	7	1595	A. Aulbach	31.33
7	1512	Andrew Coulter	61.33	7	1596	James Aitken	61.33
7	1513	S. Comegys	61.33	7	1598	William F. Berry	61.33
7	1514	Peter Demitz	61.33	7	1599	Samuel Bunce	61.33
7	1515	James Dolan	61.33	7	1600	Robert Bell	61.33
7	1516	A. Durfee	61.33	7	1601	F. G. Burton	61.33
7	1518	S. R. Edmison	61.33	7	1602	John Brown	61.33

ABSTRACT C.—*Showing disbursements by the State of Nevada, etc.*—Continued.

Date.	War-rant.	To whom issued.	Amount.	Date.	War-rant.	To whom issued.	Amount.
1865.				1865.			
Aug. 7	1605	John Clark	$61.33	Aug. 26	1703	Ed. T. Maynard	$61.33
7	1606	Henry Curran	61.33	26	1704	John Johnson	61.33
7	1607	John Cono	61.33	26	1705	William R. Jones	48.66
7	1608	R. L. Collard	53.66	26	1706	R. C. McKenzie	61.33
7	1609	M. Duffy	61.33	26	1707	K. Flechsenhaur	61.33
7	1610	John H. Davis	61.33	26	1708	James Scull	29.16
7	1611	F. S. Dickson	9.66	26	1709	Charles Peterson	61.33
7	1612	Thomas A. Frazier	61.33	26	1711	A. E. Easterbrook	61.33
7	1613	M. J. Fouts	61.33	26	1712	Thomas Bowman	61.33
7	1614	A. Fenstermaker	61.33	26	1713	S. V. Ables	61.33
7	1615	Reuben Ferris	9.00	26	1714	Moses Austin	61.33
7	1616	Leon Gris	61.33	26	1715	James Allen	61.33
7	1617	M. Davis	61.33	26	1716	John S. Briggs	31.33
7	1618	J. B. Greenlaw	61.33	26	1717	J. Brownstein	61.33
7	1620	Ira J. Harder	61.33	26	1718	M. Corcoran	61.33
7	1621	Abram Harder	61.33	26	1719	E. J. Davis	61.33
7	1622	John Harder	61.33	26	1720	C. Florine	61.33
7	1623	Alfred Holder	36.66	26	1721	Jos. M. Fulton	61.33
7	1624	S. Hartman	11.50	26	1722	Eli Hoyt	61.33
7	1625	S. Hayworth	9.66	26	1723	John Hopkins	61.33
7	1626	Charles Jarrett	4.16	26	1724	John N. Hamilton	61.33
7	1627	S. L. Jacobs	36.66	26	1725	Frank Hohman	33.50
7	1628	E. H. Johnson	11.50	26	1726	Job Hoxie	26.50
7	1630	B. F. Keller	40.50	26	1727	John Johnson, 2d	61.33
7	1631	George Long	37.33	26	1728	Otto Luderwig	61.33
7	1632	P. McKewon	61.33	26	1730	M. McMahon	61.33
7	1633	E. McKenzie	41.00	26	1731	P. R. McAuliffe	61.33
7	1634	George Norvitzky	61.33	26	1732	Zac. Mitchell	40.50
7	1635	William Nowlan	61.33	26	1733	John Marshall	34.00
7	1636	John R. Nugent	61.33	26	1734	L. M. Meallo	19.83
7	1637	A. M. Newton	9.83	26	1736	James C. Naff	61.33
7	1638	Felix O'Neil	61.33	26	1737	John O'Brien, 2d	43.00
7	1639	William O'Neal	9.00	26	1738	John Ratigan	61.37
7	1640	H. H. Oates	61.33	26	1739	George D. Rush	28.54
7	1641	Peter S. Post	61.33	26	1740	L. M. Spencer	61.33
7	1642	J. M. Plaisted	9.50	26	1741	Thornton Sleeth	61.33
7	1644	John Robinson, 1st	61.33	26	1742	John Sullivan	61.33
7	1645	John Robinson, 2d	15.50	26	1743	John Skelton	7.50
7	1646	William Roberts	91.33	26	1744	William Walsh	61.33
7	1647	J. W. Staples	39.50	26	1745	John Walsh	61.33
7	1648	J. Schuster	61.33	26	1746	Henry Ward	61.33
7	1649	W. H. or W. Scott	61.33	26	1747	John Whalen	33.16
7	1650	R. Shoemaker	61.33	26	1748	A. C. White	28.16
7	1651	Rodney Shoemaker	61.33	26	1749	E. B. Hagnas	61.33
7	1652	James Shields	43.00	26	1750	R. D. Wadleigh	61.33
7	1653	N. L. Shaw	9.66	26	1751	William Liggett	61.33
7	1655	James S. Warren	61.33	26	1752	William H. Freeland	61.33
7	1656	James R. Young	61.33	26	1753	Mark Moyers	61.33
7	1657	Peter Campbell	56.33	26	1754	Hubert Bisat	61.33
26	1664	D. Vanderhorf	127.46	26	1755	David Thomas	61.33
26	1665	Henry Finley	61.33	26	1756	Martin Sherman	61.33
26	1667	B. F. McCready	61.33	26	1757	John Dolan	61.33
26	1668	Samuel M. Cook	61.33	26	1758	H. E. Botel	61.33
26	1670	Fred Kreitzer	61.33	26	1759	R. J. Bronson	61.33
26	1671	W. J. Palmer	56.50	26	1760	Frank Lapoint	57.83
26	1672	Thomas J. Bell	61.33	26	1761	James H. Brown	61.33
26	1673	Sam. J. Bath	61.33	26	1762	John Levings	61.33
26	1674	Peter Benedict	61.33	26	1763	James L. Sanborn	26.83
26	1675	A. Barrett	33.50	26	1764	E. B. Dunning	26.50
26	1678	Charles A. F. Deitz	34.00	26	1765	Anderson Morgan	17.16
26	1679	George Emerson	61.33	26	1766	Peter Brocha	61.33
26	1680	Morris Eastwood	34.00	26	1767	Philip Barnett	61.33
26	1681	Charles Trickker	59.16	26	1768	William J. Bartells	25.16
26	1682	G. A. Hamlin	61.33	26	1769	Charles B. Blanchard	25.16
26	1683	Jos. Kerr	61.33	26	1770	William Bowen	25.16
26	1684	Pat Kearney	57.16	26	1771	William H. Camell	61.33
26	1685	C. F. Kircher	47.16	26	1772	Lewis B. Clark	61.33
26	1686	Charles F. Lake	61.33	26	1773	John F. Cassidy	61.33
26	1687	A. Lampson	60.00	26	1774	John Cody	22.16
26	1688	H. Morris	61.33	26	1775	Charles Callahan	19.66
26	1689	H. C. Murray	55.33	26	1776	John Durkin	61.33
26	1690	Ed. McDonogh	38.66	26	1777	George W. Durham	28.83
26	1691	G. Mahler	34.00	26	1778	Alex. Dickson	23.00
26	1693	Floyd Potter	61.33	26	1779	Alonzo L. Estees	25.33
26	1694	Joseph Poss	57.33	26	1780	A. W. Faxon	61.33
26	1695	Xavier Pasquier	57.33	26	1781	John Farnan	25.16
26	1696	Alex. Prado	34.00	26	1782	Samuel Friend	61.33
26	1697	Jos. Schorb	61.33	26	1783	William Gray	61.33
26	1698	Charles D. St. Croix	57.33	26	1784	Jos. Good	61.33
26	1701	Maurice Geary	61.33	26	1785	W. D. Godfrey	61.33
26	1702	Charles Meservo	61.33	26	1786	Louis Gaisberg	23.00

ABSTRACT C.—*Showing disbursements by the State of Nevada, etc.*—Continued.

Date.	Warrant.	To whom issued.	Amount.	Date.	Warrant.	To whom issued.	Amount.
1865.				1865.			
Aug. 26	1787	Isaac Hickerson	$61.33	Aug. 26	1874	Jared Grover	$27.16
26	1788	James Hamilton	61.33	26	1875	L. Grinnell	15.00
26	1789	Samuel Hilton	25.50	26	1876	Charles L. Hardy	61.33
26	1790	George Inks	50.50	26	1877	N. F. Hedrick	13.00
26	1791	Jos. Johanningmeir	61.33	26	1878	Andrew Healey	42.50
26	1792	Charles Jones	27.33	26	1879	Edward Lade	61.33
26	1793	Charles E. Jackson	27.33	26	1880	Charles Lenard	22.50
26	1794	P. B. Kyes or Koys	23.66	26	1881	John M. Lowrie	26.00
26	1795	James W. Lee	61.33	26	1882	Abraham Long	20.66
26	1796	Charles Lynch	61.33	26	1883	Francis Miller	42.66
26	1797	John P. McCabe	61.33	26	1884	N. McNaughton	56.66
26	1798	William Mulloy	61.33	26	1885	Jacob Myers	53.83
26	1799	John Mead	61.33	26	1886	S. Marshall	61.33
26	1800	William Morat	61.33	26	1888	M. L. Mead	15.00
26	1801	Charles Martin	61.33	26	1889	J. O. Sullivan	51.50
26	1802	John McNamara	29.83	26	1890	James M. Preston	60.83
26	1803	Charles F. Murray	25.16	26	1891	Andrew Parks	27.33
26	1804	John McNemeo	25.16	26	1892	George Parker	27.33
26	1805	James E. O'Reilly	32.83	26	1893	H. W. Sawyer	61.33
26	1806	H. C. Osborn	27.33	26	1894	Wm. T. Stephens	15.33
26	1807	Galen O. Preble	61.33	26	1895	Wm. Smith	13.50
26	1808	George Pope	15.00	26	1896	S. B. Shoemaker	14.50
26	1809	William Robinson	61.33	26	1897	E. M. Shipley	13.50
26	1810	W. A. Ralston	61.33	26	1898	B. F. Settle	43.50
26	1811	Lewis Rose	61.33	26	1899	Wm. Thompson	59.56
26	1812	S. E. Robinson	16.33	26	1900	S. H. Tuttle	44.16
26	1813	H. K. Sneath	61.33	26	1901	DeWitt Taplin	15.66
26	1814	S. B. Sample	61.33	26	1902	Charles W. Thornton	15.00
26	1815	C. E. Smith, jr	29.33	26	1903	Wm. Urtel	61.33
26	1816	George W. Smith	25.50	26	1904	J. Van Dusen	61.33
26	1817	John Taylor	61.33	26	1905	A. D. Vantreese	61.33
26	1818	George M. Thomas	27.33	26	1906	L. G. Wilson	51.00
26	1819	John T. Thatcher	26.33	26	1908	Dan Winfield	27.16
26	1820	Thos. B. Wilkerson	12.83	26	1909	R. C. Wilcox	13.00
26	1821	McHenry White	27.00	26	1910	S. A. Densmore	61.33
26	1822	George M. or W.White	25.16	26	1911	Jesse Fox	50.83
26	1823	John Bossinger	49.83	26	1912	I. B. Libbey	53.00
26	1825	M. C. Bolonge	50.50	26	1913	George Brasch	50.83
26	1826	Andrew Dunn	55.16	26	1914	A. J. Grimes	45.16
26	1827	H. L. Desmerett	61.33	26	1915	Daniel Casey	46.16
26	1828	T. J. Hornett	61.33	26	1916	James Lonergan	51.33
26	1829	M. E. Kean	61.33	26	1917	William Ayer	5.33
26	1830	Fred Morlet	51.00	26	1918	William R. Appleton	3.50
26	1831	P. L. B. Massont	55.16	26	1919	George W. Bradley	56.66
26	1832	John Sherlock	52.66	26	1920	J. Boulware	48.50
26	1833	Dennis Myer	45.00	26	1921	B. S. Breeden	50.16
26	1836	H. Richards	16.66	26	1922	F. M. Buck	43.66
26	1838	M. W. Stone	21.66	26	1923	C. C. Carter	61.33
26	1839	C. H. Verschoyle	21.66	26	1924	J. Coquillot	43.33
26	1840	Aaron Wood	15.16	26	1925	John Charvis	45.00
26	1841	E. D. Sherrill	61.33	26	1926	John M. Clifford	50.33
26	1842	T. W. Roussin	50.50	26	1927	S. Campbell	61.33
26	1843	J. Kellison	60.16	26	1928	John V. Cook	6.66
26	1844	James H. Sanborn	27.16	26	1929	William J. Cook	7.66
26	1845	Jotham Burns	61.33	26	1930	Dyer James	51.66
26	1846	Harvey Pierce	14.83	26	1931	Thomas B. Fitzhugh	61.33
26	1847	F. Morlath	61.33	26	1932	F. Guilloux	51.33
26	1849	H. Huesner	61.33	26	1933	A. Harris	52.83
26	1850	Geo. H. Ackler	27.16	26	1934	L. Hoard	53.00
26	1852	Hugh Burns	54.66	26	1935	F. S. Hubbard	47.16
26	1853	George Brumfield	47.66	26	1936	Paul Hoard	7.83
26	1854	Wm. Brooks	61.33	26	1937	R. P. Knapp	54.16
26	1855	Thomas Bryson	15.00	26	1938	Benjamin E. Loosen	7.16
26	1856	Wm. C. Bell	15.66	26	1939	Joel B. Longes	10.00
26	1857	E. C. or D. Blood	15.33	26	1940	Dan McVoy	48.33
26	1858	John A. Bird	15.66	26	1941	John B. McGee	61.33
26	1859	James Crozar	43.50	26	1942	Thomas Mulloy	58.83
26	1860	J. C. G. Cregan	45.50	26	1943	John W. Martin	7.50
26	1861	B. F. Currier	47.50	26	1944	M. Masseth	7.00
26	1862	M. Dunnigan	13.00	26	1945	P. L. Nutting	4.33
26	1863	George W. Evans	61.33	26	1946	Eugene O'Neil	45.33
26	1864	Robert Elliott	61.33	26	1947	Eli D. Phelps	47.16
26	1865	W. W. Esterbrook, jr.	52.50	26	1948	M. M. Rhodes	43.66
26	1866	D. K. Ewbanks	18.66	26	1949	William Robinson	7.10
26	1867	N. W. Fish	56.00	26	1950	John I. Smith	55.83
26	1868	Gregory Ford	43.16	26	1951	William Smith	50.66
26	1869	Joseph Ferris	61.33	26	1952	M. Savage	6.83
26	1870	George W. Gould	61.33	26	1953	B. Stauffer	6.66
26	1871	W. Govenlock	61.33	26	1954	John Shaw	19.66
26	1872	I. Graham	56.00	26	1956	George B. Wallace	61.33
26	1873	N. Garlon	43.33	26	1957	James W. Warden	49.00

ABSTRACT C.—*Showing disbursements by the State of Nevada, etc.*—Continued.

Date.	Warrant.	To whom issued.	Amount.	Date.	Warrant.	To whom issued.	Amount.
1865.				1865.			
Aug. 26	1958	B. Winslow	$43.16	Nov. 29	2179	H. McOmie	$43.00
26	1959	Henry Willis	56.83	29	2180	John Morris	43.00
26	1960	Richard Williams	59.33	29	2181	George A. Miller	43.00
26	1961	James P. Wheeler	54.83	29	2182	John McConnell	43.00
26	1962	A. H. Yocum	6.66	29	2183	Henry Noyes	43.00
26	1963	E. A. Young	14.66	29	2184	C. O'Loughlin	43.00
31	1964	J. Neely Johnson	51.75	29	2185	George Peabody	43.00
Sept. 2	1977	C. C. Warner	101.66	20	2186	Dudley Phelps	43.00
2	1978	John W. Leonard	51.83	29	2187	George W. Patterson	43.00
16	1990	Thomas Williams	24.33	29	2188	Levi L. Reese	43.00
16	1991	Leo D. McDonald	20.16	29	2189	John Smith	43.00
16	1992	Alexander McGiffen	25.33	29	2190	James Taveras	43.00
16	1993	Alexander Thompson	25.16	29	2191	M. S. Eastwood	43.00
16	1994	Charles B. Aul	26.33	29	2192	H. E. Emery	43.00
16	1995	John C. Powers	28.66	29	2193	George Goodpaster	43.00
16	1996	William H. Scott	27.83	29	2194	Benjamin C. Gowan	43.00
16	1997	Justin Edwards	150.00	29	2195	Ed. Hagans	43.00
16	1998	Joel Wolverton	100.00	29	2196	Joseph Kerr	43.00
16	1999	A. B. Wells	140.00	29	2197	William C. Medbury	43.00
16	2000	J. W. Staples	23.50	29	2198	Elijah Prino	43.00
27	2024	Hugh Burns	29.19	29	2199	Reuben Parish	43.00
Nov. 10	2078	George A. Thurston	210.00	29	2200	Joseph Richards	43.00
29	2102	George W. Durham	43.00	29	2201	Moses Stoppard	43.00
29	2103	Martin Sherman	43.00	29	2202	John M. Williams	43.00
29	2104	Eli B. Dunning	43.00	Dec. 8	2209	Richard Armstrong	43.33
29	2105	John McNamara	43.00	8	2210	Charles Hodgman	39.50
29	2106	Warren Godfrey	43.00	8	2211	P. Obershaw	61.33
29	2107	Charles M. Beard	43.00	8	2212	E. J. Davis	43.50
29	2108	E. B. Hagans	43.00	8	2213	John N. Hamilton	43.33
29	2109	Henry K. Wicks	252.46	8	2214	A. B. Wells	20.70
29	2110	L. J. Whitney	50.00	8	2216	Samuel Hilton	43.00
29	2111	Justin Edwards	64.75	8	2217	H. O. Osborn	43.00
29	2112	A. B. Wells	70.00	8	2218	George M. Thomas	43.00
27	2113	W. H. Clark	150.00	8	2219	A. Koneman	1,247.00
27	2114	Wm. Wallace	241.00	8	2220	W. H. Clark	64.76
27	2115	E. B. Zabriskie	639.20	8	2221	John Littlefield	164.76
27	2135	James A. Wilkinson	100.00	8	2222	J. B. Robinson	43.33
27	2136	Albert C. White	43.50	8	2223	Wm. Rafferty	43.00
27	2137	George Inks	43.00	8	2224	Isaac Van Valkenborg	43.00
27	2138	James L. Sanborn	43.00	8	2225	James H. Sackett	43.00
27	2139	Isaac Hickerson	43.00	8	2226	A. Koneman	1,677.00
27	2140	Frank Marion	43.00	8	2227	A. Koneman	258.00
27	2141	Peter Brocha	43.00	8	2228	Solomon Gee	43.00
27	2142	Charles B. Blanchard	43.00	8	2229	James B. Jones	43.00
27	2143	Hubert Besat	43.00	19	2287	Wm. Morat	43.00
27	2144	Geo. W. Bibbins	36.83	19	2288	James E. O'Reilly	43.00
27	2145	John T. Cassidy	43.00	19	2289	William H. Desmore or Desmondes	43.00
27	2146	John Dolan	43.00				
27	2147	A. W. Faxon	43.00	19	2290	William S. Alexander	43.00
27	2148	Jos. Good	43.00	19	2291	William Ellsworth	104.33
27	2149	Jos. Johanningmier	43.00	1866.			
27	2150	Frank Lapoint	43.00	Jan. 29	2601	Milo George	391.50
27	2151	Charles Lynch	43.00	29	2602	A. J. Cisno	54.25
27	2152	Joseph W. Lee	43.00	29	2603	James A. Wilkerson	50.00
27	2153	John McNemo	43.00	29	2604	G. J. Lansing	189.75
27	2154	M. H. Myers	43.00	29	2605	D. H. Pine	89.16
27	2155	Edward Neal	36.00	29	2606	William Wallace	130.30
27	2156	S. E. Robinson	43.00	29	2607	M. Ahern	48.84
27	2157	William Robinson	43.00	29	2608	Charles G. Higgins	48.84
27	2158	H. K. Smith	43.00	29	2609	J. W. Johnson	48.84
27	2159	S. B. Sample	43.00	29	2610	J. Quigley	48.84
27	2160	George W. White	43.00	29	2611	J. Rossinger	48.84
27	2161	Henry Young	43.00	29	2612	S. M. Ballard	48.84
27	2162	John Armstrong	43.00	29	2613	S. Dunn	48.84
27	2163	Edwin Billings	43.00	29	2614	J. N. Merrett	48.84
27	2164	Joseph Cullen	43.00	29	2615	J. W. Thompson	49.50
27	2165	Samuel Chambers	43.00	29	2616	C. H. Vessahoyle	48.84
27	2166	James E. Dickerson	43.00	29	2617	T. Zacariah	48.84
27	2167	Samuel Eagles	43.00	29	2618	William Barrett	110.33
27	2168	L. W. Fye	43.00	29	2620	M. C. Bolinge	48.84
27	2169	Charles Goisbach	43.00	29	2621	J. A. Belt	48.84
27	2170	A. F. Gordon	43.00	29	2622	J. Carey	48.84
27	2171	H. Henning	43.00	29	2623	J. Craddick	48.84
27	2172	N. Hazel or Hagat	43.00	29	2624	J. Clark	48.84
27	2173	Thomas Hall	43.00	29	2625	M. Crowley	48.67
29	2174	C. H. Kibbe	43.00	29	2626	P. Kavanna	48.84
29	2175	James Lindsey	43.00	29	2627	J. S. Collins	50.50
29	2176	John Mulligan	61.33	29	2628	C. Conrad	48.84
29	2177	John Mulligan	43.00	29	2629	James Davis	48.84
29	2178	Peter Meyer	43.00				

Statement C.—*Showing disbursements by the State of Nevada, etc.*—Continued.

Date.	War-rant.	To whom issued.	Amount.	Date.	War-rant.	To whom issued.	Amount.
1866.				**1866.**			
Jan. 29	2630	J. Dronett	$48.84	Jan. 29	2711	H. Pierce	$47.50
29	2631	J. or G. W. Devers	48.84	29	2712	J. M. or W. Preston	47.50
29	2632	H. S. Desmerett	48.84	29	2713	D. Park	47.00
29	2633	A. Dunn	48.84	29	2714	G. W. Ruttan	47.50
29	2634	J. Evens	48.84	29	2715	H. W. Sawyer	47.50
29	2635	N. Gunther	48.84	29	2716	W. T. Stephens	47.50
29	2636	J. Goff or Gough	48.84	29	2717	George Sutherland	47.50
29	2637	S. Crouse	48.84	29	2718	J. O'Sullivan	47.50
29	2638	T. Green	48.84	29	2719	S. B. Shoemaker	47.50
29	2639	G. E. Gilson	48.84	29	2720	B. F. Settle	47.50
29	2640	T. F. Harrington	50.50	29	2721	E. M. Shipley	47.50
29	2641	H. M. Harris	48.84	29	2722	David Smith	47.50
29	2642	Pat Hennessy	48.84	29	2723	George H. McCallum	47.50
29	2643	Huston Williams	48.84	29	2724	J. Turnley	47.50
29	2644	H. Humphrey	48.84	29	2725	George Parker	47.50
29	2645	E. C. Lynn	48.84	29	2726	A. E. Townley, or Townsley	47.50
29	2646	F. W. Lohydo	48.84	29	2727	William Thompson	47.50
29	2647	S. W. Lawson	48.84	29	2728	Ed. Lado	47.50
29	2648	J. G. J. Lansing	12.50	29	2729	De Witt Taplan	47.50
29	2649	P. Lyon	48.84	29	2730	S. H. Tuttle	47.50
29	2650	F. Morlett	48.84	29	2731	A. D. Vantreese	47.50
29	2651	L. D. McIntosh	51.00	29	2732	J. P. Wheeler	48.84
29	2652	F. Miller	48.84	29	2733	R. C. Wilcox	47.50
29	2653	Edward Morgan	48.84	29	2734	Dan Winfield	47.50
29	2654	L. C. Nelson	48.84	29	2735	Ed. Warren	47.50
29	2655	J. H. O'Brien	48.50	29	2736	J. G. Kelley	210.00
29	2656	J. B. Robotham	48.84	29	2737	G. Vanderhorf	144.25
29	2657	M. J. Ryan	48.67	29	2738	David Love	173.34
29	2658	H. Richards	48.84	29	2739	George Broesch	48.84
29	2659	J. Richmond	48.84	29	2740	D. Casey	48.84
29	2660	M. W. Stone	48.84	29	2741	S. T. E. England	48.84
29	2661	S. Summers	48.84	29	2742	A. J. Grimes	48.84
29	2662	J. Sherlock	48.84	29	2743	J. Lonorgan	48.84
29	2663	T. H. Steen	47.84	29	2744	C. C. Mills	48.84
29	2664	I. H. or N. Sherman	47.84	29	2745	F. Woods	50.17
29	2665	G. E. Thomas	48.84	29	2746	G. E. Ball	48.84
29	2666	J. Turnbull	48.84	29	2747	L. J. Crombie	48.84
29	2667	S. W. Waddell	48.84	29	2748	S. A. Densmoro	48.84
29	2668	J. J. Woods	44.50	29	2749	N. R. Warner	48.84
29	2669	A. Wood	48.48	29	2750	E. Moreledge	48.84
29	2670	J. Wilson	48.48	29	2751	W. R. Appleton	48.84
29	2671	W. G. Seamands	187.50	29	2752	William A. Ables	48.84
29	2672	John or Jotham Burns	47.50	29	2753	John Boulware	48.84
29	2673	J. A. Bird	47.50	29	2754	G. E. Berry	48.84
29	2674	J. Kellison	47.50	29	2755	F. M. Buck	48.84
29	2675	William Golt	47.50	29	2756	Thomas Bowen	48.84
29	2676	A. Henley	47.50	29	2757	R. S. Breeden	48.84
29	2677	T. N. Roussin	47.50	29	2758	G. W. Bradley	48.84
29	2678	J. H. Sanborn	47.50	29	2759	Charles Bowring	48.84
29	2679	E. D. Sherrill	47.50	29	2760	George W. Commins	48.84
29	2680	J. M. D. Warfield	47.50	29	2761	John Chavis	48.84
29	2681	C. W. Thornton	47.50	29	2762	W. J. Cook	48.84
29	2682	G. H. Ackler	47.50	29	2763	J. V. Cook	48.84
29	2683	J. W. Brink	47.50	29	2764	S. Campbell	48.84
29	2684	A. C. Blanchard	47.50	29	2765	L. Coppers	48.84
29	2685	E. D. Blood	47.50	29	2766	W. A. Culberson	48.84
29	2686	W. Brooks	47.50	29	2767	C. C. Carter	48.84
29	2687	J. C. G. Ceregin	47.50	29	2768	J. Corquillot	48.84
29	2688	J. Crozer	47.50	29	2769	James Dyer	48.84
29	2689	B. F. Currier	47.50	29	2770	J. Diamond	48.84
29	2690	G. A. Eubanks	47.50	29	2771	C. De La Cruz	48.84
29	2691	W. W. Easterbrook, jr	47.50	29	2772	G. M. Chase	48.84
29	2692	George W. Evans	47.50	29	2773	T. B. Fitzhugh	48.84
29	2693	George Ford	47.50	29	2774	Jesse Fox	48.84
29	2694	J. Ferris	47.50	29	2775	T. Gilloux	48.84
29	2695	N. W. Fish	47.50	29	2776	R. W. Gile	48.84
29	2696	L. Grinnell	47.50	29	2777	R. Gestelle	48.84
29	2697	G. or William Gould	47.50	29	2778	N. C. Hinckley	48.84
29	2698	M. Garlon	47.50	29	2779	F. S. Hubbard	48.84
29	2699	O. L. Hardy	47.50	29	2780	A. Harris	48.84
29	2700	N. F. Hedrick	47.50	29	3781	L. Head	48.84
29	2701	J. M. Lowrie	47.50	29	2782	T. Hough	48.84
29	2702	C. Leonard	47.50	29	2783	P. Howard	48.84
29	2703	A. Long	47.50	29	2784	B. E. Hutchinson	50.17
29	2704	M. F. Mead	47.50	29	2785	R. P. Knapp	48.84
29	2705	N. McNaughton	47.50	29	2786	D. Love	11.66
29	2706	R. Morleth	47.50	29	2787	H. J. Locke	48.84
29	2707	Jacob Meyers	47.50	29	2788	William A. Lyon	45.00
29	2708	F. Miller	47.50	29	2789	J. B. Longeo	48.84
29	2709	S. Marshall	47.50	29	2790	B. E. Loron	48.84
29	2710	A. Parks	47.50				

ABSTRACT C.—*Showing disbursements by the State of Nevada, etc.*—Continued.

Date.	Warrant.	To whom issued.	Amount.
1866.			
Jan. 29	2791	M. Masseth	$48.84
29	2792	D. McVoy	48.84
29	2793	Alex. Mitchell	48.84
29	2794	M. McCoy	48.84
29	2795	J. B. McGee	48.84
29	2796	Thomas Mulloy	48.84
29	2797	P. L. Nutting	48.84
29	2798	Eugene O'Neil	48.84
29	2799	E. or G. D. Phelps	48.84
29	2800	M. N. Rhoades	48.84
29	2801	J. M. Reno	48.84
29	2802	W. Rowley	48.84
29	2803	E. Riendan	48.84
29	2804	William Robinson	48.84
29	2805	Fred Reefe	48.84
29	2806	J. J. Smith	48.84
29	2807	B. Stauffer	48.84
29	2808	John Shaw	48.84
29	2809	A. S. Kinkle	48.84
29	2810	Geo. M. or W. Sigler	48.84
29	2811	William Smith	48.84
29	2812	E. F. Scott	32.16
29	2813	William J. Tasco	48.84
29	2814	F. M. Voight	49.66
29	2815	A. S. or G. Van Meter	44.34
29	2816	A. F. W. Winter	48.84
29	2817	Richard Williams	48.84
29	2818	George B. Wallace	48.84
29	2819	B. Winstow	48.84
29	2820	James W. Warden	48.84
29	2821	Henry Wills	48.84
29	2822	A. H. Yocum	48.84
29	2823	E. A. Young	48.84
29	2824	Oscar Jewett	522.50
29	2825	James Taylor	43.00
29	2826	H. Eigenmellig	43.00
29	2827	William Young	43.00
Feb. 6	2931	Martin E. Kean	48.84
6	2935	Jacob Van Doren	47.50
6	2936	John W. Martin	48.84
6	2937	Daniel S. McKay	48.84
Mar. 7	3447	N. McGuone	48.84
7	3448	George C. Welch	48.84
7	3449	J. R. Hamilton	48.84
7	3450	Patrick Reilly	48.84
7	3451	James J. Hutchinson	48.84
7	3452	John E. Howe	47.50
7	3453	James Leonard	47.50
7	3454	Samuel C. Day	47.67
7	3455	W. Govenlock	47.50
7	3456	James Dougherty	47.50
7	3457	J. T. Leonard	47.50
7	3458	William Smith	47.50
7	3459	Robert Elliott	47.50
7	3460	Ign. Graham	47.50
7	3461	John Rogers	40.84
7	3462	J. B. Libbey	43.00
7	3463	Alex. Dickson	43.00
7	3464	James C. Palmer	43.00
7	3465	Joseph F. Hewett	43.00
21	3504	James H. Stewart	606.07
21	3505	George Brumfield	47.50
21	3506	Simon L. Coen	47.50
21	3507	Jared Grover	47.50
21	3508	Henry Heusner	47.50
21	3510	T. M. Roussin	47.50
21	3512	John U. Tolles	290.84
21	3513	William Urtel	47.50
21	3514	Samuel or Lemuel G. Wilson	47.50
21	3515	Charles H. Judd	43.00
21	3516	Henry E. Scott	43.00
21	3517	G. M. Thurlow	47.50
April 20	3559	Jno. Farnan or Farman	43.00
20	3560	James S. Warren	282.50
26	3561	E. B. Zabriskie	140.00
26	3562	R. A. Fitch	48.84
May 23	3622	Adolph Hanson	48.83
23	3623	John W. Thomas	29.50
31	3624	William Ayer	48.84

Date.	Warrant.	To whom issued.	Amount.
1866.			
May 31	3638	H. M. Ellsworth	$50.00
31	3639	Robert P. Frisbie	67.67
31	3640	L. J. Whitney	200.00
June 16	3658	Dennis Weyer	48.84
16	3659	John H. Clifford	48.84
16	3660	Michael Savage	48.84
16	3661	George A. Thurston	52.50
16	3662	A. M. Newton	60.50
16	3663	James A. Wilkinson	50.00
16	3664	James Byrne	42.00
16	3665	F. P. Blowers	65.00
16	3666	F. P. Blowers	8.66
16	3667	Isan Grogan	50.00
16	3668	J. D. Arnold	65.00
16	3669	J. D. Arnold	11.34
16	3670	S. J. Keeler	65.00
16	3671	S. J. Keeler	10.84
16	3672	H. C. Leech	65.00
16	3673	H. C. Leech	10.84
16	3674	William McCaffery	65.00
16	3675	William McCaffery	10.84
16	3676	L. Singleton	50.00
16	3677	Zebulon Stokes	50.00
16	3678	F. M. White	65.00
16	3679	F. M. White	10.00
16	3680	J. H. Marshall	65.00
16	3681	J. H. Marshall	9.33
16	3682	J. C. Quayle	65.00
16	3683	J. C. Quayle	10.34
16	3684	George Stoll	65.00
16	3685	George Stoll	10.50
16	3686	Robert Joyce	66.00
16	3687	Daniel Hughes	43.00
16	3745	Sylvester Bouch	60.84
16	3746	William F. Berry	65.00
16	3747	William F. Berry	14.33
16	3748	William H. Chipman	65.00
16	3749	William H. Chipman	12.50
16	3750	Erl Caters	65.00
16	3751	Erl Caters	12.84
16	3752	M. Duffey	65.00
16	3753	M. Duffey	12.67
16	3754	Thomas A. Frazer	65.00
16	3755	Thomas A. Frazer	14.33
16	3756	Ira J. Harder	65.00
6	3757	Ira J. Harder	13.16
6	3758	F. M. Mounts	65.00
6	3759	F. M. Mounts	14.00
6	3760	J. J. Anderson	65.00
6	3761	J. J. Anderson	11.34
6	3762	William Bronson	65.00
6	3763	William Bronson	12.00
6	3764	James Blaslin	65.00
6	3765	James Blaslin	11.67
6	3766	Andrew Coulter	65.00
6	3767	Andrew Coulter	10.00
6	3768	E. C. Dunning	65.00
6	3769	E. C. Dunning	11.00
6	3770	James Dolan	65.00
6	3771	James Dolan	11.67
6	3772	Peter Demitz	65.00
6	3773	Peter Demitz	11.16
6	3774	S. R. Edmisson	65.00
6	3775	S. R. Edmisson	13.50
6	3776	James P. Fagan	65.00
6	3777	James P. Fagan	13.33
6	3778	Dayton Field	65.00
6	3779	Dayton Field	12.00
6	3780	Thomas Fitzpatrick	65.00
6	3781	Thomas Fitzpatrick	13.16
6	3782	Richard Grace	65.00
6	3783	Richard Grace	10.16
6	3784	F. J. Haight	65.00
6	3785	F. J. Haight	11.50
6	3786	M. Handlin	65.00
6	3787	M. Handlin	11.16
6	3788	M. J. Hay	65.00
6	3789	M. J. Hay	11.16
6	3790	William M. Huptill	65.00
6	3791	William M. Huptill	13.16

Abstract C.—*Showing disbursements by the State of Nevada, etc.*—Continued.

Date.	Warrant.	To whom issued.	Amount.	Date.	Warrant.	To whom issued.	Amount.
1866. July 6	3792	G. R. Kellogg	$65.00	1866. Aug. 4	3914	John McDonald	$17.00
6	3793	G. R. Kellogg	13.50	4	3915	William C. Matlock	65.00
6	3794	B. F. Logan	325.00	4	3916	William C. Matlock	16.00
6	3795	Henry McQuaid	65.00	4	3917	John L. Nelson	65.00
6	3796	Henry McQuaid	11.50	4	3918	John L. Nelson	17.00
6	3797	James Mullett	65.00	4	3919	Isaac Sanderson	65.00
6	3798	James Mullett	12.00	4	3920	Isaac Sanderson	17.00
6	3799	George W. Norton	65.00	4	3921	Smith Stewart	65.00
6	3800	George W. Norton	12.67	4	3922	Smith Stewart	15.33
6	3801	C. Ottman	65.00	4	3923	Pat Walsh	65.00
6	3802	C. Ottman	11.34	4	3924	Pat Walsh	17.00
6	3803	George Peterson	65.00	4	3925	Jos. M. Westwood	65.00
6	3804	George Peterson	12.16	4	3926	Jos. M. Westwood	17.00
6	3805	J. F. Pennoyer	65.00	4	3927	James S. Warren	25.00
6	3806	J. F. Pennoyer	11.18	4	3928	James S. Warren	85.00
6	3807	Thomas Ryan	65.00	4	3929	James Atkins	65.00
6	3808	Thomas Ryan	11.50	4	3930	James Atkins	17.00
6	3809	John Rush	65.00	4	3931	Frank Bauer	65.00
6	3810	John Rush	13.33	4	3932	Frank Bauer	17.00
6	3811	G. W. Smith	65.00	4	3933	Samuel Bunce	65.00
6	3812	G. W. Smith	10.84	4	3934	Samuel Bunce	13.33
6	3813	E. P. Thomas	65.00	4	3935	Robert Bell	65.00
6	3814	E. P. Thomas	— 10.67	4	3936	Robert Bell	15.00
6	3815	R. C. Payne	37.66	4	3937	F. G. Burton	65.00
6	3816	William C. Bell	47.50	4	3938	F. G. Burton	17.00
6	3817	Thomas Bryson	47.50	4	3939	William H. Bennett	65.00
24	3818	B. F. Logan	63.33	4	3940	William H. Bennett	17.00
24	3819	James K. Young	65.00	4	3941	John Clark	65.00
24	3820	James K. Young	9.16	4	3942	John Clark	17.00
24	3821	Philip Bonham	65.00	4	3943	Henry Curren	65.00
24	3822	Philip Bonham	13.33	4	3944	Henry Curren	17.00
24	3823	J. F. Barrett or Barnett	65.00	4	3945	John Cono	65.00
24	3824	J. F. Barrett or Barnett	13.33	4	3946	John Cono	17.00
24	3825	Samuel Comeggs	65.00	4	3947	F. S. Dickson	65.00
24	3826	Samuel Comeggs	14.66	4	3948	F. S. Dickson	17.00
24	3827	A. Durfee	65.00	4	3949	John H. Davis	65.00
24	3828	A. Durfee	13.33	4	3950	John H. Davis	17.00
24	3829	M. B. Hoyt	65.00	4	3951	Reuben Ferris	55.00
24	3830	M. B. Hoyt	13.33	4	3952	Reuben Ferris	17.00
24	3831	George J. Jones	65.00	4	3953	M. J. Fontz	65.00
24	3832	George J. Jones	8.84	4	3954	M. J. Fontz	17.00
24	3833	S. McCall	65.00	4	3955	Sol Hayworth	65.00
24	3834	S. McCall	13.33	4	3956	Sol Hayworth	17.00
24	3835	A. Opelesley	65.00	4	3957	Samuel Hartman	48.50
24	3836	A. Opelesley	14.67	4	3958	Samuel Hartman	16.50
24	3837	Charles Perry	65.00	4	3959	Samuel Hartman	17.00
24	3838	Charles Perry	13.50	4	3960	John Harder	65.00
24	3839	John Thoroughman	65.00	4	3961	John Harder	17.00
24	3840	John Thoroughman	11.00	4	3962	Alfred Holder	65.00
24	●3841	S. V. Ables	65.00	4	3963	Alfred Holder	17.00
24	3842	S. V. Ables	17.00	4	3964	Abram Harder	65.00
24	3843	Moses Austin	65.00	4	3965	Abram Harder	17.00
24	3844	Moses Austin	17.00	4	3966	E. H Johnson	65.00
24	3845	Rasmus Berry	65.00	4	3967	E. H. Johnson	17.00
24	3846	Rasmus Berry	17.00	4	3968	Charles Jarrett	65.00
24	3847	John J. Briggs	65.00	4	3969	Charles Jarrett	17.00
24	3848	John J. Briggs	17.00	4	3970	Otis W. Johnson	60.00
24	3849	John Hopkins	65.00	4	3971	S. L. Jacobs	65.00
24	3850	John Hopkins	17.00	4	3972	S. L. Jacobs	17.00
24	3851	Otto Ludderwig	65.00	4	3973	Peter McKeown	65.00
24	3852	Otto Ludderwig	17.00	4	3974	Peter McKeown	17.00
24	3853	James C. Neff	65.00	4	3975	Ed. McKenzie	65.00
24	3854	James C. Neff	15.83	4	3976	Ed. McKenzie	17.00
24	3855	Alex Thompson	65.00	4	3977	John R. Nugent	65.00
24	3856	Alex Thompson	17.00	4	3978	John R. Nugent	17.00
Aug. 4	3898	Noyes Baldwin	520.00	4	3979	Henry Nutt	62.33
4	3899	E. B. Zabriskie	105.00	4	3980	Henry Nutt	17.00
4	3900	John Andrew	65.00	4	3981	Felix O'Neil	65.00
4	3901	John Andrew	16.84	4	3982	Felix O'Neil	16.00
4	3902	Charles B. Dunn	48.84	4	3983	William O'Neil	30.00
4	3903	Leon Gris	65.00	4	3984	William O'Neil	30.84
4	3904	Leon Gris	15.84	4	3985	J. M. Plaisted	65.00
4	3905	F. W. Iserman	65.00	4	3986	J. M. Plaisted	17.00
4	3906	F. W. Iserman	17.00	4	3987	John Robinson	65.00
4	3907	James C. Logan	65.00	4	3988	John Robinson	17.00
4	3908	James C. Logan	17.00	4	3989	A. S. Robertson	65.00
4	3909	Pat Mooney	65.00	4	3990	A. S. Robertson	17.00
4	3910	Pat Mooney	15.84	4	3991	William Roberts	65.00
4	3911	Pat McNickle	65.00	4	3992	William Roberts	17.00
4	3912	Pat McNickle	7.00	4	3993	Rodney Shoemaker	65.00
4	3913	John McDonald	65.00	4	3994	Rodney Shoemaker	17.00

ABSTRACT C.—*Showing disbursements by the State of Nevada, etc.*—Continued.

Date.	War-rant.	To whom issued.	Amount.	Date.	War-rant.	To whom issued.	Amount.
1886.				1886.			
Aug. 4	3995	Aug. Schneider	$65.00	Aug. 4	4074	Thomas Bowman	$17.00
4	3996	Aug. Schneider	17.00	4	4075	J. Brownstine	65.00
4	3997	James Shields	65.00	4	4076	J. Brownstine	17.00
4	3998	James Shields	17.00	4	4077	M. Corcoran	65.00
4	3999	John Schaster	65.00	4	4078	M. Corcoran	17.00
4	4000	John Schaster	17.00	4	4079	Jos. Davis	65.00
4	4001	N. L. Shaw	65.00	4	4080	Jos. Davis	17.00
4	4002	N. L. Shaw	17.00	4	4081	George R. Day	65.00
4	4003	William H. Scott	65.00	4	4082	George R. Day	17.00
4	4004	William H. Scott	17.00	4	4083	Max Delstberg	65.00
4	4005	James H. Mathewson	430.50	4	4084	Max Delstberg	17.00
4	4006	James H. Mathewson	119.00	4	4085	A. E. Easterbrook	65.00
4	4007	James H. Stewart	25.00	4	4086	A. E. Easterbrook	17.00
4	4008	James H. Stewart	79.16	4	4087	William Edwards	65.00
4	4009	L. C. Cornell	65.00	4	4088	William Edwards	17.00
4	4010	L. C. Cornell	10.00	4	4089	K. Fleesenhaur	65.00
4	4011	James C. McGuire	65.00	4	4090	K. Fleesenhaur	17.00
4	4012	James C. McGuire	15.16	4	4091	C. Florino	65.00
4	4013	Sol M. Taylor	65.00	4	4092	C. Florino	17.00
4	4014	Sol M. Taylor	11.50	4	4093	P. W. Fisher	65.00
4	4015	George R. Hellerman	65.00	4	4094	P. W. Fisher	15.00
4	4016	George R. Hellerman	17.00	4	4095	David Hoge	65.00
4	4017	M. Jernegan	65.00	4	4096	David Hoge	17.00
4	4018	M. Jernegan	17.00	4	4097	Frank Hohman	65.00
4	4019	Jesse Jentry, or Gentry.	65.00	4	4098	Frank Hohman	17.00
				4	4099	Ed. Holsko	65.00
4	4020	Jesse Jentry, or Gentry.	17.00	4	4100	Ed. Holsko	17.00
				4	4101	A. J. Keith	65.00
4	4021	J. J. Jackson	65.00	4	4102	A. J. Keith	17.00
4	4022	J. J. Jackson	17.00	4	4103	William Killion	65.00
4	4023	John Kyle	65.00	4	4104	William Killion	17.00
4	4024	John Kyle	13.00	4	4105	Foster Lincoln	65.00
4	4025	Andrew Koontz	65.00	4	4106	Foster Lincoln	17.00
4	4026	Andrew Koontz	17.00	4	4107	Zac. Mitchell	65.00
4	4027	B. J. Lee	65.00	4	4108	Zac. Mitchell	17.00
4	4028	B. J. Lee	8.33	4	4109	John Marshall	65.00
4	4029	James Munroe	65.00	4	4110	John Marshall	17.00
4	4030	James Munroe	17.00	4	4111	M. McMahon	65.00
4	4031	William Minner	65.00	4	4112	M. McMahon	17.00
4	4032	William Minner	17.00	4	4113	R. P. McAuliffe	65.00
4	4033	L. A. Myers	65.00	4	4114	R. P. McAuliffe	17.00
4	4034	L. A. Myers	17.00	4	4115	L. M. Mealio	40.33
4	4035	F. M. Norval	65.00	4	4116	P. Martin	65.00
4	4036	F. M. Norval	17.00	4	4117	P. Martin	17.00
4	4037	Jos. R. Robinson	65.00	4	4118	George D. Rush	65.00
4	4038	Jos. R. Robinson	17.00	4	4119	George D. Rush	17.00
4	4039	Jos. Read	65.00	4	4120	Charles Reiz	65.00
4	4040	Jos. Read	17.00	4	4121	Charles Reiz	17.00
4	4041	John A. Silvers	65.00	4	4122	John Ratigan	65.00
4	4042	John A. Silvers	17.00	4	4123	John Ratigan	15.16
4	4043	J. A. Stewart	65.00	4	4124	John Sullivan	65.00
4	4044	J. A. Stewart	17.00	4	4125	John Sullivan	17.00
4	4045	G. D. Scholl	65.00	4	4126	Thornton Sleeth	65.00
4	4046	G. D. Scholl	17.00	4	4127	Thornton Sleeth	17.00
4	4047	John A. Spencer	30.00	4	4128	James Scull	65.00
4	4048	John A. Spencer	30.50	4	4129	James Scull	17.00
4	4049	S. B. Stamper	65.00	4	4130	B. M. Smedley	65.00
4	4050	S. B. Stamper	17.00	4	4131	B. M. Smedley	17.00
4	4051	Richard C. White	65.00	4	4132	Henry Waters	65.00
4	4052	Richard C. White	17.00	4	4133	Henry Waters	17.00
4	4053	John H. Dalton	35.00	4	4134	John Whelan	65.00
4	4054	John H. Dalton	119.00	4	4135	John Whelan	17.00
4	4055	D. R. Firman	275.00	4	4136	Henry Ward	65.00
4	4056	D. R. Firman	85.00	4	4137	Henry Ward	17.00
4	4057	L. P. Howell	65.00	4	4138	John Walsh	65.00
4	4058	L. P. Howell	17.00	4	4139	John Walsh	17.00
4	4059	William R. Jones	65.00	4	4140	Oscar Jewott	161.34
4	4060	William R. Jones	17.00	4	4141	Oscar Jewott	129.50
4	4061	John Johnson	65.00	4	4142	W. W. Boatwright	65.00
4	4062	John Johnson	17.00	4	4143	W. W. Boatwright	18.50
4	4063	B. J. W. Koontz	65.00	4	4144	M. L. Courtney	65.00
4	4064	B. J. W. Koontz	17.00	4	4145	M. L. Courtney	18.50
4	4065	Charles Meserve	65.00	4	4146	Charles Frickler	65.00
4	4066	Charles Meserve	17.00	4	4147	Charles Frickler	18.50
4	4067	R. C. McKenzie	65.00	4	4148	M. S. Fry	65.00
4	4068	R. C. McKenzie	17.00	4	4149	M. S. Fry	18.50
4	4069	Thomas H. Aikins	65.00	4	4150	Henry Finley	65.00
4	4070	Thomas H. Aikins	15.84	4	4151	Henry Finley	18.50
4	4071	Benjamin Brown	126.33	4	4152	M. Gehrum	65.00
4	4072	Benjamin Brown	17.00	4	4153	M. Gehrum	18.50
4	4073	Thomas Bowman	65.00	4	4154	Ed. Harris	65.00

ABSTRACT C.—*Showing disbursements by the State of Nevada, etc.*—Continued.

Date	War-rant	To whom issued.	Amount.	Date	War-rant	To whom issued.	Amount.
1866.				1866.			
Aug. 4	4155	Ed. Harris............	$18.50	Aug. 4	4253	Edward J. Soulsby....	$12.00
4	4156	B. F. McCready......	65.00	4	4254	John Campbell	65.00
4	4157	B. F. McCready......	18.50	4	4255	John Campbell	17.00
4	4158	Jackson Mowbray....	65.00	4	4256	Maurice Geary	65.00
4	4159	Jackson Mowbray....	18.50	4	4257	Maurice Geary	17.00
4	4160	Jos. J. Miesen	65.00	4	4258	E. Lewitzky	65.00
4	4161	Jos. J. Miesen	18.50	4	4259	E. Lewitzky	17.00
4	4162	William J. Palmer....	65.00	4	4260	E. P. Maynard	65.00
4	4163	William J. Palmer ..	18.50	4	4261	E. P. Maynard	17.00
4	4164	A. Aldrich..........	65.00	4	4262	John O'Brien	65.00
4	4165	A. Aldrich	18.50	4	4263	John O'Brien	17.00
4	4166	Peter Benedict	65.00	4	4264	L. M. Spencer	65.00
4	4167	Peter Benedict	18.50	4	4265	L. M. Spencer	17.00
4	4168	A. Barrett	65.00	4	4266	William Walsh......	65.00
4	4169	A. Barrett	18.50	4	4267	William Walsh......	17.00
4	4170	M. G. Bannister......	65.00	4	4268	George Emmerson....	65.00
4	4171	M. G. Bannister......	18.50	4	4269	George Emmerson....	18.50
4	4172	Peter Campbell......	65.00	27	4270	H. E. Murray	65.00
4	4173	Peter Campbell......	18.50	27	4271	H. E. Murray	18.50
4	4174	Charles H. Dietz.....	65.00	27	4272	Xavier Pasqueir......	65.00
4	4175	Charles H. Dietz.....	18.50	27	4273	Xavier Pasqueir......	18.50
4	4176	David B. Davis	65.00	27	4332	Adam Aulbuch	65.00
4	4177	David B. Davis	18.50	27	4333	Adam Aulbuch	17.00
4	4178	John C. Egan........	65.00	27	4334	George Nowitzkie....	65.00
4	4179	John C. Egan........	18.50	27	4335	George Nowitzkie	13.00
4	4180	A. G. Grant..........	65.00	27	4336	Peter S. Port	65.00
4	4181	A. G. Grant..........	18.50	27	4337	Peter S. Port......	16.16
4	4182	William F. Johnson ..	65.00	27	4338	Charles P. Frost......	65.00
4	4183	William F. Johnson ..	18.50	27	4339	Charles P. Frost......	11.16
4	4184	Conrad F. Kircher	65.00	27	4340	George F. Kibling	65.00
4	4185	Conrad F. Kircher	18.50	27	4341	George F. Kibling	13.00
4	4186	Pat Kearney..........	65.00	27	4342	James Dill	65.00
4	4187	Pat Kearney	18.50	27	4343	James Dill	17.00
4	4188	Amasa Lahair	65.00	27	4344	James C. Flynn......	65.00
4	4189	Amasa Lahair	18.50	27	4345	James C. Flynn......	17.00
4	4190	Charles F. Lake	65.00	27	4346	J. M. Fulton	65.00
4	4191	Charles F. Lake	18.50	27	4347	J. M. Fulton........	17.00
4	4192	Amos Lamson	65.00	27	4348	John Skelton........	65.00
4	4193	Amos Lamson	18.50	27	4349	John Skelton........	17.00
4	4194	N. P. Lake..........	65.00	27	4350	Thomas Shortreed....	65.00
4	4195	N. P. Lake..........	18.50	27	4351	Thomas Shortreed....	17.00
4	4196	H. Morris	65.00	27	4353	John C. Deaner......	65.00
4	4197	H. Morris	18.50	27	4354	John C. Deaner......	18.50
4	4198	Ed. McDonegh	65.00	27	4355	G. Mahler	65.00
4	4199	Ed. McDonegh	18.50	27	4356	G. Mahler	18.50
4	4200	George Millard	65.00	27	4357	George W. Rogers....	65.00
4	4201	George Millard	18.50	27	4358	George W. Rogers....	18.50
4	4202	James Nugent	65.00	27	4359	Charles D. St. Croix..	65.00
4	4203	James Nugent	18.50	27	4360	Charles D. St. Croix..	18.50
4	4204	William Olthe	65.00	27	4361	Joseph Scherb	65.00
4	4205	William Olthe	18.50	Oct. 9	4362	Joseph Scherb......	18.50
4	4206	Floyd Potter	65.00	9	4363	John C. Shelby......	65.00
4	4207	Floyd Potter	18.50	9	4364	John C. Shelby......	18.50
4	4208	Oliver R. Pyatt, or Platt	65.00	Nov. 13	4411	Job Hoxie	65.00
4	4209	Oliver R. Pyatt, or Platt	18.50	13	4412	Job Hoxie	17.00
4	4210	Joseph Poss..........	65.00	20	4413	James A. Wilkinson..	17.22
4	4211	Joseph Poss..........	18.50	20	4414	William Mulloy	43.00
4	4212	Joseph K. Ross	65.00	Dec. 11	4460	James F. Byrnes	65.00
4	4213	Joseph K. Ross	18.50	11	4461	James F. Byrnes	17.00
4	4214	James Scott	65.00	1867.			
4	4215	James Scott	18.50	Apr. 6	572	Thomas P. Hess......	65.00
4	4216	A. B. Silvera	65.00	6	573	Thomas P. Hess	15.84
4	4217	A. B. Silvera	18.50	6	574	William A. Rodd......	51.67
4	4218	Robert B. Wynd......	65.00	6	575	A. Fenstermaker	65.00
4	4219	Robert B. Wynd......	18.50	6	576	A. Fenstermaker	14.50
4	4220	Theodore Wettergren	65.00	6	577	St. L. McNaughton ...	65.00
4	4221	Theodore Wettergren	18.50	6	578	St. L. McNaughton...	15.84
4	4222	John B. Wilson......	65.00	6	579	E. Langham..........	58.00
4	4223	John B. Wilson......	18.50	6	580	E. Langham..........	2.00
4	4224	Frederick White	65.00	6	581	M. O. Garra..........	65.00
4	4225	Frederick White	18.50	6	582	M. O. Garra..........	17.00
4	4226	Noyes Baldwin	148.00	6	583	George W. Smith.....	43.00
4	4227	E. B. Zabriskie.......	110.84	6	584	H. M. Barnes........	30.33
4	4246	Michael Davis.......	65.00	6	585	Thomas J. Bell	65.00
4	4247	Michael Davis.......	6.84	6	586	Thomas J. Bell......	18.50
4	4249	H. H. Oates	65.00	6	587	Samuel McCook	65.00
4	4250	H. H. Oates	16.84	6	588	Samuel McCook	18.50
4	4251	Jos. H. Matthewson...	325.83	6	589	Fred Kreitzer	65.00
4	4252	Edward J. Soulsby....	65.00	6	590	Fred Kreitzer........	18.50
				6	591	Alex Prado..........	65.00
				6	592	Alex Prado..........	18.50

ABSTRACT C.—*Showing disbursements by the State of Nevada, etc.*—Continued.

Date.	War-rant.	To whom issued.	Amount.	Date.	War-rant.	To whom issued.	Amount.
1867.				1869.			
Apr. 15	650	Paul Sherman	$65. 00	May 25	866	Isaac Barton..........	$65. 00
15	651	Paul Sherman........	11. 00	25	867	Isaac Barton	18. 50
June 6	770	William Nolan	65. 00	Oct. 27	1183	Wm. S. McCormick ..	10. 50
6	771	William Nolan	15. 83	27	1184	Wm. S. McCormick...	65. 00
Aug. 8	935	George F. Austin....	36. 33	1870.			
Sept. 23	1010	Isaac W. Godfrey....	75. 00	Sept. 8	558	Thomas J. Davis	82. 00
23	1011	A. N. Gray...........	30. 00	1871.			
23	1012	A. N. Gray...........	35. 00	Dec. 10	2178	William Aikens	65. 16
23	1013	A. N. Gray...........	17. 00	1872.			
1868.				May 18	429	Michael Dunnigan ...	47. 50
Feb. 29	96	John W. Cummings ..	65. 00				
29	97	John B. Babnis	65. 00			Grand total......	96,054. 78
29	177	John W. Cummings .	17. 00				
29	118	John B. Babnis.......	17. 00				

ABSTRACT D.—*Showing liabilities assumed by the State of Nevada, and as successor to the Territory of Nevada, on account of costs, charges, and expenses for monthly pay to volunteer and military forces in the Territory and State of Nevada, in the service of the United States, and employed in the defense of the United States during the war of the rebellion.*

Date.	No. war-rant.	Name—to whom issued.	Remarks.	Amount.
1865.				
June 28	1312	Fred Hosli....................	Certificate of service filed..........	$36. 50
31	1402	B. Fawcett...................	See 1448 for certificate filed........	61. 33
31	1441	Joseph Segur.................	......do	27. 83
Aug. 7	1517	A. D. Zelin..................	See 1489 for certificate filed........	61. 33
7	1571	James Williams	See 1489 power attorney filed	11. 33
7	1590	Edwin White.................	See 1573 for certificate filed........	8. 50
7	1597	Samuel Ayres	.... do	8. 83
7	1603	S. Bouck	See 1573 power attorney filed........	8. 50
7	1604	Frank Bauer	See 1573 for certificate filed........	4. 16
7	1619	S. Garrison	......do	19. 66
7	1629	Thomas Jewell	......do	11. 33
7	1643	A. G. Robertson	......do ...../......................	2. 33
7	1654	Francis Sands	......do	9. 50
26	1666	G. Whitehead	See 1865 for certificate filed........	61. 33
26	1669	F. M. Blair..................	......do	58. 50
26	1676	B. S. Clements	......do	56. 33
26	1677	N. B. Common	......do	34. 00
26	1692	John McClusky....., ...	......do	13. 16
26	1699	H. Schlischting	......do	12. 66
26	1700	John Tindle	......do	13. 83
26	1710	John B. Babin	See 1701 for certificate filed	19. 00
26	1729	George Latham....	......do	61. 33
26	1735	Hugh Miller.................	......do	16. 00
26	1824	W. J. Johnson	See 1823 for certificate filed	61. 33
26	1834	Joseph Boley	......do	6. 66
26	1835	Joseph Payett	......do	17. 00
26	1837	Davis Steel..................	......do	21. 66
26	1848	George W. Thurlow	See 1841 for certificate filed	14. 83
26	1851	E. Beamingthal	......do	61. 33
26	1887	William I. McGinnis	......do	13. 16
26	1907	A. J. Whitbeck	See 1841 for power attorney filed.....	52. 83
26	1955	Albert Sumpter..............	See 1910 for certificate filed	3. 00
Dec. 8	2215	Joel Wolverton...............	Certificate of service filed..........	50. 00
1886.				
Jan. 29	2619	J. Boley.....................	......do	48. 84
Mar. 21	3509	Harry Pierce.................	......do	47. 50
	3511	James H. Sanborn	......do	47. 50
Aug. 27	4248	Richard A. Fitch	......do	48. 84
Oct. 9	4352	William M. Liggett...........	......do	43. 00
		Total ....- .....-	....-.......	1,153. 75

ABSTRACT E.—*Showing disbursements by the State of Nevada, and as successor to the Territory of Nevada, on account of costs, charges, and expenses for pay as salary to the adjutant-general of the volunteer and military forces in the Territory and State of Nevada, in the service of the United States, and employed in defense of the United States during the war of the rebellion.*

Date.	Warrant.	To whom issued.	Amount.	Remarks.
1862.				
May 1	85 and 86	H. P. Russell......................	$250.00	
Aug. 2	134	H. P. Russell......................	250.00	
Nov. 7	159	H. P. Russell......................	250.00	
1863.				
Feb. 6	{ 323 / 324 }	H. P. Russell......................	250.00	
Mar. 31	349	H. P. Russell......................	233.00	
July 1	375	H. P. Russell......................	250.00	
Oct. 1	422	H. P. Russell......................	250.00	
1864.				
Jan. 5	490	H. P. Russell......................	250.00	
Apr. 2	692	H. P. Russell......................	250.00	
July 1	743	H. P. Russell......................	250.00	Paid in State bond No. 3.
Sept. 30	801	H. P. Russell......................	250.00	Paid in State bond No. 195.
Oct. 30	840	H. P. Russell......................	81.00	Paid in State bonds Nos. 7 to 111.
1865.				
Apr. 3	1073	John Cradlebaugh...............	116.66	
	1159	John Cradlebaugh...............	500.00	
	1160	John Cradlebaugh...............	500.00	
	1330	John Cradlebaugh...............	300.00	
	1331	John Cradlebaugh...............	200.00	
	2035	John Cradlebaugh...............	500.00	
Dec. 31	2313	John Cradlebaugh...............	500.00	
1866.				
Mar. 31	3533	John Cradlebaugh...............	250.00	
	3538	John Cradlebaugh...............	250.00	
	3704	John Cradlebaugh...............	250.00	
	4291	John Cradlebaugh...............	500.00	
	4538	John Cradlebaugh...............	500.00	
			7,431.16	

ABSTRACT F.—*Showing disbursements of the State of Nevada and as successor to the Territory of Nevada, on account of costs, charges, and expenses for transportation, on account of the volunteer and military forces in the Territory and State of Nevada, in the service of the United States and employed in defense of the United States, during the war of the rebellion.*

Date.	No. warrant.	Name—to whom issued.	Remarks.	Amount.
July 1, 1864	741	G. L. Gibson..............	Transportation of arms..........	$29.00
Apr. 29, 1865	1161	Shaw's F. F. & Ex. Co....	Transportation of blanks........	8.00
	1162	......do...................	Transportation of stationery....	23.00
				60.00

ABSTRACT G.—*Showing the amount actually paid by the State of Nevada and as successor to the Territory of Nevada on account of interest money on disbursements and liabilities for Nevada volunteers in the service of the United States, and employed in the defense of the United States during the war of the rebellion.*

	Amount.
First—Interest paid on $46,050.12 from February 10, 1865, to March 3, 1866, at 2 per cent. per month.. [See acts legislature of Nevada for 1864–'65, page 82, act January 4, 1865.]	$11,925.33
Second—Interest paid on $46,950.12 from March 3, 1866, to May 30, 1867, at 15 per cent. per annum.. [See acts legislature of Nevada for 1866, page 47, act January 10, 1866.]	8,744.40
Third—Interest paid on $119,800.12 from May 30, 1867, to March 28, 1872, at 15 per cent. per annum.. [See acts legislature of Nevada for 1867, pages 50 and 65, act February 6, 1867.]	86,755.25
Fourth—Interest paid on $119.800.12 from March 28, 1872, to January 1, 1883, at 9½ per cent. per annum.. [See acts legislature of Nevada for 1871, page 84, act of February 27, 1871.]	122,472.33
	229,897.37

RECAPITULATION.

[For the war of the rebellion.]

	Amount.
Abstract A : Enrolling, recruiting, etc...	$11,986.05
Abstract B : Supplying..	3,114.38
Abstract C : Pay to troops..	96,054.78
Abstract D : Liabilities assumed...	1,153.75
Abstract E : Pay of salary of adjutant-general.....................................	7,431.16
Abstract F : Transportation...	60.00
	119,800.12
Abstract G : Interest actually paid..	229,897.37
Total..	349,697.49

S. Rep. 1286——6

The United States in account current with the State of Nevada, and as successor to the Territory of Nevada, for the expenses of the United States during the war of the rebellion.

DR.

	Amount.
1. The amount disbursed by the State of Nevada, and as successor to the Territory of Nevada, on account of recruiting, enlisting, organizing, and enrolling Nevada volunteers in the service of the United States in the war of the rebellion, as per abstract A.	$11,986.05
2. To amount disbursed by the State of Nevada, and as successor to the Territory of Nevada, on account of supplying Nevada volunteers in the service of the United States in the war of the rebellion, as per abstract B	3,114.38
3. To amount disbursed by the State of Nevada, and as successor to the Territory of Nevada, on account of pay to Nevada volunteers in the service of the United States in the war of the rebellion, as per abstract C	96,054.78
4. To amount of liabilities assumed by the State of Nevada, and as successor to the Territory of Nevada, on account of pay to Nevada volunteers in the service of the United States in the war of the rebellion, as per abstract D	1,153.75
5. The amount disbursed by the State of Nevada, and as successor to the Territory of Nevada, on account of salary of adjutant-general of Nevada volunteers in the service of the United States during the war of the rebellion, as per abstract E	7,431.16
6. To amount disbursed by the State of Nevada, and as successor to the Territory of Nevada, on account of transportation of Nevada volunteers in the service of the United States during the war of the rebellion, as per abstract F	60.00
7. To amount of interest actually paid by the State of Nevada, and as successor to the Territory of Nevada, on disbursements and liabilities on account of Nevada volunteers during the war of the rebellion, as per abstract G	229,897.37
Total	349,697.49

CR.

	Amount.

CONTROLLER'S CERTIFICATE.

STATE OF NEVADA, CONTROLLER'S DEPARTMENT,
Carson City, November 1, 1882.

I, J. F. Hallock, State controller of the State of Nevada, hereby certify that the foregoing account current sets forth a full, true, and correct statement of the claim of the State of Nevada, and as successor to the Territory of Nevada, on account of the matters enumerated in the several abstracts A, B, C, D, E, F, and G therein referred to, and that no part thereof has ever been paid by the United States to the Territory or to the State of Nevada, nor by any officer thereof, and that the same is now due and payable by the United States to the State of Nevada

J. F. HALLOCK,
State Controller of the State of Nevada.

GOVERNOR'S CERTIFICATE.

STATE OF NEVADA, EXECUTIVE DEPARTMENT,
Carson City, November 1, 1882.

I, John H. Kinkead, governor of the State of Nevada, hereby certify that the foregoing account current sets forth a full, true, and correct statement of the claims of the State of Nevada, and as successor to the Territory of Nevada, on account of the matters enumerated in the several abstracts A, B, C, D, E, F, and G therein referred to, and that no part thereof has ever been paid by the United States to the Territory or to the State of Nevada, nor by any officer thereof, and that the same is now due and payable by the United States to the State of Nevada.

JOHN H. KINKEAD,
Governor of the State of Nevada.

EXHIBIT No. 14.

DECISION OF THE SECRETARY OF WAR DISALLOWING CLAIM OF NEVADA FOR INTEREST AND EXTRA PAY TO NEVADA VOLUNTEERS.

WAR DEPARTMENT,
Washington City, February 8, 1887.

SIR: The Department has received your communications of December 31, 1886, and January 28, 1887, submitting arguments in the claim of the State of Nevada, under the act of June 27, 1882, for re-imbursement of amounts paid by the State for "extra pay" and for interest. Also, your communication of the 2d instant, inclosing a resolution of the senate and assembly of Nevada, requesting favorable and early action on said claim.

In reply, I have the honor to inform you that after a careful consideration of the subject, I am of opinion that neither the extra pay nor the interest can, under the provisions of the act, be allowed.

Very respectfully,

WILLIAM C. ENDICOTT,
Secretary of War.

JOHN MULLAN, Esq.,
Agent of the State of Nevada, 1101 G Street N. W., City.

The following is the argument submitted in support of the two propositions adversely decided by the Secretary of War in the foregoing:

BEFORE THE HONORABLE SECRETARY OF WAR.

In the matter of the claim of the State of Nevada to be re-imbursed by the United States the money actually paid out by her for interest on certain money by her borrowed to defray certain expenses by her incurred on account of the troops called into the service of the United States, and also for the monthly pay made by her to her said troops for certain times between April 15, 1861, and June 27, 1862, arising under the act of Congress approved June 27, 1882 (U. S. Statutes, vol. 22, page 111).

Honorable Secretary of War:

SIR: Under leave by you granted me to be heard why the claim of the State of Nevada to be re-imbursed the money which she has heretofore paid out for interest on certain money by her borrowed to defray certain expenses by her incurred on account of the troops by her raised and called into the service of the United States, and raised in said State between April 15, 1861, and June 27, 1882, and in the service of the United States for a portion of the time during that period; and also why the money paid out as "monthly pay" by her to said troops during said period, when said troops were in the service of the United States, should be now allowed to her by you when acting thereon under the provisions of the act of Congress approved June 27, 1882, I have the honor to now respectfully submit to you as follows, to wit:

First, that whereas section No. 3489 of the United States Revised Statutes is in words as follows, to wit:

"No claim against the United States for collecting, drilling, or organizing volunteers for the war of the rebellion shall be audited or paid unless presented before the thirtieth day of June, eighteen hundred and seventy-four. No claims for horses lost prior to the first day of January, eighteen hundred and seventy-two, shall be audited or paid unless presented before the thirtieth day of June, eighteen hundred and seventy-four."

Second, and whereas the State of Nevada had sundry claims against the United States for collecting, drilling, and organizing volunteers for the war of the rebellion, and for horses and equipments lost by said forces, etc., she had not, however, presented same prior to January 1, 1874, that being the date named in said section No. 3489, Revised Statutes.

Third, and whereas the State of Nevada, between 1st January, 1874, and June 27, 1882, conceiving, as she did, that said first-named claims were barred by the limitations as named and provided for in said section of the Revised Statutes, did seek by appropriate means at the hands of Congress for an adequate remedy in said premises, and for re-imbursement of such other proper expenses as she had incurred in various ways in behalf of the United States in these premises; and the prayer of her said petition resulted in the passage of the act of Congress of June 27, 1882.

The State of Nevada, therefore, now respectfully submits to you that it was the intention of Congress in said act of June 27, 1882, to re-imburse to her all moneys which she has in good faith expended in behalf of the United States for organizing, arming, equipping, supplying, clothing, subsisting, transporting, and paying the volunteer and militia forces of said State in the service of the United States between April 15, 1861, and the date of the passage of said act of June 27, 1882, and including all other proper expense necessarily incurred by said State by virtue of said troops having been so called into active service of the United States as aforesaid. And said act of June 27, 1882, in section 2 thereof, provided that the rate to be allowed to said State for such proper expenses was to be the same as were paid by the United States for similar expenses during that same period of time. Now the State of Nevada respectfully submits to you that the United States had to go into the markets of the world to borrow money in order to raise the principal with which to pay for similar classes of expenditures as named in said act, and the United States had to pay interest on such loans at the rate of at least 6 per cent. per annum, and the record of the claim of the State of Nevada before you shows that when the United States called upon her for troops (she being then only a Territory) her Territorial treasury was bankrupt, but nevertheless, as a Territory only, she promised to pay, and all of which promises the future State of Nevada fully redeemed and did pay dollar for dollar, and in doing so did incur very great financial embarrassments, but she maintained her credit at both home and abroad at all hazards. And the State of Nevada therefore submits that as she had to go into the markets of the world and borrow money in a similar way and for similar reasons as did the United States, that therefore Congress in said act of June 27, 1882, intended to place Nevada upon exactly the same place as to this proper expense as the United States had occupied as to the interest she had to pay out during the same period.

There can not be, certainly there ought not to be, any question that said expense of interest was a proper expense, and because it was a necessary expense, and it was necessary because it was proper; and it was proper because it was necessary; and without this dernier resort Nevada might have been powerless to respond to the call made upon her by the United States for troops; for if this absolutely necessary step had not been resorted to, it might have been a serious question whether Nevada could have done as promptly and efficiently as she finally succeeded in doing in behalf of the United States in these premises.

Again, while this particular claim against the United States is one for interest paid out by the State of Nevada to John Doe and Richard Roe for the use of their own private money, the same as if it had been paid out to them for the use of any other species of their own private property, yet it is none the less a part of the principal which Nevada was compelled to finally pay, and which constituted an advance to and in behalf of the United States for her own purposes.

A matter similar to this having been before the honorable Second Comptroller of the Treasury in 1869, that officer declared therein as follows, to wit: "Interest can in no case be allowed by the accounting officer upon claims against the Government, either in favor of a State or an individual. But in cases where the claimant has been compelled to pay interest for the benefit of the Government, it then becomes a part of the principal of his claim, and, as such, is allowable. Such is the case of a State which has been obliged to raise money upon interest for the suppression of hostilities against which the United States should protect her. In such cases the amount of interest actually and necessarily paid will be allowed, without reference to the rate of it." Section 997, Dec. 2d., Comp. Ed. 1869, p. 137.

In addition, the State of Nevada submits that such a ruling as made by the Second Comptroller is in perfect harmony with the long line of precedents as established by Congress, beginning in 1812 and ending in July 8, 1870, in the cases of Massachusetts and Maine (16 Stats., page 198), and is one of the many cases cited by Senator Hoar of Massachusetts, in a report to Congress, as late as December 6, 1885, made to the Senate from the Committee on Claims, in behalf of a general bill to re-imburse the States for interest paid out by them on war loans not heretofore provided for, and copy of which Senate report No. 2 is as follows:

"The policy of the United States to refund to the States interest on money expended by them in aid of the General Government for military purposes in time of war is settled. It has been applied to all such expenditures incurred by the States in aid of the war of 1812 (see Virginia, act March 3, 1825, 4 Stat. at Large, p. 132; Maryland, act of May 13, 1826, 4 Stat. at Large, p. 151; Delaware, act of May 20, 1826, 4 Stat. at Large, p. 175; New York, act of May 22, 1826, 4 Stat. at Large, p. 192; Pennsylvania, act of March 3, 1827, 4 Stat. at Large, p. 241; South Carolina, act of March 22, 1832, 4 Stat. at Large, p. 499; Maine, act of March 31, 1851, 9 Stat. at Large, p. 626; Massachusetts and Maine, act of July 8, 1870, 16 Stat. at Large, p. 198); in aid of various Indian wars (see Alabama, act January 26, 1849, 9 Stat. at Large, p. 344; Georgia, act of March 31, 1851, 9 Stat. at Large, p. 626; Washington Territory, act March 3, 1859, 11 Stat. at Large, p. 429; New Hampshire, act January 27. 1852, 10 Stat. at Large, p. 1; California, act August 5, 1854, 10 Stat. at Large, p. 582; California, act August 18, 1856, 11 Stat. at Large, p. 91; California, act June 23, 1860, 12 Stat. at Large, p. 104; California, act July 25, 1868, 15 Stat. at Large, p. 175; California, act March 3, 1881, 21 Stat. at Large, p. 510); and in aid of the Mexican war. See statute of June 2, 1848, which is as follows:

AN ACT to refund money for expenses incurred, subsistence and transportation furnished for the use of volunteers during the present war, before being mustered into the service of the United States.

Be it enacted by the Senate and House of Representatives of the United States of America in Congress assembled, That the provisions of the joint resolution approved March third, eighteen hundred and forty-seven, entitled "A resolution to refund money to the States which have supplied volunteers and furnished them transportation during the present war, before being mustered and received into the service of the United States," be, and the same are hereby, extended so as to embrace all cases of expenses heretofore incurred in organizing, subsisting, and transporting volunteers, previous to their being mustered and received into the service of the United States, for the present war, whether by States, counties, corporations, or individuals, either acting with or without the authority of the State: Provided, however, That proof shall be made to the satisfaction of the Secretary of War of the amount thus expended, and that the same was necessary and proper for the troops aforesaid.

SEC. 2. And be it further enacted, That an amount sufficient to refund said expenses so incurred be, and the same is hereby, appropriated out of any money in the Treasury not otherwise appropriated.

SEC. 3. And be it further enacted, That in refunding moneys under this act and the resolution which it amends, it shall be lawful to pay interest at the rate of six per centum per annum on all sums advanced [advanced] by States, corporations, or individuals in all cases where the State, corporation, or individual paid or lost the interest, or is liable to pay it.

Approved June 2, 1848.

"Mr. Chase, Secretary of the Treasury, recognized the obligation imposed by these precedents in a communication to the State auditor of Ohio in the following language:

If Ohio raises money by loan at a discount, the United States can not refund such discount to the State, but only the amount of the debt with interest, unless Congress specially provide otherwise.

"This was two days after the passage of the statute of July 27, 1861, which is as follows:

That the Secretary of the Treasury be, and is hereby, directed out of any money in the Treasury not otherwise appropriated, to pay to the governor of any State, or to his duly-authorized agents, the costs, charges, and expenses properly incurred by such State for enrolling, subsisting, clothing, supplying, arming, equipping, paying, and transporting its troops employed in aiding to suppress the present insurrection against the United States, to be settled upon proper vouchers to be filed and passed upon by the proper accounting officers of the Treasury.

"By a resolution passed March 8, 1862, the above provision is to be construed to apply to expenses incurred as well after as before the date of the approval thereof.

"It is held by the accounting officers of the Treasury that they are not warranted in the allowance of interest to the States by the existing law. This question was submitted to Attorney-General Brewster, who says, in his opinion, July 23, 1883:

Undoubtedly the interest paid by the State of New York on money borrowed and applied to the objects specified in the act of July 27, 1861, forms a part of the burden borne by that State for the general public defense, and constitutes a just charge against the United States; and the obligation to re-imburse for payments of that kind, made under similar circumstances, has frequently been recognized by Congress, as appears by statutes above cited.

"This opinion is in accord with that of his predecessors, Mr. Wirt and Mr. Crittenden. Mr. Wirt says:

The expenditure thus incurred forms a debt against the United States which they are bound to re-imburse. If the expenditures made for such purpose are supplied from the treasury of the State, the United States re-imburse the principal without interest; but if, being unable itself from the condition of its own finances to meet the emergency, such State has been obliged to borrow money for the purpose, and thus to incur a debt on which she herself has had to pay interest, such debt is essentially a debt due by the United States, and both the principal and interest are to be paid by the United States. (See Opinions of Attorneys-General, vol. 1, p. 174.)

" Mr. Crittenden says :

The act of the 27th of February, 1851, is intended to indemnify the State against loss or damage. Re-imbursing means repairing the loss or expenses by an equivalent. If the State of Florida has contracted obligations bearing interest, or has paid money, with interest, for the use and benefit, in necessary and proper supplies, for the troops called into service in 1849, to refund to the State of Florida the principal sum only, without the interest, would not re-imburse the State, would not save the State from loss and damage, would not be an equivalent for the expense the State has incurred for the United States. There is no public policy, no saving to the public Treasury, no virtue, no laudable end consulted in order to cut down the claims of the several States in opposition to the intention of Congress and the good faith of the Government.

" We append, for the information of the Senate, House Report No. 1102, made at the last session, and recommend the passage of the bill, with sundry amendments.

Mr. Rowell, from the Committee on War Claims, submitted the following report, to accompany bill H. R. 2463 :

By the act of July 27, 1861, and the joint resolution of March 8, 1862, the Secretary of the Treasury was directed to pay to the governor of any State, or his duly-authorized agents, " the costs, charges, and expenses properly incurred by such States for enrolling, subsisting, clothing, supplying, arming, equipping, paying, and transporting its troops employed in aiding to suppress the present insurrection against the United States, to be settled upon proper vouchers, to be filed and passed upon by the proper accounting officers of the Treasury."

By the joint resolution of March 8, 1862, payments were directed to be made for expenditures made subsequent to as well as before the passage of the act. Under this act disbursements have been made to the States amounting to the sum of $43,296,938.22; and there yet remain unsettled or disallowed claims amounting to several millions of dollars.

Many, if not all, of the States were obliged to borrow money to pay the expenses incurred, but in adjusting and allowing their claims the accounting officers of the Treasury have rejected all claims for interest paid out by the States, holding that the law did not authorize such payment.

The bill under consideration provides for re-imbursing the States for interest paid or lost on account of expenses incurred and repaid under the act of July 27, 1861. By its provisions interest is only to be paid on such sums as have been refunded or may hereafter be refunded under the authority of the act of Congress and explanatory resolutions; no interest is to be paid unless it was actually paid out or lost by the States, and then only up to the time of repayment by the Government, and limited to 6 per cent.

Claims for interest have been filed amounting to $3,188,887.25 ; but these claims are based upon a higher rate of interest than that provided in the bill; other States have not filed interest claims, owing to the ruling of the Department, but if the bill becomes law they will have proper claims.

Your committee are of opinion that these interest claims, at a rate such as the General Government was obliged to pay, are a just and proper charge against the Government. Immediately after the passage of the acts, Mr. Chase, then Secretary of the Treasury, in a communication to the auditor of the State of Ohio, gave assurances that interest would be paid. Laws were passed after the war of 1812 to re-imburse the several States for moneys expended in that war, with similar provisos to the law under which the payments herein considered have been made.

Subsequently Congress passed laws to pay interest, as is provided in this bill. A similar bill was passed by Congress to re-imburse States for expenses incurred on account of the Indian war, with like necessity of subsequent legislation to authorize the payment of interest.

It seems to be the history of all the legislation of Congress for the re-imbursement of States for war expenditures that the initial statutes have always failed to provide for the payment of interest, but in every instance previous to 1861 subsequent acts provided for the payment of interest.

It may therefore be regarded as the settled policy of Congress to repay to the several States not only the principal sums expended by them in aid of the General Government in times of war, but also to repay interest actually paid out not exceeding the rate paid by the General Government during the same period.

Your committee therefore recommend that the bill do pass.

The State of Nevada respectfully submits that the act of Congress approved June 27, 1882, made, and intended to make, special and ample provision for the specific States named therein in regard to this proper expense, to wit, that of interest among other proper expenses. Nevada being one of the States specifically named in said statute, she respectfully submits that when she had been compelled to pay interest for the benefit of the Government of the United States, such interest became a part of the principal of her claim against the United States, and as such is now allowable to her by you under said act of June 27, 1882. And she further submits to you that, when she had been obliged to raise money upon interest for the suppression of hostilities against which the United States should have protected her, as in this case, the amount of interest actually and necessarily paid out by her is now allowable to her by you under said act of June 27, 1882.

The State of Nevada respectfully submits that this is not a case of a claim for interest on money which she had already on hand in her own State treasury and disbursed therefrom for the benefit of the United States, but, on the contrary, it is one where she had to go out publicly into the open money markets of the world, to borrow the very principal which she expended for the benefit of the United States; so that it ought to appear self-evident, and as not needing argument to show, that it is a case of even a more legitimate claim against the United States than even for the principal itself, and under the circumstances it is even a higher order of claim, and the two factors are merged into one and the same claim, because said interest has become as completely merged in the principal as a coupon is merged into and becomes a part of the bond to which it is attached, and of which, it has ever been held, it forms a constituent part.

The State of Nevada, therefore, respectfully submits to you that the act of June 27, 1882, interpreted in the light of the unvarying and uniform policy of Congress from 1842 to date, and as held by the honorable Second Comptroller, should be now construed by the honorable Secretary of War as allowing interest to her, either in the sum she has actually and necessarily paid out as interest during the period named in said statute, or if not that, then such interest as the United States was compelled to pay out on money she borrowed during such period (which rate of interest was 6 per cent. per annum), should be now, as an alternative allowance, made by you to her under said act of June 27, 1882, and not otherwise.

Second. In regard to the pay of Nevada Territorial and State troops, as made by the State of Nevada, and which troops were raised therein for the service exclusively of the United States during the war of the rebellion, and which pay was the sum of $5 per month, the State of Nevada respectfully submits that it was the intention of Congress, in said act of Congress of June 27, 1882, to re-imburse her, as the successor of the Territory of Nevada, such monthly pay as she had made to her own troops while in the service of the United States; provided such monthly pay did not exceed the sum per month that the United States were then paying for similar services to other troops.

The State of Nevada respectfully submits that Congress in enacting this statute took full cognizance of the public condition of things as same existed in the Territory and State of Nevada in 1861, 1862, 1863, 1864, and 1865, when there were no railroads therein, and when the Federal troops had all been withdrawn therefrom, and when Nevada's Territorial and State troops had to guard the overland mail route (as well as the general Indian frontier therein) from Salt Lake, Utah, to Sacramento, Cal., and when everything, always theretofore very expensive, was rendered more so for the troops in the field and for their families at home by virtue of peculiar exigencies of her situation. The State of Nevada further submits that Congress is presumed to have taken cognizance of these public facts, and in view of these causes as promises, she had duly enacted a law under and by which her own Territorial troops while in the service of the United States should receive a monthly pay from her own Territorial Treasury of $5 per month, and against which the United States not only never demurred, but the payment of which she duly facilitated; and it is submitted that such monthly pay of $5 per month to said troops was not only a proper and necessary expense, but in some cases was a boon to the United States, whose credit was strained to the utmost, and Nevada will not, for she can not, assume that any construction will be placed upon this statute of June 27, 1882, such as would be equivalent to a repudiation of an obligation incurred in behalf of the United States, and under circumstances so peculiar as those under which this obligation was contracted.

The State of Nevada submits that the only limitation prescribed by the statute of June 27, 1882, is that such monthly pay should not exceed the monthly pay made by the United States to its other troops during this same period. The said act of June 27, 1882, contains all the exceptions that Congress intended it to contain or to apply to the several States when their said claims were being finally adjusted, and it is respectfully submitted that the honorable Secretary of War will not interpolate this statute with any exception not found upon the face thereof. Now, for instance, said statute provides "that no allowance shall be made for the services of any person in more than one capacity at the same time." In the absence of such provision as the foregoing the Secretary of War could, and probably would, allow a soldier pay as such, and also pay as an artificer, or a hospital steward, or a company clerk, or such like, provided, always, such soldier served in any one of such capacities.

In this case of pay of troops the State of Nevada respectfully submits that Congress is presumed to have taken into consideration the condition of the troops therein and made special provision for them in said statute of June 27, 1882, and such as the peculiar public exigencies in that locality and at that time fully justified, and of none of which was Congress ignorant. This pay was not in the nature of a bounty as an encouragement to enlist, and because it applied only to troops in the active service of the United States, and it was paid by the month and was to terminate, and did terminate, whenever said troops ceased to be in the service of the United States.

The State of Nevada respectfully submits that she has acted in perfect good faith in all these premises, and that to make this monthly pay to her troops was not only necessary by virtue of the foregoing recitals, but also by virtue of the fact that the only rich silver mines then being extensively and successfully worked in the United States—principally on the Comstock lodes—rendered available men few and services high, and when the very miners were getting by the day a sum fully equal to this pay received by her troops in the field per month, and that too only when they were in the services of the United States.

The State of Nevada further submits that all these public and notorious facts were well known to Congress when enacting said statute of June 27, 1882, and that such expense must have been regarded by Congress as a proper expense, and as such was intended to be allowed to her by the Secretary of War when adjusting her claim presented under the aforesaid statute.

Wherefore, the State of Nevada, in her own behalf, and as the successor to the Territory of Nevada, in view of these recitals and of said act of Congress of June 27, 1882, and of the intent thereof, and of the equitable and liberal construction that should now be placed upon this remedial statute by you, as the administrator of the law of the United States, for whose use and benefit all such expenses in good faith have been incurred, now respectfully submits her claim for re-imbursement thereof, and prays that same may be allowed her in the adjustment of the several claims presented by her under the said act of June 27, 1882.

In conclusion, the State of Nevada submits an extract from Senate Report No. 575, relating to Nevada's war claims, made to the Senate on May 12, 1882, by its Committee on Military Affairs, recommending the payment of said claims, and which, having had the serious attention of Congress, resulted in the passage of said act of June 27, 1882, and which extract is as follows, to wit:

"*Nevada.*—It appears by the report of the Adjutant-General, U. S. Army, of February 25, 1882, that one regiment of cavalry and one battalion of infantry were raised in the late Territory of Nevada during the late war of the rebellion, and that the expenses of raising, organizing, and placing in the field said forces were never paid by said Territory, but were assumed and paid by the State of Nevada, and that none of said expenses so incurred by said Territory, and assumed and paid by said State, have ever been re-imbursed the State of Nevada by the United States, and that no claims therefor have ever been heretofore presented by either said Territory or said State for audit and payment by the United States. Under section 3489 of the Revised Statutes, hereinbefore referred to, the payment of these claims is barred by limitation.

"These forces were raised to guard the overland mail route and emigrant road to California, east of Carson City, and to do other military service in Nevada, and were called out by the governor of the late Territory of Nevada, upon requisitions therefor by the commanding general of the Department of the Pacific, and under authority of the War Department, as appears by copies of official correspondence furnished to your committee by the Secretary of War and the general commanding the Division of the Pacific; and it further appears that there are some unadjusted claims of the State of Nevada for expenses growing out of the so-called White Pine Indian war of 1875, and aggregating $17,650.98, and of the so-called Elko Indian war of 1878 therein, and aggregating $4,654.64, and which sums, it appears by the official statement of the controller of said State of Nevada, were expended and paid out of the treasury of said State."

Respectfully,

JOHN MULLAN,
State Agent for Nevada.

Senate joint memorial and resolution No. 4, relative to war claims of the State of Nevada against the United States.

[Introduced by committee on ways and means January 17, 1887.]

Read first time, rules suspended, read second time by title, considered engrossed, placed on its third reading and passed by the following vote: Yeas, 19; nays, none.

CHAS. E. LAUGHTON,
Assistant Secretary.

January 18, 1887: Received from senate January 19—Read first time, rules suspended, read second time by title, and referred to committee on federal relations. January 21—Returned from the committee favorably and passage recommended and placed on general file. January 24—Read third time and passed. Yeas, 38; nays, none.

R. L. THOMAS,
Assistant Clerk.

Received from assembly January 24—To enrolling committee.

Whereas claims of the State of Nevada against the United States growing out of the late war of the rebellion have been properly made out, authenticated, and forwarded to the proper authorities of the Government for allowance and payment; and

Whereas it appears from correspondence between the agent of this State at Washington City and the State controller that there is danger of great delay in respect to final action upon said claims, if not of their ultimate rejection and non-payment, in part, if not wholly; and

Whereas it has been established that said claims are most just and equitable and ought to be paid without further delay:

Therefore, the senate and assembly of the State of Nevada hereby jointly memorialize our Senators and Representative in Congress, and do most respectfully and urgently request them, and each of them, to use all proper means and efforts before the honorable Secretary of War, before Congress, or any other department, body or officer, so far as necessary to secure the earliest possible allowance and payment of our said war claims against the United States; and

Be it resolved by the senate and assembly, jointly, That his excellency the governor be, and he hereby is, respectfully requested to forward by mail a certified copy of the *foregoing* (to be accompanied by a printed copy of the recent argument of Capt. John Mullan before the honorable Secretary of War upon the allowance of said claims), to each of our Senators and Representative in Congress, at the earliest practicable date, and that he and Hon. J. F. Hallock immediately telegraph to Capt. John Mullan that said memorial and argument will be so forwarded without delay.

EXHIBIT No. 15.

REPORT OF THE MAJORITY OF THE BOARD OF WAR CLAIMS EXAMINERS.

WAR DEPARTMENT,
Washington, D. C., February 9, 1887.

SIR: The undersigned, examiners of State and Territorial war claims, appointed by paragraph 4, Special Orders No. 232, Adjutant-General's Office, October 6, 1886, to examine the claims submitted under the acts of Congress of June 27, 1882, and August 4, 1886, have the honor to submit herewith their report upon the claims presented by the governor of Nevada, under said acts.

The examiners believe that the wording of the first section of the act of 1882 *assumes* the necessity of the calls for troops from the State by the proper authorities thereof, and that the second section of said act of 1882 refers to the *necessity* of the expenditures and the rate of allowances therefor, and they report the amounts which should be *allowed* under the act of 1882 as *proper* and *necessary*, and the amounts which should be *disallowed* as *improper, unnecessary,* and *unauthorized* by law.

The examiners, in acting upon the claims for subsistence stores, have taken into consideration the fact that the supplies were purchased in open market, and that the prices are not as low as might have been obtained by the U. S. Army, under its contract system, and bought in cities at a great distance from Nevada, and they believe that there can be no just comparison between the systematized purchases of the Government and the open market purchases made during an Indian excitement, and that the amounts expended may be somewhat more than was actually needed owing to the inability to determine the duration of the campaigns.

The vouchers are not of the form demanded by Army and Treasury regulations, for the reason that the State of Nevada had not had the experience of the United States in such matters, and the examiners are of the opinion that it was the real intent of the act of August 4, 1886, to take the vouchers away from the exacting scrutiny of the Treasury Department in order that they might be examined solely on their merits, as in their present shape they would not be likely to pass the crucial test of a bureau examination. Most of them have already passed an examination by a State board of audit of Nevada, and the examiners have no reason to doubt the integrity of that board, while their liberality has been curtailed by the present examiners where the expenditures were found to be *excessive* or *injudicious.*

The examiners have allowed the same rate for pay and clothing as was allowed by the United States for its troops for the same period, and 40 cents per day for use of each enlisted man's own horse, instead of the pay and clothing allowed by the State where the State paid a greater amount for services than the United States Army rates.

The pay of the adjutant-general of Nevada was allowed under decision of Second Comptroller, viz:

"Under the act of Congress of July 17 and 27, 1861, the amount paid by the several States for their adjutant-general, down to August 20, 1866, may be refunded, provided the maximum of allowance shall not exceed \$3,000 per annum" (Sec. 1122, p. 387, Digest 2d Comp., vol. 2).

The examiners deem it just that the State should receive the amount claimed for pay of its adjutant-general *prior* to August 20, 1866, from January 1, 1862, although the first call for troops was not made upon the State till April, 1863, yet the war had been in progress since April, 1861, and it was *necessary* and *proper* that the State should have an adjutant-general's office in readiness to supply the volunteers promptly at the first call. The amount paid by the State for the time *prior* to April, 1863, was at the small rate of $1,000 per annum.

Bounty or premium for each enlistment has been disallowed. This bounty was paid to captains for expenses incurred by them in enlisting, lodging, and subsisting the men of their companies *prior* to their entering the United States service, in *lieu* thereof, as is shown by the fact that no other bills are presented for those expenses, and, under the circumstances, this expense was economical; but this claim having been submitted by the State of Nevada as a premium or bounty, the examiners are debarred from considering it, as, under the second section of the act of 1882, no higher rate can be allowed than was paid by the United States, which was $2 per enlistment, and that amount has already been paid by the United States for these enlistments.

Interest was disallowed under decision from the Secretary of War.

*   *   *   *   *   *   *

Very respectfully, your obedient servants,

JAMES BIDDLE,
Major Sixth Cavalry, U. S. Army, Senior Examiner.
H. J. FARNSWORTH,
Major and Inspector-General, U. S. Army, Examiner.
FRANK WEST,
First Lieutenant Sixth Cavalry, U. S. Army, Secretary to the Board.

The SECRETARY OF WAR.

EXHIBIT No. 16.

REPORT OF THE MINORITY OF THE BOARD OF WAR CLAIMS EXAMINERS.

WAR DEPARTMENT,
Washington, D. C., February 9, 1887.

SIR: I have the honor to submit that I have made a careful examination of the claims of the Territory and State of Nevada presented for examination and investigation under the acts of Congress approved June 27, 1882, and August 4, 1886, and that as just and impartial a statement thereof as required by said act of 1882 as it is possible for your examiner to make will be found in the following:

*   *   *   *   *   *   *

From the wording of the first section of the act of 1882 it is believed the Congress assumed the necessity of the calls into active service of the troops of Nevada, by the proper authorities thereof, for the wars for which these claims are presented. Evidence that the calls were made in each instance by the proper authorities will be found in the fact that in the war of the rebellion the call was made by the governor of the Territory, upon the authority of the United States War Department, and in each of the Indian wars for which claims are presented the call was by the governor of the State of Nevada (see letter of General Wright, dated April 2, 1863; third and fourth biennial messages of the governor of Nevada, and biennial report of the adjutant-general of Nevada for 1877–'78).

In my examination of these war claims of Nevada, I have not attempted to apply rigorously the requirements of the Army Regulations, for the reason that this method would prove an insuperable bar to their adjustment, and allowance has been made for the exigencies under which the expenses were incurred, and for a lack of familiarity with army methods of keeping accounts on the part of those intrusted with the record and preservation of the war expenses of the State. Full and impartial consideration has been given to the merits of these claims, and in ascertaining the amounts believed to be fairly and justly due the State of Nevada; the restrictions imposed in the second section of the act of 1882 have been complied with as far as was possible.

The rates paid by the Government for supplies, transportation, rents, * * * for the Army in the localities and during the periods of time for which these claims are made have been, where they could be ascertained, the standard by which has been determined the reasonableness of every charge.

At the outset of the investigation of the claims of the war of the rebellion the difficulty was met to determine whether or not it was required by the act of 1882 to consider and adjust the demands of Nevada for re-imbursement of "bounties," "extra pay," "premium" and "interest." In this important question there is involved more than two-thirds of the entire amount claimed by Nevada. I have disallowed Nevada's claim for re-imbursement for amounts disbursed under the provisions of an act of the legislature approved February 20, 1864, entitled "An act to encourage enlistments and give bounties and extra pay to our volunteer soldiers," as being a higher rate than was allowed and paid by the United States for similar services in the same grade and for the same time in the U. S. Army serving in Nevada. The troops of Nevada (war of the rebellion) received the bounties and pay allowed by the United States to her Army, and to repay the State her expenditure on account of "bounty" and "extra pay" would be, in my opinion, a violation of the law under which this examination is made.

The claim for interest is disallowed for the reason that the acts of Congress under which the examination is made do not *specifically* provide for the consideration of a claim of this character.

A second difficulty met in the examination of the claims of the war of the rebellion was to determine a just and impartial time for which to allow re-imbursement for salary paid an adjutant-general of the Territory. After mature consideration of this subject, I believe the proper dates between which to allow re-imbursement for such expense are *April* 2, 1863 (the date General Wright called on Nevada for troops), and *August* 20, 1866, the *official* date of the close of the war. A principal reason for fixing on the time of General Wright's call as the proper date from which to reckon said allowance, is found in the fact that there is no evidence furnished that Nevada, previous to this date (April 2, 1863), had a single soldier (volunteer or militia) in the field, or even on paper.

This call was for troops to protect from Indians the overland travel, and I find no evidence that, previous to the time of this call, Nevada had in anticipation a call from the President to furnish a quota for the war of the rebellion. The act of Congress of March 2, 1864, organizing the Territory of Nevada makes no mention of an office of adjutant-general. The act of the legislature providing for the organization and enrollment of the militia was passed March 4, 1865, and (March 3, 1866) was so amended as to make the secretary of state *ex officio* adjutant-general. From a careful examination of the evidence I am constrained to believe that from her organization as a Territory to the spring of 1863 (time of the call for troops) "there was no necessity at the time and under all circumstances" for an adjutant-general of Nevada, and further, that the labor performed by such officer during the period referred to does not, under the terms of the act of 1882, entitle the Territory to re-imbursement of his salary for such period (see acts referred to and report of adjutant-general of Nevada for 1865).

For the reasons above given, I have *disallowed* the claim of $1,233.50 contained in vouchers 1 to 5, inclusive, Abstract B, it being for salary of an adjutant-general for 1862 and part of 1863.

A summary, in brief, of the result of my examination of Nevada's claim for the war of the rebellion is as follows:

Amount claimed	$349,697.49
Amount allowed	$8,559.61
Amount disallowed	341,137.88
	349,697.49

*   *   *   *   *   *   *

Very respectfully, your obedient servant,

EDWARD HUNTER,
Captain First Cavalry, U. S. Army,
Examiner of State and Territorial War Claims.

The SECRETARY OF WAR.

EXHIBIT No. 17.

TABLE PREPARED BY BOARD OF WAR CLAIMS EXAMINERS SHOWING AMOUNTS OF CLAIM OF NEVADA ALLOWED, AND THOSE DISALLOWED, AND REASONS ASSIGNED THEREFOR.

Abstract of the claims of the Territory and State of Nevada (first, second, and third installments) submitted under acts approved June 27, 1882, and August 4, 1886.

WAR OF THE REBELLION—FIRST INSTALLMENT.

Abstract.	No. of voucher.	Date.	In whose favor.	Nature of claim.	Amount claimed.	Amount allowed.	Amount disallowed.	Remarks.
A	*1-24	1863, 1864, 1865, 1866	Bounties paid to commanding officers of companies, of $10 per capita for each recruit		$11,840.00		$11,840.00	Unauthorized by act of June 27, 1882.
A	25	Sept. 22, 1863	John Church & Co	Printing	30.00	$30.00		
A	26	Dec. 6, 1863	....do	....do	25.00	25.00		
A	27	Oct. 19, 1864	Daily Evening Post	....do	18.00	18.00		
A	28	Jan. 2, 1865	Gold Hill Daily News	....do	34.30	34.30		
A	29	Oct. 29, 1864	E. B. Wilson	....do	13.75	13.75		
A	30	Dec. 3, 1863	Daily Independent	....do	20.00	20.00		
A	31	Oct. 29, 1864	Lyon County Sentinel	....do	5.00	5.00		
			Total Abstract A		11,986.05	146.05	11,840.00	
B	1	Apr. 3, 1865	Gillig, Mott & Co	Furniture for adjutant-general's office.	37.00	37.00		
B	2	May 24, 1865	W. E. Shun	Repairing and putting down carpet, etc.	6.00	6.00		
B	3	Apr. 20, 1865	E. Barker	Seal for adjutant-general's office.	26.00	26.00		
B	4	Apr. 10, 1865	Cowing & Co.	Sign for adjutant's office.	18.00	18.00		
B	5	Mar. 26, 1865	John G. Fox	Stationery for adjutant-general's office.	43.00	43.00		
B	6	Apr. 22, 1865	B. F. Small, postmaster	Postage, etc., for adjutant-general's office.	21.00	21.00		
B	7	May 1, 1865	P. Caravauth	Rent for adjutant-general's office	83.33	45.00	38.33	A double charge.
B	8	Apr. 1, 1865	Silas Caulkins	Clerk, adjutant-general's office	125.00	125.00		
B	9	Apr. 1, 1865	....do	Traveling expenses, adjutant-general's office.	50.00	50.00		
B	10	May 24, 1865	John G. Fox	Stationery, adjutant-general's office.	41.00	41.00		
B	11	May 7, 1865	Daily Morning Post	Printing.	10.00	10.00		

Abs.	No.	Date	To whom paid	For what	Amount claimed	Amount allowed	Disallowed	Remarks
B	12	May 31, 1865	Silas Caulkins	Clerk	125.00	125.00		
B	13	June 30, 1865	...do...	...do...	125.00	125.00		
B	14	July 1, 1865	John Church	Printing	35.00	35.00		
B	15	July 30, 1865	Silas Caulkins	Clerk	50.00	50.00		
B	16	Apr. 28, 1865	F. Foster	Stationery	85.00	60.00	25.00	Printing of bounty certificates unauthorized
B	17	Apr. 20, 1865	Edwards & Co	Rent	448.75	448.75		
B	18	Aug. 29, 1865	C. Tiller	Clerk	120.00	120.00		
B	19	Aug. 31, 1865	Silas Caulkins	Rollers	50.00	50.00		
B	20	Nov. 20, 1865	...do...	Clerk	5.00	5.00		
B	21	Dec. 18, 1865	Mason, Huff & Co.	Oil	200.00	200.00		
B	22	Dec. 6, 1865	E. B. Rail	Hardware	10.00	10.00		
B	23	Dec. 18, 1865	John G. Fox	Stationery	38.75	38.75		
B	24	Dec. 4, 1865	John Cradlebaugh	Rent	27.75	27.75		
B	25	Jan. 1, 1866	Charles S. Hammer	Oil and glass	105.00	105.00		
B	26	May 29, 1866	R. C. Crandall	Wood	11.00	11.00		
B	27	Dec. 19, 1866	R. F. Small, postmaster	Postage	52.50	52.50		
B	28	Dec. 31, 1866	Mason, Huff & Co.	Oil	23.25	23.25		
B	29	Mar. 1, 1865	E. B. Rail	Spittoons	10.50	10.50		
B	30	Mar. 5, 1866	John G. Fox	Stationery	9.50	9.50		
B	31	Mar. 31, 1866	Carson Appeal	Printing	3.00	3.00		
B	32	Apr. 23, 1866	John G. Fox	Stationery	14.00	14.00		
B	33	...do...	B. F. Small, postmaster	Postage, etc.	3.50	3.50		
B	34	Apr. 30, 1866	John Church	Printing	35.10	35.10		
B	35	Apr. 7, 1866	Mason, Huff & Co	Oil, etc.	52.00	52.00		
B	36	June 30, 1866	B. F. Small, postmaster	Box-rent, adjutant-general's office	11.81	11.81		
B	37	Oct. 8, 1866	...do...	...do...	8.70	8.70		
B	38	Jan. 1, 1867	E. B. Rail	Lamps	8.40	8.40		
B	39	May 21, 1866	J. Cradlebaugh	Rent	2.50	2.50		
B	40	Jan. 1, 1867	...do...	...do...	270.00	230.00	40.00	Allowed rent up to August 20, 1860, end of war.
B	41	...do...	...do...	...do...	90.00		90.00	Do.
B	42	...do...	C. N. Noteware	Cartage	5.00	5.00		
B	43	Dec. 31, 1867	...do...	Premium on gold to pay soldiers' warrants.	42.92		42.92	Premium on gold to pay extra pay and bounties disallowed.
B	44	Nov. 28, 1863	Daily Independent	Printing military commercial note warrants.	30.00	30.00		
B	45	Jan. 5, 1864	H. P. Russell	Office desk, $25; stationery, $10.	45.00	45.00		
B	46	May 1, 1866	...do...	Rent of adjutant-general's office and stationery.	500.00	500.00		
				Total Abstract B	3,114.38	2,876.13	236.25	
C	*7-1513	1863,1864,1865	Volunteer soldiers	Extra pay for Nevada volunteers	96,054.78		96,054.78	Disallowed by section 2, act June 27, 1882.
				Total Abstract C	96,054.78		96,054.78	
D	*1-10	1863,1864,1865	Volunteer soldiers	Extra pay for Nevada volunteers	1,153.75		1,153.75	Disallowed by section 2, act June 27, 1882.
				Total Abstract D	1,153.75		1,153.75	

* Inclusive.

Abstract of the claims of the Territory and State of Nevada, etc.—Continued.

WAR OF THE REBELLION—FIRST INSTALLMENT—Continued.

Abstract	No. of voucher.	Date.	In whose favor.	Nature of claim.	Amount claimed.	Amount allowed.	Amount disallowed.	Remarks.
E	1	Apr. 7, 1862	H. P. Russell	Salary as adjutant-general	$250.00	$250.00		These amounts were allowed by the majority of the board of examiners, but were disallowed by the minority for the reason that "the amounts of these vouchers (1–5 inclusive) are disallowed on account of being salary paid before April 2, 1863, the time the Territory was called upon by the United States for troops." These items constitute the entire difference between the allowances of the majority and minority. (Note by Committee on Military Affairs.)
E	2	July 31, 1862	do	do	250.00	250.00		
E	3	Aug. 7, 1862	do	do	250.00	250.00		
E	4	Jan. 7, 1863	do	do	250.00	250.00		
E	5	Apr. 1, 1863	do	do	233.50	233.50		
E	6	July 1, 1863	do	do	250.00	250.00		
E	7	Oct. 1, 1863	do	do	250.00	250.00		
E	8	Jan. 1, 1864	do	do	250.00	250.00		
E	9	Apr. 1, 1864	do	do	250.00	250.00		
E	10	July 1, 1864	do	do	250.00	250.00		
E	11	Oct. 1, 1864	do	do	250.00	250.00		
E	12	Oct. 31, 1864	do	do	81.00	81.00		
E	13	Mar. 31, 1865	John Craillebaugh	Contingent expenses of adjutant-general	116.66	116.66		
E	14, 15	Apr. 29, 1865	do	do	1,000.00	1,000.00		
E	16, 17	June 30, 1865	do	Salary as adjutant-general	500.00	500.00		
E	18, 19	Dec. 31, 1865	do	do	1,000.00	1,000.00		
E	20, 21	Mar. 31, 1865	do	do	500.00	500.00		
E	22	June 30, 1866	do	do	500.00	500.00		
E	23	Sept. 30, 1866	do	do	500.00	277.77	$222.23	This disallowance is from August 20, 1866, end of the war, according to decision Supreme Court; also see decision Second Comptroller dated February 6, 1877, page 387, vol 2, Digest Second Comptroller.
E	24	Dec. 31, 1866	do	do	500.00		500.00	
			Total Abstract E		7,431.16	6,708.93	722.23	

F	July 1, 1864	G. L. Gibson	Transportation of arms	29.00	29.00
F	Apr. 28, 1865	Shaw's Fast Freight and Express Company.	Transportation of blank	8.00	8.00
F	Apr. 27, 1865	do	Transportation of stationery	23.00	23.00
			Total Abstract F	60.00	60.00
G	Mar. 3, 1866	State of Nevada	Interest paid on $46,950.12 from February 10, 1865, to March 3, 1866, at 2 per cent. per month.	11,925.33	11,925.33
G	May 30, 1867	do	Interest paid on $46,950.12 from March 3, 1866, to May 30, 1867, at 15 per cent. per annum.	8,744.46	8,744.46
G	Mar. 28, 1872	do	Interest paid on $119,800.12 from May 30, 1867, to March 28, 1872, at 15 per cent. per annum.	86,755.25	86,755.25
G	Jan. 1 1883	do	Interest paid on $119,800.12 from March 28, 1872, to January 1, 1883, at 9½ per cent. per annum.	122,472.33	122,472.33
			Total Abstract G	229,897.37	229,897.37

RECAPITULATION.

A	1865 to 1866	State of Nevada	Enrolling, recruiting, etc	$11,986.05	$146.05	$11,840.00
B	1863 to 1867	do	Supplying	3,114.38	2,875.13	236.25
C	1863 to 1865	do	Pay to troops	96,154.78		96,054.78
D	1863 to 1866	do	Pay to troops (liabilities)	1,153.75		1,153.75
E	1862 to 1866	do	Pay of salary of adjutant-general	7,431.16	6,708.93	722.23
F	1864 and 1865	do	Transportation	60.00	60.00	
G	1866,1867,1872, and 1883.	do	Interest actually paid	229,897.57		229,897.37
			Total	349,697.49	9,793.11	339,904.38

The undersigned examiners of State and Territorial war claims certify on honor that the foregoing is a just and impartial statement of the claim of the State of Nevada, as determined by them after examination and consideration according to the acts of June 27, 1882, and August 4, 1886.

JAMES BIDDLE,

Major Sixth Cavalry, U. S. Army, Senior Officer and Examiner.

H. J. FARNSWORTH,

Major and Inspector-General, U. S. Army, Examiner.

WAR DEPARTMENT,
   OFFICE OF THE STATE AND TERRITORIAL WAR CLAIMS,
              Washington, D. C., February 9, 1887.

NOTE.—The total amount allowed by the minority of the board of examiners was $8,559.61. This allowance was approved by the Secretary of War, and has since been paid to the State of Nevada. The amount disallowed by said minority report was $341,137.88, and this disallowance was also approved by the Secretary of War. On 27th April, 1888, Hon. C. C. Stevenson, then and now governor of Nevada, to whom was paid by the Secretary of the Treasury said sum of $8,559.61, so allowed by said minority member of said board of war-claim examiners, receipted to said Secretary for said sum ON ACCOUNT-ONLY, and as a payment PRO TANTO ONLY of said claim, and on May 8, 1888, Governor Stevenson served upon the Secretary and upon the proper accounting officers of the Treasury at Washington an official notice to that effect.

EXHIBIT No. 18.

PRECEDENTS OF CASES ALLOWED BY CONGRESS TO STATES FOR MONEYS BY THEM EXPENDED FOR TROOPS FOR THE USE AND BENEFIT OF THE UNITED STATES AFTER HAVING BEEN DISALLOWED BY ACCOUNTING OFFICERS OF THE TREASURY, AND FOR INTEREST ON SIMILAR CLAIMS PRESENTED WHICH WERE ALLOWED WITHOUT INTEREST.

Claims for payments made by the several States on account of expenses incurred for enrolling, subsisting, clothing, supplying, arming, equipping, paying, and transporting volunteers and militia called into the service of the United States in the war of 1812 were audited and settled under the supervision of the Secretary of War in pursuance of general laws, and paid by the United States.

Claims were afterwards presented by the several States to Congress and provision made for their payment on account of expenses which were disallowed by the accounting officers, and for interest on claims which had been presented and allowed without interest, as follows:

1. By an act approved April 2, 1830, the Secretary of the Treasury was authorized to cause to be paid to the mayor and city council of Baltimore the sum of $7,434.53 in full for their claim against the United States for money borrowed and expended by them in defense of said city in the war of 1812, and by the second section of said act the Secretary of the Treasury was directed to cause to be paid interest on said sum according to the provisions and regulations of "the act to authorize payment of interest due the city of Baltimore," approved May 20, 1826.

2. By an act approved May 31, 1830, the proper accounting officers of the Treasury, under the superintendence of the Secretary of War, were authorized and directed to audit and settle the claims of the State of Massachusetts against the United States for services of her militia during the war of 1812, in the following cases:

(1.) Where the militia of said State were called out to repel actual invasion or under a well-founded apprehension of invasion, provided their numbers were not in undue proportion to the exigency.

(2.) Where they were called out by the authority of the State and afterwards recognized by the Federal Government.

(3.) Where they were called out by and served under the requisition of the President of the United States or of any officer thereof.

3. By a joint resolution approved May 14, 1836, entitled "A resolution to authorize the Secretary of War to receive additional evidence in support of claims of Massachusetts and other States of the United States for disbursements, services," etc., during the war of 1812, the Secretary of War was authorized, in preparing his report pursuant to the resolution of House of Representatives agreed to the 24th of February, 1832, without regard to existing rules and requirements to receive such evidence as was on file, and any further proofs which might be offered tending to establish the validity of the claims of Massachusetts upon the United States, or any part thereof, for services,

disbursements, and expenditures during the war with Great Britain; and in all cases where such evidence should, in his judgment, prove the truth of the items of the claim, or any part thereof, to act on the same in like manner as if the proof consisted of such vouchers and evidence as was required by existing rules and regulations touching the allowance of such claims; and it was provided that in the settlement of claims of other States upon the United States for services, disbursements, and expenditures during the war with Great Britain, the same kind of evidence, vouchers, and proof should be received as therein provided for in relation to the claim of Massachusetts.

4. By the sixth section of an act approved March 31, 1837, an appropriation was made for paying the claims of the State of Connecticut for the services of her militia during the war of 1812, to be audited and settled by the proper accounting officers of the Treasury under the superintendence of the Secretary of War in the following cases:

(1.) Where the militia of said State were called out to repel actual invasion or, under a well-founded apprehension of invasion, provided their numbers were not in undue proportion to the exigency.

(2.) Where they were called out by the authorities of the State and afterwards recognized by the Federal Government; and

(3.) Where they were called out and served under the requisition of the President of the United States or of any officer thereof.

5. By an act approved August 14, 1848, the proper accounting officers of the Treasury were directed to settle the claims for one month's service of the officers and soldiers of the Fourth Regiment in the Second Brigade of the Third Division of the militia of the State of Vermont, who served at the battle of Plattsburgh on the 11th of September, 1814, for their military services on that occasion.

6. By act approved March 3, 1853, making appropriations for the civil and diplomatic expenses of the Government for the year ending June 30, 1854, an appropriation of $10,334.31 was made for arrearages of pay, subsistence, and clothing due to Capt. Richard McRae's Company of Virginia Volunteers, which served in the war with Great Britain in 1812–'13, to be paid to the officers and soldiers of said company or their legal representatives, under the order of the Secretary of War, upon the production of proof as to the identity of said officers and soldiers, and that they have not been paid.

7. By an act approved August 31, 1852 (Army appropriation), the Secretary of War was required to pay to the State of South Carolina such sums of money as were paid by said State in 1838, 1839, and 1840 for services, losses, and damage sustained by her volunteers in the Florida war of 1836, 1837, and 1838, while in the service of the United States, and on their return from said service, as were ascertained and allowed by the board of commissioners appointed for that purpose by the act of the legislature of said State in 1837, with the proviso that no interest should be allowed upon moneys paid to the State of South Carolina under the provisions of said act. And it was by said act further provided that in the settlement of the claims of the State of Georgia, under the act of August 11, 1842, providing for the settlement of the claims of that State for the service of her militia, which had theretofore been suspended or disallowed, the accounting officers of the Treasury Department should allow and pay, upon proof that the State had allowed and paid the same, all accounts for forage, subsistence, hospital stores, medical service, and transportation which had not theretofore been allowed by the United States. And it was further provided by said act that in the adjustment of the accounts of the State of Maine, under the act of June 13, 1842, the proper accounting officers of the Treasury should include and allow the claims which had theretofore been presented under said act, provided it should be satisfactorily shown that said claims had been actually allowed and paid by said State.

8. By an act approved March 3, 1853, second section, the proper accounting officers of the Treasury Department were authorized to settle the claims of the State of Florida for services of her troops under the act of February 27, 1851, by the provision stated for the settlement of the claims of the State of Georgia for like services, under the act approved August 31, 1851 (Army appropriation bill).

9. By the eighth section of an act approved March 3, 1853, the Secretary of the Treasury was directed to pay to the State of Georgia her claims remaining unpaid for moneys paid by the State in suppressing hostilities of the Cherokee, Creek, and Seminole Indians in the year 1835 and since, upon proof that the same was paid by the State, and that the provisions of the act relative to the settlement of the claims of Georgia for military service, approved March 3, 1851, should be extended to payments under said act.

The Secretary of the Treasury was also by said act required to pay the State of Alabama, under the provisions of the acts of Congress of August 16, 1842, and January 26, 1849, the balance due said State, growing out of the Creek Indian hostilities of 1836 and 1837; and by the twelfth section of said act it was provided that in the adjustment of the accounts of the State of Virginia under the twelfth section of the act of August 31, 1852, the Secretary of War should follow the provisions of the act of June 2, 1848, providing for refunding to the several States the amounts expended by them in raising regiments of volunteers for the Mexican war.

10. By an act approved January 26, 1849, the Secretary of War was directed to pay interest upon the advances made by the State of Alabama for the use of the United States Government in the suppression of hostilities by the Creek Indians in 1836 and 837, at the rate of 6 per cent. per annum from the time of the advances until the principal of the same was paid by the United States to the State. And in ascertaining the amount of interest it was provided that interest should not be computed on any sum which Alabama had not expended for the use and benefit of the United States, as evidenced by the amount refunded to the State of Alabama by the United States, and that no interest should be paid on any sum on which the State of Alabama did not either pay or lose interest, as aforesaid.

11. By an act approved March 3, 1851, the Secretary of War was authorized to allow to the State of Georgia for advances made to the United States for the suppression of hostilities of the Creek, Seminole, and Cherokee Indians in the years 1835, 1836, 1837, and 1838, with interest at the rate of 6 per cent. per annum on all sums allowed and paid to the State of Georgia and that might thereafter be allowed and paid for any moneys advanced by the State for the purposes aforesaid, from the date of such advances until the principal sums were or might be paid by the United States, with the proviso that no interest should be paid on any sum on which Georgia did not either pay or lose interest.

12. By an act passed the same day as the above act, the proper accounting officers of the Treasury were directed to settle the claim of the State of Maine against the United States, being for interest on money borrowed and actually expended by her for the protection of the northeastern frontier of said State during the years 1839, 1840, and 1841, the amount of such interest to be ascertained under the following rules:

"(1.) Interest not to be computed on any sum not expended by the State for the use and benefit of the United States, as evidenced by the amount refunded or paid to the State by the United States.

"(2.) No interest to be paid on any sum on which the State did not either pay or lose interest."

13. By act approved July 21, 1852, making appropriations to supply deficiencies in the appropriations for the year ending June 30, 1852, the sum of $50,741 was appropriated for pay of five companies of Texas mounted volunteers.

14. By act approved March 3, 1859, for the purpose of executing the resolution of May 14, 1836, the Secretary of War was directed to pay to Massachusetts $227,176.48, reported to be due said State by Secretary of War J. R. Poinsett, in report dated December 23, 1837, made to House of Representatives December 27, 1837, and it was provided that in lieu of payment in money the Secretary of the Treasury might, at his discretion, issue to said State United States stock bearing 5 per cent. per annum, and redeemable at the end of ten years, or sooner, at the pleasure of the President.

EXHIBIT No. 19.

SENATE REPORT IN SUPPORT OF THE PROPOSITION THAT PRINCIPAL AND INTEREST ARE THE TWO ELEMENTS CONSTITUTING ONE AND THE SAME UNIT OF A COMPLETE INDEMNITY OF A CLAIM.

[Senate Report No. 1060, Forty-ninth Congress, first session.]

The Committee on Claims, to whom was referred the bill (S. 1651) "authorizing the Secretary of the Treasury to make final adjustment of claims of certain foreign steam-ship companies arising from the illegal exaction of tonnage dues," have had the same under consideration and respectfully report as follows:

This claim has been considered and favorably reported by the Committee on Foreign Relations to the House of Representatives of the Forty-sixth and Forty-eighth Congresses. It has likewise been favorably reported by the Committee on Claims of the House of Representatives at the present session.

The report of the Committee on Foreign Affairs of the Forty-eighth Congress, embodying the report of the same committee of the Forty-sixth Congress, is able and exhaustive, and is adopted, as follows:

[House Report No. 1568, Forty-eighth Congress, first session.]

The Committee on Foreign Affairs, to whom was referred the bill (H. R. 1062) authorizing the Secretary of the Treasury to make final adjustment of claims of certain foreign steam-ship companies, arising from the illegal exaction of tonnage duties, respectfully report:

The matters arising herein were thoroughly and exhaustively considered by this committee in the Forty-sixth Congress, and a very able report made thereon, by Hon. Mr. Rice, then and now a member of the committee, was favorably considered by the committee.

The ninth article of the treaty of 1827 between the United States and the Hanseatic Republic is as follows:

"ART. 9. The contracting parties, desiring to live in peace and harmony with all the other nations of the earth by means of a policy frank and equally friendly with all, engage mutually not to grant any particular favor to other nations in respect of commerce and navigation which shall not immediately become common to the other party, who shall enjoy the same freely, if the concession was freely made, or on allowing the same compensation, if the concession was conditional."

This treaty is still in force. (See letter Secretary of State in H. Rep. No. 124, part 2, page 29, second session Forty-fifth Congress.)

Subsequently a treaty was ratified with Belgium, July 18, 1858, article 4 of which is in the following words:

"Steam-vessels of the United States and Belgium engaged in regular navigation between the United States and Belgium shall be exempt in both countries from the payment of duties of *tonnage, anchorage,* buoys and light-houses."

This treaty was abrogated July 1, 1875. (See notes to Treaties and Conventions concluded since May 1, 1870, p. 1261.)

From this it will appear that the United States agreed not to grant any particular favor to other nations in respect of commerce and navigation which should not immediately become common to the Hanseatic Republics.

By the fourth article of the treaty of July 17, 1858, with Belgium, quoted above, the United States directly stipulated that steam-vessels engaged in regular navigation between them and Belgium should be exempt from the payment of duties on tonnage, anchorage, buoys, and light-house charges. This favor having been extended to Belgium, it immediately attached, under the foregoing ninth article of the Hanseatic treaty, to the steam-ships of the lines above referred to, both plying between the ports of Bremen and Hamburg (Hanseatic Republics) and ports of the United States. It is manifest that after July 17, 1858, the lines of steam-ships from Belgium and the Hanseatic Republics were upon precisely the same footing.

For thirty years anterior to July, 1862, tonnage duties were not levied or collected by the United States on vessels of foreign countries. The necessities of the Government at this time, however, compelled the imposition of tonnage duties, when an act was passed July 14, 1862, entitled "An act increasing temporarily the duties on imports, and for other purposes," providing—

"That upon all ships, vessels, or steamers, which, after the 31st day of December, 1862, shall be entered at any custom-house in the United States, whether ships or vessels of the United States or belonging wholly or in part to subjects of foreign powers, there shall be paid a tax or tonnage duty of ten cents per ton of the measurement of said vessel in addition to any tonnage duty now imposed by law. * * * *Provided,* That nothing in this act contained shall be deemed in any wise to impair any rights and privileges which have been or may be acquired by any foreign nation under the laws and treaties of the United States relative to the duty on tonnage of vessels."

The act of March 3, 1865, amended the foregoing act by inserting *thirty* cents per ton in lieu of "ten" cents.

It was the manifest duty of the Secretary of the Treasury, upon the passage of the above law and before proceeding to administer it, to have caused a careful examination of the treaties with various foreign nations to learn what countries, if any, were exempt from the imposition of such duties.

The Secretary of the Treasury, however, immediately on the passage of the act of July 14, 1862, issued his instructions, in the form of circulars, to the collectors of the ports of New York, Baltimore, and New Orleans, making no exception of the vessels so exempted, but required the tonnage-tax to be levied and collected indiscriminately upon these vessels, notwithstanding the Attorney-General (Opinions, vol. 10, p. 481) had advised the Secretary of certain exemptions from the operation of said act by virtue of certain treaties.

The North German Lloyd Steamship Company accordingly paid, at the ports of New York, Baltimore, and New Orleans, as tonnage duties on vessels of their line thus exempted, the sum of $130,800.09, and the Hamburg-American Packet Company also paid the sum of $130,119, covering the period in both cases from December 31, 1862, to July 1, 1875, as appears by the books of the Treasury Department and by House Ex. Doc. No. 76, third session Forty-fifth Congress.

No laches can be imputed to the claimants in not having made prompt demand upon the United States for restitution.

The tax was first paid in 1863. Until 1867 the claimants had no knowledge that their lines were exempt. They were naturally misled by the Secretary of the Treasury, whose instructions to collectors were to levy tonnage indiscriminately.

The exemption depended as much upon the fourth article of the treaty with Belgium as upon the treaty with the Hanseatic Republics, since only by their concurrent operation was this privilege conferred. The exemption was nevertheless a plain and positive one, and the officers of the United States were clearly in the wrong in imposing and enforcing the collection of such duties. This is now admitted on all hands. We find no necessity of setting forth here the various diplomatic correspondence on the subject, and the decisions of the Secretary of State, and Secretary of the Treasury, and the Attorney-General, all of which hold that the treaty obligations of the United States were clearly violated. These are fully set forth in House Ex. Doc. No. 62, first session Forty-fourth Congress, and in House Report No. 124, second session Forty-fifth Congress, parts 1 and 2.

On the 19th June, 1878, Congress passed the following act, the bill having been maturely considered by the Committee on Foreign Affairs of the House of Representatives and the Committee on Finance in the Senate:

"AN ACT to amend section twenty-nine hundred and thirty-one of the Revised Statutes of the United States so as to allow repayment by the Secretary of the Treasury of the tonnage tax, where it has been exacted in contravention of treaty provisions.

"*Be it enacted by the Senate and House of Representatives of the United States of America in Congress assembled*, That the provisions of section twenty-nine hundred and thirty-one, of chapter six, title thirty-four of the Revised Statutes, shall not apply to cases of the payment of tonnage tax on vessels where the Secretary of the Treasury and Attorney-General shall be satisfied that the exaction of such tax was in contravention of treaty provisions; and he may draw his warrant for the refund of the tax so illegally exacted, as is provided in section three thousand twelve and one-half of said statutes: *Provided*, That this act shall not be construed to authorize the refunding of any tonnage duties whatever exacted prior to the first day of June, eighteen hundred and sixty-two; nor shall it apply to cases of the payment of tonnage tax heretofore made on vessels other than those of the Hanseatic Republics, and Sweden and Norway."

The object of this act was to authorize the refund of the tonnage duties so illegally exacted from the companies in question, relieving them from the necessity of making protest against payment within the thirty days required by the act of June 30, 1862, above referred to.

Under this act the North German Lloyd Company presented its claim for $139,785, as principal of duties paid, and $80,737.50, as interest at 6 per cent. per annum to August 8, 1878; and the Hamburg American Packet Company presented its claim for $130,119, as principal of duties paid, and for $75,069.27, as interest on the same at 6 per cent. per annum to July 1, 1878.

In August last the amounts named as principal were paid by the Treasury Department to the two companies and accepted by them under protest, and the question now before your committee is the one embracing this claim for interest, referred to it by the letter of the Secretary of the Treasury, to be determined under the principles of international law; and the inquiry presented is, what shall be the just measure of reparation for an injury inflicted upon a foreign and friendly power in contravention of the solemn treaty obligations of the United States.

It is one of the highest national importance, not because it demands a considerable sum of money, but because it involves a question of national honor, and its determination will sanction a principle to which the Government will henceforth stand committed in the enforcement of its own demands against foreign powers.

The cause of said act of Congress authorizing a refund was the fact that the United States had violated treaty obligations by the exaction of moneys it had no right to receive. It has held these moneys for years, depriving the lawful owners of their use, benefit, and profit. We think it very plain that the United States, according to principles of public law, can not make just or complete reparation for this wrong without now determining that it will pay interest, at a reasonable rate, on the moneys thus wrongfully exacted and withheld to the injury of the other party to the compact.

Pending the consideration of the bill in the Senate, the Hon. Justin S. Morrill, chairman of the Committee on Finance (from which committee the bill was reported), in a letter addressed to the Secretary of the Treasury under date of April 8, 1878, submitted, among others, the following inquiry: "Again, let me ask you whether, if nothing is said in the act as to the payment of interest, you would pay any?" To this the Secretary of the Treasury, under date of April 15, 1878, replied:—

"You further inquire whether, if nothing be said in the act about payment of interest, this Department would pay interest on the amounts originally exacted. I reply that the question whether interest should be paid on the original claim would depend on the obligations of the Government under the treaty stipulations referred to, as such stipulations are ordinarily construed by the law of nations."

Nevertheless, the Secretary of the Treasury, on more mature consideration, and after obtaining the decision of the Attorney-General thereon, determined that he was not permitted to pay the interest under the peculiar phraseology of the act, and recommended further legislation by Congress.

It only remains to show, by the recognized authorities on international law, what the just obligations of the United States are under the treaty stipulations referred to, " as such stipulations are ordinarily construed by the law of nations."

It is sometimes asserted that "the Government never pays interest." This assumption doubtless arises from two ideas, namely : the principle that interest is often allowed in the nature of damage for money wrongfully withheld; and the common-law fiction, that the sovereign can do no wrong and can be guilty of no laches ; therefore, the Government can not be chargeable with interest. The idea may also have obtained acceptance from the custom and usage of the accounting officers and Departments refusing to allow interest generally in their accounts with disbursing officers, and in the settlement of unliquidated domestic claims arising out of dealings with the Government. It will hardly be pretended, however, that this custom or usage is so "reasonable," well-known, and "certain" as to give it the force and effect of law.

But it is submitted that even were it true that the Government, as a rule, pays no interest to its own citizens, the fiction that " the sovereign can do no wrong" can be invoked only in its relation to its own subjects, and has no application whatever in its dealings with a foreign power, for both stand on the same footing of national equality.

By the principles of the public law, interest is always allowed as indemnity for the delay of payment of an ascertained and fixed demand. There is no conflict of authority upon this question among the writers on public law.

This rule is laid down by Rutherford in these terms :

" In estimating the damages which any one has sustained, when such things as he has a perfect right to are unjustly taken from him, or withholden, or intercepted, we are to consider not only the value of the thing itself, but the value likewise of the fruits or profits that might have arisen from it. He who is the owner of the thing is likewise the owner of the fruits or profits. So that it is properly a damage to be deprived of them as it is to be deprived of the thing itself." (Rutherford's Institutes, Book I, chap. 17, sec. 5.)

In laying down the rule for the satisfaction of injuries in the case of reprisals, in making which the strictest caution is enjoined not to transcend the clearest rules of justice, Mr. Wheaton, in his work on the law of nations, says:

" If a nation has taken possession of that which belongs to another, if it refuses to pay a debt, to repair an injury, or to give adequate satisfaction for it, the latter may seize something of the former and apply it to [his] its advantage till it obtains payment of what is due, together with interest and damages." (Wheaton on International Law, p. 341.)

Domat thus states the law of reason and justice on this point :

" It is a natural consequence of the general engagement to do wrong to no one that they who cause any damages, by failing in the performance of that engagement, are obliged to repair the damage which they have done. Of what nature soever the damage may be, and from what cause soever it may proceed, he who is answerable for it ought to repair it by an amende proportionable either to his fault or to his offense or other cause on his part, and to the loss which has happened thereby." (Domat, Part I, Book III, Title V, 1900, 1903.)

" Interest" is, in reality, in justice, in reason, and in law, too, a part of the debt due. It includes, in Pothier's words, the loss which one has suffered and the gain which he has failed to make. The Roman law defines it as " quantum mea interfruit ; id est, quantum mihi abest, quantumque lucrari potui." The two elements of it were termed " lucrum cessans et damnum emergens." The payment of both is necessary to a complete indemnity.

" Interest," Domat says, " is the reparation or satisfaction which he who owes a sum of money is bound to make to his creditor for the damage which he does him by not paying him the money he owes him."

It is because of the universal recognition of the justice of paying for the retention of moneys indisputably due and payable immediately, a rate of interest considered to be a fair equivalent for the loss of its use, that judgments for money everywhere bear interest. The creditor is deprived of this profit and the debtor has it. What greater wrong could the law permit than that the debtor should be at liberty indefinitely to delay payment, and, during the delay, have the use of the creditor's money for nothing ? They are none the less the creditor's moneys because the debtor wrongfully withholds them. He holds them, in reality and essentially, in trust ; and a trustee is always bound to pay interest upon moneys so held.

In closing these citations from the public law, the language of Chancellor Kent seems eminently appropriate. He says:

" In cases where the principal jurists agree the presumption will be very great in favor of the solidity of their maxims, and no civilized nation that does not arrogantly

S. Rep. 6——22

set all ordinary law and justice at defiance will venture to disregard the uniform sense of established writers on international law," (1 Kent Com., 19.)

The practice of the United States in discharging obligations resulting from treaty stipulations has always been in accord with these well-established principles. It has exacted the payment of interest from other nations in all cases where the obligation to make payment resulted from treaty stipulations, and it has acknowledged that obligation in all cases where a like liability was imposed upon it.

The most important and leading cases which have occurred are those which arose between this country and Great Britain—the first under the treaty of 1794, and the other under the first article of the treaty of Ghent. In the latter case the United States claimed compensation for slaves and other property taken away from the country by the British forces at the close of the war in 1815. A difference arose between the two Governments, which was submitted to the arbitrament of the Emperor of Russia, who decided that "the United States of America are entitled to a just indemnification from Great Britain for all private property carried away by the British forces." A joint commission was appointed for the purpose of hearing the claims of individuals under this decision. At an early stage of the proceedings the question arose as to whether interest was a part of that "just indemnification" which the decision of the Emperor of Russia contemplated. The British commissioner denied the obligation to pay interest. The American commissioner, Langdon Cheves, insisted upon its allowance, and, in the course of his argument upon this question, said:

"Indemnification means a re-imbursement of a loss sustained. If the property taken away on the 17th of February, 1815, were returned now uninjured, it would not re-imburse the loss sustained by the taking away and consequent detention; it would not be an indemnification. The claimant would still be unindemnified for the loss of the use of his property for ten years, which, considered as money, is nearly equivalent to the original value of the principal thing."

Again, he says:

"If interest be an incident usually attendant on the delay of payment of debts, damages are equally an incident attendant on the withholding an article of property."

In consequence of this disagreement, the commission was broken up; but the claims were subsequently compromised by the payment of $1,204,960, instead of $1,250,000, as claimed by Mr. Cheves; and of the sum paid by Great Britain, $418,000, was expressly for interest.

The propriety of this claim for interest was subsequently submitted to William Wirt, then Attorney-General, for his opinion. Mr. Wirt said:

"I am of the opinion that the just indemnification awarded by the Emperor involves not merely the return of the value of the specific property, but a compensation also for the subsequent use and wrongful detention of it in the nature of damages. * * * I am of opinion that the interest, according to the usage of nations, is a necessary part of the just indemnification awarded by the Emperor of Russia." (Opinions Attorney-General, vol. 2, p. 33.)

An earlier case, in which this principle of interest was involved, arose under the treaty of 1794 between the United States and Great Britain, in which there was a stipulation on the part of the British Government in relation to certain losses and damages sustained by American merchants and other citizens by reason of illegal or irregular capture of their vessels or other property by British cruisers; and the seventh article provided in substance that "full and complete compensation for the same will be made by the British Government to said claimants."

A joint commission was instituted under this treaty, which sat in London, and by which these claims were adjudicated. Mr. Pinckney and Mr. Gore were commissioners on the part of the United States, and Dr. Nicholl and Dr. Swabey on the part of Great Britain; and it is believed that in all instances this commission allowed interest as a part of the damage. In the case of The Betsey, one of the cases which came before the board, Dr. Nicholl stated the rule of compensation as follows:

"To re-imburse the claimants the original cost of their property, and all the expenses they have actually incurred, together with interest on the whole amount, would, I think, be a just and adequate compensation. This, I believe, is the measure of compensation usually made by all belligerent nations, and accepted by all neutral nations, for losses, costs, and damages occasioned by illegal capture." (Vide Wheaton's Life of Pinckney, p. 198; also p. 205; note, p. 371.)

By reference to the American State Papers (Foreign Relations, vol. 2, pages 119, 120), it will be seen by a report of the Secretary of State of the 16th of February, 1798, laid before the House of Representatives, that interest was awarded and paid on such of these claims as had been submitted to the award of Sir William Scott and Sir John Nicholl, as it was in all cases by the board of commissioners. In consequence of some difference of opinion between the members of this commission, their proceedings were suspended until 1802, when a convention was concluded between the two Governments, and the commission re-assembled, and then a question arose as to the allowance of interest on the claims during the suspension. This the American commissioners claimed, and though it was at first resisted by the British commissioners, yet it was finally yielded, and interest was allowed and paid. (See Mr. King's three letters to the Secretary of State, of 25th March, 1803, 23d April, 1803, and 30th April, 1803, American State Papers, Foreign Relations, vol. 2, pp. 387, 388.)

Another case in which this principle was involved arose under the treaty of the 27th October, 1795, with Spain, by the twenty-first article of which, "In order to terminate all differences on account of the losses sustained by citizens of the United States in consequence of their vessels and cargoes having been taken by the subjects of His Catholic Majesty during the late war between Spain and France, it is agreed that all such cases shall be referred to the final decision of commissioners, to be appointed in the following manner," etc. The commissioners were to be chosen, one by the United States, one by Spain, and the two were to choose a third, and the award of the commissioners, or any two of them, was to be final, and the Spanish Government to pay the amount in specie. This commission awarded interest as part of the damages. (See American State Papers, vol. 2, Foreign Relations, p. 283.)

So, in the case of claims of American citizens against Brazil, settled by Mr. Tudor, United States minister, interest was claimed and allowed. (See House Ex. Doc. No. 32, first session Twenty-fifth Congress, p. 249.)

Again, in the convention with Mexico of the 11th of April, 1839, by which provision was made by Mexico for the payment of claims of American citizens for injuries to persons and property by the Mexican authorities, a mixed commission was provided for, and this commission allowed interest in all cases (House Ex. Doc. No. 291, Twenty-seventh Congress, second session).

So, also, under the treaty with Mexico of February 2, 1848, the board of commissioners for the adjustment of claims under that treaty allowed interest in all cases from the origin of the claim until the day when the commission expired.

So, also, under the convention with Colombia, concluded February 10, 1864, the commission for the adjudication of claims under that treaty allowed interest in all cases as a part of the indemnity.

So, under the recent convention with Venezuela, the United States exacted interest upon the awards of the commission from the date of the adjournment of the commission until the payment of the awards.

The recent Mixed American and Mexican Commission allowed interest in all cases from the origin of the claim, and the awards were paid with interest.

The distinguished tribunal at Geneva, under the treaty of Washington, allowed interest on the claims of the United States against Great Britain as being "just and reasonable."

In discussing the measure for determining damages to be awarded against Great Britain by the tribunal at Geneva, the eminent counsel of the United States, Mr. Evarts, Mr. Cushing, and Mr. Waite, contended as follows:

"The counsel assume that interest will be awarded by the tribunal as an element of the damage. We conceive this to be conformable to public law and to be required by paramount considerations of equity and justice."

The counsel thereupon cited the then recent decision by Sir Edward Thornton, the British minister at Washington, as umpire of a claim on part of the United States against Brazil, which held that the claimants were entitled to interest by the same right that entitled them to reparation—the interest allowed being $45,077, nearly half the total award of $100,740. The counsel for the United States further relied upon the awards under the treaty of Ghent and the Jay treaty, herein elsewhere referred to, as marked precedents for the allowance of interest.

The counsel on behalf of Great Britain, while objecting to the principle urged by the United States as not being applicable to unliquidated claims, nevertheless admitted its reason or justice as to liquidated or ascertained claims in the following words:

"Interest, in the proper sense of that word, can only be allowed where there is a principal debt of liquidated and ascertained amount detained and withheld by the debtor from the creditor after the time when it was absolutely due and ought to have been paid, the fault of the delay in payment resting with the debtor, or where the debtor has wrongfully taken possession of and exercised dominion over the property of a creditor. In the former case, from the time when the debt ought to have been paid, the debtor has had the use of the creditor's money and may justly be presumed to have employed it for his own profit and advantage. He has thus made a gain corresponding with the loss which the creditor has sustained by being deprived, during the same period of time, of the use of his money; and it is evidently just that he should account to the creditor for the interest, which the law takes as the measure of this reciprocal gain and loss. In the latter case the principle is exactly the same; it is, ordinarily, to be presumed that the person who has wrongfully taken possession of the property of another has enjoyed the fruits of it; and if instead of this he has dostroyed it, or kept it unproductive, it is still just to hold him responsible for interest on its value, because his own acts, after the time when he assumed control over it, are the causes why it has remained unfruitful. In all these cases it is the actual or virtual possession of the money or property belonging to another, which is the foundation of the liability of interest. The person liable is either *lucratus* by the detention of what is not his own, or is justly accountable as if he were so."

And in pursuance of the principles thus asserted, the exalted tribunal at Geneva allowed interest on the demands of the United States against Great Britain in the following words:

"And whereas it is just and reasonable to allow interest at a reasonable rate." (See decision and award of the arbitrators.)

In Judge Hale's report of November, 1873, to the Secretary of State, of claims before the American British Mixed Commission under article 12 of the treaty of 8th of May, 1871, he says:

"The commission ordinarily allowed interest at the rate of 6 per cent. per annum from the date of the injury to the anticipated date of the final award" (Ex. Doc., part 1, 1st session, 43d Congress. Part 2, Foreign Affairs, p. 21).

It can hardly be necessary to pursue these precedents further. They sufficiently and clearly show the practice of the Government of the United States with foreign nations or with claimants under treaties.

Aside from considerations of international character, it will be found upon examination of the precedents where Congress has passed acts for the relief of citizens of the United States, that in almost every case where the Government has withheld a sum of money which had been decided by competent authority to be due, or where the amount due was ascertained, fixed, and definite, Congress has directed the payment of interest together with the principal. (See "Law of Claims against Governments," being Report No. 134, 2d sess. 43d Congress.)

Nor has the recovery of interest as against foreign powers depended upon arbitration or joint commissions for recognition of the principle. Such claims for interest have been directly and successfully urged by the diplomatic representatives of the United States as a matter of right under principles of established international law.

The cases are innumerable where claims have been enforced in behalf of citizens of the United States against foreign governments with interest, and where, too, the damages were unliquidated and rested even in tort. These cases may be found stated at length in Senate Ex. Doc. No. 18, second session Thirty-fifth Congress. But confining ourselves rigidly to precedents established by the Government of the United States, like case now presented, we find numerous instances.

The United States presented a claim against Portugal for loss by seizure in 1820, at Lisbon, of specie belonging to James Hall and J. Shepherd, citizens of the former Government, which was being shipped contrary to law. Restitution was subsequently made, $17,741.98 being allowed to the United States, of which sum $7,652.98 was expressly allowed as interest.

Claims asserted against Mexico in behalf of Jonas P. Levy for illegal duties exacted in 1843–'46, where $3,675 was recovered, including interest. Case of William B. Hatch for overcharge of tonnage duties, where $277.65 was recovered, with interest.

The case against Brazil of William W. Harper, administrator, for fine paid customhouse at Maranham, interest, etc., where $1,130.40 was recovered. The case of John Devereux, for anchorage and tonnage dues unlawfully imposed on the bark *Globe*, where, including interest, $196.99 was recovered.

The case of Foster & Elliott, for fine exacted on ship *Louisiana*, at Rio, in January, 1835, where $577.94 was recovered, including interest. The case of Francis A. Gray, for illegal exaction of fine at Rio in the same year, where $1,453.94 was recovered, including interest. The case of Hyman Gratz, president Pennsylvania Insurance Company, for interest (only) on customs duty illegally exacted and previously refunded by Brazilian Government $500.65 was allowed and recovered.

The United States claimed certain indemnity from the Government of Brazil in the matter of the brig *Caroline*, which was paid. Subsequently, on review by this Government, the conclusion was reached that the money had been unjustly demanded and received, and in a letter of Secretary Fish to Señor de Barros, of the Brazilian legation, dated Department of State, June 26, 1874, he says:

"I now have the honor to inform you that the President, after a careful examination of the case, has come to the conclusion that the Government of Brazil is not justly responsible for the damages in this case. It is understood that the Government of His Majesty the Emperor of Brazil is of the same opinion respecting it. Under these circumstances the President regards it as the duty of the United States to repay to Brazil the amount thus received by their minister at Rio, with interest thereon at 6 per cent. per annum. * * * "

Here the sum of $96,405.73 was accordingly paid, covering the amount originally exacted, with 6 per cent. interest thereon, as being a just reparation for moneys wrongfully exacted from a foreign power. (See Foreign Relations United States, 2d sess. 43d Congress, No. 63, page 95.)

It will thus be seen that no principle is now urged that has not hitherto been repeatedly and successfully enforced by the United States in behalf of its own citizens against foreign governments.

The Federal courts of the United States have repeatedly determined, where an illegal tax has been collected, that in a suit against the collector, the person so paying the tax is entitled to interest from the time of the illegal exaction (Erskine *vs.* Van Arsdale, 15 Wall., 77; Howland *vs.* Maxwell, 3 Blatchf., 147; Harrison *vs.* Same, *ibid.*, 421).

Reason furnishes no distinction in this regard between the collector who first receives it and the Secretary of the Treasury to whom it is ultimately paid. They are equally the representative of the Government. Besides, the latter stands in the attitude of an accessory after the fact, and for this reason, of itself, should be held accountable.

As to the rule for the construction of treaties and the determination of rights thereby guarantied, the engagements and obligations are to be interpreted in accordance with the principles of the public law, and not in accordance with any municipal code or executive regulation. No statement of this proposition can equal the clearness or force with which Mr. Webster declares it in his opinion on the Florida claims, attached to the report in the case of Letitia Humphreys (Senate Report No. 93, 1st sess. 36th Congress, p. 10). Speaking of the obligation of a treaty, he said:

"A treaty is the supreme law of the land. It can neither be limited, nor restrained, nor modified, nor altered. It stands on the ground of national contract, and is declared by the Constitution to be the supreme law of the land, and this gives it a character higher than any act of ordinary legislation. It enjoys an immunity from he operation and effect of all such legislation.

"A second general proposition, equally certain and well established, is that the terms and the language used in a treaty are always to be interpreted according to the law of nations, and not according to any municipal code. This rule is of universal application. When two nations speak to each other they use the language of nations. Their intercourse is regulated, and their mutual agreements and obligations are to be interpreted, by that code only which we usually denominate the public law of the world. This public law is not one thing at Rome, another at London, and a third at Washington. It is the same in all civilized states, everywhere speaking with the same voice and the same authority."

Again, in the same opinion, Mr. Webster used the following language:

"We are construing a treaty, a solemn compact between nations. This compact between nations, this treaty, is to be construed and interpreted throughout its whole length and breadth, in its general provisions, and in all its details, in every phrase, sentence, word, and syllable in it, by the settled rules of the law of nations. No municipal code can touch it, no local municipal law affect it, no practice of an administrative department come near it. Over all its terms, over all its doubts, over all its ambiguities, if it have any, the law of nations 'sits arbitress.'"

The levying of tonnage taxes on the vessels of these companies being unlawful, the exaction of the money on such unlawful levies was wrongful; and we think the wrongful taking of money excuses the necessity of a demand for the repayment. It therefore follows, in accordance with the principles of well-adjudicated cases, irrespective of the international rule, that if the money was wrongfully taken by the United States from these companies, it is bound to allow and pay interest on the money from the time it was so wrongfully taken.

The general doctrine which prevails on the subject of interest was elaborately discussed and correctly expounded in Reid *vs.* Rensselaer Glass Factory (3 How., 436). Ch. J. Savage, after a full examination of the cases, asserts that interest is allowed: 1. Upon a special agreement; 2. Upon an implied agreement; 3. When money is withheld against the will of the owner; 4. By way of punishment for an illegal conversion or use of another's property; 5. Upon advances in cash.

It has been the invariable practice, at the circuits, for more than a quarter of a century, to allow interest in cases like the present. So well settled has our practice been in this respect, that the question of interest on a debt which is withheld after it is due, without the assent of the creditor, rarely passes into the reports unless some more important question is connected with it.

These tonnage duties being paid under duress and without warrant of law, and being immediately transferred to the Secretary of the Treasury, they came into the hands of these officers unlawfully, the taking was tortious and a conversion *per se*, and no demand for repayment was necessary to sustain trover or assumpsit for the value.

Where the property came lawfully in the defendant's possession there must be a demand and refusal to sustain trover or assumpsit for the value (Spoor *vs.* Newall, 3 Hill, 307).

Where the taking is tortious no demand is necessary (Connah *vs.* Hale, 23 Wend., 471; Bates *vs.* Conkling, 10 Wend., 391).

To maintain an action for the wrongful conversion of property, it is enough that the rightful owner has been deprived of it by the unauthorized act of another assuming dominion over it (Boyce *et al. vs.* Brockway, 31 N. Y., 490).

In accordance with the law of these cases, there was tortious taking, conversion *per se,* at the date of exaction of these tonnage duties. The date of conversion, where the taking is lawful, is fixed from the date of the demand for the goods or money lawfully held, and by refusal to surrender them the possession becomes unlawful; and in assumpsit for the value this owner is entitled to the value at the time of taking, with interest from the same date.

This rule gives interest from the date of seizure, where the taking is tortious or the plaintiff is wrongfully deprived of his money. As, in an action against a public officer to recover damages for a tort, it was held:

"The plaintiff has a vested right to the amount of the assessment. The interest thereon is but an incident—an outgrowth from that right. The defendant's wrongful act has prevented him from realizing his money. It was a willful, because an intentional wrong, and a plain violation of a legal duty which the defendant owed to the plaintiff. If entitled to sustain this action at all, the plaintiff should *obtain complete satisfaction*" (Clark *vs.* Miller, 47 Barb., 43).

The correct rule of damages is its value at the time of taking an interest (N. Y. Guaranty and Indemnity Co. *vs.* Flynn, 65 Barb., 368).

Having ascertained what plaintiff's damage was, the referee properly allowed interest on the amount thereof from the time plaintiff became entitled to payment of the same. Without the interest plaintiff would not have secured full indemnity (Muller *vs.* Express Propellor Line, 61 N. Y., 316).

The same rule is affirmed in Wehle *vs.* Haviland *et al.*, 66 N. Y., 450; Prince *vs.* Connor, 69 N. Y., 608.

This is the rule as to illegal exactions by revenue officers (Erskine *vs.* Van Arsdale, 15 Wall., 77).

Interest is chargeable from the time the money was wrongfully obtained or wrongfully detained, and not from the time of demand (Wood *vs.* Robbins, 11 Mass., 506; Atlantic Nat. Bank *vs.* Harris, 118 Mass., 147).

The cases cited from Massachusetts reports are based upon the same principle, which was clearly laid down as the law by Judge Story, in the United States circuit court, in the case of Ricketson *et al. vs.* Wright *et al.*, 3 Sumner, 336.

In this case the proceeds of a cargo belonging to the plaintiffs had been taken under legal process by the defendants, the consignees, in Rio de Janerio, for the debts of prior owners of the ship.

The court held the taking was unlawful, but that the tort had been waived by bringing assumpsit. The question arose as to the time from which interest should be computed, whether from the time of the actual receipt of the money by the defendants at Rio, or from the time when the same would have been received as cash by the plaintiffs in Boston, if remitted in the ordinary course of business.

The plaintiffs insisted that the defendants, having had the money and the use of it, should pay interest from the time of its receipt. The defendants held that the interest, being in the nature of damages for the detention of the money, must date from the time when the defendants were bound to have it paid over.

The court held:

"The question is not without difficulty; but from the best consideration which I have been able to give it, my opinion is that interest ought to run from the receipt of the money by the defendants. If this were the case of an ordinary transaction and sale by consignees, who had sold property on account of consignors in violation of their orders, and held the proceeds for and on account of their principals, I should have no doubt that the plaintiffs, by bringing assumpsit for the proceeds, had affirmed the sale and proceedings throughout, and that the acts of the consignees, being done by them throughout for and on account of the principals, must be all deemed to be adopted by the principals. But here the case is entirely otherwise. The defendants, so far from attaching or selling the property on account of the plaintiffs and retaining the proceeds for their account, professedly acted throughout adversely to the plaintiffs and on their own sole account. They insisted upon the right to hold the proceeds for themselves, as their own property, rightfully acquired; and although the plaintiffs, by bringing assumpsit for the proceeds, have waived the tort, it is impossible to say that they have adopted or ratified the acts of the defendants in retaining the proceeds for their (the defendants') own use and account. That would be to defeat their own right to recover in this very suit upon the merits. I think, therefore, that the defendants must still be deemed to have received and held the proceeds adversely to the plaintiffs, and, of course to have had possession of the funds, and to have used them for their own benefit. And, if so, they ought to pay interest for the same from the time when the funds were appropriated to their own use. In the com-men case of an illegal conversion of property by a defendant acting adversely and for his own interests in the sale of the property, the plaintiff does not, by waiving the tort and bringing assumpsit for the proceeds, do more than affirm the sale.

"The defendant is still liable for interest upon the amount from the time of receiving the proceeds of the sale; for he has received and detained them, not for the plaintiff, but for himself. And the presumption of law is, that the defendant in such a case has derived a benefit from the use of the funds equivalent to the interest; or, what is equally potent, that the plaintiff has lost the use of his money from the time of the receipt thereof by the defendant by the unlawful and wrongful detention of the defendant. In the present case it is perfectly clear that the plaintiffs never could have drawn a bill for the funds which would have been honored, nor could they have insisted successfully upon a remittance of them. And up to the very time of the trial of the present cause the defendants have claimed the proceeds as their own, not recognizing, but absolutely repudiating, the title of the plaintiffs. It seems to me that interest, therefore, belongs to the plaintiff during all the time of the detention.

"When money is wrongfully and illegally exacted, it is received without any legal right or authority to receive it; and the law at the very time of payment creates the obligation to refund it (Bank of the United States vs. Bank of Washington, 6 Pet., 19).

Even were this of the class of cases where demand is necessary to carry interest, the peculiar circumstances here would in all equity and fairness relieve it from such requirement. Had the exactions of these moneys been in direct violation of the provisions of the treaty with these Hanseatic Republics, patent upon the face of the treaty itself, then there might be some laches attributable to these companies in not having protested against their respective payments at the time and failing to demand an immediate return of the money. But the United States, in disregard of its obligations, at first unlawfully exacted these duties, even as against Belgium, whose treaty on its face carried like exemption, and a refund to subjects of that Government was made in February, 1872; but the restitution being promptly made and the amount being small, no claim for interest was set forth. The case is much stronger with the Hanseatic Republic. The United States gave them no notice that by virtue of a treaty with Belgium (made 30 years subsequent to their own), to which those republics were utter strangers, certain commercial rights had accrued to them which they could not anticipate; and it would be unreasonable, as well as unjust, to hold these republics of a knowledge of treaty privileges thus conferred which it seems our own officials, specially charged with their administration, had utterly overlooked and disregarded.

The diplomatic correspondence herein referred to, however, shows that demand was made upon this Government for the refund of these moneys as soon as the authorities of the Hanseatic Republics became advised concerning the character of the indirect concession made to them, viz, as early as 1872, and the official correspondence also shows a consistent and uninterrupted claim to these moneys from the beginning.

The concluding consideration is at what rate the interest should be allowed and paid. With this the committee find little or no difficulty, since this Government, from the earliest years, has established the rate at 6 per cent., by decisions of the Federal courts and by the multitude of cases we have examined, as the measure of lawful interest for moneys unjustly held. Nor would this rate of interest work any hardship upon this Government. These moneys were withheld from the year 1862 to the year 1878, when the United States was a borrower of money at a rate largely in excess of 6 per cent. During all this period the United States Government, unhappily, was not a creditor among nations, but an anxious borrower, and it is plain that, as a borrower, the needs of the Government were relieved to the extent of these moneys wrongfully exacted and withheld.

These moneys, from the beginning being those of another, should have been restored immediately. Had they been thus restored and by the owners loaned to the United States for a period covering most of the years they were retained, a much larger sum as interest would have accrued on any of the then current public loans than the simple interest at 6 per cent. to be now allowed. We think, therefore, that the rate thus sanctioned by a long current of judicial decisions and by acts of Congress may well be adhered to in the present instance.

From the facts in the case it appears:

1st. The United States, by treaty of 1827 with the Hanseatic Republics, engaged not to grant any particular favor to any other nation in respect of commerce and navigation that should not immediately become common to these republics.

2d. That by treaty of 1858 with Belgium, the steam-ships of that country were exempt from payment of tonnage duties in ports of the United States.

3d. That, by operation of these treaties taken together, the steam-ships of the Hanseatic ports were also exempted so long as both treaties should remain in force.

4th. That, notwithstanding such exemption by treaty, and the proviso in the act of 1862 "that nothing in this act contained shall be deemed in anywise to impair any rights and privileges which have been or may be acquired by any foreign nation under the laws and treaties of the United States relative to the duty on tonnage of vessels," nevertheless these provisions were totally disregarded by the United States officers, and large sums of money were exacted from companies thus exempt.

5th. That such exactions were made in contravention of the treaty stipulations of the United States has been decided by the Attorney-General, by the Secretary of State, and by the Secretary of the Treasury, and, lastly, determined by Congress, by the act of June 19, 1878, under construction of which the precise sum exacted has been refunded and no more (although claim was made for interest); the United States having the uninterrupted use of such moneys for a period varying from three to fifteen years.

6th. That such refund was taken under protest, with a distinct declaration on part of claimants that claims for interest would be urged before Congress. Under these circumstances your committee are clearly of the opinion that a just reparation for the injury committed alone by the United States can not be made by returning to the innocent party simply the money wrongfully exacted without an allowance for its use. The United States would otherwise derive a large pecuniary benefit from its wrongful act, and an innocent friendly power would sustain a corresponding pecuniary loss. For the United States to claim such a benefit would violate one of the fundamental axioms of the common law as well as a cardinal principle of morality, that no one should be permitted to derive an advantage from his own wrong to the detriment of another.

It should not be forgotten that during the entire period of these exactions all steam-vessels of the United States entering the ports of Bremen and Hamburg were wholly exempt from the payment of like duties, and that not a dollar has been levied upon American tonnage to excuse or justify the exactions of the United States, and that perfect reciprocity could have existed only on exemption by the United States.

The obligations of the United States, construed as they must be in this instance by rules and precedents of an international character, are not and can not be properly discharged without the payment of interest on these claims. This Government must and should uncomplainingly submit to the administration of such rules of international law as it has aided to establish for the determination of rights between itself and other powers. It could not now with propriety and for the purpose of a temporary and pecuniary gain ask other nations to change a rule to which it has long and consistently adhered, and by which its citizens have hitherto been repeatedly benefited. As we have said before, the question is one of the highest national importance, as it involves a consideration of national honor, and its determination will sanction a principle to which the United States will henceforth stand committed in the enforcement of its own demands against foreign powers.

The time will surely come when American commerce will again, as in the past, maintain its supremacy upon the seas, and when kindred questions affecting commercial concessions to us under treaties will receive the interpretation which a liberal and enlightened judgment has hitherto invoked for the determination of questions arising between friendly powers.

It would be unjust, unwise, and unstatesmanlike to deviate in the present instance from uniform precedents, and such course would most likely be found at no remote day to have been a humiliating and unprofitable evasion of just obligations, the fulfillment of which has been already too long delayed.

Your committee adopt the said report made to the Forty-sixth Congress, so far as herein set forth, and recommend the passage of said bill (H. R. 1062) as amended and attached to this report.

That the claim is considered just by the Treasury Department is apparent from the following letter from Assistant Secretary Fairchild to the Secretary of State, under date March 4, 1886, to wit:

TREASURY DEPARTMENT, *March* 4, 1886.

SIR: I have the honor to acknowledge the receipt of your letter of the 3d instant, submitting for the consideration of this Department a translation of a note, under date of the 16th ultimo, from the minister of Germany at this capital in relation to the claim of certain German steam-ship companies for the payment of interests on certain moneys which were exacted from said companies in contravention of treaty provisions and heretofore refunded to them under the act of July 19, 1878.

You request the views of this Department as to the justice of the claim of the German steam-ship companies.

I have the honor to reply that the companies referred to in the note of the German minister are the North German Lloyd, the Hamburg-American Packet Company, and the Eagle Line. The amounts paid to these several companies will be found tabulated in Senate Executive Document No. 30 of the second session of the Forty-eighth Congress, a copy of which was transmitted to the Department of State in a communication from this Department of the 16th of January last, relating to claims for repayment of tonnage duties on French vessels.

I would say in this connection that a special claim for the refund of the tonnage tax paid on a steam-ship of the Lloyd Line with interest was presented to this Department in 1875, and was rejected solely on the ground of a lack of protests and appeal, and not on the ground that it was not a just claim. In January, 1873, these German steamships were declared exempt by order of this Department from payment of tonnage dues on account of the exaction of such dues being in contravention of treaty stipulations. The sheer inability of this Department to refund tonnage dues illegally exacted in the absence of a proper protest and appeal led to the passage of the act of July 19, 1878. The justice of the claim to the original sum never was disputed or doubted by this Department. In a communication of the Secretary of the Treasury to the chairman of the Committee on Finance of the Senate, under date of April 15, 1878, it was declared that "the money (the tonnage exactions) of which refund is demanded was taken in violation of law and in contravention of treaty stipulations." Congress admitted the justice of the original claims by the passage of the act of July 19, 1878. In the letter of this Department above referred to it was said, in response to the question whether interest could be paid on the original claims, that, that would depend upon the obligations of this Government under its treaty stipulations with the Hanseatic towns, "as such stipulations are ordinarily construed by the law of nations." It is not for this Department to decide what usage may require in this class of cases, but it is known that this Government demanded interest in the settlement of the Alabama claims, and has paid interest on claims of foreign Governments where such claims had no basis in justice more clearly evident than those of these German companies.

The original moneys were taken and have been long held from the original claimants, simply because the power of this Department to cut off interest was so restricted by the law requiring protest and appeal. The refusal to pay interest in cases of this character might be a detrimental precedent should claims of a similar character arise or be discovered where this Government might be claimant.

Respectfully yours,

C. S. FAIRCHILD,
Acting Secretary.

The honorable the SECRETARY OF STATE.

The Imperial Government of Germany, through its minister resident, is pressing upon the proper Department the payment of this claim. It requires legislative action. In view of the favorable reports made from time to time upon the claim, and of its palpable merits, it hardly comports with the dignity and justice of such a Government as ours that favorable and final action upon it should be longer deferred.

The committee reports back the bill with the recommendation that it do pass.

EXHIBIT No. 20.

PRECEDENTS OF CASES WHERE INTEREST WAS ALLOWED IN THE SAME ACT ALLOWING PRINCIPAL TO STATES BY THEM EXPENDED FOR TROOPS DOING MILITARY SERVICE FOR THE UNITED STATES.

REFERENCES TO ACTS AUTHORIZING PAYMENT OF CLAIMS OF STATES FOR EXPENSES ON ACCOUNT OF THE WAR WITH MEXICO.

1. By a joint resolution approved March 3, 1847 (Stats. at Large, vol. 9, p. —), the Secretary of War was authorized and required to cause to be refunded to the several States or to individuals for services rendered, acting under the authority of any State, the amount of expenses incurred by them in organizing, subsisting, and transporting volunteers previous to their being mustered and received into the service of the United States for the war with Mexico, and for subsisting troops in the service of the United States.

2. By an act approved June 2, 1848, the provisions of said joint resolution were extended so as to embrace all cases of expenses theretofore incurred in organizing, subsisting, and transporting volunteers previous to their being mustered and received into the United States for the war with Mexico, whether by States, counties, corporations, or individuals, either acting with or without the authority of any State, and that in refunding moneys under said act and said joint resolution it should be lawful to pay interest at the rate of 6 per cent. per annum on all sums advanced by States, corporations, or individuals in all cases where the State, corporation, or individual paid or lost the interest or was liable to pay it.

3. By act approved August 5, 1854, the sum of $924,259.65 was appropriated to re-imburse the State of California for expenditures "in the suppression of Indian hostilities within the State prior to the 1st day of January, 1854." (See U. S. Stats. at Large for 1853 and 1854.)

4. By act approved August 18, 1856 (section 8), the Secretary of War was authorized and directed to pay to the holders of the war bonds of the State of California the amount of money appropriated by act of Congress approved May [August] 5, 1854, in payment of expenses incurred and actually paid by the State of California for the suppression of Indian hostilities within the said State prior to the 1st day of January, 1854, under the following restrictions and regulations:

Before any bonds were redeemed by the Secretary of War they were required to be presented to the board of commissioners appointed under an act of the legislature of said State, approved April 19, 1856, and the amount due and payable upon each bond indorsed thereon by said commissioners; the amounts in the aggregate not to exceed the amount appropriated by act of August 5, 1854.

———

PRECEDENTS OF CASES AUTHORIZING PAYMENT OF INTEREST ON PRINCIPAL EXPENDED BY STATES FOR TROOPS FOR THE USE AND BENEFIT OF THE UNITED STATES DURING THE WAR OF 1812 WHERE THE PRINCIPAL HAD BEEN ALREADY PAID AT PRIOR DATES.

1. By act approved March 3, 1825, the accounting officers of the Treasury Department were authorized and directed to settle the claim of the State of Virginia against the United States for interest upon loans on moneys borrowed and actually expended by her for the use and benefit of the United States during the war of 1812.

2. By this act it was provided that, in ascertaining the amount of interest, as aforesaid, due to the State of Virginia, the following rules should be understood as applicable to and governing the case, to wit: First, that interest should not be computed on any sum which Virginia had not expended for the use and benefit of the United States as evidenced by the amount refunded or repaid to Virginia by the United States. Second, that no interest should be paid on any sum on which she had not paid interest. Third, that when the principal, or any part of it, had been paid, or refunded by the United States, or money placed in the hands of Virginia for that purpose, the interest on the sum or sums so paid or refunded should cease, and not be considered as chargeable to the United States any longer than up to the re-payment, as aforesaid.

The mode of computing interest provided by the above act appears to have been satisfactory at the time to all the States, and their claims against the General Government were authorized to be adjusted, and were adjusted under the same rules for computing interest.

3. By an act approved May 13, 1826, entitled "An act authorizing the payment of interest due to the State of Maryland," the accounting officers of the Treasury Department were authorized and directed to liquidate and settle the claim of the State of Maryland against the United States, for interest upon loans on moneys borrowed and actually expended by her for the use and benefit of the United States, during the late war with Great Britain, and the same rules for computing the interest was provided by the act as in the case of the State of Virginia.

4. By an act approved May 20, 1826, entitled "An act authorizing the payment of interest due to the State of Delaware," the accounting officers of the Treasury Department were authorized and directed to take similar action in regard to the settlement of the claim of the State of Delaware against the United States as that directed to be taken in the case of the claim of Maryland, and to be governed by the same rules.

5. By act approved May 20, 1826, the proper accounting officers of the Treasury Department were directed to settle the claim of the city of Baltimore against the United States, for interest on money borrowed and actually expended by the city in its defense during the war of 1812; and the act further provided that the amount due should be ascertained under rules which were the same as those provided by the foregoing act for the adjustment of the accounts in the cases of Virginia, Maryland, and Delaware.

6. By an act approved May 22, 1826, entitled "An act authorizing the payment of interest due to the State of New York," the accounting officers of the Treasury Department were authorized and directed to take similar action and to be governed by the same rules as in the cases of Virginia, Maryland, and Delaware.

7. By an act approved March 3, 1827, the accounting officers of the Treasury Department were authorized and directed to settle the claim of the State of Pennsylvania in the same manner as in the cases of Maryland, Delaware, and New York.

8. By an act approved March 22, 1832, entitled "An act for the adjustment and settlement of the claims of the State of South Carolina against the United States," the accounting officers of the Treasury were authorized and directed to liquidate and settle the claim of the State of South Carolina against the United States for interest upon money actually expended by her for military stores for the use and benefit of the United States, and on account of her militia, whilst in the service of the United

States, during the late war with Great Britain, the money so expended having been drawn by the State from a fund upon which she was then receiving interest. The act designates upon what sums interest shall be paid, and recites in detail other claims of the State theretofore disallowed, which shall be adjusted and settled, such as claims for cannon-balls, transportation of troops and supplies, pay to certain staff officers, blankets ($7,500 being the amount of this item), and muskets.

9. By an act approved March 3, 1857, a re-examination and re-adjustment of the account of the State of Maryland was directed to be made, and it was provided that in the calculation of interest the following rules should be observed:

"Interest shall be calculated up to the time of any payment made. To this interest the payment shall be first applied, and if it exceeds the interest due, the balance shall be applied to diminish the principal; if the payment fall short of the interest, the balance of interest shall not be added to the principal so as to produce interest. Second, interest shall be allowed on such sums only on which the State either paid interest or lost interest by the transfer of an interest-bearing fund."

Under this act Maryland received the additional sum of $275,770.23.

10. By section 7 of said act (March 1, 1837), an appropriation was made to pay all the claims of North Carolina for the services of her militia during the war of 1812 with Great Britain in the cases enumerated in the act approved May 31, 1830, entitled "An act to authorize the payment of the claims of the State of Massachusetts for certain services of her militia during the war of 1812," and also the claims of said State for disbursements in the purchase of munitions or other supplies on account of the war and expended therein.

11. On the 8th day of July, 1870, an act was passed directing the account between the United States and Massachusetts and Maine to be re-opened and re-adjusted, and Massachusetts received the sum of $678,362.42, of which one-third was allotted to the State of Maine as an integral part of Massachusetts when the advances were made.

The ninth section of an act approved June 12, 1858, entitled "An act making appropriations for civil service" (11 Stat. at Large, p. 326), is as follows:

"And be it further enacted, That the Secretary of the Treasury be instructed to report to Congress, at its next regular session, all applications made by State authority of the States and cities for the re-opening and re-examination of the settlements heretofore made with such States and cities and upon the principle of re-adjustment upon which such claims are based, and the amount thereof; and the Secretary of the Treasury is further instructed to report to Congress, at its next regular session, the gross amount that will be required to pay such claims to the States and cities of the United States."

The Secretary of the Treasury made his report at the next session of Congress, showing an aggregate, computing interest down to the date of his report, January 8, 1859, of $1,588,521.69, as follows:

South Carolina	$202,230.90
Virginia	1,076,683.35
Delaware	18,540.97
New York	48,896.21
Pennsylvania	218,507.71
City of Baltimore	23,662.55
Total	1,588,521.69

(See H. Ex. Doc. No. 35, second session, Thirty-fifth Congress, vol. 5.)

12. At the first session of the present Congress a bill was introduced in the House of Representatives (H. R. 5431) to apply to the above States the same rule of computing interest which was applied to the cases of Maryland, Massachusetts, and Maine. The bill was reported favorably by Mr. Broadhead May 29, 1884, from the Committee on the Judiciary.

EXHIBIT No. 21.

CONGRESSIONAL REPORTS CITING AUTHORITIES IN SUPPORT OF CLAIM FOR INTEREST UPON PRINCIPAL EXPENDED BY STATES TO FURNISH AND PAY TROOPS DOING MILITARY SERVICE FOR THE UNITED STATES.

[House Report No. 1670, Forty-eighth Congress, first session.]

The Committee on the Judiciary, to whom was referred the bill (H. R. 5431) directing the Secretary of the Treasury to examine and settle the accounts of certain States and the city of Baltimore, growing out of moneys expended by said States and the city of Baltimore for military purposes, during the war of 1812, have had the same under consideration, and ask leave to submit the following report :

During the war of 1812-'14 with Great Britain the States of Massachusetts, New York, Pennsylvania, Delaware, Maryland, Virginia, South Carolina, and the city of Baltimore expended certain moneys for military purposes. After many years the United States acknowledging the debt to be just and payable with interest, refunded the money with interest; but the rule of casting interest that was applied was to compute interest on the sum advanced by the State from the date of advancement up to the time of refunding to the State by the United States any portion of the sum advanced, deduct the sum refunded from the advancement, and then compute interest on the balance; and so on until the final payment of the principal. The aggregate of the interest columns so computed was the amount of interest paid (see Second Auditor's Report of October 30, 1858). In other words, the payments were applied, first to the payment of the principal, and, after the principal was wholly extinguished, then to the several items in the column of interest.

Against this mode of computing interest the States formally protested (S. Doc., 2d session, 22d Congress, 1832-'33). It was a plain neglect and refusal of the United States to refund the whole amount borrowed. To illustrate: Suppose, in the emergency of war, Virginia, one of the States, should borrow a million of dollars at 6 per cent., and advance the amount to the United States. Sixteen years afterward, when the interest would about equal the principal, the United States should refund a million, but insist that it shall be applied to the payment of the principal. Sixteen years afterward another million is refunded, and it is applied to the payment of the item of interest; the interest not bearing interest, the whole debt, principal and interest, would be paid, according to this mode of adjustment. Meanwhile Virginia has paid her creditors one million of interest during the first sixteen years, another million during the second period of sixteen years, and still owes the million of principal. Virginia, in the case supposed, paid out a million dollars more than the United States refunded. If one borrowed a thousand at 6 per cent. to lend a friend in distress, and after sixteen years the friend should repay a thousand dollars, but compelled the lender to accept it in full of the principal, and sixteen years afterward should pay another thousand dollars in full of the interest, leaving his friend still in debt for the principal, what court would sanction such a settlement, and what justice would there be in it? Yet such is the treatment received by the States that made advances to the United States in the war of 1812-'14. It is evident that the United States have not refunded in full the advances made by the States embraced in this bill.

It was not until the act of March 3, 1857, that partial redress was obtained. By that act a re-examination and re-adjustment of the account of the State of Maryland was directed to be made, and it was provided that in the calculation of interest the following rules should be observed :

"Interest shall be calculated up to the time of any payment made. To this interest the payment shall be first applied; and, if it exceeds the interest due, the balance shall be applied to diminish the principal; if the payment fall short of the interest, the balance of interest shall not be added to the principal so as to produce interest. Second, interest shall be allowed on such sums only on which the State either paid interest or lost interest by the transfer of an interest-bearing fund."

Under this act Maryland received the additional sum of $275,770.23.

And on the 8th of July, 1870, an act was passed directing the accounts between the United States and Massachusetts and Maine to be re-opened and re-adjusted, and Massachusetts received the sum of $678,362.42, of which one-third was allotted to the State of Maine as an integral part of Massachusetts when the advances were made.

Previously to this period, however, the account between the United States and the State of Alabama had been settled on the basis of the Maryland settlement. Indeed, the bill now under consideration passed the Senate of the United States by a vote of 33 yeas to 19 nays, on the —— day of ——, 1857. It went to the House of Representatives, which substituted for this bill the following, which was subsequently concurred in by the Senate, and stands as the ninth section of the act of that session:

"*And be it further enacted*, That the Secretary of the Treasury be instructed to report to Congress at its next regular session all applications made by State authority of the States and cities for the re-opening and re-examination of the settlements heretofore made with such States and cities and upon the principle of re-adjustment upon which such claims are based, and the amount thereof; and the Secretary of the Treasury is further instructed to report to Congress, at its next regular session, the gross amount that will be required to pay such claims to the States and cities of the United States. (11 Stat. at-Large, p. 326, an act making appropriations for civil service, approved June 12, 1858.)"

The Secretary of the Treasury made his report at the next session of Congress, showing an aggregate, computing interest down to the date of his report, of $1,588,521.69, as follows:

South Carolina	$202,230.90
Virginia	1,076,683.35
Delaware	18,540.97
New York	48,896.21
Pennsylvania	218,507.71
City of Baltimore	23,662.55
Total	1,588,521.69

(See Ex. Doc., second session Thirty-fifth Congress, vol. 5.)

These are the States embraced in this bill. None others have unsettled accounts with the Government of the United States growing out of moneys expended during the war of 1812.

This bill proposes to apply to the above States that made similar advances the same rule of computing interest which was applied in the case of Maryland—a rule which has been long and firmly established by the decisions of the Supreme Court of the United States, by the practice of every State in the Union, and adopted for many years past by the accounting officers of the Treasury.

The bill gives simple (not compound) interest on any balance of principal that may be found unpaid, upon the proposed basis of settlement, until its payment by the United States. It provides for any and all proper offsets which the United States may have against any of the States hereby entitled. Both Virginia and South Carolina are largely indebted to the United States, and will receive but a part of what is reported in their favor.

In conclusion, the committee recommend a settlement of the accounts of the United States with the other States by the same rule of computing interest that was applied in the case of Maryland. It makes this recommendation because the rule itself is just and equitable—because, otherwise, the money advanced will not be fully repaid; because the rule has been applied to some of the States, and if applied to one should be applied to all; and because the rule has been repeatedly approved by the Supreme Court of the United States and sanctioned by the practice of every State in the Union, and for many years past followed in similar cases by the accounting officers of the Treasury.

Therefore the committee report the accompanying bill and respectfully recommend its passage, and ask leave to submit as a part of this report the following extracts from debate in the United States Senate on this subject. (See Congressional Globe, vol. 36, part 3, p. 2540, first session, Twenty-fifth Congress.)

IN SENATE, MAY 31, 1858.

Mr. IVERSON. No, sir; no more than was the case of the State of Maryland. The act in relation to Maryland directs that "the proper accounting officers of the Treasury be, and they are hereby, authorized and directed to re-examine the accounts between the United States and the State of Maryland, as the same was from time to time adjusted under the act," etc.

That proposed a re-examination of an account which had been adjusted, did it not? Precisely. Whether the account had been closed or not, whether it had been adjusted or not, whether it was still in existence or not, this act directed the accounting officers to re-examine the account for interest, and make the computation on a particular basis. It was done in the case of Alabama. I desire to apply the same rule to all the States. It is just, equitable, and proper, if you apply it to two States, that you should give it to all. I do not know that my State is interested to any great extent. The State of South Carolina is interested, and her account has not been settled.

The comptroller of that State, in his report to the governor, made a few years ago, states the difficulties between the accounting officers of the United States and himself. That account is still lying open. The State of South Carolina protested against the settlement by its officers at the time. This amendment will meet that case, and authorize the accounting officers to re-adjust the accounts of South Carolina on the basis applied to the State of Maryland. This amendment simply directs that the provisions and principles applied under the twelfth section of the act of 1857 to Maryland shall be applied to all the States. It does not re-open accounts.

Mr. BENJAMIN. Will the Senator from Georgia give us some information on one or two points suggested by his amendment? First, in what way this matter comes before the committee of which he is the organ? Is there a claim from the States? Has it been referred to the committee on behalf of the States?

Mr. IVERSON. Yes, sir; a memorial from the State of South Carolina was referred to the Committee on Claims, and it was upon that memorial that the committee have predicated their amendment.

Mr. BENJAMIN. A general section?

Mr. IVERSON. Yes, a general section, believing that it was equitable to apply the rule to all the States.

Mr. BENJAMIN. The next question I would desire to ask the Senator is: If he has any idea what the amount involved in this appropriation will be?

Mr. IVERSON. I have no idea. The comptroller of the State of South Carolina alleges, in his report to the governor of that State, which I have in my hand, that in the settlement between him and the accounting officers of the United States the State of South Carolina lost $55,000 in interest. That is the difference between the mode of computation of the accounting officers and the mode of accounting as regulated by the act in relation to Maryland. I do not know how other States may be affected. I do not suppose the amounts are very large. I expect that the amount of the State of South Carolina is larger than that of any other State.

Mr. BENJAMIN. It does not seem to me that this section is liable to the objection made by the Senator from Virginia. This is not to pay a private claim of the State of South Carolina. It is a general rule by which the Treasury is to be guided in its settlements with the States; and we having already sanctioned the payments to some of the States on this basis, this section provides that even in cases which have already been closed by the Comptroller of the Treasury, not to the satisfaction of the State, as the Senator from Virginia suggests, but to the dissatisfaction of the State, the account shall be re-opened and examined, and settled according to principles which we have declared to be just. The idea of applying a payment made at any time by the Government of the United States to the extinction of a part of the capital of the debt due to a State whilst there remains interest unsatisfied, is contrary to all principle, to every rule by which computation of payments is made. The State of South Carolina having presented this memorial, if the proposition of the Senator from Georgia, now, was to pay the claim, I admit it would be a private claim; but the committee, instead of treating this as a private claim, preferred to report a section which amounts to a general law, for the very reason that they are not willing to act upon the claim of one State as a private claim. My State has no interest in this question; but I do think that justice requires that the adjustment of these accounts with the States should be made all upon the same footing; and as it has already been made on this footing with the States of Alabama and Maryland, I can not conceive why South Carolina should be made an exception, or any other State which has had accounts to adjust with the General Government. It is a general rule now provided by Congress for the settlement of accounts with States, and the mode of adjusting the interests that arise in accounts with States. It is not an appropriation for the benefit of the State of South Carolina. The committee, it appears to me, have carefully avoided reporting a private claim, and have ex industria changed the legislation into a general law. I do not see that it comes under the rule of the Senate which has been cited, and I shall vote for the amendment.

The PRESIDING OFFICER. Inasmuch as authority is given by the rules to take the opinion of the Senate on questions of this sort, and inasmuch as the facts in this case are disputed, the Chair will submit the question of order to the Senate.

Mr. HAMLIN. I think the matter has been so clearly and so well stated by the Senator from Louisiana, that really there can be no doubt about it. Certainly there is none in my mind; and I have only risen for the purpose of inviting the attention of the Senate to its action on other cases which I think are very similar, if not entirely parallel to this. We pass pension laws, in which we prescribe the time of service; we prescribe the rules which shall entitle a person to a pension. We find, outside of that class of pensions, a very large class of cases that come very nearly up to the rules we have prescribed; they come here, and what is done? Our Committee on Pensions recommend this special case, and that special case, and they are passed. By and by we see there are so many special cases that we remove the limitation by general law, and it has been done in appropriation bills, precisely in the way now proposed.

I will cite an instance. We removed the limitations as to the time or mode of proof required at the Department, and that takes in a whole class of cases. True, if each one came here and asked action separately by itself, it would be a private claim; but you make a general law to include all cases. That is precisely this case.

I refer, now, to an instance in my mind, with regard to those who drew pensions for Revolutionary service. You prescribed, originally, that only those widows of Revolutionary soldiers should draw a pension who were married previous to 1783, I think. Then you limited it to 1794; and then you limited it to 1800, because you found such a large number of cases coming so nearly up to the time, that it was deemed advisable to extend it. The last amendment I recollect distinctly, because I drew it, was ingrafted on an appropriation bill in 1853, and it was to meet a class of special cases here pending.

Mr. GREEN. I will inquire when the rule is to apply under the resolution adopted this morning, for a recess, to-day or to-morrow.

The PRESIDING OFFICER. To-morrow.

Mr. GREEN. Then I move that the Senate do now adjourn.

Mr. HUNTER. I hope that we shall get through with this bill.

Mr. GREEN. We can not get through, because I have an amendment to offer, and so have others.

Mr. HUNTER. Let us hear them.

The motion to adjourn was not agreed to.

The PRESIDING OFFICER. Will the Senate receive the amendment proposed by the Senator from Georgia?

The amendment was received.

The PRESIDING OFFICER. The question now is on agreeing to the amendment.

Mr. HUNTER. The amendment is a proposition which certainly ought to receive some examination before it is passed. We ought to know how much money it will take from the Treasury; we ought to know what changes it is to make in the principles on which accounts have been settled with States. I apprehend it will be found that it makes other changes besides the one which has been referred to by the Senator from Louisiana the mode of stating the account as to interest and principal. I believe there have been some rules as to whether interest shall be allowed to States at all, and upon which settlements have been made with most of the States, and that will be changed if this provision be adopted; and it is probable that under the change it will be found that very large sums will be due to the States of this Union. I have no doubt that most of the old States would come in if this amendment be adopted, and some of them might claim very largely. This is eminently a subject for separate legislation. We ought to know what changes are made. We ought to know whether, under this amendment, we shall not pay to some States interest on claims on which interest has never been voted.

The first deviation, if I remember, was in the case of Alabama; but there it was determined to make certain allowances of interest, because the State had paid the interest, because it had sold stocks, as was done in Maine; and an exception was made in the case of Alabama for that reason. I believe that was the case, also, in Maryland, where the allowance was on the principle of the Alabama case. Unless you treat this as having arisen out of those exceptional circumstances, you will re-open all the settlements that have been made with the States; and you will pass out of the Treasury a large sum of money, in my opinion. I speak, though, only from general recollection; I have had no time to examine the amendment particularly; but I am afraid it will be found when we come to see the effect of it—if it should be adopted—that it will go much further than any of us suppose.

Mr. FESSENDEN. The Senator from Virginia, if he would take the pains to read the amendment, would see that it is not open to the objections he has stated. It does not provide, if I read it rightly, for the payment of any interest to a State, in any case whatever, where interest has not been allowed heretofore. It does not make any new claim in that respect. The whole amount of it is simply this: The Treasury, as I understand, has adopted the rule that where a certain amount of debt is owing to a State, and a certain amount of interest has accumulated on that debt, and where the principal thus owing bears interest, and the interest thus owing does not, if the claim is paid in part, they apply that part payment to the principal which bears interest, instead of to the interest which does not, thus reversing the rule which exists in every State in the Union and operating most unjustly towards the States themselves. For instance, suppose a debt is due to a State, which debt bears interest, and by the law at the same time there is an amount of interest accumulated upon it which does not bear interest—let us call one $50,000 and the other $30,000, the $50,000 bearing interest and the $30,000 not bearing interest. The Government, in these circumstances, instead of paying the whole, pay up $30,000. Then, instead of applying it to the amount which does not bear interest against the Government, and which the State has paid, they apply it to the principal, reducing the claim which bears interest to $20,000, and leaving the State to lose its interest on $30,000.

Mr. TOOMBS. It is worse than that.

Mr. FESSENDEN. That is bad enough. The provision is, in regard to all these claims which the States have where the United States will not pay accumulating interest, as they ought to do, that the partial payment shall first go to sink the interest that is due. If a 'man owes me money and interest has been accumulating year after year which he has failed to pay, and especially if I am in debt for it, as is very often the case with the States, he ought to indemnify me; but the rule adopted by the Treasury is worse than that. They say they will not only not indemnify me and leave me to pay my interest, but when they do make a payment it shall not go to sink the interest, but to sink the principal, leaving the interest to stand. That is unjust. It does not apply in the case of any private claim anywhere, but has been arbitrarily adopted by the accounting officers of the Treasury. In the case of Maryland, which was precisely similar, Maryland remonstrated, and at the last session Congress said that account should be adjusted upon proper principles—the same principles that exist in every State of the Union between man and man—that where principal and interest are due and the Government paid any part, that payment should be applied to the interest first; if it paid it off, very well; if it overbalanced it, the balance should be so much towards the principal. This was on the common, ordinary principles of justice.

In the case of the State of South Carolina, if I understand it, the officers went so far as to keep an account with the State, crediting her with interest accumulating on the principal, and if there was any left they then took the part they had paid, cast interest on that, and then offset the two! That is to say, they paid their interest in part and retained to themselves the right of offsetting the interest which accrued on their own payment of money due to the State to pay the rest of the debt with. [Laughter.]

It does not do to make it a matter of account current between the two, because the account is really all on one side; but the Treasury officers apply the principle of accounts current to it as if so much was due from Maryland and so much from the United States, and cast interest on both and then offset the two; but, instead of that, it is all due from the United States. They say, "We will owe you the interest; we will pay you part of the principal; we will cast interest on the money we allow you and pay you interest with it." That is the principle they have adopted. This is simply to set that right and to say that where these things exist the Government shall do what is proper. * * * Why, sir, what difference will it make how much money it amounts to? If there be more or less, the Government ought to pay, and pay it at once, without the slightest hesitation, and calculate the interest upon proper principles.

The Maryland provision came from the Senator's own Committee on Finance and was agreed to by the Senate. If it was proper in that case, why is it not in every other?

Mr. HUNTER. I have stated that was made under peculiar circumstances; that I do not recollect perfectly. The Senator from Maryland can explain them. It will be found, I think, that they do not apply to other cases.

Mr. PEARCE. I will state the facts in relation to the claim of Maryland. The State of Maryland advanced large sums of money to the Government of the United States during the war of 1812, and some time after the close of that war the United States re-imbursed the principal. In 1812, an act was passed for the payment of interest to the State of Maryland, and the interest was paid upon a mode of calculation novel to me, though I find it has been adopted as the usual rule of computation in such cases at the Treasury. That is to say, having determined to settle the accounts, and commenced to make payments on it, the first payment was applied to the reduction of the principal, the interest being made to stand aside; and so payments were made from time to time, until the whole of the principal was liquidated; and then they went back to the period when they began to pay, and ascertained what the amount of interest due at the time was, and paid that sum without any interest on it. In 1829, or 1830, an act was passed through both houses of Congress authorizing the payment of interest to the State of Maryland upon the proper principle, such as prevailed in mercantile transactions, and it was vetoed by General Jackson, and the veto came in at the next session of Congress, on the ground that it was disturbing the usual mode of settlement. [Laughter.]

After I became a member of the Senate, I revived this claim of Maryland, under instructions from my State legislature, and I introduced a general bill, providing for the liquidation of the interest due to the different States of the Union, which had made such advances in a body. It was objected to by a gentleman, then a Senator from Alabama, who preferred that each State should have its own claim rest on his own basis. He introduced another bill for the benefit of the State of Alabama, and it was passed through the Senate, and under that bill the State of Alabama was paid according to the old mode of computation. The Senate will remark, however, that this rule was always adopted in the allowance of interest. The Government of the United States never paid interest, except where the State had paid interest itself upon its advance, or had lost interest, and Alabama obtained her allowance of interest because the funds which she had applied to aid the General Government were taken from a bank which was her property, and she had thus been obliged to contract her line of discounts, and so lost interest. The State of Maryland obtained interest because she had liquidated the bonds which she had given to her creditors for the money she applid for the service of the Government during the war, by selling United States stock of which she was owner, thus transferring to the liquidation of this obligation an interest-bearing fund. The principle was that the United States would pay no interest, except where interest had actually been paid or lost by the State.

As the State of Maryland came within that category she was entitled to interest, and after long years of dispute on the subject, the Congress of the United States at the last session passed the act which has been referred to, providing for the re-examination and re-adjustment of the account of the State of Maryland, and directing that the interest should be calculated according to certain rules laid down by the Supreme Court of the United States for that purpose; that is to say, first applying the payments to the interest, and when the interest was all liquidated then applying them to the principal; and under that act I think the State of Maryland received after the last session of Congress about two hundred and seventy thousand dollars. There are several Stat 's interested in like manner; I do not recollect how many; but when I originally introduced the bill I carefully noticed the States interested and their number, and no doubt the amount will be very large. Delaware, South Carolina, Virginia, and several other States are interested, and the amount is very large; but I do not know that magnitude of the obligation is any defense against the passage of an act for payment according to the principles of equity which have been applied to the State of Maryland. This is an inconvenient time, it is true, for us to be dunned for this money; but I think we ought to settle fairly, if we do nothing else. If we can not pay the money we ought, at least, to acknowledge the obligation.

[Second session Thirty-fifth Congress.]

IN SENATE, FEBRUARY —, 1859.

The army bill being under consideration—
Mr. IVERSON. I am instructed by the Committee on Claims to offer the following amendment:
"That all the States which have had or shall have refunded to them by the United States moneys expended by such States for military purposes during or since the war of 1812 with Great Britain, which have not already been allowed interest upon the moneys so expended, shall now be allowed interest, so far as they have themselves paid or lost it, said interest to be computed by the proper accounting officers of the Treasury according to the provisions and principles directed to be applied to the case of Maryland by the twelfth section of the act of March 3, 1857, entitled 'An act making appropriations for certain civil expenses of the Government for the year ending the 30th of June, 1858,' and that all the States which have been allowed interest upon claims against the United States accruing during or since said war of 1812 shall be entitled to have their interest accounts re-examined and restated by the proper accounting officers of the Treasury according to the provisions and principles of the twelfth section of said act of March 3, 1857, and that those provisions and principles shall govern the computation of interest in all cases in which interest may hereafter be allowed to any of the States. Any money found to be due to any State, as directed by this section to be computed and ascertained, shall be paid to such State out of any money in the Treasury not otherwise appropriated: Provided, That, in lieu of the payment of money, the Secretary of the Treasury may allow the State of Maryland interest on such sums only on which the said State either paid interest or lost interest by the transfer of an interest-bearing fund."

This provision was applied by that act to the State of Maryland, and under it the accounts of that State were re-opened and re-adjusted at the Treasury Department, and she was paid back, if I remember aright, the sum of $272,000. The amendment which I now propose simply puts all the States precisely on the footing that the act of 1857 put the State of Maryland. It is just and proper that the rule, if applied to one State, should be applied to all; and the rule is itself just and proper. Heretofore the mode of calculating interest at the Treasury Department has been the old one which was in vogue some half century or century ago, and which has long since been exploded in every civilized country. They calculated the interest upon the principal up to the time of the settlement, and they calculated interest upon the various payments up to the time of the settlement, and struck a balance. That mode of calculating interest has been exploded in every State in the Union. Not a single State now adheres to it, although it was, in early days, when I was a boy, the mode of calculating interest. The mode now is that applied to the accounts of the State of Maryland, first to compute interest up to the time of the first payment, and then apply the payment, in the first place, to the extinguishment of the interest, and then apply any surplus to the extinguishment of the principal, and so on of each payment of interest. That is the principle on which the accounts of Maryland have been settled, and I propose to apply it to all the States of the Union. It is just and proper.

The amendment, you will perceive, does not give the States interest unless they paid it themselves or lost it by the transfer of an interest-bearing fund. It is just and proper that every State should be put on the same footing as the State of Maryland. And the principle of settlement proposed is just and proper in itself. It is the mode adopted by every State in the Union in the calculation of interest. I have put in the amendment a provision that the Secretary of the Treasury shall pay these amounts to the States in 5 per cent. bonds of the United States, redeemable in ten years, or sooner, at the discretion of the President. The States, I understand, are perfectly willing to take 5 per cent. bonds of the United States instead of the money. In the present embarrassed condition of the country we think it prudent and proper to make this provision. With this explanation of the case I hope the Senate will adopt the amendment.

Mr. HUNTER. At the last session I voted against the provision when it was introduced, but I believe the opinion of the State which I represent is, that she is entitled to the money ; and although I would never have used my official position to introduce it, I feel bound to vote for it as her representative. I suppose, in justice, if we were settling the account originally, this would be the proper mode of doing it. I do not think it well to re-open these old accounts, which have been settled, and with the settlements of which the States were satisfied in former times ; but the precedent which has been set in the case of Maryland has made all the States desire the application of the same principle to them, and I believe most of them have agents here, and are insisting upon it.

    *   *   *   *   #   *

Mr. IVERSON called for the yeas and nays, and they were ordered.

Mr. FESSENDEN. I wish to say a word about this proposition; because I think, when the Senate understands it, there will be no difficulty in passing it. I think there can be no dispute about it. I advocated this provision last year against the opposition of the chairman of the Committee on Finance ; and I have no sort of disposition to change my action because it turns out that the State of West Virginia is so largely interested as she is. I do not mean to say that that affects his action, because everbody knows that he is not influenced in that way. I mean simply to say, in regard to myself, that Virginia has a large claim under this provision, much larger than it was supposed any State could have; but that does not affect my action, or induce me to change my vote. I have no doubt, from the honorable Senator's well-known habit of looking out for the Treasury, that if Virginia would let him alone he would vote against the amendment, although his State will be so much benefited by it.

But, sir, the principle of settlement proposed is a very simple one, and a perfectly honest one. In settling these claims the Government officers have heretofore acted on the principle of applying partial payments to the discharge of the principal, and letting the interest accumulate. It is no question about paying interest ; that is settled. This *class of claims always carry interest, and it is always allowed.* The Government let the interest run on until it got to be as large as the principal. They then paid a certain amount ; but instead of applying that amount to the interest which was due, they applied it to the principal and let the interest stand, which did not carry interest ; that is to say, they paid the principal before the interest. They did worse than that in many cases, as I understand ; when they came to settle up fairly they charged interest on the payment of the principal up to the time of the settlement, and allowed no interest on the interest existing. Thus they made the payment of the principal eat up the interest.

This mode of settlement was grossly unjust, and as great an outrage as anything could be. It was contrary to the mode in which interest is computed between individual and individual. Maryland applied for a recomputation, and Congress passed a law to allow it. All that is now asked is to place every other State on the same footing—there may be some half dozen of them—that advanced money on the same foundation on which you placed Maryland, not only to do the thing equally as between the States, but to do the just thing, and pay money which is absolutely due without any sort of question.

The following thirty-four Senators voted *in favor* of the amendment, viz, twenty-six in 1858, and eight *others* in 1859 :

Bayard,	Dixon,	Harlan,	Rice,
Benjamin,	Doolittle,	Hunter,	Seward,
Bigler,	Durkee,	Iverson,	Simmons,
Bright,	Fessenden,	Kennedy,	Thomson,
Brown,	Fitch,	Mallory,	Toombs,
Chestnut,	Foot,	Mason,	Wade,
Clark,	Foster,	Pearce,	Wilson,
Collamer,	Hamlin,	Polk,	Yulee—34.
Crittenden,	Hammond,		

The amendment prevailed in the Senate, but failed in the House of Representatives in a close vote, when avowed friends, enough to have carried it, voted in the negative, because of the then condition of the Treasury.

[House Report No. 303, Forty-ninth Congress, first session.]

The Committee on Claims, to whom was referred the bill (H. R. 3877) to authorize the Secre tary of the Treasury to settle the claim of the State of Florida on account of expenditures made in suppressing Indian hostilities, beg leave to submit the following report :

In accordance with the requirements of the joint resolution of Congress approved March 3, 1881, the Secretary of War has investigated, audited, and made a report to Congress, May 22, 1882, of the amount due the State of Florida for expenditures made in suppressing Indian hostilities in that State between the 1st day of December, 1855, and the 1st day of January, 1860 (Ex. Doc. 203, Forty-seventh Congress, first session).

The expenditures grew out of the Seminole war of 1855, 1856, and 1857, the State authorities being compelled, in the presence of an anticipated and subsequently actual outbreak of the Indians, to call forth the militia of the State, the force of United States troops then on duty being inadequate to the protection of the people. The report of the Secretary of War (Ex. Doc. 203) fully sets forth in detail the items of expenditure allowed and disallowed, the total amount found due the State being the sum of $224,648.09.

It is established that the funds at the command of the executive of the State of Florida in the years referred to were insufficient to equip, supply, and pay the troops in the field; and, relying upon the approval given by the President of the United States, through the Secretary of War, on the 21st day of May, 1857, of the services of these volunteers, the State legislature, in order to provide their equipment and maintenance, authorized the issue of 7 per cent. bonds.

A portion of the bonds, amounting to $132,000, was sold by the governor to the Indian trust fund of the United States, and the proceeds of such sale were disbursed by the treasurer of the State for the "expenses of Indian hostilities," as appears from his report to the legislature for the year ending October 31, 1857 (Ex. Doc. 203, Forty-seventh Congress, first session). Another portion was hypothecated to the banks of South Carolina and Georgia as security for a loan of $222,015, and $192,331 of this loan was disbursed directly by a disbursing agent of the State in payment of "expenses of Indian hostilities," including pay of volunteers (Ex. Doc. 203, Forty-seventh Congress, first session).

This case is one where the Government, through the President of the United States by the Secretary of War, promised to pay these troops when mustered into the United States service, and they would have been long since paid by the Government if so mustered, but the mustering officer arrived in the State after they had been mustered out, and the State was compelled to borrow money with which to pay them. (See letter of Secretary of War hereto appended.)

Congress has universally paid interest to the States where they have paid interest. We cite the cases where interest has been allowed and paid for moneys advanced during the war of 1812–'15, as follows : Virginia, act March 3, 1825 (4 Stat. at L., p. 132); Maryland, act May 13, 1826 (4 Stat. at L., p. 161); Delaware, act May 20, 1826 (4 Stat. at L., p. 175); New York, act May 22, 1826 (4 Stat. at L., p. 192); Pennsylvania, act March 3, 1827 (4 Stat. at L., p. 241); South Carolina, act March 22, 1832 (4 Stat. at L., p. 499); Maine, act of March 31, 1851 (9 Stat. at L., p. 626); Massachusetts and Maine, act of July 8, 1870 (16 Stat. at L., p. 198).

For advances for Indian and other wars the same rule has been observed in the following cases: Alabama, act January 26 (4 Stat. at L., p. 344); Georgia, act March 31, 1851 (9 Stat. at L., p. 626); Georgia, act March 3, 1870 (20 Stat. at L., p. 385); Washington Territory, act March 3, 1859 (11 Stat. at L., p. 429); New Hampshire, act January 27, 1852 (10 Stat. at L., p. 1); California, act August 5, 1854 (10 Stat. at L., p. 582); California, act August 18, 1856 (11 Stat. at L., p. 91); California, act June 23, 1860 (12 Stat. at L., p. 104); California, act July 25, 1868 (15 Stat. at L., p. 175); California, March 3, 1881 (21 Stat. at L., p. 510); and in aid of the Mexican war. (See statute of June 2, 1848.)

Attorney-General Wirt, in his opinion on an analogous case, says:

"The expenditure thus incurred forms a debt against the United States which they are bound to re-imburse. If the expenditures made for such purposes are supplied from the treasury of the State, the United States re-imburse the principal without interest ; but if being unable itself, from the condition of its own finances, to meet the emergency, such State has been obliged to borrow money for the purpose, and thus to incur a debt on which she herself has had to pay interest, such debt   essentially a debt due by the United States, and both the principal and interest are to be paid by the United States. (See Opinions of Attorneys-General, vol. 1, p. 174.)"

Thus it will be seen that the precedent for the payment of interest, under the rule adopted for the settlement of claims of war of 1812–'15, and Indian wars above cited, is well established.

The committee are of the opinion that the urgent necessity for the services of these troops, and the action of the President and the Secretary of War, are well established, and create an equitable obligation on the part of the General Government, and as it is clearly shown by Ex. Doc. 203, Forty-seventh Congress, that the State of Florida not only borrowed money from the Indian trust fund, but also from the banks of the States of Georgia and South Carolina, for their payment, upon which the State has since paid interest, your committee have concluded to recommend the passage of the bill, with the following amendments:

In line 18 of section 1, after the word "it," insert the words "upon said claim or claims."

In line 8 of section 2 strike out the words "and to pay such sum so ascertained due the said State," and insert the words "and shall adjust and settle the claim of the State therefor, and shall pay such sum as may be ascertained to be due the State thereon."

WAR DEPARTMENT,
Washington, D. C., May 21, 1857.

SIR: I have the honor to acknowledge the receipt of your letter of the 8th instant, asking an approval of the services of certain volunteers called out by you, and in reply to inform you that the explanations as to the necessity of their services is satisfactory, and orders have been issued to the officer commanding in Florida to muster them in and out of the service of the United States.

Very respectfully, your obedient servant,

JOHN B. FLOYD,
Secretary of War.

His Excellency JAMES E. BROOME,
Governor of Florida.

[House Report No. 3126, Forty-ninth Congress, first session.]

The Committee on Claims, to whom was referred the bill (H. R. 1125) for the relief of the First National Bank of Newton, Mass., having considered the same, respectfully report:

That this bill was favorably reported by the Committee on Claims of the Senate in the Forty-eighth Congress, and after an exhaustive discussion passed that body. It has again been favorably reported by the Committee on Claims of the Senate, the report being made by Senator Jackson, which we adopt, as follows:

That on and prior to February 28, 1867, Julius F. Hartwell was cashier of the United States sub-treasury in Boston, Mass. While acting as such cashier he embezzled a large amount of the Government's money by lending the same to the firm of Mellon, Ward & Co., who were extensively engaged in stock speculations. As the time for the examination of the funds in the sub-treasury approached, March 1, 1867, when Hartwell's accounts would have to be passed, some plan had to be devised by the guilty parties to prevent or delay exposure. The device resorted to and put in operation was to procure funds and assets of innocent third parties to be placed temporarily on deposit in the sub-treasury till the examination was had, and then to be immediately withdrawn again, and thus tide Hartwell and his associates in the embezzlement over the crisis. Edward Carter, the active financial member of said firm of Mellon, Ward & Co., who concocted this scheme with Hartwell, was a director in the First National Bank of Newton, and seems to have possessed not only the confidence of, but unlimited influence over, E. Porter Dyer, the cashier of said bank. By means of this confidence and influence, and in execution of his and Hartwell's fraudulent conspiracy, Carter procured from Dyer the money, bonds, securities, and checks of the First National Bank of Newton, to the amount of $371,025, which were deposited in the sub-treasury on February 28, 1867, Hartwell giving a receipt therefor, as cashier, that the deposit was "to be returned on demand in Governments, or bills, or its equivalent." This receipt, being in the name of Mellon, Ward & Co., was immediately indorsed by Carter, as follows: "Pay only to the order of E. Porter Dyer, jr., cashier," and signed Mellon, Ward & Co.

This deposit of its funds and assets was made without the knowledge and consent of the president and directors of the First National Bank of Newton. Hartwell's default was discovered on the night of February 28, and on March 1, 1867, when Dyer presented the above receipt and demanded its redemption, payment was refused, and the bank's funds and securities were held and applied by the Government to make good Hartwell's default. The capital stock of the bank was $150,000. It was doing and for years had done a prosperous and profitable business; but this fraudulent misapplication and appropriation of its assets ruined the institution, and on March 11, 1867, it was placed in the hands of a receiver, and to make good its losses and provide the means to discharge its debts the stockholders were compelled to pay in a second time the amount of their respective holdings of its capital stock. On February 24, 1873, the First National Bank of Newton filed its petition in the Court of Claims against the United States to recover the amount of its funds and assets so deposited in the sub-treasury and appropriated by the Government. The case was heard in December, 1880, and judgment was rendered in favor of the bank January 24, 1881, for the full amount of principal claimed, viz, $371,025. The full details of the conspiracy and transaction by which the Government, through the fraud of its agent, wrongfully got possession of the bank's assets, are clearly set forth in 10 Court of Claims Reports, p. 519; 96 United States Supreme Court Reports, 30; and 16 Court of Claims Reports, p. 54, to which reference is here made for a more complete statement of the facts than hereinabove stated. In delivering the opinion of the Court of Claims in the bank's suit, Chief-Justice Drake characterized the taking of its assets as a "villainous scheme," and the transaction as "simply a case of a bank being robbed, and of its stolen assets being put into the hands of the cashier of the sub-treasury for a purpose which by no possible view could in law be held to effect a transfer of the bank's right of property in them either to him or to the United States." That the United States could not derive a benefit from the fraudulent act of their cashier, or lawfully withhold the funds thus obtained, admitted of no question, either in law or morals. After referring to many of the authorities on the question, the Supreme Court (96 U. S. Reports, p. 36) say, in conclusion:

"But surely it ought to require neither argument nor authority to support the proposition that where the money or property of an innocent person has gone into the coffers of the nation by means of a fraud to which its agent was a party, such money or property can not be held by the United States against the claim of the wronged and injured party. The agent was agent for no such purpose. His doings were vitiated by the underlying dishonesty and could confer no rights upon his principal."

On the 28th of April, 1881, a duly certified copy of the bank's judgment against the United States was presented to the Secretary of the Treasury, as provided by law. Before its payment the now Attorney-General of the United States, in March, 1881, entered an appeal to the Supreme Court. This appeal seems to have been taken for the purpose of enabling him to examine the case. After making such examination and finding the case undistinguishable from that reported in 96 United States Reports above cited, the appeal, which had been in the mean time entered in the Supreme Court, was, on his motion, dismissed in that court October 25, 1881.

Thereafter, on October 29, 1881, the sum of $260,000 was paid on account of this judgment, by the Treasurer of the United States, that being the only amount available under the appropriation then existing. The balance of $111,025 was paid August 30, 1882.

Such is the brief history of the case. The bill under consideration proposes to pay the bank interest on the amount of its funds so taken and appropriated by the United States, from date of conversion to time of payment. The Court of Claims was not authorized to award such interest, its jurisdiction in the matter of "interest" being confined to cases of contract expressly stipulating for the payment of interest. It will hardly be insisted that this restriction upon one of its tribunals settles either the question of the Government's liability or the measure of its duty in a case like the present, where the contract relation is not voluntarily assumed by the party making the claim. The Government may with propriety refuse to recognize any obligation to pay interest to those who voluntarily deal with it, without expressly stipulating for the payment of interest. But the question of its obligation to make indemnity by the allowance of interest, where the creditor relation is forced upon the individual by the wrongful act of the Government or its agents, stands upon a different footing and should be determined by the general principles of the public law and the rules of natural justice and equity applicable to the facts and circumstances of the particular case. Ordinarily the Government can not, and should not be made responsible to the extent of individuals for the wrongful acts of its officers or agents. But this rule can not be justly invoked to shield or protect the Government from the measure of responsibility applied to private persons where it has adopted such wrongful acts and derived an advantage and benefit therefrom. Where the Government has profited by the fraud of its agent, why should it deny to the injured party the full redress that courts of equity would afford as between individuals and private corporations? In the jurisprudence of all civilized countries the general doctrine is well settled that any one—except a "bona fide" purchaser for value and without notice—who obtains possession of property which has been procured from the owner by *fraudulent* means or practices is converted by the courts into a *trustee*, and ordered to account as such; or, as stated by Perry on Trusts, § 166, the principle "denotes that the parties defrauded, or beneficially entitled, have the same right and remedies against him as they would be entitled to against an express trustee who had fraudulently committed a breach of trust." Whenever the principal adopts the fraudulent act of his agent, or attempts to reap an advantage therefrom, his liability is properly measured by this rule. Indeed (says Perry on Trusts, 172), the doctrine has been thus broadly stated :

"That when once a fraud has been committed, not only is the person who committed the fraud precluded from deriving any benefit from it, but every innocent person is so likewise, unless he has innocently acquired a subsequent interest ; for a third person by seeking to derive any benefit under such a transaction, or to retain any benefit resulting therefrom, becomes 'participes criminis,' however innocent of the fraud in the beginning."

It would not admit of a moment's doubt that in the present case interest would have been awarded the bank as against the agent committing the fraud. It is also clear that as against any private principal occupying the position of the Government the bank could and would have received interest. Why should not the Government, standing as it does under this transaction in the attitude of a trustee, if not a "participes criminis," be held to the same measure of responsibility and redress ? Nothing short of this will meet the justice of the case or afford the equitable relief to which the bank is justly entitled. A great Government like ours, with unlimited resources and revenues at its command, should above all things deal justly with its citizens. It should not stand upon technicalities in withholding property or funds which may have wrongfully come into its possession. It should never make for itself a profit or secure and retain an advantage through the fraud of its agents or by any breach of trust which has worked a wrong or injury. It should in such cases make such reparation as its courts would enforce as between individuals.

The American consul at Geneva successfully claimed interest upon the amounts awarded to the United States against Great Britain. The counsel for Great Britain, while objecting to the application of the principle allowing interest, distinguished between cases where, in their view, it should and should not be allowed, in language strikingly applicable here ; and attention is called to it as being a concession, on the part of a party objecting to the allowance of interest, which covers the present case, as follows :

"Interest, in the proper sense of that word, can only be allowed where there is a principal debt of liquidated and ascertained amount detained and withheld by the debtor from the creditor after the time when it was absolutely due and ought to have been paid, the fault of the delay in payment resting with the debtor ; or where the debtor has wrongfully taken possession of and exercised dominion over the property of the creditor. In the former case, from the time when the debt ought to have been paid, the debtor has had the use of the creditor's money, and may be justly presumed to have employed it for his own profit and advantage. He has thus made a gain corresponding with the loss which the creditor has sustained by being deprived, during the same period of time, of the use of his money ; and it is evidently just that he should account to the creditor for the interest which the law takes as the measure of this reciprocal gain and loss. In the latter case the principle is exactly the same. It is ordinarily to be presumed that the person who has wrongfully taken possession of the property of another has enjoyed the fruits of it ; and if, instead of this, he has destroyed it or kept it unproductive, it is still just to hold him responsible for interest on its value, because his own acts, after the time when he assumed control over it, are the causes why it has remained unfruitful. In all these cases *it is the actual or virtual possession of the money or property belonging to another* which is the foundation of the liability of interest. The person liable is either *lucratus* by the detention of what is not his own, or is justly accountable as if he were so."

In the case under consideration, the funds of the bank—an amount fixed and liquidated—have been wrongfully withheld for many years, during which the Government has retained and used them, and to that extent has made or saved interest, of which the bank throughout the same period lost such interest. In allowing interest at a low rate the bank will receive only (or less than) what it was unjustly deprived of, while the United States will only yield up what it has received or saved that rightfully belonged to the bank, for it can not be questioned that the use of the principal sum has put the Government in receipt of additional funds to the amount of the value of such use. The claim is thus brought within the general principle so clearly and forcibly stated in the above-quoted extract from the counsel of Great Britain.

In this statement of the proposition which should govern the present case it is hardly necessary to say that the committee do not wish to be understood as even suggesting that the same rule could or should be applied to that large class of cases known as war claims. They stand entirely u pon a different footing. Every man woman, and child residing, during the war, in the insurrectionary territory, became thereby an enemy of the United States. The Government could have asserted against each and all of them the extremest measures conceded by the public law to belligerents. That it did not adopt this policy, but modified the harsher rules of war, by which it waived some of its belligerent rights, could not be made in any case the basis of a claim for interest, nor lay the ground for the payment of interest. Take, for illustration, the captured and abandoned property cases. This property and its proceeds, under the modern rules of war, could have been appropriated to the absolute use of the Government. Instead of pursuing this course, the Government, in a spirit of liberality, adopted the generous policy of making itself a depository of these funds, to be held for the benefit of the real owners. The proposition to allow interest on such claims should not and would not be entertained for a moment.

It can not be properly urged as an objection to this claim for interest that the bank should be held responsible to some extent for the unfaithfulness of the cashier whom it had selected and intrusted with certain well-defined duties in respect to its funds and assets. No want of care is shown in making the selection. There was nothing in his previous conduct to excite suspicion or put the bank upon inquiry or notice so as to charge it with any degree of negligence in retaining him in its employ. The doctrine of contributory negligence is sometimes looked to and considered in the determination of the better equity as between two innocent parties who have been defrauded by a *third party who has been trusted by both*. If there had been no previous default on the part of Hartwell, and he had on the night of February 28, 1867, embezzled the funds and assets of the bank that day deposited with him by Carter and Dyer, the Government and the bank might then have occupied the position of two innocent parties, whose equities would have to be determined and settled to some extent by the question of negligence in the employment of unfaithful agents. But that is not the present case. The Government had already lost its money by the previous embezzlement of its cashier of the sub-treasury, and then through the corrupt influence of that same agent and his confederate, the bank's agent is tempted by a "villainous scheme" into a breach of his trust, by means of which the Government obtains possession of the bank's entire assets, and wrongfully appropriates them in making good its previous losses. It would be shocking to every sense of right and justice for the Government now to urge that the unfaithfulness of the bank's trusted agent was a bar or valid defense to its liability and duty to refund either the principal or interest of the funds so procured and converted to its own use. Your committee have too much regard for the honor and good name of the Government to allow it to occupy a position so questionable. It should be observed, too, that the decision of its own courts declaring that the Government could not rightfully hold the assets so fraudulently obtained has really disposed of this question of negligence, which applied with equal force to the recovery of the principal as to the interest.

To the objection that the allowance of this claim for interest will establish a bad precedent, the reply of Mr. Sumner to a similar objection is a complete answer:

"If the claim is just, the precedent of paying it is one which our Government should wish to establish. Honesty and justice are not precedents of which either Government or individuals should be afraid" (Senate Report No. 4, Forty-first Congress, first session, p. 10).

But it is respectfully submitted that there are abundant precedents, both in the judicial and in the legislative branches of the Government, to support the present application for the allowance of interest. The prevalent idea that "the Government never pays interest" has grown up from the *practice* of the *Departments* which do not allow *interest* except where it is specially provided for in cases of contracts or expressly authorized by law. But this usage and custom of the Executive Departments can not be properly regarded as the settled rule and policy of the Government, for its action upon the subject of interest has not from the earliest time conformed to such usage. On the contrary, it will be found, upon an examination of the precedents where Congress has passed acts for the relief of private citizens, that in almost every case, except those growing out of the late war, Congress has directed the payment of interest where the United States had withheld a sum of money which had been decided by competent authority to be due, or where the amount due was ascertained, fixed, and certain. The highest court of the country has also affirmed this to be not only the practice of the Government but the measure of its duty. Thus, in 15 Wallace, p. 77, where the suit was against a United States collector for the recovery of taxes illegally collected, the Supreme Court used the following language upon the subject of interest allowed on the claim, viz:

"The third exception is to the instruction that if the jury found for plaintiff they might add interest. This was not contested upon the argument, and we think it clearly correct. The *ground for the refusal to allow interest is the presumption that* the *Government is always ready and willing to pay its ordinary debts*. Where an *illegal* tax has been collected, the citizen who has paid it and has been obliged to bring suit against the collector is *entitled* to *interest* in the event of recovery from the time of the alleged exaction."

On June 8, 1872, Congress referred the claim of the heirs of Francis Vigo to the Court of Claims, in the following language:

"The claim of the heirs and legal representatives of Col. Francis Vigo, deceased, late of Terre Haute, Ind., for money and supplies furnished the troops under command of General George Rogers Clarke, in the year 1778, during the Revolutionary war, be, and the same hereby is, referred, along with all the papers and official documents belonging thereto, to the Court of Claims, with full jurisdiction to adjust and settle the same; and in making such adjustment and settlement, the said court *shall be governed* by the *rules* and *regulations* heretofore adopted by the United States in the settlement of like cases, giving proper consideration to official acts, if any have heretofore been had in connection with this claim, and without regard to the statutes of limitation."

The Court of Claims allowed the claim with interest thereon from the time it accrued, and, among other facts, found that—

"No rules and regulations have heretofore been adopted by the United States in the settlement of like cases except such as may be inferred from the policy of Congress when passing private acts for the relief of various persons. When passing such private acts, Congress has allowed interest upon the claim up to the time that the relief was granted."

The Attorney-General appealed from this judgment, awarding interest, but the decision of the court below was affirmed by the Supreme Court at the October term, 1875. (See 91 U. S. Rep., p. 443 *et seq.*) In delivering the opinion of the Supreme Court, Mr. Justice Miller says:

"It has been the general rule of the officers of Government, in adjusting and allowing *unliquidated* and *disputed* claims against the United States, to refuse to give interest. That this rule is sometimes at variance with that which governs the acts of private citizens in a court of justice would not authorize us to depart from it in this case. The rule, however, is not uniform ; and especially is it not so in regard to claims allowed by special acts of Congress, or referred by such acts to some Department or officer for settlement."

This was said in reference to unliquidated and unadjusted claims. Where the Government, by and through the fraud of its agents, gets possession and withholds from the rightful owner an ascertained, fixed, and certain amount, the claim for interest certainly stands upon higher equitable grounds than in the cases cited. The finding by the Court of Claims that the policy of the Government, as shown by the general rule pursued by Congress in passing acts for the relief of private claims, was to allow interest, is supported by the precedents.

Your committee, upon this proposition, beg leave to refer to and adopt this portion of House Report 391, Forty-third Congress, first session, which discusses the subject of *interest* as follows :

THE OBLIGATION TO PAY INTEREST ON THE AMOUNT AWARDED THE CHOCTAW NATION.

Your committee have given this question a most careful examination, and are obliged to admit and declare that the United States can not, in equity and justice, nor without national dishonor, refuse to pay interest upon the moneys so long withheld from the Choctaw Nation. Some of the reasons which force us to this conclusion are as follows :

1. The United States acquired the lands of the Choctaw Nation on account of which the said award was made on the 27th day of September, 1830, and it has held them for the benefit of its citizens ever since.

2. The United States had in its Treasury, many years prior to the first day of January, 1859, the proceeds resulting from the sale of the said lands, and have enjoyed the use of such moneys from that time until now.

3. The award in favor of the Choctaw Nation was an award under a treaty, and made by a tribunal whose adjudication was final and conclusive (Comegys *v.* Vasse, 1 Peters, 193).

4. The obligations of the United States, under its treaties with Indian nations, have been declared to be equally sacred with those made by treaties with foreign nations. (Worcester *v.* The State of Georgia, 6 Peters, 582.) And such treaties, Mr. Justice Miller declares, are to be construed liberally (The Kansas Indians, 5 Wall., 737-760).

5. The engagements and obligations of a treaty are to be interpreted in accordance with the principles of the public law, and not in accordance with any municipal code or executive regulation. No statement of this proposition can equal the clearness or force with which Mr. Webster declares it in his opinion on the Florida claims, attached to the report in the case of Letitia Humphreys (Senate report No. 93,

first session, Thirty-sixth Congress, page 16). Speaking of the obligation of a treaty, he said:

"A treaty is the supreme law of the land. It can neither be limited nor restrained nor modified nor altered. It stands on the ground of national contract, and is declared by the Constitution to be the supreme law of the land, and this gives it a character higher than any act of ordinary legislation. It enjoys an immunity from the operation and effect of all such legislation.

"A second general proposition, equally certain and well established, is that the terms and the language used in a treaty are always to be interpreted according to the law of nations, and not according to any municipal code. This rule is of universal application. When two nations speak to each other they use the language of nations. Their intercourse is regulated, and their mutual agreements and obligations are to be interpreted by that code only which we usually denominate the public law of the world. This public law is not one thing at Rome, another at London, and a third at Washington. It is the same in all civilized States; everywhere speaking with the same voice and the same authority."

Again, in the same opinion, Mr. Webster used the following language:

"We are construing a treaty, a solemn compact between nations. This compact between nations, this treaty, is to be construed and interpreted throughout its whole length and breadth, in its general provisions and in all its details, in every phrase, sentence, word, and syllable in it, by the settled rules of the law of nations. No municipal code can touch it, no local municipal law affect it, no practice of administrative department come near it. Over all its terms, over all its doubts, over all its ambiguities, if it had any, the law of nations 'sits arbitress.'"

6. By the principles of the public law interest is always allowed as indemnity for the delay of payment of an ascertained and fixed demand. There is no conflict of authority upon this question among the writers on public law.

This rule is laid down by Rutherford in these terms:

"In estimating the damages which any one has sustained, when such things as he has a perfect right to are unjustly taken from him, or WITHHOLDEN, or intercepted, we are to consider not only the value of the thing itself, but the value likewise of the fruits or profits that might have arisen from it. He who is the owner of the thing is likewise the owner of the fruits or profits. So that it is as properly a damage to be deprived of them as it is to be deprived of the thing itself" (Rutherford's Institutes, Book I, chap. 17, sec. 5).

In laying down the rule for the satisfaction of injuries in the case of reprisals, in making which the strictest caution is enjoined not to transcend the clearest rules of justice, Mr. Wheaton, in his work on the law of nations, says:

"If a nation has taken possession of that which belongs to another, IF IT REFUSES TO PAY A DEBT, to repair an injury, or to give adequate satisfaction for it, the latter may seize something of the former and apply it to his or its advantage till it obtains payment of what is due, together with INTEREST and damages" (Wheaton on International Law, p. 341).

A great writer, Domat, thus states the law of reason and justice on this point:

"It is a natural consequence of the general engagement to do wrong to no one that they who cause any damages by failing in the performance of that engagement are obliged to repair the damage which they have done. Of what nature soever the damage may be, and from what cause soever it may proceed, he who is answerable for it ought to repair it by an *amende* proportionable either to his fault, or to his offense, or other cause on his part, and to the loss which has happened thereby" (Domat, Part I, Book III, Tit. V., 1900, 1903.)

"Interest," is, in reality, in justice, in reason, and in law, too, a part of the debt due. It includes, in Pothier's words, the loss which one has suffered, and the gain which he has failed to make. The Roman law defines it as "quantum mea interfuit; id est, quantum mihi abest, quantumque lucrari potui." The two elements of it were termed "lucrum cessans et damnum emergens." The payment of both is necessary to a complete indemnity.

Interest, Domat says, is the reparation or satisfaction which he who owes a sum of money is bound to make to his creditor for the damage which he does him by not paying him the money he owes him.

It is because of the universal recognition of the justice of paying, for the retention of moneys indisputably due and payable immediately, a rate of interest considered to be a fair equivalent for the loss of its use, that judgments for money everywhere bear interest. The creditor is deprived of this profit, and the debtor has it. What greater wrong could the law permit than that the debtor should be at liberty indefinitely to delay payment, and, during the delay, have the use of the creditor's moneys for nothing? They are none the less the creditor's moneys because the debtor wrongfully withholds them. *He holds them, in reality and essentially, in trust; and a trustee is always bound to pay interest upon moneys so held.*

In closing these citations from the public law, the language of Chancellor Kent seems eminently appropriate. He says: "In cases where the principal jurists agree, the presumption will be very great in favor of the solidity of their maxims, and no *civilized nation that does not arrogantly set all ordinary law and justice at defiance will venture to disregard the uniform sense of established writers on international law.*"

7. The *practice* of the United States in discharging obligations resulting from treaty stipulations has always been in accord with these well-established principles. It has exacted the payment of *interest* from other nations in all cases where the obligation to make payment resulted from treaty stipulations, and it has acknowledged that obligation in all cases where a like liability was imposed upon it.

The most important and leading cases which have occurred are those which arose between this country and Great Britain; the first under the treaty of 1794, and the other under the first article of the treaty of Ghent. In the latter case the United States, under the first article of the treaty, claimed compensation for slaves and other property taken away from the country by the British forces at the close of the war in 1815. A difference arose between the two Governments which was submitted to the arbitrament of the Emperor of Russia, who decided that "the United States of America are entitled to a just indemnification from Great Britain for all private property carried away by the British forces." A joint commission was appointed for the purpose of hearing the claims of individuals under this decision. At an early stage of the proceedings the question arose as to whether *interest* was a part of that *"just indemnification"* which the decision of the Emperor of Russia contemplated. The British commissioner denied the obligation to pay interest. The American commissioner, Langdon Cheves, insisted upon its allowance, and in the course of his argument upon this question said:

'Indemnification means a re-imbursement of a loss sustained. If the property taken away on the 17th of February, 1815, were returned now uninjured it would not re-imburse the loss sustained by the taking away and consequent detention; it would not be an indemnification. The claimant would still be unindemnified for the loss of the use of his property for ten years, which, considered as money, is nearly equivalent to the original value of the principal thing."

Again he says:

"If interest be an incident usually attendant on the delay of payment of debts, damages are equally an incident attendant on the withholding an article of property."

In consequence of this disagreement the commission was broken up, but the claims were subsequently compromised by the payment of $1,204,960, instead of $1,250,000, as claimed by Mr. Cheves; and of the sum paid by Great Britain $418,000 was expressly for interest.

An earlier case, in which this principle of interest was involved, arose under the treaty of 1794, between the United States and Great Britain, in which there was a stipulation on the part of the British Government in relation to certain losses and damages sustained by American merchants and other citizens by reason of the illegal or irregular capture of their vessels or other property by British cruisers; and the seventh article provided in substance that "full and complete compensation for the same will be made by the British Government to the said claimants."

A joint commission was instituted under this treaty, which sat in London, and by which these claims were adjudicated. Mr. Pinckney and Mr. Gore were commissioners on the part of the United States, and Dr. Nicholl and Dr. Swabey on the part of Great Britain; and it is believed that in all instances this commission allowed interest as a part of the damage. In the case of *The Betsy*, one of the cases which came before the board, Dr. Nicholl stated the rule of compensation as follows:—

To re-imburse the claimants the original cost of their property and all the expenses they have actually incurred, together with interest on the whole amount, would, I think, be a just and adequate compensation. This, I believe, is the measure of compensation usually made by all belligerent nations, and accepted by all neutral nations, for losses, costs, and damages occasioned by illegal captures (Vide Wheaton's Life of Pinckney, page 198; also 265, note, and page 371).

By a reference to the American State Papers, Foreign Relations, vol. 2, pages 119, 120, it will be seen by a report of the Secretary of State of the 16th February, 1798, laid before the House of Representatives, that interest was awarded and paid on such of these claims as had been submitted to the award of Sir William Scott and Sir John Nicholl, as it was in all cases by the board of commissioners. In consequence of some difference of opinion between the members of this commission their proceedings were suspended until 1802, when a convention was concluded between the two Governments, and the commission re-assembled, and then a question arose as to the allowance of interest on the claims during the suspension. This the American commissioners claimed, and though it was at first resisted by the British commissioners, yet it was finally yielded, and interest was allowed and paid (See Mr. King's three letters to the Secretary of State, of 25th of March, 1803, 23d April, 1803, and 30th April, 1803, American State Papers, Foreign Relations, vol. 2, pages 387 and 388).

Another case in which this principle was involved arose under the treaty of the 27th October, 1795, with Spain; by the twenty-first article of which, "in order to terminate all differences on account of the losses sustained by citizens of the United States in consequence of their vessels and cargoes having been taken by the subjects of His Catholic Majesty during the late war between Spain and France, it is agreed that all such cases shall be referred to the final decision of commissioners, to be appointed in the following manner," etc. The commissioners were to be chosen, one by the United States, one by Spain, and the two were to choose a third, and the award of the commissioners, or any two of them, was to be final, and the Spanish Government to pay the amount in specie.

This commission awarded interest as part of the damages (See American State Papers, vol. 2, Foreign Relation, page 283). So in the case of claims of American citizens against Brazil, settled by Mr. Tudor, United States minister, interest was claimed and allowed. (See Ex. Doc., first session Twenty-fifth Congress, House Reps., Doc. 32, page 249.)

Again, in the convention with Mexico of the 11th of April, 1839, by which provision was made by Mexico for the payment of claims of American citizens for injuries to persons and property by the Mexican authorities, a mixed commission was provided for, and this commission allowed interest in all cases. (House Ex. Doc. 291, 27th Congress, 2d session.

So also under the treaty with Mexico of February 2, 1848, the board of commissioners for the adjustment of claims under that treaty allowed interest in all cases from the origin of the claim until the day when the commission expired.

So also under the convention with Colombia, concluded February 10, 1864, the commission for the adjudication of claims under that treaty allowed interest in all cases as a part of the indemnity.

So under the recent convention with Venezuela, the United States exacted interest upon the awards of the commission, from the date of the adjournment of the commission until the payment of the awards.

The mixed American and Mexican Commission, now in session here, allow interest in all cases from the origin of the claim, and the awards are payable with interest.

Other cases might be shown in which the United States or their authorized diplomatic agents have claimed interest in such cases, or where it has been paid in whole or in part. (See Mr. Russell's letter to the Count de Engstein of October 5, 1818, American State Papers, vol. 4, p. 639, and proceedings under the convention with the Two Sicilies of October, 1835, Elliott's Dip. Code, p. 625.)

It can hardly be necessary to pursue these precedents further. They sufficiently and clearly show the practice of this Government with foreign nations, or with claimants under treaties.

8. The practice of the United States in its dealings with the various Indian tribes or nations has been in harmony with these principles.

In all cases where money belonging to Indian nations has been retained by the United States it has been so invested as to produce *interest*, for the benefit of the nation to which it belongs; and such interest is *annually* paid to the nation who may be entitled to receive it.

9. The United States in adjusting the claim of the Cherokee Nation for a balance due as purchase money upon lands ceded by that nation to the United States in 1858, allowed interest upon the balance due then, being $189,422.76, until the same was paid.

The question was submitted to the Senate of the United States, as to whether interest should be allowed them. The Senate Committee on Indian Affairs, in their report upon this subject, used the following language:

"By the treaty of August, 1846, it was referred to the Senate to decide, and that decision to be final, whether the Cherokees shall receive interest on the sums found due them from a misapplication of their funds to purposes with which they were not chargeable, and on account of which improper charges the money has been withheld from them. It has been the uniform practice of this Government to pay and demand interest in all transactions with foreign governments, which the Indian tribes have always been said to be, both by the Supreme Court and all other branches of our Government, in all matters of treaty or contract. The Indians, relying upon the prompt payment of their dues, have in many cases contracted debts upon the faith of it, upon which they have paid, or are liable to pay, interest. If, therefore, they do not now receive interest on their money so long withheld from them they will in effect have received nothing." (Senate Report No. 176, first session Thirty-first Congress, p. 78).

10th. That upon an examination of the precedents where Congress had passed acts for the relief of private citizens, it will be found that in almost every case, Congress has directed the payment of interest, where the United States had withheld a sum of money which had been decided by competent authority to be due, or where the amount due was ascertained, fixed, and certain.

no

The following precedents illustrate and enforce the correctness of this assertion, and sustain this proposition:

1. An act approved January 14, 1793, provided that lawful interest from the 16th of May, 1776, shall be allowed on the sum of $200 ordered to be paid to Return J. Meigs, and the legal representatives of Christopher Greene, deceased, by a resolve of the United States, in Congress assembled, on the 28th of September, 1785 (6 Stats. at Large, p. 11).

2. An act approved May 31, 1794, providing for a settlement with Arthur St. Clair, for expenses while going from New York to Fort Pitt and till his return, and for services in the business of Indian treaties, and "allowed interest on the balance found to be due him" (6 Stats. at Large, p. 46).

3. An act approved February 27, 1795, authorized the officers of the Treasury to issue and deliver to Angus McLean, or his duly authorized attorney, certificates for the amount of $254.43, bearing interest at 6 per cent., from the first of July, 1783, being for his services in the Corps of Sappers and Miners during the late war (6 Stats. at Large, p. 20).

4. An act approved January 23, 1798, directing the Secretary of the Treasury to pay General Kosciusko an interest at the rate of six per cent. per annum on the sum of $12,280.54, the amount of a certificate due to him from the United States from the 1st of January, 1793, to the 31st of December, 1797 (6 Stats. at Large, p. 32).

5. An act approved May 3, 1802, provided that there be paid Fulwar Skipwith the sum of $4,550, advanced by him for the use of the United States, with interest at the rate of six per cent. per annum from the first of November, 1795, at which time the advance was made (6 Stats at Large, p. 48).

6. An act for the relief of John Coles, approved January 14, 1804, authorized the proper accounting officers of the Treasury to liquidate the claim of John Coles, owner of the ship *Grand Turk*, heretofore employed in the service of the United States, for the detention of said ship at Gibraltar from the 10th of May to the 4th of July, 1801, inclusive, and that he be allowed demurrage at the rate stipulated in the charter-party, together with the interest thereon (6 Stat. at L., p. 50).

7. An act approved March 3, 1807, provided for the settlement of the accounts of Oliver Pollock, formerly commercial agent for the United States at New Orleans, allowing him certain sums and commissions, with interest until paid (6 Stat. at L., p. 65.)

8. An act for the relief of Stephen Sayre, approved March 3, 1807, provided that the accounting officers of the Treasury be authorized to settle the account of Stephen Sayre, as secretary of legation at the court of Berlin, in the year 1777, with interest on the whole sum until paid (6. Stat. at L., p. 65).

9. An act approved April 25, 1810, directing the accounting officers of the Treasury to settle the account of Moses Young, as secretary of legation to Holland in 1780, and providing that after the deduction of certain moneys paid him, the balance, with interest thereon, should be paid (6 Stat. at L., p. 89).

10. An act approved May 1, 1810, for the relief of P. C. L'Enfant, directed the Secretary of the Treasury to pay to him the sum of six hundred and sixty-six dollars, with legal interest thereon from March 1, 1792, as a compensation for his services in laying out the plan of the city of Washington (6 Stat. at L., p. 92).

11. An act approved January 10, 1812, provided that there be paid to John Burnham the sum of $126.72, and the interest on the same since the 30th of May, 1796, which, in addition to the sum allowed him by the act of that date, is to be considered a re-imbursement of the money advanced by him for his ransom from captivity in Algiers (6 Stat. at L., p. 101).

12. An act approved July 1, 1812, for the relief of Anna Young, required the War Department to settle the account of Col. John Durkee, deceased, and to allow said Anna Young, his sole heiress and representative, said seven years' half-pay, and interest thereon (6 Stat. at L., p. 110).

13. An act approved February 25, 1813, provided that there be paid to John Dixon the sum of $320.84 with 6 per cent. per annum interest thereon from the first of January, 1785, "being the amount of a final-settlement certificate, No. 596, issued by Andrew Dunscomb, late commissioner of accounts for the State of Virginia, on the 22d of December, 1786, to Lucy Dixon, who transferred the same to John Dixon" (6 Stat. at L., p 117).

14. An act approved February 25, 1813, required the accounting officers of the Treasury to settle the account of John Murray, representative of Dr. Henry Murray, and that he be allowed the amount of three loan certificates for $1,000, with interest from the 20th of March, 1782, issued in the name of said Murray, signed Francis Hopkinson, treasurer of loans (6 Stat. at L., p. 117).

15. An act approved March 3, 1813, directed the accounting officers of the Treasury to settle the accounts of Samuel Lapsley, deceased, and that they be allowed the amount of two final-settlement certificates, No. 78,446, for one thousand dollars, and No. 78,447, for one thousand three hundred dollars, and interest from the 22d day of

March, 1783, issued in the name of Samuel Lapsley, by the commissioner of army accounts for the United States on the 1st day of July, 1784 (6 Stat. at L., p 119).

16. An act approved April 13, 1814, directed the officers of the Treasury to settle the account of Joseph Brevard, and that he be allowed the amount of a final-settlement certificate for $183.23, dated February 1, 1785, and bearing interest from the 1st of January, 1783, issued to said Brevard by John Pierce, commissioner for settling army accounts (6 Stat. at L., p. 134).

17. An act approved April 18, 1814, directed the receiver of public moneys at Cincinnati to pay the full amount of moneys, with interest, paid by Dennis Clark, in discharge of the purchase money for a certain fractional section of land purchased by said Clark (6 Stat. at L., 141).

18. An act for the relief of William Arnold, approved February 2, 1815, allowed interest on the sum of six hundred dollars due him from January 1, 1783 (6 Stat. at L., 146).

19. An act approved April 26, 1816, directing the accounting officers of the Treasury to pay to Joseph Wheaton the sum of eight hundred and thirty-six dollars and forty-two cents, on account of interest due him from the United States upon sixteen hundred dollars and eighty-four cents, from April 1, 1807, to December 21, 1815, pursuant to the award of George Youngs and Elias B. Caldwell, in a controversy between the United States and the said Joseph Wheaton (6 Stat. at L., 166).

20. An act approved April 26, 1816, authorized the liquidation and settlement of the claim of the heirs of Alexander Roxburgh, arising on a final-settlement certificate issued on the 18th of August, 1878, for $480.87, by John Pierce, commissioner for settling Army accounts, bearing interest from the 1st of January, 1782 (6 Stat. at L., 167).

21. An act approved April 14, 1818, authorized the accounting officers of the Treasury Department "to review the settlement of the account of John Thompson," made under the authority of an act approved the 11th of May, 1812, and "to allow the said John Thompson interest at six per cent. per annum from the 4th of March, 1787, to the 20th of May, 1812, on the sum which was found due to him, and paid under the act aforesaid" (6 Stat. at L., 208).

22. An act approved May 11, 1820, directed the proper officers of the Treasury to pay to Samuel B. Beall the amount of two final-settlement certificates issued to him on the 1st of February, 1785, for his services as a lieutenant in the Army of the United States during the Revolutionary war, together with interest on the said certificates, at the rate of 6 per cent. per annum, from the time they bore interest, respectively, which said certificates were lost by the said Beall, and remain yet outstanding and unpaid (6 Laws of U. S., 510 ; 6 Stat. at L., 249).

23. An act approved May 15, 1820, required that there be paid to Thomas Leiper the specie value of four loan-office certificates, issued to him by the commissioner of loans for the State of Pennsylvania, on the 27th of February, 1779, for one thousand dollars each ; and also the specie value of two loan-certificates, issued to him by the said commissioner on the 2d day of March, 1779, for one thousand dollars each, with interest at six per cent. annually (6 Stat. at L., 252).

24. An act approved May 7, 1822, provided that there be paid to the legal representatives of John Guthry, deceased, the sum of $123.30, being the amount of a final-settlement certificate, with interest at the rate of six per cent. per annum from the 1st day of January, 1788 (6 Stat. at L., 269).

25. An act for the relief of the legal representatives of James McClung, approved March 3, 1823, allowed interest on the amount due at the rate of six per cent. per annum from January 1, 1788 (6 Stat. at L., 284).

26. An act approved March 3, 1823, for the relief of Daniel Seward, allowed interest to him for money paid to the United States for land to which the title failed, at the rate of six per cent. per annum from January 29, 1814 (6 Stat. at L., 286).

27. An act approved May 5, 1824, directed the Secretary of the Treasury to pay to Amasa Stetson the sum of $6,215, "being for interest on moneys advanced by him for the use of the United States, and on warrants issued in his favor, in the years 1814 and 1815, for his services in the Ordnance and Quartermaster's Department for superintending the making of Army clothing and for issuing the public supplies" (6 Stat. at L., 298).

28. An act approved March 3, 1824, directed the proper accounting officers of the Treasury to settle and adjust the claims of Stephen Arnold, David and George Jenks, for the manufacture of three thousand nine hundred and twenty-five muskets, with interest thereon from the 26th day of October, 1813 (6 Stat. at L., 331).

29. An act approved May 20, 1826, directed the proper accounting officers of the Treasury to settle and adjust the claim of John Stemman and others for the manufacture of four thousand one hundred stand of arms, and to allow interest on the amount due from October 26, 1813 (6 Stat. at L., 345).

30. An act approved May 20, 1826, for the relief of Ann D. Taylor, directed the payment to her of the sum of three hundred and fifty-four dollars and fifteen cents, with

interest thereon at a rate of six per cent. per annum from December 30, 1786, until paid (6 Stat. at L., 351).

31. An act approved March 3, 1827, provided that the proper accounting officers of the Treasury were authorized to pay B. J. V. Valkenborg the sum of $597.24, "being the amount of fourteen indents of interest, with interest thereon from the 1st of January, 1791, to the 31st of December, 1826" (6 Stat. at L., 365).

In this case the United States paid interest on interest.

32. An act approved May 19, 1828, provided that there be paid to the legal representatives of Patience Gordon the specie value of a certificate issued in the name of Patience Gordon by the commissioner of loans for the State of Pennsylvania, on the 7th of April, 1778, with interest at the rate of 6 per cent. per annum from the 1st day of January, 1783 (7 Stat. at L., p. 378).

33. An act approved May 29, 1830, required the Treasury Department "to settle the accounts of Benjamin Wells, as deputy commissary of issues at the magazine at Monster Mills, in Pennsylvania, under John Irvin, deputy commissary-general of the Army of the United States, in said State, in the Revolutionary war"; and that "they credit him with the sum of $574.04, as payable February 9, 1779, and $326.67, payable July 20, 1780, in the same manner, and with such interest, as if these sums, with their interest from the times respectively as aforesaid, had been subscribed to the loan of the United States (6 Stats. at Large, 447).

34. An act approved May 19, 1832, for the relief of Richard G. Morris, provided for the payment to him of two certificates issued to him by Timothy Pickering, quartermaster-general, with interest thereon from the 1st of September, 1781 (6 Stats. at Large, 486).

35. An act approved July 4, 1832, for the relief of Aaron Snow, a Revolutionary soldier, provided for the payment to him of two certificates issued by John Pierce, late commissioner of Army accounts, and dated in 1784, with interest thereon (6 Stats. at Large, 503).

36. An act approved July 4, 1832, provided for the payment to W. P. Gibbs of a final-settlement certificate dated January 30, 1784, with interest at 6 per cent. from the 1st of January, 1783, up to the passage of the act. This act went behind the final certificate and provided for the payment of interest anterior to its date (6 Stats. at Large, 504).

37. An act approved July 14, 1832, directed the payment to the heirs of Ebenezer L. Warren of certain sums of money illegally demanded and received from the United States from the said Warren as one of the sureties of Daniel Evans, former collector of direct taxes, with interest thereon at the rate of six per cent. per annum from September 9, 1820 (6 Stats. at Large, 373).

38. An act for the relief of Hartwell Vick, approved July 14, 1832, directed the accounting officers of the Treasury to refund to the said Vick the money paid by him to the United States for a certain tract of land which was found not to be property of the United States, with interest thereon at the rate of six per centum per annum, from the 23d day of May, 1818 (6 Stats. at Large, 523).

39. An act approved June 18, 1834, for the relief of Martha Bailey and others, directed the Secretary of the Treasury to pay to the parties therein named the sum of four thousand eight hundred and thirty-seven dollars and sixty-one cents, being the amount of interest upon the sum of two hundred thousand dollars, part of a balance due from the United States to Elbert Anderson on the 26th day of October, 1814; also the further sum of nine thousand five hundred and ninety-five dollars and thirty-six cents, being the amount of interest accruing from the deferred payment of warrants issued for balances due from the United States to said Anderson from the date of such warrants until the payment thereof; also the further sum of two thousand and eighteen dollars and fifty cents admitted to be due from the United States to the said Anderson by a decision of the Second Comptroller, with interest on the sum last mentioned from the period of such decision until paid (6 Stats. at Large, 562).

40. An act approved June 10, 1834, directed the Secretary of the Treasury to pay balance of damages recovered against William C. H. Waddell, United States marshal for the southern district of New York, for the illegal seizure of a certain importation of brandy, on behalf of the United States, with legal interest on the amount of said judgment from the time the same was paid by the said Waddell (6 Stats. at Large, 594).

41. An act approved February 17, 1836, directed the payment of the sum therein named to Marinus W. Gilbert, being the interest on money advanced by him to pay off troops in the service of the United States, and not repaid when demanded (6 Stats. at Large, 622).

42. An act approved February 17, 1836, for the relief of the executor of Charles Wilkins, directed the Secretary of the Treasury to settle the claim of the said executor, for interest on a liquidated demand in favor of Jonathan Taylor, James Morrison, and Charles Wilkins, who were lessees of the United States of the salt works in the State of Illinois (6 Stats. at Large, 626).

43. An act approved July 2, 1836, for the relief of the legal representatives of David Caldwell, directed the proper accounting officers of the Treasury to settle the claim of the said David Caldwell for fees and allowances, certified by the circuit court of the United States for the eastern district of Pennsylvania, for official services to the United States, and to pay on that account the sum of four hundred and ninety-six dollars and thirty-eight cents, with interest thereon at the rate of six per centum from the 25th day of November, 1830, till paid (6 Stats. at Large, 664).

44. An act approved July 2, 1836, provided that there be paid Don Carlos Delossus interest at the rate of six per centum per annum on three hundred and thirty-three dollars, being the amount allowed him under the act of July 14, 1832, for his relief, on account of moneys taken from him at the capture of Baton Rouge, La., on the 23d day of September, 1810, being the interest to be allowed from the said 23d day of September, 1810, to the 14th day of July, 1832 (6 Stats. at Large, 672).

In this case the interest was directed to be paid four years after the principal had been satisfied and discharged.

45. An act approved July 7, 1838, provided that the proper officers of the Treasury be directed to settle the accounts of Richard Harrison, formerly consular agent of the United States at Cadiz, in Spain, and to allow him, among other items, the interest on the money advanced, under agreement with the minister of the United States, in Spain, for the relief of destitute and distressed seamen, and for their passages to the United States, from the time the advances, respectively, were made to the time at which the said advances were re-imbursed (6 Stats. at Large, 734).

46. An act approved August 11, 1842, directed the Secretary of the Treasury to pay to John Johnson the sum of seven hundred and fifty-six dollars and eighty-two cents, being the amount received from the said Johnson upon a judgment against him in favor of the United States, together with the interest thereon from the time of such payment (6 Stats. at Large, 856).

47. An act approved August 3, 1846, authorized the Secretary of the Treasury to pay to Abraham Horbach the sum of five thousand dollars, with lawful interest from the 1st of January, 1836, being the amount of a draft drawn by James Reeside on the Post-Office Department, dated April 18, 1835, payable on the 1st of January, 1836, and accepted by the treasurer of the Post-Office Department, which said draft was indorsed by said Abraham Horbach, at the instance of the said Reeside, and the amount drawn from the Bank of Philadelphia, and, at maturity, said draft was protested for non-payment, and said Horbach became liable to pay, and, in consequence of his indorsement, did pay the full amount of said draft (9 Stats. at Large, 677).

48. An act approved February 5, 1859, authorized the Secretary of War to pay to Thomas Laurent, as surviving partner, the sum of $15,000, with interest at the rate of six per cent. yearly, from the 11th of November, 1847, it being the amount paid by the firm on that day to Major-General Winfield Scott, in the City of Mexico, for the purchase of a house in said city, out of the possession of which they were since ousted by the Mexican authorities (11 Stats. at Large, 558).

49. An act approved March 2, 1847, directed the Secretary of the Treasury to pay the balance due to the Bank of Metropolis for moneys due upon the settlement of the account of the bank with the United States, with interest thereon from the 6th day of March, 1838 (9 Stats. at Large, 689).

50. An act approved July 20, 1852, directed the payment to the legal representative of James C. Watson, late of the State of Georgia, the sum of fourteen thousand six hundred dollars, with interest at the rate of six per cent. per annum, from the 8th day of May, 1838, till paid, being the amount paid by him, under the sanction of the Indian agent, to certain Creek warriors, for slaves captured by said warriors while they were in the service of the United States against the Seminole Indians in Florida (10 Stats. at Large, 734).

51. An act approved July 29, 1854, directed the Secretary of the Treasury to pay to John C. Fremont one hundred and eighty-three thousand eight hundred and twenty-five dollars, with interest thereon from the 1st day of June, 1851, at the rate of ten per cent. per annum, in full for his account for beef delivered to Commissioner Barbour, for the use of the Indians in California, in 1851 and 1852 (10 Stats. at Large, 804).

52. An act approved July 8, 1870, directed the Secretary of the Treasury to make proper payments to carry into effect the decree of the district court of the United States for the district of Louisiana, bearing date the *fourth* of June, 1867, in the case of the British brig *Volant* and her cargo; and also another decree of the same court, bearing date the *eleventh* of June, in the same year, in the case of the British bark *Science*, and cargo, vessels illegally seized by a cruiser of the United States, such payments to be made as follows, viz: To the several persons named in such decrees, or the legal representatives, the several sums awarded to them respectively, *with interest to each person from the date of the decree under which he receives payment* (16 Stats. at Large, 650).

53. An act approved July 8, 1870, directed the Secretary to make the proper pay-

ments to carry into effect the decree of the district court of the United States for the district of Louisiana, bearing date July 13, 1867, in the case of the British brig *Dashing Wave*, and her cargo, illegally seized by a cruiser of the United States, which decree was made in pursuance of the decision of the Supreme Court, *such payments to be made with interest from the date of the decree* (16 Stats. at Large, 651).

An examination of these cases will show that, subsequent to the seizure of these several vessels, they were each sold by the United States marshal for the district of Louisiana as prize, and the proceeds of such sales deposited by him in the First National Bank of New Orleans. The bank, while the proceeds of these sales were on deposit there, became insolvent. The seizures were held illegal, and the vessels not subject to capture as prize. But the proceeds of the sales of these vessels and their cargoes could not be restored to the owners in accordance of the decrees of the district court, because the funds had been lost by the insolvency of the bank. In these cases, therefore, Congress provided indemnity for losses resulting from the acts of its agents, and made the indemnity complete by providing for the payment of interest.

Your committee have directed attention to these numerous precedents for the purpose of exposing the utter want of foundation of the often repeated assumption that "the Government never pays interest." It will readily be admitted that there is no statute law to sustain this position. The idea has grown up from the custom and usage of the accounting officers and Departments refusing to allow interest generally in their accounts with disbursing officers, and in the settlement of unliquidated domestic claims arising out of dealings with the Government. It will hardly be pretended, however, that this custom or usage is so "reasonable," well-known, and "certain," as to give it the force and effect of law, and to override and trample under foot the law of nations and also the well-settled practice of the Government itself in its intercourse with other nations.

11th. Interest was allowed and paid to the State of Massachusetts because the United States delayed the payment of the principal for twenty-two years after the amount due had been ascertained and determined. The amount appropriated to pay this interest was $678,362.41, more than the original principal (16 Stats. at Large 198).

Mr. Sumner, in his report upon the memorial introduced for that purpose, discussing this question of interest, said:

"It is urged that the payment of this interest would establish a bad precedent. If the claim is just, the precedent of paying it is one of which our Government should wish to establish. Honesty and justice are not precedents of which either Government or individuals should be afraid" (Senate Report 4, Forty-first Congress, first session, p. 10).

14th. Interest has always been allowed to the several States for advances made to the United States for military purposes.

The claims of the several States for advances during the Revolutionary war were adjusted, and settled under the provision of the acts of Congress of August 5, 1790, and of May 31, 1794. By these acts interest was allowed to the States, whether they had advanced money on hand in their treasuries or obtained by loans.

In respect to the advances of States during the war of 1812–'15, a more restricted rule was adopted, viz : That States should be allowed interest only so far as they had themselves paid it by borrowing, or had lost it by the sale of interest-bearing funds.

Interest, according to this rule, has been paid to all the States which made advances during the war of 1812–'15, with the exception of Massachusetts. Here are the cases :

Virginia, U. S. Stats. at Large, vol. 4, p. 161.
Delaware, U. S. Stats. at Large, vol. 4, p. 175.
New York, U. S. Stats. at Large, vol. 4, p. 192.
Pennsylvania, U. S. Stats. at Large, vol. 4, p. 241.
South Carolina, U. S. Stats. at Large, vol. 4, p. 499.
In Indian and other wars the same rule has been observed, as in the following cases :

Alabama, U. S. Stats. at Large, vol. 9, p. 344.
Georgia, U. S. Stats. at Large, vol. 9, p. 626.
Washington Territory, U. S. Stats. at Large, vol. 11, p. 429.
New Hampshire, U. S. Stats. at Large, vol. 10, p. 1.
13th. The Senate Committee on Indian Affairs, in the report to which reference has heretofore been made, speaking of this award and of the obligation of the United States to pay interest upon the balance remaining due and unpaid thereon, used the following language :

"Your committee are of opinion that this sum should be paid them with accrued interest from the date of said award, deducting therefrom $250,000, paid to them in money, as directed by the act of March 2, 1861 ; and, therefore, find no sufficient reason for further delay in carrying into effect that provision of the aforenamed act, and the act of March 3, 1871, by the delivery of the bonds therein described, with accrued interest from the date of the act of March 8, 1861.

" Your committee have discussed this question with an anxious desire to come to such a conclusion in regard to it as would do no injustice to that Indian nation whose rights are involved here, nor establish such a precedent as would be inconsistent with the practice or duty of the United States in such cases. Therefore, your committee have considered it not only by the light of those principles of the public law—always in harmony with the highest demands of the most perfect justice—but also in the light of those numerous precedents which this Government in its action in litigation has furnished for our guidance. Your committee can not believe that the payment of interest on the moneys awarded by the Senate to the Choctaw Nation would either violate any principle of law or establish any precedent which the United States would not wish to follow in any similar case, and your committee can not believe that the United States are prepared to repudiate these principles, or to admit that because their obligation is held by a weak and powerless Indian nation it is any the less sacred or binding than if held by a nation able to enforce its payment and secure complete indemnity under it. Could the United States escape the payment of *interest* to Great Britain, if it should refuse or neglect, after the same became due, to pay the amount awarded in favor of British subjects by the recent joint commission which sat here? Could we delay payment of the amount awarded by that commission for fifteen years, and then escape by merely paying the principal? The Choctaw Nation asks the same measure of justice which we *must* accord to Great Britain; and your committee can not deny that demand unless they shall ignore and set aside those principles of the public law which it is of the utmost importance to the United States to always maintain inviolate.

"Your committee are not unmindful that the amount due the Choctaw Nation under the award of the Senate is large. They are not unmindful, either, that the discredit of refusing payment is increased in proportion to the amount withheld and the time during which refusal has been continued."

Few, if any, of the foregoing cases presented as strong and meritorious grounds for the allowance of interest as the claim now under consideration. Following these precedents, and for the reasons above set forth, the committee deem the present a proper case for the payment of interest on the sum converted ($371,025) from date of conversion to date of payment. This interest they fix at the rate of four and a half (4½) per centum per annum, that being about the average rate paid by the Government between 1867 and 1881, and which it may be fairly assumed was saved or made by it for the use of the funds during the period of detention. On this basis the interest allowed will amount to the sum of $249,039.95.

The committee accordingly recommend that the bill be amended as follows: In line one of section 2 strike out the words "seventy-five" and insert in lieu thereof "forty-nine," and in line second of said second section, after the word "thousand," insert the words "and thirty-nine and ninety-five hundredths." And as thus amended that the bill be passed by the Senate.

In addition to the precedents cited in the foregoing Senate report, the committee refer to the following cases in which interest has been allowed by act of Congress or paid by the Treasury Department:

Case of—	Date of act.	Statutes at Large.	
		Volume.	Page.
Baron de Glaubeck	Sept. 29, 1789	6	1
Captain Markley	Aug. 11, 1790	6	4
Lieutenant Brewster	Aug. 11, 1790	6	4
John Stevens	Aug. 11, 1790	6	4
James Derry	Aug. 11, 1790	6	4
Benjamin Hardison	Aug. 11, 1790	6	4
Widow of General Lord Stirling	Aug. 11, 1790	6	4
Child of Colonel Laurens	Aug. 11, 1790	6	5
Oliver Pollock	Dec. 23, 1791		
Widow of Colonel Roberts	Mar. 27, 1792	6	6
Widow of Captain White	Mar. 27, 1792	6	6
Widow of Colonel Elliott	Mar. 27, 1792	6	6
Widow of Major Wise	Mar. 27, 1792	6	6
Widow of Major Huger	Mar. 27, 1792	6	6
Widow of Lieutenant Bush	Mar. 27, 1792	6	6
Widow of Major Motte	Mar. 27, 1792	6	6
Captain McIntire	Mar. 27, 1792	6	7
Colonel Pannill	Mar. 27, 1792	6	7
General De Haas	Mar. 27, 1792	6	7
Dr. Debevere	Mar. 27, 1792	6	7
Lieutenant King	Mar. 27, 1792	6	7
Sailingmaster Sherman	Mar. 27, 1792	6	7
General Nathaniel Greene	Apr. 27, 1792	6	9

Case of—	Date of act.	Statutes at Large.	
		Volume.	Page.
Colonel Dubois	June 4, 1794	6	16
Moses White	Mar. 2, 1803	6	50
Widow of Thomas Flinn	Mar. 3, 1805	6	57
De Beaumarchais	Apr. 18, 1806		
Thomas Barclay	Apr. 18, 1808	6	72
Mary Rippleyea	Feb. 2, 1815	6	146
John Holkar	Apr. 29, 1816	6	175
Joshua Barney	Mar. 2, 1840	9	700
Nicholas Vreeland	Apr. 5, 1820	6	238
John Crute	May 7, 1822	6	270
Walter S. Chandler	Mar. 3, 1825	6	320
John Crain	Mar. 3, 1825	6	334
Heirs of John W. Baylor and others	May 20, 1826	6	351
Robert Johnson	May 20, 1828	6	392
Benjamin Wells	May 20, 1830	6	447
A. D. Baylor	May 20, 1830	6	437
Charles Yates's executor	May 29, 1830	6	440
Ward & Brothers	May 31, 1830	6	450
Lucian Harper	Mar. 2, 1831	6	457
Heirs of General Hazen	Mar. 3, 1831	6	466
Lieutenant Vawtes	May 25, 1832	6	489
Major Roberts	May 25, 1832	6	490
Lieutenant Hillary	May 25, 1832	6	490
Dr. Carter	May 25, 1832	6	490
Colonel Baylor	May 25, 1832	6	491
Lieutenant Brooke	May 25, 1832	6	491
Ichabod Ward	June 15, 1832	6	490
Dr. Axson	June 15, 1832	6	491
Dr. Knight	June 15, 1832	6	495
John B. Taylor	July 13, 1832	6	507
J. & J. Pettigrew	July 14, 1832		
A. McKnight	July 14, 1832		
Heirs of Colonel Harrison	July 14, 1832		
Lieutenant Jacob	July 14, 1832	6	516
The Union Bank of Florida	Mar. 3, 1849	9	778
William Greer	Mar. 26, 1852	10	731
Gray, McMurdo & Co	Mar. 27, 1854	10	776
John S. Wilson	July 27, 1854	10	701
Charles Cooper & Co	July 27, 1854	10	705
James Dunning	July 27, 1854	10	706
John Frazier and John G. Clendenin	July 29, 1854	10	803
Phineas M. Nightingale, administrator	Aug. 1, 1854	10	808
Thomas H. Baird	Aug. 18, 1856	11	467
The legal representatives of Thomas Gordon	Aug. 23, 1856	11	483
Mary Reeside	Feb. 7, 1857	11	495
Joseph D. Beers	Feb. 10, 1857	11	496
John Hamilton	Mar. 16, 1858	11	527
Rufus Dwinell	June 1, 1858	11	536
Heirs of Richard D. Rowland	June 3, 1858	11	538
Henry Hubbard	Feb. 9, 1859	11	559
Francis Huttman	Apr. 13, 1860	12	837
Nott & Co	Feb. 22, 1869	15	440
British schooner *Flying Scud*	July 7, 1870	16	640
British steamer *Labuan*	July 7, 1870	16	640
James F. Joy	May 25, 1872	17	663
John N. Hall	Mar. 3, 1877	19	542
Executors of Samuel P. Fearou	June 18, 1878	20	576
Manhattan Savings Institution	Dec. 19, 1878	20	580
Commercial Bank of Knoxville	Feb. 28, 1878	20	602
Henry Page	Feb. 18, 1880	21	535
Albert Elsberg, administrator	Aug. 8, 1882	22	726
Robert Stodart Wyld	Jan. 5, 1883	22	752
German National Bank of Louisville	Mar. 3, 1883	22	805
Captain Davenport	July 14, 1832	6	518
Gertrude Gates	July 14, 1832	6	521
John Peck	July 14, 1832	6	524
John Laurens	July 14, 1832	6	514
Colonel Thornton	Feb. 9, 1833	6	533
Son of Alexander Brownlee	Feb. 9, 1833	6	533
Heirs of John Wilson	Feb. 27, 1833	6	537
Riddle, Becktle, Headington & Co	Feb. 27, 1833	6	537
Captain Thomas	Mar. 2, 1833	6	540
Lieutenant Foster	Mar. 2, 1833	6	540
Dr. Lodyard	Mar. 2, 1833	6	542
Col. John Ely	Mar. 2, 1833	6	543
Captain Triplett	Mar. 2, 1833	6	544
Lieutenant Wagnon	Mar. 2, 1833	6	546
William Price	Mar. 2, 1833	6	551
Philip Slaughter	Mar. 2, 1833	6	551
James Barnett	Mar. 2, 1833	6	551
Archibald Watts	Feb. 47, 1833	6	537

Case of—	Date of act.	Statutes at Large.	
		Volume.	Page.
Captain Gibbon	Mar. 2, 1833	3	551
Philip Bush	Mar. 2, 1833	6	540
Eleanor Courts	Mar. 2, 1833	6	542
Dr. John Berrien	June 19, 1834	6	565
The legal representatives of Christian Ish	June 27, 1834	6	570
Joseph Falconer	June 28, 1834	6	574
Samuel Gibbs	June 28, 1834	6	576
Benjamin Bird	June 28, 1834	6	576
Grove Pomeroy	June 28, 1834	6	576
The representatives of General Lord Stirling	June 30, 1834	6	587
John Peck	June 30, 1834	6	582
Capt. George Hurlburt	June 30, 1834	6	589
Alvarez Fisk	Apr. 10, 1840	6	796
Matthew Lyon	July 4, 1840	6	802
John Johnston	Aug. 11, 1842	6	856
Felix St. Vrain	Aug. 3, 1846	9	653
Lewis C. Sartori	Mar. 3, 1847	9	704
The legal representatives of Simon Spaulding	Mar. 3, 1847	9	694

Every fact in the present case has been officially found by the Court of Claims, and that court in delivering judgment (16 Court of Claims Reports, 73) characterized the transaction as "simply a case of a bank being robbed, and of its stolen assets being put into the hands of the cashier of the sub-treasury for a purpose which by no possible view could in law be held to effect a transfer of the bank's right of property in them either to him or to the United States." Demand was immediately made for the return of the money, but it remained in the hands of the Government for fifteen years, and then repayment of the principal was made. So that the United States was able to hold property, which its courts has declared it had no right to hold, until it earned enough at 6 per cent. to pay for it. Surely reparation should be made in such a case. The principle of repaying interest under such circumstances seems to be established, in the language of several distinguished committees of this House, as follows:

"It will be found, upon examination of the precedents where Congress has passed acts for the relief of citizens of the United States, that in almost every case where the Government has withheld a sum of money which had been decided by competent authority to be due, or where the amount due was ascertained, fixed, and definite, Congress has directed the payment of interest, together with the principal. (Report No. 17, Forty-sixth Congress, first session; Report No. 1568, Forty-eighth Congress, first session; Report No. 661, Forty-ninth Congress, first session.)"

For a stronger reason should this be so in the present case, where not only was the amount ascertained, fixed, and definite, but where, also, the creditor relation was not voluntary, but was forced upon the claimants by the United States, who became, therefore, tort debtors.

There is abundant proof to show that at the time the property of the bank was transferred to the sub-treasury of the United States the bank was earning from 8 to 10 per cent. upon its assets, being in a very prosperous condition. The bill calls for the payment of 5 per cent. interest, but the Senate committee have found that 4½ per cent. was about the average rate of interest paid by the Government between 1867 and 1881, and accordingly your committee, recognizing the fact that the Government ought not to pay a higher rate of interest on this claim than they were in the habit of paying to other creditors, recommend that the bill be amended by striking out in lines 1 and 2 of section 2 the words "two hundred and seventy-five thousand dollars," and inserting in lieu thereof the words "two hundred and forty-nine thousand thirty-nine dollars and ninety-five cents," and thus amended, recommend its passage.

[Senate Report No. 183, Forty-ninth Congress, first session.]

The Committee on Military Affairs, to whom was referred the bill (S. 1293 "to authorize the Secretary of the Treasury to settle and pay the claim of the State of Florida on account of expenditures made in suppressing Indian hostilities, and for other purposes," have considered the same and they beg leave to report:

That in the Forty-eighth Congress they had under consideration the same subject, and they reported by bill to the Senate. A report accompanied the bill, and this report, now annexed, is adopted. They recommend the indefinite postponement of bill 1293, and the substitution of a bill hereby reported, that being the bill reported favorably by the committee in the Forty-eighth Congress.

[Senate Report No. 100, Forty-eighth Congress, first session.]

The Committee on Military Affairs, to whom was referred the bill (S. 230) "to authorize the Secretary of the Treasury to settle the claim of the State of Florida on account of expenditures made in suppressing Indian hostilities," beg leave to submit the following report:

In accordance with the requirements of the joint resolution of Congress approved March 3, 1881, the Secretary of War has investigated, audited, and made a report to Congress, May 22, 1882, of the amount due the State of Florida for expenditures made in suppressing Indian hostilities in that State between the 1st day of December, 1855, and the 1st day of January, 1860. (Ex. Doc. 203, 47th Congress, first session.)

The expenditures grew out of the Seminole war of 1855, 1856, and 1857, the State authorities being compelled, in the presence of an anticipated and subsequently actual outbreak of the Indians, to call forth the militia of the State, the force of United States troops then on duty being inadequate to the protection of the people. The report of the Secretary of War (Ex. Doc. 203) fully sets forth in detail the items of expenditure allowed and disallowed, the total amount found due the State being the sum of $224,648.09.

It is established that the funds at the command of the executive of the State of Florida in the years referred to were insufficient to equip, supply, and pay the troops in the field, and, relying upon the approval given by the President of the United States and the Secretary of War, on the 21st day of May, 1857, of the services of these volunteers, the State legislature, in order to provide their equipment and maintenance, authorized the issue of 7 per cent. bonds.

A portion of the bonds, amounting to $132,000, was sold by the governor to the Indian trust fund of the United States, and the proceeds of such sale were disbursed by the treasurer of the State for the "expenses of Indian hostilities," as appears from his report to the legislature for the year ending October 31, 1857. Another portion was hypothecated to the banks of South Carolina and Georgia as security for a loan of $222,015, and $192,331 of this loan was disbursed directly by a disbursing agent of the State in payment of "expenses of Indian hostilities," including pay of volunteers.

The portion of the bonds sold to the United States for the "Indian trust fund" is still held by that fund and accrued interest since 1857

The State of Florida paid out through a disbursing agent, as shown by
War Department report $193,330.16
And through warrants from State treasurer 78,056.11
                                                                      —————————
Total 271,386.27
Interest on this sum from January 1, 1857, to April 1, 1883.......... 498,672.27
                                                                      —————————
Total cost to the State to date..................................... 770,058.54

We quote from a statement made by the United States Treasurer of the State indebtedness to the "Indian trust fund," June 12, 1882, as follows:

Loan on 7 per cent. bonds of the State of Florida............:....... $132,000
Coupons due and unpaid January 1, 1877.............................. 138,040
Interest to July 1, 1882, from January 1, 1857...................... 50,820
Interest from July 1, 1882, to April 1, 1883 6,930
                                                                      —————————
                                                                      327,790.00
                                                                      —————————
Due the State... 442,268.54

There appears, therefore, lawfully due the State of Florida, according to the State treasurer's account, the sum of $770,058.54, being the principal and interest of the sums which she borrowed and expended on behalf of the United States.

If from this sum be deducted the amount loaned the State by the Indian trust fund, principal and interest, $327,790, there still remains due the State the sum of $442,268.54.

In auditing the accounts of the State, however, the Secretary of War has disallowed many items under the rules and regulations governing payments to the regular forces, and yet, with all his disallowances, after an exhaustive examination, he finds due $224,648.09. Now, if we add the interest on this sum from January 1, 1857, to April 1, 1883, to wit, $412,790.86, we have $637,438.95. Now, if we deduct the amount due the Indian trust fund, to wit, $327,790, there is still due the State the sum of $309,648.95.

This case is one where the Government, through the President of the United States and Secretary of War, promised to pay these troops when mustered into the United States service, and they would have been long since paid by the Government, if so mustered, but the mustering officer arrived in the State after they had been mustered out, and the State was compelled to borrow money with which to pay them.

Congress has universally paid interest to the States where they have paid interest We cite the cases where interest has been allowed and paid for moneys advanced during the war of 1812-'15 as follows: Virginia, act March 3, 1825 (4 Stat. at L., p. 132); Maryland, act May 13, 1826 (4 Stat. at L., p. 161); Delaware, act May 20, 1826 (4 Stat. at L., p. 175); New York, act May 22, 1826 (4 Stat. at L., p. 192); Pennsylvania, act March 3, 1827 (4 Stat. at L., p. 241); South Carolina, act March 22, 1832 (4 Stat. at L., p. 499; Massachusetts, July 8, 1870 (16 Stat. at L., p. 198).

For advances for Indian and other wars the same rule has been observed in the following cases: Alabama, act January 26, 1849 (4 Stat. at L., p. 344); Georgia, act March 31, 1851 (9 Stat. at L., p. 626); Georgia, act March 3, 1879 (20 Stat. at L., p. 385); Washington Territory, act March 3, 1859 (11 Stat. at L., p. 429); New Hampshire, act January 27, 1852 (10 Stat. at L., p. 1).

Thus it will be seen that the precedent for the payment of interest under the rule adopted for the settlement of claims of war of 1812-'15 is well established.

The committee are of the opinion that the urgent necessity for the services of these troops and the action of the President and the Secretary of War create an equitable obligation on the part of the General Government; and as the State of Florida not only borrowed money from the Indian trust fund, but also from the banks of the States of Georgia and South Carolina, for their payment, upon which the State has since paid interest, your committee have concluded to recommend the sum of $92,648.09 as a full payment to the State of all Indian war-claims, this being the difference after deducting the sum borrowed by the State from the Indian trust fund ($132,000) from the amount found due the State by the Secretary of War ($224,648.09), and to further recommend the delivery to the State of all bonds and coupons held by the trustee of the Indian trust fund.

The committee have amended the bill in accordance with the views expressed in this report, and they recommend the passage of the bill as thus amended. Accompanying the report is a communication from the Secretary of War, explaining the origin and the present condition of the claim of the State of Florida against the Government of the United States.

[House Report No. 309, Fiftieth Congress, first session.]

The Committee on War Claims, to whom was referred the bill (H. R. 1474) to reimburse the several States for interest on moneys expended by them on account of raising troops employed in aiding the United States in suppressing the late insurrection against the United States, beg leave to report the same back to the House, with the recommendation that it do pass.

This recommendation is founded upon the precedents which Congress has heretofore established of paying interest on moneys advanced by States on account of the war of 1812; also, Indian wars of 1835, 1836, 1837, and 1838, and the northeast frontier of the State of Maine, as evidenced by the following acts of Congress:

To re-imburse Virginia, act of March 3, 1825, Stat. at Large, vol. 4, p. 132.
To re-imburse Maryland, act of May 13, 1826, Stat. at Large, vol. 4, p. 161.
To re-imburse city of Baltimore, act of May 20, 1826, Stat. at Large, vol. 4, p. 177.
To re-imburse Delaware, act of May 20, 1826, Stat. at Large, vol. 4, p. 175.
To re-imburse New York, act of May 22, 1826, Stat. at Large, vol. 4, pp. 192, 193.
To re-imburse Pennsylvania, act of March 3, 1827, Stat. at Large, vol. 4, pp. 240, 241.
To re-imburse South Carolina, act of March 22, 1832, Stat. at Large, vol. 4, p. 499.
To re-imburse Alabama, act of January 26, 1849, Stat. at Large, vol. 6, p. 344.
To re-imburse Georgia, act of March 3, 1851, Stat. at Large, vol. 6, p. 646.
To re-imburse Maine, act of March 3, 1851, Stat. at Large, vol. 6, p. 626.
To re-imburse New Hampshire, act of January 27, 1852, Stat. at Large, vol. 10, pp. 1, 2.
To re-imburse Massachusetts, act of July 8, 1870, Stat. at Large, vol. 16, pp. 197, 198.

The President, by authority of Congress, called upon the governors of the States of Maine, New Hampshire, Vermont, Massachusetts, Rhode Island, Connecticut, New York, New Jersey, Pennsylvania, Delaware, Maryland, Virginia, West Virginia, Ohio, Kentucky, Michigan, Indiana, Illinois, Wisconsin, Minnesota, Iowa, Missouri, Kansas, Nebraska, Nevada, Oregon, and California to furnish volunteers and militia troops to aid the United States in suppressing the late insurrection against it, and these States expended various sums of money which were advanced to the Government in enrolling, equipping, subsisting, clothing, supplying, arming, paying, and transporting regiments and companies employed by the Government in suppressing the late insurrection, and it matters not to the Government from what sources these States obtained the moneys advanced by them for the benefit of the Government, they are equally and justly entitled to be paid interest on such advances from the time they presented their claims to the Government for payment to the time when the same were refunded by the Secretary of the Treasury.

These States incurred heavy obligations of indebtedness on account of raising these troops, on which they paid interest, and many of them are still paying interest on their bonded indebtedness.

As the Government had the use and benefit of these advances made by these States, above mentioned, and that, too, at a time when greatly needed, and added largely to the maintaining of the credit of the Government, it is deemed by your committee but equitable and just that interest should be allowed equally to all the States on moneys advanced by them to aid the Government in furnishing troops.

[Senate Report No. 618, Fiftieth Congress, first session.]

The Committee on Military Affairs, to whom was referred the bill (S. 1364) to declare the sense of an act entitled "An act to re-imburse the State of Pennsylvania for moneys advanced Government for war purposes," and to authorize a re-examination of the settlement made by the Secretary of War thereunder, having had the same under consideration, beg leave to submit the following report:

The object of this bill is to carry out the provisions of the act of April 12, 1866 (14 Stats., p. 32), entitled "An act to re-imburse the State of Pennsylvania for moneys advanced Government for war purposes," and to indemnify the State for the loss sustained by the non-fulfillment thereof.

The origin of this indebtedness is fully explained in the special message of Governor Curtin of April 30, 1864 (see copy herewith, marked Exhibit A), from which it appears that when the militia, called out by the governor under the proclamation of the President of June 15, 1863, were disbanded, the appropriation in the Treasury of the United States from which the militia were paid had been exhausted, and the Secretary of War requested the governor to borrow the money needed to pay them for services rendered the United States, assuring him at the same time that he would secure from Congress at the next session the appropriation to pay the parties from whom the money was obtained the expense incurred.

That upon the faith of this assurance the governor, with the sanction of the Secretary of War, induced a committee of bankers in Philadelphia, of which Charles H. Rogers was chairman, to borrow on their personal credit the amount required, with the understanding that if the United States failed to indemnify them, he would ask the legislature to do so, and the militia were paid by said committee in August and September, 1863, from funds thus obtained, the sum of $671,476.43, the vouchers for which were forwarded to the War Department for payment in December, 1863, through the adjutant-general of the State.

Congress failed to make the appropriation promised by the Secretary of War, but the legislature promptly responded to the governor's request to redeem the pledge that he had made, and the Rogers committee were on the 8th of September, 1864, paid by the State treasurer their account of expenses incurred in paying off the militia in full to date, as follows:

For amount paid the militia in August and September, 1863 .... $671,476.43
For interest on the money borrowed to September 8, 1864 .... 41,890.71
For expenses 52.47
                                                                    _____
    Making a total of 713,419.61
(See official report of State treasurer for 1864, p. 421.)

The legislature of Pennsylvania, by joint resolution approved February 3, 1865, requested the governor to make a formal demand upon the United States for the payment of this sum with interest from September 8, 1864, and instructed the Senators and Representatives of the State in Congress to vote for and urge an appropriation to pay the same (State laws of 1865, p. 361; see copy appended to this report marked Exhibit B). This exhibit also contains a copy of the act of Congress of April 12, 1866.

This resolution was introduced in Congress the next session after its passage, and became, as the record shows, the inducing cause that brought about the passage of the act of April 12, 1866.

A bill, which is the counterpart of said act, differing therefrom in nothing essential, was reported from the Committee on Ways and Means, on the 21st of March, 1866, appropriating $800,000 to re-imburse the State for money expended.

In reporting the same Mr. Stevens said, mentioning the amount paid to the militia by the Rogers committee:

"It is that amount, with the interest due to these individuals, which has since been paid by the State, that it is proposed to pay. Pennsylvania has paid it, and that State is now substituted for those individuals (Congressional Globe, Thirty-ninth Congress, first session, part 2, p. 1553).

In making this declaration Mr. Stevens was simply repeating what is conclusively established by the history of the times when said act was passed, and which occasioned its passage, hereinbefore recited, which the Supreme Court has said may not only be recurred to in construing a statute, but that a recurrence thereto "is frequently necessary in order to ascertain the reason as well as the meaning of particular provisions in it" (3 Howard, p. 24; 1 Wheaton, p. 120, and 91 U. S. R., p. 72).

In this particular case such recurrence is indispensable, for otherwise the statute is unintelligible.

The transaction was in substance the borrowing of so much money by the United States through the agency of the State of Pennsylvania, upon the credit of the latter, the whole of which was paid by the latter as quasi security for the former, and as the former recognizes its liability to pay the principal, no part of the transaction can be repudiated, but interest as well as principal should be paid by the party for whose benefit and at whose request the loan was made.

From the large amount appropriated in excess of the principal expended by the State ($713,419.61) the reasonable inference would be that Congress intended to include the interest thereon from September 8, 1864, as claimed in the joint resolution of February 3, 1865, which, if added, would very nearly exhaust the amount appropriated ($800,000), as shown by the following statement:

Amount expended by the State September 8, 1864....................... $713,419.61
Interest to June 18, 1866 (1 year 9 months and 10 days), date when the
award of Secretary of War was made.................................... 78,841.77

Amount due 792,361.38

Assuming, however, that a strict interpretation of the statute only authorized a return of the principal expended by the State, which is probably all the language employed—namely, "to re-imburse the State of Pennsylvania for money expended"—would warrant, and deducting therefrom the amount paid by the United States, the account would stand as follows:

Amount expended by the State September 8, 1864 .... $713,419.61
Amount paid June 18, 1866, under the settlement of the Secretary of War 667,074.35

Balance due the State June 18, 1866............................... 46,345.26

The State subsequently applied to the War Department for said balance, payment whereof was refused, upon the ground that the Secretary of War had no authority to review the settlement made by his predecessor, except to correct an error of computation therein, and that the State was concluded by the governor's acceptance of the payment made.

The plea that a State could be concluded by a payment made to any one of its officers, not authorized to bind the State, of a part only of what was due under the statute, or that the remedy provided by the statute could be exhausted by such a settlement as the record shows was made in this case, is certainly a novel one. It was not such a settlement as the statute contemplated. The statute authorized payment, and consequently settlement of the claim therein described, namely, the claim of the State for money expended by the State; that is to say, the claim presented to Congress, described in the joint resolution of the legislature of February 3, 1865.

The claim settled by the Secretary of War was the claim that the Rogers committee had presented to the War Department in December 1863, and the amount paid was a portion of that claim.

Furthermore, as shown by recently discovered testimony, the settlement of the Secretary of War was not intended to be a re-imbursement in full of the payment authorized by the statute, but only an advance pro tanto of the account due the State thereunder (see Exhibit 'C, appended to this report, consisting of a letter from the Register of the Treasury, dated December 31, 1887, transmitting copy of warrant No. 8447, of June 18, 1866).

This was the warrant issued in payment of the award made by the Secretary of War, and thereon appears the following indorsement:

"This payment, approved by the Secretary of War, is made as an advance to the State of Pennsylvania. The account as approved by the Secretary of War, not having been fully stated and passed by the accounting officers of the Treasury Department, will be subject to a re-examination and final settlement at this Department hereafter.

" H. McCULLOCH,
" Secretary."

It is very evident from the facts stated that the settlement made by the Secretary of War was not a final settlement of the claim of the State of Pennsylvania for which re-imbursement was provided by the act of Congress approved April 12, 1866, nor so intended, and that the State has not received the full amount authorized by said act.

Your committee, therefore, beg leave to report the bill back to the Senate with an amendment in the nature of a substitute, and, as amended, recommend its passage.

EXHIBIT A.

[April 30, 1864, Journal of the senate.]

The secretary of the Commonwealth being introduced, presented a message from the governor, which was read as follows, viz:

EXECUTIVE CHAMBER,
Harrisburg, April 30, 1864.

To the senate and house of representatives of the Commonwealth of Pennsylvania:

GENTLEMEN: On the 15th of June last, in consequence of the advance of the rebel army north of the Potomac, the President issued his proclamation calling for militia from this State to repel the invasion. I immediately issued my proclamation, of the same date, calling on the militia to come forward. When the men began to assemble under this call of the President, some difficulties arose from their unwillingness to be mustered into the service of the United States, as mischievous persons made themselves busy in misrepresenting the consequences of such muster. In this state of affairs I suggested to the President the expediency of my calling the militia so as to remove the difficulties which had been thus created. The President approved of the suggestion, and for the purpose of attaining the end proposed by his proclamation, directed me to make a State call for militia. I accordingly, on the 26th day of June, 1863, issued my call for the militia. The United States clothed, equipped, and subsisted the men thus called into service, but declined to pay them, on the ground that Congress had made no appropriation for that purpose. Assurances were, however, received from the War Department, that if the money to pay these troops should be advanced by corporations or individuals, application would be made to Congress, on its meeting, to make the necessary appropriations to refund the money thus advanced. Copies of two telegraphic dispatches from the Secretary of War are herewith submitted—one addressed to me, dated July 22, 1863, and the other addressed to a member of a committee of the Union League in Philadelphia, dated July 21, 1863, and which was immediately communicated to me. On the faith of these assurances I proposed that the moneyed institutions of the State should advance the money, there being no State appropriation for the purpose. I pledged myself that if the money should be so advanced I would recommend an appropriation by the legislature to refund it, in case Congress should fail to do so. A copy of my letter on this subject, dated July 22, 1863, is herewith submitted. This not being entirely satisfactory to the gentlemen composing the committee of banks, they had an interview with me here, and I finally handed to them the paper dated 24th July, 1863, a copy of which is also herewith submitted. Several of the banks, and other corporations in the State, acting with their accustomed spirit and patriotism, promptly came forward and agreed to advance the necessary funds, and the troops were accordingly paid. The disbursements were made, and the pay accounts were so faithfully, as well as formally, kept by gentlemen who acted entirely without compensation, that they were settled by the adjutant-general of the State with the accounting officers at Washington, without any objections arising.

The sums thus advanced amount, with interest, at the present time, to about $700,000. It ought to be added that little more than one-half of this sum was required to pay the troops during the existence of the emergency. The remainder was expended in paying such of them as, against my remonstrance, were detained afterwards by the United States for the purpose of enforcing the draft.

The assurances given by the Secretary of War were, of course, sanctioned by the President. The pay of these troops was in fact a debt of the United States, and the faith of the Government was pledged to do all in its power to procure the proper appropriation by Congress to refund the money. I regret to say that the President has not considered it to be his duty to lay the matter openly before Congress by a message. A bill, it is true, has been introduced and is now pending in Congress, providing the necessary appropriation, but it has met with opposition, and in the absence of some public declaration by the Executive of the pledges made by Government, it may possibly be defeated.

Meanwhile, as your session is drawing to a close, I feel bound to redeem the faith of the executive department of Pennsylvania, and do therefore earnestly recommend the passage of a law providing for the repayment of the sums advanced as hereinbefore stated, if Congress should fail to provide therefor at its present session. Our own good faith will be thus preserved, and it can be in no other manner.

A. G. CURTIN.

WASHINGTON, *July* 21, 1863.

J. R. FRY,
　　Chairman Union League, Philadelphia:

All that is necessary is that the governor of Pennsylvania should see that the company pay-rolls are properly made out and certified. This being done, the amount due is readily ascertained, and can be paid, and the pay-rolls will furnish the proper official voucher of the payment. This Department will lay before Congress, at the commencement of the session, an estimate to cover the amount, and request the appropriation. The matter has been arranged in this way in other States, and has been productive of no delay or complaint where the governors have given their attention to it, and seen that the muster-rolls are properly made out.

EDWIN M. STANTON,
Secretary of War.

WASHINGTON, July 22, 1863.

To His Excellency Governor A. G. CURTIN :

Your telegrams respecting the pay of militia called out under your proclamation of the 27th of June have been referred to the President for instructions, and have been under his consideration. He directs me to say that while no law or appropriation authorizes the payment by the General Government of troops that have not been mustered into the service of the United States, he will recommend to Congress to make an appropriation for the payment of troops called into State service to repel an actual invasion, including those of the State of Pennsylvania. If in the mean time you can raise the necessary amount, as has been done in other States, the appropriation will be applied to refund the advance to those who made it.

Measures have been taken for the payment of troops mustered into the United States service as soon as the muster and pay rolls are made out.

The answer of this Department to you, as governor of the State, will be given directly to yourself whenever the Department is prepared to make answer.

EDWIN M. STANTON,
Secretary of War.

EXECUTIVE CHAMBER,
Harrisburg, Pa., July 22, 1863.

GENTLEMEN: In my interview with you on the 19th instant I had the honor to lay before you and the presidents of the other banks of the city of Philadelphia the difficulties which surround the militia of Pennsylvania called into service for the defense of the State, and more especially the want of any appropriation of money by the National or State Government for their payment. I proposed at the time that the money necessary for that purpose be raised from banks and other corporations, relying upon Congress for an appropriation at the next session, or, on failure, upon the legislature of our own State. I refer, with great pleasure, to the promptness and unanimity with which the gentlemen present expressed their willingness to respond to the call made upon them.

I inclose a copy of a telegram received this morning from the Secretary of War, which you notice is fully up to the expectations we entertained at the time of our meeting, and pledges the Government of the United States so far as it is possible in the absence of Congress. I can not give you a correct estimate of the amount of money we may require. I do not think, however, it can exceed $700,000. Of that amount, the city of Philadelphia having appropriated $150,000 to the payment of volunteers raised in the city, it would seem just and proper that it should be refunded in the same manner and made part of the fund to be disbursed.

I propose that your committee immediately address banks and other corporations throughout the State, requesting them to contribute in some just proportion, which I leave to your discretion.

Inasmuch as the money thus raised could not go into the treasury of the State, and if in could not be drawn out without authority of law, I suggest that gentlemen of known character be selected to pay the regiments as they pass out of service. In the mean time we will have the proper muster-rolls prepared, so that under the laws of the United States and regulations of the War Department the proper vouchers will be presented with our claim on the Government.

If there should be any failure on the part of the Government of the United States to refund the money raised as proposed, I will ask the legislature at the opening of the next session to make an appropriation to refund it, with interest.

You will excuse me for again reminding you that we should act promptly in this matter, as it is not only just to the men who have cheerfully taken up arms in defense of the State, but important to the Government, if it should be necessary to make any such calls in the future.

I am, gentlemen, very respectfully, your obedient servant,

A. G. CURTIN.

Messrs. Charles H. Rogers (chairman), Edwin M. Lewis, Joseph Patterson, Thomas Smith, John Jordan, B. B. Comegys, and John B. Austin, committee of the banks of Philadelphia.

EXECUTIVE CHAMBER,
Harrisburg, July 24, 1863.

I ask the banks and other corporations in Pennsylvania to advance money to pay the militia called into service under my proclamation of the 26th of June, 1863, for the defense of the State, there being no appropriation made by the legislature for that purpose.

When the legislature meets in January I will ask and recommend an appropriation to refund the money thus advanced, with interest.

It will be noticed that the Secretary of War, by a telegram to me, dated the 22d of July, commits the Government of the United States to the payment of this money, so far as it is possible in the absence of Congress.

Having had an interview with the presidents of the banks in Philadelphia, and a correspondence on this subject, I request that if the money can be raised, the committee appointed by that body collect and disburse the fund through paymasters nominated by me.

A. G. CURTIN,
Governor of Pennsylvania.

Messrs. Charles H. Rogers (chairman), Edwin M. Lewis, Joseph Patterson, Thomas Smith, John Jordan, B. B. Comegys, and John B. Austin, committee of the banks of Philadelphia.

Laid on the table.

———

EXHIBIT B.

No. 4.—JOINT RESOLUTION relative to the repayment by the United States of certain moneys advanced by the Commonwealth of Pennsylvania to pay the volunteer militia of eighteen hundred and sixty-three.

Whereas the United States are indebted to the Commonwealth of Pennsylvania in the sum of seven hundred and thirteen thousand dollars, with interest on the same from the eighth day of September, anno Domini one thousand eight hundred and sixty-four, for money advanced to pay the volunteer militia of eighteen hundred and sixty-three, which was promised to be paid by the General Government, as appears by the telegram of the Secretary of War to Governor Curtin, bearing date the twenty-second day of July, anno Domini eighteen hundred and sixty-three: Therefore be it

Resolved by the senate and house of representatives of the Commonwealth of Pennsylvania in general assembly met, That the President is hereby requested to recommend Congress to make the necessary appropriation to pay the said sum. And we further request the Senators and Representatives of this State in the Congress of the United States to earnestly urge and vote for an appropriation to pay the same.

That the governor be, and he is hereby, requested to cause a copy of the foregoing preamble and resolutions to be transmitted to the President and each of the Senators and Representatives of this State in the Congress of the United States.

ARTHUR G. OLMSTEAD,
Speaker of the House of Representatives.
WILLIAM J. TURRELL,
Speaker of the Senate.

Approved the 3d day of February, A. D. 1865.

A. G. CURTIN.

(Laws of 1865, p. 861.)

———

Copy of act of Congress approved April 12, 1866.

CHAP. XL. AN ACT to reimburse the State of Pennsylvania for moneys advanced Government for war purposes.

Be it enacted by the Senate and House of Representatives of the United States of America in Congress assembled, That to supply a deficiency in paying the Army under the act of March fourteenth, eighteen hundred and sixty-four, and to reimburse the State of Pennsylvania for money expended for payment of militia in the service of the United States, the sum of eight hundred thousand dollars, or so much thereof as may be necessary, is hereby appropriated out of any money in the Treasury not otherwise appropriated: *Provided,* That before the same is paid the claim of the State shall be again examined and settled by the Secretary of War. (14 Stats. at Large, p. 32.)

Memorandum.

As stated in report, the bill which brought about the passage of the act of April 12, 1866, was reported to the House March 21, 1866.

In addition to the remarks of Mr. Stevens, quoted in the brief, explanatory of the object of the bill, the reference given (Cong. Globe, 1st sess. 39th Congress, 1865-1866, Part 2, page 1553, also contains copies of the correspondence between Secretary Stanton and Gov'r Curtin and J. R. Fry, chairman of the Union League, Philada., and between Secretary Stanton and Congress. The history of the legislation in the 39th Congress with the bill introduced, appropriating $700,000.00 to pay the parties from whom the money was borrowed, is also explained.

EXHIBIT C.

Transcript certificate.

TREASURY DEPARTMENT, REGISTER'S OFFICE,
Washington, D. C., December 30, 1887.

Pursuant to section 886 of the Revised Statutes of the United States, I, W. S. Rosecrans, Register of the Treasury Department, do hereby certify that the annexed are true copies of warrant and draft in favor of Hon. Andrew G. Curtin, governor, on file in this Department.

W. S. ROSECRANS,
Register.

Be it remembered that William S. Rosecrans, esq., who certified the annexed transcript, is now, and was at the time of doing so, Register of the Treasury of the United States, and that full faith and credit are due to his official attestations.

In testimony whereof, I, Charles S. Fairchild, Secretary of the Treasury of the United States, have hereunto subscribed my name and caused to be affixed the seal of this Department, at the city of Washington, this 30th day of December, in the year of our Lord 1887.

[SEAL.]

C. S. FAIRCHILD,
Secretary of the Treasury.

[Warrant, War Dep't, No. 8447. Appropriation.]

TREASURY DEPARTMENT.

To the Treasurer of the United States, greeting:

Pay to Hon. Andrew G. Curtin, governor, present, or order, out of the appropriation named in the margin, six hundred and sixty-seven thousand and seventy-four dollars and thirty-five cents, due the State of Pennsylvania on settlement, approved by the Secretary of War, pursuant to requisition No. 4195 of the Secretary of War, dated 16 June, 1866, countersigned by the Second Comptroller of the Treasury, and registered by the 2d Auditor. For so doing this shall be your warrant.

Given under my hand and the seal of the Treasury this 18th day of June, in the year of our Lord one thousand eight hundred and sixty-6, and of Independence the ninety-th.

H. McCULLOCH,
Secretary of the Treasury.

Countersigne ` '8.
$667,074.35.

R. W. TAYLER,
Comptroller.

...ecorded, 18.
[SEAL.]

J. A. GRAHAM,
Assistant Register.

NOTE.—This payment, approved by the Secretary of War, is made as an advance to the State of Pennsylvania. The accounts, *as* approved by the Secretary of War, not having been fully stated and passed by the accounting officers of the Treasury Department, will be subject to re-examination and final settlement at this Department hereafter.

H. McCULLOCH,
Secretary.

To re-imburse the State of Pennsylvania for money expended for payment of militia in the service of the United States. Act app'd April 12, 1866.

Received for the above warrant the following draft, No. 3878, on A. T., Phila.:
Draft No. 3878 on War.]   Warrant No. 8447.
$667,074.38/100.   D. F.

TREASURY OF THE UNITED STATES,
Washington, June 18, 1866.

At sight, pay to Hon. Andrew G. Curtin, governor, etc., or order, six hundred sixty-seven thousand seventy-four dollars 38/100.
Registered June 18, 1866.

J. A. GRAHAM,
Asst. Register of the Treasury,
[$667,074.38/100]
To ASST. TREASURER U. S.,
Philadelphia, Pa.   F. E. SPINNER,
No. 3878.]   *Treasurer of the United States.*

DECEMBER 31, 1887.

DEAR SIR: In accordance with your request of 20th instant, I transmit herewith a copy of warrant No. 8447, dated June 18, 1866, in favor of Hon. A. G. Curtin, governor.

Respectfully,

W. S. ROSECRANS,
Register.

L. S. WELLS, Esq.

The Committee on War Claims in the House of Representatives having had under consideration the above Senate bill, reported the same back to the House, with a favorable recommendation, and that the same do pass—no amendment whatsoever having been suggested by said House War Claims Committee—and submitted House Report No. 2198, Fiftieth Congress, first session, of which report the following is a copy:

[House Report No. 2198, Fiftieth Congress, first session.]

The Committee on War Claims, to whom was referred the bill (S. 2329) to authorize the Secretary of the Treasury to re-examine and re-audit the claim of the State of Pennsylvania for advances made and money borrowed by said State to pay the militia called into the military service by the governor, report as follows:

The facts out of which this bill for relief arises will be found stated in Senate report from the Committee on Military Affairs of the present Congress, a copy of which is hereto annexed for information.

Your committee adopt the said report as their own, and report back the bill and recommend its passage.

The report so adopted by the House Committee on War Claims is the foregoing Senate Report No. 518, Fiftieth Congress, first session.

CLAIMS OF THE STATE OF NEVADA. 145

[House Report No. 1179, Fiftieth Congress, first session.]

The Committee on Claims, to whom was referred the petition of Joseph W. Parish for relief, have examined the same and make the following report:

On the 5th of March, 1863, Mr. Parish, in company with one William L. Huse, under the firm-name of J. W. Parish & Co., contracted with Henry Johnson, a medical store-keeper, acting on behalf of the United States, and under the direction of the then Surgeon-General, William Hammond, to "deliver at Memphis, Tenn., Nashville, Tenn., Saint Louis, Mo., and Cairo, Ill., the whole amount of ice required to be consumed at each respective point and vicinity during the remainder of the year 1863." The price to be paid for the ice, as the same should be delivered at these various points, was stipulated in the contract, and the quantity left to be determined by the wants of the Government.

Very soon after this contract was made Huse withdrew from the firm, and the entire interest on the part of the contractors became vested in said Parish.

On the 25th of March following the date of the contract, Col. R. C. Wood, the assistant surgeon-general stationed at Saint Louis, directed Parish, in writing, to furnish 5,000 tons of ice each at Saint Louis and Cairo, and 10,000 tons each at Memphis and Nashville; 30,000 tons in all. Twenty thousand tons of this were to be furnished without delay. The contractor at once commenced the purchase of ice, and within a week had succeeded in securing sufficient to fill the order. Large portions of this were purchased at Ogdensburgh and Kingston, on the St. Lawrence River, and at Lake Pepin, in Minnesota.

After such purchases were all made and the contractor stood ready to fulfill his contract, he was notified by the said Assistant Surgeon-General Wood that the Surgeon-General of the Army had directed that the order above referred to should be suspended "until further instructions." That suspension was never removed. From that time to the close of the year 1863 (the date of the termination of the contract) the contractor was called upon by the proper medical officers to deliver only about 12,670 tons of ice, although it appears he was during all the time ready and desirous to deliver the full amount of 30,000 tons as Surgeon Wood had directed. The contract terminated, and the balance of the ice melted away and was a total loss.

The claimant at first applied to the executive department of the Government for relief. After the delays incident to the prosecution of a claim before the Departments, and utterly failing in his efforts in that direction, he applied to Congress.

On May 30, 1872, an act was approved which authorized the Court of Claims to hear and determine his claim. A large amount of testimony was taken at great expense, and the case finally brought to a hearing. The court entered a decree dismissing the petition, on the ground that Assistant Surgeon-General Wood had no authority to determine the quantity of ice that would be required, and that his action therein was wholly nugatory.

From this decree an appeal was taken to the Supreme Court. The decision below was reversed, the Supreme Court holding that the acts of the assistant surgeon-general were the acts of the Surgeon-General, having the same validity until countermanded or revoked.

In the Court of Claims, however, Parish had claimed as his measure of damages the contract price of the ice less the expense of delivering the same, and all his testimony had been taken on that theory. But the Supreme Court laid down another doctrine as to the measure of damages. It held that the claimant "was entitled to recover what he paid for the ice that was lost and what expense he was at in making the purchase and in keeping it until it was lost."

Thereupon the case was returned to the Court of Claims, to ascertain the damages under this new rule and to render judgment accordingly. But the testimony having been taken under another theory, there were only fragmentary and incidental proofs as to the cost of the ice or the expense of purchasing and keeping the same. Therefore a motion was made on the part of the claimant for leave to take further testimony. This the court denied, and gave judgment in the gross sum of $10,444.91. This judgment a former committee of this House has characterized as follows:

"The action of the Court of Claims on this mandate, to the mind of your committee, was somewhat strange and inexplicable. The report of the Surgeon-General, which is made a part of this report, shows that upon application the court declined to allow any additional testimony to be taken, believing, perhaps, that it could not be regularly done under a mandate; it declined, upon request, to find the facts required by the rules, whereby the right of appeal was cut off under the rules. In allowing a mere fractional part of the claim, it declined, or rather omitted, to state any reasons whatever, either in writing or orally, as the grounds of its decision, leaving the parties wholly in the dark as to the data upon which it gave judgment. The effect of all this was to deny to the claimant a day in court, in the true and proper sense of that term, on the question or right of recovery as laid down by the Supreme Court."
(House Report No. 1956, Forty-seventh Congress, second session).

S. Rep. 1286——10

The only entry of this judgment in any printed report is found in 16 C. Cls., 642, in the following words, after giving title of the case:

"Mandate of Supreme Court. Contract to furnish ice. Amount awarded, $10,444.91."

The claimant avers that he was advised by his counsel that a further appeal to the Supreme Court would be useless, as the technical assumption would be that the Court of Claims had obeyed the mandate of the Supreme Court, and the amount allowed was found in pursuance of the rule of damages established on the former appeal.

The claimant again promptly appealed to Congress for redress. At the succeeding term he secured the introduction of bills in both houses. The Committee on Claims in the Forty-seventh Congress sent the matter to the Secretary of War for a report. The Secretary referred it to Surgeon-General Barnes, who, on the 25th of May, 1882, made a very full report of the whole case to the Secretary, who reported the same to Congress. A copy will be found appended hereto.

General Barnes, after examining the case in the light of the testimony which was before the Court of Claims and some additional testimony submitted by the committee, and after applying the rule laid down by the Supreme Court, finds that there was due the contractor, on the termination of his contract, $69,261.11. Then, after deducting from this amount the amount of the award by the Court of Claims and two small items for ice and lumber sold, he finds that there was still due at the date of his report $58,341.85.

Upon the receipt of this report from the Surgeon-General, the committees of the Senate and House of the Forty-seventh Congress having the bills in charge reported them to their respective houses, recommending that the claim for above amount be allowed and paid. These bills were not reached on the Calendars for action. At each succeeding Congress favorable reports were made to both houses. In March last an act was approved providing that the balance of the principal sum due Mr. Parish on his contract, amounting to $58,341.85, be paid.

The petitioner now claims interest. From the foregoing history of the matter it will be seen that he has been vigilant and persistent in his efforts to collect the amount due him. The claim has been constantly prosecuted before some Department of the Government. Congress and the Supreme Court have fully acknowledged its justice, and the principal sum, after a delay of more than twenty years, has finally been paid.

And right here it should be added that the rule applied by the Supreme Court was a hard, technical one, which reduced the claim to the lowest minimum amount. Equitably the claimant should have recovered the contract price of the ice ordered to be furnished, less the cost of delivering the same. This would have given him more than three times the amount which he finally received.

Your committee find: (1) That the original claim is based upon a written contract legally made with the Government by the petitioner—this point is res adjudicata; (2) that the petitioner is not chargeable with laches in the prosecution of his claim; (3) that the delay in making payment of the principal is solely chargeable to the refusal or neglect of the various Departments of the Government.

The question then arises upon these propositions whether the Government should pay interest on the sum which was due on the 1st day of January, 1864, and which it did not finally pay until March, 1886. Your committee are of the opinion that it should.

If the contention was between two individuals there could be no possible question. Where there is a principal debt, either liquidated or depending for liquidation upon some act of the debtor, which is withheld from the creditor without fault on his part, the debtor should pay interest from inception of the debt until the same is paid; or, in the language of Mr. Parsons (Par. Contr. 2, 380), "where it is that money ought now to be paid, and ought to have been paid long since, the law, in general, implies conclusively that for the delay in the payment of the money, the debtor promised to pay legal interest" (Silleck v. French, 1 Conn., 32; 3 Cow., 393, and other authorities given by the author).

In fact as between man and man, this is hornbook law. No need to cite authorities. Every lawyer admits it as a sound legal principle, and every layman recognizes it as just and right.

The rule is equally applicable in every respect when the Government is the debtor. That the Government never pays interest is a saying more or less common among the people. It is wrong in principle and untrue in fact. It probably had its origin in the fact that the officers of the Executive Department, being strictly limited in their function by statutory law, can not pay interest to claimants unless the same is specially directed by Congress. The Government goes into the market to borrow money with an interest-bearing bond in its hand. It exacts interest of its citizens when they are debtors. It pays interest on claims of foreign nations. It insists upon interest from foreign nations. It pays interest to the Indian tribes.

The debtor is as much entitled to pay for the use of his principal as to the principal itself. For the Government to take the citizen's money without interest would be a violation of the spirit, if not the letter, of the Constitution where it provides "nor shall private property be taken for public use without just compensation,"

In Erskine v. Van Arsdale (15 Wall., 75), which was a case against the Government, Erskine being a collector of internal revenue, Chief-Justice Chase, in delivering the unanimous opinion of the court, says:

"The court (below) also charged the jury that if they found for the plaintiff they might add interest. This was not contested upon the argument, and we think it clearly correct. The ground for the refusal to allow interest is the presumption that the Government is always ready and willing to pay its ordinary debts. Where an illegal tax has been collected, the citizen who has paid it, and has been obliged to bring suit against the collector, is, we think, entitled to interest in the event of recovery, from the time of the illegal exaction."

Here, the court says, the ground for the refusal to allow interest is the presumption that the Government is always ready and willing to pay its ordinary debts; a presumption which the court at once shows must give way when the Government forces the citizen to the delay and expense of a suit to recover the debt.

In Cochran et al, v. Schell, collector of customs (17 Otto, 625), which is a case where judgment was obtained in the United States circuit court against a collector of customs in his official capacity (virtually against the United States), and the solicitor-general took it on writ of error to the Supreme Court. The latter tribunal, on affirming the decision of the lower court, ordered interest on the judgment until paid. In this case the judgment below was for damages and interest; and now comes the Supreme Court and orders interest on this judgment, which, in effect, is, as to a portion of the judgment, interest upon interest. The theory of the whole case is that the Government forced the creditor to bring suit to enforce his claim; hence when judgment went for claimant he was entitled to interest from the date of his claim to date of judgment; and again, when further delay in payment was made by appealing, the Supreme Court says the judgment creditor must have interest on his judgment. (See also Barber v. Schell, 17 Otto, 617, and Schell v. Dodge et al., Ib., 629.)

The Congressional precedents for paying interest on claims are very numerous. Attached to the petition on file with the claim is a report of Senator Jackson, from the Senate Committee on Claims, submitted to the first session of the Forty-eighth Congress (S. Report 326), in which is noted a long list of acts of Congress allowing interest to every class of claimants. That report will also be found in the appendix hereto.

We earnestly call attention, not only to the laws there cited, but also to the able argument it contains in favor of interest on a claim similar in its principles to the one we now present. The report was unanimously made by the Committee on Claims, and the bill passed the Senate providing for interest alone where the principal had previously been paid by Congress.

If Congress is authorized to do partial justice, it is authorized to do complete justice. It can not consistently hand over to Mr. Parish a portion of what is due him and retain the balance. For twenty-two years he besought payment of his claim. It is now admitted beyond dispute that during the whole of this time the Government was his debtor. He has been forced to the expenditure of large sums in prosecuting the matter in the courts and before Congress. There is absolutely nothing to be alleged against this claim for interest except the trite saying that the Government never pays interest. If the claimant were a tribe of Indians or a foreign nation, instead of one of our citizens, no question would be raised.

Suppose the Government had taken from one of its citizens interest-bearing securities, and for twenty-two years collected and appropriated the interest on them, could there be any question that when it came to make restitution it would, in very decency, be compelled to restore both interest and principal? But, upon principle, the case cited does not differ from the one which we now report. The Government has had the use of this claimant's money, and, by retaining it, deprived him of the benefits resulting from such use.

Your committee is therefore of the opinion that the prayer of the petitioner should be granted; and accordingly report the accompanying bill directing the Secretary of the Treasury to ascertain the amount of interest found due on the several sums awarded the claimant by the Court of Claims and the Congress and pay the same to the petitioner.

NOTE.

Senator Jackson's report (Senate, No. 326, Forty-eighth Congress, first session) herein referred to, and printed as a part of the foregoing House Report No. 1179, will be found printed in the appendix hereto, pages 120 to 135.

IN THE SENATE OF THE UNITED STATES.

AUGUST 10, 1888.—Ordered to be printed.

Mr. STEWART, from the Committee on Military Affairs, submitted the
following

REPORT:

[To accompany bill S. 3420.]

*The Committee on Military Affairs, to whom was referred the bill (S. 3420)
authorizing the Secretary of War to ascertain what amount of money has
been expended by the States of California, Oregon, and Nevada for military purposes in aid of the Government of the United States during the
war of the rebellion, having considered the same, report as follows:*

During the war of the rebellion the States of California, Oregon, and
Nevada were separated from the Atlantic States by over 1,500 miles of
almost uninhabited country. Much apprehension was felt on account
of the exposed condition of those distant States, and the Government
called upon them to assist in guarding the overland mail and emigrant
routes, in preventing Indian outbreaks in the States, and to aid the United
States in various ways during the war of the rebellion.

At the beginning of the war Nevada was a Territory, and was admitted into the Union as a State in 1864; but for the purposes of this report Nevada will hereafter be referred to as a State.

These States complied promptly with all the requirements of the General Government, and volunteered all the aid in their power to assist
the United States. On the Pacific coast during this time, and particularly in Nevada, prices of all commodities (and also the price of labor)
were exceedingly high, and as a mining excitement existed in these
States it became necessary to extend aid in many ways in organizing,
arming, equipping, furnishing, and maintaining volunteer soldiers and
militia beyond the amount required for those purposes in the Eastern
States. California, Oregon, and Nevada passed numerous acts to organize and equip soldiers in compliance with the requests of the Government, for which they were compelled to expend large sums of money.
They were also compelled to borrow money, upon which a large amount
of interest has been paid.

An examination of all the facts connected with these claims, a statement of accounts showing for what the money was paid, and under what
authority involves too much detail for a committee of Congress to investigate. They, therefore, recommend the passage of the accompanying bill, which simply provides for an examination and report upon the
facts of the claims of each of these States, so as to enable Congress to
take such action as may be just and proper in the premises.

The bill does not commit Congress to the payment of these claims in
advance, nor a settlement upon any particular theory. It does not

commit Congress in advance to re-imburse these States for bounty or extra money expended by them in furnishing troops to assist the United States in suppressing the war of the rebellion, nor to the payment of interest on moneys borrowed. It simply provides for an ascertainment of such facts as to enable Congress to legislate intelligently.

A bill for the payment of the claims of Nevada has already been reported by a majority of your committee and is now on the Calendar of the Senate. The report in that case is very elaborate, and some members of your committee desire, before action is taken on it, a more authoritative statement of the case, which will be obtained by the examination now proposed. The claims of California and Oregon are of a similar character to those of Nevada. All these States were differently situated during the rebellion from the other States of the Union, and your committee, therefore, thought proper to have the same investigation and report made in each case and have them all incorporated in one bill. The writer of this report has prepared an elaborate statement of the claims of California and Oregon, which has been printed, by order of the Senate, for the use of the committee.

The report on the Nevada claim, known as Senate Report No. 1286, and dated May 14, 1888, and the statement with regard to the claims of California and Oregon will assist the War Department in collecting the laws and orders under which these States expended the money in question, and your committee desire to call the attention of the Secretary of War to these documents in case this bill should become a law.

The laws that have been passed for the investigation of claims of other States are not applicable to the peculiar conditions of these States during the war of the rebellion, and there is no authority under them for the ascertainment of the necessary facts to enable Congress to determine what allowances should be made under the peculiar circumstances which surrounded these States at the time in question.

Your committee report the bill back with an amendment, and when so amended recommend that it do pass.

O

WAR CLAIMS OF CALIFORNIA, OREGON, AND NEVADA.

JUNE 25, 1890.—Committed to the Committee of the Whole House on the state of the Union and ordered to be printed.

Mr. STONE, of Kentucky, from the Committee on War Claims, submitted the following

REPORT:

[To accompany H. R. 7430.]

The Committee on War Claims, to whom was referred the bill (H. R. 7430) to reimburse the States of California, Oregon, and Nevada for moneys by them expended in the suppression of the rebellion, report as follows:

The facts out of which this bill for relief arises will be found stated in Senate Report No. 644, from the Committee on Military Affairs of the present Congress, which report is hereto annexed and made part of this report. Your committee adopt the said report as their own, and report back the bill (H. R. 7430) with an amendment, to wit: Strike out lines 8 to 18, inclusive, and in lieu thereof insert as follows, to wit:

To the State of California, the sum of two million four hundred and fifty-one thousand three hundred and sixty-nine dollars and fifty-six cents.

To the State of Oregon, the sum of two hundred and twenty-four thousand five hundred and twenty-six dollars and fifty-three cents.

To the State of Nevada, the sum of four hundred and four thousand forty dollars and seventy cents, being the sums of money shown by the reports of the Secretary of War to have been paid by said States in the suppression of the rebellion.

When so amended, your committee recommend the passage of said bill.

Senate Report No. 644, Fifty-first Congress, first session.

IN THE SENATE OF THE UNITED STATES.

APRIL 10, 1890.—Ordered to be printed.

Mr. STEWART, from the Committee on Military Affairs, submitted the following

REPORT:

[To accompany S. 2416.]

The Committee on Military Affairs, to whom was referred the bill (S. 2416) to re-imburse the States of California, Oregon, and Nevada for moneys by them expended in the suppression of the rebellion, having duly considered the same, respectfully report as follows:

The larger portions of the claims of these States are for extra pay and bounty paid by them during the war of the rebellion.

The circumstances under which the expenditures provided for in this bill were made by these States being exceptional, and their re-imbursement not being provided for by any existing law, general or special, prior to June 27, 1882, Senator Grover, of Oregon, on December 12, 1881, introduced Senate joint resolution No. 10, and Senator Fair, of Nevada, on December 13, 1881, introduced Senate joint resolution No. 13, providing for the equitable adjustment of these State war claims of Oregon and Nevada, which resolutions were referred to the Senate Committee on Military Affairs.

That committee, instead of reporting back said joint resolutions, reported back, May 12, 1882, in lieu thereof a substitute in the form of a bill to wit: S. 1673, Forty-seventh Congress, first session, providing for the payment of certain war claims, to wit, those only of Texas, Oregon, and Nevada, and of the Territories of Idaho and Washington, and which bill, after having been amended in the Senate so as to include the State war claims of Colorado, Nebraska, and California, and amended in the House so as to include the State war claims of Kansas, finally resulted in the passage of the act approved June 27, 1882. (22 U. S. Stats., 111.)

It was then no doubt the intention of Congress to equitably provide for the re-imbursement of all moneys which California, Oregon, and Nevada, and Nevada when a Territory, had actually expended during the war of the rebellion, on account of the several matters recited in S. bill 3420, Fiftieth Congress, first session. This bill (S. 1673, Forty-seventh Congress, first session) was accompanied by a report (S. No. 575, Forty-seventh Congress, first session) made by Senator Grover May 12, 1882, from which the following is quoted; and which renders said intention of Congress quite evident.

OREGON.

It appears by the report of the Adjutant-General U. S. Army, of April 3, 1882, that one regiment of calvary, one regiment of infantry, and one independent company of cavalry were raised in the State of Oregon during the late war of the rebellion, and that the expenses incident thereto have never been re-imbursed said State by the United States: and that the claims therefor have never been heretofore presented by said State for audit and payment by the United States, as per report of the Secretary of War of April 15, 1882, and of the Third Auditor of the Treasury of April 8, 1882. Under section 3489 of the Revised Statutes, the claim for expenditures so incurred by said State can not now be presented for audit and payment without legislation by Congress. In addition thereto there are some unadjusted claims of said State growing out of the Bannock and Umatilla Indian hostilities therein in 1877 and 1878, evidenced by a communication of the Secretary of War of date last aforesaid, and some unadjusted balances pertaining to the Modoc war, not presented for audit to General James A. Hardie, approximating the sum of $5,000.

NEVADA.

It appears by the report of the Adjutant-General, U. S. Army, of February 25, 1882, that one regiment of cavalry and one battalion of infantry were raised in the late Territory of Nevada during the late war of the rebellion, and that the expenses of raising, organizing, and placing in the field said forces were never paid by said Territory, but were assumed and paid by the State of Nevada, and that none of said expenses so incurred by said Territory, and assumed and paid by said State, have ever been re-imbursed the State of Nevada by the United States, and that no claims therefor have ever been heretofore presented by either said Territory or said State for audit and payment by the United States. Under section 3489 of the Revised Statutes, hereinbefore referred to, the payment of these claims is barred by limitation.

These forces were raised to guard the overland mail route and emigrant road to California, east of Carson City, and to do other military service in Nevada, and were called out by the governor of the late Territory of Nevada, upon requisitions therefor by the commanding general of the Department of the Pacific, and under authority of the War Department, as appears by copies of official correspondence furnished to your committee by the Secretary of War and the general commanding the Division of the Pacific. * * *

The Senate Committee on Military Affairs did not at that time make any report in relation to the State war claims of the State of California, but when this substitute bill (S. 1673, Forty-seventh Congress, first session) reported from that committee was under consideration in the Senate, Senator Miller, of California, called attention to the fact that California had war claims unprovided for, and on his motion this bill (S. 1673, Forty-seventh Congress, first session) was amended in the Senate so as to include these State war claims of the State of California. It is alleged by California, Oregon, and Nevada that this act of June 27, 1882, which they believed was intended by Congress to be an act for their relief and benefit and an equitable statute to be liberally construed, has been found to be an act "so well and carefully and closely guarded by restrictions" that, when construed by those who have been called upon to execute it, has proven to be completely inoperative as an equitable relief measure, so much so as to amount to a practical denial of justice so far as the present State war claims of these States now provided for in this bill were or are concerned.

PRESENTATION BY CALIFORNIA, OREGON, AND NEVADA OF THEIR STATE WAR CLAIMS TO THE UNITED STATES.

The aforesaid bill (S. 1673, Forty-seventh Congress, first session) having become a law June 27, 1882, the State war claims of California, Oregon, and Nevada were thereafter duly transmitted for presentation to the proper authorities of the United States, those of Oregon by Hon. R. P. Earhart, and Hon. George W. McBride, secretary of state for Oregon and *ex officio* adjutant-general. Those for Nevada by Hon. J. F. Hallock, controller of Nevada. Those for California by Hon. John

Dunn, controller, assisted by his deputy, Hon. M. J. O'Reilly, and by Hon. D. I. Oullahan and Hon. Adam Herold, State treasurers, and General George B. Crosby, adjutant-general of California, aided therein by Hon. George Stoneman, Governor of California, and his private secretary, Hon. W. W. Moreland, and by Hon. W. C. Hendricks, secretary, and General H. B. Davidson, assistant secretary of state of California.

These State war claims of these three States, accompanied with proper original vouchers and evidence in support thereof, in each case were thereafter duly delivered by the aforesaid State authorities of California, Oregon, and Nevada, or by those duly authorized therein, to Capt. John Mullan, the duly appointed agent and authorized special counsel for each of said three States, by whom they were put in abstracts and proper shape and thereafter submitted by him to the Secretary of the Treasury and Secretary of War, as provided for in said act of Congress approved June 27, 1882.

DELAY OF THE UNITED STATES IN THE EXAMINATION OF CALIFORNIA, OREGON, AND NEVADA STATE WAR CLAIMS AND THE CAUSES THEREOF.

These State war claims, with said vouchers and evidence, so originally presented to the Secretary of the Treasury and Secretary of War for examination, remained of record in the Treasury and War Departments unacted on up to and after August 4, 1886, because, as was stated to Congress by Hon. Robert T. Lincoln, the Secretary of War, required the aid of at least three army officers to assist his Department in making a proper examination thereof, and he requested Congress to make an appropriation of $25,000 to defray the expenses of such examination of these State and Territorial war claims presented and others to be presented under said act of June 27, 1882. Congress delayed action upon these repeated requests of the Secretary of War until August 4, 1886, on which date acts were passed by Congress providing for a board of three army officers, as asked for, and also appropriating $10,000 to defray the expenses of a full and exhaustive examination (see vol. 24, Stats. at Large, pages 217 and 249) of these State war claims.

SECRETARY LINCOLN'S CONSTRUCTION OF THIS ACT OF JUNE 27, 1882, FOR THE RELIEF OF NEVADA, ETC.

Prior to any action by the War Department on these State war claims of the States of California, Oregon, and Nevada, and prior to any action by Congress on said request of the Secretary of War for a board of army officers to aid him to examine said claims, a bill, S. 657, Forty-eighth Congress, first session, was introduced in Congress by Senator Jones, of Nevada, providing for the payment of certain individual claims of citizens of Nevada on account of Indian hostilities in Nevada in 1860, and was referred by the Senate Committee on Military Affairs to the Secretary of War and of the Treasury for reports, and upon which the Secretary of War reported as follows:

WAR DEPARTMENT,
Washington City, January 26, 1884.

SIR: In response to so much of your communication of the 22d ultimo as requests information concerning Senate bill 657, "to authorize the Secretary of the Treasury to adjust and settle the expenses of Indian wars in Nevada," I have the honor to invite your attention to the following report of the Third Auditor of the Treasury, to whom your request was duly referred:

"The State of Nevada has filed in the office abstracts and vouchers for expenses in-

curred on account of raising volunteers for the United States to aid in suppressing the late rebellion, amounting to $349,697.49, and for expenses on account of her militia in the 'White Pine Indian war' of 1875, $17,650.98. Also, expenses of her militia in the 'Elko Indian war' of 1878, amounting to $4,654.64, presented under act of Congress approved June 27, 1882 (22 Statutes 111, 112).

"These abstracts and vouchers will be sent to your Department for examination and report as soon as they can be stamped, as that statute requires a report from the Secretary of War as to the necessity and reasonableness of the expenses incurred. This statute is deemed sufficiently broad enough to embrace all proper claims of said State and Territory of Nevada."

Very respectfully, your obedient servant,

ROBERT T. LINCOLN,
Secretary of War.

Hon. S. B. MAXEY,
Of Committee on Military Affairs, United States Senate.

In accordance with this report and opinion of the Secretary of War the Senate Committee on Military Affairs reported back this bill so referred to (S. 657, Forty-eighth Congress, first session), and asked that it be indefinitely postponed, and because of the explanation made to the Senate by said committee, and based upon said report and construction of said act and said opinion of the then Secretary of War, Hon. Robert T. Lincoln, as follows, to wit:

It will be observed that it is deemed by the War Department that the act approved June 27, 1882, is sufficiently broad to embrace all proper claims of Nevada, whether as State or Territory.

For convenience of reference the above act accompanies this report, and an examination thereof, and of the construction thereon, satisfies the committee that no additional legislation is necessary.

The State of Kansas presented her State war claim to Secretary Lincoln under this very act, which claim was by him examined, audited, and allowed for almost exactly the sum that Kansas had actually expended for the use and benefit of the United States, and all of which allowance has since been paid to Kansas by the United States, and aggregating the sum of $322,308.13 (23 U. S. Stats., 474) as allowed and paid to said State by the United States. So, too, the State of Nebraska under similar circumstances was allowed and paid the sum of $18,081.23 under this same act of June 27, 1882.

AFTER OVER FOUR YEARS' DELAY, SUBSEQUENT TO THE PASSAGE OF THE ACT OF JUNE 27, 1882, THE UNITED STATES TAKES UP NEVADA'S STATE WAR CLAIM FOR EXAMINATION, WHEN THE VERY FIRST QUESTION RAISED IS ONE OF JURISDICTION, AND WHICH IS DECIDED AGAINST NEVADA.

After the passage of said act of August 4, 1886, the War Department detailed a board of three Army officers under Special Orders No. 232, dated October 6, 1886, to proceed to examine the claims provided for under said act of June 27, 1882, and in the manner contemplated in said act. The State war claims of the State of Nevada were the first examined by said board. This board being in doubt whether, under the terms of said act of June 27, 1882, they could allow a re-imbursement to Nevada of the amount of money by her expended for interest and extra pay to her troops while in the military service of the United States, duly referred these two questions to the Secretary of War for his decision. On February 8, 1887, after argument was submitted to said Secretary in support of these two elements of Nevada's State war claims against the United States, that officer decided "that, after a careful consideration of the subject, he was of opinion that neither the extra pay nor the interest can, under the provisions of the act, be allowed," meaning the act of June 27, 1882, and refused the same, as appears from the correspondence following, to wit:

DECISION OF THE SECRETARY OF WAR DISALLOWING THE STATE WAR CLAIM OF NEVADA FOR INTEREST AND EXTRA PAY TO NEVADA VOLUNTEERS.

WAR DEPARTMENT,
Washington City, February 8, 1887.

SIR: The Department has received your communications of December 31, 1886, and January 28, 1887, submitting arguments in the claim of the State of Nevada, under the act of June 27, 1882, for re-imbursement of amounts paid by the State for "extra pay" and for interest. Also, your communication of 2d instant, inclosing a resolution of the senate and assembly of Nevada, requesting favorable and early action on said claim.

In reply, I have the honor to inform you that after a careful consideration of the subject I am of opinion that neither the extra pay nor the interest can, under the provisions of the act, be allowed.

Very respectfully,
WILLIAM C. ENDICOTT,
Secretary of War.

JOHN MULLAN, Esq.,
Agent of the State of Nevada, 1101 *G street, N. W., City.*

It therefore fully appears that on January 26, 1884, Secretary Lincoln, when construing said act of June 27, 1882, was of opinion that it was sufficiently broad to embrace all proper war claims of the State of Nevada; whereupon the Senate Committee on Military Affairs, in consequence thereof, reported to the Senate that said committee was satisfied that no additional legislation was necessary in regard thereto, while Secretary Endicott, on February 8, 1887, construing this same act and deciding thereunder, held that these war claims of the States and Territories named in said act for expenditure for interest and extra pay to their troops while in the service of the United States could not be allowed by him under said act.

This decision of Secretary Endicott in the case of the State of Nevada, to the effect that "under the provisions of the act of June 27, 1882, he had no jurisdiction to allow interest paid by that State upon the principal by her expended, nor the extra pay made by her to the State troops while they were in the service of the United States," became practically a decision in the case of the State war claims of the State of California, and effectually disposed of these two similar items in the war claims of that State. In addition thereto the Secretary of War, Mr. Endicott, on November 8, 1887, upon a statement made to him by the chief of said board of war claims examiners, also decided that he had no jurisdiction to adjudicate Oregon's State war claim, which claim also contained similar items for interest and extra pay, and thus Secretary Endicott's aforesaid decision in the Nevada case also practically disposed of these two similar items in Oregon's claim so far as his Department was concerned.

In consequence, therefore, of these conflicting decisions of two Secretaries of War upon one and the same act of June 27, 1882, rendering it absolutely nugatory so far as the adjustment of these State war claims of these three States were concerned, made and makes additional remedial legislation by Congress absolutely necessary in order to deal equitably with these States and their claims for re-imbursement of money by them expended in good faith for the common defense during a period of war and at the instance of the authorities of the United States.

The Senate Committee on Military Affairs, therefore, during the Fiftieth Congress, first session, had first under consideration a bill (S. 2918) "to re-imburse the State of Nevada for moneys expended on obligations incurred by said State and the Territory of Nevada, and afterwards assumed and paid by said State, in the suppression of the war of the

rebellion, and for guarding the overland mail and emigrant route," and
a majority of the committee made a favorable report thereon. (S. R.
No. 1286, Fiftieth Congress, first session.)

Your committee thereafter, having under due consideration similar
claims for California and Oregon, reported a general bill, to wit, S. 3420,
Fiftieth Congress, first session, accompanied by Senate Report No. 2014,
Fiftieth Congress, first session, made August 10, 1888, for the investigation of all the war claims of California, Oregon, and Nevada substantially in the same language as recited in the resolution afterwards
passed by the Senate and hereinafter set forth. A full statement of
these war claims was made and submitted to your committee, but not
reported to the Senate at the same time that said resolution for investigation was approved by your committee. That statement is printed in
the report of the war claims examiners on the claims of the State of
California, commencing after the report and after page 95 of Ex. Doc.
No. 11, Fifty-first Congress, first session, and also in Senate Ex. Docs.
Nos. 10 and 17, Fifty-first Congress, first session. Senate Report No.
2014, Fiftieth Congress, first session, does not seem to appear in said
reports, Senate Ex. Docs. 10, 11, 17, although said bill S. 3420 passed
the Senate and was favorably reported in the House September 4,
1888, in House Report No. 3396, Fiftieth Congress, first session, as follows, to wit:

Mr. Stone, of Kentucky, from the Committee on War Claims, submitted the following report (to accompany bill S. 3420).

The Committee on War Claims, to whom was referred the bill (S. 3420) authorizing
the Secretary of War to ascertain what amount of money has been expended by the
States of California, Oregon, and Nevada for military purposes in aid of the Government of the United States during the war of the rebellion, report as follows:

The facts out of which this bill for relief arises will be found stated in Senate report from the Committee on Military Affairs of the present Congress, which report is
hereto annexed and made a part of this report. Your committee adopt the said report as their own, and report back the bill and recommend its passage.

[Senate Report No. 2014, Fiftieth Congress, first session.]

The Committee on Military Affairs, to whom was referred the bill (S. 3420) authorizing the Secretary of War to ascertain what amount of money has been expended
by the States of California, Oregon, and Nevada for military purposes in aid of the
Government of the United States during the war of the rebellion, having considered
the same, report as follows:

During the war of the rebellion the States of California, Oregon, and Nevada were
separated from the Atlantic States by over 1,500 miles of almost uninhabited country.
Much apprehension was felt on account of the exposed condition of those distant
States, and the Government called upon them to assist in guarding the overland mail
and emigrant routes, in preventing Indian outbreaks in the States, and to aid the
United States in various ways during the war of the rebellion.

At the beginning of the war Nevada was a Territory, and was admitted into the
Union as a State in 1864; but for the purposes of this report Nevada will hereafter be
referred to as a State.

These States complied promptly with all the requirements of the General Government, and volunteered all the aid in their power to assist the United States. On the
Pacific coast during this time, and particularly in Nevada, prices of all commodities
(and also the price of labor) were exceedingly high, and as a mining excitement existed in these States it became necessary to extend aid in many ways in organizing,
arming, equipping, furnishing, and maintaining volunteer soldiers and militia beyond
the amount required for those purposes in the Eastern States. California, Oregon,
and Nevada passed numerous acts to organize and equip soldiers in compliance with
the requests of the Government, for which they were compelled to expend large sums
of money. They were also compelled to borrow money, upon which a large amount
of interest has been paid.

An examination of all the facts connected with these claims, a statement of accounts showing for what the money was paid and under what authority, involves too

much detail for a committee of Congress to investigate. They therefore recommend the passage of the accompanying bill, which simply provides for an examination and report upon the facts of the claims of each of these States, so as to enable Congress to take such action as may be just and proper in the premises.

The bill does not commit Congress to the payment of these claims in advance, nor a settlement upon any particular theory. It does not commit Congress in advance to re-imburse these States for bounty or extra money expended by them in furnishing troops to assist the United States in suppressing the war of the rebellion, nor to the payment of interest on moneys borrowed. It simply provides for an ascertainment of such facts so as to enable Congress to legislate intelligently.

A bill for the payment of the claims of Nevada has already been reported by a majority of your committee and is now on the Calendar of the Senate. The report in that case is very elaborate, and some members of your committee desire, before action is taken on it, a more authoritative statement of the case, which will be obtained by the examination now proposed. The claims of California and Oregon are of a similar character to those of Nevada. All these States were differently situated during the rebellion from the other States of the Union, and your committee therefore thought proper to have the same investigation and report made in each case and have them all incorporated in one bill. The writer of this report has prepared an elaborate statement of the claims of California and Oregon, which has been printed by order of the Senate for the use of the committee.

The report on the Nevada claim, known as Senate Report No. 1286, and dated May 14, 1888, and the statement with regard to the claims of California and Oregon will assist the War Department in collecting the laws and orders under which these States expended the money in question, and your committee desire to call the attention of the Secretary of War to these documents in case this bill should become a law.

The laws that have been passed for the investigation of claims of other States are not applicable to the peculiar conditions of these States during the war of the rebellion, and there is no authority under them for the ascertainment of the necessary facts to enable Congress to determine what allowances should be made under the peculiar circumstances which surrounded these States at the time in question.

Your committee report the bill back with an amendment, and when so amended recommend that it do pass.

No action having been taken in the House on said Senate bill 3420 after said House Report No. 3396 was made, and it being deemed important that Congress at its present session should have before it in an official form all the data, facts, and the results of a full, exhaustive, and official examination of these State war claims to be made by the War Department, which then had and now has official custody of all these claims, and of all evidence relating thereto filed in support thereof, and in order that the Secretary of War should have the full benefit and aid of said Board of Army Officers, which was then still in session at Washington, D. C., and which Board Congress had specially created in said act of August 4, 1886 (24 U. S. Stats., 217), to aid the Secretary of War to make a full, exhaustive, and official examination of these State war claims of these three States, so that the Secretary of War could officially and intelligently report upon the same to Congress, or to either branch thereof, for its information and action, as contemplated in said Senate bill 3420, Fiftieth Congress, first session, the Senate therefore, on the 27th of February, 1889, passed the following resolution:

Resolved, That the Secretary of War, through the board of war claims examiners, appointed under section 2 of the act of Congress entitled "An act for the benefit of the States of Texas, Colorado, Oregon, Nebraska, California, Kansas, and Nevada, and the Territories of Washington and Idaho, and Nevada, when a Territory," approved August 4, 1886, be, and he is hereby, authorized and directed to examine all accounts, papers, and evidence which heretofore have been, or which hereafter may be, submitted to him in support of the war claims of the States of California, Oregon, and Nevada, and Nevada when a Territory, growing out of the war of the rebellion, and in suppressing Indian hostilities and disturbances during the war of the rebellion, and in guarding the overland mail and emigrant routes during and subsequent to the war of the rebellion, and to ascertain and state what amount of money each of said States, and Nevada when a Territory, actually expended, and what obligations they incurred for the purposes aforesaid, whether such expenditures were made or obligations incurred in actual warfare or in recruiting, enlisting, enrolling, organizing, arming, equipping, supplying, clothing, subsisting, drilling, furnishing, transporting,

and paying their volunteers, militia, and home guards, and for bounty, extra pay, and relief paid to their volunteers, militia, and home guards, and in preparing their volunteers, militia, and home guards in camp and field to perform military service for the United States.

The Secretary of War is also directed to ascertain what amount of interest has been paid by each of said States, and Nevada when a Territory, on obligations incurred for purposes above enumerated. The Secretary of War shall report to Congress the amount of money which may be thus ascertained to have been actually paid by each of said States, and Nevada when a Territory, on account of the matters above enumerated, and also the amount of interest actually paid or assumed by each of said States, and Nevada when a Territory, on moneys borrowed for the purposes above enumerated. And the Secretary of War shall also report the circumstances and exigencies under which, and the authority by which, such expenditures were made, and what payments have been made on account thereof by the United States.

In response to this resolution the honorable Secretary of War, having theretofore fully completed, with the aid of said Army Board, a thorough, and exhaustive official examination of all these war claims of said three States, transmitted in December, 1889, his report to the Senate in each of the cases of California, Oregon, and Nevada, as required by said resolution, and which reports are as follows, to wit: Senate Ex. Docs. Nos. 10, 11, 17, Fifty-first Congress, first session. These reports and the exhibits attached thereto, respectively, are in great detail, and contain a very full history of the important part taken by the Pacific States and Territories during the rebellion in defense of the Union. These reports are in full compliance with said Senate resolution, showing the actual amount of money expended by each of said States, and of Nevada when a Territory, during the war of the rebellion in aid of the United States, and the authority, State, Territorial, and national, and also the special circumstances and exigencies under which the expenditures reported upon by said Secretary and said board therein respectively were made. The following tables, taken from the reports of said war claims examiners, show the several sums of money actually expended and paid out as principal and interest by each of said States:

CALIFORNIA.

[Senate Ex. Doc. No. 11, Fifty-first Congress, first session, page 27.]

Amount expended in recruiting California volunteers (Abstract F)....	$24,260.00
Amount expended in payment of adjutant-general, etc. (Abstract H)...	38,083.17
Amount expended in organizing volunteers (Abstract M)...............	5,639.34
Amount expended in pay of volunteer officers (Abstract N)...........	23,277.34
Amount expended in extra pay to enlisted men of California volunteers (Abstract P)..	1,459,270.21
Amount expended in bounty to enlisted men (Abstract Q).............	900,839.50
Total expense of volunteers, and not repaid the State by the United States..	2,451,369.56
Amount expended in payment of interest on moneys borrowed to carry out the provisions of the acts of April 27, 1863, and April 4, 1864.....	1,500,545.86
Aggregate expenses incurred on account of volunteers, principal and interest..	3,951,915.42
Amount expended on account of militia.............................	468,976.54
Grand total of expenses on account of volunteers and militia....	4,420,891.96

OREGON.

[Senate Ex. Doc. No. 17, Fifty-first Congress, first session, page 20.]

Amount expended in payment of adjutant-general, etc. (Abstract E)...	$3,973.49
Amount expended in extra pay to enlisted men (Abstract G)...........	90,476.32
Amount expended in bounty to enlisted men (Abstract H).............	129,241.02
Amount expended for advertising calls for redemption of bonds (Abstract K)...	835.70

Amount expended in payment of interest on moneys borrowed to carry out the provisions of the acts of October 24, 1864 (Abstract L)....... $110,626.35

Total amount expended on account of volunteers and not repaid State by United States 335,152.88
Amount expended on account of militia............................ 21,118.73

Aggregate expenses incurred on account of militia and volunteers..... 356,271.61

NEVADA.

[Senate Ex. Doc. No. 10, Fifty-first Congress, first session, page 8.]

Amount actually paid out on account of volunteers raised in Nevada.... $118,667.49
Amount of interest paid on moneys borrowed and so expended.......... 289,685.59
Amount of liabilities assumed on account of volunteers raised in Nevada. 1,133.92
Amount of interest paid on liabilities assumed 3,113.31

Total amount expended or assumed............................... 412,600.31
Amount already paid to Nevada by the United States upon an examination under the provisions of the act of June 27, 1882................... 8,559.61

Amount expended or assumed and not repaid by the United States.. 404,040.70

INTEREST.

In said Ex. Doc. No. 10, Fifty-first Congress, first session, page 15, it is declared that—

Interest paid by California, Oregon, and Nevada is in reality, in justice, in reason, and in law a proper part of the debt due them by the United States, the payment of which, together with that of the principal, is necessary to a complete indemnity.

The United States has generally refused to pay interest on claims against the Government. This rule sometimes works great hardship and wrong; but the inconveniences that might arise from a departure from it may be very great. There is one exception, however, to this rule which has been uniformly recognized and acted upon; that is, when a State has claims against the Government for expenditures made for the United States, and a part of such claims consists of interest paid out or assumed by the State, the interest so paid out or assumed has been treated eventually so far as the adjustment thereof was concerned as if it had been originally presented as a part of the principal, although Congress has always treated the interest as a separate, independent, and distinct claim apart from the principal, which sometimes is adjusted when adjusting the principal, depending no doubt in part upon the special circumstances of the cases presented to Congress and at other times adjusted after the principal is paid, but always adjusting it some time in all proper cases. The rule is well stated in the Decisions of the Second Comptroller for 1869, page 137, as follows:

Interest can in no case be allowed by the accounting officers upon claims against the Government, either in favor of a State or an individual. But in cases where the claimant has been compelled to pay interest for the benefit of the Government it then becomes a part of the principal of the claim, and as such is allowable.

Such is the case of a State which has been obliged to raise money upon interest for the suppression of hostilities against which the United States should protect her.

In such cases the amount of interest actually and necessarily paid will be allowed, without reference to the rate of it.

There are many cases to sustain this ruling of the Second Comptroller, of which the following are cited as precedents where Congress first authorized the adjustment and payment of the principal and then subsequently adjusted and thereafter paid the interest:

1. By an act approved April 2, 1830, the Secretary of the Treasury was authorized to cause to be paid to the mayor and city council of Baltimore the sum of $7,434.63 in full for their claim against the United States for money borrowed and expended by

them in defense of said city in the war of 1812, and by the second section of said act the Secretary of the Treasury was directed to cause to be paid interest on said sum according to the provisions and regulations of " the act to authorize payment of interest due the city of Baltimore," approved May 20, 1826.

2. By an act approved May 31, 1830, the proper accounting officers of the Treasury, under the superintendence of the Secretary of War, were authorized and directed to audit and settle the claims of the State of Massachusetts against the United States for services of her militia during the war of 1812, in the following cases:

(1) Where the militia of said State were called out to repel actual invasion, or under a well-founded apprehension of invasion, provided their numbers were not in undue proportion to the exigency.

(2) Where they were called out by the authority of the State and afterwards recognized by the Federal Government.

(3) Where they were called out by and served under the requisition of the President of the United States or of any officer thereof.

3. By a joint resolution approved May 14, 1836, entitled " A resolution to authorize the Secretary of War to receive additional evidence in support of claims of Massachusetts and other States of the United States for disbursements, services," etc , during the war of 1812, the Secretary was authorized, in preparing his report pursuant to the resolution of House of Representatives agreed to the 24th of February, 1832, without regard to existing rules and requirements to receive such evidence as was on file, and any further proofs which might be offered tending to establish the validity of the claims of Massachusetts upon the United States, or any part thereof, for services, disbursements, and expenditures during the war with Great Britain; and in all cases where such evidence should, in his judgment, prove the truth of the items of the claim, or any part thereof, to act on the same in like manner as if the proof consisted of such vouchers and evidence as was required by existing rules and regulations touching the allowance of such claims; and it was provided that in the settlement of claims of other States upon the United States for services, disbursements, and expenditures during the war with Great Britain, the same kind of evidence, vouchers, and proof should be received as therein provided for in relation to the claim of Massachusetts.

4. By the sixth section of an act approved March 31, 1837, an appropriation was made for paying the claims of the State of Connecticut for the services of her militia during the war of 1812, to be audited and settled by the proper accounting officers of the Treasury under the superintendence of the Secretary of War in the following cases:

(1) Where the militia of said State were called out to repel actual invasion or under a well-founded apprehension of invasion, provided their numbers were not in undue proportion to the exigency.

(2) Where they were called out by the authorities of the State and afterwards recognized by the Federal Government, and

(3) Where they were called out and served under the requisition of the President of the United States or of any officer thereof.

5. By an act approved August 14, 1848, the proper accounting officers of the Treasury were directed to settle the claims for one month's service of the officers and soldiers of the Fourth Regiment in the Second Brigade of the Third Division of the militia of the State of Vermont, who served at the battle of Plattsburgh on the 11th of September, 1814, for their military services on that occasion.

6. By act approved March 3, 1853, making appropriations for the civil and diplomatic expenses of the Government for the year ending June 30, 1854, an appropriation of $10,334.31 was made for arrearages of pay, subsistence, and clothing due to Capt. Richard McRae's Company of Virginia Volunteers, which served in the war with Great Britain in 1812–'13 to be paid to the officers and soldiers of said company or their legal representatives, under the order of the Secretary of War, upon the production of proof as to the identity of said officers and soldiers, and that they have not been paid.

7. By an act approved August 31, 1852 (Army appropriation), the Secretary of War was required to pay to the State of South Carolina such sums of money as were paid by said State in 1838, 1839, and 1840 for services, losses, and damages sustained by her volunteers in the Florida war of 1836, 1837, and 1838, while in the service of the United States, and on their return from said service, as were ascertained and allowed by the board of commissioners appointed for that purpose by the act of the legislature of said State in 1837, with the proviso that no interest should be allowed upon moneys paid to the State of South Carolina under the provisions of said act. And it was by said act further provided that, in the settlement of the claims of the State of Georgia, under the act of August 11, 1842, providing for the settlement of the claims of that State for the service of her militia, which had theretofore been suspended or disallowed, the accounting officers of the Treasury Department should allow and pay, upon proof that the State had allowed and paid the same, all accounts for forage, subsistence, hospital stores, medical service, and transportation which had not there-

tofore been allowed by the United States. And it was further provided by said act that in the adjustment of the accounts of the State of Maine, under the act of June 13, 1842, the proper accounting officers of the Treasury should include and allow the claims which had theretofore been presented under said act, provided it should be satisfactorily shown that said claims had been actually allowed and paid by said State.

8. By an act approved March 3, 1853, second section, the proper accounting officers of the Treasury Department were authorized to settle the claims of the State of Florida for services of her troops under the act of February 27, 1851, by the provision stated for the settlement of the claims of the State of Georgia for like services, under the act approved August 31, 1851 (Army appropriation bill).

9. By the eighth section of an act approved March 3, 1853, the Secretary of the Treasury was directed to pay to the State of Georgia her claims remaining unpaid for moneys paid by the State in suppressing hostilities of the Cherokee, Creek, and Seminole Indians in the year 1835 and since, upon proof that the same was paid by the State, and that the provisions of the act relative to the settlement of the claims of Georgia for military service, approved March 3, 1851, should be extended to payments under said act.

The Secretary of the Treasury was also by said act required to pay the State of Alabama, under the provisions of the acts of Congress of August 16, 1842, and January 26, 1849, the balance due said State, growing out of the Creek Indian hostilities of 1836 and 1837; and by the twelfth section of said act it was provided that in the adjustment of the accounts of the State of Virginia under the twelfth section of the act of August 31, 1852, the Secretary of War should follow the provisions of the act of June 2, 1848, providing for refunding to the several States the amounts expended by them in raising regiments of volunteers for the Mexican war.

10. By an act approved January 26, 1849, the Secretary of War was directed to pay interest upon the advances made by the State of Alabama for the use of the United States Government in the suppression of hostilities by the Creek Indians in 1836 and 1837, at the rate of 6 per cent. per annum from the time of the advances until the principal of the same was paid by the United States to the State. And in ascertaining the amount of interest it was provided that interest should not be computed on any sum which Alabama had not expended for the use and benefit of the United States, as evidenced by the amount refunded to the State of Alabama by the United States, and that no interest should be paid on any sum on which the State of Alabama did not either pay or lose interest as aforesaid.

11. By an act approved March 3, 1851, the Secretary of War was authorized to allow to the State of Georgia for advances made to the United States for the suppression of hostilities of the Creek, Seminole, and Cherokee Indians in the years 1835, 1836, 1837, and 1838, with interest at the rate of 6 per cent. per annum on all sums allowed and paid to the State of Georgia and that might thereafter be allowed and paid for any moneys advanced by the State for the purposes aforesaid, from the date of such advances until the principal sums were or might be paid by the United States, with the proviso that no interest should be paid on any sum on which Georgia did not either pay or lose interest.

12. By an act passed the same day as the above act, the proper accounting officers of the Treasury were directed to settle the claim of the State of Maine against the United States, being for interest on money borrowed and actually expended by her for the protection of the northeastern frontier of said State during the years 1839 1840, and 1841, the amount of such interest to be ascertained under the following rules:

"(1) Interest not to be computed on any sum not expended by the State for the use and benefit of the United States, as evidenced by the amount refunded or paid to the State by the United States.

"(2) No interest to be paid on any sum on which the State did not either pay or lose interest."

13. By act approved July 21, 1852, making appropriations to supply deficiencies in the appropriations for the year ending June 30, 1852, the sum of $20,741 was appropriated for pay of five companies of Texas mounted volunteers.

14. By act approved March 3, 1859, for the purpose of executing the resolution of May 14, 1836, the Secretary of the Treasury was directed to pay to Massachusetts $227,176.48, reported to be due said State by Secretary of War J. R. Poinsett, in report dated December 23, 1837, made to the House of Representatives December 27, 1837, and it was provided that in lieu of payment in money the Secretary of the Treasury might, at his discretion, issue to said State United States stock bearing 5 per cent. per annum, and redeemable at the end of ten years, or sooner, at the pleasure of the President.

15. By act approved March 3, 1825, the accounting officers of the Treasury Department were authorized and directed to settle the claim of the State of Virginia against the United States for interest upon loans on moneys borrowed and actually expended by her for the use and benefit of the United States during the war of 1812.

16. By this act it was provided that, in ascertaining the amount of interest, as aforesaid, due to the State of Virginia, the following rules should be understood as applicable to and governing the case, to wit: First, that interest should not be computed on any sum which Virginia had not expended for the use and benefit of the United States, as evidenced by the amount refunded or repaid to Virginia by the United States. Second, that no interest should be paid on any sum on which she had not paid interest. Third, that when the principal, or any part of it, had been paid, or refunded by the United States, or money placed in the hands of Virginia for that purpose, the interest on the sum or sums so paid or refunded should cease, and not be considered as chargeable to the United States any longer than up to the repayment, as aforesaid.

The mode of computing interest provided by the above act appears to have been satisfactory at the time to all the States, and their claims against the General Government were authorized to be adjusted, and were adjusted under the same rules for computing interest.

17. By an act approved May 13, 1826, entitled "An act authorizing the payment of interest due to the State of Maryland," the accounting officers of the Treasury Department were authorized and directed to liquidate and settle the claim of the State of Maryland against the United States, for interest upon loans on moneys borrowed and actually expended by her for the use and benefit of the United States, during the late war with Great Britain, and the same rules for computing the interest was provided by the act as in the case of the State of Virginia.

18. By an act approved May 20, 1826, entitled "An act authorizing the payment of interest due to the State of Delaware," the accounting officers of the Treasury Department were authorized and directed to take similar action in regard to the settlement of the claim of the State of Delaware against the United States as that directed to be taken in the case of the claim of Maryland, and to be governed by the same rules.

19. By act approved May 20, 1826, the proper accounting officers of the Treasury Department were directed to settle the claim of the city of Baltimore against the United States, for interest on money borrowed and actually expended by the city in its defense during the war of 1812; and the act further provided that the amount due should be ascertained under rules which were the same as those provided by the foregoing act for the adjustment of the accounts in the cases of Virginia, Maryland, and Delaware.

20. By an act approved May 22, 1826, entitled "An act authorizing the payment of interest due to the State of New York," the accounting officers of the Treasury Department were authorized and directed to take similar action and to be governed by the same rules as in the cases of Virginia, Maryland, and Delaware.

21. By an act approved March 3, 1827, the accounting officers of the Treasury Department were authorized and directed to settle the claim of the State of Pennsylvania in the same manner as in the cases of Maryland, Delaware, and New York.

22. By an act approved March 22, 1832, entitled "An act for the adjustment and settlement of the claims of the State of South Carolina against the United States," the accounting officers of the Treasury were authorized and directed to liquidate and settle the claim of the State of South Carolina against the United States for interest upon money actually expended by her for military stores for the use and benefit of the United States, and on account of her militia, whilst in the service of the United States, during the late war with Great Britain, the money so expended having been drawn by the State from a fund upon which she was then receiving interest. The act designates upon what sums interest shall be paid, and recites in detail other claims of the State theretofore disallowed, which shall be adjusted and settled, such as claims for cannon-balls, transportation of troops and supplies, pay to certain staff officers, blankets ($7,500 being the amount of this item), and muskets.

23. By an act approved March 3, 1857, a re-examination and re-adjustment of the account of the State of Maryland was directed to be made, and it was provided that in the calculation of interest the following rules should be observed:

"Interest shall be calculated up to the time of any payment made. To this interest the payment shall be first applied, and if it exceeds the interest due, the balance shall be applied to diminish the principal; if the payment fall short of the interest, the balance of interest shall not be added to the principal so as to produce interest. Second, interest shall be allowed on such sums only on which the State either paid interest or lost interest by the transfer of an interest-bearing fund."

Under this act Maryland received the additional sum of $275,770.23.

24. By section 7 of said act (March 1, 1837), an appropriation was made to pay all the claims of North Carolina for the services of her militia during the war of 1812 with Great Britain in the cases enumerated in the act approved May 31, 1830, entitled "An act to authorize the payment of the claims of the State of Massachusetts for certain services of her militia during the war of 1812," and also the claims of said State for disbursements in the purchase of munitions or other supplies on account of the war and expended therein.

25. On the 8th day of July, 1870, an act was passed directing the account between the United States and Massachusetts and Maine to be re-opened and re-adjusted, and Massachusetts received the sum of $678,362.42, of which one-third was allotted to the State of Maine as an integral part of Massachusetts when the advances were made.

In the foregoing cases the principal was first re-imbursed, and subsequently the interest was adjusted and then paid by the United States. The following cases are cited as precedents, where both the principal and interest were authorized by Congress to be paid at one and the same time and in and under one and the same act:

1. By a joint resolution approved March 3, 1847 (Stats. at Large, vol. 9, p. —), the Secretary of War was authorized and required to cause to be refunded to the several States or to individuals for services rendered, acting under the authority of any State, the amount of expenses incurred by them in organizing, subsisting, and transporting volunteers previous to their being mustered and received into the service of the United States for the war with Mexico, and for subsisting troops in the service of the United States.

2. By an act approved June 2, 1848, the provisions of said joint resolution were extended so as to embrace all cases of expenses theretofore incurred in organizing, subsisting, and transporting volunteers previous to their being mustered and received into the United States for the war with Mexico, whether by States, counties, corporations, or individuals, either acting with or without the authority of any State, and that in refunding moneys under said act and said joint resolution it should be lawful to pay interest at the rate of 6 per cent. per annum on all sums advanced by States, corporations, or individuals in all cases where the State, corporation, or individual paid or lost the interest or was liable to pay it.

3. By act approved August 5, 1854, the sum of $924,259.65 was appropriated to re-imburse the State of California for expenditures "in the suppression of Indian hostilities within the State prior to the 1st day of January, 1854." (See U. S. Stats. at Large for 1853 and 1854.)

4. By act approved August 18, 1856 (section 8), the Secretary of War was authorized and directed to pay to the holders of the war bonds of the State of California the amount of money appropriated by act of Congress approved May [August] 5, 1854, in payment of expenses incurred and actually paid by the State of California for the suppression of Indian hostilities within the said State prior to the 1st day of January, 1854, under the following restrictions and regulations:

Before any bonds were redeemed by the Secretary of War they were required to be presented to the board of commissioners appointed under an act of the legislature of said State, approved April 19, 1856, and the amount due and payable upon each bond indorsed thereon by said commissioners; the amounts in the aggregate not to exceed the amount appropriated by act of August 5, 1854.

All the States, except California, Oregon, and Nevada, have been re-imbursed by the United States all or nearly all of the principal of the moneys expended by them in the suppression of the rebellion. None of them have as yet been re-imbursed for interest which they paid to obtain said principal.

The following table shows the amount of money already paid by the United States as principal to the several States for the suppression of the rebellion, as shown by the books of the Treasury Department:

[Senate Ex. Doc. No. 11, Fifty-first Congress, first session, p. 63.]

States.	Amount.	States.	Amount.
Connecticut	$2,096,950.46	Minnesota	$71,075.20
Massachusetts	3,668,091.95	Kansas	384,138.15
Rhode Island	723,530.15	Nebraska	475.00
Maine	1,027,185.00	Colorado	55,238.84
New Hampshire	976,531.92	Missouri	7,580,421.43
Vermont	832,557.40	Michigan	814,262.53
New York	4,156,935.50	Delaware	31,088.96
New Jersey	1,517,020.79	Maryland	133,140.99
Pennsylvania	3,871,710.59	Virginia	48,469.97
Ohio	3,245,319.58	West Virginia	471,063.94
Wisconsin	1,035,059.17	Kentucky	3,504,466.57
Iowa	1,030,759.45		
Illinois	3,080,412.51	Total	44,137,590.34
Indiana	3,741,738.20		

In addition to the payment of said war claims to the several States on account of the war of the rebellion, as shown by the foregoing table, the claims of the following-named States for expenses in the suppression of Indian hostilities, etc., have been settled by the Third Auditor of the Treasury under the said act of June 27, 1882, and all of which have heretofore been paid by the United States:

States.	Amount.
Kansas	$332,308.13
Nebraska	18,081.23
Nevada	8,559.61
California	11,723.04
Texas	927,177.40
Total	1,297,850.01

An additional sum of $148,615.97 has been allowed the State of Texas by the Third Auditor, and the settlement is now pending before the Second Comptroller of the Treasury, under said act of June 27, 1882. The said State war claims of California, Oregon, and Nevada during the war of the rebellion reported on by the honorable Secretary of War and said board of war claims examiners under said resolution of the Senate of February 27, 1889, were never before properly or fully considered for want of jurisdiction, as hereinbefore shown, until they were so reported upon by the present Secretary of War, Hon. Redfield Proctor, aided by said Army board in said Senate Ex. Docs. 10, 11, 17.

Your committee recognize and approve the precedents which treat interest paid by a State on money borrowed or advanced for suppressing rebellion or repelling invasion in aid of the United States as a legitimate charge against the Government in every case where the Government is equitably liable for the principal; but inasmuch as none of the States have as yet been re-imbursed for any claim for interest paid out by them on money borrowed or advanced and expended by them on account of the war of the rebellion, your committee recommend that this bill be amended so as to omit at this time the claim for interest presented by California and Oregon in the two cases examined herein and reported upon in Senate Ex. Docs., Nos. 11 and 17, Fifty-first Congress, first session.

The claim of Nevada, however, for the re-imbursement of the interest actually paid out by her on the principal by her borrowed and in good faith expended for the common defense, and at the behest of the authorities of the United States, presents a question different from that of the other States. Nevada was a Territory at the time when the greater part of these expenditures were made. The necessity for these expenditures was imperative. The settlements in Nevada were isolated and separated from California by the Sierra Nevada Mountains, which cut off all means of transportation for several consecutive months in each year. There were no railroads. Transportation of freights was confined to teams and pack animals. The Indians along the overland route became hostile and cut off communication between the Atlantic and Pacific States. It was under these circumstances that the Territory of Nevada was called upon by the United States authorities to raise volunteer troops and furnish supplies for them. Labor was excessively high on account of the new mines, and supplies scarce and exceedingly dear. This Territory had no money to comply with these demands made upon her by the United States military authorities, and was forced to borrow money as best she could.

When the Territory of Nevada became a State the State of Nevada assumed the indebtedness of the Territory, including these war claims, and inserted a provision in her constitution in the following language:

All debts and liabilities of the Territory of Nevada lawfully incurred, and which remain unpaid at the time of the admission of this State into the Union, shall be assumed by and become the debt of the State of Nevada. (Compiled Laws of Nevada, vol. 1, page 133.)

Under these exceptional circumstances your committee recommend the payment of both principal and interest in the case of Nevada.

EXTRA PAY AND BOUNTIES.

As we have already seen, the larger portion of the claims of each of the States of California, Oregon, and Nevada were expended for extra pay and bounties. This was an absolute necessity for two reasons: First, the expenses of living and wages of labor in the Pacific coast States were during the rebellion at least 50 per cent., and in many cases 200 per cent., higher than in the Atlantic States; second, the Pacific States and Territories maintained the gold standard continuously throughout the war. The United States paid said volunteer troops in Treasury notes, although they had on deposit at the sub-treasury at San Francisco at all times a large amount of gold. The discount which the soldiers were compelled to pay to convert their greenbacks into gold was from 30 to 60 per cent.

This added largely to the cost of living.

Extra pay was found necessary to provide for the support of the families of the soldiers. This extra allowance, however, in the shape of extra pay and bounty did not exceed the extra compensation which the Government had theretofore paid the officers of the Army and Navy and the enlisted soldiers and sailors stationed on the Pacific coast between the dates of the acquisition of California and the breaking out of the rebellion. The Pacific coast States and Territories had a right to assume that the United States would continue or resume such extra pay and compensation during the war of the rebellion. Certainly the necessity for it was much greater in war than in peace, and, as a matter of fact, it was imperative.

On the 17th of June, 1850, an act was passed, the third section of which reads as follows:

SEC. 3. *And be it further enacted,* That whenever enlistments are made at, or in the vicinity of, the said military posts, and remote and distant stations, a bounty equal in amount to the cost of transporting and subsisting a soldier from the principal recruiting depot in the harbor of New York, to the place of such enlistment, be, and the same is hereby, allowed to each recruit so enlisted, to be paid in unequal installments at the end of each year's service, so that the several amounts shall annually increase, and the largest be paid at the expiration of each enlistment. (U. S. Stat., vol. 9, p. 439.)

On the 23d of September, 1850, the following provision was inserted in the Army appropriation bill:

For extra pay to the commissioned officers and enlisted men of the Army of the United States, serving in Oregon or California, three hundred and twenty-five thousand eight hundred and fifty-four dollars, on the following basis, to wit: That there shall be allowed to each commissioned officer as aforesaid, whilst serving as aforesaid, a per diem, in addition to their regular pay and allowances, of two dollars each, to each enlisted man as aforesaid, whilst serving as aforesaid, a per diem, in addition to their present pay and allowances, equal to the pay proper of each as established by existing laws, said extra pay of the enlisted men to be retained until honorably discharged. This additional pay to continue until the first of March, eighteen hundred and fifty-two, or until otherwise provided. (U. S. Stat., vol. 9, p. 504.)

The first of these acts was continued in force until August 3, 1861 (U. S. Stat., vol. 12, p. 288, sec. 9), on which date it was repealed. During the time when the last of said acts was in existence the United States soldiers and sailors on the Pacific coast received nearly double pay.

During the five years immediately prior to the rebellion the United States Army serving in the Pacific coast States and Territories was composed, first, of men transported from New York, via the Isthmus of Panama, at an aggregate cost to the United States of not less than $390,103, or at an average cost for each officer of $293, and for each enlisted man of $151 when landed in Oregon; or $275 for each officer and $115 for each enlisted man, when landed in California; and when discharged, all said enlisted men were entitled to an amount of money equal to the actual cost of their traveling expenses and subsistence back to New York; estimated by the War Department to be $142, making a total aggregate cost for each enlisted man of $293 and $256, respectively; or second, said army was composed of men enlisted in the Pacific coast States and Territories, at an expense to the United States of $142 per capita, paid to each enlisted man as a bounty under said act of Congress approved June 17, 1850 (9 U. S. Stat., 439), which payments were made continuously from June 17, 1850, to August 3, 1861. (U. S. Stat., vol. 12, p. 288.)

During the first year of the war of the rebellion the larger portion of this United States military force was transported from the Pacific coast States and Territories back to New York, via the Isthmus of Panama, at an aggregate cost to the United States of not less than $303,380, or at an average cost for each enlisted man of $145 from Oregon and of $125 from California.

Details of these various items of cost to the United States for thus transporting said military force to and from New York to the Pacific coast States and Territories are set forth in a table, prepared under the direction of the honorable Secretary of War as follows, to wit:

H. Rep. 2553——2-

Statement of number of officers and enlisted men of the United States Army transported at the expense of the United States from New York City to various points in California and Washington Territory via the Isthmus of Panama, in the years 1856, 1857, 1858, 1859, and 1860; also the amount paid for similar services from April 15, 1861, to December, 1861, between Oregon, Washington, California, and Nevada to New York, via the Isthmus of Panama, showing the total and the average cost per capita of each, so far as shown by the records of this office.

Destination.	Year.	Officers.	Cost.	Enlisted men.	Cost.	Total cost.	Average cost per officer.	Average cost per man.
New York City to San Francisco, Cal., via the Isthmus.........	1856	3	$750	396	$39,600	$40,350		
Do	1857	9	2,700	470	58,750	61,450		
Do	1858	2	600	34	493	1,093	$267.80	$109.83
Do	1859*	..						
Do	1860	21	6,325	441	44,000	49,325		
Total	......	35	9,375	1,341	142,843	152,218		
New York City to Benicia, Cal., via the Isthmus	1857	18	5,000	689	79,525	84,525	284.00	121.10
Do	1858	7	2,100	445	57,875	59,975		
Total	......	25	7,100	1,134	137,400	144,400		
New York City to Fort Vancouver, Wash., and near Portland, Oregon, via the Isthmus	1858	15	4,500	400	61,500	66,000	293.12	151.09
Do	1859	1	190	14	1,050	1,240		
Total	......	16	4,690	414	62,550	67,240		
Fort Vancouver, Wash., to Benicia, Cal	1856	1	60	50	1,750	1,810	60.00	35.00
San Francisco, Cal., to Fort Vancouver, Wash...............	1858	18	1,000	787	23,345	24,345	55.56	29.60
San Francisco, Cal., to New York City, via the Isthmus........	1861	49	12,250	1,495	186,875	199,125	250.00	125.00
San Pedro, Cal., to New York City, via the Isthmus	1861	15	3,750	500	62,500	66,250	250.00	125.00
San Francisco, Cal., to Fort Vancouver, Wash............	1861	30	1,200	775	15,500	16,700	40.00	20.00
Fort Vancouver, Wash., to San Francisco, Cal	1861	34	1,400	960	19,900	21,300	40.00	20.73

* None found.

QUARTERMASTER-GENERAL'S OFFICE,
Washington, D. C., January 8, 1890.

In consequence of this withdrawal in 1861 of said military forces from the Pacific coast, in order that they might perform military services in the East, and in view of the circumstances and exigencies existing in the Pacific Coast States and Territories during the rebellion period, requisitions were duly made from time to time by the President of the United States and by the Secretary of War upon the proper State authorities of California, Oregon, and Nevada for volunteers to perform military service for the United States in said States and Territories, as are fully and in detail set forth in said Senate Ex. Docs., Nos. 10, 11, 17, Fifty-first Congress, first session. In compliance with the several calls so made between 1861 and 1866, inclusive,

Volunteers'

The State of California furnished 15,725
The State of Nevada furnished 1,180
The State of Oregon furnished 1,810

Making a total aggregate of 18,715

men who enlisted and were duly mustered into the military service of the United States as volunteers in said States. The same number of

troops if organized and transported from New York City to the Pacific coast States and Territories in the same manner as was done by the United States War Department from June 17, 1850, to August 3, 1861, would have cost the United States at that time the sum of about $5,483,385 for *transportation alone.*

The reports of said war claims examiners upon extra pay in Nevada, California, and Oregon are as follows, to-wit:

[Senate Ex. Doc. No. 10, Fifty-first Congress, first session, p. 7.]

NEVADA.

Extra monthly pay—liabilities assumed.

It appears from the affidavit of the State comptroller (herewith, marked Exhibit No. 2), that liabilities to the amount of $1,153.75 were assumed by the State of Nevada as successor to the Territory of Nevada on account of "costs, charges, and expenses for monthly pay to volunteers and military forces in the Territory and State of Nevada in the service of the United States," and that State warrants fully covering such liabilities were duly issued. It is also shown in the affidavit that of said warrants two for the sums of $11.33 and $8.50 respectively have been paid, such payment reducing said liabilities to $1,133.92.

The circumstances and exigencies under which the Nevada legislature allowed this extra compensation to its citizens serving as volunteers in the United States Army are believed to have been substantially the same as those that impelled the legislatures of California and Oregon to a similar course of action for the relief of the contingent of troops raised in each of these States. Prices of commodities of every kind were extravagantly high during the war period in Nevada, which depended for the transportation of its supplies upon wagon roads across mountain ranges that were impassable for six months of every year; and at certain times at least during the said period, the rich yields of newly-opened mines produced an extraordinary demand for labor, largely increasing wages and salaries. These high prices of commodities and services were co-existent with, though in their causes independent of, the depreciation of the Treasury notes, which did not pass current in that section of the country, though accepted through necessity by the troops serving there; and it is safe to say that in Nevada, as in California and Oregon, the soldier could buy no more with a gold dollar than could the soldier serving in the Eastern States with the greenback or paper dollar.

On the whole, therefore, we are decided in the conviction that in granting them this extra compensation the legislature was mainly instigated by a desire to do a plain act of justice to the United States volunteers raised in the State and performing an arduous frontier service, by placing them on the same footing, as regards compensation, with the great mass of the officers and soldiers of the United States Army, serving east of the Rocky Mountains. It is true that the seven companies of infantry that were called for on October 19, 1864, had not been organized; and that on March 8, 1865, three days before the approval of the State law above noticed, the commanding general Department of the Pacific wrote as follows from his headquarters at San Francisco to the governor of Nevada (see page 287, Senate Ex. Doc. 70, Fiftieth Congress, second session):

"What progress is making in recruiting the Nevada volunteers? I will need them for the protection of the State, and trust that you may meet with success in your efforts to raise them. I hope the legislature may assist you by some such means as have been adopted by California and Oregon."

But the fact remains that the declared purpose of the monthly allowance was to give a compensation to the Nevada volunteers (see section 1 of the act last referred to), and that when measured by the current prices of the country in which they were serving, their compensation from all sources did not exceed, if indeed it was equal to, the value of the money received as pay by the troops stationed elsewhere, *i. e.*, outside of the Department of the Pacific.

[Senate Ex. Doc. No. 11, Fifty-first Congress, first session, p. 23.]

CALIFORNIA.

Extra pay to enlisted men.

By an act approved April 27, 1863, the legislature appropriated and set apart "as a soldiers' relief fund" the sum of $600,000, from which every enlisted soldier of the companies of California volunteers raised or thereafter to be raised for the service of the United States was to be paid, in addition to the pay and allowances granted him

by the United States, a "compensation" of $5 per month from the time of his enlistment to the time of his discharge. Drafted men, substitutes for drafted men, soldiers dishonorably discharged or discharged for disability existing at time of enlistment, were not to share in the benefits of the act, and, except in cases of married men having families dependent upon them for support, payment was not to be made until after discharge. Seven per cent. interest bearing bonds to the amount of $600,000, in sums of $500, with coupons for interest attached to each bond, were authorized to be issued on July 1, 1863. (Pages 349-351, Statement for Senate Military Committee.)

A few unimportant changes respecting the mode of payment in certain cases was made by act of March 15, 1864, and on March 31, 1866, the additional sum of $550,000 was appropriated for the payment of claims arising under its provisions, such sum to be transferred from the general fund of the State to the "Soldiers' Relief Fund."

Fearing that the total amount of $1,150,000 specifically appropriated might still prove insufficient to pay all the claims accruing under the act of April 27, 1863, above mentioned, the legislature directed, by an act which also took effect March 31, 1866 (page 604, Stats. of California, 1865-'66), that the remainder of such claims should be audited and allowed out of the appropriation and fund made and created by the act granting bounties to the volunteers of California approved April 4, 1864, and more fully referred to on page 19 of this report.

Upon the certificate of the adjutant-general of the State that the amounts were due under the provisions of the act and of the board of State examiners, warrants amounting to $1,459,270.21 were paid by the State treasurer, as shown by the receipts of the payees indorsed on said warrants.

It is worthy of note here that on July 16, 1863, the governor of California, replying to a communication from the headquarters Department of the Pacific, dated July 5, 1863, advising him that under a resolution of Congress adopted March 9, 1862, the payments provided for by the State law of April 27, 1863, might be made through the officers of the Pay Department of the U. S. Army, stated that the provisions of said law were such as to preclude him from availing himself of the offer.

Some information as to the circumstances and exigencies under which this money was expended may be derived from the following extract from the annual report of the adjutant-general of the State for the year 1862, dated December 15, 1862:

"The rank and file of the California contingent is made up of material of which any State might be proud, and the sacrifices they have made should be duly appreciated and their services rewarded by the State. I do most earnestly recommend therefore that the precedent established by many of the Atlantic Coast States of paying their troops in the service of the United States an additional amount monthly should be adopted by California, and that a bill appropriating, say, $10 per month to each enlisted man of the troops raised or to be raised in this State be passed. * * * This would be a most tangible method of recognizing the patriotic efforts of our soldiers, relieve many of their families from actual destitution and want, and hold out a fitting encouragement for honorable service." (Page 58, Statement for Senate Committee on Military Affairs.)

Your examiners are of the opinion that the favorable action which was taken on the above recommendation of the Adjutant-General can not be justly ascribed to any desire on the part of the legislature to avoid resort to a conscription, although the exclusion of drafted men from the benefits of the act indicates that they realized and deemed it proper to call attention to the possibility of a draft. Unlike the law of April 4, 1864, the benefits of which were confined to men who should enlist after the date of its passage and be credited to the quota of the State, the provisions of the act now under consideration extended alike to the volunteers who had already entered or had actually completed their enlistment contract and to those who were to enlist in the future. There is every reason for the belief that the predominating if not the only reason of the State authorities in enacting this measure was to allow their volunteers in the United States service such a stipend as would, together with the pay received by them from the General Government, amount to a fair and just compensation. In fact, as has already been stated, this was expressly declared to be the purpose of the act.

It appears that up to December 31, 1862, those of the United States troops serving in the Department of the Pacific who were paid at all—in some cases attachments had not been paid for a year or more—were generally paid in coin, but on February 9, 1863, instructions were issued from the Treasury Department to the Assistant Treasurer of the United States at San Francisco that "checks of disbursing officers must be paid in United States notes." (Letter of Deputy Paymaster-General George H. Ringgold, dated February 13, 1863, to Paymaster-General; copy herewith marked Exhibit No. 10.)

Before this, greenbacks had become the current medium of exchange in all ordinary business transactions in the Eastern States, but in the Pacific Coast States and the adjoining Territories, gold continued to be the basis of circulation throughout

the war. At this time the paper currency had become greatly depreciated, and on February 28, 1863, the price of gold in Treasury notes touched 170. This action of the Government in compelling troops to accept such notes as an equivalent of gold in payment for services rendered by them in a section where coin alone was current, gave rise to much dissatisfaction. For although gold could be bought in San Francisco at nearly the same price in Treasury notes as in New York, it must be remembered that the troops in the Department of the Pacific were largely stationed at remote and isolated points.

When paying in greenbacks for articles purchased by, or for services rendered to, them in these out-of-the-way places, they were obliged to submit not only to the current discount in San Francisco but also to a further loss occasioned by the desire of the persons who sold the articles, or rendered the service, to protect themselves against possible further depreciation. It admits of little doubt that by reason of his inability to realize the full value of paper money, as quoted in the money centers, and of the fact that wages and the cost of living and of commodities of every kind were abnormally high (owing in great part to the development of newly discovered mines in that region) the purchasing power of the greenback dollar in the hands of the average soldier serving in the Department of the Pacific was from the latter part of 1862 onward from 25 to 50 per cent. less than that of the same dollar paid to his fellow soldier in the East.

Representation of the great hardship the Treasury Department's instructions entailed upon the troops were promptly made. On March 10, 1863, the legislature telegraphed to Washington a resolution adopted on that date instructing the State's delegation in Congress to impress upon the Executive "the necessity which exists of having officers and soldiers of the U. S. Army, officers, seamen, and marines of the U. S. Navy, and all citizen employés in the service of the Government of the United States serving west of the Rocky Mountains and on the Pacific coast paid their salaries and pay in gold and silver currency of the United States, provided the same be paid in as revenue on this coast." (Page 46, Statement for Senate Committee on Military Affairs.)

And on March 16, 1863, Brig. Gen. G. Wright, the commander of the Department of the Pacific (comprising besides California, the State of Oregon and the Territories of Nevada, Utah, and Arizona), transmitted to the Adjutant General of the U. S. Army a letter of Maj. C. S. Drew, First Oregon Cavalry, commandant at Camp Baker, Oregon, containing an explicit statement of the effects of and a formal protest against paying his men in greenbacks. In his letter of transmittal (page 154, Ex. Doc. 70), General Wright remarked as follows:

"The difficulties and embarrassments enumerated in the major's communication are common to all the troops in this department, and I most respectfully ask the serious consideration of the General-in-Chief and the War Department to this subject. Most of the troops would prefer waiting for their pay to receiving notes worth but little more than half their face; but even at this ruinous discount, officers, unless they have private means, are compelled to receive the notes. Knowing the difficulties experienced by the Government in procuring coin to pay the Army, I feel great reluctance in submitting any grievances from this remote department; but justice to the officers and soldiers demands that a fair statement should be made to the War Department."

It was under circumstances and exigencies such as these that the legislature themselves—all appeals to the General Government having proved futile—provided the necessary relief by the law of April 27, 1863. They did not even after that relax their efforts on behalf of United States troops, other than their own volunteers, serving among them, but on April 1, 1864, adopted a resolution requesting their representatives in Congress to "use their influence in procuring the passage of a law giving to the officers and soldiers of the regular Army stationed on the Pacific coast an increase of their pay, amounting to 30 per cent. on the amount now allowed by law."

[S. Ex. Doc. No. 17, Fifty-first Congress, first session, p. 14.]

OREGON.

Extra monthly compensation to officers and enlisted men of volunteers.

The certificate of the State treasurer, duly authenticated by the secretary of state under the seal of the State, sets forth that the amounts severally paid out for the redemption of relief bonds, as shown by the books of the treasurer's office, as reported by the treasurer to the several legislative assemblies and as verified by the several joint committees (investigating commissions) of said assembly under the provisions

of a joint resolution thereof, aggregate $90,476.32.   The following books, papers, etc., are also submitted in evidence of payment:

(1) The canceled bonds.

(2) A copy of the relief bond register, the correctness of which is certified by the secretary of state and State treasurer, showing number of bond, to whom issued, date of issue, and amount of bond; also showing the date and rate of redemption. The reports of the joint committees of the legislature above mentioned, to the effect that they compared the record kept by the State treasurer with the bonds redeemed and found the amounts correct and agreeing with the amounts reported by the State treasurer to the legislative assembly, are entered in said bond register.

(3) Certificates of service given to the several Oregon volunteers upon which warrants were given entitling the holders to bonds. These certificates cover service for which the sum of $86,639.85 was due. The remainder of the certificates, the State authorities report, were not found and are probably lost or destroyed.

(4) Copies of the muster-rolls of the Oregon volunteers, certified to by the secretary of state, setting forth the entire service of each officer and enlisted man.

In all, bonds amounting to $93,637 were issued. As has been stated but $90,476.32 is found to have been expended in the redemption of these bonds, some of which were redeemed at less than their face value. Five bonds, valued at $731, have not been redeemed.

The authority by which these bonds were issued is contained in an act of the legislature, which was approved on October 24, 1864 (copy herewith), appropriating a sum not exceeding $100,000 to constitute and be known as the "commissioned officers' and soldiers' relief fund," out of which was to be paid to each commissioned officer and enlisted soldier of the companies of Oregon volunteers raised in the State for the service of the United States to aid in repelling invasion, etc., from the time of their enlistment to the time of their discharge, $5 per month in addition to the pay allowed them by the United States. Enlisted men not receiving an honorable discharge from the service, or volunteers discharged for disability existing at the time of enlistment, were not to be entitled to the benefits of the act, nor was payment under the provisions thereof to be made to an enlisted soldier until he should be honorably discharged the service; but enlisted married men having families dependent upon them were authorized to allot the whole or any portion of the monthly pay accruing to them for the support of such dependents. A bond bearing interest, payable semi-annually, at 7 per cent. per annum, redeemable July 1, 1875, with coupons for the interest attached, was to be issued by the secretary of state for such amount as the adjutant-general should certify to be due under the provisions of the act to each man, whose receipt for the amount so paid him was to be taken by the secretary of state. Said bonds were to be paid to the recipient or order.

The circumstances and exigencies that led to the enactment of the above-cited law and to the expenditures incurred under its provisions were substantially the same as those which brought about the adoption of similar measures of relief in California and Nevada. It must have been patent to every one fully acquainted with the circumstances of the case that the volunteers, that had been raised in Oregon, at this time (October 24, 1864) consisting only of the seven companies of the First Oregon Cavalry and the independent detachment of four months' men, a majority of whom had then nearly completed their term, had been greatly underpaid, considering the nature of the service performed by them and the current rate of salaries and wages realized in other pursuits of life. At the time of the enrollment and muster in of the First Oregon Cavalry and up to the latter part of 1862 the Government paid those of its troops in the Department of the Pacific, that were paid at all, in specie; but as often happened during the war a number of the companies of the regiment named, occupying remote stations, remained unpaid for a long time and were finally paid in Treasury notes, some of the members having more than a year's pay due them.

During the remainder of the war the Government paid its troops in the Department of the Pacific, as elsewhere, in greenbacks. Referring to this condition of things and to the fact that coin continued to be the ordinary medium of exchange in Oregon in private business transactions, Maj. C. S. Drew, First Oregon Cavalry, in a letter to his department commander, dated March 4, 1863 (page 154, Ex. Doc. 70), called attention to the fact that at his station (Camp Baker) Treasury notes were worth "not more than 50 or 55 cents per dollar;" that each officer and soldier of his command was serving for less than half pay, and had done so, some of them, for sixteen months past; that while capital protected itself from loss and perhaps realized better profits than under the old and better system of payment in coin, "the soldier did not have that power, and if paid in notes must necessarily receipt in full for what is equivalent to him of half pay or loss for the service he has rendered, and must continue to fulfill his part of the contract with the Government for the same reduced rate of pay until his period of service shall have terminated; and that "good men will not enlist for $6 or $7 a month while $13 is the regular pay, and, moreover, being realized by every soldier

in every other department than the Pacific." In forwarding this letter to the Adjutant-General, U. S. Army, the department commander remarked that the embarrassments enumerated in the major's communication were common to all the troops in the department, and he therefore asked "the serious consideration of the General-in-Chief and the War Department to this subject." Some months later (August 18, 1863) General Alvord, while reporting to the department commander the location of a new military post at Fort Boisé, referred to the difficulties encountered by the garrison* charged with the duty of establishing it, as follows:

"Some difficulty is experienced in building the post in consequence of the low rates of legal-tender notes. In that country they bear merely nominal value. The depreciation of the Government currency not only embarrasses the Quartermaster's Department, but also tends greatly to disaffect the men. The differences between their pay and the promises held out by the richest mines, perhaps, on the coast, the proximity of which makes them all the more tempting, is so great that many desertions occur." (Ex. Doc. 70, page 188.)

About the same time (September 1, 1863) the adjutant-general of the State complained of the inadequacy of the soldiers' pay, resulting from the depreciation of the paper currency with which they were paid. Referring to the fact that after the expiration of eight months from the date of the requisition of the United States military authorities for six additional companies for the First Oregon Cavalry but one had been raised, he said:

"And yet we are not prepared to say that it is for the want of patriotism on the part of the people of Oregon, but from other causes, partly from the deficiency in the pay of the volunteer in comparison with the wages given in the civil pursuits of life, as well as with the nature of the currency with which they are paid, the depreciation of which renders it hardly possible for the soldier to enlist from any other motive save pure patriotism. And I would here suggest that the attention of our legislature be called to this defect, and that additional pay, either in land, money, or something else, be allowed to those who have volunteered. Justice demands that this should be done."

In enacting the relief law of October 24, 1864, it is fair to presume that the legislature was largely influenced by the following statements and recommendations of the governor contained in his annual message, dated September 15, 1864:

"The Snake and other tribes of Indians in eastern Oregon have been hostile and constantly committing depredations. The regiment has spent two summers on the plains, furnishing protection to the immigration and to the trade and travel in that region of the country. During the past summer the regiment has traveled over twelve hundred miles, and the officers and men are still out on duty. The officers and most, if not all, the men joined the regiment through patriotic motives, and, while some of the time they have been traveling over rich gold fields, where laborers' wages are from $3 to $5 per day, there have been very few desertions, and that, too, while they were being paid in depreciated currency, making their wages only about $5 per month. A great many of these men have no pecuniary interest in keeping open the lines of travel, protecting mining districts and merchants and traders. The benefit of their service thus insures [inures] to the benefit of others, who should help these faithful soldiers in bearing these burdens. Oregon, in proportion to her population and wealth, has paid far less than other States for military purposes. California pays her volunteers $5 per month extra in coin. It would be but an act of simple justice for this State to make good to the members of this regiment their losses by depreciated currency." (Page 87, Statement for Senate Military Committee.)

It is to be noted here that while the officers and men who became the beneficiaries of this law had been paid in a depreciated currency, which in Oregon does not appear to have had more than two-thirds of the purchasing power it had in the East, the Government provided them with clothing, subsistence, shelter, and all their absolutely necessary wants. On the other hand, it is to be borne in mind that the legislature must have been aware of the fact noted, and that it granted the extra compensation from a sense of justice and without any purpose calculated to benefit the State at large, such as might be reasonably inferred from the granting of bounties to men "who should hereafter enlist." As has been already mentioned, the terms of the Oregon Volunteers were drawing to a close and the benefits of the law were restricted to the volunteers "raised," and did not therefore include those "to be raised."

California, as shown by the report (Senate Ex. Doc. No. 11, Fifty-first Congress, first session) of said war claims examiners, expended $468,976.54 on account of her militia during the war of the rebellion. The circumstances under which this expenditure was made present a strong case of equity for reimbursement, but inasmuch as the militia of

---

*Although the First Oregon Cavalry did not form a part of this garrison, three companies of it were at this time scouting against hostile Indians in the vicinity of the post.

California did not serve under the direct or immediate authority of the United States during the war of the rebellion, your committee do not allow it at this time, although they do not reject it for want of merit.

Oregon expended on account of her militia, as shown by the report of said war claims examiners, $21,118.73; and your committee make a similar recommendation in regard to that claim.

Some of the circumstances under which the present war claim of the State of Nevada was created are set forth in the report of the majority of the Committee on Military Affairs made in the Fiftieth Congress, first session (Senate Report No. 1286), which, without the appendix, is as follows, to wit:

Senate Report No. 1286, Fiftieth Congress, first session.

MAY 14, 1888.

Mr. STEWART, from the Committee on Military Affairs, submitted the following report:

[To accompany bill S. 2918]

OBJECT OF THIS BILL.

The object of this bill is to re-imburse the State of Nevada for moneys paid and contracted to be paid by the Territory of Nevada and afterwards assumed and paid by that State, and also for moneys actually expended by Nevada after becoming a State for the common defense and in furnishing troops to the United States during the suppression of the war of the rebellion, and for guarding the overland mail and emigrant route between the Missouri River and California, and for suppressing Indian hostilities under circumstances hereinafter set forth.

APPEAL OF PRESIDENT LINCOLN, THROUGH SECRETARY SEWARD, TO THE NATION FOR AID.

On October 14, 1861, Mr. Seward, Secretary of State, addressed a circular letter to the governors of the loyal States and Territories, calling for assistance for the General Government in suppressing hostilities in the so-called Confederate States, and for the improvement and perfection of the defenses of the loyal States respectively. A copy of this letter is printed in the appendix hereto, marked Exhibit No. 1, page 23.

ACTION TAKEN BY NEVADA IN RESPONSE TO THE FOREGOING APPEAL OF SECRETARY SEWARD.

Upon the receipt of this letter the legislative assembly of Nevada Territory at its first session passed appropriate resolutions pledging the support of the people of that Territory to the Union cause to the extent of their means, which resolutions are printed in the appendix, marked Exhibit No. 2, page 24.

On the 28th day of November, 1861, three days after the passage of the resolutions above mentioned, the legislative assembly of Nevada also passed an elaborate law for the enrollment and organization of a militia force to aid the United States when called upon in the suppression of the rebellion, and to carry out the spirit and intent of the aforesaid circular letter of Secretary Seward. This law will be found on

pages 106 to 125 of the Laws of Nevada Territory, 1861. This act provided that the militia of the Territory organized under its provisions should be subject to be called into the military service of the United States by the President, or any officer of the United States Army commanding a division or a department. A militia force was immediately organized under its provisions. H. P. Russell was appointed adjutant-general, and was succeeded by Col. John Cradlebaugh, who is mentioned in the resolutions above referred to and printed in the appendix as Exhibit No. 2, page 24.

It will thus be seen that Nevada made the necessary preparations, organized her militia, and was ready to answer any call that might be thereafter made upon her by the General Government, and also to protect the Territory against a large portion of its inhabitants who desired to join the Confederacy.

CONDITION OF AFFAIRS THAT RENDERED A CALL FOR NEVADA VOLUNTEERS NECESSARY.

The Territory of Nevada was organized by Congress on March 2, 1861, (12 U. S. Stats., 209). At the breaking out of the rebellion it became a serious question what attitude Nevada would occupy, and home guards were immediately organized. These guards afterwards formed a portion of the militia of the Territory as provided for in the aforesaid militia law, and protected the inhabitants from violence, without any expense to the Government of the United States.

In the early part of April, 1863, the overland mail and emigrant route was attacked by Indians and communication was closed between the Atlantic States and the Pacific coast. This route extended from the Missouri River to California via the Platte River, Salt Lake City, through Nevada to Sacramento, in California, and was the only means at that date of direct overland communication between the Missouri River and California. At this time the gold discoveries in California continued to invite a large immigration, the interest in which was more or less intensified by the continued extensive silver discoveries in Nevada Territory, and principally on the Comstock lode in the western part of the Territory. The routes via Cape Horn, and especially that via the Isthmus of Panama, were rendered extremely doubtful, dangerous, and expensive, on account of Confederate privateer cruisers hovering around the West India Islands and along both these sea routes, and in anticipation of other Confederate cruisers infesting the waters of the Pacific (which soon thereafter became the theater of the operations and extensive depredations of the Confederate privateer cruiser *Shenandoah*) the overland route, therefore, although in itself both dangerous and difficult, was yet considered the better and preferable route by which to reach the Pacific.

On account of a general uprising of the Indians along the entire overland route, and especially that portion between Salt Lake City, in the Territory of Utah, and the Sierra Nevada Mountains, and because of the doubts as to the loyalty of the Mormons to the Government of the United States, the maintenance and protection of the mail and emigrant route through that section of the country and along the aforesaid line was regarded by the Government as a military necessity. Apparently in anticipation of no immediate danger of attack on the Pacific coast, nearly all the troops of the regular Army at this time had been withdrawn from service throughout this entire region of country and transferred East to other fields of military operations. This left the entire coun-

try between Salt Lake City and the Sierra Nevada Mountains without adequate and efficient military protection. The Government thus having but few troops of its regular Army in that region, was therefore compelled to call upon the inhabitants of Nevada Territory to raise and organize volunteer military companies to suppress Indian disturbances which threatened the entire suspension of all mail facilities and emigration from the East, as will be hereafter shown.

At the time of the calls upon Nevada for troops the prices of labor and supplies of all descriptions in Nevada were extremely high. There were then no railroads, and the snow on the Sierra Nevada Mountains formed an almost impassable barrier against teams from about the 1st of December until about June. The average cost of freight from San Francisco, the main source of supply for western Nevada, was about $80 a ton, and it was necessary to lay in supplies during the summer and fall for the remainder of the year. A great mining excitement prevailed at this time, occasioned by the marvelous development of the great Comstock lode, and wages were from $4 to $10 a day in gold. The people who had emigrated to the new gold and silver fields went there for the purpose of mining and prospecting for mines, and were generally reluctant to enter the irregular military service of guarding the overland mail and emigrant route. Besides, on account of the extraordinary high price of supplies of every description, and also of wages and services of every kind, it was impossible for them to maintain themselves and families without involving much more expense than any compensation which could be paid them as volunteer troops under the laws of the United States, and, as will be seen by the letters of General Wright, hereafter quoted, they were expected, as volunteer troops, to furnish themselves with horses and equipments, in addition to what could be furnished by the Government.

The military authorities of the United States well knew at that time the exact condition of the country and of the roads across the mountains leading thereto and of the cost of transportation and of the prices of labor and of supplies and of their own inability to furnish either horses or equipments for a military service that required mounted troops.

FIRST CALL BY THE UNITED STATES FOR NEVADA VOLUNTEERS.

In view of the necessities of the situation, and with all the facts fully known to the military authorities of the United States, General Wright, commanding the Department of the Pacific, was authorized by the War Department to raise volunteer military companies in Nevada Territory for the protection of said overland mail and emigrant route, and on April 2, 1863, he addressed the following requisition for troops to the Governor of the Territory:

HEADQUARTERS DEPARTMENT OF THE PACIFIC,
San Francisco, Cal., April 2, 1863.

His Excellency O. CLEMENS,
Governor of Nevada Territory, Carson City, Nev.:

SIR: I have been authorized by the War Department to raise volunteer companies in Nevada Territory for the purpose of moving east on the overland mail route in the direction of Great Salt Lake City. If it is possible to raise three or four companies in the Territory for this service I have to request your excellency may be pleased to have them organized. I should be glad to get two companies of cavalry and two of infantry. The mounted troops to furnish their own horses and equipments. Arms, ammunition, etc., will be furnished by the United States. Should your excellency consider it improbable that this volunteer force can be raised, even one company will be

accepted. I will send you a plan of organization, and an officer with the necessary instructions for mustering them into the service.

With great respect, I have the honor to be, your most obedient servant,

G. WRIGHT,
Brigadier-General, U. S. Army, Commanding.

Official copy.

J. C. KELTON,
Colonel, A. A. G.

While correspondence was being conducted between the Governor of Nevada and General Wright as to the method of organizing Nevada's troops, the following telegram was dispatched by General H. W. Halleck, general-in-chief of the U. S. Army, to General Wright:

HEADQUARTERS OF THE ARMY,
Washington, D. C., April 15, 1863.

Brig. Gen. G. WRIGHT,
San Francisco, Cal. :

The Secretary of War authorizes you to raise additional regiments in California and Nevada to re-enforce General Conner and protect overland route. Can not companies be raised in Nevada and pushed forward immediately? General Conner may be able to raise some companies in Utah or out of emigrant trains.

H. W. HALLECK,
General-in-Chief.

———

Whereupon General Wright addressed the governor of Nevada Territory the following communication:

HEADQUARTERS DEPARTMENT OF THE PACIFIC,
San Francisco, Cal., April 16, 1863.

His Excellency ORION CLEMENS,
Governor of Nevada Territory, Carson City, Nev. :

SIR: I have the honor to acknowledge the receipt of your excellency's communication of the 9th instant.

The Indian disturbances along the line of the overland mail route, east of Carson City, threaten the entire suspension of our mail facilities, as well as preventing any portion of the vast immigration approaching from the east reaching Nevada. The interest and prosperity of your Territory depend much upon maintaining free and safe access to it from all directions. My force immediately available for operation on that line is small. A company of cavalry stationed at Fort Churchill, and under orders to move towards Ruby Valley, I was compelled to divert for temporary service to assist in quelling an Indian outbreak in the Owen's Lake district. As soon as the services of this company can be dispensed with there, it will operate on the mail and emigrant line. Some infantry companies will also be thrown forward from this side of the mountains as soon as transportation can be prepared and the roads are in order. In the mean time it is of such importance to keep the mail and emigrant route east of you open, that I would earnestly recommend that one or two companies of cavalry be promptly organized and prepared for muster into the service of the United States. It is impossible for us at this moment to purchase horses and equipments. Each man would have to furnish his own.

I can furnish arms, ammunition, forage, clothing, provisions, etc.; in fact, everything except horses and equipments.

The organization of a company or troop of cavalry is: one captain, one first lieutenant, one second lieutenant, one first sergeant, one quartermaster-sergeant, one commissary sergeant, five sergeants, eight corporals, two teamsters, two farriers or blacksmiths, one saddler, one wagoner, and seventy-eight privates.

This is the first appeal that has been made to Nevada Territory, a Territory soon to add another star to that glorious galaxy which adorns our beautiful banner, and I doubt not this call will be nobly responded to by the loyal and patriotic citizens of the Territory.

With great respect, your excellency's most obedient servant,

G. WRIGHT,
Brigadier-General U. S. Army, Commanding.

Official copy.

J. C. KELTON.
Colonel, A. A. G.

NEVADA'S RESPONSE TO THE FOREGOING CALL FOR TROOPS BY THE UNITED STATES.

Immediately upon the receipt of the foregoing requisition for troops the governor of Nevada issued the following proclamation:

PROCLAMATION.

EXECUTIVE DEPARTMENT,
Carson City, April 24, 1863.

Whereas Brigadier-General George Wright, United States Army, commanding officer of the Department of the Pacific, has, by authority of the War Department called upon me for two companies of infantry and two companies of cavalry to serve three years, or during the war:

Now, therefore, I, Orion Clemens, governor of the Territory of Nevada and commander-in-chief of the militia thereof, do hereby authorize and call upon the citizens of the Territory, as many as shall be necessary to fill up the preceding requisition, to immediately organize themselves into companies as required hereby.

In witness whereof I have hereunto set my hand and affixed the great seal of the Territory.

Done at Carson City, Territory of Nevada, this 24th day of April, in the year of our Lord one thousand eight hundred and sixty-three.

ORION CLEMENS,
Secretary and Acting Governor.

In answer to these calls and requisitions of General Wright and said proclamation of the governor of Nevada four companies of cavalry were completely organized, two of which were sent to Camp Douglas, Utah Territory, for military service, and the remaining two were sent to station Fort Churchill, Nev.

SECOND CALL AND REQUISITION OF THE UNITED STATES FOR NEVADA VOLUNTEERS.

Thereafter General Wright made a further requisition upon the governor of Nevada for two additional companies of cavalry and a regiment of infantry, as will appear from the following:

HEADQUARTERS DEPARTMENT OF THE PACIFIC,
San Francisco, December 22, 1863.

SIR: The four companies of cavalry called for from the Territory of Nevada have completed their organization; two of the companies have reached Camp Douglas, Utah, and the remaining two are at Fort Churchill, Nev. On the representations of Governor Nye that additional troops can be raised in Nevada, I have, under the authority conferred upon me by the War Department, called upon the governor for a regiment of infantry and two more companies of cavalry.

Very respectfully, your obedient servant,

G. WRIGHT,
Brig. Gen., U. S. Army, Commanding.

ADJUTANT-GENERAL, U. S. ARMY,
Washington, D. C.

WHAT WAS DONE BY NEVADA UNDER THE SECOND CALL AND REQUISITION BY THE UNITED STATES FOR NEVADA VOLUNTEERS.

In response to General Wright's second requisition for troops made in the latter part of November, 1863, the governor of Nevada issued the following proclamation:

PROCLAMATION.

Whereas a requisition having been made upon me by Brig. Gen. George Wright, U. S. Army, commanding the Department of the Pacific, for one regiment of volunteer infantry and two companies of cavalry, for service in the employ of the General Government of the United States;

Now, therefore, I, James W. Nye, governor of the Territory of Nevada and com-

mander-in-chief of the militia thereof, by virtue of the authority in me vested, do issue this my proclamation, calling upon the people of this Territory to forthwith proceed to organize a regiment of infantry, consisting of ten companies, and two companies of cavalry, in full compliance of said requisition.

All applicants for line officers will present themselves before the Army examining board for examination, and report to me with certificate of such examination as soon as practicable.

Given under my hand and seal at Carson, Nev., this 4th day of December, A. D. 1863.

JAMES W. NYE,
Governor of the Territory of Nevada.

Attest:
OLION CLEMENS,
Secretary of the Territory.

Under this last requisition of General Wright and last proclamation of the governor of Nevada two additional cavalry companies and the First Battalion Nevada Infantry Volunteers, composed of four companies, were raised and assigned to duty to such fields of military service in Utah and Nevada as were determined upon by General Wright, as will appear from the correspondence printed in the appendix, marked "Exhibit 3, pages 24 to 29.

It will thus be seen that the people of the Territory of Nevada responded promptly to and complied fully with the appeals of the United States Government for troops and in accordance with the requisitions and calls of the War Department. The action of the people of Nevada was reported to Mr. Seward, Secretary of State, by the governor of Nevada on March 25, 1864. He wrote to Mr. Seward the condition of affairs in the Territory, which letter was transmitted to the Senate by President Lincoln on April 29, 1864 (see Senate Ex. Doc. No. 41, 38th Cong., 1st sess.). In his report Governor Nye said:

We have raised in the Territory within the last two years one company of infantry, now attached to a California regiment, a battalion of cavalry, consisting of six companies, four of which are in the field; the remaining two will be there also as soon as they can be mounted. In addition we are raising a regiment of infantry, now in a good state of forwardness, and we can raise a brigade easily if necessary.

SOME OF THE DUTIES OF THE TROOPS CALLED TO AID THE UNITED STATES AT THIS TIME.

The first duty of these troops was to open and guard the overland mail and emigrant route from the Sierra Nevada Mountains to Utah. The campaign in which this was accomplished was under the command of General Conner. The volunteer troops under this gallant officer had already conducted a most successful campaign against the Indians of eastern Nevada, Utah, and Idaho, in the region where the Mormon influence was most potential, conquered many Indian tribes, and secured lasting peace.

The Secretary of War, in reporting to Congress the condition of things in that region of country, then under the military command of General Conner, said as follows, to wit:

DEPARTMENT OF THE PACIFIC.

This department has been most signally exempt from the evils of civil war, and consequently has enjoyed unexampled prosperity. Some thefts and robberies having been committed by roving bands of Indians on the overland stage route in January last, General Conner marched with a small force to Bear River, Idaho, where, on the 26th, he overtook and completely defeated them in a severe battle, in which he killed 224 of the 300 and captured 175 of their horses. His own loss in killed and wounded was 63 out of 200. Many of his men were severely injured by the frost. Since this severe punishment the Indians in that quarter have ceased to commit depredations on the whites. (Secretary of War's report, first session Thirty-eighth Congress.)

ADDITIONAL CAUSES THAT LED TO A THIRD CALL AND REQUISITION BY THE UNITED STATES FOR NEVADA VOLUNTEERS.

Congress having on July 1, 1862, chartered the Union Pacific Railroad Company, to which, and also to the Central Pacific Railroad Company, aid was given to build one continuous line of railroad from the Missouri River to the Pacific Ocean through this region of country, did, on July 2, 1864, still further foster these enterprises by additional grants. These two companies thereupon placed in the field numerous corps of surveyors, civil engineers, and employés to explore said country in the effort to discover the most practicable and economical railroad route from the Missouri River to the Pacific, and to run trial lines and definitely locate the lines of the two subdivisions of said railroad route. In regard to these roads the Secretary of War, in his annual report for 1864–'65, page 144, said:

It is, in a military sense, of the utmost importance that the Pacific Railroad should be pressed to the earliest possible completion.

The exploration and location for a Pacific railroad through that region of country then mostly uninhabited except by large tribes and roving bands of hostile Indians, called for additional military protection and rendered it necessary for the United States to again call upon Nevada to raise additional troops. Accordingly General McDowell, commanding the Department of the Pacific, made the following call on October 13, 1864, upon the Governor of Nevada Territory:

HEADQUARTERS DEPARTMENT OF THE PACIFIC,
Virginia City, October 13, 1864.

SIR: I have the honor to acquaint you that I have received authority from the War Department to call on you, from time to time, as the circumstances of the service may require, for not to exceed in all, at any one time, one regiment of volunteer infantry and one regiment of volunteer cavalry, to be mustered into service of the United States as other volunteer regiments, under existing laws and regulations.

Under this authority I have to request you will please raise, as soon as possible, enough companies of infantry to complete, with those already in service from Nevada, a full regiment of infantry.

Brigadier-General Wason will confer with you and give all the information necessary to details for this service.

I have the honor to be, governor, very respectfully, your most obedient servant,
IRWIN McDOWELL,
Major-General, Commanding Department.

His Excellency JAMES W. NYE,
Governor of Nevada Territory.

WHAT WAS DONE BY NEVADA IN RESPONSE TO THIS CALL.

The governor of Nevada responded to this call by issuing the following proclamation:

PROCLAMATION.

TERRITORY OF NEVADA, EXECUTIVE DEPARTMENT,
Carson City, October 19, 1864.

Whereas I have received a requisition from Maj. Gen. Irwin McDowell, commanding Department of the Pacific, the same having been made under authority from the War Department, to raise, as soon as possible, enough companies of infantry to complete, with those already in service from Nevada, a full regiment of infantry:

Now, therefore, I, James W. Nye, governor of the Territory of Nevada, and commander-in-chief of the militia thereof, do hereby call upon the citizens of this Territory to organize themselves into seven companies, sufficient to fill the battalion of infantry now in service from this Territory, and the requirements of said requisition.

In witness whereof I have hereunto set my hand and caused the great seal of the

Territory of Nevada to be affixed. Done at Carson City this 19th day of October, 1864.

JAMES W. NYE,
Governor and Commander-in-Chief of the Territory of Nevada.

Attest:
ORION CLEMENS,
Secretary of the Territory.

Afterward the Indians became troublesome between Utah and the Missouri River. During the years 1865-'66 the Nevada cavalry were actively engaged in Colorado, Wyoming, Kansas, and Nebraska in the Indian wars in that region. The writer of this report crossed the continent in the summer of 1865, and met several small detachments of Nevada cavalry in active service against the Indians, and was much gratified to learn that they were quite celebrated for their gallantry and faithful services in that kind of warfare, which subjects the soldier to the severest test of endurance, and requires individual exertion and watchfulness unknown in civilized war.

METHOD RECOGNIZED BY NEVADA FOR THE ENROLLMENT OF HER TROOPS CALLED INTO THE MILITARY SERVICE OF THE UNITED STATES AND HER MODE OF DEFRAYING THE EXPENSES OF SUCH ENROLL-MENT FOR SUCH SERVICE.

The citizens of Nevada were never drafted, nor did they ever hire substitutes, but were organized into military companies by commanding officers, most of whom had undergone an examination for commission before military boards instituted for that purpose and satisfactory to the general of the United States Army commanding the military Department of the Pacific.

As a compensation to and a reimbursement intended for all the costs by them incurred for raising and organizing said volunteer military companies, and in lieu of all other kinds of expenses necessarily incident to enrolling and enlisting the members of said companies for the military service of the United States, the legislature of Nevada passed an act providing for the payment to the commanding officers of said companies of $10 per capita for each volunteer soldier by them for said purposes enrolled and enlisted, aggregating the sum of $11,840. This provision in said statute was improperly called a "bounty;" but this expenditure was not in any sense whatsoever a "bounty," but, on the contrary, it was an actual disbursement by Nevada to cover all the legitimate expenses of every kind incident to enrolling and enlisting Nevada's troops to perform military service for the United States.

The history of this expenditure and of this mode of enrollment of troops by the Territory of Nevada, and the economy and reasons therefor, are all fully set forth in a memorial to Congress signed by all the State officers of Nevada, which is printed in the appendix, marked Exhibit No. 4, page 29.

METHOD ADOPTED BY NEVADA TO PAY THE TROOPS CALLED INTO THE MILITARY SERVICE OF THE UNITED STATES BY THE TERRITORY OF NE-VADA, AND THE EXTENT TO WHICH THE STATE OF NEVADA PLEDGED HER FAITH TO PAY THE OBLIGATIONS CONTRACTED BY THE TERRI-TORY OF NEVADA TO AID THE UNITED STATES.

This same act of the legislature of Nevada, among other things, provided that each citizen of Nevada so volunteering and enlisting as a private soldier for the military service of the United States, not being

drafted or acting as a substitute for another, should, during each and every month while honorably serving the United States, be paid out of the treasury of Nevada the sum of $5 per month, gold coin. It further provided that, in the case of an enlisted married man, an allotment of the whole or a portion of the extra monthly pay could be drawn by his family dependent upon him for support (see Laws of Nevada Territory, 1864, page 81, or appendix, Exhibit No. 5, page 31).

On March 11, 1865, after Nevada became a State, an act similar to this Territorial act, but more liberal in its provisions, was passed, to take the place of the Territorial law. The State legislature having deemed the situation so important to maintain the good faith of the Territory, that had been pledged to aid the United States, it passed this act *over the veto of Governor Blasdel*, who alleged in his veto message his fear that the expense might exceed the constitutional limit, etc.

This act provided for the assumption and payment by the State of Nevada of all obligations of every kind that had been incurred and contracted to be paid by the Territory for the enlistments, enrollments, bounties, extra pay, etc., of volunteer soldiers that had been theretofore called into the military service of the United States. The bonds now outstanding and still due by Nevada, though at a smaller rate of interest than that named in the original issue and still drawing interest, were issued under the provisions of this latter act (see Statutes, Nevada, 1864-'65, page 389, or appendix, Exhibit No. 6, page 34).

RESULTS OF THE FOREGOING LEGISLATION BY NEVADA.

By these legislative enactments of Nevada substantial and effectual aid was given and guaranteed by Nevada, both as a Territory and State, to the Government of the United States in guarding its overland mail and emigrant route and the line of the proposed transcontinental railroad in furnishing troops during the war of the rebellion and for suppressing Indian hostilities and maintaining peace in the country inhabited by the Mormons, and for the common defense as contemplated in said circular letter of Secretary Seward along an exposed, difficult, and hostile Indian frontier, and then but sparsely populated. These enactments were fully known to the authorities of the United States and to Congress; they have ever been acquiesced in and met with the sanction and practical indorsement of the United States, in whose interest and for whose benefit they were made. As a partial compensation to these volunteers for this irregular, hazardous, and exposed service in the mountains and on the desert plains, and to aid them to a small extent to maintain families dependent upon them for support, first the Territory and afterwards the State of Nevada offered and paid this small stipend, never suspecting that the United States would not promptly and willingly respond when asked to re-imburse the same. These citizens of Nevada who volunteered and enlisted and did military service for the United States were compelled in many cases to abandon their employments, in which their wages were always lucrative and service continuous, so that nothing less than the individual patriotism of these volunteers enabled the Territory and State of Nevada to cheerfully and promptly respond to every call and requisition made upon them for troops by the United States.

The records of the War Department, in addition to what is already quoted and referred to in substantiation of the facts herein stated, are printed in the appendix, marked Exhibit No. 3, pages 24 to 29.

THE BASIS AND AUTHORITY OF NEVADA'S CLAIM AGAINST THE UNITED
STATES AND THE PRECEDENTS IN SUPPORT THEREOF.

These enactments of Nevada both as a Territory and a State, and
various acts done under them in and execution thereof, when complying
according to her own methods with the various calls and requisitions of
the United States for troops, have resulted in the expenditure of a large
sum of money which constitutes the present claim of Nevada against
the United States. The authority upon which this claim rests is found
in the fourth section of the fourth article of the Constitution of the
United States, which provides that—

The United States shall guaranty to every State in the Union a republican form of
government, and shall protect each of them against invasion, and, on application of
the legislature, or of the executive (when the legislature can not be convened),
against domestic violence.

And upon the latter part of the tenth section of the first article of
the Constitution; which is as follows:

No State shall, without the consent of Congress, lay any duty on tonnage, keep
troops or ships of war in time of peace, enter into any agreement or compact with
another State, or with a foreign power, or engage in war, unless actually invaded or
in such imminent danger as will not admit of delay.

And also upon the act of July 28, 1795, chapter 36, section 1, page
424, now section No. 1642, U. S. Revised Statutes, which provides
that—

Whenever the United States are invaded or are in imminent danger of invasion
from any foreign nation or Indian tribe, or of rebellion against the authority of the
Government of the United States, it shall be lawful for the President to call forth such
number of the militia of the State or States most convenient to the place of danger
or scene of action, as he may deem necessary to repel such invasion or to suppress such
rebellion, and to issue his orders for that purpose to such officer of the militia as he
may think proper.*

In reference to the foregoing the courts have held that—

When a particular authority is confided to a public officer, to be exercised by him
in his discretion, upon an examination of the facts of which he is made the appropriate judge, his decision upon the facts in the absence of any controlling provision,
is absolutely conclusive as to the existence of those facts (Allen vs. Blunt, 3 Story,
U. S. Circuit Court Reports, 745).*

And again the supreme court of the State of New York (Hon. Chancellor Kent presiding as chief justice) held in the case of Vanderheyden
vs. Young, 11 Johnson's New York Reports, 157, that—

It is a general and sound principle that when the law vests any person with a
power to do an act, and constitutes him a judge of the evidence on which that act
may be done, and at the same time contemplates that the act is to be carried into
effect through the instrumentality of agents, the person thus clothed with power is
invested with discretion and is quoad hoc a judge.
His mandates to his legal agents on his declaring the event to have happened will
be a protection to those agents, and it is not their duty or business to investigate the
facts thus referred to their superior, and to rejudge his determination.*

The United States Supreme Court in Martin vs. Mott, 12 Wheaton,
19, unanimously held—

That the authority to decide upon what occasions and upon what emergencies Federal calls should be made and Federal assistance given, "belongs exclusively to the
President, and that his decision is conclusive upon all other persons."*

And Chief Justice Taney, in Luther vs. Borden, 7 Howard, referred
approvingly to the opinion of the United States Supreme Court in Martin vs. Mott, as expressed in these words:

That whenever a statute gives a discretionary power to any person to be exercised
by him upon his own opinion of certain facts, it is a sound rule of construction that
the statute constitutes him the sole and exclusive judge of the existence of those facts.*

* NOTE.—The acts of heads of Departments of the Government are in law the acts
of the President (Wilcox vs. Jackson, 13 Peters., 498).
H. Rep. 2553——3

The obligations arising under these provisions of the Constitution and laws and decisions have been recognized by the Government from its foundation, as will fully appear from the authorities cited by Senator Dolph in a report made by him from the Senate Committee on Claims on February 25, 1885 (Forty-eighth Congress, second session), Report No. 1438. These authorities are printed in the appendix, marked Exhibit No. 7, page 37 *et sequiter*.

NEVADA'S DILIGENCE IN THESE PREMISES.

The State of Nevada has not slept upon her rights in any of these premises nor been guilty of any *laches*; on the contrary, at all proper times she has respectfully brought the same to the attention of Congress by memorials of her legislature and of her State authorities, and through her representatives in Congress. On March 29, 1867, her legislature first asked for the payment of the claims of the State by a joint resolution, which is printed in the appendix, marked Exhibit No. 8, page 64. And again, on February 1, 1869, the legislature of Nevada passed a memorial and joint resolution renewing her prayer in these premises, which is also so printed in the appendix, marked Exhibit No. 9, page 65.

The Journals of the United States Senate show that on March 10, 1868, the writer of this report presented the first-mentioned memorial and resolution to the Senate, accompanied with an official statement of the amount of the claims of the State referred to therein. These papers were referred to the Committee on Claims, but the records fail to show that any action was ever taken upon them. On May 29 of the same year the writer of this report introduced a joint resolution (S. 138) providing for the appointment of a board of examiners to examine the claims of the State of Nevada against the United States, and on June 18 of the same year the Committee on Claims, to whom this joint resolution was referred, was discharged from its further consideration. The official statement of the moneys expended by the State of Nevada on account of the United States, and presented to the Senate on March 10, 1868, can not now be found on the files of the Senate.

On February 11, 1885, and January 26, 1887, the legislature of Nevada, renewing its prayer for a re-imbursement of the money by her expended for the use and benefit of the United States, further memorialized Congress, asking for the settlement of her claims, which are printed in the appendix and marked Exhibits Nos. 10 and 11, pages 65 and 66.

PROCEEDINGS IN CONGRESS TO REDEEM THE OBLIGATIONS OF THE
UNITED STATES DUE TO NEVADA IN THIS CASE.

The circumstances under which these expenditures were made by the Territory and State of Nevada being exceptional, and their re-imbursement not being provided for by any existing law, general or special, Senator Fair, of Nevada, on December 13, 1881, introduced a joint resolution in the Senate providing for the equitable adjustment of these claims of Nevada now under consideration, which was referred to the Committee on Military Affairs. A copy of said resolution will be found in the appendix, marked Exhibit 12, page 67.

This committee, instead of reporting back this joint resolution, reported back a substitute in the form of a bill providing for the payment of the claims of several States and Territories, including the State of Nevada, and which bill finally resulted in the act of June 27, 1882. This bill was reported on May 12, 1882, by Hon. L. F. Grover, and

Nevada believed then and believes now that it was then the intention of Congress to equitably and explicitly provide for the re-imbursement to her of the amount of money which she had actually and in good faith expended in these premises. This bill was accompanied by a report in which the following statement is made in relation to the claims of the State of Nevada:

NEVADA.

It appears by the report of the Adjutant-General U. S. Army, of February 25, 1882, that one regiment of cavalry and one battalion of infantry were raised in the late Territory of Nevada during the late war of the rebellion; and that the expenses of raising, organizing, and placing in the field said forces were never paid by said Territory, but were assumed and paid by the State of Nevada, and that none of said expenses so incurred by said Territory, and assumed and paid by said State, have ever been re-imbursed the State of Nevada by the United States, and that no claims therefor have ever been heretofore presented by either said Territory or said State for audit and payment by the United States. Under section 3489 of the Revised Statutes, hereinbefore referred to, the payment of these claims is barred by limitation.

These forces were raised to guard the overland mail route and emigrant road to California, east of Carson City, and to do other military service in Nevada, and were called out by the governor of the late Territory of Nevada upon requisitions therefor by the commanding general of the Department of the Pacific, and under authority of the War Department, as appears by copies of official correspondence furnished to your committee by the Secretary of War and the general commanding the Division of the Pacific. * * *

PRESENTATION BY NEVADA TO THE UNITED STATES OF HER CLAIM.

This bill reported from this committee having become a law in an amended form on June 27, 1882, thereupon the governor and controller of the State of Nevada transmitted to the Secretary of the Treasury and Secretary of War a detailed account of the moneys actually expended and actual indebtedness assumed and paid by the State of Nevada on account of the volunteer military forces enrolled by the Territory and State of Nevada, as shown by the books of the State controller.

This statement of the claim of Nevada against the United States was prepared with great care by the proper officers of the State of Nevada, being first submitted by them to the legislature thereof in printed form at the expense of the State, and thereafter transmitted, as above stated, with proper original vouchers and evidence of every kind then in her possession, to the authorities of the Government of the United States and as provided for in said act of June 27, 1882. This statement is printed in the appendix, marked Exhibit No. 13, page 67.

DELAY OF THE UNITED STATES IN THE EXAMINATION OF NEVADA'S CLAIM AND THE CAUSES THEREOF.

This claim, with said vouchers and evidence, was first presented to the Secretary of the Treasury in 1883, where, being properly stamped, it was duly transmitted to the Secretary of War for examination and action thereon. It remained of record in the War Department unacted on up to and after August 4, 1886, because, as was stated to Congress by Hon. Robert T. Lincoln, Secretary of War, he required the aid of a board of at least three army officers to assist his Department in such examination, and he requested Congress to make an appropriation of $25,000 to defray the expenses of the examination of the different State and Territorial claims presented under the act of June 27, 1882. Congress delayed action upon these requests of the Secretary of War until August 4, 1886, on which date acts were passed providing for said board of

army officers, as asked for, and also appropriated $10,000 to defray the expenses of said examinations (see vol. 24, Stats. at Large, pages 217 and 249.)

SECRETARY LINCOLN'S CONSTRUCTION OF THIS ACT OF JUNE 27, 1882, FOR THE RELIEF OF NEVADA, ETC.

Prior to any action by the War Department on this claim of the State of Nevada, and prior to any action by Congress on the request of the Secretary of War for a board of Army officers to examine said claim, a bill was introduced in Congress by Senator Jones, of Nevada, and referred to the Secretary of War for report, providing for the payment of certain individual claims of citizens of Nevada on account of Indian hostilities in Nevada in 1860, upon which the Secretary of War reported as follows:

WAR DEPARTMENT,
Washington City, January 26, 1884.

SIR: In response to so much of your communication of the 22d ultimo as requests information concerning Senate bill 657, "to authorize the Secretary of the Treasury to adjust and settle the expenses of Indian wars in Nevada," I have the honor to invite your attention to the following report of the Third Auditor of the Treasury, to whom your request was duly referred:

"The State of Nevada has filed in the office abstracts and vouchers for expenses incurred on account of raising volunteers for the United States to aid in suppressing the late rebellion amounting to $349,697.49, and for expenses on account of her militia in the 'White Pine Indian war' of 1875, $17,650.98. Also, expenses of her militia in the 'Elko Indian war' of 1878, amounting to $4,654.64, presented under act of Congress approved June 27, 1882 (22 Statutes, 111, 112).

"These abstracts and vouchers will be sent to your Department for examination and report as soon as they can be stamped, as that statute requires a report from the Secretary of War as to the necessity and reasonableness of the expenses incurred. This statute is deemed sufficiently broad enough to embrace all proper claims of said State and Territory of Nevada."

Very respectfully, your obedient servant,

ROBERT T. LINCOLN,
Secretary of War.

Hon. S. B. MAXEY,
Of Committee on Military Affairs, United States Senate.

In accordance with this letter the Committee on Military Affairs reported back the bill referred to (S. 657), and asked that it be indefinitely postponed, and because of the explanation made by said committee, as follows, to wit:

It will be observed that it is deemed by the War Department that the act approved June 27, 1882, is sufficiently broad to embrace all proper claims of Nevada, whether as State or Territory.

For convenience of reference the above act accompanies this report, and an examination thereof, and of the construction thereon, satisfies the committee that no additional legislation is necessary.

The State of Kansas presented her claim to Secretary Lincoln under this act, which claim was by him examined, audited, and allowed for almost exactly the sum that Kansas had actually expended for the use and benefit of the United States, and all of which allowance has since been paid to Kansas by the United States, and aggregating the sum of $332,308.13 (23 U. S. Stats., 474).

AFTER OVER FOUR YEARS DELAY, SUBSEQUENT TO THE PASSAGE OF THE ACT OF JUNE 27, 1882, THE UNITED STATES TAKES UP NEVADA'S CLAIM FOR EXAMINATION, WHEN THE VERY FIRST QUESTION RAISED IS ONE OF JURISDICTION, AND WHICH IS DECIDED AGAINST NEVADA.

After the passage of said act of August 4, 1886, the War Department detailed a board of three Army officers under Special Orders No. 232,

dated October 6, 1886, to proceed to examine the claims arising under
the act of June 27, 1882, and in the manner contemplated and as provided for in said acts. The claim of the State of Nevada was the first
claim submitted to and examined by said board. This board being in
doubt whether, under the terms of said act of June 27, 1882, they could
allow a re-imbursement to Nevada of the amount by her expended for
interest and extra pay to her troops while in the military service of the
United States, referred these two questions to the Secretary of War for
his decision. On February 8, 1887, after argument was submitted to
him in support of these two elements of Nevada's claim against the
United States, the Secretary of War decided "that after a careful consideration of the subject" he was "of opinion that neither the extra pay
nor the interest can, under the provisions of the act, be allowed," meaning the act of June 27, 1882, and refused the same (see appendix, Exhibit
No. 14, page 83).

TWO SEPARATE REPORTS (A MAJORITY AND MINORITY) MADE BY THE
ARMY BOARD OF WAR CLAIMS EXAMINERS, THE MINORITY REPORT
ALLOWING ONLY ABOUT 2½ PER CENT. OF THE AMOUNT ACTUALLY EX-
PENDED BY NEVADA, AND WHICH MINORITY REPORT IS APPROVED
BY THE SECRETARY OF WAR.

It will be borne in mind that on January 26, 1884, Secretary Lincoln
was of opinion that the act of June 27, 1882, was sufficiently broad to
embrace all proper claims of the State of Nevada, and the Committee
on Military Affairs, in consequence thereof, reported to the Senate
that that committee was satisfied that no additional legislation was
necessary in regard thereto, while Secretary Endicott, on February 8,
1887, decided that the claims for expenditure for interest and extra
pay to said troops while in the service of the United States could not
be allowed by him under said act, and further, by approving the
award made by the minority examiner, and, as will hereinafter be
more particularly referred to, also disallowed the amount expended by
Nevada and by her paid as her costs for the enrollment of those very
troops so called into the service of the United States.

The day following the decision of the Secretary of War, to wit,
February 9, 1887, and contrary to a practice usual in similar cases, said
board of Army officers, instead of submitting one report to the Secretary of War, submitted two separate and independent reports, one
signed by the majority of said board and the other in the nature of a
minority report. These two reports are submitted herewith, and printed
in the Appendix, marked Exhibits Nos. 15, 16, and 17, pages 89 to 90.

The total of this particular claim of the State of Nevada so presented
to said board amounted to $349,697.49. The amount thereof that was
allowed in said minority report was only $8,559.61. This minority
report was approved by the Secretary of War, thereby disallowing or
suspending all of Nevada's claim except the paltry sum of about 2½ per
cent. of the money actually expended by Nevada for troops called into
the service of the United States and at the urgent solicitation of the
Government of the United States in its hour of need, while this same
board allowed nearly $1,000,000 of the claim of Texas, to wit, $927,242.30,
being about 50 per cent. of the claim of that State of $1,867,259.13, as
presented for re-imbursement for the expenses of her Indian wars, which
occurred since the rebellion, and prosecuted chiefly, if not solely, for
the protection of the inhabitants of the State of Texas. It is worthy
of remark that no minority report was submitted in the case of Texas.

It will be observed by a perusal of the reports of the board of war claims examiners that the great mass of this claim of the State of Nevada for re-imbursement for moneys, expended under very extraordinary circumstances, was rejected by the board of examiners on either purely technical grounds or for an alleged want of jurisdiction to make an award under what has since been admitted and found to be the most restrictive act that was ever drawn since 1789 intended as an "act of relief."

Only $8,559.61 was finally awarded to Nevada by the Secretary of War.

The want of specific information on the part of the officer making the minority report which reduced the amount of the claim to the sum named may be shown in part by the mistakes made in reference to the statutes of Nevada, which are in several public libraries here, and could have been easily examined. For example, he seems to have inferred that the act of the Nevada legislature of March 4, 1865, was the first act of the Territory providing for the organization of its militia, whereas, as we have already shown, there was an elaborate act for that purpose passed by the Territorial legislature as early as November 28, 1861, and apparently on the assumption that there was no law creating the office of adjutant-general prior to 1865, and upon the fact that no evidence was furnished that Nevada previous to April 2, 1863, had soldiers, that therefore the salary of that officer ought not to commence prior to the time when the volunteers were actually called for service into the Army. But it will be observed that he was mistaken as to the time the law was passed creating the office of adjutant-general. The second section of the act of November 28, 1861, provides that—

The adjutant-general shall be appointed by the commander-in-chief, and shall hold his office for the term of two years. He shall be *ex officio* chief of staff, quartermaster-general, commissary-general, inspector-general, and chief of ordnance. He shall receive a salary of $1,000 annually, to be paid out of moneys appropriated for that purpose. He shall reside at the seat of government, and shall keep his office open for the transaction of business every day (Sundays excepted) from 10 o'clock a. m. to 3 o'clock p. m.

The minority examiner is again mistaken if he assumed that the secretary of state of Nevada became *ex officio* adjutant-general on March 3, 1866. It is true that an act devolving the duties of adjutant-general upon the secretary of state was passed on that date, but the second section of said act provides that—

This act shall take effect and be in force from and after the first day of January, 1867 (Stats. Nev., 1866, p. 206).

Thus it appears that the secretary of state did not in fact or in law become *ex officio* adjutant-general until January 1, 1867. The original section of the militia law of 1861 in regard to the office of adjutant-general was afterward amended, changing the length of time that officer was to hold office and increasing his salary to $2,000 per annum, but the abolishment of the office did not take effect until January, 1867.

PROBABLY CONFOUNDING THE ACT OF JUNE 27, 1882, WITH THE ACT OF JULY 27, 1861.

The minority examiner in terminating the salary of adjutant-general on August 20, 1866, undoubtedly had in mind the act of July 27, 1861, and not the act of June 27, 1882, under which last act alone said board was authorized to make an examination and award; otherwise he would not have limited the salary to August 20, 1866, the end of the war of the rebellion, as heretofore officially declared, but would have certainly al-

lowed Nevada a re-imbursement for the money actually paid by her as salary to that officer until his services terminated, and the Indian wars on the plains were actually suppressed and the office of adjutant-general abolished, which was done on December 31, 1866, since which time either the secretary of state or lieutenant-governor has acted as *ex officio* adjutant-general.

Attention is called to these discrepancies simply to show that the minority examiner apparently fell into error, unintentionally, of course, in his examination of the statutes of Nevada, or failed to consider all the circumstances under which this claim of the State arose. The majority of the board who made the same award and allowance as the minority, with the exception of $1,233.50 for salary of adjutant-general prior to the time when the troops were mustered in the service, made a very thorough examination of all the vouchers showing each item of expenditure made by the State, and this examination may be assumed as correct and as establishing the fact that the State expended all the moneys for which this claim is made, leaving the question as to the liability of the Government to re-imburse the State to the discretion of Congress. There is but one item stated in the account by the board of examiners which appears to have been charged by mistake. It was undoubtedly paid by the State, but if the board are correct, it was such a palpable mistake of the State officers that the State ought to lose it. It was a double charge for rent, amounting to $38.33. This amount, together with the $8,559.61 allowed by the minority of the board of examiners, and already paid to the State, making a total of $8,597.94, should be deducted from the claim now presented by the State. The State, however, should have the benefit of the fact that no other error in the accounts was discovered. All the other disallowed claims were rejected, not because the State did not pay the money, but because the board of examiners thought they were not authorized to allow the same under the act of June 27, 1882. We print in the appendix, Exhibit No. 17, page 92, the table accompanying report of the majority of the board of war claims examiners showing the amounts allowed and disallowed, together with the reasons therefor.

The question is now presented in this case whether it is the duty of the Government to re-imburse the State for moneys honestly expended, at the request of the United States, under circumstances which rendered it impossible for the Territory and State of Nevada to comply with such request without making the expenditures in question. It must be conceded that if the State or Territory made larger expenditures than would have been required to secure like services in any other section of the country, the services secured by these expenditures at the time, place, and under the circumstances were a necessity and could not have been furnished by the State on more favorable terms, and it seems that the State and Territory did not make any expenditure that appeared at the time unnecessary.

WHAT NEVADA THOUGHT WAS INTENDED BY CONGRESS TO BE AN ACT FOR HER RELIEF AND BENEFIT IS NOW FOUND TO BE AN ACT "SO WELL AND CAREFULLY AND CLOSELY GUARDED" BY RESTRICTIONS THAT WHEN CONSTRUED BY THOSE CALLED UPON TO EXECUTE IT, IS FOUND TO BE INOPERATIVE AS A RELIEF MEASURE, AND A PRACTICAL DENIAL OF JUSTICE.

We fully concur with the officer who made the minority report, that "the restrictions imposed in the second section of the act of June 27,

1882, have been complied with as far as was possible," whatever question there may be as to his complying with the provisions of the act itself. The argument that the Government might have bought supplies cheaper under its contract system than were furnished in Nevada is one which your committee are unwilling to urge under the circumstances. The Government was not situated so as to obtain troops or supplies by contract or otherwise, but was compelled to call upon the Territory to furnish both troops and supplies. All prices of all supplies, and also of all services, at that time in Nevada were on a gold basis, and coin was the only circulating medium. The roads over the mountains were blocked by snow and no considerable amount of supplies could be transported over them. The supplies in the Territory had been carried there during the previous summer for the use of the inhabitants, and the troops had to be furnished from the limited stock of individuals found in the Territory, and at a moment's notice. The Government could not wait to advertise. The overland mail route was closed and immediate action was required. The cheapest, most effective, and in fact the only immediate relief that could be had was furnished by the militia and volunteer troops of Nevada, who, leaving their workshops and employments of every character, and the high wages for their services, were organized and marched immediately in the direction of Salt Lake City to open the mail and emigrant route. They subsequently joined General Conner's forces from California, subdued the Indians, fortified Camp Douglas, overlooking Salt Lake City, and were in the field, subject to call, to go wherever ordered or needed.

PAYMENT BY THE UNITED STATES OF ABOUT 2½ PER CENT. OF THIS CLAIM ON ACCOUNT IS NOT A VALID BASIS FOR THE UNITED STATES TO REPUDIATE THE BALANCE THEREOF, OR TO REFUSE TO PAY THE SAME, AND SHOULD NOT, IN GOOD CONSCIENCE, BE EVER PLEADED BY AN HONEST DEBTOR, FOR WHOSE RELIEF AND AT WHOSE URGENT SOLICITATION SUCH DEBT WAS INCURRED.

The fact that a small fraction only of this claim has been allowed and paid on account, to wit, about 2½ per cent., and the great bulk thereof rejected for want of jurisdiction only, is no valid objection to an authorization by Congress for the payment of what is honestly due the State of Nevada, and for this there are numerous precedents, some of which are cited in the appendix in Exhibit No. 18, pages 96 to 98.

"INTEREST" PAID IN THIS CASE BY NEVADA IS IN REALITY, IN JUSTICE, IN REASON, AND IN LAW A PROPER PART OF THE DEBT DUE NEVADA BY THE UNITED STATES, THE PAYMENT OF WHICH, TOGETHER WITH THAT OF THE PRINCIPAL IS NECESSARY TO A COMPLETE INDEMNITY.

The embarrassments under which Nevada paid the principal of the money involved in this claim is shown by the enormous rates of interest which the Territory and State were compelled to pay in order to raise money to fully comply with these calls and requisitions made for troops and as hereinbefore recited. The rates of interest which were actually paid by Nevada are shown by the official statement of her controller and as furnished to the Secretary of the Treasury and the Secretary of War, as before stated, as follows:

ABSTRACT G.—*Showing the amount actually paid by the State of Nevada and as successor to the Territory of Nevada on account of interest money on disbursements and liabilities for Nevada volunteers in the service of the United States, and employed in the defense of the United States during the war of the rebellion.*

	Amount.
First—Interest paid on $46,950.12 from February 10, 1865, to March 3, 1866, at 2 per cent. per month	$11, 925. 33
[See acts legislature of Nevada for 1864–'65, page 82, act January 4, 1865.]	
Second—Interest paid on $46,950.12 from March 3, 1866, to May 30, 1867, at 15 per cent. per annum	8, 744. 46
[See acts legislature of Nevada for 1866, page 47, act January 19, 1866.]	
Third—Interest paid on $119,800.12 from May 30, 1867, to March 28, 1872, at 15 per cent. per annum	86, 755. 25
[See acts legislature of Nevada for 1867, pages 50 and 65, act February 6, 1867.]	
Fourth—Interest paid on $119, 800.12 from March 28, 1872, to January 1, 1883, at 9½ per cent. per annum	122, 472. 33
[See acts legislature of Nevada for 1871, page 84, act February 27, 1871.]	
	229, 897. 37

Your committee, however, deem it unwise to establish a precedent under any circumstances, however extraordinary, and they admit that the recitals in support of this claim render it one extraordinary in character, of refunding interest to the full extent as paid by the Territory and State of Nevada, and as shown by the foregoing statement. The legal rate of interest of the Territory and State of Nevada was, at all the times herein stated, 10 per cent. per annum where no different rate was fixed by contract.

Your committee therefore do not feel warranted in recommending re-imbursing the State of Nevada for a higher rate of interest than the legal rate fixed by her own statutes during the period of time in which these disbursements were made, and including the period up to the date of the re-imbursement of the principal by the United States, and for that reason they have incorporated in this bill, herewith reported, a provision that the aggregate of interest accruing to Nevada between the date of the expenditure by her of the principal and of the date of the re-imbursement of such principal by the United States shall not exceed the actual amount of interest paid by the State and Territory, nor the amount of interest which would accrue to her on said principal if interest thereon were calculated during said period at the legal rate as established by the statutes of the Territory and State of Nevada. In support of the proposition that interest and principal are simply but two elements of one and the same unit and constituting a complete indemnity, your committee cite Senate Report 1069, made by Senator Spooner during the first session of the Forty-ninth Congress from the Committee on Claims (see appendix, Exhibit No. 19, pages 98 to 109.)

PRECEDENTS FOR THE PAYMENT TO STATES OF INTEREST ON THE PRINCIPAL BY THEM EXPENDED FOR THE USE AND BENEFIT OF THE UNITED STATES UNDER SIMILAR CIRCUMSTANCES.

The United States has in all cases, where the question has been properly presented, re-imbursed States for interest paid by such States on moneys by them borrowed and expended for the purpose of either enrolling, subsisting, clothing, supplying, arming, equipping, paying, furnishing, or transporting volunteer and militia forces called into the service of the United States. If it be suggested that the bill under consideration providing for the payment of both principal and interest is against precedent, we answer that, in the opinion of your committee, it is the better

practice to deal with a case in its entirety in a single act, and your committee state that there are abundant precedents for this practice, some
of which your committee cite in the appendix, Exhibit 20 on page 109.

We call particular attention to the precedents collected in the appendix, authorizing the payment of claims of States for interest on moneys
by them expended for the use and benefit of the United States (see appendix, Exhibits Nos. 18, 19, 20, and 21, pages 96 to 149).

In addition to the authorities cited in the appendix in support of
Nevada's claim for interest, your committee also refer to the case before
the Second Comptroller of the Treasury in 1869, in which that officer
made the following decision:

Interest can in no case be allowed by the accounting officer upon claims against the
Government either in favor of a State or an individual. But in cases where the claimant has been compelled to pay interest for the benefit of the Government, it then becomes a part of the principal of his claim, and as such is allowable. Such is the case
of a State which has been obliged to raise money upon interest for the suppression of
hostilities against which the United States should protect her. In such cases the
amount of interest actually and necessarily paid will be allowed, without reference
to the rate of it (section 997, Dec. 2, Comp. Ed. 1869, p. 137).

This ruling is in harmony with a long line of precedents established
by Congress, beginning in 1812, and printed in the appendix hereto
attached and marked Exhibit Nos. 18 to 21, inclusive, pages 96 to 145.

In addition to the foregoing, your committee cite in support of Nevada's claim for interest the following, to wit:

1. Forty-eighth Congress, first session, House Report No. 1670,
from Committee on Judiciary (see appendix, Exhibit 21,
page 112).
2. Forty-eighth Congress, second session, House Report No. 1102,
from Committee on War Claims (published in Exhibit No.
14, page 86).
3. Forty-ninth Congress, first session, Senate Report No. 183,
from the Committee on Military Affairs (see appendix, Exhibit 21, page 135).
4. Forty-ninth Congress, first session, Senate Report No. 2, from
the Committee on Claims (published in Exhibit No. 14,
page 85).
5. Forty-ninth Congress, first session, House Report No. 303,
from Committee on Claims (see appendix, Exhibit 21, page
119).
6. Forty-ninth Congress, first session, House Report No. 3126,
from Committee on Claims (see appendix, Exhibit 21, page
120).
7. Fiftieth Congress, first session, Senate Report No. 518, from
the Committee on Military Affairs (see appendix, Exhibit
21, page 138).
8. Fiftieth Congress, first session, House Report No. 309, from
the Committee on War Claims (see appendix, Exhibit 21,
page 137).
9. Fiftieth Congress, first session, House Report No. 1179, from
the Committee on Claims (see appendix, Exhibit 21, page
145).
10. Fiftieth Congress, first session, House Report No. 2198, from
the Committee on War Claims (see appendix, Exhibit 21,
page 144).

The precedents cited or referred to in the appendix herewith abundantly establish the fact that the United States has paid the claims of
States incurred under circumstances such as those in which Nevada ex-

pended her money for the benefit of the United States, and that in all cases properly presented to Congress, where the States were compelled to borrow money and pay interest thereon and expended the same for the use and benefit of the United States, that either at the time of providing payment for the principal or subsequently the United States has invariably assumed and paid such interest.

As before stated, the claim of the State of Nevada, provided for in this bill, has been thoroughly examined by a board of Army officers appointed for that purpose. The evidence upon which this claim was founded was submitted to said board, and the evidences of payment found by them to be correct; but said board of war-claims examiners, while finding these facts, did not, under the very restrictive and prohibitory provisions and conditions of the acts of June 27, 1882, and August 4, 1886, recommend an award to Nevada of the amount of money which they found that Nevada had actually expended for the use and benefit of the United States and in the manner as set forth in the claim as presented by Nevada for the examination of and allowance by the Treasury and War Departments; and under the terms of these acts, as construed and declared by the Secretary of War, the proper accounting officers of the Treasury could not allow Nevada any sum, either as principal or interest, not allowed by the War Department as assisted by said Army board of war-claims examiners.

COST OF TRANSPORTATION OF ARMY SUPPLIES FROM FORT LEAVENWORTH WESTWARD IN 1864-'66.

It is evident that the supplies and services furnished could not at the times and places have been obtained on more reasonable terms. And in support of this statement your committee refer to the report of the Secretary of War made during that period, and in reference to a region of country much more favorably situated than was even Nevada at that time, to wit:

The troops operating on the great western plains and in the mountain regions of New Mexico, Colorado, Utah, and Idaho are supplied principally by the trains of the Quartermaster's Department from depots established on the great routes of overland travel, to which depots supplies are conveyed by contract. * * *

Travelers by the stage from Denver to Fort Leavenworth, a distance of 683 miles, in the month of July, 1865, were never out of sight of wagons trains belonging either to emigrants or to the merchants who transport supplies for the War Department, for the Indian Department, and for the miners and settlers of the central Territories.

The cost of transportation of a *pound* of corn, hay, clothing, subsistence, lumber, or any other necessary from Fort Leavenworth—

To Fort Riley is	$0. 0244
To Fort Union, the depot for New Mexico	.1425
To Santa Fé, N. Mex	.1685
To Fort Kearny	.0644
To Fort Laramie	.1410
To Denver City, Colo	.1542
To Salt Lake City, Utah	.2784

The cost of a bushel of corn purchased at Fort Leavenworth and delivered at each of these points was as follows:

Fort Riley	$2. 79
Fort Union	9. 44
Santa Fé	10. 84
Fort Kearny	5. 03
Fort Laramie	9. 26
Denver City	10. 05
Great Salt Lake City	17. 00

(Secretary of War's report, 1865-'66, part 1, pages 23 and 112; also see General Halleck to Adjutant-General, and General McDowell to Adjutant-General U. S. Army, report of Secretary of War, October 18, 1866, pages 31 and 32.)

This table is cited to show the costs of maintaining troops in that section of the country, and also to show the comparative costs of furnishing troops and supplies in Nevada and the points immediately east thereof during the periods of time involved herein.

The details concerning the peculiar and difficult and expensive service on the plains and mountains by the troops doing military service, similar in all respects to those performed by these Nevada volunteers, are fully set forth in the report of the Secretary of War respecting the protection of the overland mail and emigrant route to the Pacific from the molestations and depredations by hostile Indians, and set forth in Ex. Docs. Nos. 9 to 24, second session Thirty-ninth Congress, 1866-'67.

CONCLUSIONS AND RECOMMENDATIONS.

Nevada has not demanded a bounty, nor presented a claim against the United States for re-imbursement of any expenditure she did not in good faith actually make for the use and benefit of the United States, and made, too, only subsequent to the date of the aforesaid appeal of Secretary Seward to the nation, and made, too, in consequence of said appeal and of the subsequent calls and requisitions made upon her then scanty resources and sparse population, and wherein the good faith of the United States was to be relied upon to make to her ungrudgingly a just re-imbursement whenever the United States found itself in a condition to redeem all its obligations.

Nevada has been diligent in making her claim known to Congress, but she has not with an indecorous speed demanded her pound of flesh, but has waited long and patiently, believing upon the principle that the higher obligations between States, like those among men, are not always "set down in writing, signed and sealed in the form of a bond, but reside rather in honor," and that the obligation of the United States due her in this case was as sacred as if it had originally been in the form of a 4 per cent. United States bond, now being redeemed by the United States at $1.27 upon each $1 of this particular form of its unpaid obligations.

Nevada has not solicited any charity in this case, but, on the contrary, by numerous petitions and memorials she has respectfully represented to Congress why the taxes heretofore levied upon her people and paid out of her own treasury to her volunteer troops in gold and silver coin to aid the United States at its own solicitation to protect itself and maintain the general welfare should be now returned to her by the General Government.

Congress should not forget that during the long period of the nation's peril the citizens of Nevada, like those of California (when not engaged in the military or naval service of the United States) not only guarded the principal gold and silver mines of the country then discovered, and prevented them from falling into the hands of the public enemy, but also worked them so profitably for the general welfare as to enable the United States to make it possible to resume specie payment, and to redeem its bonds at 27 per cent. above par, and to repay all its money-lenders at a high rate of interest, and that, too, not in the depreciated currency with which it paid Nevada's volunteer troops, but in gold coin of standard value.

As these expenditures were honestly made by the Territory and State of Nevada, your committee do not think that, under all the peculiar and exceptional circumstances of this case, the action of the Territory and State of Nevada should be hewn too nicely or too hypercritically by the United States at this late date. These expenditures were

all made in perfect good faith and for patriotic purposes, and secured effectual aid to the United States which otherwise could not have been obtained without a much larger expenditure. The State of Nevada in good faith assumed and paid all the obligations of the Territory of Nevada to aid the United States, and issued and sold its own bonds for their payment, upon which bonds it has paid interest until the present time. The only question now for consideration is, shall the United States in equal good faith and under all the circumstances herein recited relieve the State of Nevada from this obligation, or shall the United States insist and require it to be paid by the people of that State alone?

CALIFORNIA.

The total amount paid by California, as shown by said report of said war claims examiners, is $4,420,891.96. Of this amount $1,500,545.86 was interest, and $468,976.54 was expended on account of militia. Deducting these amounts and we have the expenditure of California, excluding interest and expenses of militia, $2,451,369.56.

OREGON.

The total amount paid by Oregon, as shown by said report of said war claims examiners, is $356,271.61. Of this amount $110,626.35 was interest, and $21,118.73 was expended on account of militia. Deducting these amounts and we have the expenditure of Oregon, excluding interest and expenses of militia, of $224,526.53.

NEVADA.

The total amount paid by Nevada as principal and interest, as shown by said report of said war claims examiners, is $404,040.70.

With these amendments your committee therefore recommend the passage of this bill, which, so amended, is as follows, to-wit:

A BILL to re-imburse the States of California, Oregon, and Nevada for moneys by them expended in the suppression of the rebellion.

Be it enacted by the Senate and House of Representatives of the United States of America in Congress assembled, That there is hereby appropriated, out of any money in the Treasury not otherwise appropriated, the sums hereinafter mentioned to re-imburse and to be paid to the States of California, Oregon, and Nevada for moneys by them expended in aid of the United States in the war of the rebellion, to wit:

To the State of California, the sum of two million four hundred and fifty-one thousand three hundred and sixty-nine dollars and fifty-six cents.

To the State of Oregon, the sum of two hundred and twenty-four thousand five hundred and twenty-six dollars and fifty-three cents.

To the State of Nevada, the sum of four hundred and four thousand forty dollars and seventy cents, being the sums of money shown by the reports of the Secretary of War to have been paid by said States in the suppression of the rebellion.

WAR CLAIMS OF CALIFORNIA, OREGON, AND NEVADA.

IN THE SENATE OF THE UNITED STATES.

APRIL 10, 1890.—Ordered to be printed.

Mr. STEWART, from the Committee on Military Affairs, submitted the following

REPORT:

[To accompany S. 2416.]

The Committee on Military Affairs, to whom was referred the bill (S. 2416) to re-imburse the States of California, Oregon, and Nevada for moneys by them expended in the suppression of the rebellion, having duly considered the same, respectfully report as follows:

The larger portions of the claims of these States are for extra pay and bounty paid by them during the war of the rebellion.

The circumstances under which the expenditures provided for in this bill were made by these States being exceptional, and their re-imbursement not being provided for by any existing law, general or special, prior to June 27, 1882, Senator Grover, of Oregon, on December 12, 1881, introduced Senate joint resolution No. 10, and Senator Fair, of Nevada, on December 13, 1881, introduced Senate joint resolution No. 13, providing for the equitable adjustment of these State war claims of Oregon and Nevada, which resolutions were referred to the Senate Committee on Military Affairs.

That committee, instead of reporting back said joint resolutions, reported back, May 12, 1882, in lieu thereof a substitute in the form of a bill to wit: S. 1673, Forty-seventh Congress, first session, providing for the payment of certain war claims, to wit, those only of Texas, Oregon, and Nevada, and of the Territories of Idaho and Washington, and which bill, after having been amended in the Senate so as to include the State war claims of Colorado, Nebraska, and California, and amended in the House so as to include the State war claims of Kansas, finally resulted in the passage of the act approved June 27, 1882. (22 U. S. Stats., 111.)

It was then no doubt the intention of Congress to equitably provide for the re-imbursement of all moneys which California, Oregon, and Nevada, and Nevada when a Territory, had actually expended during the war of the rebellion, on account of the several matters recited in S. bill 3420, Fiftieth Congress, first session. This bill (S. 1673, Forty-seventh Congress, first session) was accompanied by a report (S. No. 575, Forty-seventh Congress, first session) made by Senator Grover May 12, 1882, from which the following is quoted; and which renders said intention of Congress quite evident.

S. Rep. 3——1

OREGON.

It appears by the report of the Adjutant-General U. S. Army, of April 3, 1882, that one regiment of calvary, one regiment of infantry, and one independent company of cavalry were raised in the State of Oregon during the late war of the rebellion, and that the expenses incident thereto have never been re-imbursed said State by the United States: and that the claims therefor have never been heretofore presented by said State for audit and payment by the United States, as per report of the Secretary of War of April 15, 1882, and of the Third Auditor of the Treasury of April 8, 1882. Under section 3489 of the Revised Statutes, the claim for expenditures so incurred by said State can not now be presented for audit and payment without legislation by Congress. In addition thereto there are some unadjusted claims of said State growing out of the Bannock and Umatilla Indian hostilities therein in 1877 and 1878, evidenced by a communication of the Secretary of War of date last aforesaid, and some unadjusted balances pertaining to the Modoc war, not presented for audit to General James A. Hardie, approximating the sum of $5,000.

NEVADA.

It appears by the report of the Adjutant-General, U. S. Army, of February 25, 1882, that one regiment of cavalry and one battalion of infantry were raised in the late Territory of Nevada during the late war of the rebellion, and that the expenses of raising, organizing, and placing in the field said forces were never paid by said Territory, but were assumed and paid by the State of Nevada, and that none of said expenses so incurred by said Territory, and assumed and paid by said State, have ever been re-imbursed the State of Nevada by the United States, and that no claims therefor have ever been heretofore presented by either said Territory or said State for audit and payment by the United States. Under section 3489 of the Revised Statutes, hereinbefore referred to, the payment of these claims is barred by limitation.

These forces were raised to guard the overland mail route and emigrant road to California, east of Carson City, and to do other military service in Nevada, and were called out by the governor of the late Territory of Nevada, upon requisitions therefor by the commanding general of the Department of the Pacific, and under authority of the War Department, as appears by copies of official correspondence furnished to your committee by the Secretary of War and the general commanding the Division of the Pacific. * * *

The Senate Committee on Military Affairs did not at that time make any report in relation to the State war claims of the State of California, but when this substitute bill (S. 1673, Forty-seventh Congress, first session) reported from that committee was under consideration in the Senate, Senator Miller, of California, called attention to the fact that California had war claims unprovided for, and on his motion this bill (S. 1673, Forty-seventh Congress, first session) was amended in the Senate so as to include these State war claims of the State of California. It is alleged by California, Oregon, and Nevada that this act of June 27, 1882, which they believed was intended by Congress to be an act for their relief and benefit and an equitable statute to be liberally construed, has been found to be an act " so well and carefully and closely guarded by restrictions" that, when construed by those who have been called upon to execute it, has proven to be completely inoperative as an equitable relief measure, so much so as to amount to a practical denial of justice so far as the present State war claims of these States now provided for in this bill were or are concerned.

PRESENTATION BY CALIFORNIA, OREGON, AND NEVADA OF THEIR STATE WAR CLAIMS TO THE UNITED STATES.

The aforesaid bill (S. 1673, Forty-seventh Congress, first session) having become a law June 27, 1882, the State war claims of California, Oregon, and Nevada were thereafter duly transmitted for presentation to the proper authorities of the United States, those of Oregon by Hon. R. P. Earhart, and Hon. George W. McBride, secretary of state for Oregon and ex officio adjutant-general. Those for Nevada by Hon. J. F. Hallock, controller of Nevada. Those for California by Hon. John

Dunn, controller, assisted by his deputy, Hon. M. J. O'Reilly, and by Hon. D. I. Oullahan and Hon. Adam Herold, State treasurers, and General George B. Crosby, adjutant-general of California, aided therein by Hon. George Stoneman, Governor of California, and his private secretary, Hon. W. W. Moreland, and by Hon. W. C. Hendricks, secretary, and General H. B. Davidson, assistant secretary of state of California.

These State war claims of these three States, accompanied with proper original vouchers and evidence in support thereof, in each case were thereafter duly delivered by the aforesaid State authorities of California, Oregon, and Nevada, or by those duly authorized therein, to Capt. John Mullan, the duly appointed agent and authorized special counsel for each of said three States, by whom they were put in abstracts and proper shape and thereafter submitted by him to the Secretary of the Treasury and Secretary of War, as provided for in said act of Congress approved June 27, 1882.

DELAY OF THE UNITED STATES IN THE EXAMINATION OF CALIFORNIA, OREGON, AND NEVADA STATE WAR CLAIMS AND THE CAUSES THEREOF.

These State war claims, with said vouchers and evidence, so originally presented to the Secretary of the Treasury and Secretary of War for examination, remained of record in the Treasury and War Departments unacted on up to and after August 4, 1886, because, as was stated to Congress by Hon. Robert T. Lincoln, the Secretary of War, required the aid of at least three army officers to assist his Department in making a proper examination thereof, and he requested Congress to make an appropriation of $25,000 to defray the expenses of such examination of these State and Territorial war claims presented and others to be presented under said act of June 27, 1882. Congress delayed action upon these repeated requests of the Secretary of War until August 4, 1886, on which date acts were passed by Congress providing for a board of three army officers, as asked for, and also appropriating $10,000 to defray the expenses of a full and exhaustive examination (see vol. 24. Stats. at Large, pages 217 and 249) of these State war claims.

SECRETARY LINCOLN'S CONSTRUCTION OF THIS ACT OF JUNE 27, 1882, FOR THE RELIEF OF NEVADA, ETC.

Prior to any action by the War Department on these State war claims of the States of California, Oregon, and Nevada, and prior to any action by Congress on said request of the Secretary of War for a board of army officers to aid him to examine said claims, a bill, S. 657, Forty-eighth Congress, first session, was introduced in Congress by Senator Jones, of Nevada, providing for the payment of certain individual claims of citizens of Nevada on account of Indian hostilities in Nevada in 1860, and was referred by the Senate Committee on Military Affairs to the Secretary of War and of the Treasury for reports, and upon which the Secretary of War reported as follows:

WAR DEPARTMENT,
Washington City, January 26, 1884.

SIR: In response to so much of your communication of the 22d ultimo as requests information concerning Senate bill 657, "to authorize the Secretary of the Treasury to adjust and settle the expenses of Indian wars in Nevada," I have the honor to invite your attention to the following report of the Third Auditor of the Treasury, to whom your request was duly referred:

"The State of Nevada has filed in the office abstracts and vouchers for expenses in-

curred on account of raising volunteers for the United States to aid in suppressing the late rebellion, amounting to $349,697.49, and for expenses on account of her militia in the 'White Pine Indian war' of 1875, $17,650.98. Also, expenses of her militia in the 'Elko Indian war' of 1878, amounting to $4,654.64, presented under act of Congress approved June 27, 1882 (22 Statutes 111, 112).

"These abstracts and vouchers will be sent to your Department for examination and report as soon as they can be stamped, as that statute requires a report from the Secretary of War as to the necessity and reasonableness of the expenses incurred. This statute is deemed sufficiently broad enough to embrace all proper claims of said State and Territory of Nevada."

Very respectfully, your obedient servant,

ROBERT T. LINCOLN,
Secretary of War.

Hon. S. B. MAXEY,
Of Committee on Military Affairs, United States Senate.

In accordance with this report and opinion of the Secretary of War the Senate Committee on Military Affairs reported back this bill so referred to (S. 657, Forty-eighth Congress, first session), and asked that it be indefinitely postponed, and because of the explanation made to the Senate by said committee, and based upon said report and construction of said act and said opinion of the then Secretary of War, Hon. Robert T. Lincoln, as follows, to wit:

It will be observed that it is deemed by the War Department that the act approved June 27, 1882, is sufficiently broad to embrace all proper claims of Nevada, whether as State or Territory.

For convenience of reference the above act accompanies this report, and an examination thereof, and of the construction thereon, satisfies the committee that no additional legislation is necessary.

The State of Kansas presented her State war claim to Secretary Lincoln under this very act, which claim was by him examined, audited, and allowed for almost exactly the sum that Kansas had actually expended for the use and benefit of the United States, and all of which allowance has since been paid to Kansas by the United States, and aggregating the sum of $322,308.13 (23 U. S. Stats., 474) as allowed and paid to said State by the United States. So, too, the State of Nebraska under similar circumstances was allowed and paid the sum of $18,031.23 under this same act of June 27, 1882.

AFTER OVER FOUR YEARS' DELAY, SUBSEQUENT TO THE PASSAGE OF THE ACT OF JUNE 27, 1882, THE UNITED STATES TAKES UP NEVADA'S STATE WAR CLAIM FOR EXAMINATION, WHEN THE VERY FIRST QUESTION RAISED IS ONE OF JURISDICTION, AND WHICH IS DECIDED AGAINST NEVADA.

After the passage of said act of August 4, 1886, the War Department detailed a board of three Army officers under Special Orders No. 232, dated October 6, 1886, to proceed to examine the claims provided for under said act of June 27, 1882, and in the manner contemplated in said act. The State war claims of the State of Nevada were the first examined by said board. This board being in doubt whether, under the terms of said act of June 27, 1882, they could allow a re-imbursement to Nevada of the amount of money by her expended for interest and extra pay to her troops while in the military service of the United States, duly referred these two questions to the Secretary of War for his decision. On February 8, 1887, after argument was submitted to said Secretary in support of these two elements of Nevada's State war claims against the United States, that officer decided "that, after a careful consideration of the subject, he was of opinion that neither the extra pay nor the interest can, under the provisions of the act, be allowed," meaning the act of June 27, 1882, and refused the same, as appears from the correspondence following, to wit:

DECISION OF THE SECRETARY OF WAR DISALLOWING THE STATE WAR CLAIM OF NEVADA FOR INTEREST AND EXTRA PAY TO NEVADA VOLUNTEERS.

WAR DEPARTMENT,
Washington City, February 8, 1887.

SIR: The Department has received your communications of December 31, 1886, and January 28, 1887, submitting arguments in the claim of the State of Nevada, under the act of June 27, 1882, for re-imbursement of amounts paid by the State for "extra pay" and for interest. Also, your communication of 2d instant, inclosing a resolution of the senate and assembly of Nevada, requesting favorable and early action on said claim.

In reply, I have the honor to inform you that after a careful consideration of the subject I am of opinion that neither the extra pay nor the interest can, under the provisions of the act, be allowed.

Very respectfully,

WILLIAM C. ENDICOTT,
Secretary of War.

JOHN MULLAN, Esq.,
Agent of the State of Nevada, 1101 *G street, N. W., City.*

It therefore fully appears that on January 26, 1884, Secretary Lincoln, when construing said act of June 27, 1882, was of opinion that it was sufficiently broad to embrace all proper war claims of the State of Nevada; whereupon the Senate Committee on Military Affairs, in consequence thereof, reported to the Senate that said committee was satisfied that no additional legislation was necessary in regard thereto, while Secretary Endicott, on February 8, 1887, construing this same act and deciding thereunder, held that these war claims of the States and Territories named in said act for expenditure for interest and extra pay to their troops while in the service of the United States could not be allowed by him under said act.

This decision of Secretary Endicott in the case of the State of Nevada, to the effect that "under the provisions of the act of June 27, 1882, he had no jurisdiction to allow interest paid by that State upon the principal by her expended, nor the extra pay made by her to the State troops while they were in the service of the United States," became practically a decision in the case of the State war claims of the State of California, and effectually disposed of these two similar items in the war claims of that State. In addition thereto the Secretary of War, Mr. Endicott, on November 8, 1887, upon a statement made to him by the chief of said board of war claims examiners, also decided that he had no jurisdiction to adjudicate Oregon's State war claim, which claim also contained similar items for interest and extra pay, and thus Secretary Endicott's aforesaid decision in the Nevada case also practically disposed of these two similar items in Oregon's claim so far as his Department was concerned.

In consequence, therefore, of these conflicting decisions of two Secretaries of War upon one and the same act of June 27, 1882, rendering it absolutely nugatory so far as the adjustment of these State war claims of these three States were concerned, made and makes additional remedial legislation by Congress absolutely necessary in order to deal equitably with these States and their claims for re-imbursement of money by them expended in good faith for the common defense during a period of war and at the instance of the authorities of the United States.

The Senate Committee on Military Affairs, therefore, during the Fiftieth Congress, first session, had first under consideration a bill (S. 2918) "to re-imburse the State of Nevada for moneys expended on obligations incurred by said State and the Territory of Nevada, and afterwards assumed and paid by said State, in the suppression of the war of the

rebellion, and for guarding the overland mail and emigrant route," and a majority of the committee made a favorable report thereon. (S. R. No. 1286, Fiftieth Congress, first session.)

Your committee thereafter, having under due consideration similar claims for California and Oregon, reported a general bill, to wit, S. 3420, Fiftieth Congress, first session, accompanied by Senate Report No. 2014, Fiftieth Congress, first session, made August 10, 1888, for the investigation of all the war claims of California, Oregon, and Nevada substantially in the same language as recited in the resolution afterwards passed by the Senate and hereinafter set forth. A full statement of these war claims was made and submitted to your committee, but not reported to the Senate at the same time that said resolution for investigation was approved by your committee. That statement is printed in the report of the war claims examiners on the claims of the State of California, commencing after the report and after page 95 of Ex. Doc. No. 11, Fifty-first Congress, first session, and also in Senate Ex. Docs. Nos. 10 and 17, Fifty-first Congress, first session. Senate Report No. 2014, Fiftieth Congress, first session, does not seem to appear in said reports, Senate Ex. Docs. 10, 11, 17, although said bill S. 3420 passed the Senate and was favorably reported in the House September 4, 1888, in House Report No. 3396, Fiftieth Congress, first session, as follows, to wit:

Mr. Stone, of Kentucky, from the Committee on War Claims, submitted the following report (to accompany bill S. 3420).

The Committee on War Claims, to whom was referred the bill (S. 3420) authorizing the Secretary of War to ascertain what amount of money has been expended by the States of California, Oregon, and Nevada for military purposes in aid of the Government of the United States during the war of the rebellion, report as follows:

The facts out of which this bill for relief arises will be found stated in Senate report from the Committee on Military Affairs of the present Congress, which report is hereto annexed and made a part of this report. Your committee adopt the said report as their own, and report back the bill and recommend its passage.

[Senate Report No. 2014, Fiftieth Congress, first session.]

The Committee on Military Affairs, to whom was referred the bill (S. 3420) authorizing the Secretary of War to ascertain what amount of money has been expended by the States of California, Oregon, and Nevada for military purposes in aid of the Government of the United States during the war of the rebellion, having considered the same, report as follows:

During the war of the rebellion the States of California, Oregon, and Nevada were separated from the Atlantic States by over 1,500 miles of almost uninhabited country. Much apprehension was felt on account of the exposed condition of those distant States, and the Government called upon them to assist in guarding the overland mail and emigrant routes, in preventing Indian outbreaks in the States, and to aid the United States in various ways during the war of the rebellion.

At the beginning of the war Nevada was a Territory, and was admitted into the Union as a State in 1864; but for the purposes of this report Nevada will hereafter be referred to as a State.

These States complied promptly with all the requirements of the General Government, and volunteered all the aid in their power to assist the United States. On the Pacific coast during this time, and particularly in Nevada, prices of all commodities (and also the price of labor) were exceedingly high, and as a mining excitement existed in these States it became necessary to extend aid in many ways in organizing, arming, equipping, furnishing, and maintaining volunteer soldiers and militia beyond the amount required for those purposes in the Eastern States. California, Oregon, and Nevada passed numerous acts to organize and equip soldiers in compliance with the requests of the Government, for which they were compelled to expend large sums of money. They were also compelled to borrow money, upon which a large amount of interest has been paid.

An examination of all the facts connected with these claims, a statement of accounts showing for what the money was paid and under what authority, involves too

much detail for a committee of Congress to investigate. They therefore recommend the passage of the accompanying bill, which simply provides for an examination and report upon the facts of the claims of each of these States, so as to enable Congress to take such action as may be just and proper in the premises.

The bill does not commit Congress to the payment of these claims in advance, nor a settlement upon any particular theory. It does not commit Congress in advance to re-imburse these States for bounty or extra money expended by them in furnishing troops to assist the United States in suppressing the war of the rebellion, nor to the payment of interest on moneys borrowed. It simply provides for an ascertainment of such facts so as to enable Congress to legislate intelligently.

A bill for the payment of the claims of Nevada has already been reported by a majority of your committee and is now on the Calendar of the Senate. The report in that case is very elaborate, and some members of your committee desire, before action is taken on it, a more authoritative statement of the case, which will be obtained by the examination now proposed. The claims of California and Oregon are of a similar character to those of Nevada. All these States were differently situated during the rebellion from the other States of the Union, and your committee therefore thought proper to have the same investigation and report made in each case and have them all incorporated in one bill. The writer of this report has prepared an elaborate statement of the claims of California and Oregon, which has been printed by order of the Senate for the use of the committee.

The report on the Nevada claim, known as Senate Report No. 1286, and dated May 14, 1888, and the statement with regard to the claims of California and Oregon will assist the War Department in collecting the laws and orders under which these States expended the money in question, and your committee desire to call the attention of the Secretary of War to these documents in case this bill should become a law.

The laws that have been passed for the investigation of claims of other States are not applicable to the peculiar conditions of these States during the war of the rebellion, and there is no authority under them for the ascertainment of the necessary facts to enable Congress to determine what allowances should be made under the peculiar circumstances which surrounded these States at the time in question.

Your committee report the bill back with an amendment, and when so amended recommend that it do pass.

No action having been taken in the House on said Senate bill 3420 after said House Report No. 3396 was made, and it being deemed important that Congress at its present session should have before it in an official form all the data, facts, and the results of a full, exhaustive, and official examination of these State war claims to be made by the War Department, which then had and now has official custody of all these claims, and of all evidence relating thereto filed in support thereof, and in order that the Secretary of War should have the full benefit and aid of said Board of Army Officers, which was then still in session at Washington, D. C., and which Board Congress had specially created in said act of August 4, 1886 (24 U. S. Stats., 217), to aid the Secretary of War to make a full, exhaustive, and official examination of these State war claims of these three States, so that the Secretary of War could officially and intelligently report upon the same to Congress, or to either branch thereof, for its information and action, as contemplated in said Senate bill 3420, Fiftieth Congress, first session, the Senate therefore, on the 27th of February, 1889, passed the following resolution:

Resolved, That the Secretary of War, through the board of war claims examiners, appointed under section 2 of the act of Congress entitled "An act for the benefit of the States of Texas, Colorado, Oregon, Nebraska, California, Kansas, and Nevada, and the Territories of Washington and Idaho, and Nevada, when a Territory," approved August 4, 1886, be, and he is hereby, authorized and directed to examine all accounts, papers, and evidence which heretofore have been, or which hereafter may be, submitted to him in support of the war claims of the States of California, Oregon, and Nevada, and Nevada when a Territory, growing out of the war of the rebellion, and in suppressing Indian hostilities and disturbances during the war of the rebellion, and in guarding the overland mail and emigrant routes during and subsequent to the war of the rebellion, and to ascertain and state what amount of money each of said States, and Nevada when a Territory, actually expended, and what obligations they incurred for the purposes aforesaid, whether such expenditures were made or obligations incurred in actual warfare or in recruiting, enlisting, enrolling, organizing, arming, equipping, supplying, clothing, subsisting, drilling, furnishing, transporting,

and paying their volunteers, militia, and home guards, and for bounty, extra pay, and relief paid to their volunteers, militia, and home guards, and in preparing their volunteers, militia, and home guards in camp and field to perform military service for the United States.

The Secretary of War is also directed to ascertain what amount of interest has been paid by each of said States, and Nevada when a Territory, on obligations incurred for purposes above enumerated. The Secretary of War shall report to Congress the amount of money which may be thus ascertained to have been actually paid by each of said States, and Nevada when a Territory, on account of the matters above enumerated, and also the amount of interest actually paid or assumed by each of said States, and Nevada when a Territory, on moneys borrowed for the purposes above enumerated. And the Secretary of War shall also report the circumstances and exigencies under which, and the authority by which, such expenditures were made, and what payments have been made on account thereof by the United States.

In response to this resolution the honorable Secretary of War, having theretofore fully completed, with the aid of said Army Board, a thorough, and exhaustive official examination of all these war claims of said three States, transmitted in December, 1889,his report to the Senate in each of the cases of California, Oregon, and Nevada, as required by said resolution, and which reports are as follows, to wit: Senate Ex. Docs. Nos. 10, 11, 17, Fifty-first Congress, first session. These reports and the exhibits attached thereto, respectively, are in great detail, and contain a very full history of the important part taken by the Pacific States and Territories during the rebellion in defense of the Union. These reports are in full compliance with said Senate resolution, showing the actual amount of money expended by each of said States, and of Nevada when a Territory, during the war of the rebellion in aid of the United States, and the authority, State, Territorial, and national, and also the special circumstances and exigencies under which the expenditures reported upon by said Secretary and said board therein respectively were made. The following tables, taken from the reports of said war claims examiners, show the several sums of money actually expended and paid out as principal and interest by each of said States:

CALIFORNIA.

[Senate Ex. Doc. No. 11, Fifty-first Congress, first session, page 27.]

Amount expended in recruiting California volunteers (Abstract F)....	$24,260.00
Amount expended in payment of adjutant-general, etc. (Abstract H)...	38,083.17
Amount expended in organizing volunteers (Abstract M)...............	5,639.34
Amount expended in pay of volunteer officers (Abstract N)...........	23,277.34
Amount expended in extra pay to enlisted men of California volunteers (Abstract P)...	1,459,270.21
Amount expended in bounty to enlisted men (Abstract Q).............	900,839.50
Total expense of volunteers, and not repaid the State by the United States..	2,451,369.56
Amount expended in payment of interest on moneys borrowed to carry out the provisions of the acts of April 27, 1863, and April 4, 1864	1,500,545.86
Aggregate expenses incurred on account of volunteers, principal and interest...	3,951,915.42
Amount expended on account of militia................................	468,976.54
Grand total of expenses on account of volunteers and militia....	4,420,891.96

OREGON.

[Senate Ex. Doc. No. 17, Fifty-first Congress, first session, page 20.]

Amount expended in payment of adjutant-general, etc. (Abstract E). .	$3,973.49
Amount expended in extra pay to enlisted men (Abstract G)...........	90,476.32
Amount expended in bounty to enlisted men (Abstract H).............	129,241.02
Amount expended for advertising calls for redemption of bonds (Abstract K)	835.70

Amount expended in payment of interest on moneys borrowed to carry out the provisions of the acts of October 24, 1864 (Abstract L) $110,626.35

Total amount expended on account of volunteers and not repaid State by United States 335,152.88
Amount expended on account of militia............................. 21,118.73

Aggregate expenses incurred on account of militia and volunteers..... 356,271.61

NEVADA.

[Senate Ex. Doc. No. 10, Fifty-first Congress, first session, page 8.]

Amount actually paid out on account of volunteers raised in Nevada.... $118,667.49
Amount of interest paid on moneys borrowed and so expended.......... 289,645.59
Amount of liabilities assumed on account of volunteers raised in Nevada. 1,133.92
Amount of interest paid on liabilities assumed 3,143.31

Total amount expended or assumed............................. 412,600.31
Amount already paid to Nevada by the United States upon an examination under the provisions of the act of June 27, 1882................. 8,559.61

Amount expended or assumed and not repaid by the United States.. 404,040.70

INTEREST.

In said Ex. Doc. No. 10, Fifty-first Congress, first session, page 15, it is declared that—

Interest paid by California, Oregon, and Nevada is in reality, in justice, in reason, and in law a proper part of the debt due them by the United States, the payment of which, together with that of the principal, is necessary to a complete indemnity.

The United States has generally refused to pay interest on claims against the Government. This rule sometimes works great hardship and wrong; but the inconveniences that might arise from a departure from it may be very great. There is one exception, however, to this rule which has been uniformly recognized and acted upon; that is, when a State has claims against the Government for expenditures made for the United States, and a part of such claims consists of interest paid out or assumed by the State, the interest so paid out or assumed has been treated eventually so far as the adjustment thereof was concerned as it it had. been originally presented as a part of the principal, although Congress has always treated the interest as a separate, independent, and distinct claim apart from the principal, which sometimes is adjusted when adjusting the principal, depending no doubt in part upon the special circumstances of the cases presented to Congress and at other times adjusted after the principal is paid, but always adjusting it some time in all proper cases. The rule is well stated in the Decisions of the Second Comptroller for 1869, page 137, as follows:

Interest can in no case be allowed by the accounting officers upon claims against the Government, either in favor of a State or an individual. But in cases where the claimant has been compelled to pay interest for the benefit of the Government it then becomes a part of the principal of the claim, and as such is allowable.

Such is the case of a State which has been obliged to raise money upon interest for the suppression of hostilities against which the United States should protect her.

In such cases the amount of interest actually and necessarily paid will be allowed, without reference to the rate of it.

There are many cases to sustain this ruling of the Second Comptroller, of which the following are cited as precedents where Congress first authorized the adjustment and payment of the principal and then subsequently adjusted and thereafter paid the interest:

1. By an act approved April 2, 1830, the Secretary of the Treasury was authorized to cause to be paid to the mayor and city council of Baltimore the sum of $7,434.53 in full for their claim against the United States for money borrowed and expended by

them in defense of said city in the war of 1812, and by the second section of said act the Secretary of the Treasury was directed to cause to be paid interest on said sum according to the provisions and regulations of "the act to authorize payment of interest due the city of Baltimore," approved May 20, 1826.

2. By an act approved May 31, 1830, the proper accounting officers of the Treasury, under the superintendence of the Secretary of War, were authorized and directed to audit and settle the claims of the State of Massachusetts against the United States for services of her militia during the war of 1812, in the following cases:

(1) Where the militia of said State were called out to repel actual invasion, or under a well-founded apprehension of invasion, provided their numbers were not in undue proportion to the exigency.

(2) Where they were called out by the authority of the State and afterwards recognized by the Federal Government.

(3) Where they were called out by and served under the requisition of the President of the United States or of any officer thereof.

3. By a joint resolution approved May 14, 1836, entitled "A resolution to authorize the Secretary of War to receive additional evidence in support of claims of Massachusetts and other States of the United States for disbursements, services," etc , during the war of 1812, the Secretary was authorized, in preparing his report pursuant to the resolution of House of Representatives agreed to the 24th of February, 1832, without regard to existing rules and requirements to receive such evidence as was on file, and any further proofs which might be offered tending to establish the validity of the claims of Massachusetts upon the United States, or any part thereof, for services, disbursements, and expenditures during the war with Great Britain; and in all cases where such evidence should, in his judgment, prove the truth of the items of the claim, or any part thereof, to act on the same in like manner as if the proof consisted of such vouchers and evidence as was required by existing rules and regulations touching the allowance of such claims; and it was provided that in the settlement of claims of other States upon the United States for services, disbursements, and expenditures during the war with Great Britain, the same kind of evidence, vouchers, and proof should be received as therein provided for in relation to the claim of Massachusetts.

4. By the sixth section of an act approved March 31, 1837, an appropriation was made for paying the claims of the State of Connecticut for the services of her militia during the war of 1812, to be audited and settled by the proper accounting officers of the Treasury under the superintendence of the Secretary of War in the following cases:

(1) Where the militia of said State were called out to repel actual invasion or under a well-founded apprehension of invasion, provided their numbers were not in undue proportion to the exigency.

(2) Where they were called out by the authorities of the State and afterwards recognized by the Federal Government, and

(3) Where they were called out and served under the requisition of the President of the United States or of any officer thereof.

5. By an act approved August 14, 1848, the proper accounting officers of the Treasury were directed to settle the claims for one month's service of the officers and soldiers of the Fourth Regiment in the Second Brigade of the Third Division of the militia of the State of Vermont, who served at the battle of Plattsburgh on the 11th of September, 1814, for their military services on that occasion.

6. By act approved March 3, 1853, making appropriations for the civil and diplomatic expenses of the Government for the year ending June 30, 1854, an appropriation of $10,334.31 was made for arrearages of pay, subsistence, and clothing due to Capt. Richard McRae's Company of Virginia Volunteers, which served in the war with Great Britain in 1812–'13 to be paid to the officers and soldiers of said company or their legal representatives, under the order of the Secretary of War, upon the production of proof as to the identity of said officers and soldiers, and that they have not been paid.

7. By an act approved August 31, 1852 (Army appropriation), the Secretary of War was required to pay to the State of South Carolina such sums of money as were paid by said State in 1838, 1839, and 1840 for services, losses, and damages sustained by her volunteers in the Florida war of 1836, 1837, and 1838, while in the service of the United States, and on their return from said service, as were ascertained and allowed by the board of commissioners appointed for that purpose by the act of the legislature of said State in 1837, with the proviso that no interest should be allowed upon moneys paid to the State of South Carolina under the provisions of said act. And it was by said act further provided that in the settlement of the claims of the State of Georgia, under the act of August 11, 1842, providing for the settlement of the claims of that State for the service of her militia, which had theretofore been suspended or disallowed, the accounting officers of the Treasury Department should allow and pay, upon proof that the State had allowed and paid the same, all accounts for forage, subsistence, hospital stores, medical service, and transportation which had not there-

tofore been allowed by the United States. And it was further provided by said act that in the adjustment of the accounts of the State of Maine, under the act of June 13, 1842, the proper accounting officers of the Treasury should include and allow the claims which had theretofore been presented under said act, provided it should be satisfactorily shown that said claims had been actually allowed and paid by said State.

8. By an act approved March 3, 1853, second section, the proper accounting officers of the Treasury Department were authorized to settle the claims of the State of Florida for services of her troops under the act of February 27, 1851, by the provision stated for the settlement of the claims of the State of Georgia for like services, under the act approved August 31, 1851 (Army appropriation bill).

9. ˙By the eighth section of an act approved March 3, 1853, the Secretary of the Treasury was directed to pay to the State of Georgia her claims remaining unpaid for moneys paid by the State in suppressing hostilities of the Cherokee, Creek, and Seminole Indians in the year 1835 and since, upon proof that the same was paid by the State, and that the provisions of the act relative to the settlement of the claims of Georgia for military service, approved March 3, 1851, should be extended to payments under said act.

The Secretary of the Treasury was also by said act required to pay the State of Alabama, under the provisions of the acts of Congress of August 16, 1842, and January 26, 1849, the balance due said State, growing out of the Creek Indian hostilities of 1836 and 1837; and by the twelfth section of said act it was provided that in the adjustment of the accounts of the State of Virginia under the twelfth section of the act of August 31, 1852, the Secretary of War should follow the provisions of the act of June 2, 1848, providing for refunding to the several States the amounts expended by them in raising regiments of volunteers for the Mexican war.

10. By an act approved January 26, 1849, the Secretary of War was directed to pay interest upon the advances made by the State of Alabama for the use of the United States Government in the suppression of hostilities by the Creek Indians in 1836 and 1837, at the rate of 6 per cent. per annum from the time of the advances until the principal of the same was paid by the United States to the State. And in ascertaining the amount of interest it was provided that interest should not be computed on any sum which Alabama had not expended for the use and benefit of the United States, as evidenced by the amount refunded to the State of Alabama by the United States, and that no interest should be paid on any sum on which the State of Alabama did not either pay or lose interest as aforesaid.

11. By an act approved March 3, 1851, the Secretary of War was authorized to allow to the State of Georgia for advances made to the United States for the suppression of hostilities of the Creek, Seminole, and Cherokee Indians in the years 1835, 1836, 1837, and 1838, with interest at the rate of 6 per cent. per annum on all sums allowed and paid to the State of Georgia and that might thereafter be allowed and paid for any moneys advanced by the State for the purposes aforesaid, from the date of such advances until the principal sums were or might be paid by the United States, with the proviso that no interest should be paid on any sum on which Georgia did not either pay or lose interest.

12. By an act passed the same day as the above act, the proper accounting officers of the Treasury were directed to settle the claim of the State of Maine against the United States, being for interest on money borrowed and actually expended by her for the protection of the northeastern frontier of said State during the years 1839 1840, and 1841, the amount of such interest to be ascertained under the following rules:

"(1) Interest not to be computed on any sum not expended by the State for the use and benefit of the United States, as evidenced by the amount refunded or paid to the State by the United States.

"(2) No interest to be paid on any sum on which the State did not either pay or lose interest."

13. By act approved July 21, 1852, making appropriations to supply deficiencies in the appropriations for the year ending June 30, 1852, the sum of $80,741 was appropriated for pay of five companies of Texas mounted volunteers.

14. By act approved March 3, 1859, for the purpose of executing the resolution of May 14, 1836, the Secretary of the Treasury was directed to pay to Massachusetts $227,176.48, reported to be due said State by Secretary of War J. R. Poinsett, in report dated December 23, 1837, made to the House of Representatives December 27, 1837, and it was provided that in lieu of payment in money the Secretary of the Treasury might, at his discretion, issue to said State United States stock bearing 5 per cent. per annum, and redeemable at the end of ten years, or sooner, at the pleasure of the President.

15. By act approved March 3, 1825, the accounting officers of the Treasury Department were authorized and directed to settle the claim of the State of Virginia against the United States for interest upon loans on moneys borrowed and actually expended by her for the use and benefit of the United States during the war of 1812.

16. By this act it was provided that, in ascertaining the amount of interest, as aforesaid, due to the State of Virginia, the following rules should be understood as applicable to and governing the case, to wit: First, that interest should not be computed on any sum which Virginia had not expended for the use and benefit of the United States, as evidenced by the amount refunded or repaid to Virginia by the United States. Second, that no interest should be paid on any sum on which she had not paid interest. Third, that when the principal, or any part of it, had been paid, or refunded by the United States, or money placed in the hands of Virginia for that purpose, the interest on the sum or sums so paid or refunded should cease, and not be considered as chargeable to the United States any longer than up to the repayment, as aforesaid.

The mode of computing interest provided by the above act appears to have been satisfactory at the time to all the States, and their claims against the General Government were authorized to be adjusted, and were adjusted under the same rules for computing interest.

17. By an act approved May 13, 1826, entitled "An act authorizing the payment of interest due to the State of Maryland," the accounting officers of the Treasury Department were authorized and directed to liquidate and settle the claim of the State of Maryland against the United States, for interest upon loans on moneys borrowed and actually expended by her for the use and benefit of the United States, during the late war with Great Britain, and the same rules for computing the interest was provided by the act as in the case of the State of Virginia.

18. By an act approved May 13, 1826, entitled "An act authorizing the payment of interest due to the State of Delaware," the accounting officers of the Treasury Department were authorized and directed to take similar action in regard to the settlement of the claim of the State of Delaware against the United States as that directed to be taken in the case of the claim of Maryland, and to be governed by the same rules.

19. By act approved May 20, 1826, the proper accounting officers of the Treasury Department were directed to settle the claim of the city of Baltimore against the United States, for interest on money borrowed and actually expended by the city in its defense during the war of 1812; and the act further provided that the amount due should be ascertained under rules which were the same as those provided by the foregoing act for the adjustment of the accounts in the cases of Virginia, Maryland, and Delaware.

20. By an act approved May 22, 1826, entitled "An act authorizing the payment of interest due to the State of New York," the accounting officers of the Treasury Department were authorized and directed to take similar action and to be governed by the same rules as in the cases of Virginia, Maryland, and Delaware.

21. By an act approved March 3, 1827, the accounting officers of the Treasury Department were authorized and directed to settle the claim of the State of Pennsylvania in the same manner as in the cases of Maryland, Delaware, and New York.

22. By an act approved March 22, 1832, entitled "An act for the adjustment and settlement of the claims of the State of South Carolina against the United States," the accounting officers of the Treasury were authorized and directed to liquidate and settle the claim of the State of South Carolina against the United States for interest upon money actually expended by her for military stores for the use and benefit of the United States, and on account of her militia, whilst in the service of the United States, during the late war with Great Britain, the money so expended having been drawn by the State from a fund upon which she was then receiving interest. The act designates upon what sums interest shall be paid, and recites in detail other claims of the State theretofore disallowed, which shall be adjusted and settled, such as claims for cannon-balls, transportation of troops and supplies, pay to certain staff officers, blankets ($7,500 being the amount of this item), and muskets.

23. By an act approved March 3, 1857, a re-examination and re-adjustment of the account of the State of Maryland was directed to be made, and it was provided that in the calculation of interest the following rules should be observed:

"Interest shall be calculated up to the time of any payment made. To this interest the payment shall be first applied, and if it exceeds the interest due, the balance shall be applied to diminish the principal; if the payment fall short of the interest, the balance of interest shall not be added to the principal so as to produce interest. Second, interest shall be allowed on such sums only on which the State either paid interest or lost interest by the transfer of an interest-bearing fund."

Under this act Maryland received the additional sum of $275,770.23.

24. By section 7 of said act (March 1, 1837), an appropriation was made to pay all the claims of North Carolina for the services of her militia during the war of 1812 with Great Britain in the cases enumerated in the act approved May 31, 1830, entitled "An act to authorize the payment of the claims of the State of Massachusetts for certain services of her militia during the war of 1812," and also the claims of said State for disbursements in the purchase of munitions or other supplies on account of the war and expended therein.

25. On the 8th day of July, 1870, an act was passed directing the account between the United States and Massachusetts and Maine to be re-opened and re-adjusted, and Massachusetts received the sum of $678,362.42, of which one-third was allotted to the State of Maine as an integral part of Massachusetts when the advances were made.

In the foregoing cases the principal was first re-imbursed, and subsequently the interest was adjusted and then paid by the United States. The following cases are cited as precedents, where both the principal and interest were authorized by Congress to be paid at one and the same time and in and under one and the same act:

1. By a joint resolution approved March 3, 1847 (Stats. at Large, vol. 9, p. —), the Secretary of War was authorized and required to cause to be refunded to the several States or to individuals for services rendered, acting under the authority of any State, the amount of expenses incurred by them in organizing, subsisting, and transporting volunteers previous to their being mustered and received into the service of the United States for the war with Mexico, and for subsisting troops in the service of the United States.

2. By an act approved June 2, 1848, the provisions of said joint resolution were extended so as to embrace all cases of expenses theretofore incurred in organizing, subsisting, and transporting volunteers previous to their being mustered and received into the Unite States for the war with Mexico, whether by States, counties, corporations, or individuals, either acting with or without the authority of any State, and that in refunding moneys under said act and said joint resolution it should be lawful to pay interest at the rate of 6 per cent. per annum on all sums advanced by States, corporations, or individuals in all cases where the State, corporation, or individual paid or lost the interest or was liable to pay it.

3. By act approved August 5, 1854, the sum of $924,259.65 was appropriated to reimburse the State of California for expenditures "in the suppression of Indian hostilities within the State prior to the 1st day of January, 1854." (See U. S. Stats. at Large for 1853 and 1854.)

4. By act approved August 18, 1856 (section 8), the Secretary of War was authorized and directed to pay to the holders of the war bonds of the State of California the amount of money appropriated by act of Congress approved May [August] 5, 1854, in payment of expenses incurred and actually paid by the State of California for the suppression of Indian hostilities within the said State prior to the 1st day of January, 1854, under the following restrictions and regulations:

Before any bonds were redeemed by the Secretary of War they were required to be presented to the board of commissioners appointed under an act of the legislature of said State, approved April 19, 1856, and the amount due and payable upon each bond indorsed thereon by said commissioners; the amounts in the aggregate not to exceed the amount appropriated by act of August 5, 1854.

All the States, except California, Oregon, and Nevada, have been re-imbursed by the United States all or nearly all of the principal of the moneys expended by them in the suppression of the rebellion. None of them have as yet been re-imbursed for interest which they paid to obtain said principal.

The following table shows the amount of money already paid by the United States as principal to the several States for the suppression of the rebellion, as shown by the books of the Treasury Department:

[Senate Ex. Doc. No. 11, Fifty-first Congress, first session, p. 63.]

States.	Amount.	States.	Amount.
Connecticut	$2,006,950.46	Minnesota	$71,075.20
Massachusetts	3,608,091.95	Kansas	384,138.15
Rhode Island	723,530.15	Nebraska	485.00
Maine	1,027,185.00	Colorado	55,238.84
New Hampshire	976,531.92	Missouri	7,580,421.43
Vermont	832,557.40	Michigan	814,262.53
New York	4,156,935.50	Delaware	31,988.06
New Jersey	1,517,026.79	Maryland	133,140.99
Pennsylvania	3,871,710.59	Virginia	48,469.97
Ohio	3,245,319.58	West Virginia	471,063.94
Wisconsin	1,035,059.17	Kentucky	3,504,466.57
Iowa	1,039,759.45		
Illinois	3,080,442.51	Total	44,137,596.34
Indiana	3,741,738.29		

In addition to the payment of said war claims to the several States on account of the war of the rebellion, as shown by the foregoing table, the claims of the following-named States for expenses in the suppression of Indian hostilities, etc., have been settled by the Third Auditor of the Treasury under the said act of June 27, 1882, and all of which have heretofore been paid by the United States:

States.	Amount.
Kansas	$332,308.13
Nebraska	18,081.23
Nevada	8,559.01
California	11,723,64
Texas	927,177.40
Total	1,297,850.01

An additional sum of $148,615.97 has been allowed the State of Texas by the Third Auditor, and the settlement is now pending before the Second Comptroller of the Treasury, under said act of June 27, 1882.

The said State war claims of California, Oregon, and Nevada during the war of the rebellion reported on by the honorable Secretary of War and said board of war claims examiners under said resolution of the Senate of February 27, 1889, were never before properly or fully considered for want of jurisdiction, as hereinbefore shown, until they were so reported upon by the present Secretary of War, Hon. Redfield Proctor, aided by said Army board in said Senate Ex. Docs. 10, 11, 17.

Your committee recognize and approve the precedents which treat interest paid by a State on money borrowed or advanced for suppressing rebellion or repelling invasion in aid of the United States as a legitimate charge against the Government in every case where the Government is equitably liable for the principal; but inasmuch as none of the States have as yet been re-imbursed for any claim for interest paid out by them on money borrowed or advanced and expended by them on account of the war of the rebellion, your committee recommend that this bill be amended so as to omit at this time the claim for interest presented by California and Oregon in the two cases examined herein and reported upon in Senate Ex. Docs., Nos. 11 and 17, Fifty-first Congress, first session.

The claim of Nevada, however, for the re-imbursement of the interest actually paid out by her on the principal by her borrowed and in good faith expended for the common defense, and at the behest of the authorities of the United States, presents a question different from that of the other States. Nevada was a Territory at the time when the greater part of these expenditures were made. The necessity for these expenditures was imperative. The settlements in Nevada were isolated and separated from California by the Sierra Nevada Mountains, which cut off all means of transportation for several consecutive months in each year. There were no railroads. Transportation of freights was confined to teams and pack animals. The Indians along the overland route became hostile and cut off communication between the Atlantic and Pacific States. It was under these circumstances that the Territory of Nevada was called upon by the United States authorities to raise volunteer troops and furnish supplies for them. Labor was excessively high on account of the new mines, and supplies scarce and exceedingly dear. This Territory had no money to comply with these demands made upon her by the United States military authorities, and was forced to borrow money as best she could.

When the Territory of Nevada became a State the State of Nevada assumed the indebtedness of the Territory, including these war claims, and inserted a provision in her constitution in the following language:

All debts and liabilities of the Territory of Nevada lawfully incurred, and which remain unpaid at the time of the admission of this State into the Union, shall be assumed by and become the debt of the State of Nevada. (Compiled Laws of Nevada, vol. 1, page 133.)

Under these exceptional circumstances your committee recommend the payment of both principal and interest in the case of Nevada.

EXTRA PAY AND BOUNTIES.

As we have already seen, the larger portion of the claims of each of the States of California, Oregon, and Nevada were expended for extra pay and bounties. This was an absolute necessity for two reasons: First, the expenses of living and wages of labor in the Pacific coast States were during the rebellion at least 50 per cent., and in many cases 200 per cent., higher than in the Atlantic States; second, the Pacific States and Territories maintained the gold standard continuously throughout the war. The United States paid said volunteer troops in Treasury notes, although they had on deposit at the sub-treasury at San Francisco at all times a large amount of gold. The discount which the soldiers were compelled to pay to convert their greenbacks into gold was from 30 to 60 per cent.

This added largely to the cost of living.

Extra pay was found necessary to provide for the support of the families of the soldiers. This extra allowance, however, in the shape of extra pay and bounty did not exceed the extra compensation which the Government had theretofore paid the officers of the Army and Navy and the enlisted soldiers and sailors stationed on the Pacific coast between the dates of the acquisition of California and the breaking out of the rebellion. The Pacific coast States and Territories had a right to assume that the United States would continue or resume such extra pay and compensation during the war of the rebellion. Certainly the necessity for it was much greater in war than in peace, and, as a matter of fact, it was imperative.

On the 17th of June, 1850, an act was passed, the third section of which reads as follows:

SEC. 3. And be it further enacted, That whenever enlistments are made at, or in the vicinity of, the said military posts, and remote and distant stations, a bounty equal in amount to the cost of transporting and subsisting a soldier from the principal recruiting depot in the harbor of New York, to the place of such enlistment, be, and the same is hereby, allowed to each recruit so enlisted, to be paid in unequal installments at the end of each year's service, so that the several amounts shall annually increase, and the largest be paid at the expiration of each enlistment. (U. S. Stat., vol. 9, p. 439.)

On the 23d of September, 1850, the following provision was inserted in the Army appropriation bill:

For extra pay to the commissioned officers and enlisted men of the Army of the United States, serving in Oregon or California, three hundred and twenty-five thousand eight hundred and fifty-four dollars, on the following basis, to wit: That there shall be allowed to each commissioned officer as aforesaid, whilst serving as aforesaid, a per diem, in addition to their regular pay and allowances, of two dollars each, to each enlisted man as aforesaid, whilst serving as aforesaid, a per diem, in addition to their present pay and allowances, equal to the pay proper of each as established by existing laws; said extra pay of the enlisted men to be retained until honorably discharged. This additional pay to continue until the first of March, eighteen hundred and fifty-two, or until otherwise provided. (U. S. Stat., vol. 9, p. 504.)

The first of these acts was continued in force until August 3, 1861 (U. S. Stat., vol. 12, p. 288, sec. 9), on which date it was repealed. During the time when the last of said acts was in existence the United States soldiers and sailors on the Pacific coast received nearly double pay.

During the five years immediately prior to the rebellion the United States Army serving in the Pacific coast States and Territories was composed, first, of men transported from New York, via the Isthmus of Panama, at an aggregate cost to the United States of not less than $390,103, or at an average cost for each officer of $293, and for each enlisted man of $154 when landed in Oregon; or $275 for each officer and $115 for each enlisted man, when landed in California; and when discharged, all said enlisted men were entitled to an amount of money equal to the actual cost of their traveling expenses and subsistence back to New York; estimated by the War Department to be $142, making a total aggregate cost for each enlisted man of $293 and $256, respectively; or second, said army was composed of men enlisted in the Pacific coast States and Territories, at an expense to the United States of $142 per capita, paid to each enlisted man as a bounty under said act of Congress approved June 17, 1850 (9 U. S. Stat., 439), which payments were made continuously from June 17, 1850, to August 3, 1861. (U. S. Stat., vol. 12, p. 288.)

During the first year of the war of the rebellion the larger portion of this United States military force was transported from the Pacific coast States and Territories back to New York, via the Isthmus of Panama, at an aggregate cost to the United States of not less than $303,380, or at an average cost for each enlisted man, of $145 from Oregon and of $125 from California.

Details of these various items of cost to the United States for thus transporting said military force to and from New York to the Pacific coast States and Territories are set forth in a table, prepared under the direction of the honorable Secretary of War as follows, to wit:

Statement of number of officers and enlisted men of the United States Army transported at the expense of the United States from New York City to various points in California and Washington Territory via the Isthmus of Panama, in the years 1856, 1857, 1858, 1859, and 1860; also the amount paid for similar services from April 15, 1861, to December, 1861, between Oregon, Washington, California, and Nevada to New York, via the Isthmus of Panama, showing the total and the average cost per capita of each, so far as shown by the records of this office.

Destination.	Year.	Officers.	Cost.	Enlisted men.	Cost.	Total cost.	Average cost per officer.	Average cost per man.
New York City to San Francisco, Cal., via the isthmus.........	1856	3	$750	396	$39,600	$40,350		
Do......................	1857	9	2,700	470	58,750	61,450		
Do......................	1858	2	600	34	493	1,093	} $267.86	$109.83
Do......................	1859*							
Do......................	1860	21	5,325	441	44,000	49,325		
Total	......	35	9,375	1,341	142,843	152,218		
New York City to Benicia, Cal., via the isthmus..............	1857	18	5,000	689	79,525	84,525	} 284.00	121.16
Do......................	1858	7	2,100	445	57,875	59,975		
Total	......	25	7,100	1,134	137,400	144,490		
New York City to Fort Vancouver, Wash., and near Portland, Oregon, via the isthmus......	1858	15	4,500	400	61,500	66,000	} 293.12	151.09
Do......................	1859	1	190	14	1,050	1,240		
Total	......	16	4,690	414	62,550	67,240		
Fort Vancouver, Wash., to Benicia, Cal.....................	1856	1	60	50	1,750	1,810	60.00	35.00
San Francisco,Cal., to Fort Vancouver, Wash...............	1858	18	1,000	787	23,345	24,345	55.56	29.66
San Francisco,Cal.,to New York City, via the isthmus.........	1861	49	12,250	1,495	186,875	199,125	250.00	125.00
San Pedro, Cal., to New York City, via the isthmus	1861	15	3,750	500	62,500	66,250	250.00	125.00
San Francisco, Cal., to Fort Vancouver, Wash...............	1861	30	1,200	775	15,500	16,700	40.00	20.00
Fort Vancouver, Wash., to San Francisco, Cal	1861	34	1,400	960	19,900	21,300	40.00	20.73

* None found.

QUARTERMASTER-GENERAL'S OFFICE,
Washington, D. C., January 8, 1890.

In consequence of this withdrawal in 1861 of said military forces from the Pacific coast, in order that they might perform military services in the East, and in view of the circumstances and exigencies existing in the Pacific Coast States and Territories during the rebellion period, requisitions were duly made from time to time by the President of the United States and by the Secretary of War upon the proper State authorities of California, Oregon, and Nevada for volunteers to perform military service for the United States in said States and Territories, as are fully and in detail set forth in said Senate Ex. Docs., Nos. 10, 11, 17, Fifty-first Congress, first session. In compliance with the several calls so made between 1861 and 1866, inclusive,

Volunteers'

The State of California furnished 15,725
The State of Nevada furnished 1,180
The State of Oregon furnished 1,810

Making a total aggregate of 18,715

men who enlisted and were duly mustered into the military service of the United States as volunteers in said States. The same number of

18   WAR CLAIMS OF CALIFORNIA, OREGON, AND NEVADA.

troops if organized and transported from New York City to the Pacific coast States and Territories in the same manner as was done by the United States War Department from June 17, 1850, to August 3, 1861, would have cost the United States at that time the sum of about $5,483,385 for *transportation alone.*

The reports of said war claims examiners upon extra pay in Nevada, California, and Oregon are as follows, to-wit:

[Senate Ex. Doc. No. 10, Fifty-first Congress, first session, p. 7.]

NEVADA.

Extra monthly pay—liabilities assumed.

It appears from the affidavit of the State comptroller (herewith, marked Exhibit No. 2), that liabilities to the amount of $1,153.75 were assumed by the State of Nevada as successor to the Territory of Nevada on account of "costs, charges, and expenses for monthly pay to volunteers and military forces in the Territory and State of Nevada in the service of the United States," and that State warrants fully covering such liabilities were duly issued. It is also shown in the affidavit that of said warrants two for the sums of $11.33 and $8.50 respectively have been paid, such payment reducing said liabilities to $1,133.92.

The circumstances and exigencies under which the Nevada legislature allowed this extra compensation to its citizens serving as volunteers in the United States Army are believed to have been substantially the same as those that impelled the legislatures of California and Oregon to a similar course of action for the relief of the contingent of troops raised in each of these States. Prices of commodities of every kind were extravagantly high during the war period in Nevada, which depended for the transportation of its supplies upon wagon roads across mountain ranges that were impassable for six months of every year; and at certain times at least during the said period, the rich yields of newly-opened mines produced an extraordinary demand for labor, largely increasing wages and salaries. These high prices of commodities and services were co-existent with, though in their causes independent of, the depreciation of the Treasury notes, which did not pass current in that section of the country, though accepted through necessity by the troops serving there; and it is safe to say that in Nevada, as in California and Oregon, the soldier could buy no more with a gold dollar than could the soldier serving in the Eastern States with the greenback or paper dollar.

On the whole, therefore, we are decided in the conviction that in granting them this extra compensation the legislature was mainly instigated by a desire to do a plain act of justice to the United States volunteers raised in the State and performing an arduous frontier service, by placing them on the same footing, as regards compensation, with the great mass of the officers and soldiers of the United States Army, serving east of the Rocky Mountains. It is true that the seven companies of infantry that were called for on October 19, 1864, had not been organized; and that on March 8, 1865, three days before the approval of the State law above noticed, the commanding general Department of the Pacific wrote as follows from his headquarters at San Francisco to the governor of Nevada (see page 287, Senate Ex. Doc. 70, Fiftieth Congress, second session):

"What progress is making in recruiting the Nevada volunteers? I will need them for the protection of the State, and trust that you may meet with success in your efforts to raise them. I hope the legislature may assist you by some such means as have been adopted by California and Oregon."

But the fact remains that the declared purpose of the monthly allowance was to give a compensation to the Nevada volunteers (see section 1 of the act last referred to), and that when measured by the current prices of the country in which they were serving, their compensation from all sources did not exceed, if indeed it was equal to, the value of the money received as pay by the troops stationed elsewhere, *i. e.*, outside of the Department of the Pacific.

[Senate Ex. Doc. No. 11, Fifty-first Congress, first session, p. 23.]

CALIFORNIA.

Extra pay to enlisted men.

By an act approved April 27, 1863, the legislature appropriated and set apart "as a soldiers' relief fund" the sum of $600,000, from which every enlisted soldier of the companies of California volunteers raised or thereafter to be raised for the service of the United States was to be paid, in addition to the pay and allowances granted him

by the United States, a "compensation" of $5 per month from the time of his enlistment to the time of his discharge. Drafted men, substitutes for drafted men, soldiers dishonorably discharged or discharged for disability existing at time of enlistment, were not to share in the benefits of the act, and, except in cases of married men having families dependent upon them for support, payment was not to be made until after discharge. Seven per cent. interest bearing bonds to the amount of $600,000, in sums of $500, with coupons for interest attached to each bond, were authorized to be issued on July 1, 1863. (Pages 349-351, Statement for Senate Military Committee.)

A few unimportant changes respecting the mode of payment in certain cases was made by act of March 15, 1864, and on March 31, 1866, the additional sum of $550,000 was appropriated for the payment of claims arising under its provisions, such sum to be transferred from the general fund of the State to the "Soldiers' Relief Fund."

Fearing that the total amount of $1,150,000 specifically appropriated might still prove insufficient to pay all the claims accruing under the act of April 27, 1863, above mentioned, the legislature directed, by an act which also took effect March 31, 1866 (page 604, Stats. of California, 1865-'66), that the remainder of such claims should be audited and allowed out of the appropriation and fund made and created by the act granting bounties to the volunteers of California approved April 4, 1864, and more fully referred to on page 19 of this report.

Upon the certificate of the adjutant-general of the State that the amounts were due under the provisions of the act and of the board of State examiners, warrants amounting to $1,459,270.21 were paid by the State treasurer, as shown by the receipts of the payees indorsed on said warrants.

It is worthy of note here that on July 16, 1863, the governor of California, replying to a communication from the headquarters Department of the Pacific, dated July 5, 1863, advising him that under a resolution of Congress adopted March 9, 1862, the payments provided for by the State law of April 27, 1863, might be made through the officers of the Pay Department of the U. S. Army, stated that the provisions of said law were such as to preclude him from availing himself of the offer.

Some information as to the circumstances and exigencies under which this money was expended may be derived from the following extract from the annual report of the adjutant-general of the State for the year 1862, dated December 15, 1862:

"The rank and file of the California contingent is made up of material of which any State might be proud, and the sacrifices they have made should be duly appreciated and their services rewarded by the State. I do most earnestly recommend therefore that the precedent established by many of the Atlantic Coast States of paying their troops in the service of the United States an additional amount monthly should be adopted by California, and that a bill appropriating, say, $10 per month to each enlisted man of the troops raised or to be raised in this State be passed. * * * This would be a most tangible method of recognizing the patriotic efforts of our soldiers, relieve many of their families from actual destitution and want, and hold out a fitting encouragement for honorable service." (Page 58, Statement for Senate Committee on Military Affairs.)

Your examiners are of the opinion that the favorable action which was taken on the above recommendation of the Adjutant-General can not be justly ascribed to any desire on the part of the legislature to avoid resort to a conscription, although the exclusion of drafted men from the benefits of the act indicates that they realized and deemed it proper to call attention to the possibility of a draft. Unlike the law of April 4, 1864, the benefits of which were confined to men who should enlist after the date of its passage and be credited to the quota of the State, the provisions of the act now under consideration extended alike to the volunteers who had already entered or had actually completed their enlistment contract and to those who were to enlist in the future. There is every reason for the belief that the predominating if not the only reason of the State authorities in enacting this measure was to allow their volunteers in the United States service such a stipend as would, together with the pay received by them from the General Government, amount to a fair and just compensation. In fact, as has already been stated, this was expressly declared to be the purpose of the act.

It appears that up to December 31, 1862, those of the United States troops serving in the Department of the Pacific who were paid at all—in some cases attachments had not been paid for a year or more—were generally paid in coin, but on February 9, 1863, instructions were issued from the Treasury Department to the Assistant Treasurer of the United States at San Francisco that "checks of disbursing officers must be paid in United States notes." (Letter of Deputy Paymaster-General George H. Ringgold, dated February 13, 1863, to Paymaster-General; copy herewith marked Exhibit No. 10.)

Before this, greenbacks had become the current medium of exchange in all ordinary business transactions in the Eastern States, but in the Pacific Coast States and the adjoining Territories, gold continued to be the basis of circulation throughout

the war. At this time the paper currency had become greatly depreciated, and on February 28, 1863, the price of gold in Treasury notes touched 170. This action of the Government in compelling troops to accept such notes as an eqivalent of gold in payment for services rendered by them in a section where coin alone was current, gave rise to much dissatisfaction. For although gold could be bought in San Francisco at nearly the same price in Treasury notes as in New York, it must be remembered that the troops in the Department of the Pacific were largely stationed at remote and isolated points.

When paying in greenbacks for articles purchased by, or for services rendered to, them in these out-of-the-way places, they were obliged to submit not only to the current discount in San Francisco but also to a further loss occasioned by the desire of the persons who sold the articles, or rendered the service, to protect themselves against possible further depreciation. It admits of little doubt that by reason of his inability to realize the full value of paper money, as quoted in the money centers, and of the fact that wages and the cost of living and of commodities of every kind were abnormally high (owing in great part to the development of newly discovered mines in that region) the purchasing power of the greenback dollar in the hands of the average soldier serving in the Department of the Pacific was from the latter part of 1862 onward from 25 to 50 per cent. less than that of the same dollar paid to his fellow soldier in the East.

Representation of the great hardship the Treasury Department's instructions entailed upon the troops were promptly made. On March 10, 1863, the legislature telegraphed to Washington a resolution adopted on that date instructing the State's delegation in Congress to impress upon the Executive "the necessity which exists of having officers and soldiers of the U. S. Army, officers, seamen, and marines of the U. S. Navy, and all citizen employés in the service of the Government of the United States serving west of the Rocky Mountains and on the Pacific coast paid their salaries and pay in gold and silver currency of the United States, provided the same be paid in as revenue on this coast." (Page 46, Statement for Senate Committee on Military Affairs.)

And on March 16, 1863, Brig. Gen. G. Wright, the commander of the Department of the Pacific (comprising besides California, the State of Oregon and the Territories of Nevada, Utah, and Arizona), transmitted to the Adjutant General of the U. S. Army a letter of Maj. C. S. Drew, First Oregon Cavalry, commandant at Camp Baker, Oregon, containing an explicit statement of the effects of and a formal protest against paying his men in greenbacks. In his letter of transmittal (page 154, Ex. Doc. 70), General Wright remarked as follows:

"The difficulties and embarrassments enumerated in the major's communication are common to all the troops in this department, and I most respectfully ask the serious consideration of the General-in-Chief and the War Department to this subject. Most of the troops would prefer waiting for their pay to receiving notes worth but little more than half their face; but even at this ruinous discount, officers, unless they have private means, are compelled to receive the notes. Knowing the difficulties experienced by the Government in procuring coin to pay the Army, I feel great reluctance in submitting any grievances from this remote department, but justice to the officers and soldiers demands that a fair statement should be made to the War Department."

It was under circumstances and exigencies such as these that the legislature themselves—all appeals to the General Government having proved futile—provided the necessary relief by the law of April 27, 1863. They did not even after that relax their efforts on behalf of United States troops, other than their own volunteers, serving among them, but on April 1, 1864, adopted a resolution requesting their representatives in Congress to "use their influence in procuring the passage of a law giving to the officers and soldiers of the regular Army stationed on the Pacific coast an increase of their pay, amounting to 30 per cent. on the amount now allowed by law."

[S. Ex. Doc. No. 17, Fifty-first Congress, first session, p. 14.]

OREGON.

Extra monthly compensation to officers and enlisted men of volunteers.

The certificate of the State treasurer, duly authenticated by the secretary of state under the seal of the State, sets forth that the amounts severally paid out for the redemption of relief bonds, as shown by the books of the treasurer's office, as reported by the treasurer to the several legislative assemblies and as verified by the several joint committees (investigating commissions) of said assembly under the provisions

of a joint resolution thereof, aggregate $90,476.32. The following books, papers, etc., are also submitted in evidence of payment:

(1) The canceled bonds.

(2) A copy of the relief bond register, the correctness of which is certified by the secretary of state and State treasurer, showing number of bond, to whom issued, date of issue, and amount of bond; also showing the date and rate of redemption. The reports of the joint committee of the legislature above mentioned, to the effect that they compared the record kept by the State treasurer with the bonds redeemed and found the amounts correct and agreeing with the amounts reported by the State treasurer to the legislative assembly, are entered in said bond register.

(3) Certificates of service given to the several Oregon volunteers upon which warrants were given entitling the holders to bonds. These certificates cover service for which the sum of $86,639.85 was due. The remainder of the certificates, the State authorities report, were not found and are probably lost or destroyed.

(4) Copies of the muster-rolls of the Oregon volunteers, certified to by the secretary of state, setting forth the entire service of each officer and enlisted man.

In all, bonds amounting to $93,637 were issued. As has been stated but $90,476.32 is found to have been expended in the redemption of these bonds, some of which were redeemed at less than their face value. Five bonds, valued at $731, have not been redeemed.

The authority by which these bonds were issued is contained in an act of the legislature, which was approved on October 24, 1864 (copy herewith), appropriating a sum not exceeding $100,000 to constitute and be known as the "commissioned officers' and soldiers' relief fund," out of which was to be paid to each commissioned officer and enlisted soldier of the companies of Oregon volunteers raised in the State for the service of the United States to aid in repelling invasion, etc., from the time of their enlistment to the time of their discharge, $5 per month in addition to the pay allowed them by the United States. Enlisted men not receiving an honorable discharge from the service, or volunteers discharged for disability existing at the time of enlistment, were not to be entitled to the benefits of the act, nor was payment under the provisions thereof to be made to an enlisted soldier until he should be honorably discharged the service; but enlisted married men having families dependent upon them were authorized to allot the whole or any portion of the monthly pay accruing to them for the support of such dependents. A bond bearing interest, payable semi-annually, at 7 per cent. per annum, redeemable July 1, 1875, with coupons for the interest attached, was to be issued by the secretary of state for such amount as the adjutant-general should certify to be due under the provisions of the act to each man, whose receipt for the amount so paid him was to be taken by the secretary of state. Said bonds were to be paid to the recipient or order.

The circumstances and exigencies that led to the enactment of the above-cited law and to the expenditures incurred under its provisions were substantially the same as those which brought about the adoption of similar measures of relief in California and Nevada. It must have been patent to every one fully acquainted with the circumstances of the case that the volunteers, that had been raised in Oregon, at this time (October 24, 1864) consisting only of the seven companies of the First Oregon Cavalry and the independent detachment of four months' men, a majority of whom had then nearly completed their term, had been greatly underpaid, considering the nature of the service performed by them and the current rate of salaries and wages realized in other pursuits of life. At the time of the enrollment and muster in of the First Oregon Cavalry and up to the latter part of 1862 the Government paid those of its troops in the Department of the Pacific, that were paid at all, in specie; but as often happened during the war a number of the companies of the regiment named, occupying remote stations, remained unpaid for a long time and were finally paid in Treasury notes, some of the members having more than a year's pay due them.

During the remainder of the war the Government paid its troops in the Department of the Pacific, as elsewhere, in greenbacks. Referring to this condition of things and to the fact that coin continued to be the ordinary medium of exchange in Oregon in private business transactions, Maj. C. S. Drew, First Oregon Cavalry, in a letter to his department commander, dated March 4, 1863 (page 154, Ex. Doc. 70), called attention to the fact that at his station (Camp Baker) Treasury notes were worth "not more than 50 or 55 cents per dollar;" that each officer and soldier of his command was serving for less than half pay, and had done so, some of them, for sixteen months past; that while capital protected itself from loss and perhaps realized better profits than under the old and better system of payment in coin, "the soldier did not have that power, and if paid in notes must necessarily receipt in full for what is equivalent to him of half pay or less for the service he has rendered, and must continue to fulfill his part of the contract with the Government for the same reduced rate of pay until his period of service shall have terminated; and that "good men will not enlist for $6 or $7 a month while $13 is the regular pay, and, moreover, being realized by every soldier

in every other department than the Pacific." In forwarding this letter to the Adjutant-General, U. S. Army, the department commander remarked that the embarrassments enumerated in the major's communication were common to all the troops in the department, and he therefore asked "the serious consideration of the General-in-Chief and the War Department to this subject." Some months later (August 18, 1863) General Alvord, while reporting to the department commander the location of a new military post at Fort Boisé, referred to the difficulties encountered by the garrison* charged with the duty of establishing it, as follows:

"Some difficulty is experienced in building the post in consequence of the low rates of legal-tender notes. In that country they bear merely nominal value. The depreciation of the Government currency not only embarrasses the Quartermaster's Department, but also tends greatly to disaffect the men. The differences between their pay and the promises held out by the richest mines, perhaps, on the coast, the proximity of which makes them all the more tempting, is so great that many desertions occur." (Ex. Doc. 70, page 183.)

About the same time (September 1, 1863) the adjutant-general of the State complained of the inadequacy of the soldiers' pay, resulting from the depreciation of the paper currency with which they were paid. Referring to the fact that after the expiration of eight months from the date of the requisition of the United States military authorities for six additional companies for the First Oregon Cavalry but one had been raised, he said:

"And yet we are not prepared to say that it is for the want of patriotism on the part of the people of Oregon, but from other causes, partly from the deficiency in the pay of the volunteer in comparison with the wages given in the civil pursuits of life, as well as with the nature of the currency with which they are paid, the depreciation of which renders it hardly possible for the soldier to enlist from any other motive save pure patriotism. And I would here suggest that the attention of our legislature be called to this defect, and that additional pay, either in land, money, or something else, be allowed to those who have volunteered. Justice demands that this should be done."

In enacting the relief law of October 24, 1864, it is fair to presume that the legislature was largely influenced by the following statements and recommendations of the governor contained in his annual message, dated September 15, 1864:

"The Snake and other tribes of Indians in eastern Oregon have been hostile and constantly committing depredations. The regiment has spent two summers on the plains, furnishing protection to the immigration and to the trade and travel in that region of the country. During the past summer the regiment has traveled over twelve hundred miles, and the officers and men are still out on duty. The officers and most, if not all, the men joined the regiment through patriotic motives, and, while some of the time they have been traveling over rich gold fields, where laborers' wages are from $3 to $5 per day, there have been very few desertions, and that, too, while they were being paid in depreciated currency, making their wages only about $5 per month. A great many of these men have no pecuniary interest in keeping open the lines of travel, protecting mining districts and merchants and traders. The benefit of their service thus insures [inures] to the benefit of others, who should help these faithful soldiers in bearing these burdens. Oregon, in proportion to her population and wealth, has paid far less than other States for military purposes. California pays her volunteers $5 per month extra in coin. It would be but an act of simple justice for this State to make good to the members of this regiment their losses by depreciated currency." (Page 87, Statement for Senate Military Committee.)

It is to be noted here that while the officers and men who became the beneficiaries of this law had been paid in a depreciated currency, which in Oregon does not appear to have had more than two-thirds of the purchasing power it had in the East, the Government provided them with clothing, subsistence, shelter, and all their absolutely necessary wants. On the other hand, it is to be borne in mind that the legislature must have been aware of the fact noted, and that it granted the extra compensation from a sense of justice and without any purpose calculated to benefit the State at large, such as might be reasonably inferred from the granting of bounties to men "who should hereafter enlist." As has been already mentioned, the terms of the Oregon Volunteers were drawing to a close and the benefits of the law were restricted to the volunteers "raised," and did not therefore include those "to be raised."

California, as shown by the report (Senate Ex. Doc. No. 11, Fifty-first Congress, first session) of said war claims examiners, expended $468,976.54 on account of her militia during the war of the rebellion. The circumstances under which this expenditure was made present a strong case of equity for reimbursement, but inasmuch as the militia of

---

*Although the First Oregon Cavalry did not form a part of this garrison, three companies of it were at this time scouting against hostile Indians in the vicinity of the post.

California did not serve under the direct or immediate authority of the United States during the war of the rebellion, your committee do not allow it at this time, although they do not reject it for want of merit.

Oregon expended on account of her militia, as shown by the report of said war claims examiners, $21,118.73, and your committee make a similar recommendation in regard to that claim.

Some of the circumstances under which the present war claim of the State of Nevada was created are set forth in the report of the majority of the Committee on Military Affairs made in the Fiftieth Congress, first session (Senate Report No. 1286), which, without the appendix, is as follows, to wit:

Senate Report No. 1286, Fiftieth Congress, first session.

MAY 14, 1888.

Mr. STEWART, from the Committee on Military Affairs, submitted the following report:

[To accompany bill S. 2918]

OBJECT OF THIS BILL.

The object of this bill is to re-imburse the State of Nevada for moneys paid and contracted to be paid by the Territory of Nevada and afterwards assumed and paid by that State, and also for moneys actually expended by Nevada after becoming a State for the common defense and in furnishing troops to the United States during the suppression of the war of the rebellion, and for guarding the overland mail and emigrant route between the Missouri River and California, and for suppressing Indian hostilities under circumstances hereinafter set forth.

APPEAL OF PRESIDENT LINCOLN, THROUGH SECRETARY SEWARD, TO THE NATION FOR AID.

On October 14, 1861, Mr. Seward, Secretary of State, addressed a circular letter to the governors of the loyal States and Territories, calling for assistance for the General Government in suppressing hostilities in the so-called Confederate States, and for the improvement and perfection of the defenses of the loyal States respectively. A copy of this letter is printed in the appendix hereto, marked Exhibit No. 1, page 23.

ACTION TAKEN BY NEVADA IN RESPONSE TO THE FOREGOING APPEAL OF SECRETARY SEWARD.

Upon the receipt of this letter the legislative assembly of Nevada Territory at its first session passed appropriate resolutions pledging the support of the people of that Territory to the Union cause to the extent of their means, which resolutions are printed in the appendix, marked Exhibit No. 2, page 24.

On the 28th day of November, 1861, three days after the passage of the resolutions above mentioned, the legislative assembly of Nevada also passed an elaborate law for the enrollment and organization of a militia force to aid the United States when called upon in the suppression of the rebellion, and to carry out the spirit and intent of the aforesaid circular letter of Secretary Seward. This law will be found on

pages 106 to 125 of the Laws of Nevada Territory, 1861. This act provided that the militia of the Territory organized under its provisions should be subject to be called into the military service of the United States by the President, or any officer of the United States Army commanding a division or a department. A militia force was immediately organized under its provisions. II. P. Russell was appointed adjutant-general, and was succeeded by Col. John Cradlebaugh, who is mentioned in the resolutions above referred to and printed in the appendix as Exhibit No. 2, page 24.

It will thus be seen that Nevada made the necessary preparations, organized her militia, and was ready to answer any call that might be thereafter made upon her by the General Government, and also to protect the Territory against a large portion of its inhabitants who desired to join the Confederacy.

CONDITION OF AFFAIRS THAT RENDERED A CALL FOR NEVADA VOL-
UNTEERS NECESSARY.

The Territory of Nevada was organized by Congress on March 2, 1861, (12 U. S. Stats., 209). At the breaking out of the rebellion it became a serious question what attitude Nevada would occupy, and home guards were immedi..tely organized. These guards afterwards formed a portion of the militia of the Territory as provided for in the aforesaid militia law, and protected the inhabitants from violence, without any expense to the Government of the United States.

In the early part of April, 1863, the overland mail and emigrant route was attacked by Indians and communication was closed between the Atlantic States and the Pacific coast. This route extended from the Missouri River to California via the Platte River, Salt Lake City, through Nevada to Sacramento, in California, and was the only means at that date of direct overland communication between the Missouri River and California. At this time the gold discoveries in California continued to invite a large immigration, the interest in which was more or less intensified by the continued extensive silver discoveries in Nevada Territory, and principally on the Comstock lode in the western part of the Territory. The routes via Cape Horn, and especially that via the Isthmus of Panama, were rendered extremely doubtful, dangerous, and expensive, on account of Confederate privateer cruisers hovering around the West India Islands and along both these sea routes, and in anticipation of other Confederate cruisers infesting the waters of the Pacific (which soon thereafter became the theater of the operations and extensive depredations of the Confederate privateer cruiser *Shenandoah*) the overland route, therefore, although in itself both dangerous and difficult, was yet considered the better and preferable route by which to reach the Pacific.

On account of a general uprising of the Indians along the entire overland route, and especially that portion between Salt Lake City, in the Territory of Utah, and the Sierra Nevada Mountains, and because of the doubts as to the loyalty of the Mormons to the Government of the United States, the maintenance and protection of the mail and emigrant route through that section of the country and along the aforesaid line was regarded by the Government as a military necessity. Apparently in anticipation of no immediate danger of attack on the Pacific coast, nearly all the troops of the regular Army at this time had been withdrawn from service throughout this entire region of country and transferred East to other fields of military operations. This left the entire coun-

try between Salt Lake City and the Sierra Nevada Mountains without adequate and efficient military protection. The Government thus having but few troops of its regular Army in that region, was therefore compelled to call upon the inhabitants of Nevada Territory to raise and organize volunteer military companies to suppress Indian disturbances which threatened the entire suspension of all mail facilities and emigration from the East, as will be hereafter shown.

At the time of the calls upon Nevada for troops the prices of labor and supplies of all descriptions in Nevada were extremely high. There were then no railroads, and the snow on the Sierra Nevada Mountains formed an almost impassable barrier against teams from about the 1st of December until about June. The average cost of freight from San Francisco, the main source of supply for western Nevada, was about $80 a ton, and it was necessary to lay in supplies during the summer and fall for the remainder of the year. A great mining excitement prevailed at this time, occasioned by the marvelous development of the great Comstock lode, and wages were from $4 to $10 a day in gold. The people who had emigrated to the new gold and silver fields went there for the purpose of mining and prospecting for mines, and were generally reluctant to enter the irregular military service of guarding the overland mail and emigrant route. Besides, on account of the extraordinary high price of supplies of every description, and also of wages and services of every kind, it was impossible for them to maintain themselves and families without involving much more expense than any compensation which could be paid them as volunteer troops under the laws of the United States, and, as will be seen by the letters of General Wright, hereafter quoted, they were expected, as volunteer troops, to furnish themselves with horses and equipments, in addition to what could be furnished by the Government.

The military authorities of the United States well knew at that time the exact condition of the country and of the roads across the mountains leading thereto and of the cost of transportation and of the prices of labor and of supplies and of their own inability to furnish either horses or equipments for a military service that required mounted troops.

FIRST CALL BY THE UNITED STATES FOR NEVADA VOLUNTEERS.

In view of the necessities of the situation, and with all the facts fully known to the military authorities of the United States, General Wright, commanding the Department of the Pacific, was authorized by the War Department to raise volunteer military companies in Nevada Territory for the protection of said overland mail and emigrant route, and on April 2, 1863, he addressed the following requisition for troops to the Governor of the Territory:

HEADQUARTERS DEPARTMENT OF THE PACIFIC,
San Francisco, Cal., April 2, 1863.

His Excellency O. CLEMENS,
Governor of Nevada Territory, Carson City, Nev.:

SIR: I have been authorized by the War Department to raise volunteer companies in Nevada Territory for the purpose of moving east on the overland mail route in the direction of Great Salt Lake City. If it is possible to raise three or four companies in the Territory for this service I have to request your excellency may be pleased to have them organized. I should be glad to get two companies of cavalry and two of infantry. The mounted troops to furnish their own horses and equipments. Arms, ammunition, etc., will be furnished by the United States. Should your excellency consider it improbable that this volunteer force can be raised, even one company will be

accepted. I will send you a plan of organization, and an officer with the necessary instructions for mustering them into the service.

With great respect, I have the honor to be, your most obedient servant,

G. WRIGHT,
Brigadier-General, U. S. Army, Commanding.

Official copy.

J. C. KELTON,
Colonel, A. A. G.

While correspondence was being conducted between the Governor of Nevada and General Wright as to the method of organizing Nevada's troops, the following telegram was dispatched by General H. W. Halleck, general-in-chief of the U. S. Army, to General Wright:

HEADQUARTERS OF THE ARMY,
Washington, D. C., April 15, 1863.

Brig. Gén. G. WRIGHT,
San Francisco, Cal.:

The Secretary of War authorizes you to raise additional regiments in California and Nevada to re-enforce General Conner and protect overland route. Can not companies be raised in Nevada and pushed forward immediately? General Conner may be able to raise some companies in Utah or out of emigrant trains.

H. W. HALLECK,
General-in-Chief.

———

Whereupon General Wright addressed the governor of Nevada Territory the following communication:

HEADQUARTERS DEPARTMENT OF THE PACIFIC,
San Francisco, Cal., April 16, 1863.

His Excellency ORION CLEMENS,
Governor of Nevada Territory, Carson City, Nev.:

SIR: I have the honor to acknowledge the receipt of your excellency's communication of the 9th instant.

The Indian disturbances along the line of the overland mail route, east of Carson City, threaten the entire suspension of our mail facilities, as well as preventing any portion of the vast immigration approaching from the east reaching Nevada. The interest and prosperity of your Territory depend much upon maintaining free and safe access to it from all directions. My force immediately available for operation on that line is small. A company of cavalry stationed at Fort Churchill, and under orders to move towards Ruby Valley, I was compelled to divert for temporary service to assist in quelling an Indian outbreak in the Owen's Lake district. As soon as the services of this company can be dispensed with there, it will operate on the mail and emigrant line. Some infantry companies will also be thrown forward from this side of the mountains as soon as transportation can be prepared and the roads are in order. In the mean time it is of such importance to keep the mail and emigrant route east of you open, that I would earnestly recommend that one or two companies of cavalry be promptly organized and prepared for muster into the service of the United States. It is impossible for us at this moment to purchase horses and equipments. Each man would have to furnish his own.

I can furnish arms, ammunition, forage, clothing, provisions, etc.; in fact, everything except horses and equipments.

The organization of a company or troop of cavalry is: one captain, one first lieutenant, one second lieutenant, one first sergeant, one quartermaster-sergeant, one commissary sergeant, five sergeants, eight corporals, two teamsters, two farriers or blacksmiths, one saddler, one wagoner, and seventy-eight privates.

This is the first appeal that has been made to Nevada Territory, a Territory soon to add another star to that glorious galaxy which adorns our beautiful banner, and I doubt not this call will be nobly responded to by the loyal and patriotic citizens of the Territory.

With great respect, your excellency's most obedient servant,

G. WRIGHT,
Brigadier-General U. S. Army, Commanding.

Official copy.

J. C. KELTON.
Colonel, A. A. G.

NEVADA'S RESPONSE TO THE FOREGOING CALL FOR TROOPS BY THE
UNITED STATES.

Immediately upon the receipt of the foregoing requisition for troops
the governor of Nevada issued the following proclamation:

PROCLAMATION.

EXECUTIVE DEPARTMENT,
Carson City, April 24, 1863.

Whereas Brigadier-General George Wright, United States Army, commanding officer of the Department of the Pacific, has, by authority of the War Department called
upon me for two companies of infantry and two companies of cavalry to serve three
years, or during the war:

Now, therefore, I, Orion Clemens, governor of the Territory of Nevada and commander-in-chief of the militia thereof, do hereby authorize and call upon the citizens
of the Territory, as many as shall be necessary to fill up the preceding requisition, to
immediately organize themselves into companies as required hereby.

In witness whereof I have hereunto set my hand and affixed the great seal of the
Territory.

Done at Carson City, Territory of Nevada, this 24th day of April, in the year of our
Lord one thousand eight hundred and sixty-three.

ORION CLEMENS,
Secretary and Acting Governor.

In answer to these calls and requisitions of General Wright and said
proclamation of the governor of Nevada four companies of cavalry
were completely organized, two of which were sent to Camp Douglas,
Utah Territory, for military service, and the remaining two were sent
to station Fort Churchill, Nev.

SECOND CALL AND REQUISITION OF THE UNITED STATES FOR NEVADA
VOLUNTEERS.

Thereafter General Wright made a further requisition upon the governor of Nevada for two additional companies of cavalry and a regiment
of infantry, as will appear from the following:

HEADQUARTERS DEPARTMENT OF THE PACIFIC,
San Francisco, December 22, 1863.

SIR: The four companies of cavalry called for from the Territory of Nevada have
completed their organization; two of the companies have reached Camp Douglas,
Utah, and the remaining two are at Fort Churchill, Nev. On the representations of
Governor Nye that additional troops can be raised in Nevada, I have, under the
authority conferred upon me by the War Department, called upon the governor for
a regiment of infantry and two more companies of cavalry.

Very respectfully, your obedient servant,

G. WRIGHT,
Brig. Gen., U. S. Army, Commanding.

ADJUTANT-GENERAL, U. S. ARMY,
Washington, D. C.

WHAT WAS DONE BY NEVADA UNDER THE SECOND CALL AND REQUI-
SITION BY THE UNITED STATES FOR NEVADA VOLUNTEERS.

In response to General Wright's second requisition for troops made
in the latter part of November, 1863, the governor of Nevada issued
the following proclamation:

PROCLAMATION.

Whereas a requisition having been made upon me by Brig. Gen. George Wright,
U. S. Army, commanding the Department of the Pacific, for one regiment of volunteer
infantry and two companies of cavalry, for service in the employ of the General Gov-
uerment of the United States;

Now, therefore, I, James W. Nye, governor of the Territory of Nevada and com-

mander-in-chief of the militia thereof, by virtue of the authority in me vested, do issue this my proclamation, calling upon the people of this Territory to forthwith proceed to organize a regiment of infantry, consisting of ten companies, and two companies of cavalry, in full compliance of said requisition.

All applicants for line officers will present themselves before the Army examining board for examination, and report to me with certificate of such examination as soon as practicable.

Given under my hand and seal at Carson, Nev., this 4th day of December, A. D. 1863.

JAMES W. NYE,
Governor of the Territory of Nevada.

Attest:
ORION CLEMENS,
Secretary of the Territory.

Under this last requisition of General Wright and last proclamation of the governor of Nevada two additional cavalry companies and the First Battalion Nevada Infantry Volunteers, composed of four companies, were raised and assigned to duty to such fields of military service in Utah and Nevada as were determined upon by General Wright, as will appear from the correspondence printed in the appendix, marked "Exhibit 3, pages 24 to 29.

It will thus be seen that the people of the Territory of Nevada responded promptly to and complied fully with the appeals of the United States Government for troops and in accordance with the requisitions and calls of the War Department. The action of the people of Nevada was reported to Mr. Seward, Secretary of State, by the governor of Nevada on March 25, 1864. He wrote to Mr. Seward the condition of affairs in the Territory, which letter was transmitted to the Senate by President Lincoln on April 29, 1864 (see Senate Ex. Doc. No. 41, 38th Cong., 1st sess.). In his report Governor Nye said:

We have raised in the Territory within the last two years one company of infantry, now attached to a California regiment, a battalion of cavalry, consisting of six companies, four of which are in the field; the remaining two will be there also as soon as they can be mounted. In addition we are raising a regiment of infantry, now in a good state of forwardness, and we can raise a brigade easily if necessary.

SOME OF THE DUTIES OF THE TROOPS CALLED TO AID THE UNITED STATES AT THIS TIME.

The first duty of these troops was to open and guard the overland mail and emigrant route from the Sierra Nevada Mountains to Utah. The campaign in which this was accomplished was under the command of General Conner. The volunteer troops under this gallant officer had already conducted a most successful campaign against the Indians of eastern Nevada, Utah, and Idaho, in the region where the Mormon influence was most potential, conquered many Indian tribes, and secured lasting peace.

The Secretary of War, in reporting to Congress the condition of things in that region of country, then under the military command of General Conner, said as follows, to wit:

DEPARTMENT OF THE PACIFIC.

This department has been most signally exempt from the evils of civil war, and consequently has enjoyed unexampled prosperity. Some thefts and robberies having been committed by roving bands of Indians on the overland stage route in January last, General Conner marched with a small force to Bear River, Idaho, where, on the 26th, he overtook and completely defeated them in a severe battle, in which he killed 224 of the 300 and captured 175 of their horses. His own loss in killed and wounded was 63 out of 200. Many of his men were severely injured by the frost. Since this severe punishment the Indians in that quarter have ceased to commit depredations on the whites. (Secretary of War's report, first session Thirty-eighth Congress.)

ADDITIONAL CAUSES THAT LED TO A THIRD CALL AND REQUISITION BY THE UNITED STATES FOR NEVADA VOLUNTEERS.

Congress having on July 1, 1862, chartered the Union Pacific Railroad Company, to which, and also to the Central Pacific Railroad Company, aid was given to build one continuous line of railroad from the Missouri River to the Pacific Ocean through this region of country, did, on July 2, 1864, still further foster these enterprises by additional grants. These two companies thereupon placed in the field numerous corps of surveyors, civil engineers, and employés to explore said country in the effort to discover the most practicable and economical railroad route from the Missouri River to the Pacific, and to run trial lines and definitely locate the lines of the two subdivisions of said railroad route. In regard to these roads the Secretary of War, in his annual report for 1864–'65, page 144, said:

It is, in a military sense, of the utmost importance that the Pacific Railroad should be pressed to the earliest possible completion.

The exploration and location for a Pacific railroad through that region of country then mostly uninhabited except by large tribes and roving bands of hostile Indians, called for additional military protection and rendered it necessary for the United States to again call upon Nevada to raise additional troops. Accordingly General McDowell, commanding the Department of the Pacific, made the following call on October 13, 1864, upon the Governor of Nevada Territory:

HEADQUARTERS DEPARTMENT OF THE PACIFIC,
Virginia City, October 13, 1864.

SIR: I have the honor to acquaint you that I have received authority from the War Department to call on you, from time to time, as the circumstances of the service may require, for not to exceed in all, at any one time, one regiment of volunteer infantry and one regiment of volunteer cavalry, to be mustered into service of the United States as other volunteer regiments, under existing laws and regulations.

Under this authority I have to request you will please raise, as soon as possible, enough companies of infantry to complete, with those already in service from Nevada, a full regiment of infantry.

Brigadier-General Wason will confer with you and give all the information necessary to details for this service.

I have the honor to be, governor, very respectfully, your most obedient servant,
IRWIN McDOWELL,
Major-General, Commanding Department.

His Excellency JAMES W. NYE,
Governor of Nevada Territory.

WHAT WAS DONE BY NEVADA IN RESPONSE TO THIS CALL.

The governor of Nevada responded to this call by issuing the following proclamation:

PROCLAMATION.

TERRITORY OF NEVADA, EXECUTIVE DEPARTMENT,
Carson City, October 19, 1864.

Whereas I have received a requisition from Maj. Gen. Irwin McDowell, commanding Department of the Pacific, the same having been made under authority from the War Department, to raise, as soon as possible, enough companies of infantry to complete, with those already in service from Nevada, a full regiment of infantry:

Now, therefore, I, James W. Nye, governor of the Territory of Nevada, and commander-in-chief of the militia thereof, do hereby call upon the citizens of this Territory to organize themselves into seven companies, sufficient to fill the battalion of infantry now in service from this Territory, and the requirements of said requisition.

In witness whereof I have hereunto set my hand and caused the great seal of the

Territory of Nevada to be affixed. Done at Carson City this 19th day of October, 1864.

JAMES W. NYE,
Governor and Commander-in-Chief of the Territory of Nevada.

Attest:
ORION CLEMENS,
Secretary of the Territory.

Afterward the Indians became troublesome between Utah and the Missouri River. During the years 1865–'66 the Nevada cavalry were actively engaged in Colorado, Wyoming, Kansas, and Nebraska in the Indian wars in that region. The writer of this report crossed the continent in the summer of 1865, and met several small detachments of Nevada cavalry in active service against the Indians, and was much gratified to learn that they were quite celebrated for their gallantry and faithful services in that kind of warfare, which subjects the soldier to the severest test of endurance, and requires individual exertion and watchfulness unknown in civilized war.

METHOD RECOGNIZED BY NEVADA FOR THE ENROLLMENT OF HER TROOPS CALLED INTO THE MILITARY SERVICE OF THE UNITED STATES AND HER MODE OF DEFRAYING THE EXPENSES OF SUCH ENROLLMENT FOR SUCH SERVICE.

The citizens of Nevada were never drafted, nor did they ever hire substitutes, but were organized into military companies by commanding officers, most of whom had undergone an examination for commission before military boards instituted for that purpose and satisfactory to the general of the United States Army commanding the military Department of the Pacific.

As a compensation to and a reimbursement intended for all the costs by them incurred for raising and organizing said volunteer military companies, and in lieu of all other kinds of expenses necessarily incident to enrolling and enlisting the members of said companies for the military service of the United States, the legislature of Nevada passed an act providing for the payment to the commanding officers of said companies of $10 per capita for each volunteer soldier by them for said purposes enrolled and enlisted, aggregating the sum of $11,840. This provision in said statute was improperly called a "bounty;" but this expenditure was not in any sense whatsoever a "bounty," but, on the contrary, it was an actual disbursement by Nevada to cover all the legitimate expenses of every kind incident to enrolling and enlisting Nevada's troops to perform military service for the United States.

The history of this expenditure and of this mode of enrollment of troops by the Territory of Nevada, and the economy and reasons therefor, are all fully set forth in a memorial to Congress signed by all the State officers of Nevada, which is printed in the appendix, marked Exhibit No. 4, page 29.

METHOD ADOPTED BY NEVADA TO PAY THE TROOPS CALLED INTO THE MILITARY SERVICE OF THE UNITED STATES BY THE TERRITORY OF NEVADA, AND THE EXTENT TO WHICH THE STATE OF NEVADA PLEDGED HER FAITH TO PAY THE OBLIGATIONS CONTRACTED BY THE TERRITORY OF NEVADA TO AID THE UNITED STATES.

This same act of the legislature of Nevada, among other things, provided that each citizen of Nevada so volunteering and enlisting as a private soldier for the military service of the United States, not being

drafted or acting as a substitute for another, should, during each and every month while honorably serving the United States, be paid out of the treasury of Nevada the sum of $5 per month, gold coin. It further provided that, in the case of an enlisted married man, an allotment of the whole or a portion of the extra monthly pay could be drawn by his family dependent upon him for support (see Laws of Nevada Territory, 1864, page 81, or appendix, Exhibit No. 5, page 31).

On March 11, 1865, after Nevada became a State, an act similar to this Territorial act, but more liberal in its provisions, was passed, to take the place of the Territorial law. The State legislature having deemed the situation so important to maintain the good faith of the Territory, that had been pledged to aid the United States, it passed this act *over the veto of Governor Blasdel*, who alleged in his veto message his fear that the expense might exceed the constitutional limit, etc.

This act provided for the assumption and payment by the State of Nevada of all obligations of every kind that had been incurred and contracted to be paid by the Territory for the enlistments, enrollments, bounties, extra pay, etc., of volunteer soldiers that had been theretofore called into the military service of the United States. The bonds now outstanding and still due by Nevada, though at a smaller rate of interest than that named in the original issue and still drawing interest, were issued under the provisions of this latter act (see Statutes, Nevada, 1864-'65, page 389, or appendix, Exhibit No. 6, page 34).

RESULTS OF THE FOREGOING LEGISLATION BY NEVADA.

By these legislative enactments of Nevada substantial and effectual aid was given and guaranteed by Nevada, both as a Territory and State, to the Government of the United States in guarding its overland mail and emigrant route and the line of the proposed transcontinental railroad in furnishing troops during the war of the rebellion and for suppressing Indian hostilities and maintaining peace in the country inhabited by the Mormons, and for the common defense as contemplated in said circular letter of Secretary Seward along an exposed, difficult, and hostile Indian frontier, and then but sparsely populated. These enactments were fully known to the authorities of the United States and to Congress; they have ever been acquiesced in and met with the sanction and practical indorsement of the United States, in whose interest and for whose benefit they were made. As a partial compensation to these volunteers for this irregular, hazardous, and exposed service in the mountains and on the desert plains, and to aid them to a small extent to maintain families dependent upon them for support, first the Territory and afterwards the State of Nevada offered and paid this small stipend, never suspecting that the United States would not promptly and willingly respond when asked to re-imburse the same. These citizens of Nevada who volunteered and enlisted and did military service for the United States were compelled in many cases to abandon their employments, in which their wages were always lucrative and service continuous, so that nothing less than the individual patriotism of these volunteers enabled the Territory and State of Nevada to cheerfully and promptly respond to every call and requisition made upon them for troops by the United States.

The records of the War Department, in addition to what is already quoted and referred to in substantiation of the facts herein stated, are printed in the appendix, marked Exhibit No. 3, pages 24 to 29.

THE BASIS AND AUTHORITY OF NEVADA'S CLAIM AGAINST THE UNITED
STATES AND THE PRECEDENTS IN SUPPORT THEREOF.

These enactments of Nevada both as a Territory and a State, and
various acts done under them in and execution thereof, when complying
according to her own methods with the various calls and requisitions of
the United States for troops, have resulted in the expenditure of a large
sum of money which constitutes the present claim of Nevada against
the United States. The authority upon which this claim rests is found
in the fourth section of the fourth article of the Constitution of the
United States, which provides that—

The United States shall guaranty to every State in the Union a republican form of
government, and shall protect each of them against invasion, and, on application of
the legislature, or of the executive (when the legislature can not be convened),
against domestic violence.

And upon the latter part of the tenth section of the first article of
the Constitution; which is as follows:

No State shall, without the consent of Congress, lay any duty on tonnage, keep
troops or ships of war in time of peace, enter into any agreement or compact with
another State, or with a foreign power, or engage in war, unless actually invaded or
in such imminent danger as will not admit of delay.

And also upon the act of July 28, 1795, chapter 36, section 1, page
424, now section No. 1642, U. S. Revised Statutes, which provides
that—

Whenever the United States are invaded or are in imminent danger of invasion
from any foreign nation or Indian tribe, or of rebellion against the authority of the
Government of the United States, it shall be lawful for the President to call forth such
number of the militia of the State or States most convenient to the place of danger
or scene of action, as he may deem necessary to repel such invasion or to suppress such
rebellion, and to issue his orders for that purpose to such officer of the militia as he
may think proper.*

In reference to the foregoing the courts have held that—

When a particular authority is confided to a public officer, to be exercised by him
in his discretion, upon an examination of the facts of which he is made the appropriate judge, his decision upon the facts in the absence of any controlling provision,
is absolutely conclusive as to the existence of those facts (Allen vs. Blunt, 3 Story,
U. S. Circuit Court Reports, 745).*

And again the supreme court of the State of New York (Hon. Chancellor Kent presiding as chief justice) held in the case of Vanderheyden
vs. Young, 11 Johnson's New York Reports, 157, that—

It is a general and sound principle that when the law vests any person with a
power to do an act, and constitutes him a judge of the evidence on which that act
may be done, and at the same time contemplates that the act is to be carried into
effect through the instrumentality of agents, the person thus clothed with power is
invested with discretion and is quoad hoc a judge.
His mandates to his legal agents on his declaring the event to have happened will
be a protection to those agents, and it is not their duty or business to investigate the
facts thus referred to their superior, and to rejudge his determination.*

The United States Supreme Court in Martin vs. Mott, 12 Wheaton,
19, unanimously held—

That the authority to decide upon what occasions and upon what emergencies Federal calls should be made and Federal assistance given, "belongs exclusively-to the
President, and that his decision is conclusive upon all other persons."*

And Chief Justice Taney, in Luther vs. Borden, 7 Howard, referred
approvingly to the opinion of the United States Supreme Court in Martin vs. Mott, as expressed in these words:

That whenever a statute gives a discretionary power to any person to be exercised
by him upon his own opinion of certain facts, it is a sound rule of construction that
the statute constitutes him the sole and exclusive judge of the existence of those facts.*

* NOTE.—The acts of heads of Departments of the Government are in law the acts
of the President (Wilcox vs. Jackson, 13 Peters., 498).

The obligations arising under these provisions of the Constitution and laws and decisions have been recognized by the Government from its foundation, as will fully appear from the authorities cited by Senator Dolph in a report made by him from the Senate Committee on Claims on February 25, 1885 (Forty-eighth Congress, second session), Report No. 1438. These authorities are printed in the appendix, marked Exhibit No. 7, page 37 *et sequiter.*

NEVADA'S DILIGENCE IN THESE PREMISES.

The State of Nevada has not slept upon her rights in any of these premises nor been guilty of any *laches*; on the contrary, at all proper times she has respectfully brought the same to the attention of Congress by memorials of her legislature and of her representatives in Congress. On March 29, 1867, her legislature first asked for the payment of the claims of the State by a joint resolution, which is printed in the appendix, marked Exhibit No. 8, page 64. And again, on February 1, 1869, the legislature of Nevada passed a memorial and joint resolution renewing her prayer in these premises, which is also so printed in the appendix, marked Exhibit No. 9, page 65.

The Journals of the United States Senate show that on March 10, 1868, the writer of this report presented the first-mentioned memorial and resolution to the Senate, accompanied with an official statement of the amount of the claims of the State referred to therein. These papers were referred to the Committee on Claims, but the records fail to show that any action was ever taken upon them. On May 29 of the same year the writer of this report introduced a joint resolution (S. 138) providing for the appointment of a board of examiners to examine the claims of the State of Nevada against the United States, and on June 18 of the same year the Committee on Claims, to whom this joint resolution was referred, was discharged from its further consideration. The official statement of the moneys expended by the State of Nevada on account of the United States, and presented to the Senate on March 10, 1868, can not now be found on the files of the Senate.

On February 11, 1885, and January 26, 1887, the legislature of Nevada, renewing its prayer for a re-imbursement of the money by her expended for the use and benefit of the United States, further memorialized Congress, asking for the settlement of her claims, which are printed in the appendix and marked Exhibits Nos. 10 and 11, pages 65 and 66.

PROCEEDINGS IN CONGRESS TO REDEEM THE OBLIGATIONS OF THE UNITED STATES DUE TO NEVADA IN THIS CASE.

The circumstances under which these expenditures were made by the Territory and State of Nevada being exceptional, and their re-imbursement not being provided for by any existing law, general or special, Senator Fair, of Nevada, on December 13, 1881, introduced a joint resolution in the Senate providing for the equitable adjustment of these claims of Nevada now under consideration, which was referred to the Committee on Military Affairs. A copy of said resolution will be found in the appendix, marked Exhibit 12, page 67.

This committee, instead of reporting back this joint resolution, reported back a substitute in the form of a bill providing for the payment of the claims of several States and Territories, including the State of Nevada, and which bill finally resulted in the act of June 27, 1882 This bill was reported on May 12, 1882, by Hon. L. F. Grover, and

Nevada believed then and believes now that it was then the intention of Congress to equitably and explicitly provide for the re-imbursement to her of the amount of money which she had actually and in good faith expended in these premises. This bill was accompanied by a report in which the following statement is made in relation to the claims of the State of Nevada:

NEVADA.

It appears by the report of the Adjutant-General U. S. Army, of February 25, 1882, that one regiment of cavalry and one battalion of infantry were raised in the late Territory of Nevada during the late war of the rebellion, and that the expenses of raising, organizing, and placing in the field said forces were never paid by said Territory, but were assumed and paid by the State of Nevada, and that none of said expenses so incurred by said Territory, and assumed and paid by said State, have ever been re-imbursed the State of Nevada by the United States, and that no claims therefor have ever been heretofore presented by either said Territory or said State for audit and payment by the United States. Under section 3489 of the Revised Statutes, hereinbefore referred to, the payment of these claims is barred by limitation.

These forces were raised to guard the overland mail route and emigrant road to California, east of Carson City, and to do other military service in Nevada, and were called out by the governor of the late Territory of Nevada upon requisitions therefor by the commanding general of the Department of the Pacific, and under authority of the War Department, as appears by copies of official correspondence furnished to your committee by the Secretary of War and the general commanding the Division of the Pacific. * * *

PRESENTATION BY NEVADA TO THE UNITED STATES OF HER CLAIM.

This bill reported from this committee having become a law in an amended form on June 27, 1882, thereupon the governor and controller of the State of Nevada transmitted to the Secretary of the Treasury and Secretary of War a detailed account of the moneys actually expended and actual indebtedness assumed and paid by the State of Nevada on account of the volunteer military forces enrolled by the Territory and State of Nevada, as shown by the books of the State controller.

This statement of the claim of Nevada against the United States was prepared with great care by the proper officers of the State of Nevada, being first submitted by them to the legislature thereof in printed form at the expense of the State, and thereafter transmitted, as above stated, with proper original vouchers and evidence of every kind then in her possession, to the authorities of the Government of the United States and as provided for in said act of June 27, 1882. This statement is printed in the appendix, marked Exhibit No. 13, page 67.

DELAY OF THE UNITED STATES IN THE EXAMINATION OF NEVADA'S CLAIM AND THE CAUSES THEREOF.

This claim, with said vouchers and evidence, was first presented to the Secretary of the Treasury in 1883, where, being properly stamped, it was duly transmitted, to the Secretary of War for examination and action thereon. It remained of record in the War Department unacted on up to and after August 4, 1886, because, as was stated to Congress by Hon. Robert T. Lincoln, Secretary of War, he required the aid of a board of at least three army officers to assist his Department in such examination, and he requested Congress to make an appropriation of $25,000 to defray the expenses of the examination of the different State and Territorial claims presented under the act of June 27, 1882. Congress delayed action upon these requests of the Secretary of War until August 4, 1886, on which date acts were passed providing for said board of

army officers, as asked for, and also appropriated $10,000 to defray the expenses of said examinations (see vol. 24, Stats. at Large, pages 217 and 249.)

SECRETARY LINCOLN'S CONSTRUCTION OF THIS ACT OF JUNE 27, 1882, FOR THE RELIEF OF NEVADA, ETC.

Prior to any action by the War Department on this claim of the State of Nevada, and prior to any action by Congress on the request of the Secretary of War for a board of Army officers to examine said claim, a bill was introduced in Congress by Senator Jones, of Nevada, and referred to the Secretary of War for report, providing for the payment of certain individual claims of citizens of Nevada on account of Indian hostilities in Nevada in 1860, upon which the Secretary of War reported as follows:

WAR DEPARTMENT,
Washington City, January 26, 1884.

SIR: In response to so much of your communication of the 22d ultimo as requests information concerning Senate bill 657, "to authorize the Secretary of the Treasury to adjust and settle the expenses of Indian wars in Nevada," I have the honor to invite your attention to the following report of the Third Auditor of the Treasury, to whom your request was duly referred:

"The State of Nevada has filed in the office abstracts and vouchers for expenses incurred on account of raising volunteers for the United States to aid in suppressing the late rebellion amounting to $349,697.49, and for expenses on account of her militia in the 'White Pine Indian war' of 1875, $17,650.98. Also, expenses of her militia in the 'Elko Indian war' of 1878, amounting to $4,654.64, presented under act of Congress approved June 27, 1882 (22 Statutes, 111, 112).

"These abstracts and vouchers will be sent to your Department for examination and report as soon as they can be stamped, as that statute requires a report from the Secretary of War as to the necessity and reasonableness of the expenses incurred. This statute is deemed sufficiently broad enough to embrace all proper claims of said State and Territory of Nevada."

Very respectfully, your obedient servant,

ROBERT T. LINCOLN,
Secretary of War.

Hon. S. B. MAXEY,
Of Committee on Military Affairs, United States Senate.

In accordance with this letter the Committee on Military Affairs reported back the bill referred to (S. 657), and asked that it be indefinitely postponed, and because of the explanation made by said committee, as follows, to wit:

It will be observed that it is deemed by the War Department that the act approved June 27, 1882, is sufficiently broad to embrace all proper claims of Nevada, whether as State or Territory.

For convenience of reference the above act accompanies this report, and an examination thereof, and of the construction thereon, satisfies the committee that no additional legislation is necessary.

The State of Kansas presented her claim to Secretary Lincoln under this act, which claim was by him examined, audited, and allowed for almost exactly the sum that Kansas had actually expended for the use and benefit of the United States, and all of which allowance has since been paid to Kansas by the United States, and aggregating the sum of $332,308.13 (23 U. S. Stats., 474).

AFTER OVER FOUR YEARS DELAY, SUBSEQUENT TO THE PASSAGE OF THE ACT OF JUNE 27, 1882, THE UNITED STATES TAKES UP NEVADA'S CLAIM FOR EXAMINATION, WHEN THE VERY FIRST QUESTION RAISED IS ONE OF JURISDICTION, AND WHICH IS DECIDED AGAINST NEVADA.

After the passage of said act of August 4, 1886, the War Department detailed a board of three Army officers under Special Orders No. 232,

dated October 6, 1886, to proceed to examine the claims arising under
the act of June 27, 1882, and in the manner contemplated and as provided for in said acts. The claim of the State of Nevada was the first
claim submitted to and examined by said board. This board being in
doubt whether, under the terms of said act of June 27, 1882, they could
allow a re-imbursement to Nevada of the amount by her expended for
interest and extra pay to her troops while in the military service of the
United States, referred these two questions to the Secretary of War for
his decision. On February 8, 1887, after argument was submitted to
him in support of these two elements of Nevada's claim against the
United States, the Secretary of War decided "that after a careful consideration of the subject" he was "of opinion that neither the extra pay
nor the interest can, under the provisions of the act, be allowed," meaning the act of June 27, 1882, and refused the same (see appen lix, Exhibit
No. 14, page 83).

TWO SEPARATE REPORTS (A MAJORITY AND MINORITY) MADE BY THE
ARMY BOARD OF WAR CLAIMS EXAMINERS, THE MINORITY REPORT
ALLOWING ONLY ABOUT 2½ PER CENT. OF THE AMOUNT ACTUALLY EX-
PENDED BY NEVADA, AND WHICH MINORITY REPORT IS APPROVED
BY THE SECRETARY OF WAR.

It will be borne in mind that on January 26, 1884, Secretary Lincoln
was of opinion that the act of June 27, 1882, was sufficiently broad to
embrace all proper claims of the State of Nevada, and the Committee
on Military Affairs, in consequence thereof, reported to the Senate
that that committee was satisfied that no additional legislation was
necessary in regard thereto, while Secretary Endicott, on February 8,
1887, decided that the claims for expenditure for interest and extra
pay to said troops while in the service of the United States could not
be allowed by him under said act, and further, by approving the
award made by the minority examiner, and, as will hereinafter be
more particularly referred to, also disallowed the amount expended by
Nevada and by her paid as her costs for the enrollment of those very
troops so called into the service of the United States.

The day following the decision of the Secretary of War, to wit,
February 9, 1887, and contrary to a practice usual in similar cases, said
board of Army officers, instead of submitting one report to the Secretary of War, submitted two separate and independent reports, one
signed by the majority of said board and the other in the nature of a
minority report. These two reports are submitted herewith, and printed
in the Appendix, marked Exhibits Nos. 15, 16, and 17, pages 89 to 90.

The total of this particular claim of the State of Nevada so presented
to said board amounted to $349,697.49. The amount thereof that was
allowed in said minority report was only $8,559.61. This minority
report was approved by the Secretary of War, thereby disallowing or
suspending all of Nevada's claim except the paltry sum of about 2½ per
cent. of the money actually expended by Nevada for troops called into
the service of the United States and at the urgent solicitation of the
Government of the United States in its hour of need, while this same
board allowed nearly $1,000,000 of the claim of Texas, to wit, $927,242.30,
being about 50 per cent. of the claim of that State of $1,867,259.13, as
presented for re-imbursement for the expenses of her Indian wars, which
occurred since the rebellion, and prosecuted chiefly, if not solely, for
the protection of the inhabitants of the State of Texas. It is worthy
of remark that no minority report was submitted in the case of Texas.

It will be observed by a perusal of the reports of the board of war claims examiners that the great mass of this claim of the State of Nevada for re-imbursement for moneys, expended under very extraordinary circumstances, was rejected by the board of examiners on either purely technical grounds or for an alleged want of jurisdiction to make an award under what has since been admitted and found to be the most restrictive act that was ever drawn since 1789 intended as an "act of relief."

Only $8,559.61 was finally awarded to Nevada by the Secretary of War.

The want of specific information on the part of the officer making the minority report which reduced the amount of the claim to the sum named may be shown in part by the mistakes made in reference to the statutes of Nevada, which are in several public libraries here, and could have been easily examined. For example, he seems to have inferred that the act of the Nevada legislature of March 4, 1865, was the first act of the Territory providing for the organization of its militia, whereas, as we have already shown, there was an elaborate act for that purpose passed by the Territorial legislature as early as November 28, 1861, and apparently on the assumption that there was no law creating the office of adjutant-general prior to 1865, and upon the fact that no evidence was furnished that Nevada previous to April 2, 1863, had soldiers, that therefore the salary of that officer ought not to commence prior to the time when the volunteers were actually called for service into the Army. But it will be observed that he was mistaken as to the time the law was passed creating the office of adjutant-general. The second section of the act of November 28, 1861, provides that—

The adjutant-general shall be appointed by the commander-in-chief, and shall hold his office for the term of two years. He shall be *ex officio* chief of staff, quartermaster-general, commissary-general, inspector-general, and chief of ordnance. He shall receive a salary of $1,000 annually, to be paid out of moneys appropriated for that purpose. He shall reside at the seat of government, and shall keep his office open for the transaction of business every day (Sundays excepted) from 10 o'clock a. m. to 3 o'clock p. m.

The minority examiner is again mistaken if he assumed that the secretary of state of Nevada became *ex officio* adjutant-general on March 3, 1866. It is true that an act devolving the duties of adjutant-general upon the secretary of state was passed on that date, but the second section of said act provides that—

This act shall take effect and be in force from and after the first day of January, 1867 (Stats. Nev., 1866, p. 206).

Thus it appears that the secretary of state did not in fact or in law become *ex officio* adjutant-general until January 1, 1867. The original section of the militia law of 1861 in regard to the office of adjutant-general was afterward amended, changing the length of time that officer was to hold office and increasing his salary to $2,000 per annum, but the abolishment of the office did not take effect until January, 1867.

PROBABLY CONFOUNDING THE ACT OF JUNE 27, 1882, WITH THE ACT OF JULY 27, 1861.

The minority examiner in terminating the salary of adjutant-general on August 20, 1866, undoubtedly had in mind the act of July 27, 1861, and not the act of June 27, 1882, under which last act alone said board was authorized to make an examination and award; otherwise he would not have limited the salary to August 20, 1866, the end of the war of the rebellion, as heretofore officially declared, but would have certainly al-

lowed Nevada a re-imbursement for the money actually paid by her as salary to that officer until his services terminated, and the Indian wars on the plains were actually suppressed and the office of adjutant-general abolished, which was done on December 31, 1866, since which time either the secretary of state or lieutenant-governor has acted as *ex officio* adjutant-general.

Attention is called to these discrepancies simply to show that the minority examiner apparently fell into error, unintentionally, of course, in his examination of the statutes of Nevada, or failed to consider all the circumstances under which this claim of the State arose. The majority of the board who made the same award and allowance as the minority, with the exception of $1,233.50 for salary of adjutant-general prior to the time when the troops were mustered in the service, made a very thorough examination of all the vouchers showing each item of expenditure made by the State, and this examination may be assumed as correct and as establishing the fact that the State expended all the moneys for which this claim is made, leaving the question as to the liability of the Government to re-imburse the State to the discretion of Congress. There is but one item stated in the account by the board of examiners which appears to have been charged by mistake. It was undoubtedly paid by the State, but if the board are correct, it was such a palpable mistake of the State officers that the State ought to lose it. It was a double charge for rent, amounting to $38.33. This amount, together with the $8,559.61 allowed by the minority of the board of examiners, and already paid to the State, making a total of $8,597.94, should be deducted from the claim now presented by the State. The State, however, should have the benefit of the fact that no other error in the accounts was discovered. All the other disallowed claims were rejected, not because the State did not pay the money, but because the board of examiners thought they were not authorized to allow the same under the act of June 27, 1882. We print in the appendix, Exhibit No. 17, page 92, the table accompanying report of the majority of the board of war claims examiners showing the amounts allowed and disallowed, together with the reasons therefor.

The question is now presented in this case whether it is the duty of the Government to re-imburse the State for moneys honestly expended, at the request of the United States, under circumstances which rendered it impossible for the Territory and State of Nevada to comply with such request without making the expenditures in question. It must be conceded that if the State or Territory made larger expenditures than would have been required to secure like services in any other section of the country, the services secured by these expenditures at the time, place, and under the circumstances were a necessity and could not have been furnished by the State on more favorable terms, and it seems that the State and Territory did not make any expenditure that appeared at the time unnecessary.

WHAT NEVADA THOUGHT WAS INTENDED BY CONGRESS TO BE AN ACT FOR HER RELIEF AND BENEFIT IS NOW FOUND TO BE AN ACT "SO WELL AND CAREFULLY AND CLOSELY GUARDED" BY RESTRICTIONS THAT WHEN CONSTRUED BY THOSE CALLED UPON TO EXECUTE IT, IS FOUND TO BE INOPERATIVE AS A RELIEF MEASURE, AND A PRACTICAL DENIAL OF JUSTICE.

We fully concur with the officer who made the minority report, that "the restrictions imposed in the second section of the act of June 27,

1882, have been complied with as far as was possible," whatever question there may be as to his complying with the provisions of the act itself. The argument that the Government might have bought supplies cheaper under its contract system than were furnished in Nevada is one which your committee are unwilling to urge under the circumstances. The Government was not situated so as to obtain troops or supplies by contract or otherwise, but was compelled to call upon the Territory to furnish both troops and supplies. All prices of all supplies, and also of all services, at that time in Nevada were on a gold basis, and coin was the only circulating medium. The roads over the mountains were blocked by snow and no considerable amount of supplies could be transported over them. The supplies in the Territory had been carried there during the previous summer for the use of the inhabitants, and the troops had to be furnished from the limited stock of individuals found in the Territory, and at a moment's notice. The Government could not wait to advertise. The overland mail route was closed and immediate action was required. The cheapest, most effective, and in fact the only immediate relief that could be had was furnished by the militia and volunteer troops of Nevada, who, leaving their workshops and employments of every character, and the high wages for their services, were organized and marched immediately in the direction of Salt Lake City to open the mail and emigrant route. They subsequently joined General Conner's forces from California, subdued the Indians, fortified Camp Douglas, overlooking Salt Lake City, and were in the field, subject to call, to go wherever ordered or needed.

PAYMENT BY THE UNITED STATES OF ABOUT 2½ PER CENT. OF THIS CLAIM ON ACCOUNT IS NOT A VALID BASIS FOR THE UNITED STATES TO REPUDIATE THE BALANCE THEREOF, OR TO REFUSE TO PAY THE SAME, AND SHOULD NOT, IN GOOD CONSCIENCE, BE EVER PLEADED BY AN HONEST DEBTOR, FOR WHOSE RELIEF AND AT WHOSE URGENT SOLICITATION SUCH DEBT WAS INCURRED.

The fact that a small fraction only of this claim has been allowed and paid on account, to wit, about 2½ per cent., and the great bulk thereof rejected for want of jurisdiction only, is no valid objection to an authorization by Congress for the payment of what is honestly due the State of Nevada, and for this there are numerous precedents, some of which are cited in the appendix in Exhibit No. 18, pages 96 to 98.

"INTEREST" PAID IN THIS CASE BY NEVADA IS IN REALITY, IN JUSTICE, IN REASON, AND IN LAW A PROPER PART OF THE DEBT DUE NEVADA BY THE UNITED STATES, THE PAYMENT OF WHICH, TOGETHER WITH THAT OF THE PRINCIPAL IS NECESSARY TO A COMPLETE INDEMNITY.

The embarrassments under which Nevada paid the principal of the money involved in this claim is shown by the enormous rates of interest which the Territory and State were compelled to pay in order to raise money to fully comply with these calls and requisitions made for troops and as hereinbefore recited. The rates of interest which were actually paid by Nevada are shown by the official statement of her controller and as furnished to the Secretary of the Treasury and the Secretary of War, as before stated, as follows:

Abstract G.—*Showing the amount actually paid by the State of Nevada and as successor to the Territory of Nevada on account of interest money on disbursements and liabilities for Nevada volunteers in the service of the United States, and employed in the defense of the United States during the war of the rebellion.*

	Amount.
First –Interest paid on $46,950.12 from February 10, 1865, to March 3, 1866, at 2 per cent. per month	$11,925.33
[See acts legislature of Nevada for 1864-'65, page 82, act January 4, 1865.]	
Second—Interest paid on $46,950.12 from March 3, 1866, to May 30, 1867, at 15 per cent. per annum	8,744.46
[See acts legislature of Nevada for 1866, page 47, act January 19, 1866.]	
Third—Interest paid on $119,800.12 from May 30, 1867, to March 28, 1872, at 15 per cent. per annum	86,755.25
[See acts legislature of Nevada for 1867, pages 50 and 65, act February 6, 1867.]	
Fourth—Interest paid on $119,800.12 from March 28, 1872, to January 1, 1883, at 9½ per cent. per annum	122,472.33
[See acts legislature of Nevada for 1871, page 84, act February 27, 1871.]	
	229,897.37

Your committee, however, deem it unwise to establish a precedent under any circumstances, however extraordinary, and they admit that the recitals in support of this claim render it one extraordinary in character, of refunding interest to the full extent as paid by the Territory and State of Nevada, and as shown by the foregoing statement. The legal rate of interest of the Territory and State of Nevada was, at all the times herein stated, 10 per cent. per annum where no different rate was fixed by contract.

Your committee therefore do not feel warranted in recommending re-imbursing the State of Nevada for a higher rate of interest than the legal rate fixed by her own statutes during the period of time in which these disbursements were made, and including the period up to the date of the re-imbursement of the principal by the United States, and for that reason they have incorporated in this bill, herewith reported, a provision that the aggregate of interest accruing to Nevada between the date of the expenditure by her of the principal and of the date of the re imbursement of such principal by the United States shall not exceed the actual amount of interest paid by the State and Territory, nor the amount of interest which would accrue to her on said principal if interest thereon were calculated during said period at the legal rate as established by the statutes of the Territory and State of Nevada. In support of the proposition that interest and principal are simply but two elements of one and the same unit and constituting a complete indemnity, your committee cite Senate Report 1069, made by Senator Spooner during the first session of the Forty-ninth Congress from the Committee on Claims (see appendix, Exhibit No. 19, pages 98 to 109.)

PRECEDENTS FOR THE PAYMENT TO STATES OF INTEREST ON THE PRINCIPAL BY THEM EXPENDED FOR THE USE AND BENEFIT OF THE UNITED STATES UNDER SIMILAR CIRCUMSTANCES.

The United States has in all cases, where the question has been properly presented, re-imbursed States for interest paid by such States on moneys by them borrowed and expended for the purpose of either enrolling, subsisting, clothing, supplying, arming, equipping, paying, furnishing, or transporting volunteer and militia forces called into the service of the United States. If it be suggested that the bill under consideration providing for the payment of both principal and interest is against precedent, we answer that, in the opinion of your committee, it is the better

practice to deal with a case in its entirety in a single act, and your committee state that there are abundant precedents for this practice, some
of which your committee cite in the appendix, Exhibit 20 on page 109.

We call particular attention to the precedents collected in the appendix, authorizing the payment of claims of States for interest on moneys
by them expended for the use and benefit of the United States (see appendix, Exhibits Nos. 18, 19, 20, and 21, pages 96 to 149).

In addition to the authorities cited in the appendix in support of
Nevada's claim for interest, your committee also refer to the case before
the Second Comptroller of the Treasury in 1869, in which that officer
made the following decision:

Interest can in no case be allowed by the accounting officer upon claims against the
Government either in favor of a State or an individual. But in cases where the claimant has been compelled to pay interest for the benefit of the Government, it then becomes a part of the principal of his claim, and as such is allowable. Such is the case
of a State which has been obliged to raise money upon interest for the suppression of
hostilities against which the United States should protect her. In such cases the
amount of interest actually and necessarily paid will be allowed, without reference
to the rate of it (section 997, Dec. 2, Comp. Ed. 1869, p. 137).

This ruling is in harmony with a long line of precedents established
by Congress, beginning in 1812, and printed in the appendix hereto
attached and marked Exhibit Nos. 18 to 21, inclusive, pages 96 to 145.

In addition to the foregoing, your committee cite in support of Nevada's claim for interest the following, to wit:

1. Forty-eighth Congress, first session, House Report No. 1670,
   from Committee on Judiciary (see appendix, Exhibit 21,
   page 112).

2. Forty-eighth Congress, second session, House Report No. 1102,
   from Committee on War Claims (published in Exhibit No.
   14, page 86).

3. Forty-ninth Congress, first session, Senate Report No. 183,
   from the Committee on Military Affairs (see appendix, Exhibit 21, page 135).

4. Forty-ninth Congress, first session, Senate Report No. 2, from
   the Committee on Claims (published in Exhibit No. 14,
   page 85).

5. Forty-ninth Congress, first session, House Report No. 303,
   from Committee on Claims (see appendix, Exhibit 21, page
   119).

6. Forty-ninth Congress, first session, House Report No. 3126,
   from Committee on Claims (see appendix, Exhibit 21, page
   120).

7. Fiftieth Congress, first session, Senate Report No. 518, from
   the Committee on Military Affairs (see appendix, Exhibit
   21, page 138).

8. Fiftieth Congress, first session, House Report No. 309, from
   the Committee on War Claims (see appendix, Exhibit 21,
   page 137).

9. Fiftieth Congress, first session, House Report No. 1179, from
   the Committee on Claims (see appendix, Exhibit 21, page
   145).

10. Fiftieth Congress, first session, House Report No. 2198, from
    the Committee on War Claims (see appendix, Exhibit 21,
    page 144).

The precedents cited or referred to in the appendix herewith abundantly establish the fact that the United States has paid the claims of
States incurred under circumstances such as those in which Nevada ex-

pended her money for the benefit of the United States, and that in all cases properly presented to Congress, where the States were compelled to borrow money and pay interest thereon and expended the same for the use and benefit of the United States, that either at the time of providing payment for the principal or subsequently the United States has invariably assumed and paid such interest.

As before stated, the claim of the State of Nevada, provided for in this bill, has been thoroughly examined by a board of Army officers appointed for that purpose. The evidence upon which this claim was founded was submitted to said board, and the evidences of payment found by them to be correct; but said board of war-claims examiners, while finding these facts, did not, under the very restrictive and prohibitory provisions and conditions of the acts of June 27, 1882, and August 4, 1886, recommend an award to Nevada of the amount of money which they found that Nevada had actually expended for the use and benefit of the United States and in the manner as set forth in the claim as presented by Nevada for the examination of and allowance by the Treasury and War Departments; and under the terms of these acts, as construed and declared by the Secretary of War, the proper accounting officers of the Treasury could not allow Nevada any sum, either as principal or interest, not allowed by the War Department as assisted by said Army board of war-claims examiners.

COST OF TRANSPORTATION OF ARMY SUPPLIES FROM FORT LEAVEN-
WORTH WESTWARD IN 1864-'66.

It is evident that the supplies and services furnished could not at the times and places have been obtained on more reasonable terms. And in support of this statement your committee refer to the report of the Secretary of War made during that period, and in reference to a region of country much more favorably situated than was even Nevada at that time, to wit:

The troops operating on the great western plains and in the mountain regions of New Mexico, Colorado, Utah, and Idaho are supplied principally by the trains of the Quartermaster's Department from depots established on the great routes of overland travel, to which depots supplies are conveyed by contract. * * *

Travelers by the stage from Denver to Fort Leavenworth, a distance of 683 miles, in the month of July, 1865, were never out of sight of wagons trains belonging either to emigrants or to the merchants who transport supplies for the War Department, for the Indian Department, and for the miners and settlers of the central Territories.

The cost of transportation of a *pound* of corn, hay, clothing, subsistence, lumber, or any other necessary from Fort Leavenworth—

To Fort Riley is	$0.0244
To Fort Union, the depot for New Mexico	.1425
To Santa Fé, N. Mex	.1685
To Fort Kearny	.0644
To Fort Laramie	.1410
To Denver City, Colo	.1542
To Salt Lake City, Utah	.2784

The cost of a bushel of corn purchased at Fort Leavenworth and delivered at each of these points was as follows:

Fort Riley	$2.79
Fort Union	9.44
Santa Fé	10.84
Fort Kearny	5.03
Fort Laramie	9.26
Denver City	10.05
Great Salt Lake City	17.00

(Secretary of War's report, 1865-'66, part 1, pages 23 and 112; also see General Halleck to Adjutant-General, and General McDowell to Adjutant-General U. S. Army, report of Secretary of War, October 18, 1866, pages 31 and 32.)

This table is cited to show the costs of maintaining troops in that section of the country, and also to show the comparative costs of furnishing troops and supplies in Nevada and the points immediately east thereof during the periods of time involved herein.

The details concerning the peculiar and difficult and expensive service on the plains and mountains by the troops doing military service, similar in all respects to those performed by these Nevada volunteers, are fully set forth in the report of the Secretary of War respecting the protection of the overland mail and emigrant route to the Pacific from the molestations and depredations by hostile Indians, and set forth in Ex. Docs. Nos. 9 to 24, second session Thirty-ninth Congress, 1866–'67.

CONCLUSIONS AND RECOMMENDATIONS.

Nevada has not demanded a bounty, nor presented a claim against the United States for re-imbursement of any expenditure she did not in good faith actually make for the use and benefit of the United States, and made, too, only subsequent to the date of the aforesaid appeal of Secretary Seward to the nation, and made, too, in consequence of said appeal and of the subsequent calls and requisitions made upon her then scanty resources and sparse population, and wherein the good faith of the United States was to be relied upon to make to her ungrudgingly a just re-imbursement whenever the United States found itself in a condition to redeem all its obligations.

Nevada has been diligent in making her claim known to Congress, but she has not with an indecorous speed demanded her pound of flesh, but has waited long and patiently, believing upon the principle that the higher obligations between States, like those among men, are not always "set down in writing, signed and sealed in the form of a bond, but reside rather in honor," and that the obligation of the United States due her in this case was as sacred as if it had originally been in the form of a 4 per cent. United States bond, now being redeemed by the United States at $1.27 upon each $1 of this particular form of its unpaid obligations.

Nevada has not solicited any charity in this case, but, on the contrary, by numerous petitions and memorials she has respectfully represented to Congress why the taxes heretofore levied upon her people and paid out of her own treasury to her volunteer troops in gold and silver coin to aid the United States at its own solicitation to protect itself and maintain the general welfare should be now returned to her by the General Government.

Congress should not forget that during the long period of the nation's peril the citizens of Nevada, like those of California (when not engaged in the military or naval service of the United States) not only guarded the principal gold and silver mines of the country then discovered, and prevented them from falling into the hands of the public enemy, but also worked them so profitably for the general welfare as to enable the United States to make it possible to resume specie payment, and to redeem its bonds at 27 per cent. above par, and to repay all its money-lenders at a high rate of interest, and that, too, not in the depreciated currency with which it paid Nevada's volunteer troops, but in gold coin of standard value.

As these expenditures were honestly made by the Territory and State of Nevada, your committee do not think that, under all the peculiar and exceptional circumstances of this case, the action of the Territory and State of Nevada should be hewn too nicely or too hypercritically by the United States at this late date.   These expenditures were

all made in perfect good faith and for patriotic purposes, and secured effectual aid to the United States which otherwise could not have been obtained without a much larger expenditure. The State of Nevada in good faith assumed and paid all the obligations of the Territory of Nevada to aid the United States, and issued and sold its own bonds for their payment, upon which bonds it has paid interest until the present time. The only question now for consideration is, shall the United States in equal good faith and under all the circumstances herein recited relieve the State of Nevada from this obligation, or shall the United States insist and require it to be paid by the people of that State alone?

CALIFORNIA.

The total amount paid by California, as shown by said report of said war claims examiners, is $4,420,891.96. Of this amount $1,500,545.86 was interest, and $468,976.54 was expended on account of militia. Deducting these amounts and we have the expenditure of California, excluding interest and expenses of militia, $2,451,369.56.

OREGON.

The total amount paid by Oregon, as shown by said report of said war claims examiners, is $356,271.61. Of this amount $110,626.35 was interest, and $21,118.73 was expended on account of militia. Deducting these amounts and we have the expenditure of Oregon, excluding interest and expenses of militia, of $224,526.53.

NEVADA.

The total amount paid by Nevada as principal and interest, as shown by said report of said war claims examiners, is $404,040.70.

With these amendments your committee therefore recommend the passage of this bill, which, so amended, is as follows, to-wit:

A BILL to re-imburse the States of California, Oregon, and Nevada for moneys by them expended in the suppression of the rebellion.

Be it enacted by the Senate and House of Representatives of the United States of America in Congress assembled, That there is hereby appropriated, out of any money in the Treasury not otherwise appropriated, the sums hereinafter mentioned to re-imburse and to be paid to the States of California, Oregon, and Nevada for moneys by them expended in aid of the United States in the war of the rebellion, to wit:

To the State of California, the sum of two million four hundred and fifty-one thousand three hundred and sixty-nine dollars and fifty-six cents.

To the State of Oregon, the sum of two hundred and twenty-four thousand five hundred and twenty-six dollars and fifty-three cents.

To the State of Nevada, the sum of four hundred and four thousand forty dollars and seventy cents, being the sums of money shown by the reports of the Secretary of War to have been paid by said States in the suppression of the rebellion.

○

REBELLION WAR CLAIMS OF CALIFORNIA, OREGON, AND NEVADA.

FEBRUARY 10, 1892.—Committed to the Committee of the Whole House on the state of the Union and ordered to be printed.

Mr. STONE, of Kentucky, from the Committee on War Claims, submitted the following

REPORT:

[To accompany H. R. 42.]

The Committee on War Claims, to whom was referred the bills (H. R. 42 and H. R. 54) to reimburse the States of California, Oregon, and Nevada for moneys by them expended in the suppression of the rebellion, report as follows:

The facts out of which these bills for relief arise are stated in House Report No. 2553, and in Senate Report No. 644, Fifty-first Congress, first session, also in House Report No. 3396 and in Senate Reports Nos. 1286 and 2014, Fiftieth Congress, first session.

Bills relating to the rebellion war claims of these States passed the Senate during the first session of the Fiftieth Congress and were favorably reported in the Senate during ths first session of the Fifty-first Congress, and were favorably reported from this committee during both the Fiftieth and the Fifty-first Congresses, but were not reached for consideration by the House during either of those two Congresses.

Sums of money shown by the reports of the Secretary of War to have been paid by said States in the suppression of the rebellion were included in the general deficiency appropriation bill as it passed the Senate during the second session of the Fifty-first Congress, for the purpose of paying the rebellion war claims of these three States, the amounts of which are the same as those now included in these bills, but said sums were omitted from said deficiency bill as it became a law.

Your committee now adopt the last report made to the House, June 25, 1890, on a similar bill, to wit, House Report 2553, Fifty-first Congress, first session, annexed hereto and made a part of this report.

These two bills are in all respects identical, but your committee, deeming it necessary to report upon only one thereof, wherefore now report back the bill (H. R. 42) without amendment and recommend its passage

---

[House Report No. 2553, Fifty-first Congress, first session.]

The Committee on War Claims, to whom was referred the bill (H. R. 7430) to reimburse the States of California, Oregon, and Nevada for moneys by them expended in the suppression of the rebellion, report as follows:

The facts out of which this bill for relief arises will be found stated in Senate Report No. 644, from the Committee on Military Affairs of the present Congress, which report is hereto annexed and made part of this report. Your committee adopt the said report as their own, and report back the bill (H. R. 7430) with an amendment, to wit: Strike out lines 8 to 18, inclusive, and in lieu thereof insert as follows, to wit:

To the State of California, the sum of two million four hundred and fifty-one thousand three hundred and sixty-nine dollars and fifty-six cents.

To the State of Oregon, the sum of two hundred and twenty-four thousand five hundred and twenty-six dollars and fifty-three cents.

To the State of Nevada, the sum of four hundred and four thousand forty dollars and seventy cents, being the sums of money shown by the reports of the Secretary of War to have been paid by said States in the suppression of the rebellion.

When so amended, your committee recommend the passage of said bill.

Senate Report No. 644, Fifty-first Congress, first session.

IN THE SENATE OF THE UNITED STATES.

APRIL 10, 1890.—Ordered to be printed.

Mr. STEWART, from the Committee on Military Affairs, submitted the following

REPORT:

[To accompany S. 2416.]

The Committee on Military Affairs, to whom was referred the bill (S. 2416) to re-imburse the States of California, Oregon, and Nevada for moneys by them expended in the suppression of the rebellion, having duly considered the same, respectfully report as follows:

The larger portions of the claims of these States are for extra pay and bounty paid by them during the war of the rebellion.

The circumstances under which the expenditures provided for in this bill were made by these States being exceptional, and their re-imbursement not being provided for by any existing law, general or special, prior to June 27, 1882, Senator Grover, of Oregon, on December 12, 1881, introduced Senate joint resolution No. 10, and Senator Fair, of Nevada, on December 13, 1881, introduced Senate joint resolution No. 13, providing for the equitable adjustment of these State war claims of Oregon and Nevada, which resolutions were referred to the Senate Committee on Military Affairs.

That committee, instead of reporting back said joint resolutions, reported back, May 12, 1882, in lieu thereof a substitute in the form of a bill to wit: S. 1673, Forty-seventh Congress, first session, providing for the payment of certain war claims, to wit, those only of Texas, Oregon, and Nevada, and of the Territories of Idaho and Washington, and which bill, after having been amended in the Senate so as to include the State war claims of Colorado, Nebraska, and California, and amended in the House so as to include the State war claims of Kansas, finally resulted in the passage of the act approved June 27, 1882.   (22 U. S. Stats., 111.)

It was then no doubt the intention of Congress to equitably provide for the re-imbursement of all moneys which California, Oregon, and Nevada, and Nevada when a Territory, had actually expended during the war of the rebellion, on account of the several matters recited in S. bill 3420, Fiftieth Congress, first session. This bill (S. 1673, Forty-seventh Congress, first session) was accompanied by a report (S. No. 575, Forty-seventh Congress, first session) made by Senator Grover May 12, 1882, from which the following is quoted; and which renders said intention of Congress quite evident.

OREGON.

It appears by the report of the Adjutant-General U. S. Army, of April 3, 1882, that one regiment of culvary, one regiment of infantry, and one independent company of cavalry were raised in the State of Oregon during the late war of the rebellion, and that the expenses incident thereto have never been re-imbursed said State by the United States: and that the claims therefor have never been heretofore presented by said State for audit and payment by the United States, as per report of the Secretary of War of April 15, 1882, and of the.Third Auditor of the Treasury of April 8, 1882. Under section 3489 of the Revised Statutes, the claim for expenditures so incurred by said State can not now be presented for audit and payment without legislation by Congress. In addition thereto there are some unadjusted claims of said State growing out of the Bannock and Umatilla Indian hostilities therein in 1877 and 1878, evidenced by a communication of the Secretary of War of date last aforesaid, and some unadjusted balances pertaining to the Modoc war, not presented for audit to General James A. Hardie, approximating the sum of $5,000.

NEVADA.

It appears by the report of the Adjutant-General, U. S. Army, of February 25, 1882, that one regiment of cavalry and one battalion of infantry were raised in the late Territory of Nevada during the late war of the rebellion, and that the expenses of raising, organizing, and placing in the field said forces were never paid by said Territory, but were assumed and paid by the State of Nevada, and that none of said expenses so incurred by said Territory, and assumed and paid by said State, have ever been re-imbursed the State of Nevada by the United States, and that no claims therefor have ever been heretofore presented by either said Territory or said State for audit and payment by the United States. Under section 3489 of the Revised Statutes, hereinbefore referred to, the payment of these claims is barred by limitation.

These forces were raised to guard the overland mail route and emigrant road to California, east of Carson City, and to do other military service in Nevada, and were called out by the governor of the late Territory of Nevada, upon requisitions therefor by the commanding general of the Department of the Pacific, and under authority of the War Department, as appears by copies of official correspondence furnished to your committee by the Secretary of War and the general commanding the Division of the Pacific. * * *

The Senate Committee on Military Affairs did not at that time make any report in relation to the State war claims of the State of California, but when this substitute bill (S. 1673, Forty-seventh Congress, first session) reported from that committee was under consideration in the Senate, Senator Miller, of California, called attention to the fact that California had war claims unprovided for, and on his motion this bill (S. 1673, Forty-seventh Congress, first session) was amended in the Senate so as to include these State war claims of the State of California. It is alleged by California, Oregon, and Nevada that this act of June 27,1882, which they believed was intended by Congress to be an act for their relief and benefit and an equitable statute to be liberally construed, has been found to be an act " so well and carefully and closely guarded by restrictions" that, when construed by those who have been called upon to execute it, has proven to be completely inoperative as an equitable relief measure, so much so as to amount to a practical denial of justice so far as the present State war claims of these States now provided for in this bill were or are concerned.

PRESENTATION BY CALIFORNIA, OREGON, AND NEVADA OF THEIR STATE WAR CLAIMS TO THE UNITED STATES.

The aforesaid bill (S. 1673, Forty-seventh Congress, first session) having become a law June 27, 1882, the State war claims of California, Oregon, and Nevada were thereafter duly transmitted for presentation to the proper authorities of the United States, those of Oregon by Hon. R. P. Earhart, and Hon. George W. McBride, secretary of state for Oregon and ex officio adjutant-general. Those for Nevada by Hon. J. F. Hallock, controller of Nevada. Those for California by Hon. John

Dunn, controller, assisted by his deputy, Hon. M. J. O'Reilly, and by Hon. D. I. Oullahan and Hon. Adam Herold, State treasurers, and General George B. Crosby, adjutant-general of California, aided therein by Hon. George Stoneman, Governor of California, and his private secretary, Hon. W. W. Moreland, and by Hon. W. C. Hendricks, secretary, and General H. B. Davidson, assistant secretary of state of California.

These State war claims of these three States, accompanied with proper original vouchers and evidence in support thereof, in each case were thereafter duly delivered by the aforesaid State authorities of California, Oregon, and Nevada, or by those duly authorized therein, to Capt. John Mullan, the duly appointed agent and authorized special counsel for each of said three States, by whom they were put in abstracts and proper shape and thereafter submitted by him to the Secretary of the Treasury and Secretary of War, as provided for in said act of Congress approved June 27, 1882.

DELAY OF THE UNITED STATES IN THE EXAMINATION OF CALIFORNIA, OREGON, AND NEVADA STATE WAR CLAIMS AND THE CAUSES THEREOF.

These State war claims, with said vouchers and evidence, so originally presented to the Secretary of the Treasury and Secretary of War for examination, remained of record in the Treasury and War Departments unacted on up to and after August 4, 1886, because, as was stated to Congress by Hon. Robert T. Lincoln, the Secretary of War, required the aid of at least three army officers to assist his Department in making a proper examination thereof, and he requested Congress to make an appropriation of $25,000 to defray the expenses of such examination of these State and Territorial war claims presented and others to be presented under said act of June 27, 1882. Congress delayed action upon these repeated requests of the Secretary of War until August 4, 1886, on which date acts were passed by Congress providing for a board of three army officers, as asked for, and also appropriating $10,000 to defray the expenses of a full and exhaustive examination (see vol. 24. Stats. at Large, pages 217 and 249) of these State war claims.

SECRETARY LINCOLN'S CONSTRUCTION OF THIS ACT OF JUNE 27, 1882, FOR THE RELIEF OF NEVADA, ETC.

Prior to any action by the War Department on these State war claims of the States of California, Oregon, and Nevada, and prior to any action by Congress on said request of the Secretary of War for a board of army officers to aid him to examine said claims, a bill, S. 657, Forty-eighth Congress, first session, was introduced in Congress by Senator Jones, of Nevada, providing for the payment of certain individual claims of citizens of Nevada on account of Indian hostilities in Nevada in 1860, and was referred by the Senate Committee on Military Affairs to the Secretary of War and of the Treasury for reports, and upon which the Secretary of War reported as follows:

WAR DEPARTMENT,
Washington City, January 26, 1884.

SIR: In response to so much of your communication of the 22d ultimo as requests information concerning Senate bill 657, "to authorize the Secretary of the Treasury to adjust and settle the expenses of Indian wars in Nevada," I have the honor to invite your attention to the following report of the Third Auditor of the Treasury, to whom your request was duly referred:

"The State of Nevada has filed in the office abstracts and vouchers for expenses in-

curred on account of raising volunteers for the United States to aid in suppressing the late rebellion, amounting to $349,697.49, and for expenses on account of her militia in the 'White Pine Indian war' of 1875, $17,650.98. Also, expenses of her militia in the 'Elko Indian war' of 1878, amounting to $4,654.64, presented under act of Congress approved June 27, 1882 (22 Statutes 111, 112).

"These abstracts and vouchers will be sent to your Department for examination and report us soon as they can be stamped, as that statute requires a report from the Secretary of War as to the necessity and reasonableness of the expenses incurred. This statute is deemed sufficiently broad enough to embrace all proper claims of said State and Territory of Nevada."

Very respectfully, your obedient servant,

ROBERT T. LINCOLN,
Hon. S. B. MAXEY, *Secretary of War.*
Of Committee on Military Affairs, United States Senate.

In accordance with this report and opinion of the Secretary of War the Senate Committee on Military Affairs reported back this bill so referred to (S. 657, Forty-eighth Congress, first session), and asked that it be indefinitely postponed, and because of the explanation made to the Senate by said committee, and based upon said report and construction of said act and said opinion of the then Secretary of War, Hon. Robert T. Lincoln, as follows, to wit:

It will be observed that it is deemed by the War Department that the act approved June 27, 1882, is sufficiently broad to embrace all proper claims of Nevada, whether as State or Territory.

For convenience of reference the above act accompanies this report, and an examination thereof, and of the construction thereon, satisfies the committee that no additional legislation is necessary.

The State of Kansas presented her State war claim to Secretary Lincoln under this very act, which claim was by him examined, audited, and allowed for almost exactly the sum that Kansas had actually expended for the use and benefit of the United States, and all of which allowance has since been paid to Kansas by the United States, and aggregating the sum of $322,308.13 (23 U. S. Stats., 474) as allowed and paid to said State by the United States. So, too, the State of Nebraska under similar circumstances was allowed and paid the sum of $18,081.23 under this same act of June 27, 1882.

AFTER OVER FOUR YEARS' DELAY, SUBSEQUENT TO THE PASSAGE OF THE ACT OF JUNE 27, 1882, THE UNITED STATES TAKES UP NEVADA'S STATE WAR CLAIM FOR EXAMINATION, WHEN THE VERY FIRST QUESTION RAISED IS ONE OF JURISDICTION, AND WHICH IS DECIDED AGAINST NEVADA.

After the passage of said act of August 4, 1886, the War Department detailed a board of three Army officers under Special Orders No. 232, dated October 6, 1886, to proceed to examine the claims provided for under said act of June 27, 1882, and in the manner contemplated in said act. The State war claims of the State of Nevada were the first examined by said board. This board being in doubt whether, under the terms of said act of June 27, 1882, they could allow a re-imbursement to Nevada of the amount of money by her expended for interest and extra pay to her troops while in the military service of the United States, duly referred these two questions to the Secretary of War for his decision. On February 8, 1887, after argument was submitted to said Secretary in support of these two elements of Nevada's State war claims against the United States, that officer decided "that, after a careful consideration of the subject, he was of opinion that neither the extra pay nor the interest can, under the provisions of the act, be allowed," meaning the act of June 27, 1882, and refused the same, as appears from the correspondence following, to wit:

DECISION OF THE SECRETARY OF WAR DISALLOWING THE STATE WAR CLAIM OF
NEVADA FOR INTEREST AND EXTRA PAY TO NEVADA VOLUNTEERS.

WAR DEPARTMENT,
Washington City, February 8, 1887.

SIR: The Department has received your communications of December 31, 1886, and January 28, 1887, submitting arguments in the claim of the State of Nevada, under the act of June 27, 1882, for re-imbursement of amounts paid by the State for "extra pay" and for interest. Also, your communication of 2d instant, inclosing a resolution of the senate and assembly of Nevada, requesting favorable and early action on said claim.

In reply, I have the honor to inform you that after a careful consideration of the subject I am of opinion that neither the extra pay nor the interest can, under the provisions of the act, be allowed.

Very respectfully,

WILLIAM C. ENDICOTT,
Secretary of War.

JOHN MULLAN, Esq.,
Agent of the State of Nevada, 1101 *G street, N. W., City.*

It therefore fully appears that on January 26, 1884, Secretary Lincoln, when construing said act of June 27, 1882, was of opinion that it was sufficiently broad to embrace all proper war claims of the State of Nevada; whereupon the Senate Committee on Military Affairs, in consequence thereof, reported to the Senate that said committee was satisfied that no additional legislation was necessary in regard thereto, while Secretary Endicott, on February 8, 1887, construing this same act and deciding thereunder, held that these war claims of the States and Territories named in said act for expenditure for interest and extra pay to their troops while in the service of the United States could not be allowed by him under said act.

This decision of Secretary Endicott in the case of the State of Nevada, to the effect that "under the provisions of the act of June 27, 1882, he had no jurisdiction to allow interest paid by that State upon the principal by her expended, nor the extra pay made by her to the State troops while they were in the service of the United States," became practically a decision in the case of the State war claims of the State of California, and effectually disposed of these two similar items in the war claims of that State. In addition thereto the Secretary of War, Mr. Endicott, on November 8, 1887, upon a statement made to him by the chief of said board of war claims examiners, also decided that he had no jurisdiction to adjudicate Oregon's State war claim, which claim also contained similar items for interest and extra pay, and thus Secretary Endicott's aforesaid decision in the Nevada case also practically disposed of these two similar items in Oregon's claim so far as his Department was concerned.

In consequence, therefore, of these conflicting decisions of two Secretaries of War upon one and the same act of June 27, 1882, rendering it absolutely nugatory so far as the adjustment of these State war claims of these three States were concerned, made and makes additional remedial legislation by Congress absolutely necessary in order to deal equitably with these States and their claims for re-imbursement of money by them expended in good faith for the common defense during a period of war and at the instance of the authorities of the United States.

The Senate Committee on Military Affairs, therefore, during the Fiftieth Congress, first session, had first under consideration a bill (S. 2918) "to re-imburse the State of Nevada for moneys expended on obligations incurred by said State and the Territory of Nevada, and afterwards assumed and paid by said State, in the suppression of the war of the

rebellion, and for guarding the overland mail and emigrant route," and a majority of the committee made a favorable report thereon. (S. R. No. 1286, Fiftieth Congress, first session.)

Your committee thereafter, having under due consideration similar claims for California and Oregon, reported a general bill, to wit, S. 3420, Fiftieth Congress, first session, accompanied by Senate Report No. 2014, Fiftieth Congress, first session, made August 10, 1888, for the investigation of all the war claims of California, Oregon, and Nevada substantially in the same language as recited in the resolution afterwards passed by the Senate and hereinafter set forth. A full statement of these war claims was made and submitted to your committee, but not reported to the Senate at the same time that said resolution for investigation was approved by your committee. That statement is printed in the report of the war claims examiners on the claims of the State of California, commencing after the report and after page 95 of Ex. Doc. No. 11, Fifty-first Congress, first session, and also in Senate Ex. Docs. Nos. 10 and 17, Fifty-first Congress, first session. Senate Report No. 2014, Fiftieth Congress, first session, does not seem to appear in said reports, Senate Ex. Docs. 10, 11, 17, although said bill S. 3420 passed the Senate and was favorably reported in the House September 4, 1888, in House Report No. 3306, Fiftieth Congress, first session, as follows, to wit:

Mr. Stone, of Kentucky, from the Committee on War Claims, submitted the following report (to accompany bill S. 3420).

The Committee on War Claims, to whom was referred the bill (S. 3420) authorizing the Secretary of War to ascertain what amount of money has been expended by the States of California, Oregon, and Nevada for military purposes in aid of the Government of the United States during the war of the rebellion, report as follows:

The facts out of which this bill for relief arises will be found stated in Senate report from the Committee on Military Affairs of the present Congress, which report is hereto annexed and made a part of this report. Your committee adopt the said report as their own, and report back the bill and recommend its passage.

———————

The Committee on Military Affairs, to whom was referred the bill (S. 3420) authorizing the Secretary of War to ascertain what amount of money has been expended by the States of California, Oregon, and Nevada for military purposes in aid of the Government of the United States during the war of the rebellion, having considered the same, report as follows:

During the war of the rebellion the States of California, Oregon, and Nevada were separated from the Atlantic States by over 1,500 miles of almost uninhabited country. Much apprehension was felt on account of the exposed condition of those distant States, and the Government called upon them to assist in guarding the overland mail and emigrant routes, in preventing Indian outbreaks in the States, and to aid the United States in various ways during the war of the rebellion.

At the beginning of the war Nevada was a Territory, and was admitted into the Union as a State in 1864; but for the purposes of this report Nevada will hereafter be referred to as a State.

These States complied promptly with all the requirements of the General Government, and volunteered all the aid in their power to assist the United States. On the Pacific coast during this time, and particularly in Nevada, prices of all commodities (and also the price of labor) were exceedingly high, and as a mining excitement existed in these States it became necessary to extend aid in many ways in organizing, arming, equipping, furnishing, and maintaining volunteer soldiers and militia beyond the amount required for those purposes in the Eastern States. California, Oregon, and Nevada passed numerous acts to organize and equip soldiers in compliance with the requests of the Government, for which they were compelled to expend large sums of money. They were also compelled to borrow money, upon which a large amount of interest has been paid.

An examination of all the facts connected with these claims, a statement of accounts showing for what the money was paid and under what authority, involves too

much detail for a committee of Congress to investigate. They therefore recommend the passage of the accompanying bill, which simply provides for an examination and report upon the facts of the claims of each of these States, so as to enable Congress to take such action as may be just and proper in the premises.

The bill does not commit Congress to the payment of these claims in advance, nor a settlement upon any particular theory. It does not commit Congress in advance to re-imburse these States for bounty or extra money expended by them in furnishing troops to assist the United States in suppressing the war of the rebellion, nor to the payment of interest on moneys borrowed. It simply provides for an ascertainment of such facts so as to enable Congress to legislate intelligently.

A bill for the payment of the claims of Nevada has already been reported by a majority of your committee and is now on the Calendar of the Senate. The report in that case is very elaborate, and some members of your committee desire, before action is taken on it, a more authoritative statement of the case, which will be obtained by the examination now proposed. The claims of California and Oregon are of a similar character to those of Nevada. All these States were differently situated during the rebellion from the other States of the Union, and your committee therefore thought proper to have the same investigation and report made in each case and have them all incorporated in one bill. The writer of this report has prepared an elaborate statement of the claims of California and Oregon, which has been printed by order of the Senate for the use of the committee.

The report on the Nevada claim, known as Senate Report No. 1286, and dated May 14, 188-, and the statement with regard to the claims of California and Oregon will assist the War Department in collecting the laws and orders under which these States expended the money in question, and your committee desire to call the attention of the Secretary of War to these documents in case this bill should become a law.

The laws that have been passed for the investigation of claims of other States are not applicable to the peculiar conditions of these States during the war of the rebellion, and there is no authority under them for the ascertainment of the necessary facts to enable Congress to determine what allowances should be made under the peculiar circumstances which surrounded these States at the time in question.

Your committee report the bill back with an amendment, and when so amended recommend that it do pass.

No action having been taken in the House on said Senate bill 3420 after said House Report No. 3396 was made, and it being deemed important that Congress at its present session should have before it in an official form all the data, facts, and the results of a full, exhaustive, and official examination of these State war claims to be made by the War Department, which then had and now has official custody of all these claims, and of all evidence relating thereto filed in support thereof, and in order that the Secretary of War should have the full benefit and aid of said Board of Army Officers, which was then still in session at Washington, D. C., and which Board Congress had specially created in said act of August 4, 1886 (24 U. S. Stats., 217), to aid the Secretary of War to make a full, exhaustive, and official examination of these State war claims of these three States, so that the Secretary of War could officially and intelligently report upon the same to Congress, or to either branch thereof, for its information and action, as contemplated in said Senate bill 3420, Fiftieth Congress, first session, the Senate therefore, on the 27th of February, 1889, passed the following resolution:

Resolved, That the Secretary of War, through the board of war claims examiners, appointed under section 2 of the act of Congress entitled "An act for the benefit of the States of Texas, Colorado, Oregon, Nebraska, California, Kansas, and Nevada, and the Territories of Washington and Idaho, and Nevada, when a Territory," approved August 4, 1886, be, and he is hereby, authorized and directed to examine all accounts, papers, and evidence which heretofore have been, or which hereafter may be, submitted to him in support of the war claims of the States of California, Oregon, and Nevada, and Nevada when a Territory, growing out of the war of the rebellion, and in suppressing Indian hostilities and disturbances during the war of the rebellion, and in guarding the overland mail and emigrant routes during and subsequent to the war of the rebellion, and to ascertain and state what amount of money each of said States, and Nevada when a Territory, actually expended, and what obligations they incurred for the purposes aforesaid, whether such expenditures were made or obligations incurred in actual warfare or in recruiting, enlisting, enrolling, organizing, arming, equipping, supplying, clothing, subsisting, drilling, furnishing, transporting.

and paying their volunteers, militia, and home guards, and for bounty, extra pay, and relief paid to their volunteers, militia, and home guards, and in preparing their volunteers, militia, and home guards in camp and field to perform military service for the United States.

The Secretary of War is also directed to ascertain what amount of interest has been paid by each of said States, and Nevada when a Territory, on obligations incurred for purposes above enumerated. The Secretary of War shall report to Congress the amount of money which may be thus ascertained to have been actually paid by each of said States, and Nevada when a Territory, on account of the matters above enumerated, and also the amount of interest actually paid or assumed by each of said States, and Nevada when a Territory, on moneys borrowed for the purposes above enumerated. And the Secretary of War shall also report the circumstances and exigencies under which, and the authority by which, such expenditures were made, and what payments have been made on account thereof by the United States.

In response to this resolution the honorable Secretary of War, having theretofore fully completed, with the aid of said Army Board, a thorough, and exhaustive official examination of all these war claims of said three States, transmitted in December, 1889, his report to the Senate in each of the cases of California, Oregon, and Nevada, as required by said resolution, and which reports are as follows, to wit: Senate Ex. Docs. Nos. 10, 11, 17, Fifty-first Congress, first session. These reports and the exhibits attached thereto, respectively, are in great detail, and contain a very full history of the important part taken by the Pacific States and Territories during the rebellion in defense of the Union. These reports are in full compliance with said Senate resolution, showing the actual amount of money expended by each of said States, and of Nevada when a Territory, during the war of the rebellion in aid of the United States, and the authority, State, Territorial, and national, and also the special circumstances and exigencies under which the expenditures reported upon by said Secretary and said board therein respectively were made. The following tables, taken from the reports of said war claims examiners, show the several sums of money actually expended and paid out as principal and interest by each of said States:

CALIFORNIA.

[Senate Ex. Doc. No. 11, Fifty-first Congress, first session, page 27.]

Amount expended in recruiting California volunteers (Abstract F)....	$24,260.00
Amount expended in payment of adjutant-general, etc. (Abstract H)...	38,083.17
Amount expended in organizing volunteers (Abstract M)..............	5,639.34
Amount expended in pay of volunteer officers (Abstract N)...........	23,277.34
Amount expended in extra pay to enlisted men of California volunteers (Abstract P)......	1,459,270.21
Amount expended in bounty to enlisted men (Abstract Q).............	900,839.50
Total expense of volunteers, and not repaid the State by the United States...	2,451,369.56
Amount expended in payment of interest on moneys borrowed to carry out the provisions of the acts of April 27, 1863, and April 4, 1864.....	1,500,545.86
Aggregate expenses incurred on account of volunteers, principal and interest..	3,951,915.42
Amount expended on account of militia.............................	468,976.54
Grand total of expenses on account of volunteers and militia....	4,420,891.96

OREGON.

[Senate Ex. Doc. No. 17, Fifty-first Congress, first session, page 20.]

Amount expended in payment of adjutant-general, etc. (Abstract E)...	$3,973.49
Amount expended in extra pay to enlisted men (Abstract G)...........	90,476.32
Amount expended in bounty to enlisted men (Abstract H).............	129,241.02
Amount expended for advertising calls for redemption of bonds (Abstract K)	835.70

Amount expended in payment of interest on moneys borrowed to carry
out the provisions of the acts of October 24, 1864 (Abstract L)....... $110,626.35

Total amount expended on account of volunteers and not repaid
State by United States 335,152.88
Amount expended on account of militia.............................. 21,118.73

Aggregate expenses incurred on account of militia and volunteers..... 356,271.61

NEVADA.

[Senate Ex. Doc. No. 10, Fifty-first Congress, first session, page 8.]

Amount actually paid out on account of volunteers raised in Nevada.... $118,667.49
Amount of interest paid on moneys borrowed and so expended.......... 289,645.59
Amount of liabilities assumed on account of volunteers raised in Nevada. 1,133.92
Amount of interest paid on liabilities assumed 3,113.31

Total amount expended or assumed................................... 412,600.31
Amount already paid to Nevada by the United States upon an examination under the provisions of the act of June 27, 1882.................. 8,559.61

Amount expended or assumed and not repaid by the United States.. 404,040.70

INTEREST.

In said Ex. Doc. No. 10, Fifty-first Congress, first session, page 15,
it is declared that—

Interest paid by California, Oregon, and Nevada is in reality, in justice, in reason,
and in law a proper part of the debt due them by the United States, the payment of
which, together with that of the principal, is necessary to a complete indemnity.

The United States has generally refused to pay interest on claims
against the Government. This rule sometimes works great hardship
and wrong; but the inconveniences that might arise from a departure
from it may be very great. There is one exception, however, to this rule
which has been uniformly recognized and acted upon; that is, when a
State has claims against the Government for expenditures made for
the United States, and a part of such claims consists of interest paid out or
assumed by the State, the interest so paid out or assumed has been treated
eventually so far as the adjustment thereof was concerned as if it had
been originally presented as a part of the principal, although Congress
has always treated the interest as a separate, independent, and distinct claim apart from the principal, which sometimes is adjusted when
adjusting the principal, depending no doubt in part upon the special
circumstances of the cases presented to Congress and at other times
adjusted after the principal is paid, but always adjusting it some time
in all proper cases. The rule is well stated in the Decisions of the Second
Comptroller for 1869, page 137, as follows:

Interest can in no case be allowed by the accounting officers upon claims against
the Government, either in favor of a State or an individual. But in cases where the
claimant has been compelled to pay interest for the benefit of the Government it
then becomes a part of the principal of the claim, and as such is allowable.

Such is the case of a State which has been obliged to raise money upon interest for
the suppression of hostilities against which the United States should protect her.

In such cases the amount of interest actually and necessarily paid will be allowed,
without reference to the rate of it.

There are many cases to sustain this ruling of the Second Comptroller, of which the following are cited as precedents where Congress
first authorized the adjustment and payment of the principal and then
subsequently adjusted and thereafter paid the interest:

1. By an act approved April 2, 1830, the Secretary of the Treasury was authorized
to cause to be paid to the mayor and city council of Baltimore the sum of $7,434.53 in
full for their claim against the United States for money borrowed and expended by

them in defense of said city in the war of 1812, and by the second section of said act the Secretary of the Treasury was directed to cause to be paid interest on said sum according to the provisions and regulations of "the act to authorize payment of interest due the city of Baltimore," approved May 20, 1826.

2. By an act approved May 31, 1830, the proper accounting officers of the Treasury, under the superintendence of the Secretary of War, were authorized and directed to audit and settle the claims of the State of Massachusetts against the United States for services of her militia during the war of 1812, in the following cases:

(1) Where the militia of said State were called out to repel actual invasion, or under a well-founded apprehension of invasion, provided their numbers were not in undue proportion to the exigency.

(2) Where they were called out by the authority of the State and afterwards recognized by the Federal Government.

(3) Where they were called out by and served under the requisition of the President of the United States or of any officer thereof.

3. By a joint resolution approved May 14, 1836, entitled "A resolution to authorize the Secretary of War to receive additional evidence in support of claims of Massachusetts and other States of the United States for disbursements, services," etc., during the war of 1812, the Secretary was authorized, in preparing his report pursuant to the resolution of House of Representatives agreed to the 24th of February, 1832, without regard to existing rules and requirements to receive such evidence as was on file, and any further proofs which might be offered tending to establish the validity of the claims of Massachusetts upon the United States, or any part thereof, for services, disbursements, and expenditures during the war with Great Britain; and in all cases where such evidence should, in his judgment, prove the truth of the items of the claim, or any part thereof, to act on the same in like manner as if the proof consisted of such vouchers and evidence as was required by existing rules and regulations touching the allowance of such claims; and it was provided that in the settlement of claims of other States upon the United States for services, disbursements, and expenditures during the war with Great Britain, the same kind of evidence, vouchers, and proof should be received as therein provided for in relation to the claim of Massachusetts.

4. By the sixth section of an act approved March 31, 1837, an appropriation was made for paying the claims of the State of Connecticut for the services of her militia during the war of 1812, to be audited and settled by the proper accounting officers of the Treasury under the superintendence of the Secretary of War in the following cases:

(1) Where the militia of said State were called out to repel actual invasion or under a well-founded apprehension of invasion, provided their numbers were not in undue proportion to the exigency.

(2) Where they were called out by the authorities of the State and afterwards recognized by the Federal Government, and

(3) Where they were called out and served under the requisition of the President of the United States or of any officer thereof.

5. By an act approved August 14, 1848, the proper accounting officers of the Treasury were directed to settle the claims for one month's service of the officers and soldiers of the Fourth Regiment in the Second Brigade of the Third Division of the militia of the State of Vermont, who served at the battle of Plattsburgh on the 11th of September, 1814, for their military services on that occasion.

6. By act approved March 3, 1853, making appropriations for the civil and diplomatic expenses of the Government for the year ending June 30, 1854, an appropriation of $10,334.31 was made for arrearages of pay, subsistence, and clothing due to Capt. Richard McRae's Company of Virginia Volunteers, which served in the war with Great Britain in 1812-'13 to be paid to the officers and soldiers of said company or their legal representatives, under the order of the Secretary of War, upon the production of proof as to the identity of said officers and soldiers, and that they have not been paid.

7. By an act approved August 31, 1852 (Army appropriation), the Secretary of War was required to pay to the State of South Carolina such sums of money as were paid by said State in 1838, 1839, and 1840 for services, losses, and damages sustained by her volunteers in the Florida war of 1836, 1837, and 1838, while in the service of the United States, and on their return from said service, as were ascertained and allowed by the board of commissioners appointed for that purpose by the act of the legislature of said State in 1837, with the proviso that no interest should be allowed upon moneys paid to the State of South Carolina under the provisions of said act. And it was by said act further provided that in the settlement of the claims of the State of Georgia, under the act of August 11, 1842, providing for the settlement of the claims of that State for the service of her militia, which had theretofore been suspended or disallowed, the accounting officers of the Treasury Department should allow and pay, upon proof that the State had allowed and paid the same, all accounts for forage, subsistence, hospital stores, medical service, and transportation which had not there-

tofore been allowed by the United States. And it was further provided by said act that in the adjustment of the accounts of the State of Maine, under the act of June 13, 1842, the proper accounting officers of the Treasury should include and allow the claims which had theretofore been presented under said act, provided it should be satisfactorily shown that said claims had been actually allowed and paid by said State.

8. By an act approved March 3, 1853, second section, the proper accounting officers of the Treasury Department were authorized to settle the claims of the State of Florida for services of her troops under the act of February 27, 1851, by the provision stated for the settlement of the claims of the State of Georgia for like services, under the act approved August 31, 1851 (Army appropriation bill).

9. By the eighth section of an act approved March 3, 1853, the Secretary of the Treasury was directed to pay to the State of Georgia her claims remaining unpaid for moneys paid by the State in suppressing hostilities of the Cherokee, Creek, and Seminole Indians in the year 1835 and since, upon proof that the same was paid by the State, and that the provisions of the act relative to the settlement of the claims of Georgia for military service, approved March 3, 1851, should be extended to payments under said act.

The Secretary of the Treasury was also by said act required to pay the State of Alabama, under the provisions of the acts of Congress of August 16, 1842, and January 26, 1849, the balance due said State, growing out of the Creek Indian hostilities of 1836 and 1837; and by the twelfth section of said act it was provided that in the adjustment of the accounts of the State of Virginia under the twelfth section of the act of August 31, 1852, the Secretary of War should follow the provisions of the act of June 2, 1848, providing for refunding to the several States the amounts expended by them in raising regiments of volunteers for the Mexican war.

10. By an act approved January 26, 1849, the Secretary of War was directed to pay interest upon the advances made by the State of Alabama for the use of the United States Government in the suppression of hostilities by the Creek Indians in 1836 and 1837, at the rate of 6 per cent. per annum from the time of the advances until the principal of the same was paid by the United States to the State. And in ascertaining the amount of interest it was provided that interest should not be computed on any sum which Alabama had not expended for the use and benefit of the United States, as evidenced by the amount refunded to the State of Alabama by the United States, and that no interest should be paid on any sum on which the State of Alabama did not either pay or lose interest as aforesaid.

11. By an act approved March 3, 1851, the Secretary of War was authorized to allow to the State of Georgia for advances made to the United States for the suppression of hostilities of the Creek, Seminole, and Cherokee Indians in the years 1835, 1836, 1837, and 1838, with interest at the rate of 6 per cent. per annum on all sums allowed and paid to the State of Georgia and that might thereafter be allowed and paid for any moneys advanced by the State for the purposes aforesaid, from the date of such advances until the principal sums were or might be paid by the United States, with the proviso that no interest should be paid on any sum on which Georgia did not either pay or lose interest.

12. By an act passed the same day as the above act, the proper accounting officers of the Treasury were directed to settle the claim of the State of Maine against the United States, being for interest on money borrowed and actually expended by her for the protection of the northeastern frontier of said State during the years 1839 1840, and 1841, the amount of such interest to be ascertained under the following rules:

"(1) Interest not to be computed on any sum not expended by the State for the use and benefit of the United States, as evidenced by the amount refunded or paid to the State by the United States.

"(2) No interest to be paid on any sum on which the State did not either pay or lose interest."

13. By act approved July 21, 1852, making appropriations to supply deficiencies in the appropriations for the year ending June 30, 1852, the sum of $80,741 was appropriated for pay of five companies of Texas mounted volunteers.

14. By act approved March 3, 1859, for the purpose of executing the resolution of May 14, 1836, the Secretary of the Treasury was directed to pay to Massachusetts $227,176.48, reported to be due said State by Secretary of War J. R. Poinsett, in report dated December 23, 1837, made to the House of Representatives December 27, 1837, and it was provided that in lieu of payment in money the Secretary of the Treasury might, at his discretion, issue to said State United States stock bearing 5 per cent. per annum, and redeemable at the end of ten years, or sooner, at the pleasure of the President.

15. By act approved March 3, 1825, the accounting officers of the Treasury Department were authorized and directed to settle the claim of the State of Virginia against the United States for interest upon loans on moneys borrowed and actually expended by her for the use and benefit of the United States during the war of 1812.

16. By this act it was provided that, in ascertaining the amount of interest, as aforesaid, due to the State of Virginia, the following rules should be understood as applicable to and governing the case, to wit: First, that interest should not be computed on any sum which Virginia had not expended for the use and benefit of the United States, as evidenced by the amount refunded or repaid to Virginia by the United States. Second, that no interest should be paid on any sum on which she had not paid interest. Third, that when the principal, or any part of it, had been paid, or refunded by the United States, or money placed in the hands of Virginia for that purpose, the interest on the sum or sums so paid or refunded should cease, and not be considered as chargeable to the United States any longer than up to the repayment, as aforesaid.

The mode of computing interest provided by the above act appears to have been satisfactory at the time to all the States, and their claims against the General Government were authorized to be adjusted, and were adjusted under the same rules for computing interest.

17. By an act approved May 13, 1826, entitled "An act authorizing the payment of interest due to the State of Maryland," the accounting officers of the Treasury Department were authorized and directed to liquidate and settle the claim of the State of Maryland against the United States, for interest upon loans on moneys borrowed and actually expended by her for the use and benefit of the United States, during the late war with Great Britain, and the same rules for computing the interest was provided by the act as in the case of the State of Virginia.

18. By an act approved May 20, 1826, entitled "An act authorizing the payment of interest due to the State of Delaware," the accounting officers of the Treasury Department were authorized and directed to take similar action in regard to the settlement of the claim of the State of Delaware against the United States as that directed to be taken in the case of the claim of Maryland, and to be governed by the same rules.

19. By act approved May 20, 1826, the proper accounting officers of the Treasury Department were directed to settle the claim of the city of Baltimore against the United States, for interest on money borrowed and actually expended by the city in its defense during the war of 1812; and the act further provided that the amount due should be ascertained under rules which were the same as those provided by the foregoing act for the adjustment of the accounts in the cases of Virginia, Maryland, and Delaware.

20. By an act approved May 22, 1826, entitled "An act authorizing the payment of interest due to the State of New York," the accounting officers of the Treasury Department were authorized and directed to take similar action and to be governed by the same rules as in the cases of Virginia, Maryland, and Delaware.

21. By an act approved March 3, 1827, the accounting officers of the Treasury De-

25. On the 8th day of July, 1870, an act was passed directing the account between the United States and Massachusetts and Maine to be re-opened and re-adjusted, and Massachusetts received the sum of $678,362.42, of which one-third was allotted to the State of Maine as an integral part of Massachusetts when the advances were made.

In the foregoing cases the principal was first re-imbursed, and subsequently the interest was adjusted and then paid by the United States. The following cases are cited as precedents, where both the principal and interest were authorized by Congress to be paid at one and the same time and in and under one and the same act:

1. By a joint resolution approved March 3, 1847 (Stats. at Large, vol. 9, p. —), the Secretary of War was authorized and required to cause to be refunded to the several States or to individuals for services rendered, acting under the authority of any State, the amount of expenses incurred by them in organizing, subsisting, and transporting volunteers previous to their being mustered and received into the service of the United States for the war with Mexico, and for subsisting troops in the service of the United States.

2. By an act approved June 2, 1848, the provisions of said joint resolution were extended so as to embrace all cases of expenses theretofore incurred in organizing, subsisting, and transporting volunteers previous to their being mustered and received into the United States for the war with Mexico, whether by States, counties, corporations, or individuals, either acting with or without the authority of any State, and that in refunding moneys under said act and said joint resolution it should be lawful to pay interest at the rate of 6 per cent. per annum on all sums advanced by States, corporations, or individuals in all cases where the State, corporation, or individual paid or lost the interest or was liable to pay it.

3. By act approved August 5, 1854, the sum of $924,259.65 was appropriated to re-imburse the State of California for expenditures "in the suppression of Indian hostilities within the State prior to the 1st day of January, 1854." (See U. S. Stats. at Large for 1853 and 1854.)

4. By act approved August 18, 1856 (section 8), the Secretary of War was authorized and directed to pay to the holders of the war bonds of the State of California the amount of money appropriated by act of Congress approved May [August] 5, 1854, in payment of expenses incurred and actually paid by the State of California for the suppression of Indian hostilities within the said State prior to the 1st day of January, 1854, under the following restrictions and regulations:

Before any bonds were redeemed by the Secretary of War they were required to be presented to the board of commissioners appointed under an act of the legislature of said State, approved April 19, 1856, and the amount due and payable upon each bond indorsed thereon by said commissioners; the amounts in the aggregate not to exceed the amount appropriated by act of August 5, 1854.

All the States, except California, Oregon, and Nevada, have been re-imbursed by the United States all or nearly all of the principal of the moneys expended by them in the suppression of the rebellion. None of them have as yet been re-imbursed for interest which they paid to obtain said principal.

The following table shows the amount of money already paid by the United States as principal to the several States for the suppression of the rebellion, as shown by the books of the Treasury Department:

[Senate Ex. Doc. No. 11, Fifty-first Congress, first session, p. 63.]

States.	Amount.	States.	Amount.
Connecticut	$2,096,950.46	Minnesota	$71,075.20
Massachusetts	3,668,091.95	Kansas	384,138.15
Rhode Island	723,530.15	Nebraska	485.00
Maine	1,027,185.00	Colorado	55,238.84
New Hampshire	976,531.92	Missouri	7,580,421.43
Vermont	832,557.40	Michigan	844,262.53
New York	4,156,935.50	Delaware	31,988.96
New Jersey	1,517,026.79	Maryland	133,140.99
Pennsylvania	3,871,710.59	Virginia	48,469.97
Ohio	3,245,319.58	West Virginia	471,063.94
Wisconsin	1,935,059.17	Kentucky	3,504,466.57
Iowa	1,039,759.45		
Illinois	3,080,442.51	Total	44,137,596.34
Indiana	3,741,738.29		

In addition to the payment of said war claims to the several States on account of the war of the rebellion, as shown by the foregoing table, the claims of the following-named States for expenses in the suppression of Indian hostilities, etc., have been settled by the Third Auditor of the Treasury under the said act of June 27, 1882, and all of which have heretofore been paid by the United States:

States.	Amount.
Kansas	$332,308.13
Nebraska	18,081.23
Nevada	8,559.61
California	11,723,04
Texas	927,177.40
Total	1,297,850.01

An additional sum of $148,615.97 has been allowed the State of Texas by the Third Auditor, and the settlement is now pending before the Second Comptroller of the Treasury, under said act of June 27, 1882. The said State war claims of California, Oregon, and Nevada during the war of the rebellion reported on by the honorable Secretary of War and said board of war claims examiners under said resolution of the Senate of February 27, 1889, were never before properly or fully considered for want of jurisdiction, as hereinbefore shown, until they were so reported upon by the present Secretary of War, Hon. Redfield Proctor, aided by said Army board in said Senate Ex. Docs. 10, 11, 17.

Your committee recognize and approve the precedents which treat interest paid by a State on money borrowed or advanced for suppressing rebellion or repelling invasion in aid of the United States as a legitimate charge against the Government in every case where the Government is equitably liable for the principal; but inasmuch as none of the States have as yet been re-imbursed for any claim for interest paid out by them on money borrowed or advanced and expended by them on account of the war of the rebellion, your committee recommend that this bill be amended so as to omit at this time the claim for interest presented by California and Oregon in the two cases examined herein and reported upon in Senate Ex. Docs., Nos. 11 and 17, Fifty-first Congress, first session.

The claim of Nevada, however, for the re-imbursement of the interest actually paid out by her on the principal by her borrowed and in good faith expended for the common defense, and at the behest of the authorities of the United States, presents a question different from that of the other States. Nevada was a Territory at the time when the greater part of these expenditures were made. The necessity for these expenditures was imperative. The settlements in Nevada were isolated and separated from California by the Sierra Nevada Mountains, which cut off all means of transportation for several consecutive months in each year. There were no railroads. Transportation of freights was confined to teams and pack animals. The Indians along the overland route became hostile and cut off communication between the Atlantic and Pacific States. It was under these circumstances that the Territory of Nevada was called upon by the United States authorities to raise volunteer troops and furnish supplies for them. Labor was excessively high on account of the new mines, and supplies scarce and exceedingly dear. This Territory had no money to comply with these demands made upon her by the United States military authorities, and was forced to borrow money as best she could.

When the Territory of Nevada became a State the State of Nevada assumed the indebtedness of the Territory, including these war claims, and inserted a provision in her constitution in the following language:

All debts and liabilities of the Territory of Nevada lawfully incurred, and which remain unpaid at the time of the admission of this State into the Union, shall be assumed by and become the debt of the State of Nevada. (Compiled Laws of Nevada, vol. 1, page 133.)

Under these exceptional circumstances your committee recommend the payment of both principal and interest in the case of Nevada.

EXTRA PAY AND BOUNTIES.

As we have already seen, the larger portion of the claims of each of the States of California, Oregon, and Nevada were expended for extra pay and bounties. This was an absolute necessity for two reasons: First, the expenses of living and wages of labor in the Pacific coast States were during the rebellion at least 50 per cent., and in many cases 200 per cent., higher than in the Atlantic States; second, the Pacific States and Territories maintained the gold standard continuously throughout the war. The United States paid said volunteer troops in Treasury notes, although they had on deposit at the sub-treasury at San Francisco at all times a large amount of gold. The discount which the soldiers were compelled to pay to convert their greenbacks into gold was from 30 to 60 per cent.

This added largely to the cost of living.

Extra pay was found necessary to provide for the support of the families of the soldiers. This extra allowance, however, in the shape of extra pay and bounty did not exceed the extra compensation which the Government had theretofore paid the officers of the Army and Navy and the enlisted soldiers and sailors stationed on the Pacific coast between the dates of the acquisition of California and the breaking out of the rebellion. The Pacific coast States and Territories had a right to assume that the United States would continue or resume such extra pay and compensation during the war of the rebellion. Certainly the necessity for it was much greater in war than in peace, and, as a matter of fact, it was imperative.

On the 17th of June, 1850, an act was passed, the third section of which reads as follows:

Sec. 3. *And be it further enacted,* That whenever enlistments are made at, or in the vicinity of, the said military posts, and remote and distant stations, a bounty equal in amount to the cost of transporting and subsisting a soldier from the principal recruiting depot in the harbor of New York, to the place of such enlistment, be, and the same is hereby, allowed to each recruit so enlisted, to be paid in unequal installments at the end of each year's service, so that the several amounts shall annually increase, and the largest be paid at the expiration of each enlistment. (U. S. Stat., vol. 9, p. 439.)

On the 23d of September, 1850, the following provision was inserted in the Army appropriation bill:

For extra pay to the commissioned officers and enlisted men of the Army of the United States, serving in Oregon or California, three hundred and twenty-five thousand eight hundred and fifty-four dollars, on the following basis, to wit: That there shall be allowed to each commissioned officer as aforesaid, whilst serving as aforesaid, a per diem, in addition to their regular pay and allowances, of two dollars each, to each enlisted man as aforesaid, whilst serving as aforesaid, a per diem, in addition to their present pay and allowances, equal to the pay proper of each as established by existing laws, said extra pay of the enlisted men to be retained until honorably discharged. This additional pay to continue until the first of March, eighteen hundred and fifty-two, or until otherwise provided. (U. S. Stat., vol. 9, p. 504.)

The first of these acts was continued in force until **August 3, 1861** (U. S. Stat., vol. 12, p. 288, sec. 9), on which date it was repealed.   During the time when the last of said acts was in existence the United States soldiers and sailors on the Pacific coast received nearly double pay.

During the five years immediately prior to the rebellion the United States Army serving in the Pacific coast States and Territories was composed, first, of men transported from New York, via the Isthmus of Panama, at an aggregate cost to the United States of not less than $390,103, or at an average cost for each officer of $293, and for each enlisted man of $151 when landed in Oregon; or $275 for each officer and $115 for each enlisted man, when landed in California; and when discharged, all said enlisted men were entitled to an amount of money equal to the actual cost of their traveling expenses and subsistence back to New York; estimated by the War Department to be $142, making a total aggregate cost for each enlisted man of $293 and $256, respectively; or second, said army was composed of men enlisted in the Pacific coast States and Territories, at an expense to the United States of $142 per capita, paid to each enlisted man as a bounty under said act of Congress approved June 17, 1850 (9 U. S. Stat., 439), which payments were made continuously from June 17, 1850, to August 3, 1861. (U. S. Stat., vol. 12, p. 288.)

During the first year of the war of the rebellion the larger portion of this United States military force was transported from the Pacific coast States and Territories back to New York, via the Isthmus of Panama, at an aggregate cost to the United States of not less than $303,380, or at an average cost for each enlisted man of $145 from Oregon and of $125 from California.

Details of these various items of cost to the United States for thus transporting said military force to and from New York to the Pacific coast States and Territories are set forth in a table, prepared under the direction of the honorable Secretary of War as follows, to wit:

H. Rep. 254——2

Statement of number of officers and enlisted men of the United States Army transported at the expense of the United States from New York City to various points in California and Washington Territory via the Isthmus of Panama, in the years 1856, 1857, 1858, 1859, and 1860; also the amount paid for similar services from April 15, 1861, to December, 1861, between Oregon, Washington, California, and Nevada to New York, via the Isthmus of Panama, showing the total and the average cost per capita of each, so far as shown by the records of this office.

Destination.	Year.	Offi-cers.	Cost.	Enlisted men.	Cost.	Total cost.	Average cost per officer.	Average cost per man.
New York City to San Francisco, Cal., via the isthmus.........	1856	3	$750	396	$39,600	$40,350	} $267.86	$109.83
Do.........................	1857	9	2,700	470	58,750	61,450		
Do.........................	1858	2	600	34	493	1,093		
Do.........................	1859*	......	....	......	....	....		
Do.........................	1860	21	5,325	441	44,000	49,325		
Total	......	35	9,375	1,341	142,843	152,218		
New York City to Benicia, Cal., via the isthmus..............	1857	18	5,000	689	79,525	84,525	} 284.00	121.16
Do.........................	1858	7	2,100	445	57,875	59,975		
Total	......	25	7,100	1,134	137,400	144,490		
New York City to Fort Vancouver, Wash., and near Portland, Oregon, via the isthmus......	1858	15	4,500	400	61,500	66,000	} 203.12	151.09
Do.........................	1859	1	190	14	1,050	1,240		
Total	......	16	4,690	414	62,550	67,240		
Fort Vancouver, Wash., to Benicia, Cal	1856	1	60	50	1,750	1,810	60.00	35.00
San Francisco, Cal., to Fort Vancouver, Wash.................	1858	18	1,000	787	23,345	24,345	55.56	29.66
San Francisco, Cal., to New York City, via the isthmus.........	1861	49	12,250	1,495	186,875	199,125	250.00	125.00
San Pedro, Cal., to New York City, via the isthmus	1861	15	3,750	500	62,500	66,250	250.00	125.00
San Francisco, Cal., to Fort Vancouver, Wash.................	1861	30	1,200	775	15,500	16,700	40.00	20.00
Fort Vancouver, Wash., to San Francisco, Cal	1861	34	1,400	960	19,900	21,300	40.00	20.73

* None found.

QUARTERMASTER-GENERAL'S OFFICE,
Washington, D. C., January 8, 1890.

In consequence of this withdrawal in 1861 of said military forces from the Pacific coast, in order that they might perform military services in the East, and in view of the circumstances and exigencies existing in the Pacific Coast States and Territories during the rebellion period, requisitions were duly made from time to time by the President of the United States and by the Secretary of War upon the proper State authorities of California, Oregon, and Nevada for volunteers to perform military service for the United States in said States and Territories, as are fully and in detail set forth in said Senate Ex. Docs., Nos. 10, 11, 17, Fifty-first Congress, first session. In compliance with the several calls so made between 1861 and 1866, inclusive,

Volunteers.
The State of California furnished 15,725
The State of Nevada furnished 1,180
The State of Oregon furnished 1,810

Making a total aggregate of 18,715

men who enlisted and were duly mustered into the military service of the United States as volunteers in said States. The same number of

troops if organized and transported from New York City to the Pacific coast States and Territories in the same manner as was done by the United States War Department from June 17, 1850, to August 3, 1861, would have cost the United States at that time the sum of about $5,483,385 for *transportation alone.*

The reports of said war claims examiners upon extra pay in Nevada, California, and Oregon are as follows, to-wit:

[Senate Ex. Doc. No. 10, Fifty-first Congress, first session, p. 7.]

NEVADA.

Extra monthly pay—liabilities assumed.

It appears from the affidavit of the State comptroller (herewith, marked Exhibit No. 2), that liabilities to the amount of $1,153.75 were assumed by the State of Nevada as successor to the Territory of Nevada on account of "costs, charges, and expenses for monthly pay to volunteers and military forces in the Territory and State of Nevada in the service of the United States," and that State warrants fully covering such liabilities were duly issued. It is also shown in the affidavit that of said warrants two for the sums of $11.33 and $8.50 respectively have been paid, such payment reducing said liabilities to $1,133.92.

The circumstances and exigencies under which the Nevada legislature allowed this extra compensation to its citizens serving as volunteers in the United States Army are believed to have been substantially the same as those that impelled the legislatures of California and Oregon to a similar course of action for the relief of the contingent of troops raised in each of these States. Prices of commodities of every kind were extravagantly high during the war period in Nevada, which depended for the transportation of its supplies upon wagon roads across mountain ranges that were impassable for six months of every year; and at certain times at least during the said period, the rich yields of newly-opened mines produced an extraordinary demand for labor, largely increasing wages and salaries. These high prices of commodities and services were co-existent with, though in their causes independent of, the depreciation of the Treasury notes, which did not pass current in that section of the country, though accepted through necessity by the troops serving there; and it is safe to say that in Nevada, as in California and Oregon, the soldier could buy no more with a gold dollar than could the soldier serving in the Eastern States with the greenback or paper dollar.

On the whole, therefore, we are decided in the conviction that in granting them this extra compensation the legislature was mainly instigated by a desire to do a plain act of justice to the United States volunteers raised in the State and performing an arduous frontier service, by placing them on the same footing, as regards compensation, with the great mass of the officers and soldiers of the United States Army, serving east of the Rocky Mountains. It is true that the seven companies of infantry that were called for on October 19, 1864, had not been organized; and that on March 8, 1865, three days before the approval of the State law above noticed, the commanding general Department of the Pacific wrote as follows from his headquarters at San Francisco to the governor of Nevada (see page 287, Senate Ex. Doc. 70, Fiftieth Congress, second session):

"What progress is making in recruiting the Nevada volunteers? I will need them for the protection of the State, and trust that you may meet with success in your efforts to raise them. I hope the legislature may assist you by some such means as have been adopted by California and Oregon."

But the fact remains that the declared purpose of the monthly allowance was to give a compensation to the Nevada volunteers (see section 1 of the act last referred to), and that when measured by the current prices of the country in which they were serving, their compensation from all sources did not exceed, if indeed it was equal to, the value of the money received as pay by the troops stationed elsewhere, i. e., outside of the Department of the Pacific.

[Senate Ex. Doc. No. 11, Fifty-first Congress, first session, p. 23.]

CALIFORNIA.

Extra pay to enlisted men.

By an act approved April 27, 1863, the legislature appropriated and set apart "as a soldiers' relief fund" the sum of $600,000, from which every enlisted soldier of the companies of California volunteers raised or thereafter to be raised for the service of the United States was to be paid, in addition to the pay and allowances granted him

by the United States, a "compensation" of $5 per month from the time of his enlistment to the time of his discharge.   Drafted men, substitutes for drafted men, soldiers dishonorably discharged or discharged for disability existing at time of enlistment, were not to share in the benefits of the act, and, except in cases of married men having families dependent upon them for support, payment was not to be made until after discharge.   Seven per cent. interest bearing bonds to the amount of $600,000, in sums of $500, with coupons for interest attached to each bond, were authorized to be issued on July 1, 1863.   (Pages 349-351, Statement for Senate Military Committee.)

A few unimportant changes respecting the mode of payment in certain cases was made by act of March 15, 1864, and on March 31, 1866, the additional sum of $550,000 was appropriated for the payment of claims arising under its provisions, such sum to be transferred from the general fund of the State to the "Soldiers' Relief Fund."

Fearing that the total amount of $1,150,000 specifically appropriated might still prove insufficient to pay all the claims accruing under the act of April 27, 1863, above mentioned, the legislature directed, by an act which also took effect March 31, 1866 (page 604, Stats. of California, 1865-'66), that the remainder of such claims should be audited and allowed out of the appropriation and fund made and created by the act granting bounties to the volunteers of California approved April 4, 1864, and more fully referred to on page 19 of this report.

Upon the certificate of the adjutant-general of the State that the amounts were due under the provisions of the act and of the board of State examiners, warrants amounting to $1,459,270.21 were paid by the State treasurer, as shown by the receipts of the payees indorsed on said warrants.

It is worthy of note here that on July 16, 1863, the governor of California, replying to a communication from the headquarters Department of the Pacific, dated July 5, 1863, advising him that under a resolution of Congress adopted March 9, 1862, the payments provided for by the State law of April 27, 1863, might be made through the officers of the Pay Department of the U. S. Army, stated that the provisions of said law were such as to preclude him from availing himself of the offer.

Some information as to the circumstances and exigencies under which this money was expended may be derived from the following extract from the annual report of the adjutant-general of the State for the year 1862, dated December 15, 1862:

"The rank and file of the California contingent is made up of material of which any State might be proud, and the sacrifices they have made should be duly appreciated and their services rewarded by the State.   I do most earnestly recommend therefore that the precedent established by many of the Atlantic Coast States of paying their troops in the service of the United States an additional amount monthly should be adopted by California, and that a bill appropriating, say, $10 per month to each enlisted man of the troops raised or to be raised in this State be passed.   *   *   *   This would be a most tangible method of recognizing the patriotic efforts of our soldiers, relieve many of their families from actual destitution and want, and hold out a fitting encouragement for honorable service."   (Page 58, Statement for Senate Committee on Military Affairs.)

Your examiners are of the opinion that the favorable action which was taken on the above recommendation of the Adjutant-General can not be justly ascribed to any desire on the part of the legislature to avoid resort to a conscription, although the exclusion of drafted men from the benefits of the act indicates that they realized and deemed it proper to call attention to the possibility of a draft.   Unlike the law of April 4, 1864, the benefits of which were confined to men who should enlist after the date of its passage and be credited to the quota of the State, the provisions of the act now under consideration extended alike to the volunteers who had already entered or *had actually* completed their enlistment contract and to those who were to enlist in the future.   There is every reason for the belief that the predominating if not the only reason of the State authorities in enacting this measure was to allow their volunteers in the United States service such a stipend as would, together with the pay received by them from the General Government, amount to a fair and just compensation.   In fact, as has already been stated, this was expressly declared to be the purpose of the act.

It appears that up to December 31, 1862, those of the United States troops serving in the Department of the Pacific who were paid at all—in some cases attachments had not been paid for a year or more—were generally paid in coin, but on February 9, 1863, instructions were issued from the Treasury Department to the Assistant Treasurer of the United States at San Francisco that "checks of disbursing officers must be paid in United States notes." (Letter of Deputy Paymaster-General George H. Ringgold, dated February 13, 1863, to Paymaster-General; copy herewith marked Exhibit No. 10.)

Before this, greenbacks had become the current medium of exchange in all ordinary business transactions in the Eastern States, but in the Pacific Coast States and the adjoining Territories, gold continued to be the basis of circulation throughout

the war. At this time the paper currency had become greatly depreciated, and on February 28, 1863, the price of gold in Treasury notes touched 170. This action of the Government in compelling troops to accept such notes as an eqivalent of gold in payment for services rendered by them in a section where coin alone was current, gave rise to much dissatisfaction. For although gold could be bought in San Francisco at nearly the same price in Treasury notes as in New York, it must be remembered that the troops in the Department of the Pacific were largely stationed at remote and isolated points.

When paying in greenbacks for articles purchased by, or for services rendered to, them in these out-of-the-way places, they were obliged to submit not only to the current discount in San Francisco but also to a further loss occasioned by the desire of the persons who sold the articles, or rendered the service, to protect themselves against possible further depreciation. It admits of little doubt that by reason of his inability to realize the full value of paper money, as quoted in the money centers, and of the fact that wages and the cost of living and of commodities of every kind were abnormally high (owing in great part to the development of newly discovered mines in that region) the purchasing power of the greenback dollar in the hands of the average soldier serving in the Department of the Pacific was from the latter part of 1862 onward from 25 to 50 per cent. less than that of the same dollar paid to his fellow soldier in the East.

Representation of the great hardship the Treasury Department's instructions entailed upon the troops were promptly made. On March 10, 1863, the legislature telegraphed to Washington a resolution adopted on that date instructing the State's delegation in Congress to impress upon the Executive "the necessity which exists of having officers and soldiers of the U. S. Army, officers, seamen, and marines of the U. S. Navy, and all citizen employés in the service of the Government of the United States serving west of the Rocky Mountains and on the Pacific coast paid their salaries and pay in gold and silver currency of the United States, provided the same be paid in as revenue on this coast." (Page 46, Statement for Senate Committee on Military Affairs.)

And on March 16, 1863, Brig. Gen. G. Wright, the commander of the Department of the Pacific (comprising besides California, the State of Oregon and the Territories of Nevada, Utah, and Arizona), transmitted to the Adjutant-General of the U. S. Army a letter of Maj. C. S. Drew, First Oregon Cavalry, commandant at Camp Baker, Oregon, containing an explicit statement of the effects of and a formal protest against paying his men in greenbacks. In his letter of transmittal (page 154, Ex. Doc. 70), General Wright remarked as follows:

"The difficulties and embarrassments enumerated in the major's communication are common to all the troops in this department, and I most respectfully ask the serious consideration of the General-in-Chief and the War Department to this subject. Most of the troops would prefer waiting for their pay to receiving notes worth but little more than half their face; but even at this ruinous discount, officers, unless they have private means, are compelled to receive the notes. Knowing the difficulties experienced by the Government in procuring coin to pay the Army, I feel great reluctance in submitting any grievances from this remote department, but justice to the officers and soldiers demands that a fair statement should be made to the War Department."

It was under circumstances and exigencies such as these that the legislature themselves—all appeals to the General Government having proved futile—provided the necessary relief by the law of April 27, 1863. They did not even after that relax their efforts on behalf of United States troops, other than their own volunteers, serving among them, but on April 1, 1864, adopted a resolution requesting their representatives in Congress to "use their influence in procuring the passage of a law giving to the officers and soldiers of the regular Army stationed on the Pacific coast an increase of their pay, amounting to 30 per cent. on the amount now allowed by law."

[S. Ex. Doc. No. 17, Fifty-first Congress, first session, p. 14.]

OREGON.

Extra monthly compensation to officers and enlisted men of volunteers.

The certificate of the State treasurer, duly authenticated by the secretary of state under the seal of the State, sets forth that the amounts severally paid out for the redemption of relief bonds, as shown by the books of the treasurer's office, as reported by the treasurer to the several legislative assemblies and as verified by the several joint committees (investigating commissions) of said assembly under the provisions

of a joint resolution thereof, aggregate $90,476.32.   The following books, papers, etc., are also submitted in evidence of payment:

(1) The canceled bonds.

(2) A copy of the relief bond register, the correctness of which is certified by the secretary of state and State treasurer, showing number of bond, to whom issued, date of issue, and amount of bond; also showing the date and rate of redemption.   The reports of the joint committees of the legislature above mentioned, to the effect that they compared the record kept by the State treasurer with the bonds redeemed and found the amounts correct and agreeing with the amounts reported by the State treasurer to the legislative assembly, are entered in said bond register.

(3) Certificates of service given to the several Oregon volunteers upon which warrants were given entitling the holders to bonds.   These certificates cover service for which the sum of $86,639.85 was due.   The remainder of the certificates, the State authorities report, were not found and are probably lost or destroyed.

(4) Copies of the muster-rolls of the Oregon volunteers, certified to by the secretary of state, setting forth the entire service of each officer and enlisted man.

In all, bonds amounting to $93,637 were issued.   As has been stated but $90,476.32 is found to have been expended in the redemption of these bonds, some of which were redeemed at less than their face value.   Five bonds, valued at $731, have not been redeemed.

The authority by which these bonds were issued is contained in an act of the legislature, which was approved on October 24, 1864 (copy herewith), appropriating a sum not exceeding $100,000 to constitute and be known as the "commissioned officers' and soldiers' relief fund," out of which was to be paid to each commissioned officer and enlisted soldier of the companies of Oregon volunteers raised in the State for the service of the United States to aid in repelling invasion, etc., from the time of their enlistment to the time of their discharge, $5 per month in addition to the pay allowed them by the United States.   Enlisted men not receiving an honorable discharge from the service, or volunteers discharged for disability existing at the time of enlistment, were not to be entitled to the benefits of the act, nor was payment under the provisions thereof to be made to an enlisted soldier until he should be honorably discharged the service; but enlisted married men having families dependent upon them were authorized to allot the whole or any portion of the monthly pay accruing to them for the support of such dependents.   A bond bearing interest, payable semi-annually, at 7 per cent. per annum, redeemable July 1, 1875, with coupons for the interest attached, was to be issued by the secretary of state for such amount as the adjutant-general should certify to be due under the provisions of the act to each man, whose receipt for the amount so paid him was to be taken by the secretary of state.   Said bonds were to be paid to the recipient or order.

The circumstances and exigencies that led to the enactment of the above-cited law and to the expenditures incurred under its provisions were substantially the same as those which brought about the adoption of similar measures of relief in California and Nevada.   It must have been patent to every one fully acquainted with the circumstances of the case that the volunteers, that had been raised in Oregon, at this time (October 24, 1864) consisting only of the seven companies of the First Oregon Cavalry and the independent detachment of four months' men, a majority of whom had then nearly completed their term, had been greatly underpaid, considering the nature of the service performed by them and the current rate of salaries and wages realized in other pursuits of life.   At the time of the enrollment and muster in of the First Oregon Cavalry and up to the latter part of 1862 the Government paid those of its troops in the Department of the Pacific, that were paid at all, in specie; but as often happened during the war a number of the companies of the regiment named, occupying remote stations, remained unpaid for a long time and were finally paid in Treasury notes, some of the members having more than a year's pay due them.

During the remainder of the war the Government paid its troops in the Department of the Pacific, as elsewhere, in greenbacks.   Referring to this condition of things and to the fact that coin continued to be the ordinary medium of exchange in Oregon in private business transactions, Maj. C. S. Drew, First Oregon Cavalry, in a letter to his department commander, dated March 4, 1863 (page 154, Ex. Doc. 70), called attention to the fact that at his station (Camp Baker) Treasury notes were worth "not more than 50 or 55 cents per dollar;" that each officer and soldier of his command was serving for less than half pay, and had done so, some of them, for sixteen months past; that while capital protected itself from loss and perhaps realized better profits than under the old and better system of payment in coin, "the soldier did not have that power, and if paid in notes must necessarily receipt in full for what is equivalent to him of half pay or less for the service he has rendered, and must continue to fulfill his part of the contract with the Government for the same reduced rate of pay until his period of service shall have terminated; and that "good men will not enlist for $6 or $7 a month while $13 is the regular pay, and, moreover, being realized by every soldier

in every other department than the Pacific." In forwarding this letter to the Adjutant-General, U. S. Army, the department commander remarked that the embarrassments enumerated in the major's communication were common to all the troops in the department, and he therefore asked "the serious consideration of the General-in-Chief and the War Department to this subject." Some months later (August 18, 1863) General Alvord, while reporting to the department commander the location of a new military post at Fort Boisé, referred to the difficulties encountered by the garrison* charged with the duty of establishing it, as follows:

"Some difficulty is experienced in building the post in consequence of the low rates of legal-tender notes. In that country they bear merely nominal value. The depreciation of the Government currency not only embarrasses the Quartermaster's Department, but also tends greatly to disaffect the men. The differences between their pay and the promises held out by the richest mines, perhaps, on the coast, the proximity of which makes them all the more tempting, is so great that many desertions occur." (Ex. Doc. 70, page 188.)

About the same time (September 1, 1863) the adjutant-general of the State complained of the inadequacy of the soldiers' pay, resulting from the depreciation of the paper currency with which they were paid. Referring to the fact that after the expiration of eight months from the date of the requisition of the United States military authorities for six additional companies for the First Oregon Cavalry but one had been raised, he said:

"And yet we are not prepared to say that it is for the want of patriotism on the part of the people of Oregon, but from other causes, partly from the deficiency in the pay of the volunteer in comparison with the wages given in the civil pursuits of life, as well as with the nature of the currency with which they are paid, the depreciation of which renders it hardly possible for the soldier to enlist from any other motive save pure patriotism. And I would here suggest that the attention of our legislature be called to this defect, and that additional pay, either in land, money, or something else, be allowed to those who have volunteered. Justice demands that this should be done."

In enacting the relief law of October 24, 1864, it is fair to presume that the legislature was largely influenced by the following statements and recommendations of the governor contained in his annual message, dated September 15, 1864:

"The Snake and other tribes of Indians in eastern Oregon have been hostile and constantly committing depredations. The regiment has spent two summers on the plains, furnishing protection to the immigration and to the trade and travel in that region of the country. During the past summer the regiment has traveled over twelve hundred miles, and the officers and men are still out on duty. The officers and most, if not all, the men joined the regiment through patriotic motives, and, while some of the time they have been traveling over rich gold fields, where laborers' wages are from $3 to $5 per day, there have been very few desertions, and that, too, while they were being paid in depreciated currency, making their wages only about $5 per month. A great many of these men have no pecuniary interest in keeping open the lines of travel, protecting mining districts and merchants and traders. The benefit of their service thus insures [inures] to the benefit of others, who should help these faithful soldiers in bearing these burdens. Oregon, in proportion to her population and wealth, has paid far less than other States for military purposes. California pays her volunteers $5 per month extra in coin. It would be but an act of simple justice for this State to make good to the members of this regiment their losses by depreciated currency." (Page 87, Statement for Senate Military Committee.)

It is to be noted here that while the officers and men who became the beneficiaries of this law had been paid in a depreciated currency, which in Oregon does not appear to have had more than two-thirds of the purchasing power it had in the East, the Government provided them with clothing, subsistence, shelter, and all their absolutely necessary wants. On the other hand, it is to be borne in mind that the legislature must have been aware of the fact noted, and that it granted the extra compensation from a sense of justice and without any purpose calculated to benefit the State at large, such as might be reasonably inferred from the granting of bounties to men "who should hereafter enlist." As has been already mentioned, the terms of the Oregon Volunteers were drawing to a close and the benefits of the law were restricted to the volunteers "raised," and did not therefore include those "to be raised."

California, as shown by the report (Senate Ex. Doc. No. 11, Fifty-first Congress, first session) of said war claims examiners, expended $468,976.54 on account of her militia during the war of the rebellion. The circumstances under which this expenditure was made present a strong case of equity for reimbursement, but inasmuch as the militia of

---

*Although the First Oregon Cavalry did not form a part of this garrison, three companies of it were at this time scouting against hostile Indians in the vicinity of the post.

California did not serve under the direct or immediate authority of the United States during the war of the rebellion, your committee do not allow it at this time, although they do not reject it for want of merit.

Oregon expended on account of her militia, as shown by the report of said war claims examiners, $21,118.73, and your committee make a similar recommendation in regard to that claim.

Some of the circumstances under which the present war claim of the State of Nevada was created are set forth in the report of the majority of the Committee on Military Affairs made in the Fiftieth Congress, first session (Senate Report No. 1286), which, without the appendix, is as follows, to wit:

Senate Report No. 1286, Fiftieth Congress, first session.

MAY 14, 1888.

Mr. STEWART, from the Committee on Military Affairs, submitted the following report:

[To accompany bill S. 2918]

OBJECT OF THIS BILL.

The object of this bill is to re-imburse the State of Nevada for moneys paid and contracted to be paid by the Territory of Nevada and afterwards assumed and paid by that State, and also for moneys actually expended by Nevada after becoming a State for the common defense and in furnishing troops to the United States during the suppression of the war of the rebellion, and for guarding the overland mail and emigrant route between the Missouri River and California, and for suppressing Indian hostilities under circumstances hereinafter set forth.

APPEAL OF PRESIDENT LINCOLN, THROUGH SECRETARY SEWARD, TO THE NATION FOR AID.

On October 14, 1861, Mr. Seward, Secretary of State, addressed a circular letter to the governors of the loyal States and Territories, calling for assistance for the General Government in suppressing hostilities in the so-called Confederate States, and for the improvement and perfection of the defenses of the loyal States respectively. A copy of this letter is printed in the appendix hereto, marked Exhibit No. 1, page 23.

ACTION TAKEN BY NEVADA IN RESPONSE TO THE FOREGOING APPEAL OF SECRETARY SEWARD.

Upon the receipt of this letter the legislative assembly of Nevada Territory at its first session passed appropriate resolutions pledging the support of the people of that Territory to the Union cause to the extent of their means, which resolutions are printed in the appendix, marked Exhibit No. 2, page 24.

On the 28th day of November, 1861, three days after the passage of the resolutions above mentioned, the legislative assembly of Nevada also passed an elaborate law for the enrollment and organization of a militia force to aid the United States when called upon in the suppression of the rebellion, and to carry out the spirit and intent of the aforesaid circular letter of Secretary Seward. This law will be found on

pages 106 to 125 of the Laws of Nevada Territory, 1861. This act provided that the militia of the Territory organized under its provisions should be subject to be called into the military service of the United States by the President, or any officer of the United States Army commanding a division or a department. A militia force was immediately organized under its provisions. H. P. Russell was appointed adjutant-general, and was succeeded by Col. John Cradlebaugh, who is mentioned in the resolutions above referred to and printed in the appendix as Exhibit No. 2, page 24.

It will thus be seen that Nevada made the necessary preparations, organized her militia, and was ready to answer any call that might be thereafter made upon her by the General Government, and also to protect the Territory against a large portion of its inhabitants who desired to join the Confederacy.

CONDITION OF AFFAIRS THAT RENDERED A CALL FOR NEVADA VOL-
UNTEERS NECESSARY.

The Territory of Nevada was organized by Congress on March 2, 1861, (12 U. S. Stats., 209). At the breaking out of the rebellion it became a serious question what attitude Nevada would occupy, and home guards were immediately organized. These guards afterwards formed a portion of the militia of the Territory as provided for in the aforesaid militia law, and protected the inhabitants from violence, without any expense to the Government of the United States.

In the early part of April, 1863, the overland mail and emigrant route was attacked by Indians and communication was closed between the Atlantic States and the Pacific coast. This route extended from the Missouri River to California via the Platte River, Salt Lake City, through Nevada to Sacramento, in California, and was the only means at that date of direct overland communication between the Missouri River and California. At this time the gold discoveries in California continued to invite a large immigration, the interest in which was more or less intensified by the continued extensive silver discoveries in Nevada Territory, and principally on the Comstock lode in the western part of the Territory. The routes via Cape Horn, and especially that via the Isthmus of Panama, were rendered extremely doubtful, dangerous, and expensive, on account of Confederate privateer cruisers hovering around the West India Islands and along both these sea routes, and in anticipation of other Confederate cruisers infesting the waters of the Pacific (which soon thereafter became the theater of the operations and extensive depredations of the Confederate privateer cruiser *Shenandoah*) the overland route, therefore, although in itself both dangerous and difficult, was yet considered the better and preferable route by which to reach the Pacific.

On account of a general uprising of the Indians along the entire overland route, and especially that portion between Salt Lake City, in the Territory of Utah, and the Sierra Nevada Mountains, and because of the doubts as to the loyalty of the Mormons to the Government of the United States, the maintenance and protection of the mail and emigrant route through that section of the country and along the aforesaid line was regarded by the Government as a military necessity. Apparently in anticipation of no immediate danger of attack on the Pacific coast, nearly all the troops of the regular Army at this time had been withdrawn from service throughout this entire region of country and transferred East to other fields of military operations. This left the entire coun-

try between Salt Lake City and the Sierra Nevada Mountains without adequate and efficient military protection. The Government thus having but few troops of its regular Army in that region, was therefore compelled to call upon the inhabitants of Nevada Territory to raise and organize volunteer military companies to suppress Indian disturbances which threatened the entire suspension of all mail facilities and emigration from the East, as will be hereafter shown.

At the time of the calls upon Nevada for troops the prices of labor and supplies of all descriptions in Nevada were extremely high. There were then no railroads, and the snow on the Sierra Nevada Mountains formed an almost impassable barrier against teams from about the 1st of December until about June. The average cost of freight from San Francisco, the main source of supply for western Nevada, was about $80 a ton, and it was necessary to lay in supplies during the summer and fall for the remainder of the year. A great mining excitement prevailed at this time, occasioned by the marvelous development of the great Comstock lode, and wages were from $4 to $10 a day in gold. The people who had emigrated to the new gold and silver fields went there for the purpose of mining and prospecting for mines, and were generally reluctant to enter the irregular military service of guarding the overland mail and emigrant route. Besides, on account of the extraordinary high price of supplies of every description, and also of wages and services of every kind, it was impossible for them to maintain themselves and families without involving much more expense than any compensation which could be paid them as volunteer troops under the laws of the United States, and, as will be seen by the letters of General Wright, hereafter quoted, they were expected, as volunteer troops, to furnish themselves with horses and equipments, in addition to what could be furnished by the Government.

The military authorities of the United States well knew at that time the exact condition of the country and of the roads across the mountains leading thereto and of the cost of transportation and of the prices of labor and of supplies and of their own inability to furnish either horses or equipments for a military service that required mounted troops.

FIRST CALL BY THE UNITED STATES FOR NEVADA VOLUNTEERS.

In view of the necessities of the situation, and with all the facts fully known to the military authorities of the United States, General Wright, commanding the Department of the Pacific, was authorized by the War Department to raise volunteer military companies in Nevada Territory for the protection of said overland mail and emigrant route, and on April 2, 1863, he addressed the following requisition for troops to the Governor of the Territory:

HEADQUARTERS DEPARTMENT OF THE PACIFIC,
San Francisco, Cal., April 2, 1863.

His Excellency O. CLEMENS,
Governor of Nevada Territory, Carson City, Nev.:

SIR: I have been authorized by the War Department to raise volunteer companies in Nevada Territory for the purpose of moving east on the overland mail route in the direction of Great Salt Lake City. If it is possible to raise three or four companies in the Territory for this service I have to request your excellency may be pleased to have them organized. I should be glad to get two companies of cavalry and two of infantry. The mounted troops to furnish their own horses and equipments. Arms, ammunition, etc., will be furnished by the United States. Should your excellency consider it improbable that this volunteer force can be raised, even one company will be

accepted. I will send you a plan of organization, and an officer with the necessary instructions for mustering them into the service.

With great respect, I have the honor to be, your most obedient servant,
G. WRIGHT,
Brigadier-General, U. S. Army, Commanding.

Official copy.

J. C. KELTON,
Colonel, A. A. G.

While correspondence was being conducted between the Governor of Nevada and General Wright as to the method of organizing Nevada's troops, the following telegram was dispatched by General H. W. Halleck, general-in-chief of the U. S. Army, to General Wright:

HEADQUARTERS OF THE ARMY,
Washington, D. C., April 15, 1863.

Brig. Gen. G. WRIGHT,
San Francisco, Cal.:

The Secretary of War authorizes you to raise additional regiments in California and Nevada to re-enforce General Conner and protect overland route. Can not companies be raised in Nevada and pushed forward immediately? General Conner may be able to raise some companies in Utah or out of emigrant trains.

H. W. HALLECK,
General-in-Chief.

Whereupon General Wright addressed the governor of Nevada Territory the following communication:

HEADQUARTERS DEPARTMENT OF THE PACIFIC,
San Francisco, Cal., April 16, 1863.

His Excellency ORION CLEMENS,
Governor of Nevada Territory, Carson City, Nev.:

SIR: I have the honor to acknowledge the receipt of your excellency's communication of the 9th instant.

The Indian disturbances along the line of the overland mail route, east of Carson City, threaten the entire suspension of our mail facilities, as well as preventing any portion of the vast immigration approaching from the east reaching Nevada. The interest and prosperity of your Territory depend much upon maintaining free and safe access to it from all directions. My force immediately available for operation on that line is small. A company of cavalry stationed at Fort Churchill, and under orders to move towards Ruby Valley, I was compelled to divert for temporary service to assist in quelling an Indian outbreak in the Owen's Lake district. As soon as the services of this company can be dispensed with there, it will operate on the mail and emigrant line. Some infantry companies will also be thrown forward from this side of the mountains as soon as transportation can be prepared and the roads are in order. In the mean time it is of such importance to keep the mail and emigrant route east of you open, that I would earnestly recommend that one or two companies of cavalry be promptly organized and prepared for muster into the service of the United States. It is impossible for us at this moment to purchase horses and equipments. Each man would have to furnish his own.

I can furnish arms, ammunition, forage, clothing, provisions, etc.; in fact, everything except horses and equipments.

The organization of a company or troop of cavalry is: one captain, one first lieutenant, one second lieutenant, one first sergeant, one quartermaster-sergeant, one commissary sergeant, five sergeants, eight corporals, two teamsters, two farriers or blacksmiths, one saddler, one wagoner, and seventy-eight privates.

This is the first appeal that has been made to Nevada Territory, a Territory soon to add another star to that glorious galaxy which adorns our beautiful banner, and I doubt not this call will be nobly responded to by the loyal and patriotic citizens of the Territory.

With great respect, your excellency's most obedient servant,
G. WRIGHT,
Brigadier-General U. S. Army, Commanding.

Official copy.

J. C. KELTON.
Colonel, A. A. G.

NEVADA'S RESPONSE TO THE FOREGOING CALL FOR TROOPS BY THE UNITED STATES.

Immediately upon the receipt of the foregoing requisition for troops the governor of Nevada issued the following proclamation:

PROCLAMATION.

EXECUTIVE DEPARTMENT,
Carson City, April 24, 1863.

Whereas Brigadier-General George Wright, United States Army, commanding officer of the Department of the Pacific, has, by authority of the War Department called upon me for two companies of infantry and two companies of cavalry to serve three years, or during the war:

Now, therefore, I, Orion Clemens, governor of the Territory of Nevada and commander-in-chief of the militia thereof, do hereby authorize and call upon the citizens of the Territory, as many as shall be necessary to fill up the preceding requisition, to immediately organize themselves into companies as required hereby.

In witness whereof I have hereunto set my hand and affixed the great seal of the Territory.

Done at Carson City, Territory of Nevada, this 24th day of April, in the year of our Lord one thousand eight hundred and sixty-three.

ORION CLEMENS,
Secretary and Acting Governor.

In answer to these calls and requisitions of General Wright and said proclamation of the governor of Nevada four companies of cavalry were completely organized, two of which were sent to Camp Douglas, Utah Territory, for military service, and the remaining two were sent to station Fort Churchill, Nev.

SECOND CALL AND REQUISITION OF THE UNITED STATES FOR NEVADA VOLUNTEERS.

Thereafter General Wright made a further requisition upon the governor of Nevada for two additional companies of cavalry and a regiment of infantry, as will appear from the following:

HEADQUARTERS DEPARTMENT OF THE PACIFIC,
San Francisco, December 22, 1863.

SIR: The four companies of cavalry called for from the Territory of Nevada have completed their organization; two of the companies have reached Camp Douglas, Utah, and the remaining two are at Fort Churchill, Nev. On the representations of Governor Nye that additional troops can be raised in Nevada, I have, under the authority conferred upon me by the War Department, called upon the governor for a regiment of infantry and two more companies of cavalry.

Very respectfully, your obedient servant,

G. WRIGHT,
Brig. Gen., U. S. Army, Commanding.

ADJUTANT-GENERAL, U. S. ARMY,
Washington, D. C.

WHAT WAS DONE BY NEVADA UNDER THE SECOND CALL AND REQUISITION BY THE UNITED STATES FOR NEVADA VOLUNTEERS.

In response to General Wright's second requisition for troops made in the latter part of November, 1863, the governor of Nevada issued the following proclamation:

PROCLAMATION.

Whereas a requisition having been made upon me by Brig. Gen. George Wright, U. S. Army, commanding the Department of the Pacific, for one regiment of volunteer infantry and two companies of cavalry, for service in the employ of the General Government of the United States;

Now, therefore, I, James W. Nye, governor of the Territory of Nevada and com-

mander-in-chief of the militia thereof, by virtue of the authority in me vested, do issue this my proclamation, calling upon the people of this Territory to forthwith proceed to organize a regiment of infantry, consisting of ten companies, and two companies of cavalry, in full compliance of said requisition.

All applicants for line officers will present themselves before the Army examining board for examination, and report to me with certificate of such examination as soon as practicable.

Given under my hand and seal at Carson, Nev., this 4th day of December, A. D. 1863.

JAMES W. NYE,
Governor of the Territory of Nevada.

Attest:
   ORION CLEMENS,
     Secretary of the Territory.

Under this last requisition of General Wright and last proclamation of the governor of Nevada two additional cavalry companies and the First Battalion Nevada Infantry Volunteers, composed of four companies, were raised and assigned to duty to such fields of military service in Utah and Nevada as were determined upon by General Wright, as will appear from the correspondence printed in the appendix, marked " Exhibit 3, pages 24 to 29.

It will thus be seen that the people of the Territory of Nevada responded promptly to and complied fully with the appeals of the United States Government for troops and in accordance with the requisitions and calls of the War Department. The action of the people of Nevada was reported to Mr. Seward, Secretary of State, by the governor of Nevada on March 25, 1864. He wrote to Mr. Seward the condition of affairs in the Territory, which letter was transmitted to the Senate by President Lincoln on April 29, 1864 (see Senate Ex. Doc. No. 41, 38th Cong., 1st sess.). In his report Governor Nye said:

We have raised in the Territory within the last two years one company of infantry, now attached to a California regiment, a battalion of cavalry, consisting of six companies, four of which are in the field ; the remaining two will be there also as soon as they can be mounted. In addition we are raising a regiment of infantry, now in a good state of forwardness, and we can raise a brigade easily if necessary.

SOME OF THE DUTIES OF THE TROOPS CALLED TO AID THE UNITED STATES AT THIS TIME.

The first duty of these troops was to open and guard the overland mail and emigrant route from the Sierra Nevada Mountains to Utah. The campaign in which this was accomplished was under the command of General Conner. The volunteer troops under this gallant officer had already conducted a most successful campaign against the Indians of eastern Nevada, Utah, and Idaho, in the region where the Mormon influence was most potential, conquered many Indian tribes, and secured lasting peace.

The Secretary of War, in reporting to Congress the condition of things in that region of country, then under the military command of General Conner, said as follows, to wit :

DEPARTMENT OF THE PACIFIC.

This department has been most signally exempt from the evils of civil war, and consequently has enjoyed unexampled prosperity. Some thefts and robberies having been committed by roving bands of Indians on the overland stage route in January last, General Conner marched with a small force to Bear River, Idaho, where, on the 26th, he overtook and completely defeated them in a severe battle, in which he killed 224 of the 300 and captured 175 of their horses. His own loss in killed and wounded was 63 out of 200. Many of his men were severely injured by the frost. Since this severe punishment the Indians in that quarter have ceased to commit depredations on the whites. (Secretary of War's report, first session Thirty-eighth Congress.)

ADDITIONAL CAUSES THAT LED TO A THIRD CALL AND REQUISITION
BY THE UNITED STATES FOR NEVADA VOLUNTEERS.

Congress having on July 1, 1862, chartered the Union Pacific Railroad Company, to which, and also to the Central Pacific Railroad Company, aid was given to build one continuous line of railroad from the Missouri River to the Pacific Ocean through this region of country, did, on
July 2, 1864, still further foster these enterprises by additional grants.
These two companies thereupon placed in the field numerous corps of
surveyors, civil engineers, and employés to explore said country in the
effort to discover the most practicable and economical railroad route
from the Missouri River to the Pacific, and to run trial lines and definitely locate the lines of the two subdivisions of said railroad route. In
regard to these roads the Secretary of War, in his annual report for
1864–'65, page 144, said:

It is, in a military sense, of the utmost importance that the Pacific Railroad should
be pressed to the earliest possible completion.

The exploration and location for a Pacific railroad through that region of country then mostly uninhabited except by large tribes and
roving bands of hostile Indians, called for additional military protection and rendered it necessary for the United States to again call upon
Nevada to raise additional troops. Accordingly General McDowell,
commanding the Department of the Pacific, made the following call on
October 13, 1864, upon the Governor of Nevada Territory:

HEADQUARTERS DEPARTMENT OF THE PACIFIC,
Virginia City, October 13, 1864.

SIR: I have the honor to acquaint you that I have received authority from the War
Department to call on you, from time to time, as the circumstances of the service
may require, for not to exceed in all, at any one time, one regiment of volunteer infantry and one regiment of volunteer cavalry, to be mustered into service of the
United States as other volunteer regiments, under existing laws and regulations.
    Under this authority I have to request you will please raise, as soon as possible,
enough companies of infantry to complete, with those already in service from Nevada,
a full regiment of infantry.
    Brigadier-General Wason will confer with you and give all the information neces-
sary to details for this service.
    I have the honor to be, governor, very respectfully, your most obedient servant,
IRWIN McDOWELL,
Major-General, Commanding Department.
His Excellency JAMES W. NYE,
    Governor of Nevada Territory.

WHAT WAS DONE BY NEVADA IN RESPONSE TO THIS CALL.

The governor of Nevada responded to this call by issuing the following proclamation:

PROCLAMATION.

TERRITORY OF NEVADA, EXECUTIVE DEPARTMENT,
Carson City, October 19, 1864.

Whereas I have received a requisition from Maj. Gen. Irwin McDowell, commanding Department of the Pacific, the same having been made under authority from
the War Department, to raise, as soon as possible, enough companies of infantry to
complete, with those already in service from Nevada, a full regiment of infantry:
    Now, therefore, I, James W. Nye, governor of the Territory of Nevada, and com-
mander-in-chief of the militia thereof, do hereby call upon the citizens of this Territory to organize themselves into seven companies, sufficient to fill the battalion of
infantry now in service from this Territory, and the requirements of said requisition.
    In witness whereof I have hereunto set my hand and caused the great seal of the

Territory of Nevada to be affixed.   Done at Carson City this 19th day of October, 1864.

JAMES W. NYE,
Governor and Commander-in-Chief of the Territory of Nevada.

Attest:
ORION CLEMENS,
Secretary of the Territory.

Afterward the Indians became troublesome between Utah and the Missouri River. During the years 1865–'66 the Nevada cavalry were actively engaged in Colorado, Wyoming, Kansas, and Nebraska in the Indian wars in that region. The writer of this report crossed the continent in the summer of 1865, and met several small detachments of Nevada cavalry in active service against the Indians, and was much gratified to learn that they were quite celebrated for their gallantry and faithful services in that kind of warfare, which subjects the soldier to the severest test of endurance, and requires individual exertion and watchfulness unknown in civilized war.

METHOD RECOGNIZED BY NEVADA FOR THE ENROLLMENT OF HER TROOPS CALLED INTO THE MILITARY SERVICE OF THE UNITED STATES AND HER MODE OF DEFRAYING THE EXPENSES OF SUCH ENROLLMENT FOR SUCH SERVICE.

The citizens of Nevada were never drafted, nor did they ever hire substitutes, but were organized into military companies by commanding officers, most of whom had undergone an examination for commission before military boards instituted for that purpose and satisfactory to the general of the United States Army commanding the military Department of the Pacific.

As a compensation to and a reimbursement intended for all the costs by them incurred for raising and organizing said volunteer military companies, and in lieu of all other kinds of expenses necessarily incident to enrolling and enlisting the members of said companies for the military service of the United States, the legislature of Nevada passed an act providing for the payment to the commanding officers of said companies of $10 per capita for each volunteer soldier by them for said purposes enrolled and enlisted, aggregating the sum of $11,840. This provision in said statute was improperly called a " bounty;" but this expenditure was not in any sense whatsoever a " bounty," but, on the contrary, it was an actual disbursement by Nevada to cover all the legitimate expenses of every kind incident to enrolling and enlisting Nevada's troops to perform military service for the United States.

The history of this expenditure and of this mode of enrollment of troops by the Territory of Nevada, and the economy and reasons therefor, are all fully set forth in a memorial to Congress signed by all the State officers of Nevada, which is printed in the appendix, marked Exhibit No. 4, page 29.

METHOD ADOPTED BY NEVADA TO PAY THE TROOPS CALLED INTO THE MILITARY SERVICE OF THE UNITED STATES BY THE TERRITORY OF NEVADA, AND THE EXTENT TO WHICH THE STATE OF NEVADA PLEDGED HER FAITH TO PAY THE OBLIGATIONS CONTRACTED BY THE TERRITORY OF NEVADA TO AID THE UNITED STATES.

This same act of the legislature of Nevada, among other things, provided that each citizen of Nevada so volunteering and enlisting as a private soldier for the military service of the United States, not being

drafted or acting as a substitute for another, should, during each and every month while honorably serving the United States, be paid out of the treasury of Nevada the sum of $5 per month, gold coin. It further provided that, in the case of an enlisted married man, an allotment of the whole or a portion of the extra monthly pay could be drawn by his family dependent upon him for support (see Laws of Nevada Territory, 1864, page 81, or appendix, Exhibit No. 5, page 31).

On March 11, 1865, after Nevada became a State, an act similar to this Territorial act, but more liberal in its provisions, was passed, to take the place of the Territorial law. The State legislature having deemed the situation so important to maintain the good faith of the Territory, that had been pledged to aid the United States, it passed this act *over the veto of Governor Blasdel*, who alleged in his veto message his fear that the expense might exceed the constitutional limit, etc.

This act provided for the assumption and payment by the State of Nevada of all obligations of every kind that had been incurred and contracted to be paid by the Territory for the enlistments, enrollments, bounties, extra pay, etc., of volunteer soldiers that had been theretofore called into the military service of the United States. The bonds now outstanding and still due by Nevada, though at a smaller rate of interest than that named in the original issue and still drawing interest, were issued under the provisions of this latter act (see Statutes, Nevada, 1864–'65, page 389, or appendix, Exhibit No. 6, page 34).

RESULTS OF THE FOREGOING LEGISLATION BY NEVADA.

By these legislative enactments of Nevada substantial and effectual aid was given and guaranteed by Nevada, both as a Territory and State, to the Government of the United States in guarding its overland mail and emigrant route and the line of the proposed transcontinental railroad in furnishing troops during the war of the rebellion and for suppressing Indian hostilities and maintaining peace in the country inhabited by the Mormons, and for the common defense as contemplated in said circular letter of Secretary Seward along an exposed, difficult, and hostile Indian frontier, and then but sparsely populated. These enactments were fully known to the authorities of the United States and to Congress; they have ever been acquiesced in and met with the sanction and practical indorsement of the United States, in whose interest and for whose benefit they were made. As a partial compensation to these volunteers for this irregular, hazardous, and exposed service in the mountains and on the desert plains, and to aid them to a small extent to maintain families dependent upon them for support, first the Territory and afterwards the State of Nevada offered and paid this small stipend, never suspecting that the United States would not promptly and willingly respond when asked to re-imburse the same. These citizens of Nevada who volunteered and enlisted and did military service for the United States were compelled in many cases to abandon their employments, in which their wages were always lucrative and service continuous, so that nothing less than the individual patriotism of these volunteers enabled the Territory and State of Nevada to cheerfully and promptly respond to every call and requisition made upon them for troops by the United States.

The records of the War Department, in addition to what is already quoted and referred to in substantiation of the facts herein stated, are printed in the appendix, marked Exhibit No. 3, pages 24 to 29.

THE BASIS AND AUTHORITY OF NEVADA'S CLAIM AGAINST THE UNITED STATES AND THE PRECEDENTS IN SUPPORT THEREOF.

These enactments of Nevada both as a Territory and a State, and various acts done under them in and execution thereof, when complying according to her own methods with the various calls and requisitions of the United States for troops, have resulted in the expenditure of a large sum of money which constitutes the present claim of Nevada against the United States. The authority upon which this claim rests is found in the fourth section of the fourth article of the Constitution of the United States, which provides that—

The United States shall guaranty to every State in the Union a republican form of government, and shall protect each of them against invasion, and, on application of the legislature, or of the executive (when the legislature can not be convened), against domestic violence.

And upon the latter part of the tenth section of the first article of the Constitution; which is as follows:

No State shall, without the consent of Congress, lay any duty on tonnage, keep troops or ships of war in time of peace, enter into any agreement or compact with another State, or with a foreign power, or engage in war, unless actually invaded or in such imminent danger as will not admit of delay.

And also upon the act of July 28, 1795, chapter 36, section 1, page 424, now section No. 1642, U. S. Revised Statutes, which provides that—

Whenever the United States are invaded or are in imminent danger of invasion from any foreign nation or Indian tribe, or of rebellion against the authority of the Government of the United States, it shall be lawful for the President to call forth such number of the militia of the State or States most convenient to the place of danger or scene of action, as he may deem necessary to repel such invasion or to suppress such rebellion, and to issue his orders for that purpose to such officer of the militia as he may think proper.*

In reference to the foregoing the courts have held that—

When a particular authority is confided to a public officer, to be exercised by him in his discretion, upon an examination of the facts of which he is made the appropriate judge, his decision upon the facts in the absence of any controlling provision, is absolutely conclusive as to the existence of those facts (Allen vs. Blunt, 3 Story, U. S. Circuit Court Reports, 745).*

And again the supreme court of the State of New York (Hon. Chancellor Kent presiding as chief justice) held in the case of Vanderheyden vs. Young, 11 Johnson's New York Reports, 157, that—

It is a general and sound principle that when the law vests any person with a power to do an act, and constitutes him a judge of the evidence on which that act may be done, and at the same time contemplates that the act is to be carried into effect through the instrumentality of agents, the person thus clothed with power is invested with discretion and is quoad hoc a judge.

His mandates to his legal agents on his declaring the event to have happened will be a protection to those agents, and it is not their duty or business to investigate the facts thus referred to their superior, and to rejudge his determination.*

The United States Supreme Court in Martin vs. Mott, 12 Wheaton, 19, unanimously held—

That the authority to decide upon what occasions and upon what emergencies Federal calls should be made and Federal assistance given, "belongs exclusively to the President, and that his decision is conclusive upon all other persons."*

And Chief Justice Taney, in Luther vs. Borden, 7 Howard, referred approvingly to the opinion of the United States Supreme Court in Martin vs. Mott, as expressed in these words:

That whenever a statute gives a discretionary power to any person to be exercised by him upon his own opinion of certain facts, it is a sound rule of construction that the statute constitutes him the sole and exclusive judge of the existence of those facts.*

* NOTE.—The acts of heads of Departments of the Government are in law the acts of the President (Wilcox vs. Jackson, 13 Peters., 498).

The obligations arising under these provisions of the Constitution and laws and decisions have been recognized by the Government from its foundation, as will fully appear from the authorities cited by Senator Dolph in a report made by him from the Senate Committee on Claims on February 25, 1885 (Forty-eighth Congress, second session), Report No. 1438. These authorities are printed in the appendix, marked Exhibit No. 7, page 37 *et sequiter.*

NEVADA'S DILIGENCE IN THESE PREMISES.

The State of Nevada has not slept upon her rights in any of these premises nor been guilty of any *laches*; on the contrary, at all proper times she has respectfully brought the same to the attention of Congress by memorials of her legislature and of her State authorities, and through her representatives in Congress. On March 29, 1867, her legislature first asked for the payment of the claims of the State by a joint resolution, which is printed in the appendix, marked Exhibit No. 8, page 64. And again, on February 1, 1869, the legislature of Nevada passed a memorial and joint resolution renewing her prayer in these premises, which is also so printed in the appendix, marked Exhibit No. 9, page 65.

The Journals of the United States Senate show that on March 10, 1868, the writer of this report presented the first-mentioned memorial and resolution to the Senate, accompanied with an official statement of the amount of the claims of the State referred to therein. These papers were referred to the Committee on Claims, but the records fail to show that any action was ever taken upon them. On May 29 of the same year the writer of this report introduced a joint resolution (S. 138) providing for the appointment of a board of examiners to examine the claims of the State of Nevada against the United States, and on June 18 of the same year the Committee on Claims, to whom this joint resolution was referred, was discharged from its further consideration. The official statement of the moneys expended by the State of Nevada on account of the United States, and presented to the Senate on March 10, 1868, can not now be found on the files of the Senate.

On February 11, 1885, and January 26, 1887, the legislature of Nevada, renewing its prayer for a re-imbursement of the money by her expended for the use and benefit of the United States, further memorialized Congress, asking for the settlement of her claims, which are printed in the appendix and marked Exhibits Nos. 10 and 11, pages 65 and 66.

PROCEEDINGS IN CONGRESS TO REDEEM THE OBLIGATIONS OF THE UNITED STATES DUE TO NEVADA IN THIS CASE.

The circumstances under which these expenditures were made by the Territory and State of Nevada being exceptional, and their re-imbursement not being provided for by any existing law, general or special, Senator Fair, of Nevada, on December 13, 1881, introduced a joint resolution in the Senate providing for the equitable adjustment of these claims of Nevada now under consideration, which was referred to the Committee on Military Affairs. A copy of said resolution will be found in the appendix, marked Exhibit 12, page 67.

This committee, instead of reporting back this joint resolution, reported back a substitute in the form of a bill providing for the payment of the claims of several States and Territories, including the State of Nevada, and which bill finally resulted in the act of June 27, 1882. This bill was reported on May 12, 1882, by Hon. L. F. Grover, and

Nevada believed then and believes now that it was then the intention of Congress to equitably and explicitly provide for the re-imbursement to her of the amount of money which she had actually and in good faith expended in these premises. This bill was accompanied by a report in which the following statement is made in relation to the claims of the State of Nevada:

NEVADA.

It appears by the report of the Adjutant-General U. S. Army, of February 25, 1882, that one regiment of cavalry and one battalion of infantry were raised in the late Territory of Nevada during the late war of the rebellion, and that the expenses of raising, organizing, and placing in the field said forces were never paid by said Territory, but were assumed and paid by the State of Nevada, and that none of said expenses so incurred by said Territory, and assumed and paid by said State, have ever been re-imbursed the State of Nevada by the United States, and that no claims therefor have ever been heretofore presented by either said Territory or said State for audit and payment by the United States. Under section 3489 of the Revised Statutes, hereinbefore referred to, the payment of these claims is barred by limitation.

These forces were raised to guard the overland mail route and emigrant road to California, east of Carson City, and to do other military service in Nevada, and were called out by the governor of the late Territory of Nevada upon requisitions therefor by the commanding general of the Department of the Pacific, and under authority of the War Department, as appears by copies of official correspondence furnished to your committee by the Secretary of War and the general commanding the Division of the Pacific. *   *   *

PRESENTATION BY NEVADA TO THE UNITED STATES OF HER CLAIM.

This bill reported from this committee having become a law in an amended form on June 27, 1882, thereupon the governor and controller of the State of Nevada transmitted to the Secretary of the Treasury and Secretary of War a detailed account of the moneys actually expended and actual indebtedness assumed and paid by the State of Nevada on account of the volunteer military forces enrolled by the Territory and State of Nevada, as shown by the books of the State controller.

This statement of the claim of Nevada against the United States was prepared with great care by the proper officers of the State of Nevada, being first submitted by them to the legislature thereof in printed form at the expense of the State, and thereafter transmitted, as above stated, with proper original vouchers and evidence of every kind then in her possession, to the authorities of the Government of the United States and as provided for in said act of June 27, 1882. This statement is printed in the appendix, marked Exhibit No. 13, page 67.

DELAY OF THE UNITED STATES IN THE EXAMINATION OF NEVADA'S CLAIM AND THE CAUSES THEREOF.

This claim, with said vouchers and evidence, was first presented to the Secretary of the Treasury in 1883, where, being properly stamped, it was duly transmitted to the Secretary of War for examination and action thereon. It remained of record in the War Department unacted on up to and after August 4, 1886, because, as was stated to Congress by Hon. Robert T. Lincoln, Secretary of War, he required the aid of a board of at least three army officers to assist his Department in such examination, and he requested Congress to make an appropriation of $25,000 to defray the expenses of the examination of the different State and Territorial claims presented under the act of June 27, 1882. Congress delayed action upon these requests of the Secretary of War until August 4, 1886, on which date acts were passed providing for said board of

army officers, as asked for, and also appropriated $10,000 to defray the expenses of said examinations (see vol. 24, Stats. at Large, pages 217 and 249.)

SECRETARY LINCOLN'S CONSTRUCTION OF THIS ACT OF JUNE 27, 1882, FOR THE RELIEF OF NEVADA, ETC.

Prior to any action by the War Department on this claim of the State of Nevada, and prior to any action by Congress on the request of the Secretary of War for a board of Army officers to examine said claim, a bill was introduced in Congress by Senator Jones, of Nevada, and referred to the Secretary of War for report, providing for the payment of certain individual claims of citizens of Nevada on account of Indian hostilities in Nevada in 1860, upon which the Secretary of War reported as follows:

WAR DEPARTMENT,
Washington City, January 26, 1884.

SIR: In response to so much of your communication of the 22d ultimo as requests information concerning Senate bill 657, "to authorize the Secretary of the Treasury to adjust and settle the expenses of Indian wars in Nevada," I have the honor to invite your attention to the following report of the Third Auditor of the Treasury, to whom your request was duly referred:

"The State of Nevada has filed in the office abstracts and vouchers for expenses incurred on account of raising volunteers for the United States to aid in suppressing the late rebellion amounting to $349,697.49, and for expenses on account of her militia in the 'White Pine Indian war' of 1875, $17,650.98. Also, expenses of her militia in the 'Elko Indian war' of 1878, amounting to $4,654.64, presented under act of Congress approved June 27, 1882 (22 Statutes, 111, 112).

"These abstracts and vouchers will be sent to your Department for examination and report as soon as they can be stamped, as that statute requires a report from the Secretary of War as to the necessity and reasonableness of the expenses incurred. This statute is deemed sufficiently broad enough to embrace all proper claims of said State and Territory of Nevada."

Very respectfully, your obedient servant,

ROBERT T. LINCOLN,
Secretary of War.

Hon. S. B. MAXEY,
Of Committee on Military Affairs, United States Senate.

In accordance with this letter the Committee on Military Affairs reported back the bill referred to (S. 657), and asked that it be indefinitely postponed, and because of the explanation made by said committee, as follows, to wit:

It will be observed that it is deemed by the War Department that the act approved June 27, 1882, is sufficiently broad to embrace all proper claims of Nevada, whether as State or Territory.

For convenience of reference the above act accompanies this report, and an examination thereof, and of the construction thereon, satisfies the committee that no additional legislation is necessary.

The State of Kansas presented her claim to Secretary Lincoln under this act, which claim was by him examined, audited, and allowed for almost exactly the sum that Kansas had actually expended for the use and benefit of the United States, and all of which allowance has since been paid to Kansas by the United States, and aggregating the sum of $332,308.13 (23 U. S. Stats., 474).

AFTER OVER FOUR YEARS DELAY, SUBSEQUENT TO THE PASSAGE OF THE ACT OF JUNE 27, 1882, THE UNITED STATES TAKES UP NEVADA'S CLAIM FOR EXAMINATION, WHEN THE VERY FIRST QUESTION RAISED IS ONE OF JURISDICTION, AND WHICH IS DECIDED AGAINST NEVADA.

After the passage of said act of August 4, 1886, the War Department detailed a board of three Army officers under Special Orders No. 232,

dated October 6, 1886, to proceed to examine the claims arising under the act of June 27, 1882, and in the manner contemplated and as provided for in said acts. The claim of the State of Nevada was the first claim submitted to and examined by said board. This board being in doubt whether, under the terms of said act of June 27, 1882, they could allow a re-imbursement to Nevada of the amount by her expended for interest and extra pay to her troops while in the military service of the United States, referred these two questions to the Secretary of War for his decision. On February 8, 1887, after argument was submitted to him in support of these two elements of Nevada's claim against the United States, the Secretary of War decided "that after a careful consideration of the subject" he was "of opinion that neither the extra pay nor the interest can, under the provisions of the act, be allowed," meaning the act of June 27, 1882, and refused the same (see appendix, Exhibit No. 14, page 83).

TWO SEPARATE REPORTS (A MAJORITY AND MINORITY) MADE BY THE ARMY BOARD OF WAR CLAIMS EXAMINERS, THE MINORITY REPORT ALLOWING ONLY ABOUT 2¼ PER CENT. OF THE AMOUNT ACTUALLY EX. PENDED BY NEVADA, AND WHICH MINORITY REPORT IS APPROVED BY THE SECRETARY OF WAR.

It will be borne in mind that on January 26, 1884, Secretary Lincoln was of opinion that the act of June 27, 1882, was sufficiently broad to embrace all proper claims of the State of Nevada, and the Committee on Military Affairs, in consequence thereof, reported to the Senate that that committee was satisfied that no additional legislation was necessary in regard thereto, while Secretary Endicott, on February 8, 1887, decided that the claims for expenditure for interest and extra pay to said troops while in the service of the United States could not be allowed by him under said act, and further, by approving the award made by the minority examiner, and, as will hereinafter be more particularly referred to, also disallowed the amount expended by Nevada and by her paid as her costs for the enrollment of those very troops so called into the service of the United States.

The day following the decision of the Secretary of War, to wit, February 9, 1887, and contrary to a practice usual in similar cases, said board of Army officers, instead of submitting one report to the Secretary of War, submitted two separate and independent reports, one signed by the majority of said board and the other in the nature of a minority report. These two reports are submitted herewith, and printed in the Appendix, marked Exhibits Nos. 15, 16, and 17, pages 89 to 90.

The total of this particular claim of the State of Nevada so presented to said board amounted to $349,697.49. The amount thereof that was allowed in said minority report was only $8,559.61. This minority report was approved by the Secretary of War, thereby disallowing or suspending all of Nevada's claim except the paltry sum of about 2¼ per cent. of the money actually expended by Nevada for troops called into the service of the United States and at the urgent solicitation of the Government of the United States in its hour of need, while this same board allowed nearly $1,000,000 of the claim of Texas, to wit, $927,242.30, being about 50 per cent. of the claim of that State of $1,867,259.13, as presented for re-imbursement for the expenses of her Indian wars, which occurred since the rebellion, and prosecuted chiefly, if not solely, for the protection of the inhabitants of the State of Texas. It is worthy of remark that no minority report was submitted in the case of Texas.

It will be observed by a perusal of the reports of the board of war claims examiners that the great mass of this claim of the State of Nevada for re-imbursement for moneys, expended under very extraordinary circumstances, was rejected by the board of examiners on either purely technical grounds or for an alleged want of jurisdiction to make an award under what has since been admitted and found to be the most restrictive act that was ever drawn since 1789 intended as an "act of relief."

Only $8,559.61 was finally awarded to Nevada by the Secretary of War.

The want of specific information on the part of the officer making the minority report which reduced the amount of the claim to the sum named may be shown in part by the mistakes made in reference to the statutes of Nevada, which are in several public libraries here, and could have been easily examined. For example, he seems to have inferred that the act of the Nevada legislature of March 4, 1865, was the first act of the Territory providing for the organization of its militia, whereas, as we have already shown, there was an elaborate act for that purpose passed by the Territorial legislature as early as November 28, 1861, and apparently on the assumption that there was no law creating the office of adjutant-general prior to 1865, and upon the fact that no evidence was furnished that Nevada previous to April 2, 1863, had soldiers, that therefore the salary of that officer ought not to commence prior to the time when the volunteers were actually called for service into the Army. But it will be observed that he was mistaken as to the time the law was passed creating the office of adjutant-general. The second section of the act of November 28, 1861, provides that—

The adjutant-general shall be appointed by the commander-in-chief, and shall hold his office for the term of two years. He shall be *ex officio* chief of staff, quartermaster-general, commissary-general, inspector-general, and chief of ordnance. He shall receive a salary of $1,000 annually, to be paid out of moneys appropriated for that purpose. He shall reside at the seat of government, and shall keep his office open for the transaction of business every day (Sundays excepted) from 10 o'clock a. m. to 3 o'clock p. m.

The minority examiner is again mistaken if he assumed that the secretary of state of Nevada became *ex officio* adjutant-general on March 3, 1866. It is true that an act devolving the duties of adjutant-general upon the secretary of state was passed on that date, but the second section of said act provides that—

This act shall take effect and be in force from and after the first day of January, 1867 (Stats. Nev., 1866, p. 206).

Thus it appears that the secretary of state did not in fact or in law become *ex officio* adjutant-general until January 1, 1867. The original section of the militia law of 1861 in regard to the office of adjutant-general was afterward amended, changing the length of time that officer was to hold office and increasing his salary to $2,000 per annum, but the abolishment of the office did not take effect until January, 1867.

PROBABLY CONFOUNDING THE ACT OF JUNE 27, 1882, WITH THE ACT OF JULY 27, 1861.

The minority examiner in terminating the salary of adjutant-general on August 20, 1866, undoubtedly had in mind the act of July 27, 1861, and not the act of June 27, 1882, under which last act alone said board was authorized to make an examination and award; otherwise he would not have limited the salary to August 20, 1866, the end of the war of the rebellion, as heretofore officially declared, but would have certainly al-

lowed Nevada a re-imbursement for the money actually paid by her as salary to that officer until his services terminated, and the Indian wars on the plains were actually suppressed and the office of adjutant gen eral abolished, which was done on December 31, 1866, since which time either the secretary of state or lieutenant-governor has acted as *ex officio* adjutant-general.

Attention is called to these discrepancies simply to show that the minority examiner apparently fell into error, unintentionally, of course, in his examination of the statutes of Nevada, or failed to consider all the circumstances under which this claim of the State arose. The ma- jority of the board who made the same award and allowance as the minority, with the exception of $1,233.50 for salary of adjutant-general prior to the time when the troops were mustered in the service, made a very thorough examination of all the vouchers showing each item of ex- penditure made by the State, and this examination may be assumed as correct and as establishing the fact that the State expended all the moneys for which this claim is made, leaving the question as to the liability of the Government to re-imburse the State to the discretion of Congress. There is but one item stated in the account by the board of examiners which appears to have been charged by mistake. It was undoubtedly paid by the State, but if the board are correct, it was such a palpable mistake of the State officers that the State ought to lose it. It was a double charge for rent, amounting to $38.33. This amount, together with the $8,559.61 allowed by the minority of the board of examiners, and already paid to the State, making a total of $8,597.94, should be deducted from the claim now presented by the State. The State, however, should have the benefit of the fact that no other error in the accounts was discovered. All the other disal- lowed claims were rejected, not because the State did not pay the money, but because the board of examiners thought they were not authorized to allow the same under the act of June 27, 1882. We print in the appendix, Exhibit No. 17, page 92, the table accompany- ing report of the majority of the board of war claims examiners show- ing the amounts allowed and disallowed, together with the reasons therefor.

The question is now presented in this case whether it is the duty of the Government to re-imburse the State for moneys honestly expended, at the request of the United States, under circumstances which rendered it impossible for the Territory and State of Nevada to comply with such request without making the expenditures in question. It must be con- ceded that if the State or Territory made larger expenditures than would have been required to secure like services in any other section of the country, the services secured by these expenditures at the time, place, and under the circumstances were a necessity and could not have been furnished by the State on more favorable terms, and it seems that the State and Territory did not make any expenditure that appeared at the time unnecessary.

WHAT NEVADA THOUGHT WAS INTENDED BY CONGRESS TO BE AN ACT FOR HER RELIEF AND BENEFIT IS NOW FOUND TO BE AN ACT "SO WELL AND CAREFULLY AND CLOSELY GUARDED" BY RESTRICTIONS THAT WHEN CONSTRUED BY THOSE CALLED UPON TO EXECUTE IT, IS FOUND TO BE INOPERATIVE AS A RELIEF MEASURE, AND A PRAC- TICAL DENIAL OF JUSTICE.

We fully concur with the officer who made the minority report, that "the restrictions imposed in the second section of the act of June 27,

1882, have been complied with as far as was possible," whatever question there may be as to his complying with the provisions of the act itself. The argument that the Government might have bought supplies cheaper under its contract system than were furnished in Nevada is one which your committee are unwilling to urge under the circumstances. The Government was not situated so as to obtain troops or supplies by contract or otherwise, but was compelled to call upon the Territory to furnish both troops and supplies. All prices of all supplies, and also of all services, at that time in Nevada were on a gold basis, and coin was the only circulating medium. The roads over the mountains were blocked by snow and no considerable amount of supplies could be transported over them. The supplies in the Territory had been carried there during the previous summer for the use of the inhabitants, and the troops had to be furnished from the limited stock of individuals found in the Territory, and at a moment's notice. The Government could not wait to advertise. The overland mail route was closed and immediate action was required. The cheapest, most effective, and in fact the only immediate relief that could be had was furnished by the militia and volunteer troops of Nevada, who, leaving their workshops and employments of every character, and the high wages for their services, were organized and marched immediately in the direction of Salt Lake City to open the mail and emigrant route. They subsequently joined General Conner's forces from California, subdued the Indians, fortified Camp Douglas, overlooking Salt Lake City, and were in the field, subject to call, to go wherever ordered or needed.

PAYMENT BY THE UNITED STATES OF ABOUT 2½ PER CENT. OF THIS CLAIM ON ACCOUNT IS NOT A VALID BASIS FOR THE UNITED STATES TO REPUDIATE THE BALANCE THEREOF, OR TO REFUSE TO PAY THE SAME, AND SHOULD NOT, IN GOOD CONSCIENCE, BE EVER PLEADED BY AN HONEST DEBTOR, FOR WHOSE RELIEF AND AT WHOSE URGENT SOLICITATION SUCH DEBT WAS INCURRED.

The fact that a small fraction only of this claim has been allowed and paid on account, to wit, about 2½ per cent., and the great bulk thereof rejected for want of jurisdiction only, is no valid objection to an authorization by Congress for the payment of what is honestly due the State of Nevada, and for this there are numerous precedents, some of which are cited in the appendix in Exhibit No. 18, pages 96 to 98.

"INTEREST" PAID IN THIS CASE BY NEVADA IS IN REALITY, IN JUSTICE, IN REASON, AND IN LAW A PROPER PART OF THE DEBT DUE NEVADA BY THE UNITED STATES, THE PAYMENT OF WHICH, TOGETHER WITH THAT OF THE PRINCIPAL IS NECESSARY TO A COMPLETE INDEMNITY.

The embarrassments under which Nevada paid the principal of the money involved in this claim is shown by the enormous rates of interest which the Territory and State were compelled to pay in order to raise money to fully comply with these calls and requisitions made for troops and as hereinbefore recited. The rates of interest which were actually paid by Nevada are shown by the official statement of her controller and as furnished to the Secretary of the Treasury and the Secretary of War, as before stated, as follows:

ABSTRACT G.—*Showing the amount actually paid by the State of Nevada and as successor to the Territory of Nevada on account of interest money on disbursements and liabilities for Nevada volunteers in the service of the United States, and employed in the defense of the United States during the war of the rebellion.*

	Amount.
First —Interest paid on $46,950.12 from February 10, 1805, to March 3, 1866, at 2 per cent. per month .... [See acts legislature of Nevada for 1864–'65, page 82. act January 4, 1865.]	$11,925.32
Second—Interest paid on $46,950.12 from March 3, 1866, to May 30, 1867, at 15 per cent. per annum .... [See acts legislature of Nevada for 1866, page 47, act January 19, 1866.]	8,744.46
Third—Interest paid on $119,880.12 from May 30, 1867, to March 28, 1872, at 15 per cent. per annum .... [See acts legislature of Nevada for 1867, pages 50 and 65, act February 6, 1867.]	86,755.25
Fourth—Interest paid on $119,800.12 from March 28, 1872, to January 1, 1883, at 0½ per cent. per annum .... [See acts legislature of Nevada for 1871, page 84, act February 27, 1871.]	122,472.33
	229,897.37

Your committee, however, deem it unwise to establish a precedent under any circumstances, however extraordinary, and they admit that the recitals in support of this claim render it one extraordinary in character, of refunding interest to the full extent as paid by the Territory and State of Nevada, and as shown by the foregoing statement. The legal rate of interest of the Territory and State of Nevada was, at all the times herein stated, 10 per cent. per annum where no different rate was fixed by contract.

Your committee therefore do not feel warranted in recommending re imbursing the State of Nevada for a higher rate of interest than the legal rate fixed by her own statutes during the period of time in which these disbursements were made, and including the period up to the date of the re-imbursement of the principal by the United States, and for that reason they have incorporated in this bill, herewith reported, a provision that the aggregate of interest accruing to Nevada between the date of the expenditure by her of the principal and of the date of the re imbursement of such principal by the United States shall not exceed the actual amount of interest paid by the State and Territory, nor the amount of interest which would accrue to her on said principal if interest thereon were calculated during said period at the legal rate as established by the statutes of the Territory and State of Nevada. In support of the proposition that interest and principal are simply but two elements of one and the same unit and constituting a complete indemnity, your committee cite Senate Report 1069, made by Senator Spooner during the first session of the Forty-ninth Congress from the Committee on Claims (see appendix, Exhibit No. 19, pages 98 to 109.)

PRECEDENTS FOR THE PAYMENT TO STATES OF INTEREST ON THE PRINCIPAL BY THEM EXPENDED FOR THE USE AND BENEFIT OF THE UNITED STATES UNDER SIMILAR CIRCUMSTANCES.

The United States has in all cases, where the question has been properly presented, re-imbursed States for interest paid by such States on moneys by them borrowed and expended for the purpose of either enrolling, subsisting, clothing, supplying, arming, equipping, paying, furnishing, or transporting volunteer and militia forces called into the service of the United States. If it be suggested that the bill under consideration providing for the payment of both principal and interest is against precedent, we answer that, in the opinion of your committee, it is the better

practice to deal with a case in its entirety in a single act, and your com·
mittee state that there are abundant precedents for this practice, some
of which your committee cite in the appendix, Exhibit 20 on page 109.

We call particular attention to the precedents collected in the appen·
dix, authorizing the payment of claims of States for interest on moneys
by them expended for the use and benefit of the United States (see appendix, Exhibits Nos. 18, 19, 20, and 21, pages 96 to 149).

In addition to the authorities cited in the appendix in support of
Nevada's claim for interest, your committee also refer to the case before
the Second Comptroller of the Treasury in 1869, in which that officer
made the following decision:

> Interest can in no case be allowed by the accounting officer upon claims against the
> Government either in favor of a State or an individual.   But in cases where the claim-
> ant has been compelled to pay interest for the benefit of the Government, it then be-
> comes a part of the principal of his claim, and as such is allowable.   Such is the case
> of a State which has been obliged to raise money upon interest for the suppression of
> hostilities against which the United States should protect her.   In such cases the
> amount of interest actually and necessarily paid will be allowed, without reference
> to the rate of it (section 997, Dec. 2, Comp. Ed. 1869, p. 137).

This ruling is in harmony with a long line of precedents established
by Congress, beginning in 1812, and printed in the appendix hereto
attached and marked Exhibit Nos. 18 to 21, inclusive, pages 96 to 145.

In addition to the foregoing, your committee cite in support of Nevada's claim for interest the following, to wit:

1. Forty-eighth Congress, first session, House Report No. 1670,
   from Committee on Judiciary (see appendix, Exhibit 21,
   page 112).
2. Forty-eighth Congress, second session, House Report No. 1102,
   from Committee on War Claims (published in Exhibit No.
   14, page 86).
3. Forty-ninth Congress, first session, Senate Report No. 183,
   from the Committee on Military Affairs (see appendix, Exhibit 21, page 135).
4. Forty-ninth Congress, first session, Senate Report No. 2, from
   the Committee on Claims (published in Exhibit No. 14,
   page 85).
5. Forty-ninth Congress, first session, House Report No. 303,
   from Committee on Claims (see appendix, Exhibit 21, page
   119).
6. Forty-ninth Congress, first session, House Report No. 3126,
   from Committee on Claims (see appendix, Exhibit 21, page
   120).
7. Fiftieth Congress, first session, Senate Report No. 518, from
   the Committee on Military Affairs (see appendix, Exhibit
   21, page 138).
8. Fiftieth Congress, first session, House Report No. 309, from
   the Committee on War Claims (see appendix, Exhibit 21,
   page 137).
9. Fiftieth Congress, first session, House Report No. 1179, from
   the Committee on Claims (see appendix, Exhibit 21, page
   145).
10. Fiftieth Congress, first session, House Report No. 2198, from
    the Committee on War Claims (see appendix, Exhibit 21,
    page 144).

The precedents cited or referred to in the appendix herewith abundantly establish the fact that the United States has paid the claims of
States incurred under circumstances such as those in which Nevada ex-

pended her money for the benefit of the United States, and that in all cases properly presented to Congress, where the States were compelled to borrow money and pay interest thereon and expended the same for the use and benefit of the United States, that either at the time of providing payment for the principal or subsequently the United States has invariably assumed and paid such interest.

As before stated, the claim of the State of Nevada, provided for in this bill, has been thoroughly examined by a board of Army officers appointed for that purpose. The evidence upon which this claim was founded was submitted to said board, and the evidences of payment found by them to be correct; but said board of war-claims examiners, while finding these facts, did not, under the very restrictive and prohibitory provisions and conditions of the acts of June 27, 1882, and August 4, 1886, recommend an award to Nevada of the amount of money which they found that Nevada had actually expended for the use and benefit of the United States and in the manner as set forth in the claim as presented by Nevada for the examination of and allowance by the Treasury and War Departments; and under the terms of these acts, as construed and declared by the Secretary of War, the proper accounting officers of the Treasury could not allow Nevada any sum, either as principal or interest, not allowed by the War Department as assisted by said Army board of war-claims examiners.

COST OF TRANSPORTATION OF ARMY SUPPLIES FROM FORT LEAVEN-
WORTH WESTWARD IN 1864–'66.

It is evident that the supplies and services furnished could not at the times and places have been obtained on more reasonable terms. And in support of this statement your committee refer to the report of the Secretary of War made during that period, and in reference to a region of country much more favorably situated than was even Nevada at that time, to wit:

The troops operating on the great western plains and in the mountain regions of New Mexico, Colorado, Utah, and Idaho are supplied principally by the trains of the Quartermaster's Department from depots established on the great routes of overland travel, to which depots supplies are conveyed by contract. * * *

Travelers by the stage from Denver to Fort Leavenworth, a distance of 683 miles, in the month of July, 1865, were never out of sight of wagons trains belonging either to emigrants or to the merchants who transport supplies for the War Department, for the Indian Department, and for the miners and settlers of the central Territories.

The cost of transportation of a *pound* of corn, hay, clothing, subsistence, lumber, or any other necessary from Fort Leavenworth—

To Fort Riley is	$0. 0244
To Fort Union, the depot for New Mexico	.1425
To Santa Fé, N. Mex	.1685
To Fort Kearny	.0644
To Fort Laramie	.1410
To Denver City, Colo	.1542
To Salt Lake City, Utah	.2784

The cost of a bushel of corn purchased at Fort Leavenworth and delivered at each of these points was as follows:

Fort Riley	$2. 79
Fort Union	9. 44
Santa Fé	10. 84
Fort Kearny	5. 03
Fort Laramie	9. 26
Denver City	10. 05
Great Salt Lake City	17. 00

(Secretary of War's report, 1865–'66, part 1, pages 23 and 112; also see General Halleck to Adjutant-General, and General McDowell to Adjutant-General U. S. Army, report of Secretary of War, October 18, 1866, pages 31 and 32.)

This table is cited to show the costs of maintaining troops in that section of the country, and also to show the comparative costs of furnishing troops and supplies in Nevada and the points immediately east thereof during the periods of time involved herein.

The details concerning the peculiar and difficult and expensive service on the plains and mountains by the troops doing military service, similar in all respects to those performed by these Nevada volunteers, are fully set forth in the report of the Secretary of War respecting the protection of the overland mail and emigrant route to the Pacific from the molestations and depredations by hostile Indians, and set forth in Ex. Docs. Nos. 9 to 24, second session Thirty-ninth Congress, 1866–'67.

CONCLUSIONS AND RECOMMENDATIONS.

Nevada has not demanded a bounty, nor presented a claim against the United States for re-imbursement of any expenditure she did not in good faith actually make for the use and benefit of the United States, and made, too, only subsequent to the date of the aforesaid appeal of Secretary Seward to the nation, and made, too, in consequence of said appeal and of the subsequent calls and requisitions made upon her then scanty resources and sparse population, and wherein the good faith of the United States was to be relied upon to make to her ungrudgingly a just re-imbursement whenever the United States found itself in a condition to redeem all its obligations.

Nevada has been diligent in making her claim known to Congress, but she has not with an indecorous speed demanded her pound of flesh, but has waited long and patiently, believing upon the principle that the higher obligations between States, like those among men, are not always "set down in writing, signed and sealed in the form of a bond, but reside rather in honor," and that the obligation of the United States due her in this case was as sacred as if it had originally been in the form of a 4 per cent. United States bond, now being redeemed by the United States at $1.27 upon each $1 of this particular form of its unpaid obligations.

Nevada has not solicited any charity in this case, but, on the contrary, by numerous petitions and memorials she has respectfully represented to Congress why the taxes heretofore levied upon her people and paid out of her own treasury to her volunteer troops in gold and silver coin to aid the United States at its own solicitation to protect itself and maintain the general welfare should be now returned to her by the General Government.

Congress should not forget that during the long period of the nation's peril the citizens of Nevada, like those of California (when not engaged in the military or naval service of the United States) not only guarded the principal gold and silver mines of the country then discovered, and prevented them from falling into the hands of the public enemy, but also worked them so profitably for the general welfare as to enable the United States to make it possible to resume specie payment, and to redeem its bonds at 27 per cent. above par, and to repay all its money-lenders at a high rate of interest, and that, too, not in the depreciated currency with which it paid Nevada's volunteer troops, but in gold coin of standard value.

As these expenditures were honestly made by the Territory and State of Nevada, your committee do not think that, under all the peculiar and exceptional circumstances of this case, the action of the Territory and State of Nevada should be hewn too nicely or too hypercritically by the United States at this late date. These expenditures were

all made in perfect good faith and for patriotic purposes, and secured effectual aid to the United States which otherwise could not have been obtained without a much larger expenditure. The State of Nevada in good faith assumed and paid all the obligations of the Territory of Nevada to aid the United States, and issued and sold its own bonds for their payment, upon which bonds it has paid interest until the present time. The only question now for consideration is, shall the United States in equal good faith and under all the circumstances herein recited relieve the State of Nevada from this obligation, or shall the United States insist and require it to be paid by the people of that State alone?

CALIFORNIA.

The total amount paid by California, as shown by said report of said war claims examiners, is $4,420,891.96. Of this amount $1,500,545.86 was interest, and $468,976.54 was expended on account of militia. Deducting these amounts and we have the expenditure of California, excluding interest and expenses of militia, $2,451,369.56.

OREGON.

The total amount paid by Oregon, as shown by said report of said war claims examiners, is $356,271.61. Of this amount $110,626.35 was interest, and $21,118.73 was expended on account of militia. Deducting these amounts and we have the expenditure of Oregon, excluding interest and expenses of militia, of $224,526.53.

NEVADA.

The total amount paid by Nevada as principal and interest, as shown by said report of said war claims examiners, is $404,040.70.

With these amendments your committee therefore recommend the passage of this bill, which, so amended, is as follows, to-wit:

A BILL to re-imburse the States of California, Oregon, and Nevada for moneys by them expended in the suppression of the rebellion.

Be it enacted by the Senate and House of Representatives of the United States of America in Congress assembled, That there is hereby appropriated, out of any money in the Treasury not otherwise appropriated, the sums hereinafter mentioned to re-imburse and to be paid to the States of California, Oregon, and Nevada for moneys by them expended in aid of the United States in the war of the rebellion, to wit:

To the State of California, the sum of two million four hundred and fifty-one thousand three hundred and sixty-nine dollars and fifty-six cents.

To the State of Oregon, the sum of two hundred and twenty-four thousand five hundred and twenty-six dollars and fifty-three cents.

To the State of Nevada, the sum of four hundred and four thousand forty dollars and seventy cents, being the sums of money shown by the reports of the Secretary of War to have been paid by said States in the suppression of the rebellion.

IN THE SENATE OF THE UNITED STATES.

FEBRUARY 7, 1893.—Referred to the Committee on Appropriations and ordered to
be printed.

The VICE-PRESIDENT presented the following

**RESOLUTION OF THE LEGISLATURE OF THE STATE OF NEVADA
IN FAVOR OF THE PASSAGE OF A LAW REIMBURSING SAID
STATE THE AMOUNT OF MONEY NOW DUE HER ON ACCOUNT OF
HER REBELLION WAR CLAIMS AGAINST THE UNITED STATES.**

CARSON, NEV., *February 7, 1893.*
PRESIDENT UNITED STATES SENATE,
Washington, D. C.:

Senate joint resolution to the Congress of the United States relative
to paying the rebellion war claims of the State of Nevada, passed February 6, 1893:

"Whereas the Territory of Nevada, under various calls made upon
her by the proper authorities of the United States, incurred a large
debt in aiding the United States during the war of the rebellion; and

" Whereas the State of Nevada, upon its admission into the Union, assumed and has heretofore paid the whole of said debt; and

"Whereas, under the proper authorities of the United States, the sum
so paid by the State of Nevada had been fully examined, correctly ascertained, and officially reported by the Secretary of War to Congress;
and

"Whereas no part of said moneys have as yet been refunded by the
United States to the State of Nevada, in consequence of which the
burden of said debt has been for many years very onerous upon her
citizens; therefore, be it

"*Resolved by the senate and assembly, conjointly,* That our Senators
and Representative in Congress be requested to urge Congress to fully
reimburse this State the amount of money now due her on account of
her rebellion war claims against the United States. *Resolved, also,*
That the governor be hereby requested to immediately telegraph this
resolution to our Senators and Representative in Congress, and to the
President of the Senate and to the Speaker of the House of Representatives."

A true copy.
Attest: O. H. GREY,
                                      Secretary of State.

WAR CLAIMS OF CALIFORNIA, OREGON, AND NEVADA.

MARCH 8, 1894.—Committed to the Committee of the Whole House on the state of
the Union and ordered to be printed.

Mr. HERMANN, from the Committee on War Claims, submitted the
following

REPORT:

[To accompany H. R. 4959.]

The Committee on War Claims, to whom was referred the bills (H.
R. 2615 and H. R. 4959) to reimburse the States of California, Oregon,
and Nevada for moneys by them expended in the suppression of the
rebellion when aiding the United States to maintain the "common
defense" on the Pacific coast, have examined the same and report as
follows:
The facts out of which the aforesaid State war claims arise have
been very fully stated in several reports heretofore made to the House
of Representatives and to the Senate, as follows, to wit, House Report
No. 254 and Senate Report No. 158, Fifty-second Congress, first session;
House Report No. 2553 and Senate Report No. 644, Fifty-first Congress, first session; and House Report No. 3396 and Senate Reports
No. 1286 and No. 2014, Fiftieth Congress, first session.
Bills relating to these State war claims of these three Pacific coast
States passed the Senate during the first session of the Fiftieth Congress, and were favorably reported to the Senate during the first session of the Fifty-first and Fifty-second Congresses and to the House
during the Fiftieth, Fifty-first, and Fifty-second Congresses, but were
not reached for consideration by the House in either thereof. These
bills were introduced in the House, to wit, H. R. No. 2615 on 11th day
of September, 1893, by Mr. Caminetti, of California, and H. R. No.
4959 on January 3, 1894, by Mr. Maguire, of California, and both
referred to the House Committee on War Claims.
Sums of money (recited in three reports made by the Hon. Secretary
of War to the Senate on these State war claims and printed as Senate
Ex. Docs. Nos. 10, 11, and 17, Fifty-first Congress, first session) proven
to the full satisfaction of the War Department to have been expended
by said States to aid the United States in the suppression of the war
of the rebellion were included in the general deficiency appropriation
bill as it passed the Senate during the second session of the Fifty-first
Congress for the purpose of indemnifying and reimbursing said States
on account and in partial liquidation of said claims, but the same were
omitted from said deficiency bill as it became a law. Senate bill No.
52 and House bills No. 54 and No. 42, Fifty-second Congress, first
session, were in all respects identical; the last of which House bills
was, on February 10, 1892, favorably reported by the House War
Claims Committee in House Report No. 254, Fifty-second Congress,
first session, and said Senate bill No. 52 was, on February 4, 1892,

favorably reported by the Senate Committee on Military Affairs in Senate Report No. 158, as follows, to wit:

[Senate Report No. 158, Fifty-second Congress, first session.]

The Committee on Military Affairs, to whom was referred the bill (S. 52) to reimburse the States of California, Oregon, and Nevada for moneys by them expended in the suppression of the rebellion, have examined the same and report as follows, to wit:

This measure was considered by this committee during the first session of the Fifty-first Congress, and was reported upon favorably (Report No. 614).

Your committee concur in the conclusions stated in that report and recommend the passage of the bill.

At a very early period of the war of the rebellion nearly all the troops of the regular Army of the United States then serving in California, Oregon, and Nevada were withdrawn from military duty in those States and transported thence by sea to New York City, at an expense to the United States of about $390,103, or at an average cost of about $284 for each commissioned officer and of about $133 for each enlisted man.

This withdrawal therefrom of said regular troops left these three Pacific coast States comparatively defenseless, and for the purpose of supplying their places, and to provide additional military forces, rendered necessary by public exigencies, calls for volunteers were made upon said States under proclamations of the President, or requisitions by the War Department, or by its highest military officers commanding the military departments on the Pacific. These calls for volunteers continued until the necessity therefor entirely ceased to exist, during which time these three Pacific coast States furnished, enlisted, equipped, enrolled, paid, and mustered into the military service of the United States 18,715 volunteers, as shown in said reports so made to the Senate by the Secretary of War.

In consequence of this withdrawal in 1861 of said military forces from the Pacific coast, in order that they might perform military service in the East, and in view of the circumstances and exigencies existing in the Pacific coast States and Territories during the rebellion period, requisitions were duly made from time to time by the President of the United States and by the Secretary of War upon the proper State authorities of California, Oregon, and Nevada for volunteers to perform military service for the United States in said States and Territories, as are fully and in great detail set forth in Senate Ex. Docs. Nos. 10, 11, and 17, Fifty-first Congress, first session. In compliance with the several calls and official requisitions so made between 1861 and 1866, inclusive—

Volunteers.

The State of California furnished 15,725
The State of Nevada furnished 1,180
The State of Oregon furnished 1,810

Making a total aggregate of 18,715

who were enlisted and were thereafter duly mustered into the military service of the United States as volunteers from said State. The same number of troops if organized in the East and transported from New York City to the Pacific coast States and Territories in the same manner as was done by the United States War Department from June 17, 1850, to August 3, 1861, would have cost the United States at that time the sum of about $5,483,385, for *transportation alone.*

The indemnification for the "costs, charges, and expenses" properly incurred by said States for enrolling, subsisting, clothing, supplying, arming, equipping, paying, transporting, and furnishing said 18,715

volunteer troops employed by the United States to aid them to maintain the "common defense," was guaranteed by the United States in
the act of Congress approved July 27, 1861 (12 U. S. Stats., 276), an
act entitled "An act to indemnify the States for expenses incurred by
them in defense of the United States."

The then Secretary of War, Hon. Redfield Proctor, now U. S. Senator from Vermont (on page 28 of his report, Senate Ex. Doc. No. 11,
Fifty-first Congress, first session), in reporting upon the military services performed by said volunteers during the rebellion, said:

> They took the places of the regular troops in California, all of which, except
> 3 batteries of artillery and 1 regiment of infantry, were withdrawn to the East
> at an early period after the outbreak of the war. Without them (and the
> Oregon and Nevada volunteers) the overland mail and emigrant routes, extending
> from the Missouri River via Great Salt Lake City to California and Oregon, and
> passing through an uninhabited and mountainous country, infested with hostile
> Indians and highwaymen, could not have been adequately protected; and yet it
> was of the first importance to have these routes kept open and safe, especially as
> rebel cruisers had made the sea routes both hazardous and expensive. Two expedi-
> tions composed of California volunteers, under the command of Brig. Gens. James
> H. Carleton and Patrick E. Connor, respectively, performed perilous and exhausting
> marches across a desert and over an almost impassable country and established
> themselves, the latter in Utah—where, besides protecting the mail routes, a watch-
> ful eye was kept on the uncertain and sometimes threatening attitude of the Mor-
> mons—and the former in Arizona and New Mexico, where Territories were thereafter
> effectually guarded in the interests of the United States against Indians and rebels.

The Secretary of War, with the assistance of the board of Army
officers, created under the authority of the act of Congress approved
August 4, 1886 (24 U. S. Stat., p. 217), and which officers were duly
selected and appointed on said board by Mr. Secretary of War, Hon. W.
C. Endicott, has heretofore found as facts, and has so officially reported
to the Senate (as printed in Senate Ex. Docs. Nos. 10, 11, 17, Fifty-
first Congress, first session), that the States of California, Oregon, and
Nevada, under appropriate laws of the legislatures thereof, respectively,
have actually paid in gold coin out of their State treasuries, on account of
the "costs, charges, and expenses" properly incurred by said three States
for enrolling, subsisting, clothing, supplying, arming, equipping, paying,
transporting, and furnishing said 18,715 volunteer troops of said three
States, which were employed by the United States to aid them to maintain
the "common defense" on the Pacific coast during the war of the rebellion, the exact sums of money as recited in said bill (H. R. 4959), the
reimbursement of which was so guaranteed to be paid to said States
as an indemnity under the aforesaid act of July 27, 1861 (12 U. S. Stat.,
276), "An act to indemnify the States for expenses incurred by them
in defense of the United States," and under the resolution of Congress
of March 8, 1862 (12 U. S. Stat., 615), "declaratory of the intent and
meaning of said act, and the resolution of March 19, 1862 (12 U. S. Stat.,
616), to authorize the Secretary of War to accept moneys appropriated
by any State for the payment of its volunteers, and to apply the same
as directed by such State," copies of which act and resolution are as
follows:

On the 27th day of July, 1861, Congress passed an act entitled "An
act to indemnify the States for expenses incurred by them in defense
of the United States," as follows:

> That the Secretary of the Treasury be, and is hereby, directed, out of any moneys
> in the Treasury not otherwise appropriated, to pay to the governor of any State, or
> its duly authorized agents, the costs, charges, and expenses properly incurred by
> said State for enrolling, subsisting, clothing, supplying, arming, equipping, paying,
> and transporting its troops employed in aiding in suppressing the present insurrec-
> tion against the United States, to be settled upon proper vouchers to be filed and
> passed upon by the proper accounting officers of the Treasury (12 Stat. L., p. 276.)

A RESOLUTION declaratory of the intent and meaning of a certain act therein named.

Whereas doubts have arisen as to the true intent and meaning of act numbered eighteen, entitled "An act to indemnify the States for expenses incurred by them in 'defense of the United States,' approved July twenty-seventh, eighteen hundred and sixty-one" (12 U. S. Stats., 276):

Be it resolved by the Senate and House of Representatives of the United States of America in Congress assembled, That the said act shall be construed to apply to expenses incurred as well after as before the date of the approval thereof.

Approved March 8, 1862 (12 U. S. Stats., 615).

A RESOLUTION to authorize the Secretary of War to accept moneys appropriated by any State for the payment of its volunteers and to apply the same as directed by such State.

Resolved by the Senate and House of Representatives of the United States of America in Congress assembled, That if any State during the present rebellion shall make any appropriation to pay the Volunteers of that State, the Secretary of War is hereby authorized to accept the same, and cause it to be applied by the Paymaster-General to the payments designated by the legislative act making the appropriation, in the same manner as if appropriated by act of Congress; and also to make any regulations that may be necessary for the disbursement and proper application of such funds to the specific purpose for which they may be appropriated by the several States.

Approved March 19, 1862 (12 U. S. Stats., 616).

AN ACT for the benefit of the States of Texas, Colorado, Oregon, Nebraska, California, Kansas, and Nevada, and the Territories of Washington and Idaho, and Nevada when a Territory.

*   *   *   *   *   *   *

SEC. 2. The Secretary of War is hereby authorized to detail three Army officers to assist him in examining and reporting upon the claims of the States and Territory named in the acts of June twenty-seventh, eighteen hundred and eighty-two, chapter two hundred and forty-one of the laws of the Forty-seventh Congress, and such officers, before entering upon said duties, shall take and subscribe an oath that they will carefully examine said claims, and that they will, to the best of their ability, make a just and impartial statement thereof, as required by said act.

Approved August 4, 1886. (24 U. S. Stat., 217.)

From the facts and laws hereinbefore recited, your committee concur in the conclusions reached and recommendations made in the several House and Senate reports which heretofore accompanied similar bills, and now reaffirm the same, and report back said bill (H. R. 4959) with a recommendation that it do pass with an amendment added thereto as follows, to wit:

That payment of said sums of money shall be made to each of said States in four equal installments, the first of which shall be paid to them respectively upon the passage of this act, the second of which shall be paid to them respectively on July 1, 1895, the third of which shall be paid to them respectively on July 1, 1896, the fourth of which shall be paid to them respectively on July 1, 1897.

O

IN THE SENATE OF THE UNITED STATES.

APRIL 23, 1894.—Ordered to be printed.

Mr. DOLPH presented the following

STATEMENT OF CALIFORNIA, OREGON, AND NEVADA RELATIVE TO THEIR STATE REBELLION WAR CLAIMS AGAINST THE UNITED STATES; MADE IN SUPPORT OF SENATE BILL NO. 101, INTRODUCED BY SENATOR STEWART, OF NEVADA, ON AUGUST 8, 1893, AND OF SENATE BILL NO. 1033, INTRODUCED ON OCTOBER 2, 1893, AND SENATE BILL NO. 1062, INTRODUCED BY SENATOR DOLPH, OF OREGON, ON OCTOBER 9, 1893, AND OF SENATE BILL NO. 1295, INTRODUCED BY SENATOR WHITE, OF CALIFORNIA, ON DECEMBER 18, 1893, AND OF HOUSE BILL NO. 2615, INTRODUCED BY REPRESENTATIVE CAMINETTI, OF CALIFORNIA, ON SEPTEMBER 11, 1893, AND OF HOUSE BILL NO. 4959, INTRODUCED JANUARY 3, 1894, BY REPRESENTATIVE MAGUIRE, OF CALIFORNIA, ALL HAVING FOR THEIR OBJECT "TO REIMBURSE THE STATES OF CALIFORNIA, OREGON, AND NEVADA FOR MONEYS BY THEM EXPENDED IN THE SUPPRESSION OF THE REBELLION WHEN AIDING THE UNITED STATES TO MAINTAIN THE 'COMMON DEFENSE' ON THE PACIFIC COAST.'"

The facts out of which the aforesaid State war claims arise have been very fully stated in several reports heretofore made in the House of Representatives and to the Senate, as follows, to wit: House Report No. 254, and Senate Report No. 158, Fifty-second Congress, first session; House Report No. 2553, and Senate Report No. 644, Fifty-first Congress, first session; and House Report No. 3396 and Senate Reports No. 1286 and No. 2014, Fiftieth Congress, first session.

Bills relating to these State war claims of these three Pacific coast States, passed the Senate during the first session of the Fiftieth Congress, and were favorably reported to the Senate during the first session of the Fifty-first and Fifty-second Congress, and to the House during the Fiftieth, Fifty-first and Fifty-second Congresses, but were not reached for consideration by the House, in either thereof. Similar Senate bills, to wit: Nos. 101, 1062, 1295, were introduced during the first and second sessions, Fifty-third Congress, by Senators Stewart, Dolph, and White, of California, and all referred to the Senate Committee on Military Affairs. Similar House bills, to wit: H. R. No. 2615 were also introduced in the House on 11th day of September, 1893, by Mr. Caminetti, of California, House bill No. 4959, on January 3, 1894, by Mr. Maguire, of California, and both referred to the House Committee on War Claims.

Sums of money (recited in three reports made by the honorable Secretary of War to the Senate, on the State war claims and printed as Senate Ex. Docs. Nos. 10, 11, and 17, Fifty-first Congress, first session) proven to the full satisfaction of the War Department to have been expended by said States to aid the United States in the suppression of the war of the rebellion were included in the general deficiency appropriation bill as it passed the Senate during the second session of the fifty-first Congress, for the purpose of indemnifying and reimbursing said States on account and in partial liquidation of said claims, but the same were omitted from said deficiency bill as it became a law. Senate bill No. 52, and House bills No. 54 and No. 42, Fifty-second Congress, first session were in all respects identical; the last of which House bills, was, on February 10, 1892, favorably reported by the House War Claims Committee in House Report No. 254, Fifty-second Congress, first session and said Senate bill No. 52, was on February 4, 1892, favorably reported by the Senate Committee on Military Affairs in Senate Report No. 158, as follows, to wit:

[Senate Report No. 158, Fifty-second Congress, first session.]

IN THE SENATE OF THE UNITED STATES.

FEBRUARY 4, 1892.—Ordered to be printed.

Mr. Davis, from the Committee on Military Affairs, submitted the following report (to accompany S. 52):

The Committee on Military Affairs, to whom was referred the bill (S. 52) to reimburse the States of California, Oregon, and Nevada for moneys by them expended in the suppression of the rebellion, have examined the same and report as follows, to wit:

This measure was considered by this Committee during the first session of the Fifty-first Congress, and was reported upon favorably (Report No. 644).

Your committee concur in the conclusions stated in that report, and recommend the passage of the bill.

At a very early period of the war of the rebellion, nearly all the troops of the regular Army of the United States, then serving in California, Oregon, and Nevada, were withdrawn from military duty in those States and transported thence by sea to New York City at an expense to the United States of about $390,103, or at an average cost of about $284 for each commissioned officer and of about $133 for each enlisted man.

This withdrawal therefrom of said regular troops left these three Pacific coast States comparatively defenseless, and for the purpose of supplying their places, and to provide additional military forces, rendered necessary by public exigencies, calls for volunteers were made upon said States under proclamations of the President, or requisitions by the War Department, or by its highest military officers commanding the military departments on the Pacific. These calls for volunteers continued until the necessity therefor entirely ceased to exist, during which time these three Pacific coast States furnished, enlisted, equipped, enrolled, paid, and mustered into military service of the United States 18,715 volunteers, as shown in said reports so made to the Senate by the Secretary of War.

In consequence of this withdrawal in 1861 of said military forces from the Pacific coast, in order that they might perform military service in the East, and in view of the circumstances and exigencies existing in the Pacific coast States and Territories during the rebellion period, requisitions were duly made from time to time by the President of the United States and by the Secretary of War upon the proper State authorities of California, Oregon, and Nevada for volunteers to perform military service for the United States in said States and Territories, as are fully and in great detail set forth in Senate Ex. Docs. Nos. 10, 11, 17, Fifty-first Congress, first session. In compliance with the several calls and official requisitions so made between 1861 and 1866, inclusive.

Volunteers.
The State of California furnished 15,725
The State of Nevada furnished 1,180
The State of Oregon furnished 1,810

Making a total aggregate of... 18,715 men who were enlisted and were thereafter duly mustered into the military service of the United States as volunteers from said States. The same number of troops if organized in the East and transported from New York City to the Pacific coast States and Territories in the same manner as was done by the United States War Department from June 17, 1850, to August 3, 1861, would have cost the United States at that time the sum of about $5,483,385, for *transportation alone.*

The indemnification for the "costs, charges, and expenses" properly incurred by said States for enrolling, subsisting, clothing, supplying, arming, equipping, paying, transporting, and furnishing said 18,715 volunteer troops employed by the United States to aid them to maintain the "common defense," was guaranteed by the United States in the act of Congress approved July 27, 1861 (12 U. S. Stats., 276), an act entitled "An act to indemnify the States for expenses incurred by them in defense of the United States."

The then Secretary of War, Hon. Redfield Proctor, now U. S. Senator from Vermont (on p. 28 of his report, Senate Ex. Doc. No. 41, Fifty-first Congress, first session), in reporting upon the military services performed by said volunteers during the rebellion, said:

They took the places of the regular troops in California, all of which, except three batteries of artillery and one regiment of infantry, were withdrawn to the east at an early period after the outbreak of the war. Without them (and the Oregon and Nevada volunteers) the overland mail and emigrant routes, extending from the Missouri River via Great Salt Lake City to California and Oregon, and passing through an uninhabited and mountainous country infested with hostile Indians and highwaymen, could not have been adequately protected; and yet it was of the first importance to have these routes kept open and safe, especially as rebel cruisers had made the sea routes both hazardous and expensive. Two expeditions composed of California volunteers, under the command of Brig. Gens. James H. Carleton and Patrick E. Connor, respectively, performed perilous and exhausting marches across a desert and over an almost impassable country and established themselves, the latter in Utah—where, besides protecting the mail routes, a watchful eye was kept on the uncertain and sometimes threatening attitude of the Mormons—and the former in Arizona and New Mexico, which Territories were thereafter effectually guarded in the interests of the United States against Indians and rebels.

On March 3, 1863 (12 U. S. Stats., 808), Congress organized the Territory of Idaho, the extensive mineral discoveries in which, attracting thousands of miners, explorers, and immigrants, naturally necessitated an additional volunteer military force to guard and protect so extended, difficult and new Indian frontier lines.

On October 14, 1861, the Secretary of State, Hon. William H. Seward, by direction of the President of the United States, issued to the governors of all the loyal States, a circular letter, wherein the attention of the proper authorities of said States was invited to the necessity of improving and perfecting the defenses of their respective States, to be done in a manner such as should thereafter be determined by the legislature of each of said States who were to rely upon Congress to sanction their action, and to reimburse all expenses by them so incurred, Mr. Secretary Seward, expressing it as his opinion, that "such proceedings by said States would require only a temporary use of their means."

Said circular letter is as follows, to wit:

DEPARTMENT OF STATE,
Washington, October 14, 1861.

SIR: The present insurrection had not even revealed itself in arms when disloyal citizens hastened to foreign countries to invoke their intervention for the overthrow of the Government and the destruction of the Federal Union. These agents are known to have made their appeals to some of the more important States without success. It is not likely, however, that they will remain content with such refusals. Indeed, it is understood that they are industriously endeavoring to accomplish their disloyal purposes by degrees and by indirection. Taking advantage of the embarrassments of agriculture, manufacture, and commerce in foreign countries, resulting from the insurrection they have inaugurated at home, they seek to involve our common country in controversies with States with which every public interest and every interest of mankind require that it shall remain in relations of peace, amity, and friendship. I am able to state, for your satisfaction, that the prospect of any such disturbance is now less serious than it has been at any previous period since the course of the insurrection. It is nevertheless necessary now, as it has hitherto been, to take every precaution that is possible to avert the evils of foreign war to be superinduced upon those of civil commotion which we are endeavoring to cure. One of the most obvious of such precautions is that our ports and harbors on the seas and lakes should be put in a condition of complete defense, for any nation may be said to voluntarily incur danger in tempestuous seasons when it fails to show that it has sheltered itself on every side from which the storm might possibly come.

The measures which the Executive can adopt in this emergency are such only as Congress has sanctioned and for which it has provided. The President is putting forth the most diligent efforts to execute these measures, and we have the great satisfaction of seeing that these efforts, seconded by the favor, aid, and support of a loyal, patriotic, and self-sacrificing people, are rapidly bringing the military and naval forces of the United States into the highest state of efficiency. But Congress was chiefly absorbed during its recent extra session with those measures and did not provide as amply as could be wished for the fortification of our sea and lake coasts. In previous wars, loyal States have applied themselves by independent and separate activity to support and aid the Federal Government in its arduous responsibilities. The same disposition has been manifested in a degree eminently honorable by all the loyal States during the present insurrection. In view of this fact, and relying upon the increase and continuance of the same disposition on the part of the loyal States, the President has directed me to invite your consideration to the subject of the improvement and perfection of the defenses of the State over which you preside, and to ask you to submit the subject to the consideration of the legislature when it shall have assembled. Such proceedings by the State would require only a temporary use of means.

The expenditures ought to be made the subject of conference with the Federal authorities. Being thus made with the concurrence of the Government for general defense, there is every reason to believe that Congress would sanction what the State should do and would provide for its reimbursement. Should these suggestions be accepted the President will direct proper agents of the Federal Government to confer with you and to superintend, direct, and conduct the prosecution of the system of defense of your State.

I have the honor to be, sir, your obedient servant,

WILLIAM H. SEWARD.

His Excellency THOMAS H. HICKS,
    Governor of the State of Maryland.

The Attorney-General of the United States, on June 11, 1891, in rendering an opinion, at the request of the honorable Secretary of the Treasury, involving a question as to the "State war claims of the State of Vermont against the United States," declared that the defense of the State of Vermont by said State during the war of the rebellion, as recited in his said opinion, was the defense of the United States, and that all expenses so incurred by said State in repelling invasion and in preparing to resist attacks, etc., constitute valid charges against the United States to be paid out of the public Treasury.

From June 17, 1850, and continuously until August 3, 1861, the practice of the War Department under the laws of Congress was to pay each soldier, enlisted, recruited, or re-enlisted in the State of California, Oregon, and Nevada, a sum of money which, while Congress termed it a "bounty," yet it in fact and effect was, and was intended to be merely extra or additional pay in the form of a constructive mileage equivalent to the cost of transporting a soldier from New York City to the place of such enlistment or re-enlistment; said sum was to be paid to each Pacific coast soldier in installments, in the amounts, at the times, and in the manner as recited in the act of Congress therefor, approved June 17, 1850, the third section of which reads as follows:

SEC. 3. *And be it further enacted,* That whenever enlistments are made at or in the vicinity of, the said military posts, and remote and distant stations, a bounty equal in amount to the cost of transporting and subsisting a soldier from the principal recruiting depot in the harbor of New York, to the place of such enlistment, be, and the same is hereby, allowed to each recruit so enlisted, to be paid in unequal installments at the end of each year's service, so that the several amounts shall annually increase, and the largest be paid at the expiration of each enlistment. (U. S. Stat., vol. 9, p. 439.)

Congress, during the rebellion, changed the manner of maintaining a military force in these three Pacific coast States by relying, to a very large degree, if not almost exclusively, upon volunteers to be enlisted and raised therein, and wherefore, on August 3, 1861, repealed said law. (12 U. S. Stats., sec. 9, p. 289.)

In consequence of the high cost of living in California and Oregon, Congress, on 28th September, 1850, passed an act paying to every commissioned officer serving in those States an extra $2 per day, and to all the enlisted men serving in the U. S. Army in those States double the pay then being paid to the troops of the regular Army. This law is as follows, to wit:

For extra pay to the commissioned officers and enlisted men of the Army of the United States, serving in Oregon or California, three hundred and twenty-five thousand eight hundred and fifty-four dollars, on the following basis, to wit: That there shall be allowed to each commissioned officer as aforesaid, whilst serving as aforesaid, a per diem, in addition to their regular pay and allowances, of two dollars each, and to each enlisted man as aforesaid, whilst serving as aforesaid, a per diem, in addition to their present pay and allowances, equal to the pay proper of each as established by existing laws, said extra pay of the enlisted men to be retained until honorably discharged. This additional pay to continue until the first of March, eighteen hundred and fifty-two, or until otherwise provided. (U. S. Stat., vol. 9, p. 504.)

It will be here noticed that under these two acts of Congress, the one of the 17th of June, 1850, and the other of the 28th of September, 1850, the so-called "extra pay" and the so-called "bounty" or constructive mileage, were both paid during one and the same period of time by the United States to its own troops serving in the regular United States Army stationed in these States.

If the necessity for this character of legislation for the regular Army of the United States recited in these two acts existed in a time of profound peace—and no one doubts but that a necessity therefor did exist—then how much greater the necessity for similar legislation in a period of actual war, when the land carriage for supplies over a distance of 2.000 miles, from the Missouri River to these Pacific coast States, was simply impossible, or at least impracticable, there not being then any overland railroads, and the two sea routes via Cape Horn and the Isthmus of Panama, as recited in the said reports of the Secretary of War, being both hazardous and expensive?

The condition of public affairs existing in these Pacific coast States in the early part of 1863 is recited on pages 25 and 26 of House Report No. 254, Fifty-second Congress, first session, in words as follows, to wit:

In the early part of April, 1863, the overland mail and emigrant route was attacked by Indians and communication was closed between the Atlantic States and the Pacific coast. This route extended from the Missouri River to California via the Platte River, Salt Lake City, through Nevada to Sacramento, in California, and was the only means at that date of direct overland communication between the Missouri River and California. At this time the gold discoveries in California continued to invite a large immigration, the interest in which was more or less intensified by the continued extensive silver discoveries in Nevada Territory, and principally on the Comstock lode, in the western part of the Territory. The routes via Cape Horn, and especially that via the Isthmus of Panama, were rendered extremely doubtful, dangerous, and expensive, on account of Confederate privateer cruisers hovering around the West India Islands and along both these sea routes, and in anticipation of other Confederate cruiser infesting the waters of the Pacific (which soon thereafter became the theater of the operations and extensive depredations of the Confederate privateer *Shenandoah*), the overland route, therefore, although in itself both dangerous and difficult, was yet considered the better and preferable route by which to reach the Pacific.

On account of a general uprising of the Indians along the entire overland route, and especially that portion between Salt Lake City, in the Territory of Utah, and the Sierra Nevada Mountains, and because of the doubts as to the loyalty of the Mormons to the Government of the United States, the maintenance and protection of the mail and emigrant route through that section of the country and along the aforesaid line was regarded by the Government as a military necessity. Apparently in anticipation of no immediate danger of attack on the Pacific coast, nearly all the troops of the regular Army at this time had been withdrawn from service throughout this entire region of country and transferred east to other fields of military operations. This left the entire country between Salt Lake City and the Sierra Nevada Mountains without adequate and efficient military protection. The Government thus having but few troops of its regular Army in that region, was therefore compelled to call upon the inhabitants of Nevada Territory to raise and organize volunteer military companies to suppress Indian disturbances which threatened the entire suspension of all mail facilities and emigration from the East, as will be hereafter shown.

At the time of the calls upon Nevada for troops the prices of labor and supplies of all descriptions in Nevada were extremely high. There were then no railroads, and the snow on the Sierra Nevada Mountains formed an almost impassable barrier against teams from about the 1st of December until about June. The average cost of freight from San Francisco, the main source of supply for western Nevada, was about $80 a ton, and it was necessary to lay in supplies during the summer and fall for the remainder of the year. A great mining excitement prevailed at this time, occasioned by the marvelous development of the great Comstock lode, and wages were from $4 to $10 a day, in gold. The people who had emigrated to the new gold and silver fields went there for the purpose of mining and prospecting for mines, and were generally reluctant to enter the irregular military service of guarding the overland mail and emigrant route. Besides, on account of the extraordinary high price of supplies of every description, and also of wages and services of every kind, it was impossible for them to maintain themselves and familes without involving much more expense than any compensation which could be paid them as volunteer troops under the laws of the United States, and, as will be seen by the letters of Gen. Wright, hereafter quoted, they were expected, as volunteer troops, to furnish themselves with horses and equipments, in addition to what could be furnished by the Government.

The military authorities of the United States well knew at that time the exact condition of the country and of the roads across the mountains leading thereto and of the cost of transportation and of the prices of labor and of supplies and of their own inability to furnish either horses or equipments for a military service that required mounted troops.

It was amid circumstances like these that the honorable Secretary of the Treasury, by telegraphic instructions to the assistant treasurer of the United States at San Francisco, Cal., under date of February 9, 1863 (on which date there was on deposit in the subtreasury at San Francisco, to the credit of the United States, a large amount of gold and silver coin), directed the paymasters of the Army to pay said volunteers in U. S. notes, commonly called greenbacks. An exemplification of the effect of such instructions is reported by the Secretary of War on pp. 40 and 41, Senate Ex. Doc. No. 11, Fifty-first Congress, first session, in words as follows, to wit:

EXHIBIT No. 10.

DEPUTY PAYMASTER-GENERAL'S OFFICE,
San Francisco, February 13, 1863.

SIR: Yesterday payment of my checks was refused by the assistant treasurer in San Francisco. In reply to a note which I addressed him, I received the following:

"OFFICE OF THE ASSISTANT TREASURER UNITED STATES,
"*San Francisco, February 2, 1863.*

"SIR: Your communication of this date relative to the check of $80,000 presented but a few minutes since by Maj. Eddy and payment declined by me, etc., is just received.'

"Under instructions from the honorable Secretary of the Treasury United States of February 9, 1863, I am advised that 'checks of disbursing officers must be paid in United States notes.' Not having notes on hand sufficient to meet the check presented and referred to you has compelled me to decline payment of the same for the time being.

"Respectfully, your obedient servant,
"D. W. CHEESEMAN,
"*Assistant Treasurer, United States.*

"GEORGE H. RINGGOLD,
"*Deputy Paymaster-General U. S. Army.*"

The effect of these instructions is abruptly to stop payment of the troops. I had drawn out a sufficiency, principally in coin, to pay the posts in Oregon and a portion of the troops in this immediate vicinity; the delay will, I fear, cause great dissatisfaction to those remaining unpaid, as there was a confident expectation that they would now be paid off and in coin.

In connection with the above statement, I deem proper to forward herewith a copy of a letter recently received from Maj. Drew, of the Oregon cavalry, which so clearly sets forth the condition of things as regards legal tenders on this coast as to make comment on my part superfluous, except simply to add that gold is the only currency here, and that U. S. Treasury notes are worth only what they will bring on the street. They are quoted at 61 to-day.

I have the honor to remain, very respectfully, your obedient servant,
GEO. H. RINGGOLD,
Deputy Paymaster-General.

Lieut. Col. T. P. ANDREWS,
Acting Paymaster-General U. S. Army.

Respectfully referred to Treasurer of the United States with the request that the funds may be sent to assistant treasurer at San Francisco to meet the drafts in favor of paymasters, and to return these papers for such other action as may be necessary.

T. P. ANDREWS,
Paymaster-General.

PAYMASTER-GENERAL'S OFFICE, *March 18, 1863.*

If the Treasurer would be kind enough to furnish us with any suggestions from the Treasury that would tend to do away the causes of complaint in this, to us, difficult case, we should feel indebted.

T. P. ANDREWS,
Paymaster-General.

PAYMASTER-GENERAL'S OFFICE, *March 18, 1863.*

TREASURER'S OFFICE, *March 19, 1863.*
Respectfully referred to the Secretary of the Treasury.
F. E. SPINNER,
Treasurer United States.

Concerning the foregoing condition of financial affairs in these three States and the effect thereof upon their volunteer troops then serving in the U. S. Army in the Department of the Pacific, the honorable Secretary of War (House Report No. 254, Fifty-second Congress, first session, p. 20) reported as follows, to wit:

It appears that up to December 31, 1862, those of the U. S. troops serving in the Department of the Pacific who were paid at all—in some cases detachments had not been paid for a year or more—were generally paid in coin, but on February 9, 1863, instructions were issued from the Treasury Department to the assistant treasurer of the United States at San Francisco that "checks of disbursing officers must be paid in United States notes." (Letter of Deputy Paymaster-General George H. Ringgold, dated February 13, 1863, to Paymaster-General; copy herewith marked Exhibit No. 10.)

Before this greenbacks had become the current medium of exchange in all ordinary business transactions in the Eastern States, but in the Pacific coast States and the adjoining Territories gold continued to be the basis of circulation throughout the war. At this time the paper currency had become greatly depreciated, and on February 28, 1863, the price of gold in Treasury notes touched 170. This action of the

Government in compelling troops to accept such notes as an equivalent of gold in payment for services rendered by them in a section where coin alone was current gave rise to much dissatisfaction; for although gold could be bought in San Francisco at nearly the same price in Treasury notes as in New York, it must be remembered that the troops in the Department of the Pacific were largely stationed at remote and isolated points.

When paying in greenbacks for articles purchased by or for services rendered to them in these out-of-way places, they were obliged to submit not only to the current discount in San Francisco, but also to a further loss occasioned by the desire of the persons who sold the articles or rendered the service to protect themselves against possible further depreciation. It admits of little doubt that by reason of his inability to realize the full value of paper money, as quoted in the money centers, and of the fact that wages and the cost of living and of commodities of every kind were abnormally high (owing in great part to the development of newly-discovered mines in that region), the purchasing power of the greenback dollar in the hands of the average soldier serving in the Department of the Pacific was from the latter part of 1862 onward from 25 to 50 per cent less than that of the same dollar paid to his fellow soldier in the East.

Representations of the great hardships the Treasury Department's instructions entailed upon the troops were promptly made. On March 10, 1863, the legislature telegraphed to Washington a resolution adopted on that date instructing the State's delegation in Congress to impress upon the Executive "the necessity which exists of having officers and soldiers of the U. S. Army, officers, seamen, and marines of the U. S. Navy, and all citizen employés in the service of the Government of the United States serving west of the Rocky Mountains and on the Pacific coast paid their salaries and pay in gold and silver currency of the United States, provided the same be paid in as revenue on this coast." (P. 46, Statement for Senate Committee on Military Affairs.)

And on March 16, 1863, Brig. Gen. G. Wright, the commander of the Department of the Pacific (comprising, besides California, the State of Oregon and the Territories of Nevada, Utah, and Arizona), transmitted to the Adjutant-General of the U. S. Army a letter of Maj. C. S. Drew, First Oregon Cavalry, commandant at Camp Baker, Oreg., containing an explicit statement of the effects of and a formal protest against paying his men in greenbacks. In his letter of transmittal (p. 154, Ex. Doc. 70), Gen. Wright remarked as follows:

"The difficulties and embarrassments enumerated in the major's communication are common to all the troops in this department, and I most respectfully ask the serious consideration of the General-in-Chief and the War Department to this subject. Most of the troops would prefer waiting for their pay to receiving notes worth but little more than half their face; but even at this ruinous discount officers, unless they have private means, are compelled to receive the notes. Knowing the difficulties experienced by the Government in procuring coin to pay the Army, I feel great reluctance in submitting any grievances from this remote department, but justice to the officers and soldiers demands that a fair statement should be made to the War Department."

The letter of Maj. C. S. Drew referred to by the honorable Secretary of War in the foregoing report is printed on p. 154, Sen. Ex. Doc. No. 17, Fifty-first Congress, first session, and is as follows, to wit:

CAMP BAKER, OREG., *March 4, 1863.*

COLONEL: I inclose herewith, for the consideration of the commanding general, the resignation of Asst. Surg. D. S. Holton, First Cavalry, Oregon Volunteers. Dr. Holton is a zealous and faithful officer, and I regret that circumstances, those which he sets forth, render it necessary for him to leave the service. But knowing the facts in the premises I must nevertheless recommend, as I now do, that his resignation be accepted. While upon the subject of resignations I beg to remark that the cause assigned by Dr. Holton for his resignation is valid and sufficient, doubtless, for its acceptance. But there is another which in its practical workings is almost as potent, and which precludes the possibility for any of the officers at this post to remain much longer in the service. I allude to their nonpayment since they entered the service, as also that of the entire command. This has borne heavily upon the officers, more especially as they have been compelled to hire money, some of them for more than a year past, with which to purchase their horses and equipments and to defray personal expenses. The act of Congress of June 18, 1862, requiring "that company officers of volunteers," and unjustly applied to the field and staff of regiments also, "shall be paid on the muster and pay rolls," has worked a great injury to the officers here, as it has, no doubt, in other portions of this department, by inhibiting the use of "pay accounts," which in our case could have been used as collaterals, at or near their face, in obtaining the money for our expenditures. But no such arrangement could be effected under the new regulations, as by its requirements the death of the officer or his removal to other and distant post would enhance the probability of a delay in payment of his indebtedness and increase the risk and expense attending its final collection. Hence the greater rate of interest charged.

But this is not all. The money borrowed has been specie, and must be paid in the same currency, while payment to the officers is liable to be made in Treasury notes, worth here not more than 50 to 55 cents per dollar, and very little sale for them even at those low figures; thus, practically, with the interest which has accrued on the amount borrowed, it will require more than $2 of the money in which the officer is paid to repay $1 of that which he owes. With this condition of things, too, each officer and soldier of this command is serving for less than half pay, and have done so, some of them, for more than sixteen months past. Under these circumstances it must be impossible for any of the officers here to serve much longer without becoming irretrievably bankrupt and bringing upon themselves all the contumely and reproach that such misfortune is always sure to create. But private injury is not all that this delay and final mode of payment inflicts. It is exceedingly detrimental to the public service generally, as without any stated market value to the notes, and no surety as to when payment in them, even, will be made, in every purchase or other expenditure made here, not only the current San Francisco discount on the notes is added to the specie value of the article or service, but, in addition to all this, a large percentage for the risk of a further depreciation in their value, and a vexatious delay in payment.

It is thus that capital protects itself from loss, and perhaps realizes better profits than under the old and better system of payment in coin. But the soldier has not this power, not even that to protect himself against loss, and if paid in notes must necessarily receipt in full for what is equivalent to him of half pay or less, for the service he has rendered, and must continue to fulfill his part of his contract with the Government for the same reduced rate of pay, until his period of service shall terminate. This, in its practical results, is making a distinction between capital and labor, or personal service, unfriendly and injurious to the latter, that I am sure was never contemplated or designed by the War Department, and its abolishment here at least would be of much advantage to the service, besides meting out but simple justice to long-deferred creditors, and at no greater cost to the Government. This delay and uncertainty about the payment of the troops at this post is also working a public injury by preventing enlistments in this part of Oregon, in any considerable number, for the new companies ordered to fill this regiment. Good men will not enlist for $6 or $7 a month while $13 is the regular pay, and moreover, being realized by every soldier in any other department than the Pacific. Men who would enlist under these circumstances are, as a general rule, entirely worthless for soldiers or anything else, and would be an incubus upon the service if permitted to join it.

I beg to be understood as reporting the condition of things actually existing here, and not as I would have them. Neither would I be understood as casting any censure whatever upon any officer of this department. I am aware that Col. Ringgold would have taken as favorable action in our case with regard to payment as he has at any other post, had it not have been for the unfortunate order of the Secretary of the Treasury that his drafts should be paid in notes, and at a time too when there were no notes on hand. I trust that the commanding general will give us a word of encouragement, if in his power, so that it may be imparted to the men of this command, many of whom are becoming somewhat alarmed as to their pay and as to the currency to be used in payment.

I am, colonel, very respectfully, your obedient servant,

C. S. DREW,
Major First Cavalry, Oregon Volunteers.

RICHARD C. DRUM,
  Assistant Adjutant-General, U. S. Army,
    Headquarters Department of the Pacific, San Francisco, Cal.

This action was had by the authorities of the United States notwithstanding the contents of General Orders No. 16 from the Headquarters of the Army, issued on September 3, 1861, which is as follows, to wit:

[General Orders, No. 16.]

HEADQUARTERS OF THE ARMY,
Washington, September 3, 1861.

The general in chief is happy to announce that the Treasury Department—to meet future payments to the troops—is about to supply, besides coin, as heretofore, Treasnry notes in fives, tens, and twenties, as good as gold at all banks and Government offices throughout the United States, and most convenient for transmission by mail from officers and men to their families at home. Good husbands, fathers, sons, and brothers, serving under the Stars and Stripes, will thus soon have the ready and safe means of relieving an immense amount of suffering which could not be reached with coin.

In making up such packages every officer may be relied upon, no doubt, for such assistance as may be needed by his men.

By command of Lieut. Gen. Scott,

E. D. TOWNSEND,
Assistant Adjutant-General.

In consequence of the foregoing, formal protests were duly forwarded to the War Department by the commanding general, Division of the Pacific, and legislative appeals by these States were made direct to Congress to come to the relief of the volunteers then serving the United States in these Pacific coast States, by increasing to living rates the pay of said troops.   But all such protests, appeals, and representations in behalf of these troops proved, in the language of the Secretary of War, " perfectly futile."

The reports of the honorable Secretary of War on this subject recite as follows, to wit:

It was under circumstances and exigencies such as these that the legislatures themselves—all appeals to the General Government having proved futile—provided the necessary relief by the law of April 27, 1863.   They did not even after that relax their efforts on behalf of the United States troops, other than their own volunteers, serving among them, but on April 1, 1864, adopted a resolution requesting their representatives in Congress to "use their influence in procuring the passage of a law giving to the officers and soldiers of the regular Army stationed on the Pacific coast an increase of their pay, amounting to 30 per cent on the amount now allowed by law." (Senate Ex. Doc. No. 17, Fifty-first Congress, first session, p. 14.)

It was under and amid national financial embarrassments like these that these three Pacific coast States (California taking the lead, and Oregon and Nevada following in due course, and California not moving therein until April 27, 1863) felt compelled to come to the relief of their own volunteers, then serving in the U. S. Army therein, and passed acts through their respective legislatures, under and by which each volunteer in each of said States was to be paid the sum of $5 per month, and in order to raise the money with which to pay the same, said States, under appropriate acts of their respective legislatures hereinafter recited, issued and sold their State gold bonds, and paid said $5 per month, in gold coin, to their said volunteers.

In 1864 the period of the three years' enlistments of the volunteers in these States who had been mustered in 1861 into the military service of the United States was approaching termination. These volunteers were in the field, scattered throughout the deserts of Arizona and New Mexico, in the South; in Washington Territory, in the North; along the Western slopes of the Rocky Mountains, in the East; and guarding the immigrant and overland mail routes and pony express lines, extending from the Missouri River to the Pacific Ocean, which duties, onerous and vexatious, were soon to be supplemented by others equally so in protecting and escorting exploring, reconnoitering, and surveying parties, about to engage in running preliminary lines of overland railroad surveys for the Central and Union Pacific railroads, rendering it necessary, not only to maintain an adequate military force, then in the field, but to provide for exigencies in the near future, which seemed to render an additional volunteer military force absolutely necessary.

The war in the East was still flagrant, and no one could then foretell the end thereof. Gen. Lee had just invaded Pennsylvania with a large army, and though defeated at Gettysburg, yet extensive and devastating raids were made into the State of Pennsylvania by the Confederate forces as late as July, 1864, by Gens. Early, Johnson, and McCausland, the effects of which are represented to have been even more disastrous to the people of that State than those arising from the raids made therein in 1862 by Gen. Zeb. Stuart, of the Confederate cavalry. Chambersburg, Pa., was burned on July 30, 1864, the Confederates destroying extensive properties in the counties of Adams, Bedford, Cumberland, Franklin, Fulton, Perry, Somerset, and York, lying along the southern border of Pennsylvania and adjoining the northern Maryland line, the value of which property so destroyed is reported to have aggregated a very large sum.

In addition to the foregoing, attention is called to the official decisions rendered in September, 1863, by the Second Comptroller of the Treasury, Hon. John M. Brodhead, to the effect that the volunteers of these and other States then serving in the Army of the United States, who should be discharged by virtue of reenlistments as veteran volunteers, *should not receive any mileage* from the places of their discharge to the places of their original enrollment. (See Second Comptroller's Decisions, September 8 and 9, 1863, vol. 25, pp. 422 and 425, printed as section 2192, on p. 283 of Digest of Second Comptroller's Decisions, vol. 1, 1861 to 1868.)

However valid these decisions may have been as declaratory of the intentions of the law as then viewed by the Treasury Department, yet the practical effect thereof was to discourage reenlistments in the case of these volunteers from California, about to be discharged in New Mexico, where they were serving at the dates of said decisions, many hundreds of miles from the places of their original enrollment. Under these decisions the United States paid a bounty or mileage to those volunteers *who did not reenlist in the U. S. Army,* but refused to pay it to those who did so reenlist.

The serious, in fact, alarming effect of these decisions of the honorable Second Comptroller upon the military condition of affairs in Arizona and New Mexico, where several regiments of these California volunteers were then serving, is shown by the great anxiety and serious concern of Brig. Gen. James H. Carleton, of the regular Army of the United States, commanding the department of New Mexico, so much so, that he made it the subject of a special report to the adjutant-general of the Army, at Washington, D. C., recited on pp. 60 and 61 (Report of Secretary of War, Senate Ex. Doc. No. 11, Fifty-first Congress, first session, in words as follows, to wit:

EXHIBIT No. 22.

HEADQUARTERS DEPARTMENT OF NEW MEXICO,
Santa Fé, N. Mex., November 29, 1863.

GENERAL: Until Mr. Brodhead's decision was made, that volunteers who should be discharged by enlistment in veteran volunteers should not receive their mileage from the place of said discharge to the place of original enrollment, I entertained hopes that many, if not most, of the First and Fifth Regiments of Infantry, of the First Cavalry California Volunteers, and First Cavalry New Mexican Volunteers, would reenlist in the veteran volunteers. But since that decision was made it is very doubtful if the California volunteers will reenlist. Their present term of office will expire next August and September. Before that time other troops will have to be sent here to take their places, unless these can be induced to reenlist. The troops in this department should be made an exception to the general rule. In my opinion an order should be made giving all volunteers who reenlist in this department the $100 due on first enlistment and an increased bounty on the second over and above the bounty paid to soldiers in the East, which would be equal to the cost of getting soldiers from the East to New Mexico. The Government in this way would lose nothing, but would rather gain, because these well-disciplined men would then remain, doubtless, and they have now become familiar with the country, and can do better service for that reason than any new comers. These men should receive their mileage on their first enlistment. In my opinion, the law clearly allows it to soldiers honorably discharged. If the Government do not deny their traveling allowances and will give the bounty named, I believe the most of these regiments can be got to remain. If the Government will not do this, I beg to give timely notice of the necessities which will exist to have troops sent to take their places in time to be in position before the term of service of these men expire.

The California troops do not wish to be sent as regiments back to California; they would rather be discharged here in case they do not reenlist. Some desire to go to the States, some to the gold fields of Arizona, some settle in New Mexico, and some go to California by whatever route they please. The true economy of the question would be promoted by making the bounties so liberal as to induce them to reenter the service for three years or during the war.

I am, general, very truly and respectfully, your obedient servant,
CHARLES H. CARLETON,
Brigadier-General, Commanding.

Brig. Gen. LORENZO THOMAS,
Adjutant-General, U. S. Army, Washington, D. C.

DEPARTMENT NEW MEXICO,
Santa Fé, N. Mex., July 12, 1865.

Official:

BEN. C. CUTLER,
Assistant Adjutant-General.

These three Pacific Coast States therefore and in consequence of the foregoing facts determined for the benefit of their respective volunteers who might reenlist (and thereby successfully retain veteran soldiers in the military service of the United States), or, who after April, 1864, should enlist for the first time in the U. S. Army, then serving in these States, to revive substantially the provisions of the aforesaid act of Congress of June 17, 1850, which had been in existence for the benefit of the U. S. Army serving on the Pacific coast, continuously from June 17, 1850, to August 3, 1861. Under the provisions of said act each volunteer soldier of these States, so enlisting or reenlisting in the U. S. Army after April 4, 1864 (the date of the California act for this specific purpose), was to be paid in installments, at the time and in the manner substantially as recited in said Congressional act of June 17, 1850, a sum of money assumed to be equal to the cost of transporting a soldier from New York City to the place of reenlistment or the enlistment of such volunteer soldier. In view of the scattered military stations of said Pacific coast volunteers—extending, as they did, from Arizona on the south, to Puget Sound on the north; and from San Francisco on the west to Salt Lake City on the east; this sum was fixed by all three of said States at $160 per each volunteer soldier, which sum at that time substantially represented about the average cost which the United States would have had to pay to transport a soldier from New York City to the places of such enlistment or reenlistment of said volunteers in said three States.

These three States, in reviving said act of Congress of June 17, 1850, in the manner and for the purposes therein recited, used substantially the identical language which Congress had used in said act, by calling said sum of money a "bounty," when, as aforesaid, it was, and was only intended to be, a *constructive mileage,* and which was paid by these States out of their respective State treasuries for the use and benefit of the United States in aid of the "common defense" during the war of the rebellion, but not beginning until after April 4, 1864, and as contemplated by said act of Congress of July 27, 1861 (12 U. S. Stats., 276), and Joint Resolution 5 of March 8, 1862 (12 U. S. Stats., 615), and of March 19, 1862 (12 U. S. Stats., 616). In reference to this matter the Secretary of War, in Senate Ex. No. 11, pp. 22 and 23, Fifty-first Congress, first session, reported to the Senate as follows, to wit:

With respect to the circumstances and exigencies under which this expenditure was incurred by the State, it appears to be plain that it was the earnest desire of the legislature that such troops as the State had been or might thereafter be called upon to furnish the General Government should be promptly supplied. The time was approaching when the terms of most of the volunteer regiments raised in California in the early part of the war would expire. These regiments were occupying important stations in the State and in Territories of Utah, Arizona, and New Mexico, and it was obvious that it would become necessary either to continue them in service by filling them up with new recruits or reenlisted veterans, or, in the event of their disbandment, to replace them by new organizations. Volunteering under the calls of the previous year had progressed tardily, while lucrative employment in the State was abundant and the material inducements for men to enter the army were small. It was probable that unless these latter were considerably increased, recruiting would come to a standstill, and a draft, as in the Eastern States, have to be resorted to. That a draft in California was considered possible, and even probable, is shown by an official letter, written January 8, 1864, to the Adjutant-General of the Army by General Wright, commanding Department of the Pacific, in which he expressed the hope "of procuring quite a number of men who would prefer volunteering to running the chance of being drafted." (P. 205, Senate Ex. Doc. 70, Fiftieth Congress, second session.) The expectation that the mere fear of a draft would sufficiently stimulate volunteering had not, some months later, been realized; and under all circumstances, and prompted by the desire above mentioned, the legislature doubtless deemed it wise to enact the bounty law of April 4, 1864.

Attention is called in "Statement for Senate Committee on Military Affairs" (p. 27) to the third section of an act of Congress (9 U. S. Stats., 439) granting to persons enlisting on the Western frontier, and at remote and distant stations, a bounty equal in amount to the cost of transporting and subsisting soldiers from the principal recruiting depot in the harbor of New York to the place of enlistment, and it is argued that if it was just, proper, and expedient to grant such a bounty to men enlisting in the regular Army in such localities in time of peace, the allowance by California of a bounty to its volunteers when they were in the actual and active service of the United States in time of war, and "while the exigencies exceeded in degree those under which the United States have heretofore paid a much larger sum to its own regular Army serving in said States (of California, Oregon, and Nevada) in a time of peace, may be deemed to have been in harmony with the policy so long and so frequently executed by the United States.

These "costs, charges and expenses" so incurred by these States were:

(1) Military expenditures for recruiting volunteers.

(2) Military expenditures in organizing and paying volunteers.

(3) Military expenditures in and for Adjutant-General's Office.

(4) Military expenditures in paying volunteer commissioned officers between date of service and date of muster-in by the proper mustering officers of the United States.

(5) Military expenditures of a general and miscellaneous character.

All "costs, charges, and expenses" for the military services of the *militia* in all these States were *suspended* by the Secretary of War and are excluded from the present claims in accordance with recommendations heretofore made by the Committee on Military Affairs in the Senate and by the Committee on War Claims in the House.

Attention is specially called to the aforesaid two important resolutions of Congress adopted, the one on the 8th and the other on the 19th of March, 1862, the object of the first of which was to explain the aforesaid act of Congress of July 27, 1861, and the object of the second was to encourage and invite appropriations of money to be made by the several States as they might deem to be appropriate in the interests of the United States and wherein the obligation existed that the United

States should indemnify by fully reimbursing the several States out of any money in the Federal Treasury not otherwise appropriated, the sums of money which such States should appropriate and expend for the uses and purposes recited in the acts of the legislature of each State so appropriating the same. (12 U. S. Stats., 615-616.) These two resolutions are in words as follows, to wit:

A RESOLUTION declaratory of the intent and meaning of a certain act therein named.

Whereas doubts have arisen as to the true intent and meaning of act numbered eighteen, entitled "An act to *indemnify* the States for expenses incurred by them in "Defence of the United States," approved July twenty-seven, eighteen hundred and sixty-one (12 U. S. Stats., 276):

Be it resolved by the Senate and House of Representatives of the United States of America in Congress assembled, That the said act shall be construed to apply to expenses incurred as well after as before the date of the approval thereof.

Approved March 8, 1862 (12 U. S. Stats., 615.)

A RESOLUTION to authorize the Secretary of War to accept moneys appropriated by any State for the payment of its volunteers and to apply the same as directed by such State.

Resolved by the Senate and House of Representatives of the United States of America in Congress assembled, That if any State during the present rebellion shall make any appropriation to pay the volunteers of that State, the Secretary of War is hereby authorized to accept the same, and cause it to be applied by the paymaster-general to the payments designated by the legislative act making the appropriation, in the same manner as if appropriated by act of Congress; and also to make any regulations that may be necessary for the disbursement and proper application of such funds to the specific purpose for which they may be appropriated by the several States.

Approved, March 19, 1862 (12 U. S. Stats., 616.)

In other words, the legislation enacted by Congress in said act and in these resolutions, taken in connection with subsequent similar legislation duly enacted by these States, constituted in effect and intendment, statutory contracts binding upon the United States. It is evident that Congress, in advance of all legislative acts, by these three States, making appropriations of money for their said volunteers, duly declared that all moneys appropriated by their respective legislatures, and paid out of their respective State treasuries, intended for the exclusive use and benefit of their said volunteers, theretofore, then, or thereafter serving in the military service of the United States, should be accepted by the United States, through the Secretary of War, and paid to the State volunteers of the States so appropriating said moneys, for the specific uses and purposes for which said States had so appropriated the same, and in the same manner, for the same purposes, and to the same extent as if said moneys had been actually paid directly out of the Federal Treasury, under acts of Congress, appropriating the same. In other words, Congress approved, ratified, and confirmed *in advance* all these appropriations of money so made by the legislatures of these three States, and in fact, intendment and effect, Congress made these State appropriation acts its own acts, the provisions of which should be duly administered by its own proper officers for the objects and purposes as recited in said State acts. These three Pacific coast States substantially conformed to this legislation of Congress, and strictly followed the same in all particulars, wherein the same was not inhibited by the State constitutions or by the State laws of said States.

A copy of this resolution of Congress, adopted March 19, 1862, was, on July 5, 1863, duly transmitted by Gen. George Wright, commanding the military department of the Pacific, to the governor of California, Hon. Leland Stanford, late Senator from California. The correspondence relating thereto is reported by the Secretary of War on page 183, Senate Ex. Doc. No. 11, Fifty-first Congress, first session, and is as follows, to wit:

HEADQUARTERS DEPARTMENT OF THE PACIFIC,
San Francisco, Cal., July 5, 1863.

His Excellency LELAND STANFORD
Governor, State of California, Sacramento City, Cal.:

SIR: Inclosed herewith I have the honor to lay before your excellency a resolution to authorize the Secretary of War to accept moneys appropriated by any State for the payment of its volunteers, and to apply the same as directed by such State, approved March 19, 1862.

Under the provisions of this resolution Lieut. Col. George H. Ringgold, deputy paymaster-general at my headquarters, will accept any moneys which have been or which may be appropriated for the purpose set forth, and cause it to be applied to the payments designated by the legislative acts.

With great respect, I have the honor to be your excellency's obedient servant,
G. WRIGHT,
Brigadier-General, Commanding.

———

STATE OF CALIFORNIA, EXECUTIVE DEPARTMENT,
Sacramento, July 16, 1863.

Gen. GEORGE WRIGHT,
Commanding Department of the Pacific:

SIR: Your favor of the 5th instant, with resolution relative to appropriations for the relief of volunteers in the several States, is at hand.

By reference to sections 3 and 4 of the act of the legislature approved April 27, 1863 (Statutes of 1863, folio 662), you will observe that the requirements of the law are such as to preclude our State officers from departing from its provisions, and would therefore be impossible to pay out the appropriations *in the manner* indicated by the resolution of Congress.

I am, general, very respectfully, your obedient servant,
LELAND STANFORD,
Governor of California.

The particular method, form, or manner of payment to these volunteers of the specific sums of money so appropriated by these States was not made the essence of these contracts. It is a fair and reasonable construction of said legislation of Congress to say that that which was anticipated was the *substance* rather than the form; that which was requisite being, only, that the moneys so appropriated by said States should in fact be paid to their said volunteers, all of which was done by paying said volunteers upon official muster rolls duly furnished their State adjutants-general by the colonels of these volunteer regiments, by and through which said moneys were paid directly to said volunteers for the uses and purposes recited in said State acts.

If Congress, in enacting its aforesaid legislation of July 27, 1861, March 8, 1862, and March 19, 1862, did not intend to indemnify and reimburse these States the money which they, in the exercise of the wise discretion of their own respective legislatures, should appropriate and cause to be paid to their volunteers serving in the Army of the United States during the war of the rebellion, it may then be very pertinently asked what object did Congress have in enacting such legislation?

It is submitted that these three States fully expected that these appropriations of money so made and advanced through their own legislatures to the United States, and paid to their said volunteers then serving in the Army of the United States as a part of the military establishment on the Pacific coast during the war of the rebellion, should be fully reimbursed to them. In addition to the foregoing these three States had been urged to make these very appropriations of money by Gen. George Wright, commanding the Department of the Pacific, and by Gen. Irwin McDowell, commanding the Division or Department of California and Nevada, and by Gen. Benjamin Alvord, commanding the Department of Oregon, for the reimbursement of all of which appropriations they relied, not only upon the public exigencies which demanded such appropriations of money on their part, but wherein they rested their action upon the legal and equitable obligations of the United States in all these premises to reimburse the same.

(1) In the recitals contained in said circular letter of the Secretary of State, Hon. William H. Seward, of October 14, 1861, addressed to the governors of the loyal States, prepared, issued, and proclaimed by order of the President of the United States. This order and act of Mr. Secretary Seward were the order and act of the President of the United States, and as such were in fact and in law the order and act of Congress itself, because Congress (12 U. S. Stats., 326) had declared—

That all the acts, proclamations, and orders of the President of the United States after the 4th of March, 1861, respecting the Army and Navy of the United States, and calling out or relating to the militia or volunteers from the States, are hereby approved and in all respects legalized and made valid to the same extent and with the same effect as if they had been issued and done under the previous express authority and direction of the Congress of the United States.

(2) In the act of Congress of July 27, 1861 (12 U. S. Stats., p. 276), as legislatively construed and explained by Congress itself in its resolution adopted March 8, 1862 (12 U. S. Stats., 615).

(3) In the unrestricted resolution adopted by Congress March 19, 1862 (12 U. S. Stats., 616).

(4) In the official acts of Gen. George Wright, U. S. Army, commanding the military Division of the Pacific, and the similar acts of Gen. Irwin McDowell, U. S. Army, commanding the military Department of California and Nevada, and the similar acts of Gen. Benjamin Alvord, U. S. Army, commanding the Department of Oregon, all of whom, as the highest commanding military officers of these Pacific coast States, duly conferred with the governors thereof, and who jointly agreed upon the manner in which the defenses of said States for the " common defense" should be improved and perfected, and which system of " common defense" so agreed upon was duly adopted by the legislatures of each as contemplated in said circular letter of Mr. Secretary Seward. These commanding generals, not in their own names, but in the names of their highest military commander, to wit, the *commander in chief of the Army*, the President of the United States, all of whose official acts were approved, legalized, and made valid by Congress as if done under previous express authority and direction of Congress.

In addition to the foregoing, these States have ever relied, and do now rely, for a full indemnity and reimbursement herein upon that general comity that has ever heretofore existed between the United States and the several States in all cases wherever or whenever the latter have been made, either expressly or impliedly, the agents of the United States in aiding to maintain the " common defense " during a period of actual war.

There was no war between *these three States* and the Confederate States, but the war of the rebellion was one between the *United States* and the Confederate States.

These war "costs, charges, and expenses" of these Pacific coast States so incurred under State and Federal authority, executive and legislative, were incurred not in defense of said States, separate and apart from the rest of the States, but were incurred in aiding *the United States to maintain the "common defense,"* and when incurred were authorized by the State legislature of each of said States, moved thereto at the urgent solicitation of the highest executive authorities of the United States, with the approval and at the direction of the President of the United States and by the sanction and indorsement of Congress, theretofore duly expressed in the aforesaid act and resolutions.

In view of these declarations, supported by the aforesaid opinion of the United States Attorney-General in the case of "The State of Vermont *v.* The United States," it is respectfully submitted that all "costs, charges, and expenses" properly incurred by these States when acting in accordance with the acts of their respective legislatures, when aiding the United States to maintain the "common defense," became, constituted, and now are valid charges against the United States, and as such should be duly appropriated for by Congress and paid to these States out of the National Treasury.

Congress, when legislating in these premises, did not undertake to determine in advance for these three States the specific kind or amount of the "costs, charges, and 'expenses' necessary for them to incur to maintain the common defense," nor did Congress authorize the War Department to issue proposals to these States to aid in the suppression of the rebellion provided it should be done by the *lowest possible bidder;* but Congress, confidently relying upon all the loyal States to come to the aid of the United States with men and money when called, left the President, as commander in chief of the Army and Navy of the United States, to fix the number of men for which he should make a requisition to aid the United States during this period of war, and very *properly left the respective States to be the judges and to determine for themselves the kind, character, and extent of the "costs, charges, and expenses" which they deemed necessary to be incurred by them when obeying the proclamations and requisitions for volunteers of the President of the United States and his proper officers* in all these premises.

Specific expenses had to be and were necessarily incurred in all these premises by all these States, and as heretofore duly reported to Congress by the Secretary of War, so that it would seem to ill-become the United States at this late day to raise the question either of consideration, or of necessity, or of cost, or of equivalent value received in any of these premises, under circumstances and amid exigencies as recited in this statement.

As a matter of fact, all moneys so appropriated by the legislatures of these States out of their respective State treasuries were raised by the sale of their State bonds and advanced by these States to the United States, and expended for the uses and purposes of their said volunteers, as declared and recited in these several State acts, to aid the United States to maintain the "common defense" during a period of actual war.

It it self-evident in these cases that this legislation pertaining to the volunteers of these States came jointly from Congress and from these three States, Congress in fact taking the lead, *but the moneys paid out to their volunteers actually came from moneys hired by their own State treasuries exclusively therefor and not otherwise.* The legislatures of these States did not act at any time in any of these premises until the demands therefor and the appeals made by the United States to their respective governors became most urgent and when the public exigencies which justified their action became of a character such as not to permit of any delay whatsoever on the part of the legislatures of said States.

House Report No. 254, Fifty-second Congress, first session, recites the years of diligent and persistent effort which have been made by these States to have these claims intelligently understood, recognized, and paid by Congress, which, finally recognizing their merits, passed the act of June 27, 1882, intended, as was then thought and expected by said States, to provide for the full and final adjudication of all these State war claims.

Legislation by Congress for such adjudication was initiated in the Senate by the introduction of certain Senate resolutions, one of which, Senate Resolution No. 10, was introduced December 12, 1881, by Senator Grover, of Oregon, to provide for these State rebellion war claims of the State of Oregon; and the other, Senate Resolution No. 13, was introduced December 13, 1881, by Senator Fair, of Nevada, to provide for these State rebellion war claims of the State of Nevada, and for both of which the Committee on Military Affairs in the Senate substituted a bill, S. 1673, which was amended in the Senate upon the motion of Senator Miller, of California, so as to provide for these rebellion war claims of the State of California, but when said bill finally passed Congress it included the State war claims of California, Oregon, Nevada, Colorado, Kansas, Nebraska, and Texas, and became the act of June 27, 1882 (22 U. S. Stats., 111).

Hon. Robert T. Lincoln was Secretary of War when this act of June 27, 1882, became a law, under the provisions of which his Department examined and audited the State war claims of the States of Kansas, Colorado, and Nebraska, all of which have been fully paid by the United States.

In a report made January 26, 1884, by Senator Maxey, of Texas, then a member of the Military Committee in the Senate, in reference to certain war claims referred to that committee upon the motion and request of Senator Jones, of Nevada, for the benefit of the people of that State, Mr. Secretary Lincoln, uniting therein with the honorable Third Auditor, declared his opinion to be that said act of June 27, 1882, was broad enough to embrace all proper war claims of Nevada—rebellion war claims of which, as recited in said letter, had theretofore been duly filed with said Third Auditor of the Treasury, and which were there then pending *sub judice*—the question as to the *necessity and cost incurred* by the States named therein having been left exclusively to the honorable Secretary of War to determine under said act, and as so decided by said Third Auditor.

It was in consequence of said opinion of Mr. Secretary Lincoln and of said Third Auditor that Senator Maxey, using said opinions and report as a basis for his action, being directed therein by the unanimous vote of the Senate Committee on Military Affairs, reported to the Senate that no further or additional legislation by Congress was needed in any of the war claims of the State of Nevada; and as a necessary corollary, no further or additional legislation was needed in the similar war claims of the States of California and Oregon, for if said act of June 27, 1882, was broad enough under which these State war claims of Nevada could be examined, it was equally broad to permit the examination of the similar war claims of California and Oregon. Mr. Secretary Lincoln, however, at about the same time duly submitted to Congress a report, that in view of the great labor involved in the proper examination and determination of matters arising under said act of June 27, 1882, and devolving thereunder upon his Department, relative to the war claims of these States, and recommended that he be duly authorized to appoint a special board of three Army officers to aid him in the examination and adjudication of the State war claims of the States named in said act, he alleging that Congress had imposed upon him special and responsible duties, but had failed to give him a corresponding force to aid him in the execution thereof.

Congress, in compliance with said recommendation and request of Mr. Secretary Lincoln, passed an act on August 4, 1886 (24 U. S. Stats., 217), wherein authority was given the Secretary of War to appoint a board of three Army officers to aid him in the work of examination of the war claims of the several States named in said act of June 27, 1882, and which officers, before entering upon their duties, were required to take and subscribe an oath that they would carefully examine said claims and, to the best of their ability, make a just and impartial statement thereof.

This act of August 4, 1886, is as follows, to wit:

AN ACT for the benefit of the States of Texas, Colorado, Oregon, Nebraska, California, Kansas, and Nevada, and the Territories of Washington and Idaho, and Nevada when a Territory.

*   *   *   *   *

SEC. 2. The Secretary of War is hereby authorized to detail three Army officers to assist him in examining and reporting upon the claims of the States and Territory named in the acts of June twenty-seventh, eighteen hundred and eighty-two, chapter two hundred and forty-one of the laws of the Forty-seventh Congress, and such officers, before entering upon said duties, shall take and subscribe an oath that they will carefully examine said claims, and that they will, to the best of their ability, make a just and impartial statement thereof as required by said act.

Approved August 4, 1886. (24 U. S. Stats., 217.)

In the meanwhile the Federal administration changed officers, Mr. Secretary Lincoln going out and Mr. Secretary Endicott coming in as Secretary of War; but nothing had been actually done by Mr. Secretary Lincoln in the way of adjudicating said war claims, outside of expressing said opinion as to said act of June 27, 1882, so that when Mr. Secretary Endicott took office he construed for himself said act of June 27, 1882 (22 U. S. Stats., 111), relative to the rebellion war claims of these three States, and he was of opinion, and on February 8, 1887, declared, that it was not broad enough to embrace these State war claims of these States. This information upon being made known to the Senate, that body unanimously adopted a resolution as follows, to wit:

Resolved, That the Secretary of War, through the board of war-claims examiners, appointed under section 2 of the act of Congress entitled "An act for the benefit of the States of Texas, Colorado, Oregon, Nebraska, California, Kansas, and Nevada, and the Territories of Washington and Idaho, and Nevada when a Territory," approved August 4, 1886, be, and is hereby, authorized and directed to examine all accounts, papers, and evidence which heretofore have been, or which hereafter may be, submitted to him in support of the war claims of the States of California, Oregon, and Nevada, and Nevada when a Territory, growing out of the war of the rebellion, and in suppressing Indian hostilities and disturbances during the war of the rebellion, and in guarding the overland mail and emigrant routes during and subsequent to the war of the rebellion, and to ascertain and state what amount of money each of said States, and Nevada when a Territory, actually expended and what obligations they incurred for the purposes aforesaid; whether such expenditures were made or obligations incurred in actual warfare or in recruiting, enlisting, enrolling, organizing, arming, equipping, supplying, clothing, subsisting, drilling, furnishing, transporting, and paying their volunteers, militia, and home guards, and for bounty, extra pay, and relief paid to their volunteers, militia, and home guards, and in preparing their volunteers, militia, and home guards in camp and field to perform military service for the United States.

The Secretary of War is also directed to ascertain what amount of interest has been paid by each of said States, and Nevada when a Territory, on obligations incurred for the purposes above enumerated. The Secretary of War shall report to Congress the amount of money which may be thus ascertained to have been actually paid by each of said States, and Nevada when a Territory, on account of the matters above enumerated, and also the amount of interest actually paid or assumed by each of said States, and Nevada when a Territory, on moneys borrowed for the purposes above enumerated. And the Secretary of War shall also report the circumstances and exigencies under which, and the authority by which, such expenditures were made, and what payments have been made on account thereof by the United States.

In response to this resolution, the honorable Secretary of War, having fully completed, with the aid of said Army board, a thorough and exhaustive official examination of all these war claims of said three States, transmitted in December, 1889, his reports to the Senate in each of these State war claims of California, Oregon, and Nevada, as required by said resolution, and which reports are as follows, to wit, Senate Ex. Docs. Nos. 10, 11, 17, Fifty-first Congress, first session. These reports and the exhibits attached thereto, respectively, are in great detail, and contain a very full history of the important part taken by the Pacific coast States and Territories during the rebellion in defense of the Union, and are in full compliance with said Senate resolution, showing the actual amount of the "costs, charges, and expenses" actually incurred by each of said States, and of Nevada when a Territory, during the war of the rebellion in aid of the United States and the authority, State, Territorial, and national, and also the special circumstances and exigencies under which the expenditures so reported upon by said Secretary and said board therein, respectively, were made.

Under this act of Congress of June 27, 1882, Mr. Secretary Lincoln examined, allowed, and stated the State war claims of the States of Kansas and Nebraska in sums as allowed and stated by him, and which have been fully appropriated by Congress. Mr. Secretary Endicott (with the aid of said Army board, appointed under said act of August 4, 1886) duly examined, audited, allowed, and stated the State war claims of the State of Texas, and of the sums so audited by the Secretary of War Congress appropriated the sum of $927,177.40 in the act entitled:

An Act to provide for certain of the most urgent deficiencies in the appropriations for the service of the Government for the fiscal year ending June the thirtieth, eighteen hundred and eighty-eight, and for other purposes.
Approved March 30, 1888. (25 U. S. Stats., 71.)

And further appropriated the sum of $148,615.97 in the act entitled:

An Act making appropriations to supply deficiencies in the appropriations for the fiscal year ending June the thirtieth, eighteen hundred and ninety, and for prior years, and for other purposes.
Approved September 30, 1890. (26 U. S. Stats., 539.)

Aggregating the sum of $1,175,793.37.
No one doubts but that all said war claims of Texas so examined and audited by the honorable Secretary of War (aided by said Army board) were valid and proper charges, against and should have been paid by the United States in the exact sums so audited by the Secretary of War, and which were so paid by Congress without any hostile opposition from any quarter as to the *merits* or *amounts of any thereof.*
In order to show the careful, painstaking, and exact manner in which the members of said Army board performed their duties when aiding the Secretary of War in the examination of these claims, attention is especially called to the views expressed in the House of Representatives by several members of the Texas delegation in Congress, to wit, those of Hon. S. W. T. Lanham, Hon. R. Q. Mills, and Hon. J. D. Sayers, at the

date when said Texas State war claims were under consideration in the House during the Fiftieth Congress, first session, wherein the reliability and the exactness of the statements of the board were shown to be in a manner not only perfectly satisfactory to them, but such in a statement and allowance in the said Texas war claims aggregating $927,-177.40, the difference between the sums so stated by said board and the sums subsequently appropriated by Congress with which to pay the same amounted only to the sum of $64.90. (*See* p. 2233, Congressional Record, March 16, 1888.)

The first installment of $927,177.40, so paid to the State of Texas in satisfaction of her said State war claims, passed as an item in the *urgent deficiency appropriation act*, approved March 30, 1888.

It is true this Texas war claim, besides being examined by the Secretary of War, was also reexamined in the Treasury Department, but that reexamination was for the purpose simply of verifying the computations in the audit of the Secretary of War, it being the duty of the Secretary of War, under said act of June 27, 1882, as decided by the Treasury Department, to report upon all matters which related to the *necessity for*, and *reasonableness* of, all expenses so incurred by said States, as appears from a letter from the honorable Third Auditor of January 24, 1884, to the honorable Secretary of War, reported by Mr. Secretary Lincoln to Senator Maxey, of Texas, under date of January 26, 1884, in a report as follows, to wit:

WAR DEPARTMENT,
Washington City, January 26, 1884.

SIR: In response to so much of your communication of the 22d ultimo as requests information concerning Senate bill 657, to "authorize the Secretary of the Treasury to adjust and settle the expenses of Indian wars in Nevada," I have the honor to invite your attention to the following report of the Third Auditor of the Treasury, to whom your request was duly referred:

"The State of Nevada has filed in this office abstracts and vouchers for expenses incurred on account of raising volunteers for the United States to aid in suppressing the late rebellion, amounting to $349,697.49, and the expenses on account of her militia in the 'White Pine Indian war' of 1875, $17,650.98; also, expenses of her militia in the 'Elko Indian war' of 1878, amounting to $4,654.64, presented under act of Congress approved June 27, 1882 (22 Statutes, 111, 112).

"These abstracts and vouchers will be sent to your Department for examination and report as soon as they can be stamped, as that statute requires a report from the Secretary of War as to the *necessity for*, and *reasonableness* of, the expenses incurred. This statute is deemed sufficiently broad enough to embrace all proper claims of said State and Territory of Nevada."

Very respectfully, your obedient servant,

ROBERT T. LINCOLN,
Secretary of War.

Hon. S. B. MAXEY,
Of Committee on Military Affairs, United States Senate.

In addition to the foregoing it appears, in a report from the War Department addressed to Hon. S. B. Maxey, U. S. Senator from Texas, under date of January 27, 1886, that the Secretary of War, Hon. W. C. Endicott, held that while the title of the act of June 27, 1882, and the wording of the first section thereof would seem to convey the impression that the claims of the States named in said act were to be adjusted by the Secretary of the Treasury, with the aid and assistance of the Secretary of War, yet, *as a matter of fact, the whole duty of examining and auditing said claims was, by section 2 of said act, imposed upon the Secretary of War, leaving the Treasury Department the simple duty of verifying the computations of the audit of the Secretary of War* therein, and as will officially and fully appear in Senate Mis. Doc. No. 54, Forty-ninth Congress, first session, as follows, to wit:

[Senate Mis. Doc. No. 54, Forty-ninth Congress, first session.]

Letter from the Secretary of War to Hon. S. B. Maxey, in relation to the claim of the State of Texas, presented under the act of June 27, 1882.

JANUARY 29, 1886.—Referred to the Committee on Appropriations and ordered to be printed.

WAR DEPARTMENT,
Washington City, January 27, 1886.

SIR: Referring to our recent conversation in regard to the claim of the State of Texas, presented under the act of June 27, 1882 (22 Stats., 111, 112), I have the honor to inform you that the first installment of the claim (amount $671,400.29) came before the Department from the Third Auditor of the Treasury July 9, 1884, and the action then taken in the matter appears in the letter from this Department to Mr. Dorn, dated July 16, 1884, copy herewith. The papers herein mentioned were returned to the agent of the State July 25, 1884. November 2, 1885, the Third Auditor of the Treasury wrote to the Department, transmitting through Mr. W. H. Pope, agent of the State, the papers in the claim, which papers were received here November 17, 1885, and they are now being stamped and marked.

In regard to the subject of the State claims mentioned in said act, I beg to inform you that the great difficulty experienced in disposing of the claim of the State of Kansas, the first one presented thereunder, has caused the Department to delay taking up the other claims pending. While the title of the act and the wording of the first section thereof would seem to convey the impression that the claims were to be adjusted by the Secretary of the Treasury, "with the aid and assistance of the Secretary of War," the whole duty of examining and auditing the claims was, by section 2, imposed upon the Secretary of War, leaving the Treasury Department the simple duty of verifying the computations of the Secretary of War.

The policy thus indicated differed widely from that prescribed in section 236 of the Revised Statutes, that "all claims and demands whatever by the United States, or against them, and all accounts whatever in which the United States are concerned, either as debtors or as creditors, shall be settled and adjusted in the Department of the Treasury," and differs also from the provisions for the adjudication of State claims under the act of July 27, 1861 (12 Stats., p. 276), which were "to be settled upon proper vouchers, to be filed, and passed upon by the proper accounting officers of the Treasury."

The claims arising under the act are said to amount to $10,000,000 (that of Texas is now stated at $1,842,443.78), and the vast labor of examining the papers, pointing out the evidence required to perfect the vouchers and show the necessity of calling out the militia, whose services are charged for, fixing the rate to be allowed on each voucher, and tabulating the same, many thousand in number, must be performed by the Secretary of War, and no provision has been provided by Congress for this laborious work.

Two years were consumed in disposing of the claim of the State of Kansas, and if the same course is to be pursued with the other claims arising under the act, it will be some time before the claim of Texas is reached, that of Nevada being next in order of receipt.

The subject of the claims was brought to the attention of Congress at the last session (*see* report of Secretary of War for 1884, pp. 4, 5, and estimates for 1886 on p. 206 of House Ex. Doc. No. 5, Forty-eighth Congress, second session), and it has again been presented in the Secretary's report for 1885 (pp. 35 and 36). An estimate to defray the cost of examining the claims will be found on p. 225 of House Ex. Doc. No. 5, Forty-ninth Congress, first session.

I inclose draft of a bill which, if enacted, will enable the Department to dispose of the matter.

Copies of the above mentioned reports are inclosed.

Very respectfully,

WM. C. ENDICOTT,
Secretary of War.

Hon. S. B. MAXEY,
    United States Senate.

This reexamination by the Treasury Department, to verify the final computations in said audit of the Secretary of War of the Texas war claim, showed, as aforesaid, an error of only $64.50 in a total allowance of $927,177.40, which sum was appropriated by Congress and paid by the United States to the State of Texas.

It is respectfully submitted that all that Congress in any case desires to know, and very properly inquires into in cases like these, is, have the claims which it is requested to pass upon been carefully computed and set forth in an official statement of account signed by the head of a Department or Bureau, whose duty it is to wholly examine and audit the same?

The dignity heretofore given by Congress to examinations not dissimilar to these is shown in the fact that year after year, since 1859, it has included in the regular deficiency appropriation bill appropriations with which to pay the Oregon and Washington Indian war claims in sundry and divers sums of money based exclusively upon *the original authority of a House resolution only*, adopted February 8, 1858, which resolution, reported in House Ex. Doc. No. 11, Thirty-sixth Congress, first session, is as follows, to wit:

[House Ex. Doc. No. 11, Thirty-sixth Congress, first session.]

Report of the Third Auditor of the Treasury, in pursuance of a resolution of the House of Representatives passed February 8, 1858.

FEBRUARY 10, 1860.—Referred to the Committee on Military Affairs and ordered to be printed.

THIRTY-FIFTH CONGRESS, SECOND SESSION,
CONGRESS OF THE UNITED STATES,
In the House of Representatives, February 8, 1859.

Resolved, That preliminary to the final settlement and adjustment of the claims of the citizens of the Territories of Oregon and Washington for expenses incurred in the years eighteen hundred and fifty-five and eighteen hundred and fifty-six in repelling Indian hostilities, it shall be the duty of the Third Auditor of the Treasury to examine the vouchers and papers now on file in his office, and make a report to the House of Representatives by the first Monday in December next of the amount respectively due to each company and individual engaged in said service, taking the following rules as his guide in ascertaining the amount so due:

1st. He shall recognize no company or individual as entitled to pay, except such as were called into service by the Territorial authorities of Oregon and Washington, or such whose services have been recognized and accepted by said authorities.

2d. He shall allow to the volunteers engaged in said service no higher pay and allowance than were given to officers and soldiers of equal grade at that period in the Army of the United States, including the extra pay of $2 per month given to the troops serving on the Pacific by the act of 1852.

3d. No person either in the military, or in the civil service of the United States, or of said Territories, shall be paid for his services in more than one employment or capacity for the same period of time, and all such double or triple allowances for pay as appears in said accounts shall be rejected.

4th. That in auditing the claims for supplies, transportation, and other services incurred for the maintenance of said volunteers, he is directed to have a due regard to the number of said troops, to their period of service, and to the prices current in the country at the time, and not to report said service beyond the time actually engaged therein, nor to recognize supplies beyond a reasonable approximation to the proportions and descriptions authorized by existing laws and regulations for such troops, taking into consideration the nature and peculiarities of the service.

5th. That all claims of said volunteers for horses, arms, and other property lost or destroyed in said service shall be audited according to the provisions of the act approved March 3d, eighteen hundred and fifty-nine.

Attest:

I. C. ALLEN, *Clerk.*

Attention is here specially called to the fact, disclosed by said Oregon and Washington resolution, that Congress when dealing with the volunteers of Washington and Oregon declared as late as February 8, 1858, that said volunteers should be paid an extra compensation, and in those particular cases the extra compensation was to be the same as provided for in the act of Congress approved August 31, 1852. (10 U. S. Stats., 108.)

The extra compensation of $2 per month as recited in said Oregon and Washington resolution is error—the exact extra compensation to be paid was one-half additional to the regular pay of officers and enlisted men.

Said provision of law by which said extra compensation was to be measured is as follows, to wit:

SEC. 3. *And be it further enacted,* that so much of the act making appropriations for the support of the Army for the year ending the 30th of June, 1851, approved the 28th of September, 1850, as provides extra pay to the commissioned officers and enlisted men of the United States serving in Oregon or California, be, and the same is hereby, continued in force for one year from the first day of March, 1852, and that the provisions of the last mentioned act be, and is hereby, extended to New Mexico during the current year provided for by this section, and that $300,000 be and is appropriated hereby for that purpose: Provided further, That said officers and men shall receive only one-half of the increased amount over the regular pay allowed by law.   (10 U. S. Stats., 108.)

Attention is here called to the fact, that in the examination and audit of the said Oregon and Washington Indian War Claims of 1855 and 1856 under the aforesaid House resolution, the Third Auditor was made the sole commissioner to examine the same, and for this extra duty under section 3, act of March 2, 1861, he was paid the sum of $1,000, and the appropriation to the said Oregon and Washington Indian War Claims, made in said act (12 U. S. Stats., 198), were based on the allowance that he, as such commissioner, made and reported to the House, February 8, 1859, under said resolution, and as printed in House Ex. Doc. No. 11, Thirty-sixth Congress, first session.

The examination of the war claims of the State of Texas were limited, as to time, to the examination of claims for the expenses incurred and arising in the said State subsequent to October 20, 1865, and were confined, as to character, exclusively to claims for expenses by her incurred for or on account of military defense against Mexican raids, against Mexican invasions, and against Indian hostilities only.   Whereas, in the cases of these three States said act of June 27, 1882, was intended to include and cover, and did include and cover all military expenses of every nature, beginning April 15, 1861, incident upon calling into the field their volunteers, beginning at the date of the commencement of the rebellion (April 15, 1861), and was not confined to claims for reimbursement of expenses incurred for defense against Indian hostilities only, but covered, and was intended to cover, all expenses of the rebellion or for repelling invasions, coming from any source whence they may, but included also those of Indian hostilities.

If there were any doubts as to the purposes and intentions of Congress as to the scope of said act of June 27, 1882, or as to the character of the claims to be examined thereunder, the expenses for which Congress intended to reimburse said States, these doubts would be removed by considering:

(1) The declarations recited in the fifth section of said act of June 27, 1882, in words as follows, to wit:

SEC. 5. That any military services performed and expenditures on account thereof incurred during the Territorial organization of Nevada, and paid for or assumed by either said Territory or said State of Nevada, shall be also included, and examined and reported to Congress in the same manner as like service and expenditures shall be examined and reported for the State of Nevada.

(2) By considering the views submitted May 12, 1882, on the bill S. 1673 by the Military Committee in the Senate, in Senate Report No. 575, Forty-seventh Congress, first session, and as reappears in Senate

Report No. 644, Fifty-first Congress, first sesion.   This Senate bill S. 1673 finally became the act of June 27, 1882, and an extract from said report made thereon is in words as follows, to wit:

The circumstances under which the expenditures provided for in this bill were made by these States being exceptional, and their reimbursement not being provided for by any existing law, general or special, prior to June 27, 1882, Senator Grover, of Oregon, on December 12, 1881, introduced Senate joint resolution No. 10, and Senator Fair, of Nevada, on December 13, 1881, introduced Senate joint resolution No. 13, providing for the equitable adjustment of these State war claims of Oregon and Nevada, which resolutions were referred to the Senate Committee on Military Affairs.

These two Senate joint resolutions, Nos. 10 and 13, Fortieth Congress, first session, are as follows, to wit:

[S. R. 10., Forty-seventh Congress, first session.

JOINT RESOLUTION to authorize the Secretary of War to ascertain and report to Congress the amount of money expended and indebtedness assumed by the State of Oregon in repelling invasions, suppressing insurrections and Indian hostilities, enforcing the laws, and protecting the public property.

Resolved by the Senate and House of Representatives of the United States of America in Congress assembled, That the Secretary of War be, and he is hereby, authorized and directed to cause to be examined and adjusted all the accounts of the State of Oregon against the United States for money expended and indebtedness assumed in organizing, arming, equipping, supplying clothing, subsisting, transporting, and paying either the volunteer or militia forces, or both, of said State called into active service by the governor thereof after the fifteenth day of April, eighteen hundred and sixty-one, to aid in repelling invasions, suppressing insurrections and Indian hostilities, enforcing the laws, and protecting the public property in said State and upon its borders, except during the Modoc war.

SEC. 2. That the Secretary of War shall also examine and adjust the accounts of the State of *Oregon* for all other expenses necessarily incurred on account of said forces having been called into active service as herein mentioned, including the claims assumed or paid by said State to encourage enlistments, and for horses and any other property lost or destroyed while in the line of duty by said forces: *Provided,* That in order to enable the Secretary of War to fully comply with the provisions of this act there shall be filed in the War Department by the governor of said State, or a duly authorized agent, an abstract accompanied with proper certified copies of vouchers or such other proof as may be required by said Secretary, showing the amount of all such expenditures and indebtedness, and the purposes for which the same were made.

SEC. 3. That the Secretary of War shall report in writing to Congress, at the earliest practicable date, for final action, the results of such examination and adjustment, together with the amounts which he may find to have been properly expended for the purposes aforesaid.

[S. R. 13, Forty-seventh Congress, first session.]

JOINT RESOLUTION to authorize the Secretary of War to ascertain and report to Congress the amount of money expended and indebtedness assumed by the State of Nevada in repelling invasions, suppressing insurrection and Indian hostilities, enforcing the laws, and protecting public property.

Resolved by the Senate and House of Representatives of the United States of America in Congress assembled, That the Secretary of War be, and he is hereby, authorized and directed to cause to be examined and adjusted all the accounts of the State of Nevada against the United States for money expended and indebtedness assumed in organizing, arming, equipping, supplying clothing, subsisting, transporting, and paying either the volunteers or militia, or both, of the late Territory of Nevada and of the State of Nevada, called into active service by the governor of either thereof after the fifteenth day of April, eighteen hundred and sixty-one, to aid in repelling invasions, suppress insurrections and Indian hostilities, enforcing the laws, and protecting the public property in said Territory and said State and upon the borders of the same.

SEC. 2. That the Secretary of War shall also examine and adjust the accounts of the late Territory of Nevada and of the State of Nevada for all other expenses necessarily incurred on account of said forces having been called into active service as herein mentioned, including the claims assumed or paid by said Territory and said

State, to encourage enlistments, and for horses and other property lost or destroyed while in the line of duty of said forces: *Provided,* That in order to enable the Secretary of War to fully comply with the provisions of this act, there shall be filed in the War Department by the governor of Nevada, or a duly authorized agent, an abstract accompanied with proper certified copies of vouchers or such other proof as may be required by said Secretary, showing the amount of all such expenditures and indebtedness and the purposes for which the same were made.

SEC. 3. That the Secretary of War shall report in writing to Congress, at the earliest practicable date, for final action, the results of such examinations and adjustment, together with the amounts which he may find to have been properly expended for the purpose aforesaid.

As recited in said Senate Report No. 644 (Fifty-first Congress, first session), that committee (to wit, Senate Committee on Military Affairs), instead of reporting back said joint resolution, reported back, May 12, 1882, in lieu thereof, a substitute in the form of a bill, to wit, Senate 1673, Forty-seventh Congress, first session, providing for the payment of certain war claims, to wit, those only of Texas, Oregon, and Nevada, and of the Territories of Idaho and Washington, and which bill, after having been amended in the Senate so as to include the State war claims of Colorado, Nebraska, and California, and amended in the House so as to include the State war claims of Kansas, finally resulted in the passage of the act approved June 27, 1882. (22 U. S. Stats., 111.)

It was then, no doubt, the intention of Congress to provide for the full indemnity and reimbursement of all moneys which California, Oregon, and Nevada, and Nevada when a Territory, had actually expended during the war of the rebellion on account of the several matters recited in Senate bill No. 1295, Fifty-third Congress, second session. Senate bill No. 1673, Forty-seventh Congress, first session, was accompanied by a report (Senate No. 575, Forty-seventh Congress, first session) made by Senator Grover, May 12, 1882, which renders said intention of Congress quite evident.

The Senate Committee on Military Affairs did not at that time make any report in relation to any of the State war claims of the State of California, but when this substitute bill (Senate 1673, Forty-seventh Congress, first session), reported from that committee, was under consideration in the Senate, Senator Miller, of California, called attention to the fact that California had similar war claims unprovided for, and on his motion this bill (Senate 1673, Forty-seventh Congress, first session) was amended in the Senate as to include the State war claims of the State of California. It it alleged by California, Oregon, and Nevada that this act of June 27, 1882, which they believed was intended by Congress to be an act for their relief and benefit and an equitable statute to be liberally construed in order to pay to these three States that indemnity " which had been so guaranteed by its aforesaid legislation, has been found to be an act ' so well and carefully and closely guarded by restrictions' " that, when construed by those who have been called upon to execute it, has proven to be completely inoperative as an equitable relief measure, so much so as to amount to a practical denial of justice so far as the present State war claims of these States now provided for in these bills were or are concerned.

Said report is as follows, to wit:

[Senate Report No. 575, Forty-seventh Congress, first session.]

MAY 12, 1882.—Ordered to be printed.

Mr. GROVER, from the Committee on Military Affairs, submitted the following report, to accompany bill S. 1673:

The Committee on Military Affairs, to whom were referred Senate bill 1144 and

Senate joint resolutions 10 and 13, "to authorize an examination and adjustment of the claims of the States of Kansas, Nevada, Oregon, and Texas, and of the Territories of Idaho and Washington, for repelling invasions and suppressing insurrection and Indian hostilities therein," submitted the following report:

Oregon.—It appears by the report of the Adjutant-General U. S. Army of April 3, 1882, that one regiment of cavalry, one regiment of infantry, and one independent company of cavalry were raised in the State of Oregon during the late war of the rebellion, and that the expenses incident thereto have never been reimbursed said State by the United States; and that the claims therefor have never been heretofore presented by said State for audit and payment by the United States, as per report of the Secretary of War of April 15, 1882, and of the Third Auditor of the Treasury of April 8, 1882. Under section 3489 of the Revised Statutes, the claim for expenditures so incurred by said State can not now be presented for audit and payment without legislation by Congress. In addition thereto there are some unadjusted claims of said State growing out of the Bannock and Umatilla Indian hostilities therein in 1877 and 1878, evidenced by a communication of the Secretary of War of date last aforesaid, and some unadjusted balances pertaining to the Modoc war, not presented for audit to Gen. James A. Hardie, approximating the sum of $5,000.

Nevada.—It appears by the report of the Adjutant-General U. S. Army, of February 25, 1882, that one regiment of cavalry and one battalion of infantry were raised in the late Territory of Nevada during the late war of the rebellion, and that the expenses of raising, organizing, and placing in the field said forces were never paid by said Territory, but were assumed and paid by the State of Nevada, and that none of said expenses so incurred by said Territory, and assumed and paid by said State, have never been reimbursed the State of Nevada by the United States, and that no claims therefor have ever been heretofore presented by either said Territory or said State for audit and payment by the United States. Under section 3489 of the Revised Statutes, hereinbefore referred to, the payments of these claims is barred by limitation.

These forces were raised to guard the overland mail route and emigrant road to California, east of Carson City, and to do other military service in Nevada, and were called out by the governor of the late Territory of Nevada upon requisitions therefor by the commanding general of the Department of the Pacific, and under authority of the War Department, as appears by copies of official correspondence furnished to your committee by the Secretary of War and the general commanding the Division of the Pacific; and it further appears that there are some unadjusted claims of the State of Nevada for expenses growing out of the so-called White River Indian war of 1875, and aggregating $17,650.98, and of the so-called Elko Indian war of 1878 therein, and aggregating $4,654.61, and which sums, it appears by the official statements of the comptroller of said State of Nevada, were expended and paid out of the treasury of said State.

Texas.—The unadjusted claims of the State of Texas provided for by this bill are those which accrued subsequent to October 14, 1865. These have been heretofore the subject-matter of much correspondence between the State authorities of Texas and the authorities of the United States, and have several times received the partial consideration of both branches of Congress, but without reaching any finality, never having been audited or fully examined, and consequently no payment on account thereof has been made.

These claims are referred to in Senate Ex. Doc. No. 74, second session, Forty-sixth Congress, and in the executive documents therein cited.

It appears by the official correspondence exhibited in the document referred to, and copies of official correspondence from the State authorities of Texas, and submitted to your committee, that the expenses for which the State of Texas claims reimbursement were incurred by the authorities thereof under its laws, and for the proper defense of the frontiers of said State against the attacks of numerous bands of Indians and Mexican marauders. These claims approximate the sum of $1,027,375.67, and were incurred between October 14, 1865, and August 31, 1877.

Washington and Idaho.—The volunteer troops in Washington and Idaho were in the field during Indian hostilities in 1877 and 1878, in said Territories, by orders of the local authorities thereof. While these volunteers were not mustered into the regular service of the U. S. Army, they were attached to the command of U. S. troops in the Department of the Columbia, and acted with said troops, rendering valuable and faithful services during said wars, under the orders and immediate command of officers of the regular Army of the United States, as appears by copies of orders in the hands of your committee.

The obligation of the General Government to defend each State is acknowledged to be included in the constitutional obligation to maintain the "common defense," by a long series of acts of Congress making appropriations to cover the expenses of States and Territories of the Union which have raised troops and have incurred liabilities in defending themselves against Indian hostilities and other disturbances.

The bill herewith reported provides for an examination of the claims and accounts of the States and Territories therein named by the Secretary of the Treasury, acting in connection with the Secretary of War, and that they report the amount of money necessarily expended and indebtedness properly assumed in organizing, supplying and sustaining volunteers and militia called into active service by each of them in repelling invasions and suppressing Indian hostilities therein, during the periods named.

This bill is carefully guarded against the assumption by the United States of unnecessary liabilities, and fixes the pay of volunteers and militia of these several States and Territories on the basis of the pay of regular troops.

Your committee therefore report the present original bill as a substitute for Senate bill 1144 and Senate joint resolutions 10 and 13, which heretofore have been under consideration by said committee, having the same objects as provided for by this bill, and recommend its passage.

The foregoing recitals clearly and fully show, so far as Oregon and Nevada were concerned, that said Report No. 575 and said Senate bill No. 1673, and said Military Committee in the first session of the Forty-seventh Congress dealt with both State rebellion war claims and State Indian war claims of the States of Oregon and Nevada and the Territory of Nevada, and when Senator Miller, of California, suggested that California had State war claims similar to those of Oregon and Nevada, said bill S. 1673 was amended upon his motion so as to also include the State rebellion war claims and the State Indian war claims of that State.

(3) By considering the views expressed by Hon. R. Q. Mills, now the junior Senator from Texas, of the purposes and intentions of said act of Congress of June 27, 1882, which were duly emphasized by his remarks thereon in the House on the date when said Texas war claim was then and there pending *sub judice* (which remarks with those submitted at the same time by Mr. Lanham and by Mr. Sayers of Texas on this same bill are printed on pp. 2126 to 2265, Congressional Record, Fiftieth Congress, first session). On that occasion Hon. R. Q. Mills declared as follows, to wit:

Mr. MILLS. Mr. Chairman, it might have been better if this claim had been held back and placed upon the regular deficiency bill. Perhaps there would have been no objection raised on either side of the House if that course had been adopted with reference to it. But the claim is now before the House, on a favorable report from the Committee on Appropriations, and it is here for action. Being before us, I do not want to see a vote against it to-day because of the fact that it has not been held back to give a red-tape examination to it.

This is an old, familiar friend of mine. I am thoroughly acquainted with it in all of its details. I introduced bills, as did my colleagues upon this floor, years ago to pay the State of Texas the money which had been expended by that State in doing that which the Government of the United States ought to have done for her. I remember the time when the Representatives from Kansas, Nevada, and Nebraska and ourselves often met together for conference and with a view to helping each other to get the Congress of the United States to do justice to our people in recognizing these claims which had been standing so long.

We united our efforts and aided in the passage of the law of 1882. That law was passed for the purpose of providing a settlement for these claims, and under it all of the claims of this class were submitted, with the evidence to substantiate them, to a board of Army officers. They have been thoroughly, patiently, exhaustively examined through a careful process of inspection covering a long period of time, and have all been reported to Congress.

There is no objection made to the payment of any of this class of claims upon the judgment of this board of officers, indorsed as it has been by the Treasury Department, except with regard to the claim of Texas; and the opposition, Mr. Chairman, is as unjust to the State of Texas as it would have been to the other States.

There is no gentleman who has challenged or will challenge the statement that not a single item has been questioned or can be pointed out in which a wrong judgment has been made by this board of officers.

But, sir, this appeal that is made here is all for delay. They say the case ought to have waited longer—as if it had not waited long enough already—and that it should have gone through some further and more patient examination; but they have not been able to point to a single item of all the items making up this sum of $927,000 which is not justly due to my State—not one of them.

Our claim is a little larger than the claim of the State of Kansas, because Kansas had a much smaller frontier, and had to guard only against the Indians, whereas we had both the Indians and the Mexicans. We had a border as long on the northern frontier of the State as the whole frontier line of the State of Kansas, and in addition to that we had all of that vast line from the thirty-second parallel of north latitude down to the Gulf of Mexico, making more than a thousand miles in addition. That is the reason why the claim of the State of Texas is larger. (Congressional Record, March 17, 1888, p. 2265.)

There is a consensus of opinion of the Treasury and War Departments as to the duties which were to be performed under said act of Congress of June 27, 1882, by the Secretary of War and by the Secretary of the Treasury, respectively, in the adjudication of the claims of the States named in said act, which were substantially to this effect, to wit: That the Secretary of War was to pass upon and decide as to the *necessity* for any expenses of any kind, and as to the *reasonableness* of all expenses so incurred by said States, for the "common defense;" and in addition thereto was to wholly examine all the claims of said States for all reimbursements provided to be paid in said act, and to wholly audit all the claims for any reimbursement to be made to any of said States under said act, and that the only duty of the honorable Secretary of the Treasury under said act was to verify the computations so made by the Secretary of War.

In the cases of the rebellion war claims of California, Oregon, and Nevada, it now fully appears that the honorable Secretary of War has thoroughly, patiently, carefully, and exhaustively examined all said rebellion war claims, rejecting any that appeared doubtful, and in so doing threw out or suspended in the case of California alone claims that aggregated $468,976.54, which had been paid by that State, and in the case of Oregon threw out or suspended claims which aggregated the sum of $21,118.73.

The Secretary of War has certified in an official itemized statement of account as the result of an exact computation, the true amount that should be paid by the United States, to each of these States, on account of the moneys by them respectively expended as "costs, charges, and expenses" to aid the United States to maintain the "common defense" on the Pacific coast during the war of the rebellion.

If therefore Congress will accord to the computations of the Secretary of War, Hon. Redfield Proctor, in these cases the same degree of confidence which it accorded to similar computations of the Secretary of War, Hon. W. C. Endicott, in the case of the State war claims of the State of Texas, then at this time it will make provision to pay the rebellion war claims of these three States in the sums as computed by the Secretary of War, Hon. Redfield Proctor, and by him so heretofore duly reported to the Senate.

The reliance that should be placed on this examination and audit by the Secretary of War of these claims of these three States may be correctly ascertained as aforesaid from the remarks in the House in support of said Texas war claims made by the distinguished Representative from Texas, now the chairman of the House Committee on Appropriations, Hon. J. D. Sayers, substantially to the effect that said computations in the Texas war claims were almost absolutely perfect (an error of only $64.50 occurring in an allowance of $927,177.40), *de minimis lex non curat.*

These claims were provided for in the same act which provided for said Texas war claims, and have had substantially a similar degree of examination by the Secretary of War, and are entitled to a similar degree of consideration by Congress.

In the deficiency appropriation bill which passed the Senate March 3, 1891, provision to pay some of these State war claims of these three States was included by the Senate without a single dissenting vote, after an explanation in support thereof had been made to the Senate in words as follows, to wit:

Mr. STEWART. I offer the amendment which I send to the desk.

The VICE-PRESIDENT. The amendment will be stated.

The CHIEF CLERK. On page 38, line 5, after the word "dollars," it is proposed to insert: •

To reimburse the States of California, Oregon, and Nevada for moneys by them expended in the suppression of the rebellion, under the act of Congress approved July 27, 1861, and acts amendatory thereof and supplementary thereto, being sums of money shown by the reports of the Secretary of War to have been paid by said States in the suppression of the rebellion:

To the State of California the sum of $2,451,369.56.

To the State of Oregon the sum of $224,526.53.

To the State of Nevada the sum of $404,040.70.

Mr. STEWART. Mr. President, there is no time to enter at length into an explanation of this claim. I would state, however, that during the war the States named in this amendment furnished 18,715 troops, who were enlisted in the U. S. Army and served on the Pacific coast. At the time the war broke out the soldiers who were stationed there were called home, and it became necessary to raise troops in those States. The Secretary of War, the President, and other officials urged these States to raise the troops, as they could not be sent from the East. These States, immediately after the rebellion closed, attempted to obtain compensation. It was a long time before they could get the accounts examined.

Finally, it was developed that these States had made an additional allowance beyond what was made in the Atlantic States. By two acts passed in 1850 a different allowance was made for troops serving on the Pacific coast. Those who were enlisted there were paid at a different rate. These acts were repealed in 1861. When it was attempted to raise troops on the Pacific coast it was found necessary to continue the old compensation on account of the very high price of living. Soldiers who had families or other obligations could not possibly serve at the reduced rates.

These States made an allowance, not up to what the Government had been in the habit of allowing, but considerably less, not more than one-fourth probably of the Government allowance. The transportation alone of the troops, without the subsistence that would have been allowed if they had been taken from New York under the regulations which had prevailed since 1850, would have amounted to $5,483,385. If the extra pay had been counted in it would have ranged something over $10,000,000, perhaps $15,000,000. If the regular United States pay which had been allowed from 1850 up to 1861, when the war broke out, had been paid these men, it would have amounted—I have not figured it out exactly—to some $10,000,000 or $15,000,000. The transportation alone would have been nearly $5,500,000.

In order that this question might be examined, several acts of Congress were passed, and a board of war claims commissioners was organized to investigate such claims. Under that war claims commission several States that came in on account of Indian depredations—Kansas, Nebraska, Nevada, California, and Texas—were paid in the aggregate $1,297,850. Texas received of that sum $927,177.40, and since that it has received and additional sum of $148,615.97.

The question of the allowance of additional pay, which has been so long urged, still remains. The Senate, after investigating it, passed a resolution to have the claims examined, so as to ascertain the exact amount that was paid. Under that resolution the war claims examiners reduced the amount stated. With great labor they went through all the papers and examined all the vouchers. The result is the amendment which I offer. There is no doubt about the equity of the case.

THE VICE-PRESIDENT. The question is on the amendment of the Senator from Nevada.

The amendment was agreed to.

(See p. 4116, Congressional Record, March 5, 1891.)

But this amendment was not retained in said bill by the conferees for reasons recited in the debate which took place thereon in the Senate, as follows, to wit:

Mr. STEWART. Mr. President, if I understand the amendments that have been agreed to and rejected, the amendment of the Senate putting in the French spoliation claims has been agreed to, and these State claims and the payment to the railroads for carrying the mails have been rejected.

Now, the position of the bill seems to be that the State claims of California, Oregon, and Nevada for money expended in the suppression of the rebellion, after all the other States have been paid, are rejected; that the judgments of the Supreme Court on the claims for the carrying of the mails, the judgment already declared that the United States is liable and owes the money and should pay it, have been rejected.

The French spoliation claims, in which there is no judgment, which is simply a finding under a law that declares that such findings shall not in any way commit the United States to the payment of the claims, and the finding of the court under such a law which has not been examined by the Committee on Claims, as the chairman stated that it had not been fully examined, but they had gone far enough to ascertain that a portion of them was unsatisfactory, and claims one hundred years old standing in that way, to a very large amount, are put into the bill.

Now, the system which produces such legislation certainly must be very defective. These appropriation bills come in and the main part of the legislation of Congress is forced into two or three days and nights, and investigation and deliberation under the pressure are denied, because we are threatened with an extra session of Congress, and we must take what the House says we shall take or we must take the consequences of an extra session. That alternative is constantly presented, and while judgments of courts binding upon the Government are ignored, while State claims cannot get consideration and are to be abandoned after consideration, claims that do not have a standing by reason of a judgment of a court or the investigation of a committee are allowed to pass.

I refer to the validity of these particular claims. I am aware that committees have held from time to time that there were equities in these French spoliation claims, but before they are paid it should be ascertained by some committee that each item that is appropriated goes to a legitimate claimant, so that when it has been neglected one hundred years we may investigate it and ascertain that the money goes to the parties entitled to it. This has not been done. I would not object to the payment of any of these claims if it were found that there was money due to a particular individual, but it comes in without that investigation, and it is to be passed in the last hours of the session, while the judgments of courts and claims of States are unceremoniously ignored. Now it goes back to the committee for further reference.

It is a serious responsibility upon a Senator who feels that he must do his duty here as to what he ought to do under such circumstances, whether he must continue from year to year to pass bills under the threat of an extra session, to which we can not give our assent conscientiously, and must stay here year after year and see legitimate claims ignored. The question is whether it is our duty to submit to it. It is a matter of grave consideration. I will not now determine what I shall do, but it seems to me if legislation can not be carried on more orderly than this it is the duty of the Senate to defeat the important bills and call a halt and rearrange the mode of doing business.

I think the Senate is, in a great measure, to blame in this matter. The Senate has the same power to originate appropriation bills that the House has. The House has got in the habit, and it goes on every season, and it always will, to send these bills here at the last moment so that they can not be considered by the Senate. I think the Senate is derelict in its duty if it does not commence early in the session to inaugurate bills and give time for consideration, that we may have our legislation in order, so that at the end of the session every Senator will not leave the Senate Chamber conscious that he has been a party to a very great wrong which the Congress of the United States allows because he did not have time to correct it.

The whole legislation of Congress has to be done in two or three nights, when it must be done hurriedly—done when jobs of all kinds can go through. Each Senator has to go home and explain it, and has to submit to it, that he can not reach it; that he could not discuss it because he was threatened with an extra session or the failure of the passage of the necessary bills to carry on the Government. It is a matter of grave consideration whether it is not my duty here to do all in my power to defeat this bill. Mr. President, I have said all I desire at this time. I have made these remarks, and I may make more before the bill becomes a law, but that is all I shall say at this time.

Mr. HALE. Mr. President, I desire to say only a word in reply to the Senator from Nevada. The instructions given to the committee on the part of the House do not apply to the State claims, but only to the railroad claims, so that in the conference which will immediately ensue the Senate conferees will not find the conference embarrassed by any action of the House aside from those claims. The committee of conference will be in session immediately, and I only repeat what I have said before, that it will endeavor to secure as much as possible of the action of the Senate upon this bill.

I want to say to the Senator from Nevada—I know that he is a reasonable man upon all these subjects—that the Senate is committed to these State claims by vote, by sentiment, and it is only a question of time when they will pass.

The present bill, aside from the matters which have been discussed, contains upon it an appropriation for pensions for soldiers amounting to $28,000,000. I do not suppose there is a Senator here who, whatever may be his feeling about other matters in the bill, would desire to wreck the bill and thereby leave the soldiers without money for the payment of their pensions during the remainder of the year. Calling the attention of the Senator to this, I leave the subject now, and hope to be able to report from the conference committee in a very short time.

Mr. CHANDLER. I ask the Senator how much is appropriated in the bill for pensions.

Mr. HALE. The appropriations for pensions are found upon page 5——

Mr. EDMUNDS. What is the total amount?

Mr. HALE. Amounting to $28,678,332.89. This money is needed at once. Without it the payments between now and June 30, of course, will cease.

DEFICIENCY APPROPRIATION BILL.

Mr. HALE submitted the following report:

The committee of conference on the disagreeing votes of the two Houses on certain amendments of the Senate to the bill (H. R. 13658) making appropriations to supply deficiencies in the appropriations for the fiscal year ending June 30, 1891, and for prior years, and for other purposes, having met, after full and free conference have agreed to recommend and do recommend to their respective Houses as follows:

That the Senate recede from its amendments numbered 22, 30, 59, 60, 84, 96, 98, 101, 103, and 104.

That the House recede from its disagreement to the amendment of the Senate, numbered 85, with an amendment as follows: In lieu of the matter proposed to be inserted by said amendment insert:

"For clerks to Committees on Patents, Coast Defenses, and Engrossed Bills, from March 4 to July 1, 1891, at the rate of $2,200 per annum each."

EUGENE HALE,
W. B. ALLISON,
F. M. COCKRELL,
Managers on the part of the Senate.
J. G. CANNON,
S. R. PETERS,
W. C. P. BRECKINRIDGE,
Managers on the part of the House.

Mr. STEWART. I should like to ask what disposition has been made of the amendments that were disagreed to.

Mr. HALE. The Senate conferees found the conferees on the part of the House entirely firm in their resistance, and declined to yield; so that it became a question of giving up the Senate amendments or giving up the bill, and mainly in consideration of the large appropriation in the bill for the pensioners, amounting to $28,000,-000, the conferees on the part of the Senate receded from the amendments and they are out of the bill.

Mr. STEWART. Mr. President, this illustrates in a very glaring form the mode of doing business between the two Houses. Appropriation bills involving more money than were ever appropriated in any one session, in time of peace at least, can not be said to have been considered by the Senate. They nearly all came here in a bunch in the last two or three days and the Senate has been compelled to work night and day. Many Senators were unable to stay here on account of their health. Old men feeble men, and men in ill health were unable to stay here and criticise these bills. They have been in the hands of a very few men who were overworked and could not give to them the attention they required.

They are not bills passed by the deliberation of this body, and it will be a marvel if there are not many things in these bills that Senators will regret and will be called upon to explain, and they will be compelled to make the explanation that there was no opportunity for any investigation of the great bulk of these bills, that it would have involved an extra session of Congress, which is regarded by the country as a calamity. We have been passing these bills under the shade of that calamity and under that threat, sitting here night and day. A large portion of the time, there could not be a quorum. Those who were engaged on conference were necessarily in their committee rooms, and what has been done is unknown to the majority of the Senate.

In this bill judgments of courts, of the Supreme Court, binding legal obligations of the Government, have been rejected. Claims of States of undoubted validity that have been long delayed have been rejected, and claims——

Mr. MORGAN. Will the Senator from Nevada allow me to ask him a question? Does the Senator desire to defeat the bill?

Mr. STEWART. I am not going to defeat the bill. I shall only occupy a few moments more, but I want to call attention to the situation. I am going to sit down in a moment. I say claims that have not the investigation or indorsement of the committee, involving millions, are in this bill. I do not complain of the conferees of the House; I do not complain of the conferees on the part of the Senate. They have labored night and day. It is a marvel to me that they have been able to perform the labor they have. They have done the best they could, and the result is that we have made these enormous appropriations of which the Senate, although responsible legally, can not be held responsible individually or morally.

I call attention to this matter now for the purpose of suggesting the necessity of earlier action on the appropriation bills and the further necessity of the Senate inaugurating appropriation bills, so that they can have them in time, that they can consider them properly, and that we can have legislation that we will understand, and that the country will understand, and not a great mass of material, involving millions and hundreds of millions that we know nothing of, forced through at the end of a session with the old excuse that we could not reach it because we had to submit and pass the bills to avoid an extra session. The Government must be carried on, I recognize that; and I do not propose to block the wheels of Government, but I appeal to Senators that in the future this work on appropriation bills shall be begun in time, and that they may be properly considered.

The PRESIDENT *pro tempore.* The question is on concurring in the conference report.

The report was concurred in.

(*See* p. 4223, Congressional Record, March 6, 1891.)

No valid reason is known to exist why Congress should not at this time authorize the payment of these State war claims of these three Pacific Coast States, and not compel them to keep knocking at its doors as petitioners, session after session, demanding payment of the same.

The volunteers of these States at the date when they were called, promptly responded to all requisitions made by the proper United States authorities upon their respective States, none waiting to be drafted or otherwise pressed into the military service of the United States, but all coming with alacrity when called.

The thorough, patient, careful, and exhaustive reports submitted to the Senate by the Secretary of War, Hon. Redfield Proctor, upon the work of the examination of the State war claims of these three States show some of the difficulties met and overcome by them when aiding the United States in these premises, and which, recited in the language of said Secretary in Senate Ex. Docs. Nos. 10, 11, and 17, Fifty-first Congress, first session, are as follows, to wit:

NEVADA.—EXTRA MONTHLY PAY TO HER STATE VOLUNTEERS—LIABILITIES ASSUMED.

[Senate Ex. Doc. No. 10, Fifty-first Congress, first session, p. 7.]

It appears from the affidavit of the State controller (herewith, marked Exhibit No. 2) that liabilities to the amount of $1,153.75 were assumed by the State of Nevada as successor to the Territory of Nevada on account of "costs, charges, and expenses for monthly pay to volunteers and military forces in the Territory and State of Nevada in the service of the United States," and that State warrants fully covering such liabilities were duly issued. It is also shown in the affidavit that of said warrants two for the sums of $11.33 and $8.50, respectively, have been paid, such payment reducing said liabilities to $1,133.92.

The circumstances and exigencies under which the Nevada legislature allowed this extra compensation to its citizens serving as volunteers in the U. S. Army are believed to have been substantially the same as those that impelled the legislatures of California and Oregon to a similar course of action for the relief of the contingent of troops raised in each of these States. Prices of commodities of every kind were extravagantly high during the war period in Nevada, which depended for the transportation of its supplies upon wagon roads across mountain ranges that were impassable for six months of every year; and at certain times, at least during the same period the rich yield of newly-opened mines produced an extraordinary demand for labor, largely increasing wages and salaries. These high prices of commodities and services were coexistent with, though in their causes independent of the depreciation of the Treasury notes, which did not pass current in that section of the country, though accepted through necessity by the troops serving there; and it is safe to say that in Nevada, as in California and Oregon, the soldier could buy no more with a gold dollar than could the soldier serving in the Eastern States with the greenback or paper dollar.

On the whole, therefore, we are decided in the conviction that in granting them this extra compensation the legislature was mainly instigated by a desire to do a plain act of justice to the U. S. volunteers raised in the State and performing an arduous frontier service, by placing them on the same footing as regards compensation, with the great mass of the officers and soldiers of the U. S. Army, serving east of the Rocky Mountains. It is true that the seven companies of infantry that were called for on October 19, 1864, had not been organized; and that on March 8, 1865, three days before the approval of the act above noticed, the commanding general Department of the Pacific wrote as follows from his headquarters at San Francisco to the governor of Nevada (see p. 287, Senate Ex. Doc. 70, Fiftieth Congress, second session):

"What progress is making in recruiting the Nevada volunteers? I will need them for the protection of the State, and trust that you may meet with success in your efforts to raise them. I hope the legislature may assist you by some such means as have been adopted by California and Oregon."

But the fact remains that the declared purpose of the monthly allowance was to give a compensation to the Nevada Volunteers (see section 1 of the act last referred to), and that when measured by the current prices of the country in which they were serving, their compensation from all sources did not exceed, if indeed it was equal to, the value of the money received as pay by the troops stationed elsewhere, i. e., outside of the Department of the Pacific.

CALIFORNIA.—EXTRA PAY TO ENLISTED MEN AS HER STATE VOLUNTEERS.

[Senate Ex. Doc. No. 11, Fifty-first Congress, first session, p. 23.]

By an act approved April 27, 1863, the legislature appropriated and set apart "as a soldiers' relief fund" the sum of $600,000, from which every enlisted soldier of the companies of California volunteers raised or thereafter to be raised for the service of the United States was to be paid, in addition to the pay and allowances granted him by the United States, a "compensation" of $5 per month from the time of his enlistment to the time of his discharge. Drafted men, substitutes for drafted men, soldiers dishonorably discharged or discharged for disability existing at time of enlistment, were not to share in the benefits of the act, and except in cases of married men having families dependent upon them for support, payment was not to be made until after discharge. Seven per cent interest-bearing bonds to the amount of $600,000, in sums of $500, with coupons for interest attached to each bond, were authorized to be issued on July 1, 1863. (Pp. 349–351, Statement for Senate Military Committee.)

A few unimportant changes respecting the mode of payment in certain cases were made by act of March 15, 1864, and on March 31, 1866, the additional sum of $550,000 was appropriated for the payment of claims arising under its provisions, such sum to be transferred from the general fund of the State to the "soldiers' relief fund."

Fearing that the total amount of $1,150,000 specifically appropriated might still prove insufficient to pay all the claims accruing under the act of April 27, 1863, above mentioned, the legislature directed, by an act which also took effect March 31, 1866 (p. 604, Stats. of California, 1865–'66), that the remainder of such claims should be audited and allowed out of the appropriation and fund made and created by the act granting bounties to the volunteers of California, approved April 4, 1864, and more fully referred to on page 19 of this report,

Upon the certificate of the adjutant-general of the State that the amounts were due under the provisions of the act and of the Board of State Examiners, warrants amounting to $1,459,270.21 were paid by the State treasurer, as shown by the receipts of the payees indorsed on said warrants.

It is worthy of note here that on July 16, 1863, the governor of California, replying to a communication from the headquarters Department of the Pacific, dated July 5, 1863, advising him that under a resolution of Congress adopted March 9, 1862, the payments provided for by the State law of April 27, 1863, might be made through the officers of the pay department of the U. S. Army, stated that the provisions of said law were such as to preclude him from availing himself of the offer.

Some information as to the circumstances and exigencies under which this money was expended may be derived from the following extract from the annual report of the adjutant-general of the State for the year 1862, dated December 15, 1862:

CALIFORNIA, OREGON, AND NEVADA WAR CLAIMS. 35

"The rank and file of the California contingent is made up of material of which any State might be proud, and the sacrifices they have made should be duly appreciated and their services rewarded by the State. I do most earnestly recommend therefore that the precedent established by many of the Atlantic coast States of paying their troops in the service of the United States an additional amount monthly should be adopted by California, and that a bill appropriating, say, $10 per month to each enlisted man of the troops raised or to be raised in this State be passed. * * * This would be a most tangible method of recognizing the patriotic efforts of our soldiers, relieve many of their families from actual destitution and want, and hold out a fitting encouragement for honorable service." (P. 58, Statement for Senate Committee on Military Affairs.)

Your examiners are of the opinion that the favorable action which was taken on the above recommendation of the adjutant-general can not be justly ascribed to any desire on the part of the legislature to avoid resort to a conscription, although the exclusion of drafted men from the benefits of the act indicates that they realized and deemed it proper to call attention to the possibility of a draft. Unlike the law of April 4, 1864, the benefits of which were confined to men who should enlist after the date of its passage and be credited to the quota of the State, the provisions of the act now under consideration extended alike to the volunteers who had already entered or *had actually* completed their enlistment contract and to those who were to enlist in the future. There is every reason for the belief that the predominating if not the only reason of the State authorities in enacting this measure was to allow their volunteers in the United States service such a stipend as would, together with the pay received by them from the General Government, amount to a fair and just compensation. In fact, as has already been stated, this was expressly declared to be the purpose of the act.

It appears that up to December 31, 1862, those of the U. S. troops serving in the Department of the Pacific who were paid at all—in some cases detachments had not been paid for a year or more—were generally paid in coin, but on February 9, 1863, instructions were issued from the Treasury Department to the assistant treasurer of the United States at San Francisco that "checks of disbursing officers must be paid in United States notes." (Letter of Deputy Paymaster-General George H. Ringgold, dated February 13, 1863, to Paymaster-General; copy herewith marked Exhibit No. 10.)

Before this, greenbacks had become the current medium of exchange in all ordinary business transactions in the Eastern States, but in the Pacific coast States and the adjoining territories, gold continued to be the basis of circulation throughout the war. At this time the paper currency had become greatly depreciated, and on February 28, 1863, the price of gold in Treasury notes touched 170. This action of the Government in compelling troops to accept such notes as an equivalent of gold in payment for services rendered by them in a section where coin alone was current, gave rise to much dissatisfaction. For although gold could be bought in San Francisco at nearly the same price in Treasury notes as in New York, it must be remembered that the troops in the Department of the Pacific were largely stationed at remote and isolated points.

When paying in greenbacks for articles purchased by or for services rendered by them in these out-of-the-way places, they were obliged to submit not only to the current discount in San Francisco, but also to a further loss occasioned by the desire of the persons who sold the articles or rendered the service, to protect themselves against possible further depreciation. It admits of little doubt that by reason of his inability to realize the full value of paper money, as quoted in the money centers, and of the fact that wages and the cost of living and of commodities of every kind were abnormally high (owing in great part to the development of newly-discovered mines in that region), the purchasing power of the greenback dollar in the hands of the average soldier serving in the Department of the Pacific was from the latter part of 1862 onward from 25 to 50 per cent less than that of the same dollar paid to his fellow soldier in the East.

Representation of great hardship which the Treasury Department's instructions entailed upon the troops were promptly made. On March 10, 1863, the legislature telegraphed to Washington a resolution adopted on that date instructing the State's delegation in Congress to impress upon the Executive "the necessity which exists of having officers and soldiers of the U. S. Army, officers, seamen, and marines of the U. S. Navy, and all citizen employés in the service of the Government of the United States serving west of the Rocky Mountains and on the Pacific coast paid their salaries and pay in gold and silver currency of the United States, provided the same be paid in as revenue on this coast." (P. 46, Statement for Senate Committee on Military Affairs,)

And on March 16, 1863, Brig. Gen. G. Wright, the commander of the Department of the Pacific (comprising, besides California, the State of Oregon and the Territories of Nevada, Utah, and Arizona) transmitted to the adjutant-general of the U. S. Army a letter of Maj. C. S. Drew, First Oregon Cavalry, commandant at Camp

S. Mis. 5——33

Baker, Oregon, containing an explicit statement of the effects of and a formal protest against paying his men in greenbacks. In his letter of transmittal (p. 154, Senate Ex. Doc. 70, Fiftieth Congress, second session), General Wright remarked as follows:

"The difficulties and embarrassments enumerated in the major's communication are common to all the troops in this department, and I most respectfully ask the serious consideration of the General in Chief and the War Department to this subject. Most of the troops would prefer waiting for their pay to receiving notes worth but little more than half their face; but, even at this ruinous discount, officers, unless they have private means, are compelled to receive the notes. Knowing the difficulties experienced by the Government in procuring coin to pay the Army, I feel great reluctance in submitting any grievances from this remote department, but justice to the officers and soldiers demands that a fair statement should be made to the War Department."

It was under circumstances and exigencies such as these that the legislature themselves—all appeals to the General Government having proved futile—provided the necessary relief by the law of April 27, 1863. They did not even after that relax their efforts on behalf of U. S. troops, other than their own volunteers, serving among them, but on April 1, 1864, adopted a resolution requesting their Representatives in Congress to "use their influence in procuring the passage of a law giving to the officers and soldiers of the regular Army stationed on the Pacific coast an increase of their pay amounting to 30 per cent on the amount now allowed by law."

OREGON.—EXTRA MONTHLY COMPENSATION TO OFFICERS AND ENLISTED MEN OF HER STATE VOLUNTEERS.

[Senate Ex. Doc. No. 17, Fifty-first Congress, first session, p. 14.]

The certificate of the State treasurer, duly authenticated by the secretary of state under the seal of the State, sets forth that the amounts severally paid out for the redemption of relief bonds, as shown by the books of the treasurer's office, as reported by the treasurer to the several legislative assemblies, and as verified by the several joint committees (investigating commissions) of said assembly under the provisions of a joint resolution thereof, aggregate $90,476.32. The following books, papers, etc., are also submitted in evidence of payment:

(1) The canceled bonds.

(2) A copy of the relief bond register, the correctness of which is certified by the secretary of state and state treasurer, showing number of bond, to whom issued, date of issue, and amount of bond; also showing the date and rate of redemption. The reports of the joint committees of the legislature above mentioned, to the effect that they compared the record kept by the State treasurer with the bonds redeemed and found the amounts correct and agreeing with the amounts reported by the State treasurer to the legislative assembly, are entered in said bond register.

(3) Certificates of service given to the several Oregon volunteers upon which warrants were given entitling the holders to bonds. These certificates cover service for which the sum of $86,639.85 was due. The remainder of the certificates, the State authorities report, were not found and are probably lost or destroyed.

(4) Copies of the muster rolls of the Oregon volunteers, certified to by the secretary of state, setting forth the entire service of each officer and enlisted man.

In all, bonds amounting to 93,637 were issued. As has been stated, but $90,476.32 is found to have been expended in the redemption of these bonds, some of which were redeemed at less than their face value. Five bonds, valued at $731, have not been redeemed.

The authority by which these bonds were issued is contained in an act of the legislature, which was approved on October 24, 1864 (copy herewith), appropriating a sum not exceeding $100,000 to constitute and be known as the "commissioned officers and soldiers' relief fund," out of which was to be paid to each commissioned officer and enlisted soldier of the companies of Oregon volunteers raised in the State for the service of the United States to aid in repelling invasion, etc., from the time of their enlistment to the time of their discharge, $5 per month in addition to the pay allowed them by the United States. Enlisted men not receiving an honorable discharge from the service, or volunteers discharged for disability existing at the time of enlistment, were not to be entitled to the benefits of the act, nor was payment under the provisions thereof to be made to an enlisted soldier until he should be honorably discharged the service; but enlisted married men having families dependent upon them were authorized to allot the whole or any portion of the monthly pay accruing to them for the support of such dependents. A bond bearing interest, payable semiannually, at 7 per cent per annum, redeemable July 1, 1875, with coupons for the interest attached, was to be issued by the secretary of state for such amount as the adjutant-general should certify to be due under the provisions of the act to each man, whose receipt for the amount so paid to him was to be taken by the secretary of state. Said bonds were to be paid to the recipient or order.

The circumstances and exigencies that led to the enactment of the above-cited law, and to the expenditures incurred under its provisions, were substantially the same as those which brought about the adoption of similar measures of relief in California and Nevada. It must have been patent to every one fully acquainted with the circmstances of the case that the volunteers that had been raised in Oregon at this time (October 24, 1864), consisting only of the 7 companies of the First Oregon Cavalry and the independent detachment of four months' men, a majority of whom had then nearly completed their terms, had been greatly underpaid, considering the nature of the service performed by them and the current rate of salaries and wages realized in other pursuits of life. At the time of the enrollment and muster-in of the First Oregon Cavalry and up to the latter part of 1862 the Government paid those of its troops in the Department of the Pacific that were paid at all in specie; but, as often happened during the war, a number of the companies of the regiment named, occupying remote stations, remained unpaid for a long time, and were finally paid in Treasury notes, some of the members having more than a year's pay due them.

During the remainder of the war the Government paid its troops in the Department of the Pacific, as elsewhere, in greenbacks. Referring to this condition of things and to the fact that coin continued to be the ordinary medium of exchange in Oregon in private business transactions, Maj. C. S. Drew, First Oregon Cavalry, in a letter to his department commander, dated March 4, 1863 (p. 154, Senate Ex. Doc. 70, Fiftieth Congress, second session), called attention to the fact that at his station (Camp Baker) Treasury notes were "worth not more than 50 or 55 cents per dollar;" that each officer and soldier in his command was serving for less than half pay, and had done so, some of them, for sixteen months past; that while capital protected itself from loss and perhaps realized better profits than under the old and better system of payment in coin, "the soldier did not have that power, and if paid in notes must necessarily receipt in full for what is equivalent to him of half pay or less for the service he has rendered, and must continue to fulfil his part of his contract with the Government for the same reduced rate of pay until his period of service shall have terminated; and that "good men will not enlist for $6 or $7 a month while $13 is the regular pay, and, moreover, is being realized by every soldier in every other department than the Pacific." In forwarding this letter to the Adjutant-General, U. S. Army, the department commander remarked that the embarrassments enumerated in the major's communication were common to all the troops in the department, and he therefore asked "the serious consideration of the general in chief and the War Department to this subject." Some months later (August 18, 1863) Gen. Alvord, while reporting to the department commander the location of a new military post at Fort Boise, referred to the difficulties encountered by the garrison charged with the duty of establishing it as follows:

"Some difficulty is experienced in building the post in consequence of the low rates of legal-tender notes. In that country they bear merely nominal value. The depreciation of the Government currency not only embarrasses the Quartermaster's Department, but also tends greatly to disaffect the men. The differences between their pay and the promises held out by the richest mines, perhaps, on the coast, the proximity of which makes them all the more tempting, is so great that many desertions occur." (Senate Ex. Doc. 70, Fiftieth Congress, second session, p. 188.)

About the same time (September 1, 1863) the adjutant-general of the State complained of the inadequacy of the soldiers' pay, resulting from the depreciation of the paper currency with which they were paid. Referring to the fact that after the expiration of eight months from the date of the requisition of the United States military authorities for 6 additional companies for the First Oregon Cavalry but 1 had been raised, he said:

"And yet we are not prepared to say that it is for the want of patriotism on the part of the people of Oregon, but from other causes, partly from the deficiency in the pay of the volunteer in comparison with the wages given in the civil pursuits of life, as well as with the nature of the currency with which they are paid, the depreciation of which renders it hardly possible for the soldier to enlist from any other motive save pure patriotism. And I would here suggest that the attention of our legislature be called to this defect, and that additional pay, either in land, money, or something else, be allowed to those who have volunteered. Justice demands that this should be done,"

In enacting the relief law of October 24, 1864, it is fair to presume that the legislature was largely influenced by the following statements and recommendations of the governor, contained in his annual message, dated September 15, 1864:

"The Snake and other tribes of Indians in eastern Oregon have been hostile and constantly committing depredations. The regiment has spent two summers on the plains, furnishing protection to the immigration and to the trade and travel in that region of the country. During the past summer the regiment has traveled over 1,200 miles, and the officers and men are still out on duty. The officers and most, if not all, the men joined the regiment through patriotic motives, and, while some of the time they have been traveling over rich gold fields, where laborers' wages are from $3 to $5 per day, there have been very few desertions, and that, too, while they were being paid in depreciated currency, making their wages only about $5 per month. A great many of these men have no pecuniary interest in keeping open the lines of travel, protecting mining districts and merchants and traders. The benefit of their service thus inures to the benefit of others, who should help these faithful soldiers in bearing these burdens. Oregon, in proportion to her population and wealth, has paid far less than other States for military purposes. California pays her volunteers $5 per month extra in coin. It would be but an act of simple justice for this State to make good to the members of this regiment their losses by depreciated currency." (P. 87, Statement for Senate Military Committee.)

It is to be noted here that while the officers and men who became the beneficiaries of this law had been paid in a depreciated currency, which in Oregon does not appear to have had more than two-thirds of the purchasing power it had in the East, the Government provided them with clothing, subsistence, shelter, and all their absolutely necessary wants. On the other hand, it is to be borne in mind that the legislature must have been aware of the fact noted, and that it granted the extra compensation from a sense of justice and without any purpose calculated to benefit the State at large, such as might be reasonably inferred from the granting of bounties to men "who should hereafter enlist." As has been already mentioned, the terms of the Oregon volunteers were drawing to a close and the benefits of the law were restricted to the volunteers "raised," and did not therefore include those "to be raised."

It is very material to here call attention to certain important facts, to wit, that subsequent to the dates when these three States, through appropriate legislation enacted therefor by their respective legislatures, provided for the aforesaid extra pay to their own volunteers, Congress on June 20, 1864, increased by one-third the pay of the soldiers of the regular Army of the United States, to begin on May 1, 1864, and to continue during the rebellion (the close of which, as proclaimed by the President of the United States, was August 20, 1866 (13 U. S. Stats., 144, 145).

Nay, more, Congress on March 2, 1867, as to the soldiers, extended said act for three years from August 20, 1866, and at the same time, as to the officers of the regular Army of the United States, increased their pay by one-third for two years from July 1, 1866. (14 U. S. Stats., 422, 423.)

Nay, still more, in this act of June 20, 1864, Congress provided for the payment of bounties (or constructive mileage) to such soldiers as should reenlist, as therein recited, and which bounties had theretofore been denied payment by Second Comptroller Brodhead under his aforesaid decisions of the Treasury Department.

Nay, even still more, on March 2, 1867 (14 U. S. Stats., 487), Congress provided for the payment of mileage to the California and Nevada volunteers from the places of their discharge in New Mexico, Arizona, Utah, etc., to the places of their enlistment, etc.

So therefore it fully appears that Congress finally, though tardily, enacted for the regular Army of the United States the identical provisions which these three States prior thereto felt called upon to enact for their own volunteers, the propriety of which legislation by said States has never been questioned, and the timeliness of which served only to measure the patriotism which inspired such legislation in aid of the "common defense."

But in the meanwhile the aforesaid legislation of these three States had been duly set in motion and was actively running in full force and effect at the dates of the aforesaid legislation of Congress, and the statutory obligations of said States to their own volunteers in good faith had to be fully met according to the letter and spirit of the intention of their enactment.

These war claims of these three States are not therefore to be weighed in scales of refined technicality.

These State war claims are not private claims, but are public claims presented to Congress by three States of the Union in their corporate and political capacities, and are entitled to its highest possible consideration, because of the fact they are State claims for the reimbursement of *cash actually paid by these three States, as the "costs, charges, and expenses" in aiding th. United States, at their own solicitation, to maintain the "common defense" on the Pacific coast during a period of active war.*

Not only this, but said cash so by them expended *had to be and was hired by these three States by the sale of their State interest-bearing bonds, supported only by their own State credit.*

In order to resort to measures so extraordinary, the legislatures of these three States were compelled to avail themselves of those provisions of their State constitutions that contemplated extraordinary emergencies in public affairs, and which demanded extraordinary expenditures of money, in excess of the maximum limit provided for a condition of peace and tranquillity, and which extraordinary expenditures these three States felt justified in making in view of a state of actual war against the Union and of the obligation of the United States to indemnify and reimburse them for such expenditures as had been so guaranteed by Congress in its aforesaid legislation.

It is respectfully submitted that the aforesaid legislation of Congress and proceedings had by the Executive Departments of the United States in connection therewith, so fully executed in good faith by these three Pacific coast States, constituted and are statutory contracts which contemplate an obligation on the part of the United States to wholly indemnify these three States by fully reimbursing them the money they so advanced and expended in good faith to aid the United States to maintain the "common defense," and so hired by said States by the sale of their State interest-bearing bonds.

At the dates when the United States made the aforesaid calls or requisitions for these 18,715 volunteer troops there was no money in State treasuries of these three States which was not specifically appropriated to meet their fixed and necessary current expenses, and hence, not having any money with which to defray the "costs, charges, and expenses" of furnishing said volunteer troops for the military service of the United States, they *were compelled to raise money by hiring the same, and to do this they were compelled to sell at not less than par their State interest-bearing war bonds, principal and interest of which were paid in gold coin from money raised by taxation most extraordinary, levied upon the inhabitants of these three States.*

These statutory enactments of Congress, supplemented by these statutory enactments of the legislatures of these three States, constitute and are the highest and most solemn form of governmental contracts, and are to be construed in all cases, not as mere legislative enactments, *but as contracts* binding upon all parties thereto—in this case the United States and the States of California, Oregon, and Nevada.

Huidecooper's Lessee v. Douglas, 3 Cranch R., 1;
1 Peters' Condensed Rep., 446;
State Bank v. Knoop, 16 How., 369;
Corbin v. Board of County Comrs., 1 McCrary, 521;

Sinking Fund Cases, 99 U. S. R., 700;
Fletcher *v.* Peck, 6 Cranch, 87;
New Jersey *v.* Wilson, 7 Cranch, 166;
Dartmouth College Case, 4 Wheaton, 518;
Keith *v.* Clark, 97 U. S. R., 454.

It was impossible for these States to raise, enlist, organize, equip, and muster volunteer troops into the military service of the United States *without the immediate expenditure of cash,* and they could not expend cash which they did not have, and hence they were forced *to hire cash* in the same manner as they hired anything else, to wit, by paying for the use of such hire, to wit, interest on the principal so by them hired.

In construing the aforesaid legislation the circumstances under which the same was enacted are to be and must be taken into consideration.

In this case the emergencies were not only great, but extraordinary and imminent, not admitting in the least of any delay. The life of the nation was in peril; volunteer troops were imperatively demanded; official requisitions therefor had to be promptly obeyed; the Federal treasury was wholly empty; the State treasuries of these three States were equally empty, whatever money being on deposit therein having been appropriated and set apart for specific purposes, so that no part thereof could be constitutionally used for any other object whatsoever.

It was under circumstances like these that the Federal Government besought these three States to send them 18,715 volunteer troops, and in substance promised: "We will wholly indemnify and fully reimburse you for all proper costs, charges, and expenses incurred in our behalf therein," etc.

All these things were matters of public contemporaneous history, and were contained in the constitutions and State statutes of these three States, and presumably were well known to Congress at the dates when it enacted the aforesaid acts and adopted the aforesaid resolutions, and Congress must necessarily have contemplated that these three States, if they had not the cash, would necessarily make use of their credits, respectively, for the purpose of hiring the cash with which to immediately provide for raising said volunteer troops for the "common defense," and that whatever sums of money might be paid out by these States (both principal and interest paid for the use of said principal) would be necessarily reimbursed them by the United States.

The mere *title* of the aforesaid act of Congress of July 27, 1861, is of itself sufficient to declare the intent of Congress in these premises, to wit: "An act to indemnify the States (in this case of California, Oregon, and Nevada) for expenses incurred by them in defense of the United States," both before and after July 27, 1861.

To indemnify these States was and is "to save them harmless, to secure them against any future loss or damage, to fully make up to them for all that is past, to make good all expenditures, to fully reimburse them for all proper 'costs, charges, and expenses' incurred by them in furnishing said 18,715 volunteer troops." (Webster *et als.*)

The objects of this legislation by Congress will therefore not be wholly satisfied by a partial reimbursement to these States of these expenses so by them incurred, but the intention of Congress will be properly and wholly satisfied only by the full reimbursement to these States of the total principal of the cash by them hired, and the interest paid by them for the hire of the cash (principal) expended by them, at the request of the General Government, to aid the United States to maintain the "common defense" on the Pacific coast during the rebellion.

"The costs, charges, and expenses" contemplated by the aforesaid act of July 27, 1861, was the money which theretofore had been, or which thereafter might be "duly expended, actually laid out, in fact consumed by using, or the disbursements made, outlays paid, and charges met, as the proper expenses of war" by said three States. (Webster *et als.*)

> Sullivan *v.* Triumph Mining Company, 39 Cal., 450;
> Foster *v.* Goddard, 1 Cliff., 158;
> 1 Black, 506;
> Dashiel *v.* Mayor, etc., of Baltimore, 46 Md., 615;
> Dunwoodie *v.* The United States, 22 C. of Cls. R., 269.

There is another familiar rule of statutory construction which should be observed in the application of this act of July 27, 1861, and it is, that "what is implied in a statute is as much a part of it as what is expressed." (United States *v.* Babbitt, 1 Black, 55, 61.)

And the opinion of the court in that respect has been quoted with great emphasis in many subsequent decisions of the Supreme Court of the United States.

> Gelpcke *v.* City of Dubuque, 1 Wall., 221;
> Croxall *v.* Sherrard, 5 *id.*, 228;
> Telegraph Company *v.* Eiser, 19 *id.*, 427;
> United States *v.* Hodson, 10 *id.*, 406;
> Buckley *v.* United States, 19 *id.*, 40.

The United States have universally reimbursed all sums of money actually expended and used for the benefit of the Federal Government, not only principal, but also interest paid for the hire of any principal used for such purposes.

In this case reimbursement is asked for interest, not upon any claim which these three States have against the United States, but as a part of the "costs, charges, and expenses" incurred and actually paid out, for which, it is respectfully submitted, full reimbursement should be made by the United States to these three States.

> 6 U. S. Stats., 139, April 18, 1814;
> 3 U. S. Stats., 422, April 9, 1819;
> 3 U. S. Stats., 560, April 11, 1820;
> 5 U. S. Stats., 522, August 23, 1842;
> 5 U. S. Stats., 578, August 31, 1842;
> 5 U. S. Stats., 628, March 3, 1843;
> 5 U. S. Stats., 716, April 30, 1834;
> 5 U. S. Stats., 797, March 1, 1845;
> 9 U. S. Stats., 571, February 27, 1851;
> 2 Comptroller's decision, vol. 15, p. 137, office records, holding to the effect that interest, when paid by a State for the use and benefit of the United States, becomes a part of the principal debt of the United States due to such State and constitutes a just and legal claim of such State against the Federal Government, as much so as the principal itself;
> 1 Opinion of the U. S. Attorney-General, 542, 566;
> 2 Opinion of the U. S. Attorney-General, 841;
> 5 Opinion of the U. S. Attorney-General, 71, 108, 463.

Congress is presumed to have enacted the aforesaid legislation with a full knowledge not only of its own aforesaid acts but also of the aforesaid decisions of the Executive Department of the United States in reference to the construction and application of similar legislation theretofore duly enacted by Congress; and if there existed any ambiguity or doubt (which is denied in the premises) with reference to the true construction of such legislation by Congress, then such prior decisions and opinions of the proper Executive Departments of the United States upon such similar statutes should have a controlling weight, and said laws should be construed in harmony with such decisions and opinions.

 U. S. *v.* Moore, 95 U. S. R., 760–63;
 U. S. *v.* Pugh, 99 U. S., 265–269;
 Hahn *v.* U. S., 107 U. S. R., 402–406;
 Brown *v.* U. S., 113 U. S. R., 568;
 U. S. *v.* Philbrick, 120 U. S. R., 52;
 U. S. *v.* Hill, 120 U. S. R., 169.

The departmental construction and opinions of similar laws of Congress become part of these laws, as much so as if they had been expressly incorporated therein, and should be duly respected and adopted by Congress as is invariably done by the courts of the country.

The United States are liable for the reimbursement for the "costs, charges, and expenses" upon which these claims of these three States are founded, because the same were duly made and incurred at the request and solicitation of the United States to maintain the "common defense," on the Pacific coast while the United States were engaged in actual war, and hence these States in so making said expenditures were acting in fact as the fiscal agents of the Federal Government.

In view of the emergencies amid which, from 1861 to 1866, the Federal Government was placed, and the circumstances in which these States found themselves, it must be admitted that "the costs, charges, and expenses" for which reimbursement is now claimed were not only necessary, but it has never been at any time, by any person, or at any place, suggested that these three States could in any other manner have responded to the frequent calls and urgent demands of the United States, except by doing that which in good faith they promptly did, to wit, hire money and pay interest for such hire, implicitly relying upon the good faith, equity, and the public conscience of the United States and upon the highest order of obligation imposed upon and now resting upon the United States to wholly indemnify and fully reimburse the same.

These three States have not heretofore asked and do not now seek to recover any principal or any interest which they did not actually pay out of moneys by them hired, with which to meet "the costs, charges, and expenses" of raising, organizing, equipping, and furnishing, etc., 18,715 volunteer troops, for the military service of the Federal Government on the Pacific coast, and all of which troops were continuously engaged and employed in the field, from 1861 to 1866, inclusive, serving as far south as Arizona and as far north as the Territory of Washington, and as far east as the Territory of Utah.

The State interest-bearing war bonds of these three States were not authorized to be issued or sold and were not issued and sold, nor the cash represented thereby was not hired, and the interest paid for such hire was not paid to relieve their own people, but all of the same were done by these States to enable the Federal Government to do through their credit that which the United States did not do, and seemingly could not then otherwise do, to wit: to immediately put in the field 18,715 volunteer troops, fully equipped and prepared for military service and who, in the opinion of the United States, were immediately needed to maintain the "common defense" on the Pacific coast, and to serve as aforesaid during the period of the rebellion.

The principle contended for in these cases does not go even as far as Congress itself has heretofore gone in sundry cases, at sundry times, beginning at a very early period in the history of the Federal Government because these claims are for the reimbursement only of such cash as these three States actually hired and expended for the use and benefit of the Federal Government, during a period of active war, and at the solicitation of the United States, while Congress has at times not only authorized the reimbursement of the principal, but has also authorized the payment of interest, for the use by the Federal Government, of money, up to the dates when same was actually repaid by the United States.

As late as March 7, 1892, the War Claims Committee, in the House of Representatives, having this subject-matter under examination, made a unanimous report to the House, to wit: House Report No. 555, Fifty-second Congress, first session, to accompany H. R. 4566, which report is as follows, to wit:

[House Report, No. 555; Fifty-Second Congress, first session.]

MARCH 7, 1892.—Committed to the Committee of the Whole House and ordered to be printed.

Mr. STONE, of Kentucky, from the Committee on War Claims, submitted the following report (to accompany H. R. 4566):

The Committee on War Claims, to whom was referred the bill (H. R. 4566) to reimburse the several States for interest on moneys expended by them on account of raising troops, etc., submit the following report:

The facts out of which this bill for relief arises will be found stated in a report made by this committee to the House in the Fiftieth Congress, which is appended as a part of this report.

Your committee concur in the conclusions stated in that report and recommend the passage of the bill.

[House Report No. 309, Fiftieth Congress, first session.]

The Committee on War Claims, to whom was referred the bill (H. R. 1474) to reimburse the several States for interest on moneys expended by them on account of raising troops employed in aiding the United States in suppressing the late insurrection against the United States, beg leave to report the same back to the House with the recommendation that it do pass.

This recommendation is founded upon the precedents which Congress has heretofore established of paying interest on moneys advanced by States on account of the war of 1812; also, Indian wars of 1835, 1836, 1837, and 1838, and the northeast frontier of the State of Maine, as evidenced by the following acts of Congress:

To reimburse Virginia, act of March 3, 1825, Stat. at Large, vol. 4, 132.
To reimburse Maryland, act of May 13, 1826, Stat. at Large, vol. 4, p. 161.
To reimburse city of Baltimore, act of May 20, 1826, Stat. at Large, vol. 4, p. 177.
To reimburse Delaware, act of May 20, 1826, Stat. at Large, vol. 4, p. 175.
To reimburse New York, act of May 22, 1826, Stat. at Large, vol. 4, pp. 192, 193.
To reimburse Pennsylvania, act of March 3, 1827, Stat. at Large, vol. 4, pp. 240, 241.
To reimburse South Carolina, act of March 22, 1832, Stat. at Large, vol. 4, p. 499.
To reimburse Alabama, act of January 26, 1849, Stat. at Large, vol 6, p. 344.
To reimburse Georgia, act of March 3, 1851, Stat. at Large, vol. 6, p. 646.
To reimburse Maine, act of March 3, 1851, Stat. at Large, vol. 6, p. 626.
To reimburse New Hampshire, act of January 27, 1852, Stat. at Large, vol. 10, pp. 1, 2.
To reimburse Massachusetts, act of July 8, 1870, Stat. at Large, vol. 16, pp. 197, 198.

The President, by authority of Congress, called upon the governors of the States of Maine, New Hampshire, Vermont, Massachusetts, Rhode Island, Connecticut, New York, New Jersey, Pennsylvania, Delaware, Maryland, Virginia, West Virginia, Ohio, Kentucky, Michigan, Indiana, Illinois, Wisconsin, Minnesota, Iowa, Missouri, Kansas, Nebraska, Nevada, Oregon, and California to furnish volunteers and militia troops to aid the United States in suppressing the late insurrection against it, and these States expended various sums of money, which were advanced to the Government, in enrolling, equipping, subsisting, clothing, supplying, arming, paying, and transporting regiments and companies employed by the Government in suppressing the late insurrection, and it matters not to the Government from what sources these States obtained the moneys advanced by them for the benefit of the Government, they are equally and justly entitled to be paid interest on such advances from the time they presented their claims to the Government for payment to the time when the same were refunded by the Secretary of the Treasury.

These States incurred heavy obligations of indebtedness on account of raising these troops, on which they paid interest, and many of them are still paying interest on their bonded indebtedness.

As the Government had the use and benefit of these advances made by these States, above mentioned, and that, too, at a time when greatly needed, and added largely to the maintaining of the credit of the Government, it is deemed by your committee but equitable and just that interest should be allowed equally to all the States on moneys advanced by them to aid the Government in furnishing troops.

The same rule has been observed in the cases of several States which advanced money for the "common defense," in suppressing Indian and other wars, as follows, to wit:

Georgia, act March 3, 1879 (20 Stat. at L., p. 385); Washington Territory, act March 3, 1859 (11 Stat. at L., p. 429); New Hampshire, act January 27, 1852 (10 Stat. at L., p. 1); California, act of August 5, 1854 (10 Stat. at L., p. 582); California, act August 18, 1856 (11 Stat. at L., p. 91); California, act June 23, 1860 (12 Stat. at L., p. 104); California, act July 25, 1868 (15 Stat. at L., p. 175); California, act March 3, 1881 (21 Stat. at L., p. 510); and in aid of the Mexican war (see statute of June 2, 1848).

Attorney-General Wirt, in his opinion on an analogous case, says:

"The expenditure thus incurred forms a debt against the United States which they are bound to reimburse. If the expenditures made for such purpose are supplied from the treasury of the State, the United States reimburse the principal without interest; but if, being unable itself, from the condition of its own finances, to meet the emergency, such State has been obliged to borrow money for the purpose, and thus to incur a debt on which she herself has had to pay interest, such debt is essentially a debt due by the United States, and both the principal and interest are to be paid by the United States. (See Opinions of Attorneys-General, vol. 1, p. 174.)"

Thus it will be seen that the precedent for the payment of interest, under the rule adopted for the settlement of claims of war of 1812-'15 and Indian wars above cited, is well established.

These State war claims of these three States rest, therefore, upon a basis well founded, and, by virtue of the political relations existing between these States and the United States under the circumstances herein recited, entitle their petition to Congress for payment to prompt and just consideration.

These States have not been importunate in repeating their demands, but at all times have had a due regard for the fiscal condition of the Federal Treasury. They have been prompt, active, vigilant, and earnest in the due presentation of these State war claims against the United States, understating, if anything, rather than overstating, the exact amount thereof and asking at all times that they be reimbursed only whatever amount they actually paid to aid the United States in maintaining the "common defense," now computed and reported by the head of the War Department, under which all these military services have been performed.

The States of California, Oregon, and Nevada have not been guilty of any laches or delays tending to prejudice their said claims.

Under proper legislation of Congress, and under an appropriate resolution of the Senate, proceedings to carefully investigate these claims have been had, the amount of each and every necessary "cost charge and expense" in the case of each of these States has been heretofore fully inquired into, exactly ascertained, specifically stated, and carefully computed by the honorable Secretary of War.

This branch of the history of these State war claims is, therefore, not embarrassed by any controversy as to the facts, leaving ~~only to be~~ ~~determined by Congress~~ the just measure of the obligations resting upon the General Government resulting from these facts, fully shown in this statement and recited in said reports officially made to the Senate by the Secretary of War and repeated in the several reports made to the House and Senate by the appropriate committees of each.

The question, therefore, that naturally arises is, " What is the duty of Congress under circumstances like these in a case like this ?" These claimants are not private parties, but are States of the Union, *entitled to indemnities from the Federal Government*, who have heretofore relied and do now rely for reimbursement upon the aforesaid legislation of Congress and acts of its highest officers, wherein the amount by them expended for the "common defense" has been exactly ascertained by the Secretary of War and duly reported to the Senate. These States do not ask for reimbursement of any money which they did not pay or fully expend; but they do ask that Congress, without further delay, objection, or evasion, may now fully reimburse them the moneys heretofore by them fully paid in gold coin and appropriated and expended in good faith in aiding the United States, at their own solicitation, to maintain the "common defense," and expended too, by these States when the United States seemingly were unable to pay the same.

Other States of the Union have been reimbursed sums of money which they in good faith expended during the rebellion in aid of the "common defense," and in amounts aggregating (up to March 5, 1892) the sum of $44,725,072.38, as shown by the subjoined correspondence and table, prepared in the Treasury Department, on account of expenses incurred by the States therein named during the war of the rebellion.

This table contains the names of every State loyal during the rebellion *except the States of California, Oregon, and Nevada.* This correspondence and table are as follows, to wit:

TREASURY DEPARTMENT, *March 21, 1892.*

Hon. WILLIAM M. STEWART, *U. S. Senate:*

SIR: In reply to your communication of the 9th instant, I have the honor to transmit herewith a statement of the amounts reimbursed the several States for expenses incurred by them in behalf of the United States during the war of the rebellion, as prepared in the offices of the Second and Third Auditors of the Treasury, together with accompanying reports of said officers.

Respectfully yours,

L. CROUNSE,
Assistant Secretary.

TREASURY DEPARTMENT,
Second Auditor's Office, March 21, 1892.

Respectfully returned to the honorable Secretary of the Treasury, with the report that the amounts allowed through this office, as reimbursement to States for expenses in behalf of the United States during the war of the rebellion, are set forth in Senate Ex. Doc. No. 11, Fifty-first Congress, first session.

No additional allowances have been made.

J. H. FRANKLIN,
Acting Auditor.

TREASURY DEPARTMENT, OFFICE OF THE THIRD AUDITOR,
Washington, D. C., March 15, 1892.

HON. CHARLES FOSTER, *Secretary of the Treasury:*

SIR: I have the honor to return the communication addressed to you by Hon. William M. Stewart, U. S. Senate, on the 9th instant, respecting allowances to the several States for reimbursements of the expenses of raising troops for the United States during the war of the rebellion.

The tabular statement inclosed by him (aggregating $44,137,590.34) is taken from a "Recapitulation," on page 63 of Senate Ex. Doc. No. 11, Fifty-first Congress, first session. It included jointly allowances as shown by the records of this office and as reported by the Second Auditor from his records.

So far as the data came from this office, it is correct; but some further allowances have since been made through this office, as shown by the tabular statement herewith. But I perceive that by oversight a sum of $485 paid to Nebraska was included therein, which sum was *not* for raising troops for the United States, but was expenses in suppressing Indian hostilities. I now drop out that item.

So far as the data came from the records of the Second Auditor I presume it to be correct, but can not so certify; nor can I state officially whether any further allowances have since been made through his office.

Respectfully yours,

A. W. SHAW,
Acting Auditor.

———

Statement accompanying Third Auditor's letter to the Secretary of the Treasury, dated March 15, 1892.

State.	Allowances by Third Auditor.				
	As reported in Senate Ex. Doc. No. 1438, Fortieth Congress, second session, p. 57.	Allowances made since said list.	Total allowances by Third Auditor.	Allowances by Second Auditor as reported in Senate Ex. Doc. No. 11, Fifty-first Congress, first session, p. 63.	Total allowances up to Mar. 15, 1892.
Connecticut	$2,096,950.46	$6,014.83	$2,102,965.29	....	$2,102,965.29
Massachusetts	3,660,483.07	301,133.28	3,961,616.35	$7,608.88	3,969,225.23
Rhode Island	723,530.15	....	723,530.15	....	723,530.15
Maine	1,027,185.00	448.99	1,027,633.99	....	1,027,633.99
New Hampshire	976,081.92	476.56	976,558.48	450.00	977,008.48
Vermont	832,557.40	....	832,557.40	....	832,557.40
New York	3,957,996.98	*102,737.32	4,060,734.30	198,938.52	4,259,672.82
New Jersey	1,420,167.35	6,548.45	1,426,715.80	96,859.44	1,523,575.24
Pennsylvania	3,204,636.24	14,390.04	3,219,026.28	667,074.35	3,886,100.63
Ohio	3,245,319.58	71,348.20	3,316,667.78	....	3,316,667.78
Wisconsin	1,035,059.17	24,102.86	1,059,162.03	....	1,059,162.03
Iowa	1,039,759.45	3,705.35	1,043,464.80	....	1,043,464.80
Illinois	3,080,442.51	1,532.92	3,081,975.43	....	3,081,975.43
Indiana	2,668,520.78	....	2,668,520.78	1,073,208.51	3,741,738.29
Minnesota	70,708.45	462.45	71,260.90	276.75	71,537.65
Kansas	384,138.15	2,298.21	386,436.36	....	386,436.36
Colorado	55,238.84	....	55,238.84	....	55,238.84
Missouri	7,580,421.43	996.37	7,581,417.80	....	7,581,417.80
Michigan	844,262.53	1,493.16	845,755.69	....	845,755.69
Delaware	31,988.96	....	31,988.96	....	31,988.96
Maryland	133,140.99	3,140.65	136,281.64	....	136,281.64
Virginia	48,469.97	....	48,469.97	....	48,469.97
West Virginia	471,063.94	....	471,063.94	....	471,063.94
Kentucky	3,504,466.57	47,137.40	3,551,603.97	....	3,551,603.97
Total	42,092,668.89	587,967.04	42,680,655.93	2,044,416.45	44,725,072.38

* Included in this sum is an allowance of $10,197.42 to New York not yet actually paid, but upon the list to be reported to Congress at its present session, for a deficiency appropriation.

L. W. F.

SECOND AUDITOR'S OFFICE, *March 19, 1892 (Mail Room).*
THIRD AUDITOR'S OFFICE, *March 16, 1892.*

Many of the important facts reported to the Senate by its Committee on Military Affairs, in a statement in support and explanation of Senate bill No. 3420, Fiftieth Congress, first session, which though when reported was intended to apply only to the rebellion war claims of the Territory and State of Nevada, yet the same apply with equal force and correctness to these similar rebellion war claims of the States of California and Oregon, some of which, recited in said statement, are as follows, to wit:

RESULTS OF THE FOREGOING LEGISLATION BY NEVADA.

By these legislative enactments of Nevada substantial and effectual aid was given and guaranteed by Nevada, both as a Territory and State, to the Government of the United States in guarding its overland mail and emigrant route and the line of the proposed transcontinental railroad, in furnishing troops during the war of the rebellion, and for suppressing Indian hostilities and maintaining peace in the country inhabited by the Mormons, and for the common defense, as contemplated in said circular letter of Secretary Seward, along an exposed, difficult, and hostile Indian frontier, and then but sparsely populated. These enactments were fully known to the authorities of the United States and to Congress; they have ever been acquiesced in and met with the sanction and practical indorsement of the United States, in whose interest and for whose benefit they were made. As a partial compensation to these volunteers for this irregular, hazardous, and exposed service in the mountains and on the desert plains, and to aid them to a small extent to maintain families dependent upon them for support, first the Territory and afterwards the State of Nevada offered and paid this small stipend, never suspecting that the United States would not promptly and willingly respond when asked to reimburse the same. These citizens of Nevada who volunteered, enlisted, and did military service for the United States were compelled in many cases to abandon their employment, in which their wages were always lucrative and service continuous, so that nothing less than the individual patriotism of these volunteers enabled the Territory and State of Nevada to cheerfully and promptly respond to every call and requisition made upon them for troops by the United States.

NEVADA'S DILIGENCE IN THESE PREMISES.

The State of Nevada has not slept upon her rights in any of these premises nor been guilty of any *laches;* on the contrary, at all proper times she has respectfully brought the same to the attention of Congress by memorials of her legislature and of her State authorities, and through her representatives in Congress. On March 29, 1867, her legislature first asked for the payment of the claims of the State by a joint resolution, which is printed in the appendix, marked Exhibit No. 8, p. 64. And again, on February 1, 1869, the legislature of Nevada passed a memorial and joint resolution renewing her prayer in these premises, which is also so printed in the appendix, marked Exhibit No. 9, p. 65.

The Journals of the U. S. Senate show that on March 10, 1868, the writer of this report presented the first-mentioned memorial and resolution to the Senate, accompanied with an official statement of the amount of the claims of the State referred to therein. These papers were referred to the Committee on Claims, but the records fail to show that any action was ever taken upon them. On May 29 of the same year the writer of this report introduced a joint resolution (S. 138) providing for the appointment of a board of examiners to examine the claims of the State of Nevada against the United States, and on June 18 of the same year the Committee on Claims, to whom this joint resolution was referred, was discharged from its further consideration. The official statement of the moneys expended by the State of Nevada on account of the United States, and presented to the Senate on March 10, 1868, can not now be found on the files of the Senate.

On February 11, 1885, and January 26, 1887, the legislature of Nevada, renewing its prayer for a reimbursement of the money by her expended for the use and benefit of the United States, further memorialized Congress, asking for the settlement of her claims, which are printed in the appendix and marked Exhibits Nos. 10 and 11, pp. 65 and 66.

CONCLUSIONS AND RECOMMENDATIONS.

Nevada has not demanded a bounty nor presented a claim against the United States for reimbursement of any expenditure she did not in good faith actually make for the use and benefit of the United States, and made, too, only subsequent to the date of the aforesaid appeal of Secretary Seward to the nation, and made, too, in consequence of said appeal and of the subsequent calls and requisitions made upon her then scanty resources and sparse population, and wherein the good faith of the

United States was to be relied upon to make to her ungrudgingly a just reimbursement whenever the United States found itself in a condition to redeem all its obligations.

Nevada has been diligent in making her claim known to Congress, but she has not
with an indecorous speed demanded her pound of flesh, but has waited long and
patiently, believing upon the principle that the higher obligations between States,
like those among men, are not always "set down in writing, signed and sealed in
the form of a bond, but reside rather in honor," and that the obligation of the United
States due her in this case was as sacred as if it had originally been in the form of a
4-per cent U. S. bond, now being redeemed by the United States at $1.27 upon each
$1 of this particular form of its unpaid obligations.

Nevada has not solicited any charity in this case, but, on the contrary, by numerous petitions and memorials has respectfully represented to Congress why the taxes
heretofore levied upon her people and paid out of her own treasury to her volunteer
troops in gold and silver coin to aid the United States at its own solicitation to protect itself and maintain the general welfare should be now returned to her by the
General Government.

Congress should not forget that during the long period of the nation's peril the
citizens of Nevada, like those of California (when not engaged in the military or
naval service of the United States) not only guarded the principal gold and silver
mines of the country then discovered, and prevented them from falling into the hands
of the public enemy, but also worked them so profitably for the general welfare as
to enable the United States to make it possible to resume specie payment and to
redeem its bonds at 27 per cent above par, and to repay all its money-lenders at a
high rate of interest, and that, too, not in the depreciated currency with which it
paid Nevada's volunteer troops, but in gold coin of standard value.

As these expenditures were honestly made by the Territory and State of Nevada,
your committee do not think that, under all the peculiar and exceptional circumstances of this case, the action of the Territory and State of Nevada should be hewn
too nicely or too hypercritically by the United States at this late date. These
expenditures were all made in perfect good faith and for patriotic purposes, and
secured effectual aid to the United States which otherwise could not have been
obtained without a much larger expenditure. The State of Nevada in good faith
assumed and paid all the obligations of the Territory of Nevada to aid the United
States, and issued and sold its own bonds for their payment, upon which bonds it
has paid interest until the present time. The only question now for consideration
is, shall the United States in equal good faith and under all the circumstances
herein recited relieve the State of Nevada from this obligation, or shall the United
States insist and require it to be paid by the people of that State alone?

In support of that portion of these State war claims, which relates
to the indemnity and reimbursement of the cash paid by these three
States as *interest* for the hire and use of the principal by them borrowed,
with which to defray the "costs, charges, and expenses" of furnishing
said 18,715 volunteer troops there is submitted herewith and printed
in the appendix as Exhibit No. 1 a copy of the decision of the U. S.
Court of Claims, rendered June 8, 1891, on the petition of the State of
New York in the cause in that court entitled "The State of New York
v. The United States" (26 U. S Court Claims Reports, 467–509).

That court in adjudicating the claim so presented to it in said petition of that State for *interest* actually paid out for the hire and use of
money by it borrowed and expended to aid the United States to maintain
the "common defense," rested its opinion and entered its decree and
judgment upon principles identical in all respects with those contended
for herein, and that decision being the latest judicial declaration and
announcement of the obligation of the United States incurred under
circumstances similar to those herein recited, is entitled to the careful
and respectful consideration of Congress in these premises.

Respectfully,

JOHN MULLAN,
*Of Counsel for California, and
Attorney for Oregon and Nevada, Claimant States.*

No. 1310 CONNECTICUT AVENUE,
Washington, D. C., January 4, 1894.

CITY OF WASHINGTON,
  District of Columbia, ss:
John Mullan, on first being duly sworn, says that he is now, and for many years last past has been, of counsel for the State of California and attorney for the States of Oregon and Nevada in all matters recited and referred to in the foregoing statement, all of which he has carefully read and knows fully the contents of all thereof; that all the matters therein recited are true of his own personal knowledge, except those matters therein recited upon information and belief, and as to those matters he believes the same to be true; that the United States are now justly indebted to the State of California in the sum of $3,951,915.42, and to the State of Oregon in the sum of $335,152.88, and to the State of Nevada in the sum of $404,040.70, said sums being the identical amounts as reported to the Senate by the honorable Secretary of War, and as recited in Senate Ex. Docs. Nos. 10, 11, 17, Fifty-first Congress, first session, and in Senate bill No. 1295, and in House bill No. 4959, Fifty-third Congress, second session, which two bills are printed in the appendix herewith and marked Exhibits Nos. 2 and 3, and that no portion of any thereof has ever heretofore been paid by the United States to said States, or to either of them. That the foregoing statement* embodies substantially the same facts (errors of omission and commission excepted) as were submitted in a letter signed by all the Senators and Representatives in Congress from California, Oregon, and Nevada on March 16, 1892, addressed to the House Committee on Appropriations, in support of the joint request of said delegations to said committee to include these State war claims in the deficiency appropriation bill during the Fifty-second Congress, but which request was refused only because said claims were not recognized by the subcommittee on deficiencies of said committee as being in the nature of deficiencies, but that said State claims in the opinion of said subcommittee should otherwise be provided for.

JOHN MULLAN.

Subscribed and sworn to before me this 4th day of January, 1894.
GEO. E. TERRY,
[NOTARIAL SEAL.] *Notary Public.*

APPENDIX.

EXHIBIT No. 1.

[Court of Claims, No. 16430. The State of New York v. The United States. Decided June 8, 1891.]

FINDINGS OF FACT.

This case having been heard by the Court of Claims, the court, upon the evidence, finds the facts as follows:

I.

Between the 22d day of April, 1861, and the 4th day of July, 1861, the State of New York, by its governor, Hon. Edwin D. Morgan, who was the commander in chief of its military forces, and by its other duly authorized officers and agents, enlisted, enrolled, armed, equipped, and caused to be mustered into the military service of the United States, to aid in the suppression of the war of the rebellion, 38 regiments of troops for the period of two years, or during the war, and numbering in all 30,000 men.

---

*Exhibits Nos. 4, 5, 6, and 7 are also made parts of this statement, April 14, 1894.

II.

Such troops were so enlisted, armed, equipped, and mustered into the service of the United States, under and pursuant to the provisions of chapter 277 of the laws of the S ate of New York, passed April 15, 1861, and which act provided that all expenditures for arms, supplies, or equipments necessary for such forces should be made under the direction of the governor, lieutenant-governor, secretary of State, comptroller, State engineer and surveyor, and State treasurer, or a majority of them, and that the moneys therefor should, on the certificate of the governor, be drawn from the treasury, on the warrant of the comptroller, in favor of such person or persons as shall, from time to time, be designated by the governor, and the sum of $3,000,000, or so much thereof as might be necessary, was appropriated by the act, out of any moneys in the treasury not otherwise appropriated, to defray the expenses authorized by the act, or any other expenses of mustering the militia of the State, or any part thereof, into the service of the United States.

The act also imposes, for the fiscal year commencing on the 1st day of October, 1861, a State tax for such sum as the comptroller should deem necessary to meet the expenses thereby authorized, not to exceed two mills on each dollar of the valuation of real and personal property in the State, to be assessed, raised, levied, collected, and paid in the same manner as the other State taxes are levied, assessed, collected, and paid into the treasury. (2 Laws of New York, session of 1861, p. 631, 636.)

III.

There was no money in the treasury of the State in 1861 which was not specifically appropriated for the expenses of the State government, and no money which could be used to defray the expenses of enlisting, enrolling, arming, equipping, and mustering such troops into the service of the United States.

IV.

The fiscal year began on the first day of October and ended on the 30th day of September, and the tax rate necessary to raise the tax required for the purpose of raising the moneys necessary to defray the expenses of the State government and other expenses authorized by law, in any fiscal year, is fixed by the legislature, which convenes on the first Tuesday in January preceding the commencement of the fiscal year for which the taxes are required; that is to say: For the fiscal year beginning on the 1st day of October, 1860, and ending on the 30th day of September, 1861, the tax rate was fixed by the legislature which began its session on the first Tuesday in January, 1860, and the tax rate necessary to defray the expenditures for the fiscal year beginning October 1, 1861, and ending September 30, 1862, was fixed by the legislature which began its session on the first Tuesday of January, 1861.

V.

Under the laws of the State of New York then existing, the moneys to be collected for the State taxes could not reach the State treasury and be made applicable for use in defraying its expenditures until the months of April and May of the fiscal year for which they were levied, and in some instances not until a later date, and the moneys authorized to be raised by the act of 1861, to defray the expenses of enrolling, enlisting, arming, equipping, and mustering in such troops, did not reach the State treasury, and were not available for use by the State officers in defraying such expenses until the months of April and May, 1862.

The State comptroller, in 1861, made an apportionment of the State taxes among the several counties, and issued to the board of supervisors of each county a requisition requiring such board to cause to be levied and collected and paid into the State treasury the county's quota of such tax.

The board of supervisors were required by law to meet in the month of November for the purpose, among other things, of levying such tax and apportioning it among the several towns of the county and making out a tax roll and warrant to the collector of taxes in each town, for the levy and collection of the town's quota of the tax into the county treasury, and each town had until the 1st day of February in which to pay its quota of said tax into the county treasury, and the county treasurer had until the 1st day of May to pay the quota of the county into the State treasury, and if he failed to pay in the amount by that time the comptroller might report the matter to the attorney-general, who must wait thirty days, or until the first day of June, before proceedings could be taken to compel payment.

VI.

The total tax rate of the State, fixed at the session of the legislature beginning on the first Tuesday, 1861, was 3¼ mills, of which 1¼ mills was the amount of the tax authorized by chapter 277, and the moneys realized from this tax were paid into the State treasury as follows:

In January, 1862	$190,403.72
In February, 1862	153,792.32
In March, 1862	696,696.00
In April, 1862	170,909.34
In May, 1862	614,307.09
In June, 1862	1,345,671.61
In July, 1862	68,365.27
In August, 1862	180,023.03
In September, 1862	800,246.93
And the sum of, subsequent to October	274,590.64

VII.

The State of New York had no other means of raising the money required for the purpose of immediately defraying the expenses of enlisting, enrolling, arming, equipping, and mustering in such troops, except by borrowing money in anticipation of the collection of its State tax, and between June 3, 1861, and July 2, 1861, it issued for that purpose bonds in anticipation of such State tax, to provide for the public defense, to the amount of $1,250,000, payable on July 1, 1862, except that $100,000 was payable June 1, 1862, at the rate of 7 per cent per annum, payable quarterly, which at that time was the legal rate of interest under the laws of the State of New York.

The issue of all these bonds was necessary for the purpose of providing the money required, and the full amount of the face value of such bonds was received by the State, upon the sale thereof, and was used and applied by it, together with other moneys, in raising troops, and the entire sum expended by the State for such purpose, between the 23d day of April, 1861, and the 1st day of January, 1862, was $2,873,501.19, exclusive of any interest upon the bonds or loans made by the State for that purpose.

VIII.

In addition to the sums aforesaid, the State of New York paid, on account of interest which from time to time accrued on said bonds issued in anticipation of the tax for the public defense, the sum of $91,320.84, as follows:

1861:	
October 1	$1,750.00
Same date	2,197.20
December 27	22,331.97
1862:	
January 2	1,750.00
Same date	1,750.00
March 26	18,375.00
April 1	1,750.00
Same date	1,750.00
June 3	1,166.67
June 26	18,375.00
July 1	1,750.00
Same date	1,750.00
September 26	16,625.00
Total	91,320.84

And by chapter 192 of the laws of the State of New York of the session of 1862, passed April 12, the legislature specifically appropriated the sum of $1,250,000 "for the redemption of comptroller's bonds issued for loans to the treasury in anticipation of the State tax to provide for the public defense, imposed by chapter 277 of the laws of 1861, reimbursable, viz, $100,000 on the 1st day of June and $1,150,000 on the 1st day of July, 1862, and the further sum of $91,320.84 for the payment of the accruing interest on said bonds."

IX.

Of the remainder of the above sum of $2,873,501.19 necessarily expended by the State of New York, for the purpose aforesaid, between April, 1861, and January, 1862, after deducting the amount of $1,250,000, raised by issue of bonds, the sum of $1,623,501.19 was taken from the canal fund, so called, of the State, which fund, under the constitution of the State, is a sinking fund for the ultimate payment of what is known as the canal debt of the State.

Under the tax rate of 1860 there had been levied and collected and paid into the treasury of the State the sum of $2,039,663.06 for the benefit of and to the credit of the canal fund, which moneys reached the treasury of the State in April and May, 1861, and were then in the treasury to be invested by the State officers, pursuant to the requirements of law and the constitution of the State, in securities for the benefit of the canal fund, and the interest accruing on which must be paid into that fund, and on May 21, 1861, the lieutenant-governor, comptroller, treasurer, and the attorney-general, who constituted the commissioners of the canal fund, authorized the comptroller to use $2,000,000 of the canal-fund moneys for military purposes until the 1st day of October next, and $1,000,000 until the 1st day of January, 1862, at 5 per cent, and of this amount the sum of $1,623,501.19 was used by the comptroller for the purpose of defraying the expenses of raising and equipping such troops. The following is the order:

STATE OF NEW YORK, CANAL DEPARTMENT,
Albany, May 21, 1861.

The comptroller is to be permitted to use $2,000,000 of the canal-fund moneys for military purposes until the 1st day of October next, when the commissioners of the canal fund will invest $1,000,000 of the canal sinking fund under section 1, article 7, in the tax levied for military purposes until July 1, 1862, at 5 per cent, and the comptroller may use $1,000,000 of the tax levied to pay interest on the $12,000,000 debt until January 1, 1862, when the commissioners will, if they have the means, replace that or as large an amount as they may have the means to do it with from the toll of the next fiscal year, so as that the whole advance from the canal fund on account of the tax be $2,000,000. It is understood the comptroller will retain the taxes now in the process of collection for canal purpose until the above investments are made, paying the funds 5 per cent interest therefor.

Indorsed: We assent to the within-named arrangement. Albany, May 22, 1861.
R. CAMPBELL,
Lieutenant-Governor.
ROBERT DENNISTON,
P. DORSHEIMER,
CHS. G. MYERS,
Commissioners of the Canal Fund.

On December 28, 29, and 31, 1861, the United States repaid to the State, on account of moneys so expended, the sum of $1,113,000, leaving the sum of $510,501.19 unpaid of the moneys which had been used from the canal fund, and which sum was placed to the canal fund, with interest, on April 4, 1862.

The amount of interest at 5 per cent per annum on the moneys so used of the canal fund during the time it was used by the State for the public defense, in raising troops, was $48,187.13. But during the same time the State had received interest on portions of the money while it was lying in bank unused to the amount of $8,319.95, and the net deficiency of the State on account of interest on such moneys during the period which they were so used was $39,867.18, which sum was paid into the canal fund from the State treasury, April 4, 1861.

X.

The total amount of the sums so paid by the State of New York, for interest upon its bonds issued in anticipation of the tax for the public defense, and of the amount placed by it in the canal fund for moneys used of that fund, as aforesaid, for the purpose of defraying the expenses of raising and equipping such troops, is $131,188.02, and no part of the same has been paid to the State of New York by the United States, nor has the State been reimbursed therefor, or for any part thereof, by the United States.

XI.

On September 5, 1861, the Federal War Department, by a general order, directed all persons having authority to raise volunteer regiments, batteries, or companies in the State of New York to report to Hon. Edwin D. Morgan, governor of the State, at Albany, and they and their commands were placed under the command of Governor Morgan, who was given authority to reorganize them and prepare them for the service in such manner as he might deem most advantageous for the interests of the General Government.

The order also provided that all commissioned officers of such regiments, batteries, or companies now in service raised in the State of New York independent of the State authorities, might receive commissions from the governor of the State by reporting to the adjutant-general of the State and filing in his office a duplicate of the muster rolls of their respective organizations.

XII.

On September 28, 1861, Governor Morgan was commissioned a major-general in the military service of the United States, and on October 26, 1861, a new military department was created, to be called the Department of the State of New York, and placed under command of Governor Morgan, as major-general of volunteers in the service of the United States, with headquarters at Albany.

XIII.

On June 27, 1861, Hon. William H. Seward, Secretary of State of the United States, telegraphed to Governor Morgan acknowledging that New York had furnished 50,000 troops for service in the war of the rebellion, and thanking the governor for his efforts in that direction, and on July 25, 1861, Secretary Seward telegraphed Governor Morgan: "Buy arms and equipments as fast as you can. We pay all." And on July 27, 1861, that "Treasury notes for part advances will be furnished on your call for them." And on August 16, 1861, Hon. Simon Cameron, then Secretary of War of the United States, telegraphed to Governor Morgan: "Adopt such measures as may be necessary to fill up your regiments as rapidly as possible. We need the men. Let me know the best the Empire State can do to aid the country in the present emergency." On February 11, 1862, Hon. Edwin M. Stanton, Secretary of War, telegraphed Governor Morgan: "The Government will refund the State for the advances for troops as speedily as the Treasurer can obtain funds for that purpose."

Governor Morgan continued to be major-general of volunteers in the Federal military service until about the expiration of his term of office as governor on the first day of January, 1863, when he tendered his resignation, which was subsequently accepted.

XIV.

The moneys above specified, which were actually expended by the State of New York, were necessarily paid out and expended for the purpose of enlisting, enrolling, subsisting, clothing, supplying, arming, equipping, paying, and transporting such troops, and causing them to be mustered into the military service of the United States, where they were employed in aiding to suppress the insurrection which then existed against the Government of the United States, known as the war of the rebellion, and were so paid and expended at the request of the civil and military authorities of the United States.

XV.

A large portion of such expenditures were made and incurred by the Hon. Edwin D. Morgan, governor of the State, while acting in that capacity, and pursuant to his authority as such major-general.

XVI.

Prior to January 3, 1889, the State of New York had presented, from time to time, various claims and accounts to the Treasury Department of the United States for settlement and allowance, for the charges and expenses incurred by it in enlisting, enrolling, arming, equipping, and mustering into the military service of the United States such troops, which claims amounted in aggregate to $2,950,479.46, and included charges for all the moneys paid and placed as hereinbefore specified.

That such Department has allowed thereon, from time to time, various sums, amounting in the aggregate to $2,775,915.24, leaving a balance of $174,564.22, not allowed, and the claims and accounts for which were pending in said Department unadjusted on said 3d day of January, 1889.

That of said sum of $174,564.22 not allowed by the Treasury Department, the sums hereinbefore specified, amounting to $131,188.02, constituted a part, and on said 3d day of January, 1889, the Hon. Charles S. Fairchild, then Secretary of the Treasury of the United States, transmitted to this court, under section 1063 of the Revised Statutes of the United States, the said claim of the State of New York, so pending in said Department, for said sum of $131,188.02, together with the vouchers, proofs, and documents relating thereto on file in said Department, to be proceeded with in this court according to law.

The claim of the State of New York for expenditures and expenses in furnishing troops with clothing and munitions of war, as set forth in the foregoing findings, was filed in the Treasury Department in May, 1862, which claim included said items for interest, and said claim for interest has from said time been suspended in said Department, and was so suspended at the time the matter was transmitted to this court.

CONCLUSION OF LAW.

Upon the foregoing findings the court determines as a conclusion of law that the claimant is entitled to recover the sum of $91,320.84.

OPINION.

WELDON, J., delivered the opinion of the court.

The petition alleges that the defendants became indebted to the claimant on the 1st day of July, 1862, for money laid out and expended to and for the use of defendants, at their request, in the sum of $3,131,188.02, and of this there has been paid the sum of $3,000,000, leaving a balance due the petitioner of $131,188.02.

It is further alleged that the necessity of said expenditure grew out of the wants of the Government in the early part of the civil war, and that for the purpose of maintaining national authority, through their proper officers, said defendants requested the State of New York, in common with other States, to provide means and munitions of war for the use of the Government; that in pursuance of such request the claimant did provide and render to the United States a large number of troops, and did equip the same with arms, clothing, and munitions of war, and did also render to the Government arms and munitions in addition to such as were required for the use of troops enrolled in the State of New York; that in equipping said troops and in furnishing said material for other troops the said State expended the sum of $3,000,000; that in complying with said request so made by the defendants, in furnishing equipments for troops, the claimant was compelled to borrow a large part of said sum, there not being in the treasury of said State funds sufficient to meet said expenditure; that bonds of said State were issued upon which claimant was compelled and did pay a large amount of interest, to wit, the sum of $131,188.02; that under the act of Congress of July 27, 1861, a portion of the expenditure of said claimant has been paid by defendants, but there still remains unpaid a portion of the costs, charges, and expenses properly incurred by said State in enrolling, subsisting, clothing, supplying, arming, equipping, paying, and transporting said troops as aforesaid, to wit, the amount paid by the State of New York for interest, the said sum of $131,188.02; that after the payment of said sum, and within six years from such payment, a claim for said amount was presented to the Secretary of the Treasury and such proceedings were thereon had in the Treasury Department, and before the proper officer thereof, to wit, the Second Comptroller; that on or about the 23d day of December, 1869, the question of said claim for interest so paid by the State of New York as aforesaid against the United States was suspended, subject to future decision, and thereafter on or about the 7th day of June, 1882, the said claim and the question of the validity thereof was presented to the Attorney-General of the United States for his opinion, and said Attorney-General thereafter, and on or about the 23d day of July, 1883, rendered his opinion thereon, and the same was filed in the Treasury Department of the United States, which opinion is to the effect that said claim of the State of New York does not come within the provisions of the act of July 27, 1861. Thereafter such proceedings were had in the Treasury Department in the matter of said claim; that at the request of said claimant, by its attorney in fact, on or about the 3d day of January, 1889, the Secretary of the Treasury did, under the provisions of section 1063 of the Revised Statutes of the United States, transmit the said claim, with all the vouchers, papers, proofs, and documents pertaining thereto, to the Court of Claims, there to be proceeded in accordance with law.

The findings in substance tend to maintain the allegations of the petitions except in the amount actually paid by claimant as interest on the funds used in the purchase of material and the payment of expenses incident to the equipment of troops. Of said $131,188.02 the sum of $39,867.18 is based upon the following state of facts:

Under the tax rate of 1860 of said State there had been levied, collected, and paid into the treasury of said State the sum of $2,039,663.06 for the benefit of the canal fund, which money reached the treasury in April and May, 1861, and was then in the treasury, to be invested by certain State officers, pursuant to the law and requirements of the constitution of the State, in securities for the benefit of the canal fund.

On the 21st day of May, 1861, the lieutenant-governor, comptroller, treasurer, and attorney-general, who constituted the commissioners of the canal fund, authorized the comptroller to use $2,000,000 of the canal fund money for military purposes until the 1st day of October following, and $1,000,000 until the 1st day of January, 186? at 5 per cent, and of this amount the sum of $1,623,501.19 was used by the comptroller for the purpose of defraying the expense in raising and equipping troops as aforesaid.

On December 28, 29, and 31, 1861, the United States repaid to the State, on account of moneys so expended, the sum of $1,113,000, leaving the sum of $510,501.19 unpaid of the moneys which had been used from the canal fund, and which sum was placed to the canal fund, with interest, on April 4, 1862.

The total amount of interest on the moneys so used from the canal fund, during the time that it was used by the State for the public defense in raising troops, was $48,187.13. But during the same time the State received interest on some portions of the money while it was lying in bank to the amount of $8,319.95, and the net deficiency of the State, on account of interest on such moneys during the period which they were used is $39,867.18, which sum was paid into the canal fund from the State treasury April 4, 1862.

The order made by said State officers under and by virtue of which the money of the canal fund was appropriated is as follows:

STATE OF NEW YORK, CANAL DEPARTMENT,
Albany, May 21, 1861.

The comptroller is to be permitted to use $2,000,000 of the canal fund moneys for military purposes until the 1st day of October next, when the commissioners of the canal fund will invest $1,000,000 of the canal sinking fund under section 1, article 7, in the tax levied for military purposes until the 1st of July, 1862, at 5 per cent, and the comptroller may use $1,000,000 of the tax levied to pay interest on the $12,000,000 debt until the 1st of January, 1862, when the commissioners will, if they have the means, replace that or as large an amount as they may have the means to do it with from the toll of the next fiscal year, so as that the whole advance from the canal fund on account of the tax be $2,000,000. It is understood the comptroller will retain the taxes now in the process of collection for canal purposes until the above investments are made, paying the funds 5 per cent interest therefor.

Indorsed: We assent to the within-named arrangement. Albany, May 22, 1861.
R. CAMPBELL,
Lieutenant-Governor.
ROBERT DENNISON,
P. DORSHEIMER,
CHS. G. MYERS,
Commissioners of the Canal Fund.

The amount of money actually paid as interest on the bonds issued is $91,320.84, and the amount of interest credited to and paid into the canal fund for the money used of said canal fund is $39,867.18; those two sums make in the aggregate the sum of $131,188.02, and for that amount this proceeding was commenced and is prosecuted.

Incident to the commencement of the civil war, which was inaugurated in its hostilities by the bombardment of Fort Sumter by the Confederate forces, there arose an emergency and crisis in the history and condition of the United States which called for the most effective and vigorous measures of military preparation on the part of the Federal power to maintain its authority and to preserve from dismemberment the Union of the States. And although the requisition of the 75,000 troops provided for in the first proclamation of the President was thought to be adequate, the subsequent development and magnitude of the insurrection demonstrated the inability of that force to accomplish the purpose of reestablishing the national supremacy in the States assuming to exercise the right of secession and the maintenance of that right by military force.

At the time of the commencement of the war Congress was not in session, and the Executive Department was compelled to avail itself of all the constitutional means within its power to deal with an existing state of hostility, and for that purpose, on the 15th of April, 1861, the President issued a proclamation calling for the militia of the several States " in order to suppress combinations and cause the laws to be duly executed."

Upon the same day the legislature of New York passed an act making an appropriation of $3,000,000 to be applied in the expenditure for arms, supplies, and equipments for the soldiers mustered into the service of the United States in the suppression of the rebellion; and every assurance was given by the executive branch of the Government that the State would be reimbursed in its expenditures in complying with the requirements of the President.

The same proclamation which called for 75,000 men called an extra session of Congress for the 4th day of July following; and in pursuance of that proclamation the first session of the Thirty-seventh Congress was held.

On the 27th day of July, 1861, Congress passed an act entitled "An act to indemnify the States for expenses incurred by them in defense of the United States," as follows:

" That the Secretary of the Treasury be, and is hereby, directed, out of any moneys in the Treasury not otherwise appropriated, to pay to the governor of any State, or its duly authorized agents, the costs, charges, and expenses properly incurred by said State for enrolling, subsisting, clothing, supplying, arming, equipping, paying, and transporting its troops employed in aiding in suppressing the present insurrection against the United States, to be settled upon proper vouchers to be filed and passed upon by the proper accounting officers of the Treasury." (12 St. L., p. 276.)

On the 8th of March, 1862, Congress passed a joint resolution as follows:

" Whereas doubts have arisen as to the true intent and meaning of an act entitled 'An act to indemnify the States for expenses incurred by them in defense of the United States,' approved July 27, 1861:

" *Be it resolved by the Senate and House of Representatives in Congress assembled,* That the said act shall be construed to apply to expenses incurred as well after as before the date of the approval thereof."

Some question was made in the brief and oral argument of the counsel for the defendants as to proper pendency in this court of these proceedings because of the statute of limitations.

In the case of Finn *v.* The United States, 123 U. S. R., 227, it is decided:

" It is a condition or qualification of the right to a judgment against the United States in the Court of Claims that the claimant, when not laboring under any one of the disabilities named in the statute, voluntarily put his claim in suit or present it to the proper Department for settlement within six years after suit could be commenced thereon against the United States."

The findings in the present case show that in 1862, in less than one year after the origin of the claim, the claimant presented it to the proper Department for adjudication and payment, and that from that time until the commencement of this case it was pending in the Department as an unadjusted claim. The State never abandoned it, and the United States, through its proper officers, never formally rejected it. It was pending in the Treasury Department, within the meaning of the decisions of the Supreme Court and this court, at the time it was transmitted under the order of the Secretary of the Treasury, as shown in the record.

It was not *res judicata*, and does not come within the law laid down in the case of Jackson *v.* The United States (19 Ct. Cls., 504), and State of Illinois *v.* The United States (20 Ct. Cls., 342).

The court having jurisdiction of the claim, it must be disposed of on its merits.

It is manifest, from the legislation, that Congress intended to approve the action of the Executive Department, in the assurance, that the States would be reimbursed in their expenditures incident to the enrollment of the militia in defense of the national authority.

It is not necessary to examine and discuss the obligations of the States, in such an unprecedented condition of the Federal Government. It is sufficient to assume that the liability of the defendants in this case depends upon the construction of the act of 1861 and the joint resolution of 1862.

If the claim comes within the scope and terms of the act of 1862 the plaintiff has the right to recover; if it does not, there is no liability.

The aggregate of the demand is $131,188.02, and is composed of two items originating in different forms.

Ninety-one thousand three hundred and twenty dollars and eighty-four cents compose a claim for interest paid by the State, on bonds issued by it for the purpose of raising money to defray the expense incident to the enrollment of the soldiers for the national service.

The findings show that the Treasury of the State of New York, at the time the call was made, was deficient in the funds requisite to meet the expense, and that it was necessary to negotiate bonds at 7 per cent interest, to supply that deficiency. The said sum of $91,320 is the amount of interest paid on those bonds.

The other item, $39,867.18, of the claim is for an alleged expense growing out of the use of certain funds coming into the treasury of the State prior to October 1, 1861, and which were to be invested by the State officers pursuant to the requirements of law and the constitution of the State in securities for the benefit of the canal fund.

In connection with this item of claim it may be said that no interest was paid by the State of New York; it simply failed to realize for the benefit of the canal fund certain interest which, by the investment of the money appropriated for the use of the defendants, it might otherwise have saved to that fund.

We will consider the rights of the claimant as to each demand separately. It is contended on the part of the claimant that both items come legitimately within "costs, charges, and expenses," as provided by the act of July, 1861, while the defendants insist, that as to both items of claim, it is an attempt to compel the United States to pay interest on an alleged obligation, where they have not expressly agreed to do so.

Section 1091, R. S., provides:

"No interest shall be allowed on any claim up to the time of the rendition of judgment thereon by the Court of Claims, unless upon a contract expressly stipulating for the payment of interest."

In the case of Tillson v. United States (100 U. S. R., 43), it was in substance decided:

"Where the claim of a party for loss and damage growing out of the alleged failure of the United States to perform its contracts with him, as to time and manner of payment is, by special act of Congress, referred to the Court of Claims 'to investigate the same, and to ascertain, determine, and adjudge the amount equitably due, if any, for such loss and damage,'—*Held*, that the rules of law applicable to the adjudication of claims by that court in the exercise of its general jurisdiction must govern, and that interest, not having been stipulated for in the contracts, can not be allowed thereon."

It is not necessary to speculate upon the question of the liability of the Government, for the payment of interest as such. The statute and decisions are plain and uniform on that subject, and unless there is an express contract to that effect no interest can be recovered. If this demand is in law a claim for interest, in the common and judicial sense of that term, there being no express undertaking to pay interest, in and by the words of the statute, on which the suit is based, and from which the obligation is deduced, no liability exists. It is contended by the claimant's counsel that this is not a proceeding to recover interest as such, but that the demand comes within that clause of the statute providing indemnification to the State for "costs, charges, and expenses" incurred by it in furnishing troops under the call of the President.

A liability upon the part of the Government to pay interest can not arise from implication, for the reason the statute defining the jurisdiction of the court, expressly declares, that no interest shall be allowed on any claim up to the rendition of the judgment thereon, in the Court of Claims, unless upon a contract expressly stipulating for interest.

Regarding the statute, as having the force of a contract, it has no provision from which by construction, it can be inferred, that the defendants assumed to pay the claimant any interest as such, upon any advances made by it, in defraying the expenses of the troops furnished the United States in pursuance to the proclamation of the President.

The law being that the Government does not pay interest except where the contract or statute expressly provides for the payment of interest, it is unnecessary to examine the many cases referred to by the very able argument of the counsel for the Government. If this is a proceeding to enforce the payment of interest, then the authorities relied on by the defendants are conclusively decisive of this case, and the judgment must be for the defendants.

It was not the duty of the State of New York, as one of the States of the Federal Union, acting independently to suppress the insurrection of 1861; but it was its duty to comply with all constitutional requisitions of the central government, in its efforts to maintain the authority of the United States, and to enforce the law of federal jurisdiction.

The findings show, that in responding to the call of the President for men and means, the authorities of the State did everything in their power to comply with the Federal requisition, and in so doing not only availed themselves of the taxing power of the State, but the public credit of the State government sought the money market to replenish the treasury of the State in defraying the expenses incident to the call of the President.

In appreciation of the alacrity with which the authorities acted, Congress on the 27th of July, 1861, twenty-three days after the convention of the Houses, passed the act upon which the claimant now seeks satisfaction and compensation.

It is alleged on the part of the claimant that—
"The act of July 27, 1861, constitutes a statutory contract of indemnity on the part of the United States with the several States furnishing troops as therein specified, and the payments made by the State of New York, for which this claim is filed, having been actually and necessarily made for the purpose contemplated by that act, they became part of the expenditures made by the State which the Federal Government has obligated itself to reimburse." (Huidekoper's Lessee v. Douglas, 3 Cranch, R. 1–70.)

The demand of the claimant does not necessarily require that it should maintain the full legal import of this proposition, as the statute of our jurisdiction provides that this court shall have jurisdiction of "all claims founded upon the Constitution of the United States or on any law of Congress." (24 Stat. L., 505.)

If by the terms of the act of July, 1861, Congress assumed to pay the claimant the kind and character of charges represented by the interest paid by the State, and have not done so, the right of the State to recover is clear and unquestionable; and the only question for us to decide in this connection is, whether the payment of interest on bonds issued by the claimant comes within the terms "costs, charges, and expenses properly incurred by said State."

In determining that question, we must not lose sight of the fundamental proposition of law, that the Government is not liable for interest, unless it has expressly obligated itself to pay interest, and it is not pretended that it has done so in this matter. Whatever may be said in the construction of this statute, the fact remains, that the claimant in the payment of interest to its bondholders disbursed and expended its money, as effectually, as though it had paid money directly from the treasury, to some person from whom it had purchased clothing and munitions of war. If the State of New York had limited its effort in complying with the request of the General Government, to its actual resources of money in the Treasury, it might have been the performance of its duty literally; but if the resources of its credit were opened to it, and it did not avail itself of that resource, the spirit of its obligation would have been violated to the detriment of the public service, and perhaps to the prejudice of the final success of the Federal power. The statute, it will be observed, is broad and liberal in the use of terms defining the obligation of the United States, "costs, charges and expenses."

In the construction of a law somewhat similar to the act of July, 1861, Mr. Wirt, Attorney-General of the United States, gave an opinion stating:
"In construing this law, it is proper to advert to the principle on which it was founded, and to the object which it proposes to effect. The principle is this: The United States are bound by the relation which subsists between the General and State governments to provide the means of carrying on war, and, as a part of the business of war, to provide for the defense of the several States. When the United States fails to make such provision, and the States have to defend themselves by means of their own resources, the expenditure thus incurred forms a debt against the United States which they are bound to reimburse. If the expenditures made for such purpose are supplied from the treasury of the States, the United States reimburse the principal without interest; *but if, being itself unable, from the condition of its own finances to meet the emergency, such State has been obliged to borrow money for the purpose, and thus to incur a debt on which she herself has had to pay interest, such debt is essentially a debt due by the United States, and both the principal and interest are to be paid by the United States. So that whenever a State has had to pay interest by reason of her taking the place of the United States in time of war, such interest forms a just charge against the United States. If a State borrows the money at once, on the first occurrence of the emergency, and expends the specific money so borrowed, both the borrowing and the expenditure being* flagrante bello, *there seems to be no doubt that the claim, both for the principal and the interest, which she would have paid upon such loan, would be a fair charge against the United States on the principle of this law.*" (1 Op. Att'y Gen., 723.)

Although this opinion was given before the statute forbidding the payment of interest was passed (March 3, 1863, Revised Statutes, 1091), it is important to be considered in making a legal distinction between interest actually paid and interest on funds in the Treasury at the time the requisition was made.

"It has been the general rule of the officers of the Government in adjusting and allowing unliquidated and disputed claims against the United States to refuse to give interest. That this rule is sometimes at variance with that which governs the acts of private citizens in a court of justice would not authorize us to depart from it in this case. The rule, however, is not mere form, and especially is it not so in regard to claims allowed by special acts of Congress, or referred by such acts to some Department or officer for settlement." (McKee's Case, 91 U. S. R., 442, and 11 C. Cls. R., 72.)

In the performance of the duty under the call, the officers of the State purchased the required munitions of war so long as they had funds; and when they had no money, the Government still needing the supply, they paid out money for the use of money, in order that the State might fully discharge every possible duty in the restoration of Federal authority. The payment of interest was a cost properly incurred by the claimants under the requisition of the President, and comes within the letter of the act of July, 1861, and for that item the claimants have a right to recover.

The second item of claim for $39,867.18 originates in a different form. There was no absolute payment of interest. Under the State policy of New York a portion of the tax is devoted to what is called the canal fund, and upon this fund the State is in the habit of receiving interest, the same being loaned for the benefit of that fund.

The appropriation of the canal fund for the purpose of defraying the expense of equipping the troops of the United States was in the pursuance of the following order:

STATE OF NEW YORK, CANAL DEPARTMENT,
Albany, May 21, 1861.

The comptroller is to be permitted to use $2,000,000 of the canal-fund moneys for military purposes until the 1st day of October next, when the commissioners of the canal fund will invest $1,000,000 of the canal sinking fund, under section 1, article 7, in the tax levied for military purposes until the 1st of July, 1862, at 5 per cent, and the comptroller may use $1,000,000 of the tax levied to pay interest on the $12,000,000 debt until the 1st of January, 1862, when the commissioners will, if they have the means, replace that or as large an amount as they may have the means to do it with from the toll of the next fiscal year, so as that the whole advance from the canal fund on account of the tax be $2,000,000. It is understood the comptroller will retain the taxes now in the process of collection for canal purposes until the above investments are made, paying the funds 5 per cent interest therefor.

Indorsed: We assent to the within-named arrangement. Albany, May 22, 1861.

R. CAMPBELL,
Lieutenant Governor.
ROBERT DENNISTON,
P. DORSHEIMER,
CHAS. G. MYERS,
Commissioners of the Canal Fund.

The amount of interest on the money so used of the canal fund during the time it was used by the State for the public defense in raising troops was $48,187.13. But during the same time the State had received interest on a portion of the funds while it was lying in a bank unused to the amount of $8,319.95, and the net deficiency to the State on account of the interest on such money is $39,867.18.

Upon the payment of the money into the treasury, from which this interest would have accumulated, it became the money of the State, and would have so remained after it became a part of the canal fund. While different departments are provided in the State, as well as the National Government, they constitute a part of an indivisible unity, and transactions between the different departments are the official act of the same political power.

The money is transferred from one department to another or from one fund to another, but it can not be said that by the transfer there is a lending of money upon which, by any fiction of law-interest can be calculated. By the use of the canal fund for the purpose of defraying the expense of raising troops the State simply appropriated from a particular fund, which, if permitted to become a part of that fund, might have been loaned on interest. It can not be said that the United States borrowed the money, at the agreed rate of interest, which other customers would have paid the State, as there is no express or implied obligation to that effect. The State paid no money directly for the use of the money belonging to the canal fund. There may have been an accounting to that fund from some other financial resource of the State, but that transaction was entirely between the different departments of the government which constitute the political organization of the State of New York.

If an allowance is made for the loss on that fund, it is in effect an allowance of interest against the United States on an obligation, in and by which they have not expressly agreed to pay interest. During the time the money was diverted from the canal fund to the purposes of the United States the State simply lost the use of that amount. The interest charged on the trust fund can not be said to be an "expense incurred" within the meaning of the law of 1861, as the State did not assume any liability, nor pay any money beyond the actual funds appropriated and paid in the purchase of materials, and the payment of the expenses of the transportation of troops. In the claim for $91,320.81 a different element exists. The claimant actually paid that amount of money to creditors who had advanced money on the bonds of the State, which had been issued to defray the costs, charges, and expenses properly incurred "by the State in enrolling, subsisting, clothing, supplying, paying, and transporting" troops employed by the defendants in suppressing the insurrection against the authorities of the United States.

In the discussion and determination of the question of the liability of the United States to remunerate the claimant, we must not lose sight of what is so fundamental, not only in the laws of the United States and decisions of the Supreme Court, but in the jurisdiction of this court—that the defendants are not liable for interest as such, unless they have expressly agreed to pay interest. In subordination to that well-established principle of the law, the purpose and construction of the act of 1861 must be ascertained and determined. Whatever may be said of the liability of the defendants, in the absence of said statute, on the first item of claim, it is clear that for the second they would not be liable, because it is for interest upon an obligation in which they have not expressly agreed to pay interest.

In the legal statement of a cause of action, founded upon the transaction of 1861, between the plaintiff and defendants, the pleading must necessarily allege that the $39,867.13 was interest upon certain advances made by the State, which interest was lost by the claimant, because the money was not invested in interest-bearing obligations due the State. The marked difference between the two items of claim is, that in one there was an actual payment of money by the State, in complying with the requisition of the General Government, while in the other there was no payment but a failure to receive interest, because of a diversion of the fund as herein indicated.

It does not affirmatively appear that the fund upon which the claim of $39,867.18 is based could, for the period of time it was used by the State for the benefit of the defendants, have been loaned; and if during that period other money of that fund was unemployed, the said fund would have been a surplus in the treasury of the State, and no interest was lost to the claimant.

It has been the rule of the Department and the policy of the Government not to pay interest upon claims against the United States, founded on the reason that the Government is always ready to pay all just claims, and if such claims are not paid, it is the fault of the claimant in not presenting his claim in apt time or in not presenting in such a way as to convince the officers of the Government of its lawfulness and justice.

It will be observed that Mr. Attorney-General Wirt makes the distinction between the payment of interest upon money borrowed to enable the State to discharge its duty and fulfil its obligation and interest upon funds in the treasury of the State appropriated for the use and benefit of the United States. The allowance of interest "as expenses, charges, and costs," in the construction of the act, is in derogation of the general policy of the Government in not paying interest, and should not be extended beyond the logical limits of the act of 1861.

The Chief Justice is of opinion that—

"The claimant is seeking indirectly to recover interest contrary to Revised Statutes, section 1091, which prohibits its allowance 'unless upon a contract expressly stipulating for payment of interest.'

"The case was transmitted to this court by the Secretary of the Treasury as a claim for interest alone.

"Interest on temporary loans made to obtain money for equipping, etc., troops for the United States is no more a charge against the Government, under the act of 1861 (12 Stat. L., 276), than is interest on long-time bonds issued by many States for the same purpose, computed to time of payment by the Government, for which it is conceded the United States are not liable.

"In either case interest paid constitutes no part of the 'costs, charges, and expenses *properly incurred* by said State for enrolling, subsisting, clothing, supplying, arming, equipping, and transporting its troops' within the meaning of the act. It is paid for another purpose, to wit, for the use of money raised to supply an empty treasury; and indirect expenditure, dependent upon collateral contingencies, upon the different conditions of the treasuries, and the different and uncertain legislation of the several States; for raising money by taxation, obviously not within the contemplation of Congress, and never allowed by the Treasury Department to any State under this act.

"An unequal application of the statute in the different States could not have been intended by Congress.

"If the claim be not for interest, within the intent and meaning of Revised Statutes, section 1091, then, as a one for the cost of supplying money to the State treasury, it is not unlike a claim for the cost of assessing and collecting taxes for the same object, which, it is apprehended, nobody would contend could be maintained under the act of 1861.

"Decisions of the courts and opinions of the attorneys-general before the enactment of the prohibition against allowing interest, and before the passage of the act upon which this suit is founded, or independently of them, can have no bearing on this case, which must be governed by the existing statutes and the intention of Congress."

It is the judgment of the court that the claimant recover the sum of $91,320.84, and that the $39,867.13 be disallowed.

NOTT, *J.*, concurring:

The term interest covers two distinct things: compensation for the use of money by express agreement, damages allowed by law for the nonpayment of a debt after it has become due. It is the latter which is prohibited in this court, in suits against the Government, by the Revised Statutes, section 1091.

As to the first item of money expended in the payment of interest upon the bonds of the State which were sold to raise money for the General Government I concur in the opinion of my brother Weldon. As to the second item of money expended in the payment of interest upon a loan obtained from the canal commissioners for the use of the Government I dissent.

The grounds upon which I dissent are: (1) That in order to shield the defendants from making good this loss it is necessary to hold that a State government can do an unconstitutional act, or, to express it differently, that the unconstitutional act of State authorities must be deemed the act of the State itself; (2) that a substantial loss has been incurred here by the claimant, which the defendants are in honor and good conscience bound to make good, and the intent of the act of indemnity is that the loyal States which acted on behalf of the General Government during the civil war shall be reimbursed and made whole; (3) that the restriction of the Revised Statutes (section 1091) prohibiting the recovery of interest as damages in suits against the Government is not applicable to this case inasmuch as the contract loaning the money expressly provides for the payment of interest and was ratified by the acceptance of the money and the payment of the principal.

In the application of the act of indemnity to the case the initial fact of the transaction must be borne in mind. The State of New York was not a corporation whose business was to raise and equip troops for any government that chanced to be engaged in a civil war, but, on the contrary, the President of the United States, in the awful crises of the hour, went to the State officers and asked that the resources of the State be given in aid of the General Government. The legislature was not then in session, and the State officers had no authority, constitutional or legal, to pledge the credit of the State or involve it in financial liability. From motives of the highest patriotism they assumed an enormous responsibility and proceeded to act on behalf of the General Government. But in their action they were not the agents of the State, nor acting on its behalf, nor assuming to promote its interest. If they were anybody's agents, they were the agents of the General Government, and for their unauthorized acts the General Government is in law and morals and under the terms of this act of indemnity bound to make good the losses which the unauthorized acts of these officers caused the State.

This, then, being the status of the parties, the governor and comptroller proceeded to borrow money, not for the use and benefit of the State, nor by its authority, nor at its request, but for the use and benefit and at the request of the General Government. They borrowed from two sources, from ordinary lenders who had money to invest, by selling them the interest-bearing bonds of the State, and from a board of trustees known as the commissioners of the canal fund, who had moneys in their hands to loan on interest-bearing securities and only on interest-bearing securities. In course of time these loans matured, and the State assumed and paid them, principal and interest. The General Government under the act of indemnity has paid the principal which the State expended for its use, but has refused to pay the interest.

When the General Government requested the State officers to act in its behalf they might have proceeded in one of three different ways. They might have bought the military supplies on an indefinite credit and allowed the vendor to add the unknown and undetermined interest to the price; they might have purchased by contracts bearing interest which would run until the price should be paid by the General Government; they might have borrowed money on interest and bought the goods at the lowest price for cash. As to the first method, there can be no question that if it had been pursued the Government would have been liable for the price paid. As to the second method, there can hardly be a question as to the Government's liability for both principal and interest. As to the third method, it is the one which has occasioned the controversy of the present suit. Yet from a business point of view the first method was the worst, and the third, as every man of business knows, was the best. The eminent merchant who was then the governor of the State proceeded as he would have proceeded for a brother merchant. He raised the money, and went into the market and purchased at the lowest cash price.

The money which the State of New York, through its officers, thus expended at the request and for the use of the United States was not in its treasury, but was procured from two sources:

First, the State issued and sold its own bonds, bearing 7 per cent interest. The General Government lost nothing by that. The credit of the State was better than the credit of the General Government, and a saving was effected by the State loaning its own credit for the procurement of the necessary funds. It was able at that time both to buy and to borrow on better terms than the principal for whom it was acting. It has charged nothing for the use of its credit thus loaned, and is merely seeking to be repaid the money which it expended.

The second source from which money was procured for the use of the United States was the canal fund of the State of New York. This fund was, so far as the State was concerned, a sinking fund for the reduction of a public debt; but it was also an interest-bearing trust fund pledged to a designated class of creditors. I emphasize the statement that it was an interest-bearing fund; for it was in no sense an accumulation of idle money in one of the coffers of the State, but was in fact and in contemplation of law a mass of interest-bearing securities held and accumulated for the future liquidation of a specific debt, and was at the same time pledged to the holders of the debt. The commissioners of the fund had no right to hoard the money which came to their hands, and had no right to loan it without interest. The scope of their duties was to invest, and to invest at interest, and the purpose of the fund, the chief, if not the sole purpose, was that money from time to time accumulated for the extinction of the canal debt should not lie idle in the treasury of the State, but should be invested in securities which would yield, until the debt matured, that profit which we call interest.

If the State had issued more bonds than it did for money wherewith to serve the General Government, and the canal commissioners had gone into the market and bought these bonds, the circumlocution would doubtless have saved the State from the delay and vexation which beset this branch of the case, and would have made plain to all minds that the State had incurred obligations and loaned its credit and paid interest, not for its own use or benefit, but for the use and benefit of the General Government. Yet this circuity of procedure would not have made the State any better off *or* the General Government any worse. The principle which would have governed and the result which would have been reached would have been the same.

If this charge of interest had been a mere act of the State officers, whereby the State made interest which otherwise it would not have made, the charge would be in the nature of a profit and beyond the scope of an indemnity. But in the actual case before the court, the canal fund existed long before the General Government came to the State as a borrower. It had been created and was regulated by the constitution of the State. Whoever got money from the canal fund must take it on the terms prescribed by the constitution. Neither the State officers nor the State legislature nor the General Government nor any power known to our constitutional system could take it upon any other terms or authorize it to be taken. Neither could it be applied to any purpose or business of the State; and whatever might be received from a loan in the way of interest did not go into the treasury of the State, but returned to the fund. The State itself had no power over the canal fund. Undoubtedly the State was directly interested in the fund as a public debtor, and undoubtedly the legal title to the fund was vested in the State; but beside the State was another party equally interested in the fund, the public creditors, who had loaned money upon the faith of it and who were in law a *cestui que trust* and in equity the owners of the fund.

Accordingly when the governor and comptroller of the State, who were practically acting as agents of the United States, sought a loan from the canal fund to be expended for the uses and purposes of the General Government, they proposed and agreed to the constitutional condition of interest, and expressly agreed that the loan should bear interest at the rate of 5 per cent. The canal commissioners had no authority to make the loan without interest, and they did not assume to do so; and the State subsequently recognized the obligation which it owed to its creditors and paid the interest on this specific loan out of money raised by taxation; that is to say, the taxpayers of New York made good to the canal fund the interest which would otherwise have been realized from ordinary securities, but the United States have not yet reimbursed them for the taxes that both in form and in fact were devoted to that purpose. These are in brief the ultimate facts of the transaction; the question of law involved is whether the act of indemnity extends to them.

The act of indemnity is not a statute to regulate the purchase of supplies or to restrict the compensation of purchasing agents. If the State of New York had been a merchant selling goods for the sake of profit, or a commission merchant rendering service in consideration of a percentage, it would have to take the profits or losses which legally resulted. But the State rendered its service gratuitously; it had nothing to make and, as the result proves, a risk to bear, and it acted at the request of the Government. The obligation which would rest upon an individual in such a case would be to make the other party whole, and it would be an obligation of the strongest character, legally, equitably, morally. The General Government has recognized this obligation and has passed this act of indemnity. The purpose of an act as of an instrument of indemnity is to make the injured party whole. It is not a grant; it is not one of those statutes in which doubtful words or phrases are to be strictly construed; an interpretation which leaves the injured party without the indemnity which he ought to have is as an interpretation which fails to carry into effect the confessed purpose of the statute. If an individual or a body corporate had accepted the fruits of the loan and recognized the transaction by paying the principal, his acts would constitute a binding ratification. The act of indemnity must surely be as broad as the legal obligations of the United States.

As has been said, the State was called upon to act for the General Government and acted by borrowing money to raise and equip troops. All of this money was expended in the business and on behalf of the United States. Some of it was borrowed from ordinary lenders by the State selling its own bonds; some of it was borrowed from a trust fund of which the State was the trustee. When the interest on the bonds became due the State took the money of its taxpayers and paid it. When the interest on the other loan became due the State likewise took the money of its taxpayers and paid it also. To that extent the taxpayers of the State are just so much the worse off than they would be if the State officers had never touched the trust fund and borrowed from it for the use of the General Government. Both in form and in substance this interest was money paid. In form the transaction complies with the terms of the act of indemnity; in substance the distinction between interest lost and interest paid is too refined to be applied against the purpose of the statute.

And this distinction necessarily rests on the, constructively, illegal action of the State officers; that is to say, if the custodians of the fund acted in a constitutional and legal manner by loaning the trust moneys in their charge to the United States, through the intermediation of the governor and comptroller of the State, at an agreed rate of interest, the refunding of the interest was an expenditure for the use of the Government; but if they acted in an unconstitutional and illegal manner by diverting, misappropriating, or misapplying the trust fund to State purposes, then the State can not make money out of the transaction, and the General Government is not liable.

SCHOFIELD, J., was absent when this case was argued, and took no part in the decision.

EXHIBIT NO. 2.

[S. 1205, Fifty-third Congress, second session.]

Mr. WHITE, of California, introduced the following bill; which was read twice and referred to the Committee on Military Affairs:

A BILL to reimburse the States of California, Oregon, and Nevada for moneys by them expended in the suppression of the rebellion.

Be it enacted by the Senate and House of Representatives of the United States of America in Congress assembled, That there is hereby appropriated, out of any money in the Treasury not otherwise appropriated, the sums hereinafter mentioned, to reimburse and to be paid to the States of California, Oregon, and Nevada for moneys by them expended in aid of the United States in the war of the rebellion, to wit:

To the State of California, the sum of three million nine hundred and fifty-one thousand nine hundred and fifteen dollars and forty-two cents.

To the State of Oregon, the sum of three hundred and thirty-five thousand one hundred and fifty-two dollars and eighty-eight cents.

To the State of Nevada, the sum of four hundred and four thousand and forty dollars and seventy cents, being the sums of money, principal and interest, paid by said States in the suppression of the rebellion as shown by the reports of the Secretary of War in Senate Executive Documents Numbered ten, eleven, and seventeen, Fifty-first Congress, first session.

EXHIBIT NO. 3.

[H. R. 4959, Fifty-third Congress, second session.]

JANUARY 3, 1894.—Referred to the Committee on War Claims and ordered to be printed.

Mr. MAGUIRE introduced the following bill:

A BILL to reimburse the States of California, Oregon, and Nevada for moneys by them expended in the suppression of the rebellion.

Be it enacted by the Senate and House of Representatives of the United States of America in Congress assembled, That there is hereby appropriated, out of any money in the

Treasury not otherwise appropriated, the sums hereinafter mentioned, to reimburse and to be paid to the States of California, Oregon, and Nevada for moneys by them expended in aid of the United States in the war of the rebellion, to wit:

To the State of California, the sum of three million nine hundred and fifty-one thousand nine hundred and fifteen dollars and forty-two cents.

To the State of Oregon, the sum of three hundred and thirty-five thousand one hundred and fifty-two dollars and eighty-eight cents.

To the State of Nevada, the sum of four hundred and four thousand and forty dollars and seventy cents, being the sums of money, principal and interest, paid by said States in the suppression of the rebellion as shown by the reports of the Secretary of War in Senate Executive Documents Numbered ten, eleven, and seventeen, Fifty-first Congress, first session.

EXHIBIT NO. 4.

[House Report No. 558, Fifty-third Congress, second session.]

MARCH 8, 1894.—Committed to the Committee of the Whole House on the state of the Union and ordered to be printed.

Mr. HERMANN, from the Committee on War Claims, submitted the following report, to accompany H. R. 4959:

The Committee on War Claims, to whom was referred the bills (H. R. 2615 and H. R. 4959) to reimburse the States of California, Oregon, and Nevada for moneys by them expended in the suppression of the rebellion when aiding the United States to maintain the "common defense" on the Pacific coast, have examined the same and report as follows:

The facts out of which the aforesaid State war claims arise have been very fully stated in several reports heretofore made to the House of Representatives and to the Senate, as follows, to wit, House Report No. 254 and Senate Report No. 158, Fifty-second Congress, first session; House Report No. 2553 and Senate Report No. 644, Fifty-first Congress, first session; and House Report No. 3396 and Senate Reports No. 1286 and No. 2014, Fiftieth Congress, first session.

Bills relating to these State war claims of these three Pacific coast States passed the Senate during the first session of the Fiftieth Congress, and were favorably reported to the Senate during the first session of the Fifty-first and Fifty-second Congresses and to the House during the Fiftieth, Fifty-first, and Fifty-second Congresses, but were not reached for consideration by the House in either thereof. These bills were introduced in the House, to wit, H. R. No. 2615, on 11th day of September, 1893, by Mr. Caminetti, of California, and H. R. No. 4959, on January 3, 1894, by Mr. Maguire, of California, and both referred to the House Committee on War Claims.

Sums of money (recited in three reports made by the honorable Secretary of War to the Senate on these State war claims and printed as Senate Ex. Docs. Nos. 10, 11, and 17, Fifty-first Congress, first session) proven to the full satisfaction of the War Department to have been expended by said States to aid the United States in the suppression of the war of the rebellion were included in the general deficiency appropriation bill as it passed the Senate during the second session of the Fifty-first Congress for the purpose of indemnifying and reimbursing said States on account and in partial liquidation of said claims, but the same were omitted from said deficiency bill as it became a law. Senate bill No. 52 and House bills No. 54 and No. 42, Fifty-second Congress, first session, were in all respects identical, the last of which House bills was, on February 10, 1892, favorably reported by the House War Claims Committee in House Report No. 254, Fifty-second Congress, first session, and said Senate bill No. 52 was, on February 4, 1892, favorably reported by the Senate Committee on Military Affairs in Senate Report No. 158, as follows, to wit:

[Senate Report No. 158, Fifty-second Congress, first session.]

"The Committee on Military Affairs, to whom was referred the bill (S. 52) to reimburse the States of California, Oregon, and Nevada for moneys by them expended in the suppression of the rebellion, have examined the same and report as follows, to wit:

"This measure was considered by this committee during the first session of the Fifty-first Congress, and was reported upon favorably (Report No. 644).

"Your committee concur in the conclusions stated in that report and recommend the passage of the bill."

At a very early period of the war of the rebellion nearly all the troops of the regular Army of the United States then serving in California, Oregon, and Nevada were withdrawn from military duty in those States and transported thence by sea to New York City, at an expense to the United States of about $390,103, or an average cost of about $284 for each commissioned officer and of about $133 for each enlisted man. This withdrawal therefrom of said regular troops left these three Pacific coast States comparatively defenseless, and for the purpose of supplying their places, and to provide additional military forces, rendered necessary by public exigencies, calls for volunteers were made upon said States under proclamations of the President, or requisitions by the War Department, or by its highest military officers commanding the military departments on the Pacific. These calls for volunteers continued until the necessity therefor entirely ceased to exist, during which time these three Pacific coast States furnished, enlisted, equipped, paid, and mustered into the military service of the United States 18,715 volunteers, as shown in said reports so made to the Senate by the Secretary of War.

In consequence of this withdrawal in 1861 of said military forces from the Pacific coast, in order that they might perform military service in the East, and in view of the circumstances and exigencies existing in the Pacific coast States and Territories during the rebellion period, requisitions were duly made from time to time by the President of the United States and by the Secretary of War upon the proper State authorities of California, Oregon, and Nevada for volunteers to perform military service for the United States in said States and Territories, as are fully and in great detail set forth in Senate Ex. Docs. Nos. 10, 11, and 17, Fifty-first Congress, first session. In compliance with the several calls and official requisitions so made between 1861 and 1866, inclusive—

	Volunteers.
The State of California furnished	15,725
The State of Nevada furnished	1,180
The State of Oregon furnished	1,810
Making a total aggregate of	18,715

who were enlisted and were thereafter duly mustered into the military service of the United States as volunteers from said States. The same number of troops if organized in the East and transported from New York City to the Pacific coast States and Territories in the same manner as was done by the U. S. War Department from June 17, 1850, to August 3, 1861, would have cost the United States at that time the sum of about $5,483,385 for *transportation alone.*

The indemnification for the "costs, charges, and expenses" properly incurred by said States for enrolling, subsisting, clothing, supplying, arming, equipping, paying, transporting, and furnishing said 18,715 volunteer troops employed by the United States to aid them to maintain the "common defense," was guaranteed by the United States in the act of Congress approved July 27, 1861 (12 U. S. Stats., 276), an act entitled "An act to indemnify the States for expenses incurred by them in defense of the United States."

The then Secretary of War, Hon. Redfield Proctor, now U. S. Senator from Vermont (on page 28 of his report, Senate Ex. Doc. No. 11, Fifty-first Congress, first session), in reporting upon the military services performed by said volunteers during the rebellion, said:

"They took the places of the regular troops in California, all of which, except 3 batteries of artillery and 1 regiment of infantry, were withdrawn to the East at an early period after the outbreak of the war. Without them (and the Oregon and Nevada volunteers) the overland mail and emigrant routes, extending from the Missouri River via Great Salt Lake City to California and Oregon, and passing through an uninhabited and mountainous country, infested with hostile Indians and highwaymen, could not have been adequately protected; and yet it was of the first importance to have these routes kept open and safe, especially as rebel cruisers had made the sea routes both hazardous and expensive. Two expeditions composed of California volunteers, under the command of Brig. Gens. James H. Carleton and Patrick E. Connor, respectively, performed perilous and exhausting marches across a desert and over an almost impassable country and established themselves, the latter in Utah—where, besides protecting the mail routes, a watchful eye was kept on the uncertain and sometimes threatening attitude of the Mormons—and the former in Arizona and New Mexico, which Territories were thereafter effectually guarded in the interests of the United States against Indians and rebels."

The Secretary of War, with the assistance of the board of Army officers, created under the authority of the act of Congress approved August 4, 1886 (24 U. S. Stat., p. 217), and which officers were duly selected and appointed on said board by Mr. Secretary of War, Hon. W. C. Endicott, has heretofore found as facts, and has so officially reported to the Senate (as printed in Senate Ex. Docs. Nos. 10, 11, 17, Fifty-first Congress, first session), that the States of California, Oregon, and Nevada, under appropriate laws of the legislatures thereof, respectively, have actually paid in gold coin out of their State treasuries, on account of the "costs, charges, and expenses" properly incurred by said three States for enrolling, subsisting, clothing, supplying, arming, equipping, paying, transporting, and furnishing said 18,715 volunteer troops of said three States, which were employed by the United States to aid them to maintain the "common defense" on the Pacific coast during the war of the rebellion, the exact sums of money as recited in said bill (H. R. 4959), the reimbursement of which was so guaranteed to be paid to said States as an indemnity under the aforesaid act of July 27, 1861 (12 U. S. Stat., 276), "An act to indemnify the States for expenses incurred by them in defense of the United States," and under the resolution of Congress of March 8, 1862 (12 U. S. Stat., 615), "declaratory of the intent and meaning of said act, and the resolution of March 19, 1862 (12 U. S. Stat., 616), to authorize the Secretary of War to accept moneys appropriated by any State for the payment of its volunteers, and to apply the same as directed by such State," copies of which act and resolution are as follows:

On the 27th day of July, 1861, Congress passed an act entitled "An act to indemnify the States for expenses incurred by them in defense of the United States," as follows:

"That the Secretary of the Treasury be, and is hereby, directed, out of any moneys in the Treasury not otherwise appropriated, to pay to the governor of any State, or its duly authorized agents, the costs, charges, and expenses properly incurred by said State for enrolling, subsisting, clothing, supplying, arming, equipping, paying, and transporting its troops employed in aiding in suppressing the present insurrection against the United States, to be settled upon proper vouchers to be filed and passed upon by the proper accounting officers of the Treasury." (12 Stat. L., p. 276.)

A RESOLUTION declaratory of the intent and meaning of a certain act therein named.

Whereas doubts have arisen as to the true intent and meaning of act numbered eighteen, entitled "An act to indemnify the States, for expenses incurred by them in 'defense of the United States,' approved July twenty-seventh, eighteen hundred and sixty-one" (12 U. S. Stats., 276):

Be it resolved by the Senate and House of Representatives of the United States of America in Congress assembled, That the said act shall be construed to apply to expenses incurred as well after as before the date of the approval thereof.

Approved March 8, 1862 (12 U. S. Stats., 615).

A RESOLUTION to authorize the Secretary of War to accept moneys appropriated by any State for the payment of its volunteers and to apply the same as directed by such State.

Resolved by the Senate and House of Representatives of the United States of America in Congress assembled, That if any State during the present rebellion shall make any appropriation to pay the volunteers of that State, the Secretary of War is hereby authorized to accept the same, and cause it to be applied by the Paymaster-General to the payments designated by the legislative act making the appropriation, in the same manner as if appropriated by act of Congress; and also to make any regulations that may be necessary for the disbursement and proper application of such funds to the specific purpose for which they may be appropriated by the several States.

Approved March 19, 1862 (12 U. S. Stats., 616).

AN ACT for the benefit of the States of Texas, Colorado, Oregon, Nebraska, California, Kansas, and Nevada, and the Territories of Washington and Idaho, and Nevada when a Territory.

*　　*　　*　　*　　*　　*　　*

SEC. 2. The Secretary of War is hereby authorized to detail three Army officers to assist him in examining and reporting upon the claims of the States and Territories named in the act of June twenty-seventh, eighteen hundred and eighty-two, chapter two hundred and forty-one of the laws of the Forty-seventh Congress, and such officers, before entering upon said duties shall take and subscribe an oath that they will carefully examine said claims, and that they will, to the best of their ability, make a just and impartial statement thereof, as required by said act.

Approved August 4, 1886. (24 U. S. Stat., 217.)

From the facts and laws hereinbefore recited, your committee concur in the conclusions reached and recommendations made in the several House and Senate reports which heretofore accompanied similar bills, and now reaffirm the same, and report back said bill (H. R. 4959) with a recommendation that it do pass with an amendment added thereto as follows, to wit:

"That payment of said sums of money shall be made to each of said States in four equal installments, the first of which shall be paid to them respectively upon the passage of this act, the second of which shall be paid to them respectively on July 1, 1895, the third of which shall be paid to them respectively on July 1, 1896, the fourth of which shall be paid to them respectively on July 1, 1897."

EXHIBIT NO. 5.

CHAPTER XXXII.—SENATE JOINT RESOLUTION No. 5, relative to indebtedness of the United States Government to the State of California (adopted March 13, 1893).

Resolved by the Senate, the Assembly concurring, That the State of California urges upon its Senators and Representatives in Congress to use their best efforts in procuring the passage of the act now pending in both houses of Congress, to reimburse California for the money raised and disbursed for arming and equipping troops brought into service by requisition of the United States during the rebellion. These claims have all been passed upon and approved by the War Department, and by the committee in each house to whom they were referred, and are on their respective calendars for passage, but may fail this Congress, as in the last, for want of earnest and active presentation. For war claims, see House Report three thousand three hundred and ninety-six, and Senate Reports one thousand two hundred and eighty-six and two thousand and fourteen, first session, Fiftieth Congress; also, House Report two thousand five hundred and fifty-three, and Senate Report six hundred and forty-four, first session Fifty-first Congress; and House Report two hundred and fifty-four, and Senate Report one hundred and fifty-eight, first session Fifty-second Congress.

Resolved, That whatever money shall be received by the State from these claims, or from the claim of the State to five per cent of the cash sales of public land sold in this State by the United States, the same shall be turned into the State treasury, and credited to the school fund.

Resolved, That his excellency the governor be requested to forward a copy of these resolutions to each of the Senators and Representatives in Congress.

EXHIBIT NO. 6.

[Senate Mis. Doc. No. 51, Fifty-second Congress, second session.]

FEBRUARY 13, 1893.—Referred to the Committee on Appropriations and ordered to be printed.

Mr. DOLPH presented the following memorial of the legislature of the State of Oregon praying the payment of moneys expended in maintaining the common defense and to aid in the suppression of the rebellion:

To the Congress of the United States:

Whereas the State of Oregon has heretofore paid a large sum of money to aid the United States in maintaining the common defense in the suppression of the war of the rebellion, the amount of which has been shown by the reports of the honorable Secretary of War made to Congress; and

Whereas said debt has not yet been paid but is long since due; and

Whereas Hon. J. N. Dolph has introduced in the Senate of the United States an amendment to be proposed to the sundry civil appropriation bill, making an appropriation to pay said claim, together with similar claims of the States of California and Nevada; and

Whereas the United States has reimbursed other States of the Union for sums of money expended on account of the war of the rebellion, such payments aggregating up to March 15, 1892, the sum of $44,725,072.38, but has not paid any sum whatever on said accounts to the said States of California, Oregon, and Nevada: Therefore, be it

Resolved by the legislative assembly of the State of Oregon, That justice and equity demand that the payment of said claims should be no longer delayed by the United

States, and that an appropriation of money therefor should be made by Congress at this time; and be it further

Resolved, That this memorial be telegraphed by the secretary of state to our Senators and our Representatives in Congress, and that a written copy thereof, duly certified, shall be forwarded to the presiding officers of the Senate and House of Representatives of the United States.

Adopted by the senate February 8, 1893.

C. W. FULTON,
President of the Senate.

Concurred in by the house February 8, 1893.

W. P. KEADY,
Speaker of the House.

GEORGE W. MCBRIDE,
   Secretary of State.

EXHIBIT NO. 7.

MEMORIAL TO CONGRESS.

To the Senate and House of Representatives of the United States of America in Congress assembled:

Your memorialists, now the State executive officers of the State of Nevada (the legislature of Nevada not being now in session), most respectfully represent to your honorable bodies that the State of Nevada has heretofore presented a claim to the United States for expenses by her incurred and by her paid as "costs, charges, and expenses properly incurred for enrolling" her military forces during the war of the rebellion, in response to and under requisitions made by the officer commanding the Military Department of the Pacific, and which "costs, charges, and expenses" so incurred and paid by Nevada aggregate the sum of $11,840 for enrolling 1,184 men preliminary to their being mustered into the military service of the United States.

A claim for reimbursement by the United States for the aforesaid expenditure has been presented by the State of Nevada to the United States, and payment thereof has been refused, and because its examining and accounting and auditing officers seem to have regarded this expenditure simply as a bounty or gratuity paid by Nevada to the officers of her military forces who enrolled said 1,184 men.

Nevada selected as her enrolling agents those officers of her military forces who were to be the commanding officers of the men who might be thereafter enrolled; and there can not be any valid question as to the wisdom or economy of such a course as adopted and uniformly pursued by Nevada, and especially when we consider the importance of each commanding officer being perfectly familiar with the qualifications of those he was to command in the field, both as to their mental and physical fitness.

This method of enrollment as adopted by Nevada, and seeming to doubt to her, at the time, as the most ready and economical one for putting her troops in the field for the United States military service, in obedience to requisitions made upon her, was the one followed in all cases; and this claim for reimbursement by the United States for the "costs, charges, and expenses" so incurred was in lieu of all other "costs, charges, and expenses" that would have to be incurred and as incident to said enrollment—such, for instance, as rent, fuel, furniture, salaries of enrolling officers, subsistence, and all the other detailed and expensive paraphernalia which pertain to the regular military recruiting or enrolling office of a State or of the United States, and such as the United States would herself have been compelled to incur if she had invoked or exercised her own Federal military machinery for the same purpose in the State of Nevada.

No express method of enrolling having been designated to Nevada by the United States she was left to adopt that method of organizing, collecting, and enrolling her military forces to meet the requisitions so made upon her at the time, and such as appeared to her to be the wisest and the most practicable.

To provide for and to pay the "costs, charges, and expenses" so incurred and to be incurred by Nevada on account of said enrollment the legislature of Nevada passed a law on March 11, 1865, which provided substantially that each enrolling or recruiting agent of her army intended by her for the military service of the United States should be allowed for all expenses of said enrollment $10 per capita. The law is as follows, to wit:

The people of the State of Nevada, represented in senate and assembly, do enact as follows:

"SECTION 1. A sum not exceeding one hundred thousand dollars is hereby appropriated and set aside, to constitute a separate fund to be known as the "soldiers' fund," for the purpose of paying a compensation to the soldiers of the companies of Nevada volunteers already raised in the Territory and in the State of Nevada, and to be raised in this State, for the service of the United States, to aid in repelling invasion, suppressing insurrections, enforcing the laws, and protecting the public property, in addition to the pay allowed them by the United States.

"SEC. 2. There shall be paid out of the fund created and set apart by the first section of this act * * * a bounty of ten dollars, to be paid to the captain or commanding officer of any company, for every recruit by him enlisted and subquently mustered into the service of the United States: *Provided,* That the provisions of this section shall not be deemed applicable to any soldier who may be drafted, or enlisted as a substitute, or any person drafted into the Army of the United States. * * *

"SEC. 3. The captains or commanding officers of companies of Nevada volunteers raised, or to be raised, for service in the Army of the United States, shall, before such officers, as recruiting agents of the Army, can be entitled to secure the benefits of this act, file in the office of the adjutant-general their affidavit, setting forth the number and names of recruits enlisted by them, and accepted by the proper medical examiners (who shall in each case be named) and sworn into the service; and further setting forth that no affidavit of the same character, for the same enlisted men, has heretofore been made or filed. The adjutant-general of the State is hereby authorized and directed to certify to the controller of state the number of men enlisted by each captain or commanding officer of a company, whenever the affidavit herein required is filed in his office, endorsed by the provost marshal of this State, or the commanding officer of the post where the enlisted men referred to and enumerated in the affidavit may have been rendezvoused on enlistment. Upon the filing of the adjutant-general's certificate, above required, in the office of the controller of State, the controller shall make out a copy of said certificate, and forward the same to the State board of examiners, and if the State board of examiners shall endorse the certificate as "Approved," then the controller shall draw his warrant upon the fund herein constituted for the sum set forth in the certificate of the adjutant-general in favor of the officers, or their legal assignees, named in the certificate, for the sums respectively set forth to be due them.

"SEC. 6. For the purpose of carrying into effect the provisions of this act, and providing for the fund created by section one of this act, the treasurer of the State of Nevada shall cause to be prepared bonds of the State to the amount of one hundred thousand dollars, in sums of five hundred dollars each, redeemable at the office of the treasurer of the State on the first day of July, one thousand eight hundred and seventy. The said bonds shall bear interest, payable semiannually, at the rate of ten per cent per annum, from the date of their issuance, which interest shall be due and payable at the office of the treasurer of this State on the first day of January and July of each year: *Providing,* That the first payment of interest shall not be made sooner than the first day of January, in the year of our Lord one thousand eight hundred and sixty-six. These said bonds shall be signed by the governor, and countersigned by the controller, and endorsed by the treasurer of the State, and shall have the seal of the State affixed thereto. Such bonds shall be issued from time to time as they may be required for use. The expense of preparing such bonds and disposing of the same shall be audited as a claim against the soldiers' fund created by this act.

"SEC. 10. For the payment of the principal and interest of the bonds issued under this act there shall be levied and collected, annually, until the final payment and redemption of the same, and in the same manner as other State revenue is or may be directed by law to be levied and collected annually, a tax of twenty-five cents, in gold and silver coin of the United States, on each one hundred dollars of taxable property in the State, in addition to the other taxes for State purposes, and the fund derived from this tax shall be set apart and applied to the payment of interest accruing on the bonds herein provided for and the final redemption of the principal of said bonds; and the public faith of the State of Nevada is hereby pledged for the payment of the bonds issued by virtue of this act, and the interest thereon and, if necessary, to provide other and ample means for the payment thereof." (Statutes of Nevada, March 11, 1865, pp. 389–393.)

This small sum of $10 per capita when the peculiar condition of Nevada at that time is considered, in connection with her then limited and expensive means of travel which was then exclusively by wagon or horseback, and before any railroads were built in this State, will be considered to be not exorbitant, but, as your memorialists now submit, the same was and is very reasonable.

True, the act of the legislature termed this $10 per capita for enrollment a "bounty" to the captains or commanding officers who might organize a company to be thereafter mustered into the service of the United States, yet, as a matter of fact, it was not a bounty in the sense of a gratuity, and as is frequently used by the United States as meaning money in addition to the pay and allowances as set forth in the agreement with her commanding officers and enlisted men about to enter her military service; on the contrary, it was a lump compensation paid or to be paid by the State to her recruiting or enrolling officers in lieu of all other expenses or compensation for organizing its military forces and such as have been hereinbefore recited and covered, and was intended to cover all expense of travel, subsistence, lodging, and other incidental expenses, and such as U. S. recruiting and enrolling officers might properly incur in getting together and preparing men for the military service of the State and of the United States.

Your memorialists call attention to the fact that on March 11, 1865, Nevada did not even have in her treasury the money with which to pay this disbursement, but in section 6 of said act she was compelled to issue and to sell her own State bonds with which to raise money to pay this and other expenses of a military character in order to aid in defraying the State expenses in a time of war.

Not only this, but in section 10 of said act Nevada levied a tax in gold or silver coin of the United States upon every $100 taxable property in the State of Nevada, in addition to other taxes for State purposes, to create a fund with which to pay said expenses, and which tax was to continue until all of said bonds were wholly paid and fully redeemed; and in addition thereto the public faith of Nevada was pledged to pay said bonds and interest thereon, and, if necessary, to provide other and ample means for the payment thereof.

The public faith of Nevada was therefore pledged for the benefit of the United States, and at a time when the public credit of the United States was itself put to the test and its paper largely depreciated in parts of the country outside the limits of Nevada.

Wherefore, your memorialists (the legislature not now being in session), believing that if the attention of Congress were respectfully and properly invited to this matter, it would not permit this expenditure to be repudiated by being disallowed or payment refused, now, therefore, petition your honorable bodies to reimburse Nevada in the sum of $11,840 so by her expended and paid as "costs, charges, and expenses," and by her incurred for enrolling 1,184 men for the military service of the United States, and who did perform active United States military service during the war of the rebellion wherever their military services were needed.

Respectfully,

C. C. STEVENSON,
Governor.
H. C. DAVIS,
Lieutenant-Governor and Adjutant-General.
JOHN M. DORMER,
Secretary of State.
J. F. HALLOCK,
State Controller.
GEORGE TUFLY,
State Treasurer.
JOHN F. ALEXANDER,
Attorney-General.
JOHN E. JONES,
Surveyor-General.
W. C. DOVEY,
Superintendent Public Instruction.
J. C. HARLOW,
Superintendent State Printing.

IN THE SENATE OF THE UNITED STATES.

JANUARY 29, 1896.—Ordered to be printed

Mr. STEWART, from the Committee on Claims, submitted the following

REPORT:

[To accompany S. 1650.]

The Committee on Claims, to whom was referred the bill (S. 1650) "to reimburse the States of California, Oregon, and Nevada for moneys by them expended in the suppression of the rebellion," have examined the same, and report as follows:

The claims for which reimbursement is asked in this bill are the rebellion war claims of the States of California, Oregon, and Nevada. They arose between 1861 and 1865, inclusive, and are founded upon the act of Congress of July 27, 1861 (12 U. S. Stats., 276), "An act to indemnify the States for expenses incurred by them in defense of the United States," and under the resolution of Congress of March 8, 1862 (12 U. S. Stats., 615), "declaratory of the intent and meaning of said act of July 27, 1861," and under the resolution of Congress of March 19, 1862 (12 U. S. Stats., 616), "to authorize the Secretary of War to accept money appropriated by any State for the payment of its volunteers, and to apply the same as directed by such State," and under other acts of Congress hereinafter referred to.

These State war claims of these three States are for the reimbursement to them of the money by them actually and duly expended in defraying the "costs, charges, and expenses" by them incurred in placing at the disposal of the United States 18,715 volunteer troops, under calls and requisitions officially made upon them therefor, by the proper civil and military authorities of the United States during the rebellion, between 1861 and 1865.

The facts out of which the aforesaid State war claims of California, Oregon, and Nevada arose have been very fully, in fact almost exhaustively, stated in several favorable reports heretofore made to the Senate and to the House of Representatives to accompany similar bills, and among others are as follows, to wit:

1. Senate Report No. 1286, Fiftieth Congress, first session.
2. Senate Report No. 2014, Fiftieth Congress, first session.
3. Senate Report No. 644, Fifty-first Congress, first session.
4. Senate Report No. 158, Fifty-second Congress, first session.
5. Senate Report No. 287, Fifty-third Congress, second session.
6. House Report No. 3396, Fiftieth Congress, first session.
7. House Report No. 2553, Fifty-first Congress, first session.
8. House Report No. 254, Fifty-second Congress, second session.
9. House Report No. 558, Fifty-third Congress, second session.

The sums of money named in this bill (S. 1650) are the same as those recited in three reports made by the Secretary of War to the Senate on these same State war claims of California, Oregon, and Nevada, which reports were duly printed and are Senate Ex. Docs. Nos. 10, 11, and 17, Fifty-first Congress, first session, proven to the full satisfaction of the War Department to have been the exact sums of money to have been duly expended by said three States to aid the United States in the suppression of the war of the rebellion.

Said sums were included in the general deficiency appropriation bill which passed the Senate during the second session of the Fifty-first Congress, and also in a similar bill which passed the Senate during the third session of the Fifty-third Congress, for the purpose of reimbursing and indemnifying California, Oregon, and Nevada, on account of said rebellion war claims, but said sums for said purpose were omitted from both of said bills when they became laws.

At a very early period of the war of the rebellion nearly all the troops of the Regular Army of the United States then serving in California, Oregon, and Nevada were withdrawn from military duty in those States and transported thence by sea to New York City, at an expense to the United States of about $390,103, or at an average cost of about $284 for each commissioned officer and of about $133 for each enlisted man.

This withdrawal therefrom of said regular troops left these three Pacific Coast States comparatively defenseless, and for the purpose of supplying their places, and to provide additional military forces, rendered necessary by public exigencies, calls for volunteers were made upon said States under proclamations of the President, or requisitions by the War Department, or by its highest military officers commanding the military departments on the Pacific. These calls for volunteers continued until the necessity therefor entirely ceased to exist, during which time these three Pacific Coast States furnished, enlisted, equipped, enrolled, paid, and mustered into the military service of the United States 18,715 volunteers, as shown in said reports so made to the Senate by the Secretary of War.

In consequence of this withdrawal in 1861 of said military forces from the Pacific Coast, in order that they might perform military service in the East, and in view of the circumstances and exigencies existing in the Pacific Coast States and Territories during the rebellion period, requisitions were duly made from time to time by the President of the United States and by the Secretary of War upon the proper State authorities of California, Oregon, and Nevada for volunteers to perform military service for the United States in said States and Territories, as are fully and in great detail set forth in Senate Ex. Docs. Nos. 10, 11, and 17, Fifty-first Congress, first session. In compliance with the several calls and official requisitions so made between 1861 and 1865, inclusive—

Volunteers.
The State of California furnished.. 15,725
The State of Nevada furnished 1,180
The State of Oregon furnished 1,810

Making a total aggregate of... 18,715

who were enlisted and were thereafter duly mustered into the military service of the United States as volunteers from said three States. The same number of troops, if organized in the East and transported from New York City to the Pacific Coast States and Territories in the same manner as was done by the United States War Department from June

17, 1850, to August 3, 1861, would have cost the United States at that time the sum of about $5,483,385 for *transportation alone.*

The indemnification for the "costs, charges, and expenses" properly incurred by said States for enrolling, subsisting, clothing, supplying, arming, equipping, paying, transporting, and furnishing said 18,715 volunteer troops employed by the United States to aid them to maintain the "common defense," was guaranteed these three States by the United States under the act of Congress approved July 27, 1861 (12 U. S. Stats., 276), an act entitled "An act to indemnify the States for expenses incurred by them in defense of the United States," and under other acts and resolutions of Congress hereinafter referred to.

The Secretary of War, Hon. Redfield Proctor, now United States Senator from Vermont (on page 28 of his report, Senate Ex. Doc. No. 11, Fifty-first Congress, first session), in reporting upon the military services performed by said volunteers during the rebellion, said:

They took the places of the regular troops in California, all of which, except three batteries of artillery and one regiment of infantry, were withdrawn to the East at an early period after the outbreak of the war. Without them (and the Oregon and Nevada volunteers) the overland mail and emigrant routes, extending from the Missouri River via Great Salt Lake City to California and Oregon, and passing through an uninhabited and mountainous country infested with hostile Indians and high-waymen, could not have been adequately protected; and yet it was of the first importance to have these routes kept open and safe, especially as rebel cruisers had made the sea routes both hazardous and expensive. Two expeditions composed of California volunteers, under the command of Brig. Gens. James H. Carleton and Patrick E. Connor, respectively, performed perilous and exhausting marches across a desert and over an almost impassable country and established themselves, the latter in Utah—where, besides protecting the mail routes, a watchful eye was kept on the uncertain and sometimes threatening attitude of the Mormons—and the former in Arizona and New Mexico, which Territories were thereafter effectually guarded in the interests of the United States against Indians and rebels.

The Secretary of War, with the assistance of the Board of Army Officers, specially created under the authority of the act of Congress approved August 4, 1886 (24 U. S. Stat., p. 217), to aid the Secretary of War to find all the facts in anywise relating to these State rebellion war claims of these three States, and which officers were duly selected and appointed on said Board by Mr. Secretary of War, Hon. W. C. Endicott, has heretofore found as facts, and has so officially reported to the Senate (as printed in Senate Ex. Docs. Nos. 10, 11, 17, Fifty-first Congress, first session), that the States of California, Oregon, and Nevada, under appropriate laws of the legislatures thereof, respectively, have actually paid in gold coin out of their State treasuries, on account of the "*costs, charges, and expenses*" properly incurred by said three States for enrolling, subsisting, clothing, supplying, arming, equipping, paying, transporting, and furnishing said 18,715 volunteer troops of said three States, which were employed by the United States to aid them to maintain the "common defense" on the Pacific coast during the war of the rebellion, the exact sums of money as recited in said bill (S. 1650), the reimbursement of which was so guarantied to be paid to said States as an indemnity under the aforesaid act of July 27, 1861 (12 U. S. Stat., 276), "An act to indemnify the States for expenses incurred by them in defense of the United States," and under the resolution of Congress of March 8, 1862 (12 U. S. Stat., 615), "declaratory of the intent and meaning of said act," and the resolution of March 19, 1862 (12 U. S. Stat., 616), "to authorize the Secretary of War to accept moneys appropriated by any State for the payment of its volunteers, and to apply the same as directed by such State," copies of which acts and resolutions, with other acts of Congress, are printed in an appendix hereto.

The Secretary of War found, and has reported to the Senate, that all the "costs, charges, and expenses" so paid by said three States, and for which reimbursement is provided for in said bill (S. 1650), were incurred under laws of the legislatures of each of said States duly enacted therefor, and said Secretary transmitted to the Senate copies of all of said State laws under which said expenditures were so authorized and made, and all of which laws are printed in said Executive Documents Nos. 10, 11, and 17, Fifty-first Congress, first session.

Said "costs, charges, and expenses" having been so incurred, under the State laws of said three States, to aid the United States, at its own request, to maintain the common defense during the war of the rebellion, your committee submits and declares that they were "properly incurred" within the meaning and intent of said acts of July 27, 1861, and March 8, 1862. The meaning and intent of said acts were recently interpreted and declared by the United States Supreme Court, in its unanimous opinion, delivered on December 6, 1895, by Mr. Justice Harlan, in cases No. 45 and No. 136, appealed to that court from the United States Court of Claims, entitled "The State of New York v. The United States," and "The United States v. The State of New York," and wherein that court in said cases declared thus:

Liberally interpreted, it is clear that the acts of July 27, 1861, and March 8, 1862, created, on the part of the United States, an obligation to indemnify the States for "any costs, charges, and expenses" properly incurred for the purposes expressed in the act of 1861, the title of which shows that its object was "to indemnify the States for expenses incurred by them in the defense of the United States."

So that the only inquiry is whether, within the fair meaning of the latter act, the words "costs, charges, and expenses" properly "incurred" included interest paid by the State of New York on moneys borrowed for the purpose of raising, subsisting, and supplying troops in the suppression of the rebellion. We have no hesitation in answering this question in the affirmative.

As recited by said court in said opinion in said cases, the State of New York was not only expected, but directed, on August 16, 1861, under the provisions of said act of July 27, 1861, to "adopt such measures as may be necessary to fill up your regiments as rapidly as possible; we need the men." Buy arms and equipments as fast as you can; we pay all;" and again: "The Government will refund the State for advances for troops as speedily as the Treasurer can obtain funds for that purpose." In other words, under said acts, it was left to the State of New York, and equally to all the other loyal States of the Union, upon which similar demands and requisitions were made, to be the judges to properly determine, through their respective legislatures, the kind, character, and extent of the "costs, charges, and expenses" which they deemed to be proper and necessary to be incurred by them, when obeying the proclamations, requisitions, and calls of the President and his proper civil and military subordinates for volunteer troops to aid the United States to maintain the common defense. In a word, if *any cost, any charge, and any expense, was properly incurred for any of the purposes expressed in said act of 1861 by any of the States*, an obligation was thereupon created making it the duty of the United States to indemnify the States for the same.

The full copy of said decision of Mr. Justice Harlan will be found in an appendix hereto, but so much of same as seems to your committee pertinent at this place, and which seems conclusive of the obligation and the duty of the United States to indemnify these three States for the expenses by them properly incurred in defense of the United States, by now reimbursing them the actual sums of money by them so paid as "costs, charges, and expenses" by them properly incurred for the purposes expressed in the aforesaid acts of Congress, and as reported to the Senate by the Secretary of War, is incorporated herein, as follows:

The duty of suppressing armed rebellion having for its object the overthrow of the National Government, was primarily upon that Government and not upon the several States composing the Union. New York came promptly to the assistance of the National Government by enrolling, subsisting, clothing, supplying, arming, equipping, paying, and transporting troops to be employed in putting down the rebellion. Immediately after Fort Sumter was fired upon its legislature passed an act appropriating $3,000,000, or so much thereof as was necessary, out of any moneys in its treasury not otherwise appropriated, to defray any expenses incurred for arms, supplies, or equipments, for such forces as were raised in that State and mustered into the service of the United States. In order to meet the burdens imposed by this appropriation, the real and personal property of the people of New York were subjected to taxation. When New York had succeeded in raising 30,000 soldiers to be employed in suppressing the rebellion, the United States, well knowing that the national existence was imperiled, and that the earnest cooperation and continued support of the States was required in order to maintain the Union, solemnly declared, by the act of 1861, that "the costs, charges, and expenses properly incurred" by any State in raising troops to protect the authority of the nation would be met by the General Government. And to remove any possible doubt as to what expenditures of a State would be so met, the act of 1862 declared that the act of 1861 should embrace expenses incurred before as well as after its approval.

It would be a reflection upon the patriotic motives of Congress if we did not place a liberal interpretation upon those acts and give effect to what, we are not permitted to doubt, was intended by their passage. Before the act of July 27, 1861, was passed, the Secretary of State of the United States telegraphed to the governor of New York, acknowledging that that State had then furnished 50,000 troops for service in the war of the rebellion, and thanking the governor for his efforts in that direction. And on July 25, 1861, Secretary Seward telegraphed: "Buy arms and equipments as fast as you can. We pay all." And on July 27, 1861, that "Treasury notes for part advances will be furnished on your call for them." On August 16, 1861, the Secretary of War telegraphed to the governor of New York: "Adopt such measures as may be necessary to fill up your regiments as rapidly as possible. We need the men. Let me know the best the Empire State can do to aid the country in the present emergency." And on February 11, 1862, he telegraphed: "The Government will refund the State for the advances for troops as speedily as the Treasurer can obtain funds for that purpose." Liberally interpreted, it is clear that the acts of July 27, 1861, and March 8, 1862, created, on the part of the United States, an obligation to indemnify the States for *any* costs, charges, and expenses *properly incurred* for the purposes expressed in the act of 1861, the title of which shows that its object was "to *indemnify* the States for expenses incurred by them in defense of the United States."

So that the only inquiry is whether, within the fair meaning of the latter act, the words "costs, charges, and expenses properly incurred," included interest paid by the State of New York on moneys borrowed for the purpose of raising, subsisting, and supplying troops to be employed in suppressing the rebellion. We have no hesitation in answering this question in the affirmative. If that State was to give effective aid to the General Government in its struggle with the organized forces of rebellion, it could only do so by borrowing money sufficient to meet the emergency; for it had no money in its treasury that had not been specifically appropriated for the expenses of its own government. It could not have borrowed money any more than the General Government could have borrowed money, without stipulating to pay such interest as was customary in the commercial world. Congress did not expect that any State would decline to borrow and await the collection of money raised by taxation before it moved to the support of the nation. It expected that each loyal State would, as did New York, respond at once in furtherance of the avowed purpose of Congress, by whatever force necessary, to maintain the rightful authority and existence of the National Government.

We can not doubt that the interest paid by the State on its bonds issued to raise money for the purposes expressed by Congress constituted a part of the costs, charges, and expenses properly incurred by it for those objects. Such interest, when paid, became a principal sum, as between the State and the United States; that is, became a part of the aggregate sum properly paid by the State for the United States. The principal and interest, so paid, constitutes a debt from the United States to the State. It is as if the United States had itself borrowed the money, through the agency of the State. We therefore hold that the court below did not err in adjudging that the $91,320.84 paid by the State for interest upon its bonds issued in 1861 to defray the expenses to be incurred in raising troops for the national defense was a principal sum which the United States agreed to pay, and not interest within the meaning of the rule prohibiting the allowance of interest accruing upon claims against the United States prior to the rendition of judgment thereon.

California, Oregon, and Nevada had no money in their State treasuries between 1861 and 1865 which was not specifically appropriated by the laws of their respective legislatures to meet the fixed, current, and necessary expenses of maintaining their own State governments during said period, and hence said three States were entirely without money to give effective aid to the General Government upon its requisitions upon them for volunteer troops to aid the United States in maintaining the "common defense" on the Pacific Coast during the rebellion *without borrowing the same.*

Therefore, in order to raise the money wherewith to pay all of the "costs, charges, and expenses" properly incurred by them under their own State laws for said 18,715 volunteer troops, these three States, California, Oregon, and Nevada, were compelled to borrow, and did borrow money, to wit, by issuing their State war bonds, under the authority of their respective legislatures, by laws by them duly enacted therefor, authority to do which was vested in their said legislatures *under their State constitutions during a period of war,* and for the hire and use of which money so borrowed and so expended said States were compelled to pay, and did pay, interest, as provided for in the laws authorizing the issue of their said State war bonds.

These extraordinary war expenses, principal and interest, represented by their said State war bonds, these three States have met and fully paid, by extra, special, and burdensome taxation imposed upon their people and their property; but which was made absolutely necessary, because of the failure of the United States thus far to meet the obligations due these three States in these premises.

The interest provided for in this bill is therefore the exact amount of money, *and not otherwise,* which the Secretary of War found, declared, and heretofore reported to the Senate, which these three States had actually paid, *as interest for the hire and use of the money, by them so borrowed for the aforesaid war purposes, upon their said State war bonds, issued to secure the principal; by them expended, solely, to aid the United States in the suppression of the war of the rebellion between 1861 and 1865.*

This reimbursement by the United States to California, Oregon, and Nevada of this interest by them so paid is not only in accordance with legislative and executive precedents, but is also in strict accordance with the meaning and intent of the aforesaid acts of Congress, under which these State war claims arose, and upon which they are legally and equitably founded, as said acts on December 6, 1895, were so judicially interpreted and declared by the United States Supreme Court in the said two cases, No. 45 and No. 136, October term, 1895, theretofore appealed to that court from the United States Court of Claims, entitled therein "The State of New York v. The United States" and "The United States v. The State of New York."

These State war claims of these three States, California, Oregon, and Nevada, are similar to the State war claim of the State of New York. They arose during the same period of time, they were incurred under similar circumstances, they are legally and equitably founded upon the same acts of Congress, and in reference to which Mr. Justice Harlan, on December 6, 1895, in rendering the unanimous opinion of said court, said: "The claims of the State of New York were founded on the said act of Congress of July 27, 1861, if not on *contract* with the United States," etc.

A copy of said decision of the United States Supreme Court is incorporated as a part of a statement made to your committee by said three

States in support of this bill (S. 1650) (and of similar bills introduced in the Fifty-fourth Congress), together with copies of the memorials to Congress of the legislatures of each thereof, in relation to the subject-matter of this bill (S. 1650); and also copies of official tables, showing the sums of money heretofore paid by the United States to each of the other loyal States on account of their State rebellion war claims respectively; and the number of volunteer troops furnished to the United States during the rebellion by each of said States; and also copies of the several acts and resolutions of Congress, and sundry acts of the legislatures of said States under which said volunteer troops were raised, organized, and placed at the disposal of the United States, and in consequence of which said expenditures were incurred and paid; and all of which matters are submitted as an appendix attached hereto and made a part hereof.

Wherefore, from the facts and laws herein recited, and from the matters contained in said Senate and House reports, executive documents, Supreme Court decision, and statement of said three States, your committee concur in the conclusions reached and in the recommendations made in the several reports to the Senate and to the House of Representatives to accompany similar bills, and now reaffirm the same and report back said bill (S. 1650), with a recommendation that it pass.

A copy of this bill so recommended is as follows:

A BILL to reimburse the States of California, Oregon, and Nevada for moneys by them expended in the suppression of the rebellion.

Be it enacted by the Senate and House of Representatives of the United States of America in Congress assembled, That there is hereby appropriated, out of any money in the Treasury not otherwise appropriated, the sum hereinafter mentioned to reimburse and to be paid to States of California, Oregon, and Nevada for moneys by them expended in aid of the United States in the war of rebellion, to wit:

To the State of California, the sum of three million nine hundred and fifty-one thousand nine hundred and fifteen dollars and forty-two cents.

To the State of Oregon, the sum of three hundred and thirty-five thousand one hundred and fifty-two dollars and eighty-eight cents.

To the State of Nevada, the sum of four hundred and four thousand and forty dollars and seventy cents, being the sums of money, principal and interest, paid by said States in the suppression of the rebellion as shown by the reports of the Secretary of War in Senate Executive Documents numbered ten, eleven, and seventeen, Fifty-first Congress, first session.

APPENDIX.

Statement of California, Oregon, and Nevada relative to their State rebellion war claims against the United States, made in support of Senate bill No. 31, introduced by Senator Stewart, of Nevada, on December 3, 1895; and of Senate bill No. 53, introduced on December 3, 1895, by Senator Mitchell, of Oregon; and of Senate bill No. 1650, introduced by Senator White, of California, on January 20, 1896; and of House bill No. 31, introduced by Representative Johnson, of California, on December 3, 1895; and of House bill No. 1246, introduced December 10, 1895, by Representative Maguire, of California; and House bill No. 4778, introduced on January 27, 1896, by Representative Hermann, of Oregon, and House bill No. 4962, introduced on January 27, 1896, by Representative Newlands, of Nevada, all having for their object "to reimburse the States of California, Oregon, and Nevada for moneys by them expended in the suppression of the rebellion," when aiding the United States to maintain the "common defense" on the Pacific Coast.

The facts out of which the aforesaid State war claims arise have been very fully stated in several reports heretofore made in the House of Representatives and to the Senate, as follows, to wit: House Report No. 254, and Senate Report No. 158, Fifty-second Congress, first session; House Report No. 2553, and Senate Report No. 644, Fifty-first Congress, first session; and House Report No. 3396 and Senate Reports No. 1286 and No. 2014, Fiftieth Congress, first session, and Senate Report No. 287 and House Report No. 558, Fifty-third Congress, second session.

Bills relating to these State war claims of these three Pacific Coast States passed the Senate during the first session of the Fiftieth Congress, and were favorably reported to the Senate during the first session of the Fifty-first and Fifty-second Congress, and to the House during the Fiftieth, Fifty-first, and Fifty-second Congresses, and to both Senate and House during the second session of the Fifty-third Congress, but were not reached for consideration by the House in either thereof. Similar Senate bills, to wit: Nos. 101, 1062, 1295, were introduced during the first and second sessions, Fifty-third Congress, by Senators Stewart, Dolph, and White of California, and all referred to the Senate Committee on Military Affairs. Similar House bills, to wit: H. R. No. 2615, were also introduced in the House on the 11th day of September, 1893, by Mr. Caminetti, of California; House bill No. 4959, on January 3, 1894, by Mr. Maguire, of California, and both referred to the House Committee on War Claims.

Sums of money (recited in three reports made by the Honorable Secretary of War to the Senate, on the State war claims of these three States and printed as Senate Ex. Docs. Nos. 10, 11, and 17, Fifty-first Congress, first session) proven to the full satisfaction of the War Department to have been expended by said States to aid the United States in the suppression of the war of the rebellion were included in the general deficiency appropriation bill as it passed the Senate during the second session of the Fifty-first Congress and in a similar bill during the third session of the Fifty-third Congress, for the purpose of indemnifying and reimbursing said States on account and in partial liquidation of said claims, but the same were omitted from said deficiency bill as it became a law. Senate bill No. 52 and House bills No. 54 and No. 42, Fifty-second Congress, first session, were in all respects identical, the last of which House bills was, on February 10, 1892, favorably reported by the House War Claims Committee in House Report No. 254, Fifty-second Congress, first session, and said Senate bill No. 52, which is similar to Senate bills No. 1650, No. 31, and No. 53, was, on February 4, 1892, favorably reported by the Senate Committee on Military Affairs in Senate Report No. 158, as follows, to wit: · -

[Senate Report No. 158, Fifty-second Congress, first session.]

IN THE SENATE OF THE UNITED STATES.

FEBRUARY 4, 1892.—Ordered to be printed.

Mr. Davis, from the Committee on Military Affairs, submitted the following report (to accompany S. 52):

The Committee on Military Affairs, to whom was referred the bill (S. 52) to reimburse the States of California, Oregon, and Nevada for moneys by them expended in the suppression of the rebellion, have examined the same and report as follows, to wit:

This measure was considered by this committee during the first session of the Fifty-first Congress and was reported upon favorably (Report No. 644).

Your committee concur in the conclusions stated in that report and recommend the passage of the bill.

At a very early period of the war of the rebellion nearly all the troops of the regular Army of the United States, then serving in California, Oregon, and Nevada, were withdrawn from military duty in those States and transported thence by sea to New York City at an expense to the United States of about $390,103, or at an average cost of about $284 for each commissioned officer and of about $133 for each enlisted man.

This withdrawal therefrom of said regular troops left these three Pacific Coast States comparatively defenseless, and for the purpose of supplying their places and to provide additional military forces, rendered necessary by public exigencies, calls for volunteers were made upon said States under proclamations of the President, or requisitions by the War Department, or by its highest military officers commanding the military departments on the Pacific. These calls for volunteers continued until the necessity therefor entirely ceased to exist, during which time these three Pacific Coast States furnished, enlisted, equipped, enrolled, paid, and mustered into military service of the United States 18,715 volunteers, as shown in said reports so made to the Senate by the Secretary of War.

In consequence of this withdrawal in 1861 of said military forces from the Pacific Coast, in order that they might perform military service in the East, and in view of the circumstances and exigencies existing in the Pacific Coast States and Territories during the rebellion period, requisitions were duly made from time to time by the President of the United States and by the Secretary of War upon the proper State authorities of California, Oregon, and Nevada for volunteers to perform military service for the United States in said States and Territories, as are fully and in great detail set forth in Senate Ex. Docs. Nos. 10, 11, 17, Fifty-first Congress, first session. In compliance with the several calls and official requisitions so made between 1861 and 1866, inclusive—

	Volunteers.
The State of California furnished	15,725
The State of Nevada furnished	1,180
The State of Oregon furnished	1,810
Making a total aggregate of	18,715

men who were enlisted and were thereafter duly mustered into the military service of the United States as volunteers from said States. The same number of troops if organized in the East and transported from New York City to the Pacific Coast States and Territories in the same manner as was done by the United States War Department from June 17, 1850, to August 3, 1861, would have cost the United States at that time the sum of about $5,483,385, for *transportation alone.*

The indemnification for the "costs, charges, and expenses" properly incurred by said States for enrolling, subsisting, clothing, supplying, arming, equipping, paying, transporting, and furnishing said 18,715 volunteer troops employed by the United States to aid them to maintain the "common defense," was guaranteed by the United States in

the act of Congress approved July 27, 1861 (12 U. S. Stats., 276), an act entitled "An act to indemnify the States for expenses incurred by them in defense of the United States."
The then Secretary of War, Hon. Redfield Proctor, now U. S. Senator from Vermont (on page 28 of his report, Senate Ex. Doc. No. 41, Fifty-first Congress, first session), in reporting upon the military services performed by said volunteers during the rebellion, said:

They took the places of the regular troops in California, all of which, except three batteries of artillery and one regiment of infantry, were withdrawn to the East at an early period after the outbreak of the war. Without them (and the Oregon and Nevada volunteers) the overland mail and emigrant routes, extending from the Missouri River via Great Salt Lake City to California and Oregon, and passing through an uninhabited and mountainous country infested with hostile Indians and highwaymen, could not have been adequately protected; and yet it was of the first importance to have these routes kept open and safe, especially as rebel cruisers had made the sea routes both hazardous and expensive. Two expeditions composed of California volunteers under the command of Brig. Gens. James H. Carleton and Patrick E. Connor, respectively, performed perilous and exhausting marches across a desert and over an almost impassable country and established themselves, the latter in Utah—where, besides protecting the mail routes, a watchful eye was kept on the uncertain and sometimes threatening attitude of the Mormons—and the former in Arizona and New Mexico, which Territories were thereafter effectually guarded in the interests of the United States against Indians and rebels.

On March 3, 1863 (12 U. S. Stats., 808), Congress organized the Territory of Idaho, the extensive mineral discoveries in which, attracting thousands of miners, explorers, and immigrants, naturally necessitated an additional volunteer military force to guard and protect so extended difficult and new Indian frontier lines.
On October 14, 1861, the Secretary of State, Hon. William H. Seward, by direction of the President of the United States, issued to the governors of all the loyal States a circular letter, wherein the attention of the proper authorities of said States was invited to the necessity of improving and perfecting the defenses of their respective States, to be done in a manner such as should thereafter be determined by the legislature of each of said States who were to rely upon Congress to sanction their action, and to reimburse all expenses by them so incurred, Mr. Secretary Seward expressing it as his opinion that "such proceedings by said States would require only a temporary use of their means."
Said circular letter is as follows, to wit:

DEPARTMENT OF STATE,
Washington, October 14, 1861.

SIR: The present insurrection had not even revealed itself in arms when disloyal citizens hastened to foreign countries to invoke their intervention for the overthrow of the Government and the destruction of the Federal Union. These agents are known to have made their appeals to some of the more important States without success. It is not likely, however, that they will remain content with such refusals. Indeed, it is understood that they are industriously endeavoring to accomplish their disloyal purposes by degrees and by indirection. Taking advantage of the embarrassments of agriculture, manufacture and commerce in foreign countries, resulting from the insurrection they have inaugurated at home, they seek to involve our common country in controversies with States with which every public interest and every interest of mankind require that it shall remain in relations of peace, amity, and friendship. I am able to state, for your satisfaction, that the prospect of any such disturbance is now less serious than it has been at any previous period since the course of the insurrection. It is nevertheless necessary now, as it has hitherto been, to take every precaution that is possible to avert the evils of foreign war to be superinduced upon those of civil commotion which we are endeavoring to cure. One of the most obvious of such precautions is that our ports and harbors on the seas and lakes should be put in a condition of complete defense, for any nation may be said to voluntarily incur danger in tempestuous seasons when it fails to show that it has sheltered itself on every side from which the storm might possibly come.
The measures which the Executive can adopt in this emergency are such only as Congress has sanctioned and for which it has provided. The President is putting

forth the most diligent efforts to execute these measures, and we have the great satisfaction of seeing that these efforts, seconded by the favor, aid, and support of a loyal, patriotic, and self-sacrificing people, are rapidly bringing the military and naval forces of the United States into the highest state of efficiency. But Congress was chiefly absorbed during its recent extra session with those measures and did not provide as amply as could be wished for the fortification of our sea and lake coasts. In previous wars, loyal States have applied themselves by independent and separate activity to support and aid the Federal Government in its arduous responsibilities. The same disposition has been manifested in a degree eminently honorable by all the loyal States during the present insurrection. In view of this fact, and relying upon the increase and continuance of the same disposition on the part of the loyal States, the President has directed me to invite your consideration to the subject of the improvement and perfection of the defenses of the State over which you preside, and to ask you to submit the subject to the consideration of the legislature when it shall have assembled. Such proceedings by the State would require only a temporary use of means.

The expenditures ought to be made the subject of conference with the Federal authorities. Being thus made with the concurrence of the Government for general defense, there is every reason to believe that Congress would sanction what the State should do and would provide for its reimbursement. Should these suggestions be accepted the President will direct proper agents of the Federal Government to confer with you and to superintend, direct, and conduct the prosecution of the system of defense of your State.

I have the honor to be, sir, your obedient servant,

WILLIAM H. SEWARD.

His Excellency THOMAS H. HICKS,
Governor of the State of Maryland.

The Attorney-General of the United States, on June 11, 1891, in rendering an opinion, at the request of the Honorable Secretary of the Treasury, involving a question as to the "State war claims of the State of Vermont against the United States," declared that the defense of the State of Vermont by said State during the war of the rebellion, as recited in his said opinion, was the defense of the United States, and that all expenses so incurred by said State in repelling invasion and in preparing to resist attacks, etc., constitute valid charges against the United States to be paid out of the public Treasury.

From June 17, 1850, and continuously until August 3, 1861, the practice of the War Department under the laws of Congress was to pay each soldier, enlisted, recruited, or reenlisted in the State of California, Oregon, and Nevada, a sum of money which, while Congress termed it a "bounty," yet it in fact and effect was and was intended to be merely extra or additional pay in the form of a constructive mileage equivalent to the cost of transporting a soldier from New York City to the place of such enlistment or reenlistment; said sum was to be paid to each Pacific Coast soldier in installments, in the amounts, at the times, and in the manner as recited in the act of Congress therefor, approved June 17, 1850, the third section of which reads as follows:

SEC. 3. *And be it further enacted,* That whenever enlistments are made at or in the vicinity of the said military posts, and remote and distant stations, a bounty equal in amount to the cost of transporting and subsisting a soldier from the principal recruiting depot in the harbor of New York, to the place of such enlistment, be and the same is hereby, allowed to each recruit so enlisted, to be paid in unequal installments at the end of each year's service, so that the several amounts shall annually increase, and the largest be paid at the expiration of each enlistment. (U. S. Stat., vol. 9, p. 439.)

Congress, during the rebellion, changed the manner of maintaining a military force in these three Pacific Coast States by relying, to a very large degree, if not almost exclusively, upon volunteers to be enlisted and raised therein, and therefore, on August 3, 1861, repealed said law. (12 U. S. Stats., sec. 9, p. 289.)

In consequence of the high cost of living in California and Oregon, Congress, on 28th September, 1850, passed an act paying to every commissioned officer serving in those States an extra $2 per day, arid to all the enlisted men serving in the U. S. Army in those States double the pay then being paid to the troops of the regular Army. This law is as follows, to wit:

For extra pay to the commissioned officers and enlisted men of the Army of the United States, serving in Oregon or California, three hundred and twenty-five thousand eight hundred and fifty-four dollars, on the following basis, to wit: That there shall be allowed to each commissioned officer as aforesaid, while serving as aforesaid, a per diem, in addition to their regular pay and allowances, of two dollars each, and to each enlisted man as aforesaid, while serving as aforesaid, a per diem, in addition to their present pay and allowances, equal to the pay proper of each as established by existing laws, said extra pay of the enlisted men to be retained until honorably discharged. This additional pay to continue until the first of March, eighteen hundred and fifty-two, or until otherwise provided. (U. S. Stat., vol. 9, p. 564.)

It will be here noticed that under these two acts of Congress, the one of the 17th of June, 1850, and the other of the 28th of September, 1850, the so-called "extra pay" and the so-called "bounty" or constructive mileage, were both paid during one and the same period of time by the United States to its own troops serving in the Regular United States Army stationed in these States.

If the necessity for this character of legislation for the Regular Army of the United States recited in these two acts existed in a time of profound peace—and no one doubts but that a necessity therefor did exist—then how much greater the necessity for similar legislation in a period of actual war, when the land carriage for supplies over a distance of 2,000 miles, from the Missouri River to these Pacific Coast States, was simply impossible, or at least impracticable, there not being then any overland railroads, and the two sea routes via Cape Horn and the Isthmus of Panama, as recited in the said reports of the Secretary of War, being both hazardous and expensive?

The condition of public affairs existing in these Pacific Coast States in the early part of 1863 is recited on pages 25 and 26 of House Report No. 254, Fifty-second Congress, first session, in words as follows, to wit:

In the early part of April, 1863, the overland mail and emigrant route was attacked by Indians, and communication was closed between the Atlantic States and the Pacific Coast. This route extended from the Missouri River to California via the Platte River, Salt Lake City, through Nevada to Sacramento, in California, and was the only means at that date of direct overland communication between the Missouri River and California. At this time the gold discoveries in California continued to invite a large immigration, the interest in which was more or less intensified by the continued extensive silver discoveries in Nevada Territory, and principally on the Comstock lode, in the western part of the Territory. The routes via Cape Horn, and especially that via the Isthmus of Panama, were rendered extremely doubtful, dangerous, and expensive on account of Confederate privateer cruisers hovering around the West India Islands and along both these sea routes, and in anticipation of other Confederate cruisers infesting the waters of the Pacific (which soon thereafter became the theater of the operations and extensive depredations of the Confederate privateer *Shenandoah*), the overland route, therefore, although in itself both dangerous and difficult, was yet considered the better and preferable route by which to reach the Pacific.

On account of a general uprising of the Indians along the entire overland route, and especially that portion between Salt Lake City, in the Territory of Utah and the Sierra Nevada Mountains, and because of the doubts as to the loyalty of the Mormons to the Government of the United States, the maintenance and protection of the mail and emigrant route through that section of the country and along the aforesaid line was regarded by the Government as a military necessity. Apparently in anticipation of no immediate danger of attack on the Pacific Coast, nearly all the troops of the regular Army at this time had been withdrawn from service throughout this entire region of country and transferred east to other fields of military operations. This left the entire country between Salt Lake City and the Sierra Nevada Mountains without adequate and efficient military protection. The Government thus having but few troops of its regular Army in that region, was therefore compelled to call upon the inhabitants of Nevada Territory to raise and organize volunteer military companies to suppress Indian disturbances which threatened the entire suspension of all mail facilities and emigration from the East, as will be hereafter shown.

At the time of the calls upon Nevada for troops the prices of labor and supplies of all descriptions in Nevada were extremely high. There were then no railroads, and the snow on the Sierra Nevada Mountains formed an almost impassable barrier against teams from about the 1st of December until about June. The average cost of freight from San Francisco, the main source of supply for western Nevada, was about $80 a ton, and it was necessary to lay in supplies during the summer and fall for the remainder of the year. A great mining excitement prevailed at this time, occasioned by the marvelous development of the great Comstock lode, and wages were from $4 to $10 a day, in gold. The people who had emigrated to the new gold and silver fields went there for the purpose of mining and prospecting for mines, and were generally reluctant to enter the irregular military service of guarding the overland mail and emigrant route. Besides, on account of the extraordinary high price of supplies of every description, and also of wages and service of every kind, it was impossible for them to maintain themselves and families without involving much more expense than any compensation which could be paid them as volunteer troops under the laws of the United States, and, as will be seen by the letters of Gen. Wright, hereafter quoted, they were expected, as volunteer troops, to furnish themselves with horses and equipments, in addition to what could be furnished by the Government.

The military authorities of the United States well knew at that time the exact condition of the country and of the roads across the mountains leading thereto and of the cost of transportation and of the prices of labor and of supplies and of their own inability to furnish either horses or equipments for a military service that required mounted troops.

It was amid circumstances like these that the Honorable Secretary of the Treasury, by telegraphic instructions to the assistant treasurer of the United States at San Francisco, Cal., under date of February 9, 1863 (on which date there was on deposit in the subtreasury at San Francisco, to the credit of the United States, a large amount of gold and silver coin), directed the paymasters of the Army to pay said volunteers in U. S. notes, commonly called greenbacks. An exemplification of the effect of such instructions is reported by the Secretary of War on pp. 40 and 41, Senate Ex. Doc. No. 11, Fifty-first Congress, first session, in words as follows, to wit:

EXHIBIT NO. 10.

DEPUTY PAYMASTER-GENERAL'S OFFICE,
San Francisco, February 13, 1863.

SIR: Yesterday payment of my checks was refused by the assistant treasurer in San Francisco. In reply to a note which I addressed to him I received the following:

"OFFICE OF THE ASSISTANT TREASURER UNITED STATES,
San Francisco, February 2, 1863.

"SIR: Your communication of this date relative to the check of $80,000 presented but a few minutes since by Major Eddy and payment declined by me, etc., is just received.

"Under instructions from the Honorable Secretary of the Treasury United States of February 9, 1863, I am advised that 'checks of disbursing officers must be paid in United States notes.' Not having notes on hand sufficient to meet the check presented and referred to you has compelled me to decline payment of the same for the time being.

"Respectfully, your obedient servant,

"D. W. CHEESEMAN,
Assistant Treasurer United States.

"GEORGE H. RINGGOLD,
"*Deputy Paymaster-General U. S. Army.*"

The effect of these instructions is abruptly to stop payment of the troops. I had drawn out a sufficiency, principally in coin, to pay the posts in Oregon and a portion of the troops in this immediate vicinity; the delay will, I fear, cause great dissatisfaction to those remaining unpaid, as there was a confident expectation that they would now be paid off and in coin.

In connection with the above statement, I deem proper to forward herewith a copy of a letter recently received from Major Drew, of the Oregon cavalry, which so clearly sets forth the condition of things as regards legal tenders on this coast as to make comment on my part superfluous, except simply to add that gold is the only currency here, and that U. S. Treasury notes are worth only what they will bring on the street. They are quoted at 61 to-day.

I have the honor to remain, very respectfully, your obedient servant,

GEO. H. RINGGOLD,
Deputy Paymaster-General.

Lieut. Col. T. P. ANDREWS,
Acting Paymaster-General U. S. Army.

Respectfully referred to Treasurer of the United States with the request that the funds may be sent to assistant treasurer at San Francisco to meet the drafts in favor of paymasters, and to return these papers for such other action as may be necessary.

T. P. ANDREWS,
Paymaster-General.

PAYMASTER-GENERAL'S OFFICE, *March 18, 1863.*

If the Treasurer will be kind enough to furnish us with any suggestions from the Treasury that would tend to do away with the causes of complaint in this, to us, difficult case, we should feel indebted.

T. P. ANDREWS,
Paymaster-General.

PAYMASTER-GENERAL'S OFFICE, *March 18, 1863.*

TREASURER'S OFFICE, *March 19, 1863.*

Respectfully referred to the Secretary of the Treasury.

F. E. SPINNER,
Treasurer United States.

Concerning the foregoing condition of financial affairs in these three States and the effect thereof upon their volunteer troops then serving in the U. S. Army in the Department of the Pacific, the Honorable Secretary of War (House Report No. 254, Fifty-second Congress, first session, p. 20) reported as follows, to wit:

It appears that up to December 31, 1862, those of the U. S. troops serving in the Department of the Pacific who were paid at all—in some cases detachments had not been paid for a year or more—were generally paid in coin, but on February 9, 1863, instructions were issued from the Treasury Department to the assistant treasurer of the United States at San Francisco that "checks of disbursing officers must be paid in United States notes." (Letter of Deputy Paymaster-General George H. Ringgold, dated February 13, 1863, to Paymaster-General; copy herewith marked Exhibit No. 10.)

Before this greenbacks had become the current medium of exchange in all ordinary business transactions in the Eastern States, but in the Pacific Coast States and the adjoining Territories gold continued to be the basis of circulation throughout the war. At this time the paper currency had become greatly depreciated, and on February 28, 1863, the price of gold in Treasury notes touched 170. This action of the Government in compelling troops to accept such notes as an equivalent of gold in payment for services rendered by them in a section where coin alone was current gave rise to much dissatisfaction; for although gold could be bought in San Francisco at nearly the same price in Treasury notes as in New York, it must be remembered that the troops in the Department of the Pacific were largely stationed at remote and isolated points.

When paying in greenbacks for articles purchased by or for services rendered to them in these out-of-way places, they were obliged to submit not only to the current discount in San Francisco, but also to a further loss occasioned by the desire of the persons who sold the articles or rendered the service to protect themselves against possible further depreciation. It admits of little doubt that by reason of his inability to realize the full value of paper money, as quoted in the money centers, and of the fact that wages and the cost of living and of commodities of every kind were abnormally high (owing in great part to the development of newly-discovered mines in that region), the purchasing power of the greenback dollar in the hands of the average soldier serving in the Department of the Pacific was from the latter part of 1862 onward from 25 to 50 per cent less than that of the same dollar paid to his fellow soldier in the East.

Representations of the great hardships the Treasury Department's instructions entailed upon the troops were promptly made. On March 10, 1863, the legislature telegraphed to Washington a resolution adopted on that date instructing the State's delegation in Congress to impress upon the Executive "the necessity which exists of having officers and soldiers of the U. S. Army, officers, seamen, and marines of the U. S. Navy, and all citizen employees in the service of the Government of the United States serving west of the Rocky Mountains and on the Pacific Coast paid their salaries and pay in gold and silver currency of the United States, provided the same be paid in as revenue on this coast." (P. 46, Statement for Senate Committee on Military Affairs.)

And on March 16, 1863, Brig. Gen. G. Wright, the commander of the Department of the Pacific (comprising, besides California, the State of Oregon and the Territories of Nevada, Utah, and Arizona), transmitted to the Adjutant-General of the U. S. Army a letter of Maj. C. S. Drew, First Oregon Cavalry, commandant at Camp Baker, Oreg., containing an explicit statement of the effects of and a formal protest against paying his men in greenbacks. In his letter of transmittal (p. 154, Ex. Doc. 70) General Wright remarked as follows:

"The difficulties and embarrassments enumerated in the major's communication are common to all the troops in this department, and I most respectfully ask the serious consideration of the General-in-Chief and the War Department to this subject. Most of the troops would prefer waiting for their pay to receiving notes worth but little more than half their face; but even at this ruinous discount officers, unless they have private means, are compelled to receive the notes. Knowing the difficulties experienced by the Government in procuring coin to pay the Army, I feel great reluctance in submitting any grievances from this remote department, but justice to the officers and soldiers demands that a fair statement should be made to the War Department."

The letter of Maj. C. S. Drew referred to by the Honorable Secretary of War in the foregoing report is printed on p. 154, Sen. Ex. Doc. No. 17, Fifty-first Congress, first session, and is as follows, to wit:

CAMP BAKER, OREG., *March 4, 1863.*

COLONEL: I inclose herewith, for the consideration of the commanding general, the resignation of Asst. Surg. D. S. Holton, First Cavalry, Oregon Volunteers. Dr. Holton is a zealous and faithful officer, and I regret that circumstances, those which he sets forth, render it necessary for him to leave the service. But knowing the facts in the premises I must nevertheless recommend, as I now do, that his resignation be accepted. While upon the subject of resignations I beg to remark that the cause assigned by Dr. Holton for his resignation is valid and sufficient, doubtless, for its acceptance. But there is another which in its practical workings is almost as potent, and which precludes the possibility for any of the officers at this post to remain much longer in the service. I allude to their nonpayment since they entered the service, as also that of the entire command. This has borne heavily upon the officers, more especially as they have been compelled to hire money, some of them for more than a year past, with which to purchase their horses and equipments and to defray personal expenses. The act of Congress of June 18, 1862, requiring "that company officers of volunteers," and unjustly applied to the field and staff of regiments also, "shall be paid on the muster and pay rolls," has worked a great injury to the officers here, as it has, no doubt, in other portions of this department, by inhibiting the use of "pay accounts," which in our case could have been used as collaterals, at or near their face, in obtaining the money for our expenditures. But no such arrangement could be effected under the new regulations, as by its requirements the death of the officer or his removal to other and distant post would enhance the probability of a delay in payment of his indebtedness and increase the risk and expense attending its final collection. Hence the greater rate of interest charged.

But this is not all. The money borrowed has been specie, and must be paid in the same currency, while payment to the officers is liable to be made in Treasury notes, worth here not more than 50 to 55 cents per dollar, and very little sale for them even at those low figures; thus, practically, with the interest which has accrued on the amount borrowed, it will require more than $2 of the money in which the officer is paid to repay $1 of that which he owes. With this condition of things, too, each officer and soldier of this command is serving for less than half pay, and have done so, some of them, for more than sixteen months past. Under these circumstances it must be impossible for any of the officers here to serve much longer without becoming irretrievably bankrupt and bringing upon themselves all the contumely and reproach that such misfortune is always sure to create. But private injury is not all that this delay and final mode of payment inflicts. It is exceedingly detrimental to the public service generally, as without any stated market value to the notes, and no surety as to when payment in them, even, will be made, in every purchase or other expenditure made here, not only the current San Francisco discount on the notes is added to the specie value of the article or service, but, in addition to all this, a large percentage for the risk of a further depreciation in their value, and a vexatious delay in payment.

It is thus that capital protects itself from loss, and perhaps realizes better profits than under the old and better system of payment in coin. But the soldier has not this power, not even that to protect himself against loss, and if paid in notes must necessarily receipt in full for what is equivalent to him of half pay, or less, for the service he has rendered, and must continue to fulfill his part of his contract with the Government for the same reduced rate of pay until his period of service shall terminate. This, in its practical results, is making a distinction between capital and labor, or personal service, unfriendly and injurious to the latter, that I am sure was never contemplated or designed by the War Department, and its abolishment here, at least, would be of much advantage to the service, besides meting out but simple justice to long-deferred creditors, and at no greater cost to the Government. This delay and uncertainty about the payment of the troops at this post is also working a public injury by preventing enlistments in this part of Oregon, in any considerable number, for the new companies ordered to fill this regiment. Good men will not enlist for $6 or $7 a month while $13 is the regular pay, and, moreover, being realized by every soldier in any other department than the Pacific. Men who would enlist under these circumstances are, as a general rule, entirely worthless for soldiers or anything else, and would be an incubus upon the service if permitted to join it.

I beg to be understood as reporting the condition of things actually existing here, and not as I would have them. Neither would I be understood as casting any censure whatever upon any officer of this department. I am aware that Colonel Ringgold would have taken as favorable action in our case with regard to payment as he has at any other post had it not have been for the unfortunate order of the Secretary of the Treasury that his drafts should be paid in notes, and at a time, too, when there were no notes on hand. I trust that the commanding general will give us a word of encouragement, if in his power, so that it may be imparted to the men of this command, many of whom are becoming somewhat alarmed as to their pay and as to the currency to be used in payment.

I am, colonel, very respectfully, your obedient servant,

C. S. DREW,
Major First Cavalry, Oregon Volunteers.

RICHARD C. DRUM,
Assistant Adjutant-General, U. S. Army,
Headquarters Department of the Pacific, San Francisco, Cal.

This action was had by the authorities of the United States notwithstanding the contents of General Orders, No. 16, from the Headquarters of the Army, issued on September 3, 1861, which is as follows, to wit:

[General Orders, No. 16.]

HEADQUARTERS OF THE ARMY,
Washington, September 3, 1861.

The General in Chief is happy to announce that the Treasury Department—to meet future payments to the troops—is about to supply, besides coin, as heretofore, Treasury notes in fives, tens, and twenties, as good as gold at all banks and Government offices throughout the United States, and most convenient for transmission by mail from officers and men to their families at home. Good husbands, fathers, sons, and brothers, serving under the Stars and Stripes, will thus soon have the ready and safe means of relieving an immense amount of suffering which could not be reached with coin.

In making up such packages every officer may be relied upon, no doubt, for such assistance as may be needed by his men.

By command of Lieutenant-General Scott.

E. D. TOWNSEND,
Assistant Adjutant-General.

In consequence of the foregoing, formal protests were duly forwarded to the War Department by the commanding general, Division of the Pacific, and legislative appeals by these States were made direct to Congress to come to the relief of the volunteers then serving the United States in these Pacific Coast States, by increasing to living rates the pay of said troops. But all such protests, appeals, and representations in behalf of these troops proved, in the language of the Secretary of War, "perfectly futile."

The reports of the Honorable Secretary of War on this subject recite as follows, to wit:

It was under circumstances and exigencies such as these that the legislatures themselves—all appeals to the General Government having proved futile—provided the necessary relief by the law of April 27, 1863. They did not even after that relax their efforts on behalf of the United States troops, other than their own volunteers, serving among them, but on April 1, 1864, adopted a resolution requesting their representatives in Congress to "use their influence in procuring the passage of a law giving to the officers and soldiers of the Regular Army stationed on the Pacific Coast an increase of their pay, amounting to 30 per cent on the amount now allowed by law." (Senate Ex. Doc. No. 17, Fifty-first Congress, first session, p. 14.)

It was under and amid national financial embarrassments like these that these three Pacific Coast States (California taking the lead and Oregon and Nevada following in due course, and California not moving therein until April 27, 1863) felt compelled to come to the relief of their own volunteers, then serving in the U. S. Army therein, and passed acts through their respective legislatures, under and by which each volunteer in each of said States was to be paid the sum of $5 per month, and in order to raise the money with which to pay the same said States, under appropriate acts of their respective legislatures hereinafter recited, issued and sold their State gold bonds, and paid said $5 per month, in gold coin, to their said volunteers.

In 1864 the period of the three years' enlistments of the volunteers in these States who had been mustered in 1861 into the military service of the United States was approaching termination. These volunteers were in the field, scattered throughout the deserts of Arizona and New Mexico, in the south; in Washington Territory, in the north; along the western slopes of the Rocky Mountains, in the east; and guarding the immigrant and overland mail routes and pony express lines, extending from the Missouri River to the Pacific Ocean, which duties, onerous and vexatious, were soon to be supplemented by others equally so in protecting and escorting exploring, reconnoitering, and surveying parties, about to engage in running preliminary lines of overland railroad surveys for the Central and Union Pacific railroads, rendering it necessary, not only to maintain an adequate military force then in the field, but to provide for exigencies in the near future, which seemed to render an additional volunteer military force absolutely necessary.

The war in the East was still flagrant, and no one could then foretell the end thereof. General Lee had just invaded Pennsylvania with a large army, and though defeated at Gettysburg, yet extensive and devastating raids were made into the State of Pennsylvania by the Confederate forces as late as July, 1864, by Gens. Early, Johnson, and McCausland, the effects of which are represented to have been even more disastrous to the people of that State than those arising from the raids made therein in 1862 by Gen. Zeb. Stuart, of the Confederate cavalry. Chambersburg, Pa., was burned on July 30, 1864, the Confederates destroying extensive properties in the counties of Adams, Bedford, Cumberland, Franklin, Fulton, Perry, Somerset, and York, lying along the southern border of Pennsylvania and adjoining the northern Maryland line, the value of which property so destroyed is reported to have aggregated a very large sum.

In addition to the foregoing, attention is called to the official decisions rendered in September, 1863, by the Second Comptroller of the Treasury, Hon. John M. Brodhead, to the effect that the volunteers of these and other States then serving in the Army of the United States, who should be discharged by virtue of reenlistments as veteran volunteers, *should not receive any mileage* from the places of their discharge to the places of their original enrollment. (See Second Comptroller's Decisions, September 8 and 9, 1863, vol. 25, pp. 422 and 425, printed as section 2192, on p. 283 of Digest of Second Comptroller's Decisions, vol. 1, 1861 to 1868.)

S. Rep. 145——2

18 WAR CLAIMS OF CERTAIN STATES.

However valid these decisions may have been as declaratory of the intentions of the law as then viewed by the Treasury Department, yet the practical effect thereof was to discourage reenlistments in the case of these volunteers from California, about to be discharged in New Mexico, where they were serving at the dates of said decisions, many hundreds of miles from the places of their original enrollment. Under these decisions the United States paid a bounty or mileage to those volunteers *who did not reenlist in the U. S. Army*, but refused to pay it to those who did so reenlist.

The serious, in fact, alarming effect of these decisions of the honorable Second Comptroller upon the military condition of affairs in Arizona and New Mexico, where several regiments of these California volunteers were then serving, is shown by the great anxiety and serious concern of Brig. Gen. James H. Carleton, of the Regular Army of the United States, commanding the Department of New Mexico, so much so that he made it the subject of a special report to the Adjutant-General of the Army, at Washington, D. C., recited on pp. 60 and 61, Report of Secretary of War, Senate Ex. Doc. No. 11, Fifty-first Congress, first session, in words as follows, to wit:

EXHIBIT No. 22.

HEADQUARTERS DEPARTMENT OF NEW MEXICO,
Santa Fe, N. Mex., November 29, 1863.

GENERAL: Until Mr. Brodhead's decision was made, that volunteers who should be discharged by enlistment in veteran volunteers should not receive their mileage from the place of said discharge to the place of original enrollment, I entertained hopes that many, if not most, of the First and Fifth Regiments of Infantry, of the First Cavalry California Volunteers, and First Cavalry New Mexican Volunteers, would reenlist in the veteran volunteers. But since that decision was made it is very doubtful if the California volunteers will reenlist. Their present term of office will expire next August and September. Before that time other troops will have to be sent here to take their places, unless these can be induced to reenlist. The troops in this department should be made an exception to the general rule. In my opinion an order should be made giving all volunteers who reenlist in this department the $100 due on first enlistment and an increased bounty on the second over and above the bounty paid to soldiers in the East, which would be equal to the cost of getting soldiers from the East to New Mexico. The Government in this way would lose nothing, but would rather gain, because these well-disciplined men would then remain, doubtless, and they have now become familiar with the country, and can do better service for that reason than any newcomers. These men should receive their mileage on their first enlistment. In my opinion the law clearly allows it to soldiers honorably discharged. If the Government do not deny their traveling allowances and will give the bounty named, I believe the most of these regiments can be got to remain. If the Government will not do this, I beg to give timely notice of the necessities which will exist to have troops sent to take their places in time to be in position before the term of service of these men expires.

The California troops do not wish to be sent as regiments back to California; they would rather be discharged here in case they do not reenlist. Some desire to go to the States, some to the gold fields of Arizona, some settle in New Mexico, and some go to California by whatever route they please. The true economy of the question would be promoted by making the bounties so liberal as to induce them to reenter the service for three years or during the war.

I am, General, very truly and respectfully, your obedient servant,
CHARLES H. CARLETON,
Brigadier-General, Commanding.

Brig. Gen. LORENZO THOMAS,
Adjutant-General, U. S. Army, Washington, D. C.

DEPARTMENT NEW MEXICO,
Santa Fe, N. Mex., July 12, 1865.

Official:

BEN. C. CUTLER,
Assistant Adjutant-General.

These three Pacific Coast States therefore and in consequence of the foregoing facts determined for the benefit of their respective volunteers who might reenlist (and thereby successfully retain veteran soldiers in the military service of the United States), or, who after April, 1864, should enlist for the first time in the U. S. Army, then serving in these States, to revive substantially the provisions of the aforesaid act of Congress of June 17, 1850, which had been in existence for the benefit of the U. S. Army serving on the Pacific Coast, continuously from June 17, 1850, to August 3, 1861. Under the provisions of said act each volunteer soldier of these States, so enlisting or reenlisting in the U. S. Army after April 4, 1864 (the date of the California act for this specific purpose), was to be paid in installments, at the time and in the manner substantially as recited in said Congressional act of June 17, 1850, a sum of money assumed to be equal to the cost of transporting a soldier from New York City to the place of reenlistment or the enlistment of such volunteer soldiers. In view of the scattered military stations of said Pacific Coast volunteers—extending, as they did, from Arizona on the south to Puget Sound on the north, and from San Francisco on the west to Salt Lake City on the east, this sum was fixed by all three of said States at $160 per each volunteer soldier, which sum at that time substantially represented about the average cost which the United States would have had to pay to transport a soldier from New York City to the places of such enlistment or reenlistment of said volunteers in said three States.

These three States, in reviving said act of Congress of June 17, 1850, in the manner and for the purposes therein recited, used substantially the identical language which Congress had used in said act, by calling said sum of money a "bounty," when, as aforesaid, it was, and was only intended to be, a *constructive mileage*, and which was paid by these States out of their respective State treasuries for the use and benefit of the United States in aid of the "common defense" during the war of the rebellion, but not beginning until after April 4, 1864, and as contemplated by said act of Congress of July 27, 1861 (12 U. S. Stats., 276), and Joint Resolution 5 of March 8, 1862 (12 U. S. Stats., 615), and of March 19, 1862 (12 U. S. Stats., 616). In reference to this matter the Secretary of War, in Senate Ex. Doc. No. 11, pp. 22 and 23, Fifty-first Congress, first session, reported to the Senate as follows, to wit:

With respect to the circumstances and exigencies under which this expenditure was incurred by the State, it appears to be plain that it was the earnest desire of the legislature that such troops as the State had been or might thereafter be called upon to furnish the General Government should be promptly supplied. The time was approaching when the terms of most of the volunteer regiments raised in California in the early part of the war would expire. These regiments were occupying important stations in the State and in Territories of Utah, Arizona, and New Mexico, and it was obvious that it would become necessary either to continue them in service by filling them up with new recruits or reenlisted veterans, or, in the event of their disbandment, to replace them by new organizations. Volunteering under the calls of the previous year had progressed tardily, while lucrative employment in the State was abundant and the material inducements for men to enter the army were small. It was probable that unless these latter were considerably increased, recruiting would come to a standstill, and a draft, as in the Eastern States, have to be resorted to. That a draft in California was considered possible, and even probable, is shown by an official letter, written January 8, 1864, to the Adjutant-General of the Army by General Wright, commanding Department of the Pacific, in which he expressed the hope "of procuring quite a number of men who would prefer volunteering to running the chance of being drafted." (P. 205, Senate Ex. Doc. 70, Fiftieth Congress, second session.) The expectation that the mere fear of a draft would sufficiently stimulate volunteering had not, some months later, been realized; and under all circumstances, and prompted by the desire above mentioned, the legislature doubtless deemed it wise to enact the bounty law of April 4, 1864.

Attention is called in "Statement for Senate Committee on Military Affairs" (p, 27) to the third section of an act of Congress (9 U. S. Stats., 439) granting to persons enlisting on the Western frontier, and at remote and distant stations, a bounty equal in amount to the cost of transporting and subsisting soldiers from the principal recruiting depot in the harbor of New York to the place of enlistment, and it is argued that if it was just, proper, and expedient to grant such a bounty to men enlisting in the regular Army in such localities in time of peace, the allowance by California of a bounty to its volunteers when they were in the actual and active service of the United States in time of war, and "while the exigencies exceeded in degree those under which the United States have heretofore paid a much larger sum to its own regular army serving in said States (of California, Oregon, and Nevada) in a time of peace, may be deemed to have been in harmony with the policy so long and so frequently executed by the United States."

These "costs, charges, and expenses" so incurred by these States were:

(1) Military expenditures for recruiting volunteers.

(2) Military expenditures in organizing and paying volunteers.

(3) Military expenditures in and for Adjutant-General's Office.

(4) Military expenditures in paying volunteer commissioned officers between date of service and date of muster-in by the proper mustering officers of the United States.

(5) Military expenditures of a general and miscellaneous character.

All "costs, charges, and expenses" for the military services of the *militia* in all these States were *suspended* by the Secretary of War and are excluded from the present claims in accordance with recommendations heretofore made by the Committee on Military Affairs in the Senate and by the Committee on War Claims in the House.

Attention is specially called to the aforesaid two important resolutions of Congress adopted, the one on the 8th and the other on the 19th of March, 1862, the object of the first of which was to explain the aforesaid act of Congress of July 27, 1861, and the object of the second was to encourage and invite appropriations of money to be made by the several States as they might deem to be appropriate in the interests of the United States and wherein the obligation existed that the United States should indemnify by fully reimbursing the several States out of any money in the Federal Treasury not otherwise appropriated, the sums of money which such States should appropriate and expend for the uses and purposes recited in the acts of the legislature of each State so appropriating the same. (12 U. S. Stats., 615–616.) These two resolutions are in words as follows, to wit:

A RESOLUTION declaratory of the intent and meaning of a certain act therein named.

Whereas doubts have arisen as to the true intent and meaning of act numbered eighteen, entitled "An act to *indemnify* the States for expenses incurred by them in 'Defense of the United States,'" approved July twenty-seven, eighteen hundred and sixty-one (12 U. S. Stats., 276):

Be it resolved by the Senate and House of Representatives of the United States of America in Congress assembled, That the said act shall be construed to apply to expenses incurred as well after as before the date of the approval thereof.

Approved, March 8, 1862 (12 U. S. Stats., 615).

A RESOLUTION to authorize the Secretary of War to accept moneys appropriated by any State for the payment of its volunteers and to apply the same as directed by such State.

Resolved by the Senate and House of Representatives of the United States of America in Congress assembled, That if any State during the present rebellion shall make any appropriation to pay the volunteers of that State, the Secretary of War is hereby authorized to accept the same, and cause it to be applied by the paymaster-general to the payments designated by the legislative act making the appropriation, in the same manner as if appropriated by act of Congress; and also to make any regulations that may be necessary for the disbursement and proper application of such funds to the specific purpose for which they may be appropriated by the several States.

Approved, March 19, 1862 (12 U. S. Stats., 616).

In other words, the legislation enacted by Congress in said act and in these resolutions, taken in connection with subsequent similar legislation duly enacted by these States, constituted in effect and intendment, statutory contracts binding upon the United States. It is evident that Congress, in advance of all legislative acts, by these three States, making appropriations of money for their said volunteers, duly declared that all moneys appropriated by their respective legislatures, and paid out of their respective State treasuries, intended for the exclusive use and benefit of their said volunteers, theretofore, then, or thereafter serving in the military service of the United States, should be accepted by the United States, through the Secretary of War, and paid to the State volunteers of the States so appropriating said moneys, for the specific uses and purposes for which said States had so appropriated the same, and in the same manner, for the same purposes, and to the same extent as if said moneys had been actually paid directly out of the Federal Treasury under acts of Congress appropriating the same. In other words, Congress approved, ratified, and confirmed *in advance* all these appropriations of money so made by the legislatures of these three States, and in fact, intendment, and effect Congress made these State appropriation acts its own acts, the provisions of which should be duly administered by its own proper officers for the objects and purposes as recited in said State acts. These three Pacific Coast States substantially conformed to this legislation of Congress, and strictly ollowed the same in all particulars wherein the same was not inhibited by the State consttutions or by the State laws of said States.

A copy of this resolution of Congress, adopted March 19, 1862, was, on July 5, 1863, duly transmitted by Gen. George Wright, commanding the military department of the Pacific, to the governor of California, Hon. Leland Stanford, late Senator from California. The correspondence relating thereto is reported by the Secretary of War on page 183, Senate Ex. Doc. No. 11, Fifty-first Congress, first session, and is as follows, to wit:

HEADQUARTERS DEPARTMENT OF THE PACIFIC,
San Francisco, Cal., July 5, 1863.

His Excellency LELAND STANFORD,
Governor State of California, Sacramento City, Cal.

SIR: Inclosed herewith I have the honor to lay before your excellency a resolution to authorize the Secretary of War to accept moneys appropriated by any State for the payment of its volunteers, and to apply the same as directed by such State, approved March 19, 1862.

Under the provisions of this resolution Lieut. Col. George H. Ringgold, deputy paymaster-general at my headquarters, will accept any moneys which have been or which may be appropriated for the purpose set forth, and cause it to be applied to the payments designated by the legislative acts.

With great respect, I have the honor to be your excellency's obedient servant,
G. WRIGHT,
Brigadier-General, Commanding.

STATE OF CALIFORNIA, EXECUTIVE DEPARTMENT,
Sacramento, July 16, 1863.

Gen. GEORGE WRIGHT,
Commanding Department of the Pacific.

SIR: Your favor of the 5th instant, with resolution relative to appropriations for the relief of volunteers in the several States, is at hand.

By reference to sections 3 and 4 of the act of the legislature approved April 27, 1863 (Statutes of 1863, folio 662), you will observe that the requirements of the law are such as to preclude our State officers from departing from its provisions, and would therefore be impossible to pay out the appropriations *in the manner* indicated by the resolution of Congress.

I am, general, very respectfully, your obedient servant,
LELAND STANFORD,
Governor of California.

The particular method, form, or manner of payment to these volunteers of the specific sums of money so appropriated by these States was not made the essence of these contracts. It is a fair and reasonable construction of said legislation of Congress to say that that which was anticipated was the *substance* rather than the form; that which was requisite being, only, that the moneys so appropriated by said States should in fact be paid to their said volunteers, all of which was done by paying said volunteers upon official muster rolls duly furnished their State adjutants-general by the colonels of these volunteer regiments, by and through which said moneys were paid directly to said volunteers for the uses and purposes recited in said State acts.

If Congress, in enacting its aforesaid legislation of July 27, 1861, March 8, 1862, and March 19, 1862, did not intend to indemnify and reimburse these States the money which they, in the exercise of the wise discretion of their own respective legislatures should appropriate and cause to be paid to their volunteers serving in the Army of the United States during the war of the rebellion, it may then be very pertinently asked, what object did Congress have in enacting such legislation?

It is submitted that these three States fully expected that these appropriations of money so made and advanced through their own legislatures to the United States and paid to their said volunteers then serving in the Army of the United States as a part of the military establishment on the Pacific Coast during the war of the rebellion, should be fully reimbursed to them. In addition to the foregoing, these three States had been urged to make these very appropriations of money by Gen. George Wright, commanding the Department of the Pacific, and by Gen. Irwin McDowell, commanding the Division or Department of California and Nevada, and by Gen. Benjamin Alvord, commanding the Department of Oregon, for the reimbursement of all of which appropriations they relied, not only upon the public exigencies which demanded such appropriations of money on their part, but wherein they rested their action upon the legal and equitable obligations of the United States in all these premises to reimburse the same.

(1) In the recitals contained in said circular letter of the Secretary of State, Hon. William H. Seward, of October 14, 1861, addressed to the governors of the loyal States, prepared, issued, and proclaimed by order of the President of the United States. This order and act of Mr. Secretary Seward were the order and act of the President of the United States, and as such were in fact and in law the order and act of Congress itself, because Congress (12 U. S. Stats., 326) had declared—

That all the acts, proclamations, and orders of the President of the United States after the 4th of March, 1861, respecting the Army and Navy of the United States, and calling out or relating to the militia or volunteers from the States, are hereby approved and in all respects legalized and made valid to the same extent and with the same effect as if they had been issued and done under the previous express authority and direction of the Congress of the United States.

(2) In the act of Congress of July 27, 1861 (12 U. S. Stats., p. 276), as legislatively construed and explained by Congress itself in its resolution adopted March 8, 1862 (12 U. S. Stats., 615).

(3) In the unrestricted resolution adopted by Congress March 19, 1862 (12 U. S. Stats., 616).

(4) In the official acts of Gen. George Wright, U. S. Army, commanding the military Division of the Pacific, and the similar acts of Gen. Irwin McDowell, U. S. Army, commanding the military Department of California and Nevada, and the similar acts of Gen. Benjamin Alvord, U. S. Army, commanding the Department of Oregon, all of whom, as the

highest commanding military officers of these Pacific Coast States, duly conferred with the governors thereof, and who jointly agreed upon the manner in which the defenses of said States for the "common defense" should be improved and perfected, and which system of "common defense" so agreed upon was duly adopted by the legislatures of each as contemplated in said circular letter of Mr. Secretary Seward. These commanding generals, not in their own names, but in the names of their highest military commander, to wit, the *commander in chief of the Army*, the President of the United States, all of whose official acts were approved, legalized, and made valid by Congress as if done under previous express authority and direction of Congress.

In addition to the foregoing these States have ever relied, and do now rely, for a full indemnity and reimbursement herein upon that general comity that has ever heretofore existed between the United States and the several States in all cases wherever or whenever the latter have been made, either expressly or impliedly, the agents of the United States in aiding to maintain the "common defense" during a period of actual war.

There was no war between *these three States* and the Confederate States, but the war of the rebellion was one between the *United States* and the Confederate States.

These war "costs, charges, and expenses" of these Pacific Coast States so incurred under State and Federal authority, executive and legislative, were incurred not in defense of said States, separate and apart from the rest of the States, but were incurred in aiding *the United States to maintain the "common defense,"* and when incurred were authorized by the State legislature of each of said States, moved thereto at the urgent solicitation of the highest executive authorities of the United States, with the approval and at the direction of the President of the United States and by the sanction and indorsement of Congress, theretofore duly expressed in the aforesaid act and resolutions.

In view of these declarations, supported by the aforesaid opinion of the United States Attorney-General in the case of "The State of Vermont *v.* The United States," it is respectfully submitted that all "costs, charges, and expenses" properly incurred by these States when acting in accordance with the acts of their respective legislatures, when aiding the United States to maintain the "common defense," became, constituted, and now are valid charges against the United States, and as such should be duly appropriated for by Congress and paid to these States out of the National Treasury.

Congress, when legislating in these premises, did not undertake to determine in advance for these three States the specific kind or amount of the "costs, charges, and 'expenses' necessary for them to incur to maintain the common defense," nor did Congress authorize the War Department to issue proposals to these States to aid in the suppression of the rebellion provided it should be done by the *lowest possible bidder;* but Congress, confidently relying upon all the loyal States to come to the aid of the United States with men and money when called, left the President, as commander in chief of the Army and Navy of the United States, to fix the number of men for which he should make a requisition to aid the United States during this period of war, and very *properly left the respective States to be the judges and to determine for themselves the kind, character, and extent of the "costs, charges, and expenses" which they deemed necessary to be incurred by them when obeying the proclamations and requisitions for volunteers of the President of the United States and his proper officers* in all these premises.

Specific expenses had to be and were necessarily incurred in all these premises by all these States, and as heretofore duly reported to Congress by the Secretary of War, so that it would seem to ill-become the United States at this late day to raise the question either of consideration, or of necessity, or of cost, or of equivalent value received in any of these premises, under circumstances and amid exigencies as recited in this statement.

As a matter of fact, all moneys so appropriated by the legislatures of these States out of their respective State treasuries were raised by the sale of their State bonds and advanced by these States to the United States, and expended for the uses and purposes of their said volunteers, as declared and recited in these several State acts, to aid the United States to maintain the "common defense" during a period of actual war.

It is self-evident in these cases that this legislation pertaining to the volunteers of these States came jointly from Congress and from these three States, Congress in fact taking the lead, *but the moneys paid out to their volunteers actually came from moneys hired by their own State treasuries exclusively therefor and not otherwise.* The legislatures of these States did not act at any time in any of these premises until the demands therefor and the appeals made by the United States to their respective governors became most urgent and when the public exigencies which justified their action became of a character such as not to permit of any delay whatsoever on the part of the legislatures of said States.

House Report No. 254, Fifty-second Congress, first session, recites the years of diligent and persistent effort which have been made by these States to have these claims intelligently understood, recognized, and paid by Congress, which, finally recognizing their merits, passed the act of June 27, 1882, intended, as was then thought and expected by said States, to provide for the full and final adjudication of all these State war claims.

Legislation by Congress for such adjudication was initiated in the Senate by the introduction of certain Senate resolutions, one of which, Senate Resolution No. 10, was introduced December 12, 1881, by Senator Grover, of Oregon, to provide for these State rebellion war claims of the State of Oregon; and the other, Senate Resolution No. 13, was introduced December 13, 1881, by Senator Fair, of Nevada, to provide for these State rebellion war claims of the State of Nevada, and for both of which the Committee on Military Affairs in the Senate substituted a bill, S. 1673, which was amended in the Senate upon the motion of Senator Miller, of California, so as to provide for these rebellion war claims of the State of California, but when said bill finally passed Congress it included the State war claims of California, Oregon, Nevada, Colorado, Kansas, Nebraska, and Texas, and became the act of June 27, 1882 (22 U. S. Stats., 111).

Hon. Robert T. Lincoln was Secretary of War when this act of June 27, 1882, became a law, under the provisions of which his Department examined and audited the State war claims of the States of Kansas, Colorado, and Nebraska, all of which have been fully paid by the United States.

In a report made January 26, 1884, by Senator Maxey, of Texas, then a member of the Military Committee in the Senate, in reference to certain war claims referred to that committee upon the motion and request of Senator Jones, of Nevada, for the benefit of the people of that State, Mr. Secretary Lincoln, uniting therein with the Honorable Third Auditor, declared his opinion to be that said act of June 27, 1882, was broad enough to embrace all proper war claims of Nevada—rebellion war claims of which, as recited in said letter, had theretofore been duly filed with said Third Auditor of the Treasury, and which were there then pending *sub judice*—the question as to the *necessity and cost incurred* by the States named therein having been left exclusively to the honorable Secretary of War to determine under said act, and as so decided by said Third Auditor.

It was in consequence of said opinion of Mr. Secretary Lincoln and of said Third Auditor that Senator Maxey, using said opinions and report as a basis for his action, being directed therein by the unanimous vote of the Senate Committee on Military Affairs, reported to the Senate that no further or additional legislation by Congress was needed in any of the war claims of the State of Nevada; and as a necessary corollary, no further or additional legislation was needed in the similar war claims of the States of California and Oregon, for if said act of June 27, 1882, was broad enough under which these State war claims of Nevada could be examined, it was equally broad to permit the examination of the similar war claims of California and Oregon. Mr. Secretary Lincoln, however, at about the same time duly submitted to Congress a report, that in view of the great labor involved in the proper examination and determination of matters arising under said act of June 27, 1882, and devolving thereunder upon his Department, relative to the war claims of these States, and recommended that he be duly authorized to appoint a special board of three Army officers to aid him in the examination and adjudication of the State war claims of the States named in said act, he alleging that Congress had imposed upon him special and responsible duties, but had failed to give him a corresponding force to aid him in the execution thereof.

Congress, in compliance with said recommendation and request of Mr. Secretary Lincoln, passed an act on August 4, 1886 (24 U. S. Stats., 217), wherein authority was given the Secretary of War to appoint a board of three Army officers to aid him in the work of examination of the war claims of the several States named in said act of June 27, 1882, and which officers, before entering upon their duties, were required to take and subscribe an oath that they would carefully examine said claims and, to the best of their ability, make a just and impartial statement thereof.

This act of August 4, 1886, is as follows, to wit:

AN ACT for the benefit of the States of Texas, Colorado, Oregon, Nebraska, California, Kansas, and Nevada, and the Territories of Washington and Idaho, and Nevada when a Territory.

*   *   *   *   *   *

SEC. 2. The Secretary of War is hereby authorized to detail three Army officers to assist him in examining and reporting upon the claims of the States and Territory named in the acts of June twenty-seventh, eighteen hundred and eighty-two, chapter two hundred and forty-one of the laws of the Forty-seventh Congress, and such officers, before entering upon said duties, shall take and subscribe an oath that they will carefully examine said claims, and that they will, to the best of their ability, make a just and impartial statement thereof as required by said act.
Approved, August 4, 1886. (24 U. S. Stats., 217.)

In the meanwhile the Federal Administration changed officers, Mr. Secretary Lincoln going out and Mr. Secretary Endicott coming in as Secretary of War; but nothing had been actually done by Mr. Secretary Lincoln in the way of adjudicating said war claims, outside of expressing said opinion as to said act of June 27, 1882, so that when Mr. Secretary Endicott took office he construed for himself said act of June 27, 1882 (22 U. S. Stats., 111), relative to the rebellion war claims of these three States, and he was of opinion, and on February 8, 1887, declared, that it was not broad enough to embrace these State war claims of these States. This information upon being made known to the Senate, that body unanimously adopted a resolution as follows, to wit:

Resolved, That the Secretary of War, through the board of war-claims examiners, appointed under section 2 of the act of Congress entitled "An act for the benefit of the States of Texas, Colorado, Oregon, Nebraska, California, Kansas, and Nevada, and the Territories of Washington and Idaho, and Nevada when a Territory," approved August 4, 1886, be, and is hereby, authorized and directed to examine all accounts, papers, and evidence which heretofore have been, or which hereafter may be, submitted to him in support of the war claims of the States of California, Oregon, and Nevada, and Nevada when a Territory, growing out of the war of the rebellion, and in suppressing Indian hostilities and disturbances during the war of the rebellion, and in guarding the overland mail and emigrant routes during and subsequent to the war of the rebellion, and to ascertain and state what amount of money each of said States, and Nevada when a Territory, actually expended and what obligations they incurred for the purposes aforesaid; whether such expendi tures were made or obligations incurred in actual warfare or in recruiting, enlisting, enrolling, organizing, arming, equipping, supplying, clothing, subsisting, drilling, furnishing, transporting, and paying their volunteers, militia, and home guards, and for bounty, extra pay, and relief paid to their volunteers, militia, and home guards, and in preparing their volunteers, militia, and home guards in camp and field to per form military service for the United States.

The Secretary of War is also directed to ascertain what amount of interest has been paid by each of said States, and Nevada when a Territory, on obligations incurred for the purposes above enumerated. The Secretary of War shall report to Congress the amount of money which may be thus ascertained to have been actually paid by each of said States, and Nevada when a "erritory, on account of the mat ters above enumerated, and also the amount of interest actually paid or assumed by each of said States, and Nevada when a Territory, on moneys borrowed for the purposes above enumerated. And the Secretary of War shall also report the cir cumstances and exigencies under which, and the authority by which, such expendi tures were made, and what payments have been made on account thereof by the United States.

In response to this resolution, the Honorable Secretary of War, hav ing fully completed, with the aid of said army board, a thorough and exhaustive official examination of all these war claims of said three States, transmitted in December, 1889, his reports to the Senate in each of these State war claims of Caifornia, Oregon, and Nevada, as required by said resolution, and which reports are as follows, to wit, Senate Ex. Docs. Nos. 10, 11, 17, Fifty-first Congress, first session. These reports and the exhibits attached thereto, respectively, are in great detail, and contain a very full history of the important part taken by the Pacific Coast States and Territories during the rebellion in defense of the Union, and are in full compliance with said Senate resolution, showing the actual amount of the "costs, charges, and expenses" actually incurred by each of said States, and of Nevada when a Terri tory, during the war of the rebellion in aid of the United States and the authority, State, Territorial, and national, and also the special cir cumstances and exigencies under which the expenditures so reported upon by said Secretary and said board therein, respectively, were made.

Under this act of Congress of June 27, 1882, Mr. Secretary Lincoln examined, allowed, and stated the State war claims of the States of Kan sas and Nebraska in sums as allowed and stated by him, and which have been fully appropriated by Congress. Mr. Secretary Endicott (with the aid of said Army board, appointed under said act of August 4, 1886) duly examined, audited, allowed, and stated the State war claims of the State of Texas, and of the sums as audited by the Secretary of War Congress appropriated the sum of $927,177.40 in the act entitled:

An Act to provide for certain of the most urgent deficiencies in the appropriations for the service of the Government for the fiscal year ending June the thirtieth, eighteen hundred and eighty-eight, and for other purposes.
Approved, March 30, 1888. (25 U. S. Stats., 71.)

And further appropriated the sum of $148,615.97 in the act entitled:

An Act making appropriations to supply deficiencies in the appropriations for the fiscal year ending June the thirtieth, eighteen hundred and ninety, and for prior years, and for other purposes.
Approved, September 30, 1890. (26 U. S. Stats., 539.)

Aggregating the sum of $1,175,793.37.

No one doubts but that all said war claims of Texas so examined and audited by the honorable Secretary of War (aided by said Army board) were valid and proper charges against and should have been paid by the United States in the exact sums so audited by the Secretary of War, and which were so paid by Congress without any hostile opposition from any quarter as to the *merits* or *amounts of any thereof.*

In order to show the careful, painstaking, and exact manner in which the members of said army board performed their duties when aiding the Secretary of War in the examination of these claims, attention is especially called to the views expressed in the House of Representatives by several members of the Texas delegation in Congress, to wit, those of Hon. S. W. T. Lanham, Hon. R. Q. Mills, and Hon. J. D. Sayers, at the date when said Texas State war claims were under consideration in the House during the Fiftieth Congress, first session, wherein the reliability and the exactness of the statements of the board were shown to be in a manner not only perfectly satisfactory to them, but such that in a statement and allowance in the said Texas war claims aggregating $927,177.40 the difference between the sums so stated by said board and the sums subsequently appropriated by Congress with which to pay the same amounted only to the sum of $64.90. (See p. 2233, Congressional Record, March 16, 1888.)

The first installment of $927,177.40, so paid to the State of Texas in satisfaction of her said State war claims, passed as an item in the *urgent deficiency appropriation act* approved March 30, 1888.

It is true this Texas war claim, besides being examined by the Secretary of War, was also reexamined in the Treasury Department, but that reexamination was for the purpose simply of verifying the computations in the audit of the Secretary of War, it being the duty of the Secretary of War, under said act of June 27, 1882, as decided by the Treasury Department, to report upon all matters which related to the *necessity for*, and *reasonableness* of, all expenses so incurred by said States, as appears from a letter from the Honorable Third Auditor of January 24, 1884, to the Honorable Secretary of War, reported by Mr. Secretary Lincoln to Senator Maxey, of Texas, under date of January 26, 1884, in a report as follows, to wit:

WAR DEPARTMENT,
Washington City, January 26, 1884.

SIR: In response to so much of your communication of the 22d ultimo as requests information concerning Senate bill 657, to "authorize the Secretary of the Treasury to adjust and settle the expenses of Indian wars in Nevada," I have the honor to invite your attention to the following report of the Third Auditor of the Treasury, to whom your request was duly referred:

"The State of Nevada has filed in this office abstracts and vouchers for expenses incurred on account of raising volunteers for the United States to aid in suppressing the late rebellion, amounting to $349,697.49, and the expenses on account of her militia in the 'White Pine Indian war' of 1875, $17,650.98; also, expenses of her militia in the 'Elko Indian war' of 1878, amounting to $4,654.64, presented under act of Congress approved June 27, 1882 (22 Statutes, 111, 112).

"These abstracts and vouchers will be sent to your Department for examination and report as soon as they can be stamped, as that statute requires a report from the Secretary of War as to the *necessity for*, and *reasonableness* of, the expenses

incurred. This statute is deemed sufficiently broad enough to embrace all proper
claims of said State and Territory of Nevada."
        Very respectfully, your obedient servant,
                                    ROBERT T. LINCOLN,
                                        Secretary of War.
Hon. S. B. MAXEY,
    Of Committee on Military Affairs, United States Senate.

In addition to the foregoing it appears, in a report from the War
Department addressed to Hon. S. B. Maxey, U. S. Senator from Texas,
under date of January 27, 1886, that the Secretary of War, Hon. W. C.
Endicott, held that while the title of the act of June 27, 1882, and the
wording of the first section thereof would seem to convey the impression that the claims of the States named in said act were to be adjusted
by the Secretary of the Treasury, with the aid and assistance of the
Secretary of War, yet, *as a matter of fact, the whole duty of examining
and auditing said claims was, by section 2 of said act, imposed upon the
Secretary of War, leaving the Treasury Department the simple duty of
verifying the computations of the audit of the Secretary of War* therein,
and as will officially and fully appear in Senate Mis. Doc., No. 44, Forty-
ninth Congress, first session, as follows, to wit:

[Senate Mis. Doc. No. 54, Forty-ninth Congress, first session.]

*Letter from the Secretary of War to Hon. S. B. Maxey, in relation to the claim of the
    State of Texas presented under the act of June 27, 1882.*

JANUARY 29, 1886.—Referred to the Committee on Appropriations and ordered to be printed.

                                    WAR DEPARTMENT,
                            Washington City, January 27, 1886.
SIR: Referring to our recent conversation in regard to the claim of the State of
Texas presented under the act of June 27, 1882 (22 Stats., 111, 112), I have the honor
to inform you that the first installment of the claim (amount, $671,400.29) came before
the Department from the Third Auditor of the Treasury July 9, 1884, and the action
then taken in the matter appears in the letter from this Department to Mr. Dorn,
dated July 16, 1884, copy herewith. The papers herein mentioned were returned to
the agent of the State July 25, 1884. November 2, 1885, the Third Auditor of the
Treasury wrote to the Department, transmitting through Mr. W. H. Pope, agent of
the State, the papers in the claim, which papers were received here November 17,
1885, and they are now being stamped and marked.
    In regard to the subject of the State claims mentioned in said act, I beg to inform
you that the great difficulty experienced in disposing of the claim of the State of
Kansas, the first one presented thereunder, has caused the Department to delay
taking up the other claims pending. While the title of the act and the wording of
the first section thereof would seem to convey the impression that the claims were
to be adjusted by the Secretary of the Treasury, "with the aid and assistance of
the Secretary of War," the whole duty of examining and auditing the claims was,
by section 2, imposed upon the Secretary of War, leaving the Treasury Department
the simple duty of verifying the computations of the Secretary of War.
    The policy thus indicated differed widely from that prescribed in section 236 of
the Revised Statutes, that "all claims and demands whatever by the United States,
or against them, and all accounts whatever in which the United States are concerned,
either as debtors or as creditors, shall be settled and adjusted in the Department of
the Treasury," and differs also from the provisions for the adjudication of State
claims under the act of July 27, 1861 (12 Stat., p. 276), which were "to be settled
upon proper vouchers, to be filed, and passed upon by the proper accounting officers
of the Treasury."
    The claims arising under the act are said to amount to $10,000,000 (that of Texas
is now stated at $1,842,443.78), and the vast labor of examining the papers, pointing
out the evidence required to perfect the vouchers and show the necessity of calling
out the militia, whose services are charged for, fixing the rate to be allowed on each
voucher, and tabulating the same, many thousands in number, must be performed by
the Secretary of War, and no provision has been provided by Congress for this laborious work.
    Two years were consumed in disposing of the claim of the State of Kansas, and
if the same course is to be pursued with the other claims arising under the act, it
will be sometime before the claim of Texas is reached, that of Nevada being next
in order of receipt.

The subject of the claims was brought to the attention of Congress at the last session (*see* report of Secretary of War for 1884, pp. 4, 5, and estimates for 1886 on p. 206 of House Ex. Doc. No. 5, Forty-eighth Congress, second session), and it has again been presented in the Secretary's report for 1885 (pp. 35 and 36). An estimate to defray the cost of examining the claims will be found on p. 225 of House Ex. Doc. No. 5, Forty-ninth Congress, first session.

I inclose draft of a bill which, if enacted, will enable the Department to dispose of the matter.

Copies of the above-mentioned reports are inclosed.

Very respectfully,

WM. C. ENDICOTT,
Secretary of War.

·Hon. S. B. MAXEY,
    United States Senate.

This reexamination by the Treasury Department, to verify the final computations in said audit of the Secretary of War of the Texas war claim, showed, as aforesaid, an error of only $64.50 in a total allowance of $927,177.40, which sum was appropriated by Congress and paid by the United States to the State of Texas.

It is respectfully submitted that all that Congress in any case desires to know, and very properly inquires into in cases like these, is, have the claims which it is requested to pass upon been carefully computed and set forth in an official statement of account signed by the head of a Department or Bureau, whose duty it is to wholly examine and audit the same?

The dignity heretofore given by Congress to examinations not dissimilar to these is shown in the fact that year after year, since 1859, it has included in the regular deficiency appropriation bill appropriations with which to pay the Oregon and Washington Indian war claims in sundry and divers sums of money based exclusively upon *the original authority of a House resolution only*, adopted February 8, 1858, which resolution, reported in House Ex. Doc. No. 11, Thirty-sixth Congress, first session, is as follows, to wit:

[House Ex. Doc. No. 11, Thirty-sixth Congress, first session.]

Report of the Third Auditor of the Treasury, in pursuance of a resolution of the House of Representatives passed February 8, 1858.

FEBRUARY 10, 1860.—Referred to the Committee on Military Affairs and ordered to be printed.

THIRTY-FIFTH CONGRESS, SECOND SESSION,
CONGRESS OF THE UNITED STATES,
In the House of Representatives, February 8, 1859.

Resolved, That preliminary to the final settlement and adjustment of the claims of the citizens of the Territories of Oregon and Washington for expenses incurred in the years eighteen hundred and fifty-five and eighteen hundred and fifty-six in repelling Indian hostilities, it shall be the duty of the Third Auditor of the Treasury to examine the vouchers and papers now on file in his office, and make a report to the House of Representatives by the first Monday in December next of the amount respectively due to each company and individual engaged in said service, taking the following rules as his guide in ascertaining the amount so due:

1st. He shall recognize no company or individual as entitled to pay except such as were called into service by the Territorial authorities of Oregon and Washington, or such whose services have been recognized and accepted by said authorities.

2d. He shall allow to the volunteers engaged in said service no higher pay and allowance than were given to officers and soldiers of equal grade at that period in the Army of the United States, including the extra pay of $2 per month given to the troops serving on the Pacific Coast by the act of 1852.

3d. No person either in the military or in the civil service of the United States, or of said Territories, shall be paid for his services in more than one employment or capacity for the same period of time, and all such double or triple allowances for pay as appears in said accounts shall be rejected.

4th. That in auditing the claims for supplies, transportation, and other services incurred for the maintenance of said volunteers, he is directed to have a due regard to the number of said troops, to their period of service, and to the prices current in the country at the time, and not to report said service beyond the time actually engaged therein, nor to recognize supplies beyond a reasonable approximation to the proportions and descriptions authorized by existing laws and regulations for such troops, taking into consideration the nature and peculiarities of the service.

5th. That all claims of said volunteers for horses, arms, and other property lost or destroyed in said service shall be audited according to the provisions of the act approved March 3, eighteen hundred and fifty-nine.

Attest: I. C. ALLEN, *Clerk.*

Attention is here specially called to the fact, disclosed by said Oregon and Washington resolution, that Congress when dealing with the volunteers of Washington and Oregon declared as late as February 8, 1858, that said volunteers should be paid an extra compensation, and in those particular cases the extra compensation was to be the same as provided for in the act of Congress approved August 31, 1852. (10 U. S. Stats., 108.)

The extra compensation of $2 per month as recited in said Oregon and Washington resolution is error—the exact extra compensation to be paid was one-half additional to the regular pay of officers and enlisted men.

Said provision of law by which said extra compensation was to be measured is as follows, to wit:

SEC. 3. *And be it further enacted,* That so much of the act making appropriations for the support of the Army for the year ending the 30th of June, 1851, approved the 28th of September, 1850, as provides extra pay to the commissioned officers and enlisted men of the United States serving in Oregon or California, be, and the same is hereby, continued in force for one year from the first day of March, 1852, and that the provisions of the last mentioned act be, and is hereby, extended to New Mexico during the current year provided for by this section, and that $300,000 be and is appropriated hereby for that purpose: *Provided further,* That said officers and men shall receive only one-half of the increased amount over the regular pay allowed by law. (10 U. S. Stats., 108.)

Attention is here called to the fact, that in the examination and audit of the said Oregon and Washington Indian War Claims of 1855 and 1856 under the aforesaid House resolution, the Third Auditor was made the sole commissioner to examine the same, and for this extra duty under section 3, act of March 2, 1861, he was paid the sum of $1,000, and the appropriations to the said Oregon and Washington Indian War Claims, made in said act (12 U. S. Stats., 198), were based on the allowance that he, as such commissioner, made and reported to the House, February 8, 1859, under said resolution, and as printed in House Ex. Doc. No. 11, Thirty-sixth Congress, first session.

The examination of the war claims of the State of Texas were limited, as to time, to the examination of claims for the expenses incurred and arising in the said State subsequent to October 20, 1865, and were confined, as to character, exclusively to claims for expenses by her incurred for or on account of military defense against Mexican raids, against Mexican invasions, and against Indian hostilities only. Whereas, in the cases of these three States said act June 27, 1882, was intended to include and cover, and did include and cover, all military expenses of every nature, beginning April 15, 1861, incident upon calling into the field their volunteers, beginning at the date of the commencement of the rebellion (April 15, 1861), and was not confined to claims for reimbursement of expenses incurred for defense against Indian hostilities only, but covered, and was intended to cover, all expenses of the rebellion or for repelling invasions, coming from any source whence they may, but included also those of Indian hostilities.

If there were any doubts as to the purposes and intentions of Congress as to the scope of said act of June 27, 1882, or as to the character of the claims to be examined thereunder, the expenses for which

Congress intended to reimburse said States, these doubts would be removed by considering:

(1) The declarations recited in the fifth section of said act of June 27, 1882, in words as follows, to wit:

SEC. 5. That any military services performed and expenditures on account thereof incurred during the Territorial organization of Nevada, and paid for or assumed by either said Territory or said State of Nevada, shall be also included, and examined and reported to Congress in the same manner as like service and expenditures shall be examined and reported for the State of Nevada.

(2) By considering the views submitted May 12, 1882, on the bill S. 1673 by the Military Committee in the Senate, in Senate Report No. 575, Forty-seventh Congress, first session, and as reappears in Senate Report No. 644, Fifty-first Congress, first session. This Senate bill S. 1673 finally became the act of June 27, 1882, and an extract from said report made thereon is in words as follows, to wit:

The circumstances under which the expenditures provided for in this bill were made by these States being exceptional, and their reimbursement not being provided for by any existing law, general or special, prior to June 27, 1882, Senator Grover, of Oregon, on December 12, 1881, introduced Senate joint resolution No. 10, and Senator Fair, of Nevada, on December 13, 1881, introduced Senate joint resolution No. 13, providing for the equitable adjustment of these State war claims of Oregon and Nevada, which resolutions were referred to the Senate Committee on Military Affairs.

These two Senate joint resolutions, Nos. 10 and 13, Fortieth Congress, first session, are as follows, to wit:

[S. R. 10, Forty-seventh Congress, first session.]

JOINT RESOLUTION to authorize the Secretary of War to ascertain and report to Congress the amount of money expended and indebtedness assumed by the State of Oregon in repelling invasions, suppressing insurrections and Indian hostilities, enforcing the laws, and protecting the public property.

Resolved by the Senate and House of Representatives of the United States of America in Congress assembled, That the Secretary of War be, and he is hereby, authorized and directed to cause to be examined and adjusted all the accounts of the State of Oregon against the United States for money expended and indebtedness assumed in organizing, arming, equipping, supplying clothing, subsisting, transporting, and paying either the volunteer or militia forces, or both, of said State called into active service by the governor thereof after the fifteenth day of April, eighteen hundred and sixty-one, to aid in repelling invasions, suppressing insurrections and Indian hostilities, enforcing the laws, and protecting the public property in said State and upon its borders, except during the Modoc war.

SEC. 2. That the Secretary of War shall also examine and adjust the accounts of the State of Oregon for all other expenses necessarily incurred on account of said forces having been called into active service as herein mentioned, including the claims assumed or paid by said State to encourage enlistments, and for horses and any other property lost or destroyed while in the line of duty by said forces: *Provided,* That in order to enable the Secretary of War to fully comply with the provisions of this act there shall be filed in the War Department by the governor of said State, or a duly authorized agent, an abstract accompanied with proper certified copies of vouchers or such other proof as may be required by said Secretary, showing the amount of all such expenditures and indebtedness, and the purposes for which the same were made.

SEC. 3. That the Secretary of War shall report in writing to Congress, at the earliest practicable date, for final action, the results of such examinations and adjustment, together with the amounts which he may find to have been properly expended for the purposes aforesaid.

[S. R. 13, Forty-seventh Congress, first session.]

JOINT RESOLUTION to authorize the Secretary of War to ascertain and report to Congress the amount of money expended and indebtedness assumed by the State of Nevada in repelling invasions, suppressing insurrection and Indian hostilities, enforcing the laws, and protecting public property.

Resolved by the Senate and House of Representatives of the United States of America in Congress assembled, That the Secretary of War be, and he is hereby, authorized and directed to cause to be examined and adjusted all the accounts of the State of

Nevada against the United States for money expended and indebtedness assumed in organizing, arming, equipping, supplying clothing, subsisting, transporting, and paying either the volunteers or militia, or both, of the late Territory of Nevada and of the State of Nevada, called into active service by the governor of either thereof after the fifteenth day of April, eighteen hundred and sixty-one, to aid in repelling invasions, suppress insurrections and Indian hostilities, enforcing the laws, and protecting the public property in said Territory and said State and upon the borders of the same.

SEC. 2. That the Secretary of War shall also examine and adjust the accounts of the late Territory of Nevada and of the State of Nevada for all other expenses necessarily incurred on account of said forces having been called into active service, as herein mentioned, including the claims assumed or paid by said Territory and said State to encourage enlistments, and for horses and other property lost or destroyed while in the line of duty of said forces: *Provided*, That in order to enable the Secretary of War to fully comply with the provisions of this act, there shall be filed in the War Department by the governor of Nevada, or a duly authorized agent, an abstract accompanied with proper certified copies of vouchers or such other proof as may be required by said Secretary, showing the amount of all such expenditures and indebtedness, and the purposes for which the same were made.

SEC. 3. That the Secretary of War shall report in writing to Congress, at the earliest practicable date, for final action, the results of such examinations and adjustment, together with the amounts which he may find to have been properly expended for the purpose aforesaid.

As recited in said Senate Report No. 644 (Fifty-first Congress, first session), that committee (to wit, Senate Committee on Military Affairs), instead of reporting back said joint resolution, reported back, May 12, 1882, in lieu thereof, a substitute in the form of a bill, to wit, Senate 1673, Forty-seventh Congress, first session, providing for the payment of certain war claims, to wit, those only of Texas, Oregon, and Nevada, and of the Territories of Idaho and Washington, and which bill, after having been amended in the Senate so as to include the State war claims of Colorado, Nebraska, and California, and amended in the House so as to include the State war claims of Kansas, finally resulted in the passage of the act approved June 27, 1882. (22 U. S. Stats., 111.)

It was then, no doubt, the intention of Congress to provide for the full indemnity and reimbursement of all moneys which California, Oregon, and Nevada, and Nevada when a Territory, had actually expended during the war of the rebellion on account of the several matters recited in Senate bill No. 1295, Fifty-third Congress, second session. Senate bill No. 1673, Forty-seventh Congress, first session, was accompanied by a report (Senate No. 575, Forty-seventh Congress, first session) made by Senator Grover, May 12, 1882, which renders said intention of Congress quite evident.

The Senate Committee on Military Affairs did not at that time make any report in relation to any of the State war claims of the State of California, but when this substitute bill (Senate 1673, Forty-seventh Congress, first session), reported from that committee, was under consideration in the Senate, Senator Miller, of California, called attention to the fact that California had similar war claims unprovided for, and on his motion this bill (Senate 1673, Forty-seventh Congress, first session) was amended in the Senate to include the State war claims of the State of California. It is alleged by California, Oregon, and Nevada that this act of June 27, 1882, which they believed was intended by Congress to be an act for their relief and benefit and an equitable statute to be liberally construed in order to pay to these three States that indemnity "which had been so guaranteed by its aforesaid legislation, has been found to be an act 'so well and carefully and closely guarded by restrictions'" that, when construed by those who have been called upon to execute it, has proven to be completely inoperative as an equitable relief measure, so much so as to amount to a practical denial of justice so far as the present State war claims of these States now provided for in these bills were or are concerned.

Said report is as follows, to wit:

[Senate Report No. 575, Forty-seventh Congress, first session.]
MAY 12, 1882.—Ordered to be printed.

Mr. Grover, from the Committee on Military Affairs, submitted the following report, to accompany bill S. 1673:

The Committee on Military Affairs, to whom were referred Senate bill 1144 and Senate joint resolutions 10 and 13, "to authorize an examination and adjustment of the claims of the States of Kansas, Nevada, Oregon, and Texas, and of the Territories of Idaho and Washington, for repelling invasions and suppressing insurrection and Indian hostilities therein," submitted the following report:

Oregon.—It appears by the report of the Adjutant-General U. S Army of April 3, 1882, that one regiment of cavalry, one regiment of infantry, and one independent company of cavalry were raised in the State of Oregon during the late war of the rebellion, and that the expenses incident thereto have never been reimbursed said State by the United States; and that the claims thereof have never been heretofore presented by said State for audit and payment by the United States, as per report of the Secretary of War of April 15, 1882, and of the Third Auditor of the Treasury of April 8, 1882. Under section 3489 of the Revised Statutes, the claim for expenditures so incurred by said State can not now be presented for audit and payment without legislation by Congress. In addition thereto there are some unadjusted claims of said State growing out of the Bannock and Umatilla Indian hostilities therein in 1877 and 1878, evidenced by a communication of the Secretary of War of date last aforesaid. and some unadjusted balances pertaining to the Modoc war, not presented for audit to Gen. James-A. Hardie, approximating the sum of $5,000.

Nevada.—It appears by the report of the Adjutant-General U. S. Army, of February 25, 1882, that one regiment of cavalry and one battalion of infantry were raised in the late Territory of Nevada during the late war of the rebellion, and that the expenses of raising, organizing, and placing in the field said forces were never paid by said Territory, but were assumed and paid by the State of Nevada, and that none of said expenses so incurred by said Territory, and assumed and paid by said State, have never been reimbursed the State of Nevada by the United States, and that no claims therefor have ever been heretofore presented by either said Territory or said State for audit and payment by the United States. Under section 3489 of the Revised Statutes, hereinbefore referred to, the payments of these claims is barred by limitation.

These forces were raised to guard the overland mail route and emigrant road to California, east of Carson City, and to do other military service in Nevada, and were called out by the governor of the late Territory of Nevada upon requisitions therefor by the commanding general of the Department of the Pacific, and under authority of the War Department, as appears by copies of official correspondence furnished to your committee by the Secretary of War and the general commanding the Division of the Pacific; and it further appears that there are some unadjusted claims of the State of Nevada for expenses growing out of the so-called White River Indian war of 1875, and aggregating $17,650.98, and of the so-called Elko Indian war of 1878 therein, and aggregating $4,654.64, and which sums, it appears by the official statements of the comptroller of said State of Nevada, were expended and paid out of the treasury of said State.

Texas.—The unadjusted claims of the State of Texas provided for by this bill are those which accrued subsequent to October 14, 1865. These have been heretofore the subject-matter of much correspondence between the State authorities of Texas and the authorities of the United States, and have several times received the partial consideration of both branches of Congress, but without reaching any finality, never having been audited or fully examined, and consequently no payment on account thereof has been made.

These claims are referred to in Senate Ex. Doc. No. 74, second session, Forty-sixth Congress, and in the Executive documents therein cited.

It appears by the official correspondence exhibited in the document referred to. and copies of official correspondence from the State authorities of Texas, and submitted to your committee, that the expenses for which the State of Texas claims reimbursement were incurred by the authorities thereof under its laws, and for the proper defense of the frontiers of said State against the attacks of numerous bands of Indians and Mexican marauders. These claims approximate the sum of $1,027,375.67, and were incurred between October 14, 1865, and August 31, 1877.

Washington and Idaho.—The volunteer troops in Washington and Idaho were in the field during Indian hostilities in 1877 and 1878, in said Territories, by orders of the local authorities thereof. While these volunteers were not mustered into the regular service of the U. S. Army, they were attached to the command of U. S. troops in the Department of the Columbia, and acted with said troops, rendering valuable and faithful services during said wars, under the orders and immediate command of officers of the regular Army of the United States, as appears by copies of orders in the hands of your committee.

The obligation of the General Government to defend each State is acknowledged to be included in the constitutional obligation to maintain the "common defense" by a long series of acts of Congress making appropriations to cover the expenses of States and Territories of the Union which have raised troops and have incurred liabilities in defending themselves against Indian hostilities and other disturbances.

The bill herewith reported provides for an examination of the claims and accounts of the States and Territories therein named by the Secretary of the Treasury, acting in connection with the Secretary of War, and that they report the amount of money necessarily expended and indebtedness properly assumed in organizing, supplying, and sustaining volunteers and militia called into active service by each of them in repelling invasions and suppressing Indian hostilities therein during the periods named.

This bill is carefully guarded against the assumption by the United States of unnecessary liabilities, and fixes the pay of volunteers and militia of these several States and Territories on the basis of the pay of regular troops.

Your committee therefore report the present original bill as a substitute for Senate bill 1144 and Senate joint resolutions 10 and 13, which heretofore have been under consideration by said committee, having the same objects as provided for by this bill, and recommend its passage.

The foregoing recitals clearly and fully show, so far as Oregon and Nevada were concerned, that said Report No. 575 and said Senate bill No. 1673, and said Military Committee in the first session of the Forty-seventh Congress dealt with both State rebellion war claims and State Indian war claims of the States of Oregon and Nevada and the Territory of Nevada, and when Senator Miller, of California, suggested that California had State war claims similar to those of Oregon and Nevada, said bill S. 1673 was amended upon his motion so as to also include the State rebellion war claims and the State Indian war claims of that State.

(3) By considering the views expressed by Hon. R. Q. Mills, now the junior Senator from Texas, of the purposes and intentions of said act of Congress of June 27, 1882, which were duly emphasized by his remarks thereon in the House on the date when said Texas war claim was then and there pending *sub judice* (which remarks, with those submitted at the same time by Mr. Lanham and by Mr. Sayers, of Texas, on this same bill, are printed on pp. 2126 to 2265, Congressional Record, Fiftieth Congress, first session). On that occasion Hon. R. Q. Mills declared as follows, to wit:

Mr. MILLS. Mr. Chairman, it might have been better if this claim had been held back and placed upon the regular deficiency bill. Perhaps there would have been no objection raised on either side of the House if that course had been adopted with reference to it. But the claim is now before the House, on a favorable report from the Committee on Appropriations, and it is here for action. Being before us, I do not want to see a vote against it to-day because of the fact that it has not been held back to give a red-tape examination to it.

This is an old, familiar friend of mine. I am thoroughly acquainted with it in all of its details. I introduced bills, as did my colleagues upon this floor, years ago to pay the State of Texas the money which had been expended by that State in doing that which the Government of the United States ought to have done for her. I remember the time when the Representatives from Kansas, Nevada, and Nebraska and ourselves often met together for conference and with a view to helping each other to get the Congress of the United States to do justice to our people in recognizing these claims which had been standing so long.

We united our efforts and aided in the passage of the law of 1882. That law was passed for the purpose of providing a settlement for these claims, and under it all of the claims of this class were submitted, with the evidence to substantiate them, to a board of Army officers. They have been thoroughly, patiently, exhaustively examined through a careful process of inspection covering a long period of time, and have all been reported to Congress.

There is no objection made to the payment of any of this class of claims upon the judgment of this board of officers, indorsed as it has been by the Treasury Department, except with regard to the claim of Texas; and the opposition, Mr. Chairman, is as unjust to the State of Texas as it would have been to the other States.

There is no gentleman who has challenged or will challenge the statement that not a single item has been questioned or can be pointed out in which a wrong judgment has been made by this board of officers.

But, sir, this appeal that is made here is all for delay. They say the case ought to have waited longer—as if it had not waited long enough already—and that it should have gone through some further and more patient examination; but they have not been able to point to a single item of all the items making up this sum of $927,000 which is not justly due to my State—not one of them.

Our claim is a little larger than the claim of the State of Kansas, because Kansas had a much smaller frontier, and had to guard only against the Indians, whereas we had both the Indians and the Mexicans. We had a border as long on the northern frontier of the State as the whole frontier line of the State of Kansas, and in addition to that we had all of that vast line from the thirty-second parallel of north latitude down to the Gulf of Mexico, making more than a thousand miles in addition. That is the reason why the claim of the State of Texas is larger. (Congressional Record, March 17, 1888, p. 2265.)

There is a consensus of opinion of the Treasury and War Departments as to the duties which were to be performed under said act of Congress of June 27, 1882, by the Secretary of War and by the Secretary of the Treasury, respectively, in the adjudication of the claims of the States named in said act, which were substantially to this effect, to wit: That the Secretary of War was to pass upon and decide as to the *necessity* for any expenses of any kind, and as to the *reasonableness* of all expenses so incurred by said States, for the "common defense;" and in addition thereto was to wholly examine all the claims of said States for all reimbursements provided to be paid in said act, and to wholly audit all the claims for any reimbursement to be made to any of said States under said act, and that the only duty of the Honorable Secretary of the Treasury under said act was to verify the computations so made by the Secretary of War.

In the cases of the rebellion war claims of California, Oregon, and Nevada it now fully appears that the Honorable Secretary of War has thoroughly, patiently, carefully, and exhaustively examined all said rebellion war claims, rejecting any that appeared doubtful, and in so doing threw out or suspended in the case of California alone claims that aggregated $468,976.54, which had been paid by that State, and in the case of Oregon threw out or suspended claims which aggregated the sum of $21,118.73.

The Secretary of War has certified in an official itemized statement of account as the result of an exact computation the true amount that should be paid by the United States to each of these States on account of the moneys by them respectively expended as "costs, charges, and expenses" to aid the United States to maintain the "common defense" on the Pacific Coast during the war of the rebellion.

If, therefore, Congress will accord to the computations of the Secretary of War, Hon. Redfield Proctor, in these cases the same degree of confidence which it accorded to similar computations of the Secretary of War, Hon. W. C. Endicott, in the case of the State war claims of the State of Texas, then at this time it will make provisions to pay the rebellion war claims of these three States in the sums as computed by the Secretary of War, Hon. Redfield Proctor, and by him so heretofore duly reported to the Senate.

The reliance that should be placed on this examination and audit by the Secretary of War of these claims of these three States may be correctly ascertained as aforesaid from the remarks in the House in support of said Texas war claims made by the distinguished Representative from

Texas, now the chairman of the House Committee on Appropriations, Hon. J. D. Sayers, substantially to the effect that said computations in the Texas war claims were almost absolutely perfect (an error of only $64.50 occurring in an allowance of $927,177.40). *De minimis lex non curat.*

These claims were provided for in the same act which provided for said Texas war claims, and have had substantially a similar degree of examination by the Secretary of War, and are entitled to a similar degree of consideration by Congress.

In the deficiency appropriation bill which passed the Senate March 3, 1891, provision to pay some of these State war claims of these three States was included by the Senate without a single dissenting vote, after an explanation in support thereof had been made to the Senate in words as follows, to wit:

Mr. STEWART. I offer the amendment which I send to the desk.

The VICE-PRESIDENT. The amendment will be stated.

The CHIEF CLERK. On page 38, line 5, after the word "dollars," it is proposed to insert:

"To reimburse the States of California, Oregon, and Nevada for moneys by them expended in the suppression of the rebellion, under the act of Congress approved July 27, 1861, and acts amendatory thereof and supplementary thereto, being sums of money shown by the reports of the Secretary of War to have been paid by said States in the suppression of the rebellion:

"To the State of California the sum of $2,451,369.56.

"To the State of Oregon the sum of $224,526.53.

"To the State of Nevada the sum of $404,040.70."

Mr. STEWART. Mr. President, there is no time to enter at length into an explanation of this claim. I would state, however, that during the war the States named in this amendment furnished 18,715 troops, who were enlisted in the U. S. Army and served on the Pacific Coast. At the time the war broke out the soldiers who were stationed there were called home, and it became necessary to raise troops in those States. The Secretary of War, the President, and other officials urged these States to raise the troops, as they could not be sent from the East. These States, immediately after the rebellion closed, attempted to obtain compensation. It was a long time before they could get the accounts examined.

Finally it was developed that these States had made an additional allowance beyond what was made in the Atlantic States. By two acts passed in 1850 a different allowance was made for troops serving on the Pacific Coast. Those who were enlisted there were paid at a different rate. These acts were repealed in 1861. When it was attempted to raise troops on the Pacific Coast it was found necessary to continue the old compensation on account of the very high price of living. Soldiers who had families or other obligations could not possibly serve at the reduced rates.

These States made an allowance, not up to what the Government had been in the habit of allowing, but considerably less, not more than one-fourth, probably, of the Government allowance. The transportation alone of the troops, without the subsistence that would have been allowed if they had been taken from New York under the regulations which had prevailed since 1850, would have amounted to $5,483,385. If the extra pay had been counted in it would have ranged something over $10,000,000, perhaps $15,000,000. If the regular United States pay which had been allowed from 1850 up to 1861, when the war broke out, had been paid these men, it would have amounted—I have not figured it out exactly—to some $10,000,000 or $15,000,0000. The transportation alone would have been nearly $5,500,000.

In order that this question might be examined, several acts of Congress were passed, and a board of war claims commissioners was organized to investigate such, claims. Under that war claims commission several States that came in on account of Indian depredations—Kansas, Nebraska, Nevada, California, and Texas—were paid in the aggregate $1,297,850. Texas received of that sum $927,177.40, and since that it has received an additional sum of $148,615.97.

The question of the allowance of additional pay, which has been so long urged, still remains. The Senate, after investigating it, passed a resolution to have the claims examined, so as to ascertain the exact amount that was paid. Under that resolution the war claims examiners reduced the amount stated. With great labor they went through all the papers and examined all the vouchers. The result is the amendment which I offer. There is no doubt about the equity of the case.

THE VICE-PRESIDENT. The question is on the amendment of the Senator from Nevada.

The amendment was agreed to.
(See p. 4116, Congressional Record, March 5, 1891.)

But this amendment was not retained in said bill by the conferees for reasons recited in the debate which took place thereon in the Senate, as follows, to wit:

Mr. STEWART. Mr. President, if I understand the amendments that have been agreed to and rejected, the amendment of the Senate putting in the French spoliation claims has been agreed to, and these State claims and the payment to the railroads for carrying the mails have been rejected.

Now, the position of the bill seems to be that the State claims of California, Oregon, and Nevada for money expended in the suppression of the rebellion, after all the other States have been paid, are rejected; that the judgments of the Supreme Court on the claims for the carrying of the mails, the judgment already declared that the United States is liable and owes the money and should pay it, have been rejected.

The French spoliation claims, in which there is no judgment, which is simply a finding under a law that declares that such findings shall not in any way commit the United States to the payment of the claims, and the finding of the court under such a law which has not been examined by the Committee on Claims, as the chairman stated that it had not been fully examined, but they had gone far enough to ascertain that a portion of them was unsatisfactory, and claims one hundred years old standing in that way, to a very large amount, are put into the bill.

Now, the system which produces such legislation certainly must be very defective. These appropriation bills come in and the main part of the legislation of Congress is forced into two or three days and nights, and investigation and deliberation under the pressure are denied, because we are threatened with an extra session of Congress, and we must take what the House says we shall take or we must take the consequences of an extra session. That alternative is constantly presented, and while judgments of courts binding upon the Government are ignored, while State claims can not get consideration and are to be abandoned after consideration, claims that do not have a standing by reason of a judgment of a court or the investigation of a committee are allowed to pass.

I refer to the validity of these particular claims. I am aware that committees have held from time to time that there were equities in these French spoliation claims, but before they are paid it should be ascertained by some committe that each item that is appropriated goes to a legitimate claimant, so that when it has been neglected one hundred years we may investigate it and ascertain that the money goes to the parties entitled to it. This has not been done. I would not object to the payment of any of these claims if it were found that there was money due to a particular individual, but it comes in without that investigation, and it is to be passed in the last hours of the session, while the judgments of courts and claims of States are unceremoniously ignored. Now it goes back to the committee for further reference.

It is a serious responsibility upon a Senator who feels that he must do his duty here as to what he ought to do under such circumstances, whether he must continue from year to year to pass bills under the threat of an extra session, to which we can not give our assent conscientiously, and must stay here year after year and see legitimate claims ignored. The question is whether it is our duty to submit to it. It is a matter of grave consideration. I will not now determine what I shall do, but it seems to me if legislation can not be carried on more orderly than this it is the duty of the Senate to defeat the important bills and call a halt and rearrange the mode of doing business.

I think the Senate is, in a great measure, to blame in this matter. The Senate has the same power to originate appropriation bills that the House has. The House has got in the habit, and it goes on every season, and it always will, to send these bills here at the last moment so that they can not be considered by the Senate. I think the Senate is derelict in its duty if it does not commence early in the session to inaugurate bills and give time for consideration, that we may have our legislation in order, so that at the end of the session every Senator will not leave the Senate Chamber conscious that he has been a party to a very great wrong which the Congress of the United States allows because he did not have time to correct it.

The whole legislation of Congress has to be done in two or three nights, when it must be done hurriedly—done when jobs of all kinds can go through. Each Senator has to go home and explain it, and has to submit to it, that he can not reach it; that he could not discuss it because he was threatened with an extra session or the failure of the passage of the necessary bills to carry on the Government. It is a matter of grave consideration whether it is not my duty here to do all in my power to defeat this bill. Mr. President, I have said all I desire at this time. I have made these remarks, and I may make more before the bill becomes a law, but that is all I shall make at this time.

Mr. HALE. Mr. President, I desire to say only a word in reply to the Senator from Nevada. The instructions given to the committee on the part of the House do not apply to the State claims, but only to the railroad claims, so that in the conference which will immediately ensue the Senate conferees will not find the conference embarrassed by any action of the House aside from those claims. The committee of conference will be in session immediately, and I only repeat what I have said before, that it will endeavor to secure as much as possible of the action of the Senate upon this bill.

I want to say to the Senator from Nevada—I know that he is a reasonable man upon all these subjects—that the Senate is committed to these State claims by vote, by sentiment, and it is only a question of time when they will pass.

The present bill, aside from the matters which have been discussed, contains upon it an appropriation for pensions for soldiers amounting to $28,000,000. I do not suppose there is a Senator here who, whatever may be his feeling about other matters in the bill, would desire to wreck the bill and thereby leave the soldiers without money for the payment of their pensions during the remainder of the year. Calling the attention of the Senator to this, I leave the subject now, and hope to be able to report from the conference committee in a very short time.

Mr. CHANDLER. I ask the Senator how much is appropriated in the bill for pensions.

Mr. HALE. The appropriations for pensions are found upon page 5——

Mr. EDMUNDS. What is the total amount?

Mr. HALE. Amounting to $28,678,332.89. This money is needed at once. Without it the payments between now and June 30, of course, will cease.

DEFICIENCY APPROPRIATION BILL.

Mr. HALE submitted the following report:

The committee of conference on the disagreeing votes of the two Houses on certain amendments of the Senate to the bill (H. R. 13658) making appropriations to supply deficiencies in the appropriations for the fiscal year ending June 30, 1891, and for prior years, and for other purposes, having met, after full and free conference have agreed to recommend and do recommend to their respective Houses as follows:

That the Senate recede from its amendments numbered 22, 30, 59, 60, 84, 96, 98, 191, 103, and 104.

That the House recede from its disagreement to the amendment of the Senate numbered 85, with an amendment as follows: In lieu of the matter proposed to be inserted by said amendment insert:

"For clerks to Committees on Patents, Coast Defenses, and Engrossed Bills, from March 4 to July 1, 1891, at the rate of $2,200 per annum each."

EUGENE HALE,
W. B. ALLISON,
F. M. COCKRELL,
Managers on the part of the Senate.

J. G. CANNON,
S. R. PETERS,
W. C. P. BRECKINRIDGE,
Managers on the part of the House.

Mr. STEWART. I should like to ask what disposition has been made of the amendments that were disagreed to.

Mr. HALE. The Senate conferees found the conferees on the part of the House entirely firm in their resistance, and declined to yield; so that it became a question of giving up the Senate amendments or giving up the bill, and mainly in consideration of the large appropriation in the bill for the pensioners, amounting to $28,000,000, the conferees on the part of the Senate receded from the amendments and they are out of the bill.

Mr. STEWART. Mr. President, this illustrates in a very glaring form the mode of doing business between the two Houses. Appropriation bills involving more money than were ever appropriated in any one session, in time of peace at least, can not be said to have been considered by the Senate. They nearly all came here in a bunch in the last two or three days and the Senate has been compelled to work night and day. Many Senators were unable to stay here on account of their health. Old men, feeble men, and men in ill health were unable to stay here and criticise these bills. They have been in the hands of a very few men who were overworked and could not give to them the attention they required.

They are not bills passed by the deliberation of this body, and it will be a marvel if there are not many things in these bills that Senators will regret and will be

,alled upon to explain, and they will be compelled to make the explanation that there was no opportunity for any investigation of the great bulk of these bills, that it would have involved an extra session of Congress, which is regarded by the country as a calamity. We have been passing these bills under the shade of that calamity and under that threat, sitting here night and day. A large portion of the time there could not be a quorum. Those who were engaged on conference were necessarily in their committee rooms, and what has been done is unknown to the majority of the Senate.

In this bill judgments of courts, of the Supreme Court, binding legal obligations of the Government, have been rejected. Claims of States of undoubted validity that have been long delayed have been rejected, and claims——

Mr. MORGAN. Will the Senator from Nevada allow me to ask him a question? Does the Senator desire to defeat the bill?

Mr. STEWART. I am not going to defeat the bill. I shall only occupy a few moments more, but I want to call attention to the situation. I am going to sit down in a moment. I say claims that have not the investigation or indorsement of the committee, involving millions, are in this bill. I do not complain of the conferees of the House; I do not complain of the conferees on the part of the Senate. They have labored night and day. It is a marvel to me that they have been able to perform the labor they have. They have done the best they could, and the result is that we have made these enormous appropriations of which the Senate, although responsible legally, can not be held responsible individually or morally.

I call attention to this matter now for the purpose of suggesting the necessity of earlier action on the appropriation bills and the further necessity of the Senate inaugurating appropriation bills, so that they can have them in time, that they can consider them properly, and that we can have legislation that we will understand, and that the country will understand, and not a great mass of material, involving millions and hundreds of millions that we know nothing of, forced through at the end of a session with the old excuse that we could not reach it because we had to submit and pass the bills to avoid an extra session. The Government must be carried on, I recognize that; and I do not propose to block the wheels of Government, but I appeal to Senators that in the future this work on appropriation bills shall be begun in time, and that they may be properly considered.

The PRESIDENT pro tempore. The question is on concurring in the conference report.

The report was concurred in.

(See p. 4223, Congressional Record, March 6, 1891.)

No valid reason is known to exist why Congress should not at this time authorize the payment of these State war claims of these three Pacific Coast States, and not compel them to keep knocking at its doors as petitioners, session after session, demanding payment of the same.

The volunteers of these States at the date when they were called, promptly responded to all requisitions made by the proper United States authorities upon their respective States, none waiting to be drafted or otherwise pressed into the military service of the United States, but all coming with alacrity when called.

The thorough, patient, careful, and exhaustive reports submitted to the Senate by the Secretary of War, Hon. Redfield Proctor, upon the work of the examination of the State war claims of these three States show some of the difficulties met and overcome by them when aiding the United States in these premises, and which, recited in the language of said Secretary in Senate Ex. Docs. Nos. 10, 11, and 17, Fifty-first Congress, first session, are as follows, to wit:

NEVADA.—EXTRA MONTHLY PAY TO HER STATE VOLUNTEERS—LIABILITIES ASSUMED.

[Senate Ex. Doc. No. 10, Fifty-first Congress, first session, p. 7.]

It appears from the affidavit of the State controller (herewith, marked Exhibit No. 2) that liabilities to the amount of $1,153.75 were assumed by the State of Nevada as successor to the Territory of Nevada on account of "costs, charges, and expenses for monthly pay to volunteers and military forces in the Territory and State of Nevada in the service of the United States," and that State warrants fully covering such liabilities were duly issued. It is also shown in the affidavit that of said warrants two for the sums of $11.33 and $8.50, respectively, have been paid, such payment reducing said liabilities to $1,133.92.

The circumstances and exigencies under which the Nevada legislature allowed this extra compensation to its citizens serving as volunteers in the U. S. Army are believed to have been substantially the same as those that impelled the legislatures of California and Oregon to a similar course of action for the relief of the contingent of troops raised in each of these States. Prices of commodities of every kind were extravagantly high during the war period in Nevada, which depended for the transportation of its supplies upon wagon roads across mountain ranges that were impassable for six months of every year; and at certain times, at least, during the same period the rich yield of newly-opened mines produced an extraordinary demand for labor, largely increasing wages and salaries. These high prices of commodities and services were coexistent with, though in their causes independent of, the depreciation of the Treasury notes, which did not pass current in that section of the country, though accepted through necessity by the troops serving there; and it is safe to say that in Nevada, as in California and Oregon, the soldier could buy no more with a gold dollar than could the soldier serving in the Eastern States with the greenback or paper dollar.

On the whole, therefore, we are decided in the conviction that in granting them this extra compensation the legislature was mainly instigated by a desire to do a plain act of justice to the United States volunteers raised in the State and performing an arduous frontier service by placing them on the same footing as regards compensation with the great mass of the officers and soldiers of the United States Army serving east of the Rocky Mountains. It is true that the seven companies of infantry that were called for on October 19, 1864, had not been organized; and that on March 8, 1865, three days before the approval of the State law above noticed, the commanding general, Department of the Pacific, wrote as follows from his headquarters at San Francisco to the governor of Nevada (see p 187, S. Ex. Doc. 70, Fiftieth Congress, second session):

"What progress is making in recruiting the Nevada volunteers? I will need them for the protection of the State, and trust that you may meet with success in your efforts to raise them. I hope the legislature may assist you by some such means as have been adopted by California and Oregon."

But the fact remains that the declared purpose of the monthly allowance was to give a compensation to the Nevada Volunteers (see section 1 of the act last referred to), and that when measured by the current prices of the country in which they were serving, their compensation from all sources did not exceed, if indeed it was equal to, the value of the money received as pay by the troops stationed elsewhere, i. e., outside of the Department of the Pacific.

CALIFORNIA.—EXTRA PAY TO ENLISTED MEN AS HER STATE VOLUNTEERS.

[Senate Ex. Doc. No. 11, Fifty-first Congress, first session, p. 23.]

By an act approved April 27, 1863, the legislature appropriated and set apart "as a soldiers' relief fund" the sum of $600,600, from which every enlisted soldier of the companies of California volunteers raised or thereafter to be raised for the service of the United States was to be paid, in addition to the pay and allowances granted him by the United States, a "compensation" of $5 per month from the time of his enlistment to the time of his discharge. Drafted men, substitutes for drafted men, soldiers dishonorably discharged or discharged for disability existing at time of enlistment, were not to share in the benefits of the act, and except in cases of married men having families dependent upon them for support, payment was not to be made until after discharge. Seven per cent interest-bearing bonds to the amount of $600,000, in sums of $500, with coupons for interest attached to each bond, were authorized to be issued on July 1, 1863. (Pp. 349–351, Statement for Senate Military Committee.)

A few unimportant changes respecting the mode of payment in certain cases were made by act of March 15, 1864, and on March 31, 1866, the additional sum of $550,000 was appropriated for the payment of claims arising under its provisions, such sum to be transferred from the general fund of the State to the "soldiers' relief fund."

Fearing that the total amount of $1,500,000 specifically appropriated might still prove insufficient to pay all the claims accruing under the act of April 27, 1863, above mentioned, the legislature directed, by an act which also took effect March 31, 1866 (p. 604, Stats. of California, 1865-66), that the remainder of such claims should be audited and allowed out of the appropriation and fund made and created by the act granting bounties to the volunteers of California, approved April 4, 1864, and more fully referred to on page 19 of this report.

Upon the certificate of the adjutant-general of the State that the amounts were due under the provisions of the act and of the Board of State Examiners, warrants amounting to $1,459,270.21 were paid by the State treasurer, as shown by the receipts of the payees indorsed on said warrants.

It is worthy of note here that on July 16, 1863, the governor of California, replying to a communication from the headquarters Department of the Pacific, dated July 5, 1863, advising him that under a resolution of Congress, adopted March 9, 1862, the payments provided for by the State law of April 27, 1863, might be made through the officers of the pay department of the U. S. Army, stated that the provisions of said law were such as to preclude him from availing himself of the offer.

Some information as to the circumstances and exigencies under which this money was expended may be derived from the following extract from the annual report of the adjutant-general of the State for the year 1862, dated December 15, 1862:

"The rank and file of the California contingent is made up of material of which any State might be proud, and the sacrifices they have made should be duly appreciated and their services rewarded by the State. I do most earnestly recommend therefore that the precedent established by many of the Atlantic Coast States of paying their troops in the service of the United States an additional amount monthly should be adopted by California, and that a bill appropriating, say $10 per month to each enlisted man of the troops raised or to be raised in this State, be passed. * * * This would be a most tangible method of recognizing the patriotic efforts of our soldiers, relieve many of their families from actual destitution and want, and hold out a fitting encouragement for honorable service." (P. 58, Statement for Senate Committee on Military Affairs.)

Your examiners are of the opinion that the favorable action which was taken on the above recommendation of the adjutant-general can not be justly ascribed to any desire on the part of the legislature to avoid resort to a conscription, although the exclusion of drafted men from the benefits of the act indicates that they realized and deemed it proper to call attention to the possibility of a draft. Unlike the law of April 4, 1864, the benefits of which were confined to men who should enlist after the date of its passage and be credited to the quota of the State, the provisions of the act now under consideration extended alike to the volunteers who had already entered or *had actually* completed their enlistment contract and to those who were to enlist in the future. There is every reason for the belief that the predominating if not the only reason of the State authorities in enacting this measure was to allow their volunteers in the United States service such a stipend as would, together with the pay received by them from the General Government, amount to a fair and just compensation. In fact, as has already been stated, this was expressly declared to be the purpose of the act.

It appears that up to December 31, 1862, those of the U. S. troops serving in the Department of the Pacific who were paid at all—in some cases detachments had not been paid for a year or more—were generally paid in coin, but on February 9, 1863, instructions were issued from the Treasury Department to the assistant treasurer of the United States at San Francisco that "checks of disbursing officers must be paid in United States notes." (Letter of Deputy Paymaster-General George H. Ringgold, dated February 13, 1863, to Paymaster-General; copy herewith marked Exhibit No. 10.)

Before this, greenbacks had become the current medium of exchange in all ordinary business transactions in the Eastern States, but in the Pacific Coast States and the adjoining Territories, gold continued to be the basis of circulation throughout the war. At this time the paper currency had become greatly depreciated, and on February 28, 1863, the price of gold in Treasury notes touched 170. This action of the Government in compelling troops to accept such notes as an equivalent of gold in payment for services rendered by them in a section where coin alone was current, gave rise to much dissatisfaction. For although gold could be bought in San Francisco at nearly the same price in Treasury notes as in New York, it must be remembered that the troops in the Department of the Pacific were largely stationed at remote and isolated points.

When paying in greenbacks for articles purchased by or for services rendered by them in these out-of-the-way places, they were obliged to submit not only to the current discount in San Francisco, but also to a further loss occasioned by the desire of the persons who sold the articles or rendered the service, to protect themselves against possible further depreciation. It admits of little doubt that by reason of his inability to realize the full value of paper money, as quoted in the money centers, and of the fact that wages and the cost of living and of commodities of every kind were abnormally high (owing in great part to the development of newly discovered mines in that region), the purchasing power of the greenback dollar in the hands of the average soldier serving in the Department of the Pacific was from the latter part of 1862 onward from 25 to 50 per cent less than that of the same dollar paid to his fellow soldier in the East.

Representation of great hardship which the Treasury Department's instructions entailed upon the troops were promptly made. On March 10, 1863, the legislature telegraphed to Washington a resolution adopted on that date instructing the State's delegation in Congress to impress upon the Executive "the necessity which exists of having officers and soldiers of the U. S. Army, officers, seamen, and marines of the

U. S. Navy, and all citizen employees in the service of the Government of the United States serving west of the Rocky Mountains and on the Pacific Coast paid their salaries and pay in gold and silver currency of the United States, provided the same be paid in as revenue on this coast." (P. 46, Statement for Senate Committee on Military Affairs.)

And on March 16, 1863, Brig. Gen. G. Wright, the commander of the Department of the Pacific (comprising, besides California, the State of Oregon and the Territories of Nevada, Utah, and Arizona), transmitted to the Adjutant-General of the U. S. Army a letter of Maj. C. S. Drew, First Oregon Cavalry, commandant at Camp Baker, Oregon, containing an explicit statement of the effects of and a formal protest against paying his men in greenbacks. In his letter of transmittal (p. 154, Senate Ex. Doc. 70, Fiftieth Congress, second session), General Wright remarked as follows:

"The difficulties and embarrassments enumerated in the major's communication are common to all the troops in this department, and I most respectfully ask the serious consideration of the general in chief and the War Department to this subject. Most of the troops would prefer waiting for their pay to receiving notes worth but little more than half their face; but, even at this ruinous discount, officers, unless they have private means, are compelled to receive the notes. Knowing the difficulties experienced by the Government in procuring coin to pay the Army, I feel great reluctance in submitting any grievances from this remote department, but justice to the officers and soldiers demands that a fair statement should be made to the War Department."

It was under circumstances and exigencies such as these that the legislature themselves—all appeals to the General Government having proved futile—provided the necessary relief by the law of April 27, 1863. They did not even after that relax their efforts on behalf of U. S. troops, other than their own volunteers, serving among them, but on April 1, 1864, adopted a resolution requesting their Representatives in Congress to "use their influence in procuring the passage of a law giving to the officers and soldiers of the regular Army stationed on the Pacific Coast an increase of their pay amounting to 30 per cent on the amount now allowed by law."

OREGON.—EXTRA MONTHLY COMPENSATION TO OFFICERS AND ENLISTED MEN OF HER STATE VOLUNTEERS.

[Senate Ex. Doc. No. 17, Fifty-first Congress, first session, p. 14.]

The certificate of the State treasurer, duly authenticated by the secretary of state under the seal of the State, sets forth that the amounts severally paid out for the redemption of relief bonds, as shown by the books of the treasurer's office, as reported by the treasurer to the several legislative assemblies, and as verified by the several joint committees (investigating commissions) of said assembly under the provisions of a joint resolution thereof, aggregate $90,476.32. The following books, papers, etc., are also submitted in evidence of payment:

(1) The canceled bonds.

(2) A copy of the relief bond register, the correctness of which is certified by the secretary of state and State treasurer, showing number of bond, to whom issued, date of issue, and amount of bond; also showing the date and rate of redemption. The reports of the joint committees of the legislature above mentioned, to the effect that they compared the record kept by the State treasurer with the bonds redeemed and found the amounts correct and agreeing with the amounts reported by the State treasurer to the legislative assembly, are entered in said bond register.

(3) Certificates of service given to the several Oregon volunteers upon which warrants were given entitling the holders to bonds. These certificates cover service for which the sum of $86,639.85 was due. The remainder of the certificates, the State authorities report, were not found and are probably lost or destroyed.

(4) Copies of the muster rolls of the Oregon volunteers, certified to by the secretary of state, setting forth the entire service of each officer and enlisted man.

In all, bonds amounting to $93,637 were issued. As has been stated, but $90,476.32 is found to have been expended in the redemption of these bonds, some of which were redeemed at less than their face value. Five bonds, valued at $731, have not been redeemed.

The authority by which these bonds were issued is contained in an act of the legislature, which was approved on October 24, 1864 (copy herewith), appropriating a sum not exceeding $100,000 to constitute and be known as the "commissioned officers and soldiers' relief fund," out of which was to be paid to each commissioned officer and enlisted soldier of the companies of Oregon volunteers raised in the State for the service of the United States to aid in repelling invasion, etc., from the time of their enlistment to the time of their discharge, $5 per month in addition to the pay allowed them by the United States. Enlisted men not receiving an honorable discharge from the service, or volunteers discharged for disability existing at the time of enlistment, were not to be entitled to the benefits of the act, nor was payment under the provisions thereof to be made to an enlisted soldier until he should be honorably discharged the service; but enlisted married men having families dependent upon them were authorized to allot the whole or any portion of the monthly pay accruing to them for the support of such dependents. A bond bearing interest, payable semiannually, at 7 per cent per annum, redeemable July 1, 1875, with coupons for the interest attached, was to be issued by the secretary of state for such amount as the adjutant-general should certify to be due under the provisions of the act to each man, whose receipt for the amount so paid to him was to be taken by the secretary of state. Said bonds were to be paid to the recipient or order.

The circumstances and exigencies that led to the enactment of the above-cited law, and to the expenditures incurred under its provisions, were substantially the same as those which brought about the adoption of similar measures of relief in California and Nevada. It must have been patent to every one fully acquainted with the circumstances of the case that the volunteers that had been raised in Oregon at this time (October 24, 1864), consisting only of the 7 companies of the First Oregon Cavalry and the independent detachment of four months' men, a majority of whom had then nearly completed their terms, had been greatly underpaid, considering the nature of the service performed by them and the current rate of salaries and wages realized in other pursuits of life. At the time of the enrollment and muster-in of the First Oregon Cavalry and up to the latter part of 1862 the Government paid those of its troops in the Department of the Pacific that were paid at all in specie; but, as often happened during the war, a number of the companies of the regiment named, occupying remote stations, remained unpaid for a long time, and were finally paid in Treasury notes, some of the members having more than a year's pay due them.

During the remainder of the war the Government paid its troops in the Department of the Pacific, as elsewhere, in greenbacks. Referring to this condition of things and to the fact that coin continued to be the ordinary medium of exchange in Oregon in private business transactions, Maj. C. S. Drew, First Oregon Cavalry, in a letter to his department commander, dated March 4, 1863 (p. 154, Senate Ex. Doc. 70, Fiftieth Congress, second session), called attention to the fact that at his station (Camp Baker) Treasury notes were "worth not more than 50 or 55 cents per dollar;" that each officer and soldier of his command was serving for less than half pay, and had done so, some of them, for sixteen months past; that while capital protected itself from loss, and perhaps realized better profits than under the old and better system of payment in coin, "the soldier did not have that power, and if paid in notes must necessarily receipt in full for what is equivalent to him of half pay or less for the service he has rendered, and must continue to fulfill his part of his contract with the Government for the same reduced rate of pay until his period of service shall have terminated;" and that "good men will not enlist for $6 or $7 a month while $13 is the regular pay, and, moreover, is being realized by every soldier in every other department than the Pacific." In forwarding this letter to the Adjutant-General, U. S. Army, the department commander remarked that the embarrassments enumerated in the major's communication were common to all the troops in the department, and he therefore asked "the serious consideration of the General in Chief and the War Department to the subject." Some months later (August 18, 1863) Gen. Alvord, while reporting to the department commander the location of a new military post at Fort Boise, referred to the difficulties encountered by the garrison charged with the duty establishing it as follows:

"Some difficulty is experienced in building the post in consequence of the low rates of legal-tender notes. In that country they bear merely nominal value. The depreciation of the Government currency not only embarrasses the Quartermaster's Department, but also tends greatly to disaffect the men. The differences between their pay and the promises held out by the richest mines perhaps on the coast, the proximity of which makes them all the more tempting, is so great that many desertions occur." (Senate Ex. Doc. 70, Fiftieth Congress, second session, p. 188.)

About the same time (September 1, 1863) the adjutant-general of the State complained of the inadequacy of the soldiers' pay, resulting from the depreciation of the paper currency with which they were paid. Referring to the fact that after the expiration of eight months from the date of the requisition of the United States military authorities for 6 additional companies for the First Oregon Cavalry but 1 had been raised, he said:

"And yet we are not prepared to say that it is for the want of patriotism on the part of the people of Oregon, but from other causes, partly from the deficiency in the pay of the volunteer in comparison with the wages given in the civil pursuits of life, as well as with the nature of the currency with which they are paid, the depreciation of which renders it hardly possible for the soldier to enlist from any other motive save pure patriotism. And I would here suggest that the attention of our legislature be called to this defect, and that additional pay, either in land, money, or something else, be allowed to those who have volunteered. Justice demands that this should be done."

In enacting the relief law of October 24, 1864, it is fair to presume that the legislature was largely influenced by the following statements and recommendations of the governor, contained in his annual message, dated September 15, 1864:

"The Snake and other tribes of Indians in eastern Oregon have been hostile and constantly committing depredations. The regiment has spent two summers on the plains, furnishing protection to the immigration and to the trade and travel in that region of the country. During the past summer the regiment has traveled over 1,200 miles, and the officers and men are still out on duty. The officers and most, if not all, the men joined the regiment through patriotic motives, and, while some of the time they have been traveling over rich gold fields, where laborers' wages are from $3 to $5 per day, there have been very few desertions, and that, too, while they were being paid in depreciated currency, making their wages only about $5 per month. A great many of these men have no pecuniary interests in keeping open the lines of travel, protecting mining districts and merchants and traders. The benefit of their service thus inures to the benefit of others, who should help these faithful soldiers in bearing these burdens. Oregon, in proportion to her population and wealth, has paid far less than other States for military purposes. California pays her volunteers $5 per month extra in coin. It would be but an act of simple justice for this State to make good to the members of this regiment their losses by depreciated currency." (P. 87, Statement for Senate Military Committee.)

It is to be noted here that while the officers and men who became the beneficiaries of this law had been paid in a depreciated currency, which in Oregon does not appear to have had more than two-thirds of the purchasing power it had in the East, the Government provided them with clothing, subsistence, shelter, and all their absolutely necessary wants. On the other hand, it is to be borne in mind that the legislature must have been aware of the fact noted, and that it granted the extra compensation from a sense of justice and without any purpose calculated to benefit the States at large, such as might be reasonably inferred from the granting of bounties to men "who should hereafter enlist." As has been already mentioned, the terms of the Oregon volunteers were drawing to a close, and the benefits of the law were restricted to the volunteers "raised" and did not therefore include those "to be raised."

It is very material to here call attention to certain important facts, to wit, that subsequent to the dates when these three States, through appropriate legislation enacted therefor by their respective legislatures, provided for the aforesaid extra pay to their own volunteers, Congress on June 20, 1864, increased by one third the pay of the soldiers of the Regular Army of the United States, to begin on May 1, 1864, and to continue during the rebellion (the close of which, as proclaimed by the President of the United States, was August 20, 1866 (13 U. S. Stats., 144, 145.)

Nay, more, Congress on March 2, 1867, as to the soldiers, extended said act for three years from August 20, 1866, and at the same time, as to the officers of the Regular Army of the United States, increased their pay by one-third for two years from July 1, 1866. (14 U. S. Stats., 422, 423.)

Nay, still more, in this act of June 20, 1864, Congress provided for the payment of bounties (or constructive mileage) to such soldiers as should reenlist, as therein recited, and which bounties had theretofore been denied payment by Second Comptroller Brodhead under his aforesaid decisions of the Treasury Department.

Nay, even still more, on March 2, 1867 (14 U. S. Stats., 487), Congress provided for the payment of mileage to the California and Nevada volunteers from the places of their discharge in New Mexico, Arizona, Utah, etc., to the places of their enlistment, etc.

So, therefore, it fully appears that Congress finally, though tardily, enacted for the regular Army of the United States the identical provisions which these three States prior thereto felt called upon to enact for their own volunteers, the propriety of which legislation by said States has never been questioned, and the timeliness of which served only to measure the patriotism which inspired such legislation in aid of the "common defense."

But in the meanwhile the aforesaid legislation of these three States had been duly set in motion and was actively running in full force and effect at the dates of the aforesaid legislation of Congress, and the statutory obligations of said States to their own volunteers in good faith had to be fully met according to the letter and spirit of the intention of their enactment.

These war claims of these three States are not therefore to be weighed in scales of refined technicality.

These State war claims are not private claims, but are public claims presented to Congress by three States of the Union in their corporate and political capacities, and are entitled to its highest possible consideration, because of the fact they are State claims for the reimbursement of *cash actually paid by these three States, as the "costs, charges, and expenses" in aiding the United States, at their own solicitation, to maintain the "common defense" on the Pacific Coast during a period of active war*.

Not only this, but said cash so by them expended *had to be and was hired by these three States by the sale of their State interest-bearing bonds, supported only by their own State credit*.

In order to resort to measures so extraordinary, the legislatures of these three States were compelled to avail themselves of those provisions of their State constitutions that contemplated extraordinary emergencies in public affairs, and which demanded extraordinary expenditures of money, in excess of the maximum limit provided for a condition of peace and tranquillity, and which extraordinary expenditures these three States felt justified in making in view of a state of actual war against the Union and of the obligation of the United States to indemnify and reimburse them for such expenditures as had been so guarantied by Congress in its aforesaid legislation.

It is respectfully submitted that the aforesaid legislation of Congress and proceedings had by the Executive Departments of the United States in connection therewith, so fully executed in good faith by these three Pacific Coast States, constituted and are statutory contracts which contemplate an obligation on the part of the United States to wholly indemnify these three States by fully reimbursing them the money they so advanced and expended in good faith to aid the United States to maintain the "common defense," and so hired by said States by the sale of their State interest-bearing bonds.

At the dates when the United States made the aforesaid calls or requisitions for these 18,715 volunteer troops there was no money in the State treasuries of these three States which was not specifically appropriated to meet their fixed and necessary current expenses, and hence, not having any money with which to defray the "costs, charges, and expenses" of furnishing said volunteer troops for the military service of the United States, they *were compelled to raise money by hiring the same, and to do this they were compelled to sell at not less than par their State interest-bearing war bonds, principal and interest of which were paid in gold coin from money raised by taxation most extraordinary, levied upon the inhabitants of these three States*.

These statutory enactments of Congress, supplemented by these statutory enactments of the legislatures of these three States, constitute and are the highest and most solemn form of governmental contracts, and are to be construed in all cases, not as mere legislative enactments, *but as contracts* binding upon all parties thereto—in this case the United States and the States of California, Oregon, and Nevada.

Huidecooper's Lessee *v*. Douglass, 3 Cranch R., 1;
1 Peters's Condensed Rep., 446;
State Bank *v*. Knoop, 16 How., 369;
Corbin *v*. Board of County Comrs., 1 McCrary, 521;
Sinking Fund Cases, 99 U. S. R., 700;
Fletcher *v*. Peck, 6 Cranch, 87;
New Jersey *v*. Wilson, 7 Cranch, 166;
Dartmouth College Case, 4 Wheaton, 518;
Keith *v*. Clark, 97 U. S. R., 454.

It was impossible for these States to raise, enlist, organize, equip, and muster volunteer troops into the military service of the United States *without the immediate expenditure of cash*, and they could not expend cash which they did not have, and hence they were forced *to hire cash* in the same manner as they hired anything else, to wit, by paying for the use of such hire, to wit, interest on the principal so by them hired.

In construing the aforesaid legislation the circumstances under which the same was enacted are to be and must be taken into consideration.

In this case the emergencies were not only great, but extraordinary and imminent, not admitting in the least of any delay. The life of the nation was in peril; volunteer troops were imperatively demanded; official requisitions therefor had to be promptly obeyed; the Federal treasury was wholly empty; the State treasuries of these three States were equally empty, whatever money being on deposit therein having been appropriated and set apart for specific purposes, so that no part thereof could be constitutionally used for any other object whatsoever.

It was under circumstances like these that the Federal Government besought these three States to send them 18,715 volunteer troops, and in substance promised: "We will wholly indemnify and fully reimburse you for all proper costs, charges, and expenses incurred in our behalf therein," etc.

All these things were matters of public contemporaneous history, and were contained in the constitutions and State statutes of these three States, and presumably were well known to Congress at the dates when it enacted the aforesaid acts and adopted the aforesaid resolutions, and Congress must necessarily have contemplated that these three States, if they had not the cash, would necessarily make use of their credits, respectively, for the purpose of hiring the cash with which to immediately provide for raising said volunteer troops for the "common defense," and that whatever sums of money might be paid out by these States (both principal and interest paid for the use of said principal) would be necessarily reimbursed them by the United States.

The mere *title* of the aforesaid act of Congress of July 27, 1861, is of itself sufficient to declare the intent of Congress in these premises, to wit: "An act to indemnify the States (in this case of California, Oregon, and Nevada) for expenses incurred by them in defense of the United States," both before and after July 27, 1861.

To indemnify these States was and is "to save them harmless, to secure them against any future loss or damage, to fully make up to them for all that is past, to make good all expenditures, to fully reimburse them for all proper 'costs, charges, and expenses' incurred by them in furnishing said 18,715 volunteer troops." (Webster *et al.*)

The objects of this legislation by Congress will therefore not be wholly satisfied by a partial reimbursement to these States of these expenses so by them incurred, but the intention of Congress will be properly and wholly satisfied only by the full reimbursement to these States of the total principal of the cash by them hired, and the interest paid by them for the hire of the cash (principal) expended by them, at the request of the General Government, to aid the United States to maintain the "common defense" on the Pacific Coast during the rebellion.

"The costs, charges, and expenses" contemplated by the aforesaid act of July 27, 1861, was the money which theretofore had been, or which thereafter might be "duly expended, actually laid out, in fact consumed by using, or the disbursements made, outlays paid, and charges met, as the proper expenses of war" by said three States. (Webster *et al.*).

Sullivan *v.* Triumph Mining Company, 39 Cal., 450;
Foster *v.* Goddard, 1 Cliff., 158;
1 Black, 506;
Dashiel *v.* Mayor, etc., of Baltimore, 46 Md., 615;
Dunwoodie *v.* The United States, 22 C. of Cls. R., 269.

There is another familar rule of statutory construction which should be observed in the application of this act of July 27, 1861, and it is that "what is implied in a statute is as much a part of it as what is expressed." (United States *v.* Babbitt, 1 Black, 55, 61.)

And the opinion of the court in that respect has been quoted with great emphasis in many subsequent decisions of the Supreme Court of the United States.

Gelpcke *v.* City of Dubuque, 1 Wall., 221;
Croxall *v.* Sherrard, 5 *id.*, 228;
Telegraph Company *v.* Eiser, 19 *id.*, 427;
United States *v.* Hodson, 10 *id.*, 406;
Buckley *v.* United States, 19 *id.*, 40.

The United States have universally reimbursed all sums of money actually expended and used for the benefit of the Federal Government, not only principal, but also interest paid for the hire of any principal used for such purposes.

In this case reimbursement is asked for interest, not upon any claim which these three States have against the United States, but as a part of the "costs, charges, and expenses" incurred and actually paid out, for which, it is respectfully submitted, full reimbursement should be made by the United States to these three States.

6 U. S. Stats., 139, April 18, 1814;
3 U. S. Stats., 422, April 9, 1819;
3 U. S. Stats., 560, April 11, 1820;
5 U. S. Stats., 522, August 23, 1842;
5 U. S. Stats., 578, August 31, 1842;
5 U. S. Stats., 628, March 3, 1843;
5 U. S. Stats., 716, April 30, 1834;
5 U. S. Stats., 797, March 1, 1845;
9 U. S. Stats., 571, February 27, 1851;
2 Comptroller's Decisions, vol. 15, p. 137, office records, holding to the effect that interest, when paid by a State for the use and benefit of the United States, becomes a part of the principal debt of the United States due to such State and constitutes a just and legal claim of such State against the Federal Government, as much so as to the principal itself;
1 Opinion of the U. S. Attorney-General, 542, 566;
2 Opinion of the U. S. Attorney-General, 841;
5 Opinion of the U. S. Attorney-General, 71, 108, 463.

Congress is presumed to have enacted the aforesaid legislation with a full knowledge not only of its own aforesaid acts but also of the

aforesaid decisions of the Executive Department of the United States
in reference to the construction and application of similar legislation
theretofore duly enacted by Congress; and if there existed any ambiguity
or doubt (which is denied in the premises) with reference to the true
construction of such legislation by Congress, then such prior decisions
and opinions of the proper Executive Departments of the United States
upon such similar statutes should have a controlling weight, and said
laws should be construed in harmony with such decisions and opinions.

  U. S. *v.* Moore, 95 U. S. R., 760–63;
  U. S. *v.* Pugh, 99 U. S., 265–269;
  Hahn *v.* U. S., 107 U. S. R., 402–406;
  Brown *v.* U. S., 113 U. S. R., 568;
  U. S. *v.* Philbrick, 120 U. S. R., 52;
  U. S. *v.* Hill, 120 U. S. R., 169.

 The departmental construction and opinions of similar laws of Congress become part of these laws, as much so as if they had been expressly
incorporated therein, and should be duly respected and adopted by Congress as is invariably done by the courts of the country.

 The United States are liable for the reimbursement for the "costs,
charges, and expenses" upon which these claims of these three States
are founded, because the same were duly made and incurred at the
request and solicitation of the United States to maintain the "common
defense" on the Pacific Coast, while the United States was engaged in
actual war, and hence these States 'in so making said expenditures were
acting in fact as the fiscal agents of the Federal Government.

 In view of the emergencies amid which, from 1861 to 1866, the Federal
Government was placed, and the circumstances in which these States
found themselves, it must be admitted that "the costs, charges, and
expenses" for which reimbursement is now claimed were not only necessary, but it has never been at any time, by any person, or at any
place, suggested that these three States, could in any other manner have
responded to the frequent calls and urgent demands of the United
States, except by doing that which in good faith they promptly did, to
wit, hire money and pay interest for such hire, implicitly relying upon
the good faith, equity, and the public conscience of the United States
and upon the highest order of obligation imposed upon and now resting upon the United States to wholly indemnify and fully reimburse
the same.

 These three States have not heretofore asked and do not now seek
to recover any principal or any interest which they did not actually
pay out of moneys by them hired, with which to meet "the costs,
charges, and expenses" of raising, organizing, equipping, and furnishing, etc., 18,715 volunteer troops, for the military service of the Federal Government on the Pacific Coast, and all of which troops were
continuously engaged and employed in the field, from 1861 to 1866,
inclusive, serving as far south as Arizona and as far north as the Territory of Washington, and as far east as the Territory of Utah.

 The State interest-bearing war bonds of these three States were not
authorized to be issued or sold and were not issued and sold, nor the
cash represented thereby was not hired, and–the interest paid for such
hire was not paid to relieve their own people, but all of the same were
done by these States to enable the Federal Government to do through
their credit that which the United States did not do, and seemingly
could not then otherwise do, to wit, to immediately put in the field
18,715 volunteer troops, fully equipped and prepared for military
service, and who, in the opinion of the United States, were immediately

needed to maintain the "common defense" on the Pacific Coast, and to serve as aforesaid during the period of the rebellion.

The principle contended for in these cases does not go even as far as Congress itself has heretofore gone in sundry cases, at sundry times, beginning at a very early period in the history of the Federal Government, because these claims are for the reimbursement only of such cash as these three States actually hired and expended for the use and benefit of the Federal Government, during a period of active war, and at the solicitation of the United States, while Congress has at times not only authorized the reimbursement of the principal, but has also authorized the payment of interest, for the use of the Federal Government, of money, up to the dates when same was actually repaid by the United States.

As late as March 7, 1892, the War Claims Committee, in the House of Representatives, having this subject-matter under examination, made a unanimous report to the House, to wit: House Report No. 555, Fifty-second Congress, first session, to accompany H. R. 4566, which report is as follows, to wit:

[House Report No. 555, Fifty-second Congress, first session.]

MARCH 7, 1892.—Committed to the Committee of the Whole House and ordered to be printed.

Mr. Stone, of Kentucky, from the Committee on War Claims, submitted the following report (to accompany H. R. 4566):

The Committee on War Claims, to whom was referred the bill (H. R. 4566) to reimburse the several States for interest on moneys expended by them on account of raising troops, etc., submit the following report:

The facts out of which this bill for relief arises will be found stated in a report made by this committee to the House in the Fiftieth Congress, which is appended as a part of this report.

Your committee concur in the conclusions stated in that report and recommend the passage of the bill.

[House Report No. 309, Fiftieth Congress, first-session.]

The Committee on War Claims, to whom was referred the bill (H. R. 1474) to reimburse the several States for interest on moneys expended by them on account of raising troops employed in aiding the United States in suppressing the late insurrection against the United States, beg leave to report the same back to the House with the recommendation that it do pass.

This recommendation is founded upon the precedents which Congress has heretofore established of paying interest on moneys advanced by States on account of the war of 1812; also, Indian wars of 1835, 1836, 1837, and 1838, and the northeast frontier of the State of Maine, as evidenced by the following acts of Congress:

To reimburse Virginia, act of March 3, 1825, Stat. at Large, vol. 4, 132.
To reimburse Maryland, act of May 13, 1826, Stat. at Large, vol. 4, p. 161.
To reimburse city of Baltimore, act of May 20, 1826, Stat. at Large, vol. 4, p. 177.
To reimburse Delaware, act of May 20, 1826, Stat. at Large, vol. 4, p. 175.
To reimburse New York, act of May 22, 1826, Stat. at Large, vol. 4, pp. 192, 193.
To reimburse Pennsylvania, act of March 3, 1827, Stat. at Large, vol. 4, pp. 240, 241.
To reimburse South Carolina, act of March 22, 1832, Stat. at Large, vol. 4, p. 499.
To reimburse Alabama, act of January 26, 1849, Stat. at Large, vol. 6, p. 344.
To reimburse Georgia, act of March 3, 1851, Stat. at Large, vol. 6, p. 646.
To reimburse Maine, act of March 3, 1851, Stat. at Large, vol. 6, p. 626.
To reimburse New Hampshire, act of January 27, 1852, Stat. at Large, vol. 10, pp. 1, 2.
To reimburse Massachusetts, act of July 8, 1870, Stat. at Large, vol. 16, pp. 197, 198.

The President, by authority of Congress, called upon the governors of the States of Maine, New Hampshire, Vermont, Massachusetts, Rhode Island, Connecticut, New York, New Jersey, Pennsylvania, Delaware, Maryland, Virginia, West Virginia, Ohio, Kentucky, Michigan, Indiana, Illinois, Wisconsin, Minnesota, Iowa, Missouri, Kansas, Nebraska, Nevada, Oregon, and California to furnish volunteers and militia

S. Rep. 145——4

troops to aid the United States in suppressing the late insurrection against it, and these States expended various sums of money which were advanced to the Government, in enrolling, equipping, subsisting, clothing, supplying, arming, paying, and transporting regiments and companies employed by the Government in suppressing the late insurrection, and it matters not to the Government from what sources these States obtained the moneys advanced by them for the benefit of the Government, they are equally and justly entitled to be paid interest on such advances from the time they presented their claims to the Government for payment to the time when the same were refunded by the Secretary of the Treasury.

These States incurred heavy obligations of indebtedness on account of raising these troops, on which they paid interest, and many of them are still paying interest on their bonded indebtedness.

As the Government had the use and benefit of these advances made by these States, above mentioned, and that, too, at a time when greatly needed, and added largely to the maintaining of the credit of the Government, it is deemed by your committee but equitable and just that interest should be allowed equally to all the States on moneys advanced by them to aid the Government in furnishing troops.

The same rule has been observed in the cases of several States which advanced money for the "common defense," in suppressing Indian and other wars, as follows, to wit:

Georgia, act March 3, 1879 (20 Stat. at L., p. 385); Washington Territory, act March 3, 1859 (11 Stat. at L., p. 429); New Hampshire, act January 27, 1852 (10 Stat. at L., p. 1); California, act of August 5, 1854 (10 Stat. at L., p. 582); California, act August 18, 1856 (11 Stat. at L., p. 91); California, act June 23, 1860 (12 Stat. at L., p. 104); California, act July 25, 1868 (15 Stat. at L., p. 175); California, act March 3, 1881 (21 Stat. at L., p. 510); and in aid of the Mexican war (see statute of June 2, 1848).

Attorney-General Wirt, in his opinion on an analogous case, says:

"The expenditure thus incurred forms a debt against the United States which they are bound to reimburse. If the expenditures made for such purpose are supplied from the treasury of the State, the United States reimburse the principal without interest; but if, being unable itself, from the condition of its own finances, to meet the emergency, such State has been obliged to borrow money for the purpose, and thus to incur a debt on which she herself has had to pay interest, such debt is essentially a debt due by the United States, and both the principal and interest are to be paid by the United States. (See Opinions of Attorneys-General, vol. 1, p. 174.)"

Thus it will be seen that the precedent for the payment of interest, under the rule adopted for the settlement of claims of war of 1812-1815 and Indian wars above cited, is well established.

These State war claims of these three States rest, therefore, upon a basis well founded, and, by virtue of the political relations existing between these States and the United States under the circumstances herein recited, entitle their petition to Congress for payment to prompt and just consideration.

These States have not been importunate in repeating their demands, but at all times have had a due regard for the fiscal condition of the Federal Treasury. They have been prompt, active, vigilant, and earnest in the due presentation of these State war claims against the United States, understating, if anything, rather than overstating, the exact amount thereof and asking at all times that they be reimbursed only whatever amount they actually paid to aid the United States in maintaining the "common defense," now computed and reported by the head of the War Department, under which all these military services have been performed.

The States of California, Oregon, and Nevada have not been guilty of any laches or delays tending to prejudice their said claims.

Under proper legislation of Congress, and under an appropriate resolution of the Senate, proceedings to carefully investigate these claims have been had, the amount of each and every necessary "cost, charge, and expense" in the case of each of these State has been heretofore fully inquired into, exactly ascertained, specifically stated, and carefully computed by the honorable Secretary of War.

This branch of the history of these State war claims is, therefore, not embarrassed by any controversy as to the facts, leaving only to be determined by Congress the just measure of the obligations resting upon the General Government resulting from these facts, fully shown in this statement and recited in said reports officially made to the Senate by the Secretary of War, and repeated in the several reports made to the House and Senate by the appropriate committees of each.

The question, therefore, that naturally arises is, "What is the duty of Congress under circumstances like these in a case like this?" These claimants are not private parties, but are States of the Union, *entitled to indemnities from the Federal Government*, who have heretofore relied and do now rely for reimbursement upon the aforesaid legislation of Congress and acts of its highest officers, wherein the amount by them expended for the "common defense" has been exactly ascertained by the Secretary of War and duly reported to the Senate. These States do not ask for reimbursement of any money which they did not pay or fully expend; but they do ask (see exhibits hereto Nos. 1, 2, 3) that Congress, without further delay, objection, or evasion, may now fully reimburse them the moneys heretofore by them fully paid in gold coin and appropriated and expended in good faith in aiding the United States, at their own solicitation, to maintain the "common defense," and expended, too, by these States when the United States seemingly were unable to pay the same.

Other States of the Union (see exhibit No. 4) have been reimbursed sums of money which they in good faith expended during the rebellion in aid of the "common defense," and in amounts aggregating (up to March 5, 1892) the sum of $44,725,072.38, as shown by the subjoined correspondence and table, prepared in the Treasury Department, on account of expenses incurred by the States therein named during the war of the rebellion, and all founded upon the same acts of Congress. (See exhibits Nos. 5 and 6.)

This table, showing the sums so paid, contains the names of every State loyal during the rebellion *except the States of California, Oregon, and Nevada*. This correspondence and table are as follows, to wit:

TREASURY DEPARTMENT, *March 21, 1892.*
Hon. WILLIAM M. STEWART, *U. S. Senate.*

SIR: In reply to your communication of the 9th instant, I have the honor to transmit herewith a statement of the amounts reimbursed the several States for expenses incurred by them in behalf of the United States during the war of the rebellion, as prepared in the offices of the Second and Third Auditors of the Treasury, together with accompanying reports of said officers.

Respectfully, yours,
L. CROUNSE,
Assistant Secretary.

TREASURY DEPARTMENT,
Second Auditor's Office, March 21, 1892.

Respectfully returned to the Honorable Secretary of the Treasury, with the report that the amounts allowed through this office as reimbursement to States for expenses in behalf of the United States during the war of the rebellion are set forth in Senate Ex. Doc. No. 11, Fifty-first Congress, first session.

No additional allowances have been made.

J. H. FRANKLIN, *Acting Auditor.*

TREASURY DEPARTMENT, OFFICE OF THE THIRD AUDITOR,
Washington, D. C., March 15, 1892.

Hon. CHARLES FOSTER, *Secretary of the Treasury.*

SIR: I have the honor to return the communication addressed to you by Hon. William M. Stewart, U. S. Senate, on the 9th instant, respecting allowances to the several States for reimbursements of the expenses of raising troops for the United States during the war of the rebellion.

The tabular statement inclosed by him (aggregating $44,137,590.34) is taken from a "Recapitulation," on page 63 of Senate Ex. Doc. No. 11, Fifty-first Congress, first session. It included jointly allowances as shown by the records of this office and as reported by the Second Auditor from his records

So far as the data came from this office, it is correct; but some further allowances have since been made through this office, as shown by the tabular statement herewith. But I perceive that by oversight a sum of $485 paid to Nebraska was included therein, which sum was *not* for raising troops for the United States, but was expenses in suppressing Indian hostilities. I now drop out that item.

So far as the data came from the records of the Second Auditor I presume it to be correct, but can not so certify; nor can I state officially whether any further allowances have since been made through his office.

Respectfully, yours,   A. W. SHAW, *Acting Auditor.*

Statement accompanying Third Auditor's letter to the Secretary of the Treasury, dated March 15, 1892.

State.	Allowances by Third Auditor.				
	As reported in Senate Ex. Doc. No. 1438, Fortieth Congress, second session, p. 57.	Allowances made since said list.	Total allowances by Third Auditor.	Allowances by Second Auditor, as reported in Senate Ex. Doc. No. 11, Fifty-first Congress, first session, p. 63.	Total allowances up to Mar. 15, 1892.
Connecticut............	$2, 096, 950. 46	$6, 014. 83	$2, 102, 965. 29	....	$2, 102, 965. 29
Massachusetts..........	3, 660, 483. 07	301. 133. 28	3, 961, 616. 35	$7, 608. 88	3, 969, 225. 23
Rhode Island...........	723, 530. 15	....	723, 530. 15	....	723, 530. 15
Maine.................	1, 027. 185. 00	448. 99	1, 027, 633. 99	....	1, 027, 633. 99
New Hampshire........	976, 081. 92	476. 56	976. 558. 48	450. 00	977, 008. 48
Vermont..............	832, 557. 40	....	832, 557. 40	....	832, 557. 40
New York	3, 957, 996. 98	*102, 737. 32	4, 060, 734. 30	198. 938. 52	4, 259, 672. 82
New Jersey............	1, 420, 167. 35	6, 548. 45	1, 426, 715. 80	96, 859. 44	1, 523, 575. 24
Pennsylvania..........	3, 204, 636. 24	14, 390. 04	3, 219, 026. 28	667, 074. 35	3, 886, 100. 63
Ohio	3, 245, 319. 58	71, 348. 20	3, 316, 667. 78	....	3, 316, 667. 78
Wisconsin.............	1, 035, 059. 17	24, 102. 86	1, 059, 162. 03	....	1, 059, 162. 03
Iowa.................	1, 039, 759. 45	3, 705. 35	1, 043, 464. 80	....	1, 043, 464. 80
Illinois...............	3, 080, 442. 51	1, 532. 92	3, 081, 975. 43	....	3, 081, 975. 43
Indiana..............	2, 668, 529. 78	....	2, 668, 529. 78	1, 073, 208. 51	3, 741, 738. 29
Minnesota.............	70, 798. 45	462. 45	71, 260. 90	276. 75	71, 537. 65
Kansas	384, 138. 15	2, 298. 21	386, 436. 36	....	386, 436. 36
Colorado.............	55, 238. 84	....	55, 238. 84	....	55, 238. 84
Missouri.............	7, 580, 421. 43	996. 37	7, 581, 417. 80	....	7, 581, 417. 80
Michigan.............	844, 262. 53	1, 493. 16	845, 755. 69	....	845, 755. 69
Delaware	31, 988. 96	....	31, 988. 96	....	31, 988. 96
Maryland.............	133, 140. 99	3, 140. 65	136, 281. 64	....	136, 281. 64
Virginia	48, 469. 97	....	48, 469. 97	....	48, 469. 97
West Virginia..........	471, 063. 94	....	471, 063. 94	....	471, 063. 94
Kentucky.............	3, 504, 466. 57	47, 137. 40	3, 551. 603. 97	....	3, 551, 603. 97
Total	42, 092. 668. 89	587, 967. 04	42, 680, 655. 93	2, 044, 416. 45	44, 725, 072. 38

*Included in this sum is an allowance of $16,197.42 to New York not yet actually paid, but upon the list to be reported to Congress at its present session, for a deficiency appropriation.

L. W. F.

SECOND AUDITOR'S OFFICE, *March 19, 1892 (mail room).*
THIRD AUDITOR'S OFFICE, *March 15, 1892.*

Many of the important facts reported to the Senate by its Committee on Military Affairs, in a statement in support and explanation of Senate bill No. 3420, Fiftieth Congress, first session, which though when reported was intended to apply only to the rebellion war claims of the Territory and State of Nevada, yet the same apply with equal force and correctness to these similar rebellion war claims of the States of California and Oregon, some of which, recited in said statement, are as follows, to wit:

RESULTS OF THE FOREGOING LEGISLATION BY NEVADA.

By these legislative enactments of Nevada substantial and effectual aid was given and guaranteed by Nevada, both as a Territory and State, to the Government of the

United States in guarding its overland mail and emigrant route and the line of the proposed transcontinental railroad, in furnishing troops during the war of the rebellion, and for suppressing Indian hostilities and maintaining peace in the country inhabited by the Mormons, and for the common defense, as contemplated in said circular letter of Secretary Seward, along an exposed, difficult, and hostile Indian frontier, and then but sparsely populated. These enactments were fully known to the authorities of the United States and to Congress; they have ever been acquiesced in and met with the sanction and practical indorsement of the United States, in whose interest and for whose benefit they were made. As a partial compensation to these volunteers for this irregular, hazardous, and exposed service in the mountains and on the desert plains, and to aid them to a small extent to maintain families dependent upon them for support, first the Territory and afterwards the State of Nevada offered and paid this small stipend, never suspecting that the United States would not promptly and willingly respond when asked to reimburse the same. These citizens of Nevada who volunteered, enlisted, and did military service for the United States were compelled in many cases to abandon their employment, in which their wages were always lucrative and service continuous, so that nothing less than the individual patriotism of these volunteers enabled the Territory and State of Nevada to cheerfully and promptly respond to every call and requisition made upon them for troops by the United States.

NEVADA'S DILIGENCE IN THESE PREMISES.

The State of Nevada has not slept upon her rights in any of these premises nor been guilty of any *laches;* on the contrary, at all proper times she has respectfully brought the same to the attention of Congress by memorials of her legislature and of her State authorities and through her representatives in Congress. On March 29, 1867, her legislature first asked for the payment of the claims of the State by a joint resolution, which is printed in the appendix, marked Exhibit No. 8, p. 64. And again, on February 1, 1869, the legislature of Nevada passed a memorial and a joint resolution renewing her prayer in these premises, which is also so printed in the appendix, marked Exhibit No. 9, p. 65.

The Journals of the U. S. Senate show that on March 10, 1868, the writer of this report presented the first-mentioned memorial and resolution to the Senate, accompanied with an official statement of the amount of the claims of the State referred to therein. These papers were referred to the Comittee on Claims, but the records fail to show that any action was ever taken upon them. On May 29 of the same year the writer of this report introduced a joint resolution (S. 138) providing for the appointment of a board of examiners to examine the claims of the State of Nevada against the United States, and on June 18 of the same year the Committee on Claims, to whom this joint resolution was referred, was discharged from its further consideration. The official statement of the moneys expended by the State of Nevada on account of the United States, and presented to the Senate on March 10, 1868, can not now be found on the files of the Senate.

On February 11, 1885, and January 26, 1887, the legislature of Nevada, renewing its prayer for a reimbursement of the money by her expended for the use and benefit of the United States, further memorialized Congress, asking for the settlement of her claims, which are printed in the appendix and marked Exhibits Nos. 10 and 11, pp. 65 and 66.

CONCLUSIONS AND RECOMMENDATIONS.

Nevada has not demanded a bounty nor presented a claim against the United States for reimbursement of any expenditure she did not in good faith actually make for the use and benefit of the United States, and made, too, only subsequent to the date of the aforesaid appeal of Secretary Seward to the nation, and made, too, in consequence of said appeal and of the subsequent calls and requisitions made upon her then scanty resources and sparse population, and wherein the good faith of the United States was to be relied upon to make to her ungrudgingly a just reimbursement whenever the United States found itself in a condition to redeem all its obligations.

Nevada has been diligent in making her claim known to Congress, but she has not with an indecorous speed demanded her pound of flesh, but has waited long and patiently, believing upon the principle that the higher obligations between States, like those among men, are not always "set down in writing, signed and sealed in the form of a bond; but reside rather in honor," and that the obligation of the United States due her in this case was as sacred as if it had originally been in the form of a 4-per cent U. S. bond, now being redeemed by the United States at $1.27 upon each $1 of this particular form of its unpaid obligations.

Nevada has not solicited any charity in this case, but, on the contrary, by numerous petitions and memorials has respectfully represented to Congress why the taxes heretofore levied upon her people and paid out of her own treasury to her volunteer troops in gold and silver coin to aid the United States at its own solicitation to protect itself and maintain the general welfare should be now returned to her by the General Government.

Congress should not forget that during the long period of the nation's peril the citizens of Nevada, like those of California (when not engaged in the military or naval service of the United States) not only guarded the principal gold and silver mines of the country then discovered, and prevented them from falling into the hands of the public enemy, but also worked them so profitably for the general welfare as to enable the United States to make it possible to resume specie payment and to redeem its bonds at 27 per cent above par, and to repay all its money lenders at a high rate of interest, and that, too, not in the depreciated currency with which it paid Nevada's volunteer troops, but in gold coin of standard value.

As these expenditures were honestly made by the Territory and State of Nevada, your committee do not think that, under all the peculiar and exceptional circumstances of this case, the action of the Territory and State of Nevada should be hewn too nicely or too hypercritically by the United States at this late date. These expenditures were all made in perfect good faith and for patriotic purposes, and secured effectual aid to the United States which otherwise could not have been obtained without a much larger expenditure. The State of Nevada in good faith assumed and paid all the obligations of the Territory of Nevada to aid the United States, and issued and sold its own bonds for their payment, upon which bonds it has paid interest until the present time. The only question now for consideration is, shall the United States in equal good faith and under all the circumstances herein recited relieve the State of Nevada from this obligation, or shall the United States insist and require it to be paid by the people of that State alone?

In support of that portion of these State war claims which relates to the indemnity and reimbursement of the cash paid by these three States as *interest* for the hire and use of the principal by them borrowed with which to defray the "costs, charges, and expenses" of furnishing said 18,715 volunteer troops, there is submitted herewith a copy of the decision (see Exhibit No. 7) of the U. S. Supreme Court, rendered December 6, 1895, by Mr. Justice Harlan, in the cases of The State of New York *v.* The United States, and of The United States *v.* The State of New York on appeal from the Court of Claims on the petition of the State of New York in the cause in that court entitled "The State of New York *v.* The United States." (26 U. S. Court Claims Reports, 467–509.)

The U. S. Supreme Court in adjudicating the claims so presented in said petition of that State for *interest* actually paid out for the hire and use of money by it borrowed and expended to aid the United States to maintain the "common defense," rested its opinion and entered its decree and judgment upon principles identical in all respects with those contended for herein, and that decision being the latest judicial declaration and announcement of the obligations of the United States incurred under circumstances similar to those herein recited, is entitled to the careful and respectful consideration of Congress in these premises, and which ought to be and, it is respectfully submitted, is conclusive of both the equity and legality of these rebellion war claims of these three States.

Respectfully,　　　　　JOHN MULLAN,
Of Counsel for California, and
Attorney for Oregon and Nevada, Claimant States.

No. 1310 CONNECTICUT AVENUE,
Washington, D. C., January 28, 1896.

EXHIBIT NO. 1.

CALIFORNIA'S MEMORIAL TO CONGRESS.

CHAPTER XXXII.—SENATE JOINT RESOLUTION No. 5, relative to indebtedness of the United States Government to the State of California (adopted March 13, 1893).

Resolved by the senate, the assembly concurring, That the State of California urges upon its Senators and Representatives in Congress to use their best efforts in procuring the passage of the act now pending in both Houses of Congress to reimburse California for the money raised and disbursed for arming and equipping troops brought into service by requisition of the United States during the rebellion. These claims have all been passed upon and approved by the War Department, and by the committee in each House to whom they were referred, and are on their respective calendars for passage, but may fail this Congress, as in the last, for want of earnest and active presentation. For war claims, see House Report three thousand three hundred and ninety-six, and Senate Reports one thousand two hundred and eighty-six and two thousand and fourteen, first session Fiftieth Congress; also, House Report two thousand five hundred and fifty-three, and Senate Report six hundred and forty-four, first session Fifty-first Congress; and House Report two hundred and fifty-four and Senate Report one hundred and fifty-eight, first session Fifty-second Congress.

Resolved, That whatever money shall be received by the State from these claims, or from the claim of the State to five per cent of the cash sales of public land sold in this State by the United States, the same shall be turned into the State treasury, and credited to the school fund.

Resolved, That his excellency the governor be requested to forward a copy of these resolutions to each of the Senators and Representatives in Congress.

EXHIBIT NO. 2.

OREGON'S MEMORIAL TO CONGRESS.

[Senate Mis. Doc. No. 51, Fifty-second Congress, second session.]

FEBRUARY 13, 1893.—Referred to the Committee on Appropriations and ordered to be printed.

Mr. DOLPH presented the following memorial of the legislature of the State of Oregon praying the payment of moneys expended in maintaining the common defense and to aid in the suppression of the rebellion:

To the Congress of the United States:

Whereas the State of Oregon has heretofore paid a large sum of money to aid the United States in maintaining the common defense in the suppression of the war of the rebellion, the amount of which has been shown by the reports of the honorable Secretary of War made to Congress; and

Whereas said debt has not yet been paid but is long since due; and

Whereas Hon. J. N. Dolph has introduced in the Senate of the United States an amendment to be proposed to the sundry civil appropriation bill, making an appropriation to pay said claim, together with similar claims of the States of California and Nevada; and

Whereas the United States has reimbursed other States of the Union for sums of money expended on account of the war of the rebellion, such payments aggregating up to March 15, 1892, the sum of $44,725,072.38, but has not paid any sum whatever on said accounts to the said States of California, Oregon, and Nevada: Therefore, be it

Resolved by the legislative assembly of the State of Oregon, That justice and equity demand that the payment of said claims should be no longer delayed by the United States, and that an appropriation of money therefor should be made by Congress at this time; and be it further

Resolved, That this memorial be telegraphed by the secretary of state to our Senators and our Representatives in Congress, and that a written copy thereof, duly certified, shall be forwarded to the presiding officers of the Senate and House of Representatives of the United States.

Adopted by the senate February 8, 1893.

C. W. FULTON, *President of the Senate.*

Concurred in by the house February 8, 1893.

W. P. KEADY, *Speaker of the House.*

GEORGE W. MCBRIDE,
    Secretary of State.

To the Senate and House of Representatives of the United States of America in Congress assembled:

Your memorialists, now the State executive officers of the State of Nevada (the legislature of Nevada not being now in session), most respectfully represent to your honorable bodies that the State of Nevada has heretofore presented a claim to the United States for expenses by her incurred and by her paid as "costs, charges, and expenses properly incurred for enrolling" her military forces during the war of the rebellion, in response to and under requisitions made by the officer commanding the Military Department of the Pacific, and which "costs, charges, and expenses" so incurred and paid by Nevada aggregate the sum of $11,840 for enrolling 1,184 men preliminary to their being mustered into the military service of the United States.

A claim for reimbursement by the United States for the aforesaid expenditure has been presented by the State of Nevada to the United States, and payment thereof has been refused, and because its examining and accounting and auditing officers seem to have regarded this expenditure simply as a bounty or gratuity paid by Nevada to the officers of her military forces who enrolled said 1,184 men.

Nevada selected as her enrolling agents those officers of her military forces who were to be commanding officers of the men who might be thereafter enrolled; and there can not be any valid question as to the wisdom or economy of such a course as adopted and uniformly pursued by Nevada, and especially when we consider the importance of each commanding officer being perfectly familiar with the qualifiications of those he was to command in the field, both as to their mental and physical fitness. -

This method of enrollment as adopted by Nevada, and seeming no doubt to her at the time, as the most ready and economical one for putting her troops in the field for the United States military service, in obedience to requisitions made upon her, was the one followed in all cases; and this claim for reimbursement by the United States for the "costs, charges, and expenses" so incurred was in lieu of all other "costs, charges, and expenses" that would have to be incurred and as incident to said enrollment—such, for instance, as rent, fuel, furniture, salaries of enrolling officers, subsistence, and all the other detailed and expensive paraphernalia which pertain to the regular military recruiting or enrolling office of a State or of the United States, and such as the United States would herself have been compelled to incur if she had invoked or exercised her own Federal military machinery for the same purpose in the State of Nevada.

No express method of enrolling having been designated to Nevada by the United States she was left to adopt that method of organizing, collecting, and enrolling her military forces to meet the requisitions so made upon her at the time, and such as appeared to her to be the wisest and the most practicable.

To provide for and to pay the "costs, charges, and expenses" so incurred and to be incurred by Nevada on account of said enrollment the legislature of Nevada passed a law on March 11, 1865, which provided substantially that each enrolling or recruiting agent of her army indented by her for the military service of the United States should be allowed for all expenses of said enrollment $10 per capita. The law is as follows, to wit:

" *The people of the State of Nevada, represented in senate and assembly, do enact as follows:*

" SECTION 1. A sum not exceeding one hundred thousand dollars is hereby appropriated and set aside, to constitute a separate fund to be known as the " soldiers' fund," for the purpose of paying a compensation to the soldiers of the companies of Nevada Volunteers already raised in the Territory and in the State of Nevada, and to be raised in this State, for the service of the United States, to aid in repelling invasion, suppressing insurrections, enforcing the laws, and protecting the public property, in addition to the pay allowed them by the United States.

" SEC. 2. There shall be paid out of the fund created and set apart by the first section of this act * * * a bounty of ten dollars, to be paid to the captain or commanding officer of any company, for every recruit by him enlisted and subsequently mustered into the service of the United States: *Provided*, That the pro visions of this section shall not be deemed applicable to any soldiers who may be drafted, or enlisted as a substitute, or any person drafted into the Army of the United States. * * *

" SEC. 3. The captains or commanding officers of companies of Nevada Volunteers raised, or to be raised, for service in the Army of the United States, shall, before such officers, as recruiting agents of the Army, can be entitled to secure the benefits of this act, file in the office of the adjutant-general their affidavit, setting forth the number and names of recruits enlisted by them, and accepted by the proper medical examiners (who shall in each case be named) and sworn into the service; and further setting forth that no affidavit of the same character, for the same enlisted men, has heretofore been made or filed. The adjutant-general of the State is hereby authorized and directed to certify to the controller of state the number of men enlisted by each captain or commanding officer of a company, whenever the affidavit herein required is filed in his office, indorsed by the provost-marshal of this State, or the commanding officer of the post where the enlisted men referred to and enumerated in the affidavit may have been rendezvoused on enlistment. Upon the filing of the adjutant-general's certificate, above required, in the office of the controller of state, the controller shall make out a copy of said certificate, and forward the same to the State board of examiners, and if the State board of examiners shall indorse the certificate as "Approved," then the controller shall draw his warrant upon the fund herein constituted for the sum set forth in the certificate of the adjutant-general in favor of the officers, or their legal assignees, named in the certificate, for the sums respectively set forth to be due them.

"Sec. 6. For the purpose of carrying into effect the provisions of this act, and providing for the fund created by section one of this act, the treasurer of the State of Nevada shall cause to be prepared bonds of the State to the amount of one hundred thousand dollars, in sums of five hundred dollars each, redeemable at the office of the treasurer of the State on the first day of July, one thousand eight hundred and seventy. The said bonds shall bear interest, payable semiannually, at the rate of ten per cent per annum, from the date of their issuance, which interest shall be due and payable at the office of the treasurer of this State on the first day of January and July of each year: *Providing,* That the first payment of interest shall not be made sooner than the first day of January, in the year of our Lord one thousand eight hundred and sixty-six. These said bonds shall be signed by the governor, and countersigned by the controller, and indorsed by the treasurer of the State, and shall have the seal of the State affixed thereto. Such bonds shall be issued from time to time as they may be required for use. The expense of preparing such bonds and disposing of the same shall be audited as a claim against the soldiers' fund created by this act.

"Sec. 10. For the payment of the principal and interest of the bonds issued under this act there shall be levied and collected, annually, until the final payment and redemption of the same, and in the same manner as other State revenue is or may be directed by law to be levied and collected annually, a tax of twenty-five cents, in gold and silver coin of the United States, on each one hundred dollars of taxable property in the State, in addition to the other taxes for State purposes, and the fund derived from this tax shall be set apart and applied to the payment of interest accruing on the bonds herein provided for and the final redemption of the principal of said bonds; and the public faith of the State of Nevada is hereby pledged for the payment of the bonds issued by virtue of this act, and the interest thereon and, if necessary, to provide other and ample means for the payment thereof." (Statutes of Nevada, March 11, 1865, pp. 389–393.)

This small sum of $10 per capita when the peculiar condition of Nevada at that time is considered, in connection with her then limited and expensive means of travel which was then exclusively by wagon or horseback, and before any railroads were built in this State, will be considered to be not exorbitant, but, as your memorialists now submit, the same was and is very reasonable.

True, the act of the legislature termed this $10 per capita for enrollment a "bounty" to the captains or commanding officers who might organize a company to be thereafter mustered into the service of the United States, yet, as a matter of fact, it was not a bounty in the sense of a gratuity, and as is frequently used by the United States as meaning money in addition to the pay and allowances as set forth in the agreement with her commanding officers and enlisted men about to enter her military service; on the contrary, it was a lump compensation paid or to be paid by the State to her recruiting or enrolling officers in lieu of all other expenses or compensation for organizing its military forces and such as have been hereinbefore recited and covered, and was intended to cover all expense of travel, subsistence, lodging, and other incidental expenses, and such as U. S. recruiting and enrolling officers might properly incur in getting together and preparing men for the military service of the State and of the United States.

Your memorialists call attention to the fact that on March 11, 1865, Nevada did not even have in her treasury the money with which to pay this disbursement, but in section 6 of said act she was compelled to issue and sell her own State bonds with which to raise money to pay this and other expenses of a military character in order to aid in defraying the State expenses in a time of war.

Not only this, but in section 10 of said act Nevada levied a tax in gold or silver coin of the United States upon every $100 taxable property in the State of Nevada, in addition to other taxes for State purposes, to create a fund with which to pay said expenses, and which tax was to continue until all of said bonds were wholly paid and fully redeemed; and in addition thereto the public faith of Nevada was pledged to pay said bonds and interest thereon, and, if necessary, to provide other and ample means for the payment thereof.

The public faith of Nevada was therefore pledged for the benefit of the United States, and at a time when the public credit of the United States was itself put to the test and its paper largely depreciated in parts of the country outside the limits of Nevada.

Wherefore your memorialists (the legislature not now being in session), believing that if the attention of Congress were respectfully and properly invited to this matter it would not permit this expenditure to be repudiated by being disallowed or payment refused, now, therefore, petition your honorable bodies to reimburse Nevada in the sum of $11,840 so by her expended and paid as "costs, charges, and expenses," and by her incurred for enrolling 1,184 men for the military service of the United States, and who did perform active United States military service during the war of the rebellion wherever their military services were needed.

Respectfully,

C. C. STEVENSON,
Governor.
H. C. DAVIS,
Lieutenant-Governor and Adjutant-General.
JOHN M. DORMER,
Secretary of State.
J. F. HALLOCK,
State Controller.
GEORGE TUFLY,
State Treasurer.
JOHN F. ALEXANDER,
Attorney-General.
JOHN E. JONES,
Surveyor-General.
W. C. DOVEY,
Superintendent Public Instruction.
J. C. HARLOW,
Superintendent State Printing.

EXHIBIT NO. 4.

CALIFORNIA, OREGON, AND NEVADA WAR CLAIMS.

TREASURY DEPARTMENT, *June 21, 1894.*

SIR: In reply to your request of the 29th ultimo for a statement of the war claims of the several States, I have the honor to transmit herewith copy of a report of the Third Auditor, of the 19th instant, together with a detailed statement of the claims of the several States against the United States for the cost, charges, and expenses in aiding to maintain the "common defense" from 1861 to 1865, filed under the act of Congress of July 27, 1861 (12 Stat., p. 276), and acts supplemental thereto, or amendatory thereof.

Respectfully, yours,

S. WIKE, *Acting Secretary.*

Hon. BINGER HERMANN, *House of Representatives.*

TREASURY DEPARTMENT, OFFICE OF THE THIRD AUDITOR,
Washington, D. C., June 19, 1894.

SIR: In reply to the communication of Hon. Binger Hermann, House of Representatives, of the 29th ultimo, referred by you to me on the 1st instant for report, I have the honor to inclose a detailed statement of the claims of the several States against the United States for the cost, charges, and expenses in aiding to maintain the "common defense"—war of the rebellion, 1861–1865—filed under the act of Congress of July 27, 1861 (12 Stat., 276) and acts supplemental thereto or amendatory thereof.

The amount disallowed in each case, except claims for refund of interest, is subject to reopening and revision on presentation of new and material evidence, and then only the item or items to which such evidence applies.

Oregon, Nevada, and several other States have presented claims, some of which embrace the rebellion period; but they were filed under act of June 27, 1882 (22 Stat.,

111), for reimbursement of amounts in raising volunteer and militia forces in the suppression of Indian hostilities.

On September 21, 1887, the State of California filed a claim against the United States under the various acts of Congress for the relief of States, which was referred to the War Department for examination by a military board. That portion of the claim for expense in the suppression of Indian hostilities under act of June 27, 1882, amounting to $38,323.74, has been examined, adjusted, and finally closed. The balance of the claim is yet on the files of the War Department, and I have no knowledge as to what portion is for organizing and maintaining home guards or militia, or what portion is for recruiting and paying volunteers for the service of the United States.

Respectfully, yours,

Hon. JOHN G. CARLISLE,
    Secretary of the Treasury.

SAMUEL BLACKWELL,
Auditor.

Statement accompanying Third Auditor's letter of June 19, 1894, to the Secretary of the Treasury, in relation to the claims of the several States against the United States, for the costs, charges, and expenses in aiding to maintain the "common defense"—war of the rebellion, 1861–1865—filed under the act of Congress of July 27, 1861 (12 Stats., 276), and acts supplemental thereto or amendatory thereof.

MAINE.

No. of claim.	Date when filed.	Amount of claim.	Amount allowed and disposed of.	Amount disallowed.
1	April 25, 1862	$1,075,274.36	} $917,539.68	$226,780.22
2	July 28, 1862	15,795.25		
3	July 22, 1863	53,250.29	}	
4	February 25, 1867	157,251.88	103,385.39	53,866.49
5	August 8, 1868	6,728.96	6,728.96	
6	June 19, 1882	22,709.30		22,709.30
	Total	1,331,010.04	1,027,654.03	303,356.01

NEW HAMPSHIRE.

1	April 14, 1862	$92,046.91	} $799,443.84	$30,039.87
2	May 12, 1862	787,436.80		
3	August 10, 1863	440,228.69	136,024.04	a304,204.65
4	December 20, 1865	29,975.75	19,685.06	10,290.69
5	January 23, 1866	25,877.84	25,577.87	299.97
6	May 10, 1867	7,269.42	5,594.62	1,674.80
7	September 11, 1868	17,823.99	15,353.94	2,470.05
8	January 22, 1869	6,832.02	5,609.69	1,222.33
9	February 26, 1873	5,099.69	4,003.02	1,096.67
	Total	1,412,591.11	1,011,292.08	401,299.03

VERMONT.

1	March 8, 1862	$623,831.61	$566,614.30	$57,217.31
2	April 7, 1862	72,028.62	71,771.12	257.50
3	April 16, 1864	32,402.69	31,207.26	1,195.43
4	May 17, 1867	47,119.96	42,432.13	4,687.83
5	......do	18,788.04	b18,788.04	
6	July 11, 1868	46,169.45	46,169.45	
7	September 24, 1868	30,077.62	29,166.45	911.17
8	......do	6,672.20	6,382.85	289.35
9	......do	22,750.00	22,428.53	321.47
10	......do	4,065.02	3,755.75	309.27
11	October 3, 1868	876.56	796.69	79.87
12	June 17, 1871	19,892.04	18,271.08	1,620.96
13	February 29, 1872	61.45	61.45	
	Total	924,735.26	857,845.10	66,890.16

a Bounty.   *b* St. Albans raid, October, 1864.

Statement accompanying Third Auditor's letter of June 19, 1894, to the Secretary of the Treasury, in relation to the claims of the several States, etc.—Continued.

MASSACHUSETTS.

No. of claim.	Date when filed.	Amount of claim.	Amount allowed and disposed of.	Amount disallowed.
1	March —, 1862.............................	$1,316,344.79	$1,313 378.25	$2,966.54
2	July 2, 1852	1,848.783.06	1,845,472.35	3,310.71
3	September 22, 1863	199,982.67	195,781.05	4,201,62
4	November 28, 1864........................	101,492.46	100,726.43	766.03
5	May 1, 1865...............................	35,163.52	35,163.52	....
6	September 23, 1868	33,498.29	33,482.79	15.50
7	March 9, 1869	216,464.17	212,751.72	3,712.45
8	January 10, 1883..........................	11,754.12	11,754.12	....
9	June 13, 1883.............................	437,387.39	270,379.25	a167,008.14
10	October 30, 1884	141,656.56	85,125.54	56,531.02
	Total	4,342,527.03	4,104,015.02	238,512.01

RHODE ISLAND.

No. of claim.	Date when filed.	Amount of claim.	Amount allowed and disposed of.	Amount disallowed.
1	March 4, 1863.............................	$594,271.26	$589,614.99	b $4,656.27
2	May 18, 1867	155,252.02	154,878.95	373.07
3	December 9, 1867.........................	6,966.18	6,896.72	69.46
4	September 17, 1868	6,122.53	6,012.53	110.00
	Total...................................	762,611.99	757,403.19	5,208.80

CONNECTICUT.

No. of claim.	Date when filed.	Amount of claim.	Amount allowed and disposed of.	Amount disallowed.
1	March 14, 1862	$1,543,432.92	$1,484,163.46	c $59,369.46
2	April 16, 1863	357,297.72	350,707.19	6,590.53
3	May 30, 1865..............................	75,805.95	71,701.90	4,104.05
4	April 25, 1866	22,216.91	22,211.57	5.34
5	April 3, 1871	40,653.19	18,002.21	12,650.98
6	April 10, 1871	19,154.89	19,135.12	19.77
7	May 29, 1871	67,442.92	24,962.50	42,480.42
8	June 15, 1871.............................	129,151.44	129,128.16	23.28
9	May 8, 1872	14,975.94	14,975.94	....
10	April 30, 1879	14,831.55	9,399.59	5,431.96
11	June 24, 1881.............................	6,071.60	6,071.60	....
	Total...................................	2,291,135.03	2,160,459.24	130,675.79

NEW YORK.

No. of claim.	Date when filed.	Amount of claim.	Amount allowed and disposed of.	Amount disallowed.
1	May 22, 1862	$2,782,688.42	} $2,777,903.18	d $172,576.28
2	July 31, 1862.............................	167,791.04		
3	December 2, 1867.........................	281,845.86	267,945.25	13,900.61
4	January 2, 1872..........................	364,107.07	313,054.83	51,052.24
5	September 2, 1872........................	866,413.13	513,411.43	353,001.70
6	December 3, 1873.........................	341,580.10	115,461.50	226,118.60
7	June 30, 1874.............................	197,537.76	40,558.31	156,979.45
8	July 23, 1879.............................	21,956.11	7,460.00	14,496.11
9	June 13, 1883.............................	78,101.83	64,729.28	13,372.55
10	July 2, 1890..............................	9,066.65	6,655.55	2,411.10
11	December 28, 1891........................	65,624.24	(e)	....
12	January 3, 1894..........................	6,324.24	(f)	....
	Total....................................	5,183,036.45	4,107,179.33	1,003,908.64

a Part coast defense.
b $2,266.35 interest.
c $41,363.83 interest.
d The claim of $131,188.02, interest, is pending in the Supreme Court of the United States on appeal from Court of Claims.
e Is additional claim for interest; no action.
f No action.

Statement accompanying Third Auditor's letter of June 19, 1894, to the Secretary of the Treasury, in relation to the claims of the several States, etc.—Continued.

NEW JERSEY.

No. of claim.	Date when filed.	Amount of claim.	Amount allowed and disposed of.	Amount disallowed.
1	October 14, 1861............................	$175, 634. 08	$159, 258. 25	$16, 375. 83
2	July 17, 1862.................................	311. 855. 37	310, 166. 88	1, 688. 49
3	July 29, 1862.................................	31, 978. 96	31, 975. 96	3. 00
4	July 29, 1865.................................	33, 129. 33	33, 129 33	....
5	September 5, 1865............................	2, 094. 38	2, 094. 38	....
6	September 15, 1865...........................	602, 002. 43	600, 419. 63	1, 582. 80
7	September 18. 1865	251. 25	251. 25	....
8	November 29. 1865...........................	30, 381. 25	30, 256. 25	125. 00
9	November 1, 1866............................	14, 175. 23	14, 171. 23	4. 00
10	March 5, 1868................................	93, 944. 25	81, 648. 54	12, 295. 71
11	November 20, 1868...........................	21, 196. 44	21, 193. 89	2. 55
12	June 9. 1870.................................	36, 975. 01	34, 541. 86	2, 433. 15
13	June 13, 1870................................	6, 906. 94	6, 772. 34	134. 60
14	July 15, 1870................................	1, 479. 72	1, 479. 72	....
15	January 7, 1871..............................	6, 704. 50	6, 503. 25	201. 25
16	June 16, 1871................................	67, 035. 27	64, 940. 55	2, 094. 72
17	February 15, 1887...........................	2, 637. 00	(a)	....
	Total....................................	1, 438, 381. 41	1, 398, 803. 31	36, 941. 10

PENNSYLVANIA.

No. of claim.	Date when filed.	Amount of claim.	Amount allowed and disposed of.	Amount disallowed.
1	March 1, 1862	$1, 182, 997. 22	$1, 181, 782. 94	$1, 214. 28
2	June 11, 1862................................	854, 337. 20	834, 856. 92	19, 480. 28
3	February 20, 1863	81, 084. 91	78. 532. 60	2, 552. 31
4	May 4, 1870.................................	257, 933. 18	216, 301. 14	41, 632. 04
5	June 30, 1870...............................	762, 127. 91	677, 659. 29	84, 468. 62
6	May 25, 1871................................	33, 737. 77	31, 780. 68	1, 957. 09
7	June 18, 1874...............................	30, 163. 66	27, 657. 07	2, 506. 59
8	June 29, 1874...............................	9, 819. 30	8, 064. 21	1, 755. 09
9	June 30, 1874...............................	100, 780. 49	22, 113. 43	78, 667. 06
10	July 25, 1881................................	131, 239. 25	94, 569. 15	36, 670. 10
11	November 20, 1882...........................	75, 726. 10	33, 766. 58	41, 959. 52
12	April 21, 1884	14, 018. 14	4, 378. 30	9, 639. 84
13	December 5. 1885............................	4, 921. 04	3, 949. 53	971. 51
14	February 2, 1887	1, 300. 46	1, 001. 39	299. 07
15	April 18, 1889	14, 356. 39	7, 546. 83	6, 809. 56
16	December 5, 1892............................	b 14, 431. 80	895. 65	13, 536. 15
	Total...................................	3, 568, 974. 82	3, 224, 855. 71	344, 119. 11

DELAWARE.

No. of claim.	Date when filed.	Amount of claim.	Amount allowed and disposed of.	Amount disallowed.
1	July 27, 1864...............................	$3, 019. 20	$3, 019. 20	....
2	May 1, 1877.................................	75, 166. 63	28, 969. 76	$46, 196. 87
	Total...................................	78, 185. 83	31, 988. 96	46, 196. 87

MARYLAND.

No. of claim.	Date when filed.	Amount of claim.	Amount allowed and disposed of.	Amount disallowed.
1	January 3. 1866.............................	$23, 979. 72	$16, 692. 05	$7, 287. 67
2	May 8, 1872	10, 996. 77	1, 703. 21	9, 293. 56
3	April 30, 1874	78, 812. 60	66, 523. 74	12, 288. 86
4	September 11, 1876..........................	65, 337. 40	51, 362. 64	13, 974. 76
	Total...................................	179, 126. 49	136, 281. 64	42, 844. 85

VIRGINIA.

No. of claim.	Date when filed.	Amount of claim.	Amount allowed and disposed of.	Amount disallowed.
1	March 17, 1862	$42, 182. 01	$40, 072. 31	$2, 109. 70
2	October 16, 1865............................	11, 930. 46	8, 397. 66	3, 532. 80
	Total...................................	54, 112. 47	48, 469. 97	5, 642. 50

a Claim No. 17 withdrawn by State February 17, 1887, and refiled May 4, 1894; no action; awaiting further evidence.
b Pending in Second Comptroller's office.

Statement accompanying Third Auditor's letter of June 19, 1894, to the Secretary of the Treasury, in relation to the claims of the several States, etc.—Continued.

WEST VIRGINIA.

No. of claims.	Date when filed.	Amount of claim.	Amount allowed and disposed of.	Amount disallowed.
1	January 13, 1868......................	$456,879.03	$456,658.03	$221.00

KENTUCKY.

No. of claims.	Date when filed.	Amount of claim.	Amount allowed and disposed of.	Amount disallowed.
1	March 17, 1862......................	$753,752.47	$752,888.44	$864.03
2	March 21, 1862......................	34,457.00	31,860.55	2,596.45
3	August 4, 1862......................	340,478.63	332,408.58	8,070.05
4	March 19, 1863......................	671,257.05	648,441.48	22,815.57
5	November, 1863......................	304,638.46	296,344.49	8,293.97
6	September 16, 1864	319,788.90	312,536.09	7,252.81
7	March 27, 1865......................	47.00	....	47.00
8	August 8, 1866	193,697.71	187,888.54	5,809.17
9	....do	132,451.01	123,615.35	8,835.66
10	September 1, 1866	582,692.43	579,454.28	3,238.15
11	March 26, 1867......................	226,842.96	199,871.75	26,971.21
12	February 10, 1873	70,260.75	56,001.17	14,259.58
14	December 28, 1877......................	190,650.00	....	100,650.00
15	January 23, 1879	973,701.62	....	*a* 973,701.62
	Total	4,794,715.99	3,521,310.72	1,273,405.27

No. 13 omitted; not rebellion war claim; canal toll case, Green and Barren rivers.

OHIO.

No. of claims.	Date when filed.	Amount of claim.	Amount allowed and disposed of.	Amount disallowed.
1	November 21, 1861......................	$29,980.01	$25,490.72	$4,489.29
2	June 21, 1862......................	1,702,440.79	1,699,179.43	3,261.36
3	September 26, 1862	88,709.22	59,857.10	28,852.12
4	December 27, 1862......................	358,413.14	356,617.50	1,795.64
5	August 18, 1863	60,904.41	53,033.30	7,871.11
6	November 28, 1863......................	4,648.77	4,648.77	....
7	February 13, 1866	155,890.36	153,150.88	2,739.48
8	July 19, 1867......................	22,556.57	22,341.60	214.97
9	September 19, 1867	*b* 274,924.44	266,282.78	8,641.66
10	November 27, 1867......................	28,259.55	28,259.55	....
11	January 2, 1868......................	51,649.28	49,757.95	1,891.33
12	May 3, 1869......................	247,558.08	204,861.01	42,697.07
13	November 29, 1869......................	39,064.71	39,032.11	32.60
14	May 4, 1870......................	13,716.94	9,267.61	4,449.33
15	February 6, 1871	2,503.28	2,450.68	52.60
15½	August 3, 1864	59,449.67	57,368.77	2,080.90
16	May 8, 1871	50,928.78	41,156.09	9,772.69
17	June 8, 1871	17,305.67	16,412.23	893.44
18	June 24, 1872	49,512.79	38,644.20	10,868.59
19	August 11, 1873	36,216.72	32,604.21	36,012.51
20	July 6, 1875	89,981.67	88,127.62	1,854.05
21	January 13, 1881	53,087.44	22,977.82	30,109.62
22	May 11, 1881	452,247.89	....	*c* 452,247.89
23	June 12, 1883	4,519.26	2,856.60	1,662.66
24	....do	19,678.68	15,594.78	4,083.90
25	September 19, 1883	30,426.72	30,321.22	105.50
26	October 25, 1886	21,809.96	....	21,809.96
27	July 26, 1890	5,779.51	2,557.70	3,221.81
28	October 2, 1890	2,531.83	2,519.33	12.50
	Total	3,974,696.14	3,325,371.56	649,324.58

MICHIGAN.

No. of claims.	Date when filed.	Amount of claim.	Amount allowed and disposed of.	Amount disallowed.
1	April —, 1862	$570,839.13	$562,945.59	$7,893.54
2	July 28, 1862	62,153.16	61,455.62	697.54
3	September 29, 1865	90,326.13	75,471.51	14,854.62
4	April 23, 1868	19,174.76	19,139.91	34.85
5	October 8, 1868	30,531.70	24,707.69	5,824.01
6	February 14, 1870	59,993.00	59,688.00	305.00
7	April 27, 1877	1,579.42	347.60	1,231.82
8	October 20, 1880	4,596.75	1,675.56	2,921.19
9	June 11, 1883	364,574.27	43,845.95	*d* 320,728.32
	Total	1,203,768.32	849,277.43	354,490.89

a Interest.   *c* $320,488.32 interest.
b Expenses Morgan raid.   *d* Interest.

Statement accompanying Third Auditor's letter of June 19, 1894, to the Secretary of the Treasury in relation to the claims of the several States, etc.—Continued.

ILLINOIS.

No. of claim.	Date when filed.	Amount of claim.	Amount allowed and disposed of.	Amount disallowed.
1	March 1, 1862	$2,901,559.58		
2	June 9, 1862	544,145.70	$3,779,187.76	$24,202.13
3	June 23, 1862	237,994.44		
4	September 2, 1862	29,750.17		
5	December 19, 1865	55,902.19	52,812.13	3,090.06
6	October 14, 1867	} 693,091.92	197,874.85	a 495,217.07
	June 14, 1869			
7	June 14, 1869	21,854.51	17,896.32	3,958.19
	Total	4,574,298.51	4,047,771.06	526,527.45

WISCONSIN.

No. of claim.	Date when filed.	Amount of claim.	Amount allowed and disposed of.	Amount disallowed.
1	February 26, 1862	$215,962.03		
2	May 19, 1862	133,245.89		
3	June 12, 1862	97,080.83		
4	....do	171,820.10		
5	July 9, 1862	253,010.08	} $1,070,890.94	$70,902.87
6	September 2, 1862	173,133.91		
7	April 28, 1863	37,246.65		
8	December 9, 1863	27,215.87		
9	April 30, 1866	33,078.45		
	Total	1,141,793.81	1,070,890.94	70,902.87

INDIANA.

No. of claim.	Date when filed.	Amount of claim.	Amount allowed and disposed of.	Amount disallowed.
1	August 2, 1861	$1,053,689.51	$950,460.54	$103,228.97
2	March 20, 1862	46,370.56	36,701.18	9,678.38
3	July 29, 1862	514,740.05	442,887.16	71,852.89
5	February 27, 1865	103,877.63	83,492.51	20,385.12
6	July 10, 1865	372,730.39	275,560.68	97,169.71
7	December 17, 1866	178,680.04	99,059.91	79,620.13
8	June 8, 1868	606,979.41		b 606,979.41
9	....do	1,331.42		1,331.42
10	November 14, 1868	125,721.80	62,399.65	63,322.15
11	October 8, 1869	c 481,178.24	474,497.10	6,681.14
	Total	3,485,308.05	2,425,058.73	1,000,249.32

No. 4 withdrawn.

MINNESOTA.

No. of claim.	Date when filed.	Amount of claim.	Amount allowed and disposed of.	Amount disallowed.
1	July 19, 1862	$17,821.16	$16,291.84	$1,529.32
2	March 18, 1863	3,938.86	3,684.99	253.87
3	July 28, 1864	3,373.15	3,373.15	
4	December 14, 1866	751.51	467.70	283.81
5	....do	3,911.14	3,761.14	150.00
6	....do	11,618.11	11,503.61	114.50
7	April 6, 1868	32,678.97	32,178.47	500.50
	Total	74,092.90	71,260.90	2,832.00

IOWA.

No. of claim.	Date when filed.	Amount of claim.	Amount allowed and disposed of.	Amount disallowed.
1	February—1862	$30,824.51	$30,824.51	
2	April 15, 1863	50,287.90	} 593,084.89	$23,654.38
3	May 21, 1863	556,451.37		
4	November 26, 1867	18,988.84	18,988.84	
5	January 7, 1869	166,574.51	157,842.10	8,732.41
6	April 24, 1869	229,848.23	229,827.39	20.84
7	December 14, 1869	27,779.42	27,493.01	286.41
8	January 10, 1874	3,759.16	3,759.16	
9	June 26, 1890	789.15	633.94	155.21
	Total	1,095,303.09	1,062,453.84	32,849.25

a $433,112.03 interest and discount.   b Interest and discount.
c Expenses Morgan raid.

Statement accompanying Third Auditor's letter of June 19, 1894, to the Secretary of the Treasury, in relation to the claims of the several States, etc.—Continued.

MISSOURI.

No. of claim.	Date when filed.	Amount of claim.	Amount allowed and disposed of.	Amount disallowed.
1	January 10, 1867	$7, 236, 978. 34	$7, 220, 827. 33	$16, 151. 01
3	December 21, 1874..............................	a 2, 382, 132. 67		
4	April 5, 1880	438, 351. 72	234, 594. 10	203, 757. 62
5	May-29, 1890...................................	996. 37	996. 37	....
	Total	10, 058, 459. 10	7, 456, 417. 80	219, 908. 63

Claim No. 2 merged into No. 4.

NEBRASKA.

2	September 7, 1868	$122. 09	....	$122. 09

No. 1, war claim for expenses in suppressing Indian hostilities in the year 1864.

KANSAS.

1	April 18, 186❷..................................	$12, 351. 04	$12, 301. 22	$49. 82
2	August 2, 1872	337, 054. 38	b 337, 054. 38	....
3	January 24, 1878	470, 726. 15	369, 926. 02	100, 800. 13
	Total	820, 131. 57	719, 281. 62	100, 849. 95

OREGON.

2	August 21, 1884	$390, 820. 10	....	c $390, 820. 10

RECAPITULATION.

State.	No. of claims.	Amount of claims filed.	Amount allowed and disposed of.	Amount suspended and disallowed.	Interest and discount.
Maine	3	$1, 331, 010. 04	$1, 027, 654. 03	$303, 356. 01	....
New Hampshire..............	9	1, 412, 591. 11	1, 011, 292. 68	401, 299. 03	....
Vermont	13	924, 735. 26	857, 845. 10	66, 890. 16	....
Massachusetts	10	4, 342, 527. 03	4, 104, 015. 02	238, 512. 01	....
Rhode Island	4	762, 611. 99	757, 403. 19	5, 208. 80	$2, 266. 35
Connecticut	11	2, 291, 135. 03	2, 160. 459. 24	130, 675. 79	41, 363. 83
New York	12	5, 183, 036. 45	4, 107, 179. 33	1, 003, 908. 64	196, 812. 26
New Jersey	17	1, 438, 381. 41	1, 398, 803. 31	36, 941. 10	....
Pennsylvania	16	3, 568, 074. 82	3, 224, 855. 71	344, 119. 11	....
Delaware...................	2	78, 185. 83	31, 988. 96	46, 196. 87	....
Maryland	4	179. 126. 49	136, 281. 64	42, 844. 85	....
Virginia....................	2	54, 112. 47	48, 469. 97	5, 642. 50	....
West Virginia	1	456, 879. 03	456, 658. 03	221. 00	....
Kentucky	15	4, 794, 715. 99	3, 521, 310. 72	1, 273. 405. 27	973, 701. 62
Ohio	29	3, 974, 696. 14	3, 325, 371. 56	649, 324. 58	452, 247. 89
Michigan	9	1, 203, 768. 32	849, 277. 43	354, 490. 89	320, 488. 32
Illinois	7	4, 574, 298. 51	4, 047, 771. 06	526, 527. 45	433, 112. 03
Wisconsin	9	1, 141, 793. 81	1, 070, 890. 94	70, 902. 87	....
Indiana	10	3, 485, 308. 05	2, 425, 058. 73	1, 060, 249. 32	606, 979. 41
Minnesota	7	74, 092. 90	71, 260. 90	2, 832. 00	....
Iowa	9	1, 095, 303. 09	1, 062, 453. 84	32, 849. 25	....
Missouri	4	10, 058, 459. 10	7, 456, 417. 80	219, 908. 63	....
Nebraska	1	122. 09	....	122. 09	....
Kansas.....................	3	820, 131. 57	719, 281. 62	100, 849. 95	....
Oregon.....................	1	390, 820. 10	....	390, 820. 10	132, 183. 29
Total....................	211	53, 636, 816. 63	43, 872, 000. 21	7, 308, 098. 27	3, 159, 155. 00

Amount of claims allowed and disposed of.. $43, 872, 000. 21
Amount of claims suspended and disallowed 7, 308, 098. 27
Amount of claims—no action... 2, 456, 718. 15

Amount of claims filed... 53, 636, 816. 63

a No authority to settle.   b Repelling raid of General price in 1864.
c Of the amount disallowed, $132,183.29 is for interest.

EXHIBIT NO. 5.

ACTS OF CONGRESS TO INDEMNIFY THE STATES FOR EXPENSES INCURRED BY THEM IN DEFENSE OF THE UNITED STATES.

[12 Stat. L., p. 255.]

AN ACT to refund and remit the duties on arms imported by States.

Be it enacted by the Senate and House of Representatives of the United States of America in Congress assembled, That the Secretary of the Treasury be, and he is hereby, authorized and directed to refund and remit the duties and imposts on all arms imported into the United States since the first day of May last, or which may be imported before the first day of January next, by or for the account of any State: *Provided,* The Secretary of the Treasury shall be satisfied that the said arms are intended in good faith for the use of the troops of any State which is, or may be, engaged in aiding to suppress the insurrection now existing against the United States.

Approved, July 10, 1861.

[12 Stat. L., p. 255.]

AN ACT to provide for the payment of the militia and volunteers called into the service of the United States from the time they were called into service to the thirtieth day of June, eighteen hundred and sixty-one.

Be it enacted by the Senate and House of Representatives of the United States of America in Congress assembled, That there be, and hereby is, appropriated, out of any money in the Treasury not otherwise appropriated, the sum of five millions seven hundred and sixty thousand dollars, or so much thereof as may be necessary, to enable the Government to pay the militia and volunteers called into service of the United States, being an additional amount required for the fiscal year ending June thirtieth, eighteen hundred and sixty-one.

Approved, July 13, 1861.

[12 Stat. L., p. 274.]

AN ACT for the relief of the Ohio and other volunteers.

Whereas the War Department has decided that the term of service of the ninety days' volunteers, called out under the act of seventeen hundred and ninety-five, commenced only on the day when they were actually sworn into the service of the United States; and whereas the troops now in service of the United States from the State of Ohio were not sworn into said service until some days after their organization and acceptance as companies by the governor of said State, and that for such period, under existing laws, no payment can be made: Therefore,

Be it enacted by the Senate and House of Representatives of the United States af America in Congress assembled, That the proper disbursing officer compute and pay to the said volunteers compensation from the day of their organization and acceptance as companies by the governor of the State of Ohio, as aforesaid, until the expiration of their term of service.

SEC. 2. *And be it further enacted,* That where the militia of other States are situated similarly with those of Ohio, the War Department pay them according to the provisions of the foregoing section.

Approved, July 24, 1861.

[12 Stat. L., p. 274.]

AN ACT to refund duties on arms imported by States.

Be it enacted by the Senate and House of Representatives of the United States of America in Congress assembled, That the Secretary of the Treasury be, and is hereby, authorized to refund, out of any money in the Treasury not otherwise appropriated, the duties paid on arms imported by States under the conditions and subject to the limitation of the act approved the tenth day of July, eighteen hundred and sixty-one, entitled "An act to refund and remit the duties on arms imported by States."

Approved, July 25, 1861.

[12 Stat. L., p. 375.]

AN ACT in addition to an act to refund and remit the duties on arms imported by States, approved July ten, eighteen hundred and sixty-one.

Be it enacted by the Senate and House of Representatives of the United States of America in Congress assembled, That the authority given to the Secretary of the Treasury to refund and remit the duties and imposts on all arms imported into the United States

66   WAR CLAIMS OF CERTAIN STATES.

by or for the account of any State as provided in the act to which this is an addition shall extend to arms for which orders or contracts were made prior to the first day of January, eighteen hundred and sixty-two: *Provided,* That said Secretary shall have satisfactory proofs exhibited to him that the said arms were actually purchased in a foreign country for account of a State, and that the price paid for the same by the State was only the first cost, and the usual and customary charges attending the purchase and importation of the same, exclusive of duty.

Approved, April 2, 1862.

[12 Stat. L., p. 264.]

[Extract from an act making additional appropriations for the support of the Army for the fiscal year ending June thirtieth, eighteen hundred and sixty-two, and so forth.]

For amount required to refund to the States expenses incurred on account of volunteers called into the field, ten million dollars.

Approved, July 17, 1861.

[12 Stat. L., p. 276.]

AN ACT to indemnify the States for expenses incurred by them in defense of the United States.

Be it enacted by the Senate and House of Representatives of the United States of America in Congress assembled, That the Secretary of the Treasury be, and he is hereby, directed, out of any money in the Treasury not otherwise appropriated, to pay to the governor of any State, or to his duly authorized agents, the costs, charges, and expenses properly incurred by such State for enrolling, subsisting, clothing, supplying, arming, equipping, paying, and transporting its troops employed in aiding to suppress the present insurrection against the United States, to be settled upon proper vouchers, to be filed and passed upon by the proper accounting officers of the Treasury.

Approved, July 27, 1861.

[12 Stat. L., p. 615.]

A RESOLUTION declaratory of the intent and meaning of a certain act therein named.

Whereas doubts have arisen as to the true intent and meaning of act numbered eighteen, entitled "An act to indemnify the States for expenses incurred by them in defence of the United States," approved July twenty-seven, eighteen hundred and sixty-one:

Be it resolved by the Senate and House of Representatives of the United States of America in Congress assembled, That the said act shall be construed to apply to expenses incurred as well after as before the date of the approval thereof.

Approved, March 8, 1862.

[12 Stat. L., p. 616.]

A RESOLUTION to authorize the Secretary of War to accept moneys appropriated by any State for the payment of its volunteers, and to apply the same as directed by such State.

Resolved by the Senate and House of Representatives of the United States of America in Congress assembled, That if any State during the present rebellion shall make any appropriation to pay the volunteers of that State, the Secretary of War is hereby authorized to accept the same, and cause it to be applied by the paymaster-general to the payments designated by the legislative act making the appropriation, in the same manner as if appropriated by act of Congress; and also to make any regulations that may be necessary for the disbursement and proper application of such funds to the specific purpose for which they may be appropriated by the several States.

Approved, March 19, 1862.

[24 Stat. L., 217.]

AN ACT for the benefit of the States of Texas, Colorado, Oregon, Nebraska, California, Kansas, and Nevada, and the Territories of Washington and Idaho, and Nevada when a Territory.

*   *   *   *   *   *   *

SEC. 2. The Secretary of War is hereby authorized to detail three Army officers to assist him in examining and reporting upon the claims of the States and Territories named in the act of June twenty-seventh, eighteen hundred and eighty-two, chapter two hundred and forty-one of the laws of the Forty-seventh Congress, and such officers, before entering upon said duties, shall take and subscribe an oath that they will carefully examine said claims, and that they will, to the best of their ability, make a just and impartial statement thereof, as required by said act.

Approved August 4, 1886.

Schedule of private acts relating to State war claims (war of 1861–1865).

State.	Date of act.	Statute and page.
Pennsylvania	Apr. 12, 1866*	14 Stat., 32.
Missouri	Apr. 17, 1866	14 Stat., 38.
West Virginia	June 21, 1866	14 Stat., 68.
Vermont	June 23, 1866	14 Stat., 361.
Iowa	July 25, 1866	14 Stat., 247.
Indiana and Ohio	Mar. 29, 1867	15 Stat., 9.
Colorado	July 25, 1868	15 Stat., 175.
Iowa	Mar. 3, 1869	15 Stat., 310.
Kentucky	June 8, 1872	17 Stat., 346.
Connecticut	do	17 Stat., 343.
Connecticut	Mar. 3, 1873	17 Stat., 605.
Delaware and Maryland	Mar. 3, 1875	18 Stat., 390.
Missouri	Jan. 27, 1879	20 Stat., 266.
Kentucky	Mar. 3, 1881	21 Stat., 513.
Massachusetts	July 7, 1884	23 Stat., 204.
Missouri	Apr. 19, 1890	26 Stat., 57.

* Examined and settled by Secretary of War.
† Included authority to examine and report upon claims of the State for raising troops to defend the State against bushwhackers and Indians.
; Expenses, "Morgan raid."

NOTE.—By act approved April 12, 1866, entitled "An act to reimburse the State of Pennsylvania for moneys advanced Government for war purposes," $800,000 was appropriated to supply a deficiency in paying the Army under the act of March 14, 1864, and to reimburse the State of Pennsylvania for money expended for payment of militia in the service of the United States.

The act approved June 20, 1878, "making appropriations for sundry civil expenses of the Government for the year ending June 30, 1879, and for other purposes," contains the following clause:

"Refunding to States expenses incurred in raising volunteers: To indemnify the States for expenses incurred by them in enrolling, equipping, and transporting troops for the defense of the United States during the late insurrection, to wit: For the State of New York, $82,736.78; for the State of Pennsylvania, $29,527.23; in all, $112,264.01."

By act approved April 17, 1866, the President was authorized, by and with the advice and consent of the Senate, to appoint three commissioners to ascertain the amount of moneys expended by the State of Missouri in enrolling, equipping, subsisting, and paying such State forces as had been called into the service in said State since 24th of August, 1861, to act in concert with the United States forces in suppressing the rebellion. Said commissioners were required to proceed, subject to regulations to be prescribed by the Secretary of War, at once to examine all items of expense made by said State for the purpose, subject to certain conditions and limitations mentioned, but no allowance was authorized to be made for any troops which did not perform actual military service in full concert and cooperation with the authorities of the United States, and subject to their orders.

By act approved June 8, 1872, the Secretary of the Treasury was directed to cause to be examined, settled, and paid any proper claims of the State of Kentucky for money expended in enrolling, equipping, subsisting, and paying State forces of Kentucky called into service in said State after August 24, 1861, to act in concert with the United States forces in suppressing the rebellion, settlement to be made upon the principles and conditions and under the limitations provided in the act of Congress approved April 17, 1866, to reimburse the State of Missouri for moneys expended for like purposes.

Special acts providing for rebellion or Indian war claims, 1861–1882, and for Indian war claims and Mexican invasion claims, 1865–1882.

States.	Date.	Volume.	Page.
California	June 27, 1882 / Aug. 4, 1886	22 U. S. Stats / 24 U. S. Stats	111 / 217
Oregon	do	24 U. S. Stats	217
Nevada	do	24 U. S. Stats	217
Texas	do	24 U. S. Stats	217
Colorado	do	24 U. S. Stats	217
Kansas	do	24 U. S. Stats	217
Nebraska	do	24 U. S. Stats	217
Washington	do	24 U. S. Stats	217

68 WAR CLAIMS OF CERTAIN STATES.

EXHIBIT No. 6.

Statement of number of men called for by the President of the United States and number furnished by each State, Territory, and District of Columbia from April 15, 1861, to close of war of the rebellion.

States, etc.	Call of April 15, 1861, for 75,000 militia for 3 months.		Call of May 3, 1861 (confirmed by act approved August 6, 1861), and under acts approved July 22 and 25, 1861, for 500,000 men.						
	Quota.	Men furnished.	Quota.	Men furnished for—					Total.
				6 months.	1 year.	2 years.	3 years.		
Maine	780	771	17,560				18,104	18,104	
New Hampshire	780	779	9,234				8,338	8,338	
Vermont	780	782	8,950				9,508	9,508	
Massachusetts	1,560	3,736	34,868				32,177	32,177	
Rhode Island	780	3,147	4,955				6,286	6,286	
Connecticut	780	2,402	13,057				10,865	10,865	
New York	13,280	13,906	109,056			30,950	89,281	120,231	
New Jersey	3,123	3,123	19,152				11,523	11,523	
Pennsylvania	12,500	20,175	82,825				85,160	85,160	
Delaware	780	775	3,145				1,825	1,826	
Maryland	3,123		15,578				9,355	9,355	
West Virginia	2,340	900	8,497				12,757	12,757	
District of Columbia		4,720	1,627				1,795	1,795	
Ohio	10,153	12,357	67,365		863		83,253	84,116	
Indiana	4,683	4,686	38,832		1,698		59,643	61,341	
Illinois	4,688	4,820	47,785				81,952	81,952	
Michigan	780	781	21,357				23,546	23,546	
Wisconsin	780	817	21,753				25,499	25,499	
Minnesota	780	930	4,899		1,167		5,770	6,937	
Iowa	780	968	19,316				21,987	21,987	
Missouri	3,123	10,591	31,544	2,715	199		22,324	25,238	
Kentucky	3,123		27,237		5,129		29,966	35,095	
Kansas		650	3,235				6,953	6,953	
Tennessee	1,560								
Arkansas	780								
North Carolina	1,560								
Nebraska					91			91	
Total	71,391	91,816	611,827	2,715	9,147	30,950	657,868	700,680	

State, etc.	Men furnished in May and June, 1862, by special authority, for 3 months (no quotas).	Call of July 2, 1862, for 300,000 men for 3 years.		Call of August 4, 1862, for 300,000 militia for 9 months.		Men furnished under President's proclamation of June 15, 1863, for militia for 6 months (no quotas).
		Quota.	Men furnished.	Quota.	Men furnished.	
Maine		9,609	6,644	9,609	7,620	
New Hampshire		5,053	6,390	5,053	1,736	
Vermont		4,898	4,369	4,898	4,781	
Massachusetts		19,080	16,519	19,080	16,685	103
Rhode Island		2,712	2,742	2,712	2,059	
Connecticut		7,145	9,195	7,145	5,602	
New York	8,588	59,705	78,904	59,705	1,781	
New Jersey		10,478	5,499	10,478	10,787	
Pennsylvania		45,321	30,891	45,321	32,215	3,708
Delaware		1,720	2,508	1,720	1,799	
Maryland		8,532	3,586	8,532		1,615
West Virginia		4,650	4,925	4,650		1,148
District of Columbia		890	1,167	890		
Ohio		36,858	58,325	36,858		2,736
Indiana	1,723	21,250	30,359	21,250	337	3,767
Illinois	4,696	26,148	58,689	26,148		
Michigan		11,686	17,656	11,686		
Wisconsin		11,904	14,472	11,904	958	
Minnesota		2,681	4,626	2,681		
Iowa		10,570	24,438	10,570		
Missouri		17,269	28,324	17,269		a 3,284
Kentucky		14,905	6,463	14,905		
Kansas		1,771	2,936	1,771		
Nebraska			1,838	1,228		
Total	15,007	334,835	421,465	334,835	87,588	16,331

a Furnished in November, 1864.

Statement of number of men called for by the President of the United States and number furnished by each State, etc.—Continued.

State, etc.	Calls of October 17, 1863 (which embraces men raised by draft of 1863, and February 1, 1864, for 500,000 men for 3 years.				Call of March 14, 1864, for 200,000 men for 3 years.			
	Quota.	Men furnished.	Paid commutation.	Total.	Quota.	Men furnished.	Paid commutation.	Total.
Maine	11,803	11,958	1,986	13,944	4,721	7,042	....	7,042
New Hampshire	6,469	6,406	571	6,977	2,588	2,844	121	2,965
Vermont	5,751	6,726	1,885	8,611	2,300	1,601	89	1,690
Massachusetts	26,597	17,711	3,703	21,414	10,039	17,322	1,615	18,937
Rhode Island	3,469	3,223	463	3,686	1,388	1,906	....	1,906
Connecticut	7,919	10,326	1,513	11,839	3,168	5,294	....	5,294
New York	81,993	59,839	15,912	75,751	32,794	41,940	2,267	44,207
New Jersey	16,759	9,187	....	9,187	6,704	9,550	4,170	13,720
Pennsylvania	64,979	36,723	17,672	54,305	25,993	35,036	10,046	45,082
Delaware	2,463	2,138	435	2,573	985	652	951	1,603
Maryland	10,794	6,244	1,106	7,350	4,317	9,365	2,528	11,903
West Virginia	5,127	3,988	....	3,988	2,051	3,857	....	3,857
District of Columbia	4,256	4,570	318	4,888	1,702	1,142	....	1,142
Ohio	51,465	32,809	....	32,809	20,595	31,193	6,290	37,483
Indiana	32,521	23,023	....	23,023	13,008	14,862	....	14,862
Illinois	46,309	28,818	....	28,818	18,524	25,055	....	25,055
Michigan	19,553	17,686	1,644	19,330	7,821	7,344	323	7,667
Wisconsin	19,852	10,389	5,080	15,469	7,941	10,314	....	10,314
Minnesota	5,451	3,054	....	3,054	2,180	2,469	1,027	3,496
Iowa	16,097	8,292	....	8,292	6,439	11,579	....	11,579
Missouri	9,813	3,823	....	3,823	3,925	a10,137	....	10,137
Kentucky	14,471	4,785	....	4,785	5,789	6,488	3,241	9,689
Kansas	3,523	5,374	....	5,374	1,409	2,563	....	2,563
Total	467,434	317,092	52,288	369,380	186,981	259,515	32,678	292,193

State, etc.	Militia for 100 days, mustered into service between April 23 and July 18, 1864.		Call of July 18, 1864, for 500,000 men (reduced by excess of credits on previous calls).						
	Quota.	Men furnished.	Quota.	Men furnished for—					Total.
				1 year.	2 years.	3 years.	4 years.	Paid commutation.	
Maine	....	....	11,116	8,320	131	2,590	1	11	11,053
New Hampshire	....	b 167	4,648	1,921	25	4,027	....	....	5,973
Vermont	....	....	2,665	1,861	18	2,081	11	....	3,971
Massachusetts	4,000	6,809	21,965	6,990	108	24,641	....	....	31,739
Rhode Island	....	....	1,423	1,223	196	891	....	....	2,310
Connecticut	....	....	5,583	493	20	10,318	24	2	10,857
New York	12,000	5,640	77,539	45,089	2,128	36,547	74	5	83,843
New Jersey	....	769	14,431	9,587	1,184	4,337	....	11	15,119
Pennsylvania	12,000	7,675	49,993	44,489	433	10,416	198	171	55,707
Delaware	....	....	2,184	1,558	9	593	15	....	2,175
Maryland	....	1,207	10,947	6,198	246	3,727	64	31	10,266
West Virginia	....	....	2,717	1,726	28	202	....	....	1,956
District of Columbia	....	....	2,386	979	59	937	343	19	2,337
Ohio	30,000	36,254	27,001	25,431	748	4,644	....	176	30,999
Indiana	20,000	7,197	25,662	18,099	597	7,158	....	690	26,544
Illinois	20,000	11,328	21,997	12,558	535	2,323	....	49	15,465
Michigan	....	....	12,098	5,960	57	6,492	....	23	12,532
Wisconsin	5,000	2,134	17,590	10,905	86	5,832	....	16	16,839
Minnesota	....	....	4,018	2,701	205	239	....	3	3,238
Iowa	10,000	3,901	5,749	3,995	60	168	....	67	4,290
Missouri	....	....	25,569	7,782	1,205	14,430	....	....	23,507
Kentucky	....	....	9,871	5,060	169	10,137	....	24	15,390
Kansas	....	441	....	29	3	319	....	....	351
Total	113,000	83,612	357,152	223,044	8,340	153,049	730	1,208	386,461

a Includes militia furnished for six months 5,679; for nine months, 2,811; for one year, 1,954—credited as 2,174 three-years' men.
b Furnished for three months.

Statement of number of men called for by the President of the United States and number furnished by each State, etc.—Continued.

States, etc.	Quota.	Call of December 19, 1864, for 300,000 men.					
		Men furnished for—					Total.
		1 year.	2 years.	3 years.	4 years.	Paid commutation.	
Maine	8,389	4,898	141	1,884	3	10	6,936
New Hampshire	2,072	492	9	775	28		1,304
Vermont	1,832	902	29	550	9		1,550
Massachusetts	1,306	1,535	43	2,349	2		3,929
Rhode Island	1,459	739	92	732			1,563
Connecticut		34	7	1,282	2		1,325
New York	61,076	9,150	1,645	23,321	67	13	34,196
New Jersey	11,605	6,511	1,075	3,527	155	15	11,283
Pennsylvania	46,437	26,666	204	3,903	44	282	31,099
Delaware	968	376	5	30			411
Maryland	9,142	3,236	430	1,275		3	4,944
West Virginia	4,431	2,114	8	415			2,537
District of Columbia	2,222	692	12	116	2	1	823
Ohio	26,027	21,712	641	2,214		13	24,580
Indiana	22,582	20,642	243	2,329		94	23,308
Illinois	32,902	25,940	356	2,022		6	28,324
Michigan	10,026	6,767	41	1,034		18	7,860
Wisconsin	12,356	9,666	15	240		1	9,922
Minnesota	3,636	2,689	12	68		2	2,771
Iowa		772	15	67			854
Missouri	13,984	3,161	44	1,002			4,207
Kentucky	10,481	1,987	7	5,609			7,603
Kansas	1,222	622	36	223		2	883
Total	284,215	151,363	5,110	54,967	312	460	212,212

States, etc.	60 days.	3 months.	100 days.	4 months.	6 months.	8 months.	1 year.	3 years.	Total.
	Volunteers and militia furnished at various times for—								
Tennessee			739				6,039	24,314	31,092
Arkansas					374		213	7,702	8,289
North Carolina								3,156	3,156
California								15,725	15,725
Nevada								1,080	1,080
Oregon				42				1,768	1,810
Washington								964	964
Colorado			1,156		186			3,561	4,903
Dakota								206	206
New Mexico			1,593		803			4,165	6,561
Alabama							1,447	1,129	2,576
Florida								1,290	1,290
Louisiana		296				373		4,555	5,224
Mississippi								545	545
Texas							499	1,466	1,965
Indian Nation								3,530	3,530
Colored troops a	1,749							91,692	93,441
Total	2,045	1,593	1,895	42	1,363	373	8,198	166,848	182,357

a Colored troops organized at various stations in the States in rebellion, embracing all not specifically credited to States, and which can not be so assigned.

Statement of number of men called for by the President of the United States and number furnished by each State, etc.—Continued.

States, etc.	Aggregate.				Aggregate reduced to a three-years' standard.
	Quota.	Men furnished.	Paid commutation.	Total.	
Maine	73,587	70,107	2,007	72,114	56,776
New Hampshire	35,897	33,937	692	34,629	30,849
Vermont	32,074	33,288	1,974	35,262	29,068
Massachusetts	139,095	146,730	5,318	152,048	124,104
Rhode Island	18,898	23,236	463	23,699	17,866
Connecticut	44,757	55,864	1,515	57,379	50,623
New York	507,148	448,850	18,197	467,047	392,270
New Jersey	92,820	76,814	4,196	81,010	57,908
Pennsylvania	385,369	337,936	28,171	366,107	265,517
Delaware	13,935	12,284	1,386	13,670	10,322
Maryland	70,965	46,638	3,678	50,316	41,275
West Virginia	34,463	32,068		32,068	27,714
District of Columbia	13,973	16,534	338	16,872	11,506
Ohio	306,322	313,180	6,479	319,659	240,514
Indiana	199,788	196,363	784	197,147	153,576
Illinois	244,496	259,092	55	259,147	214,133
Michigan	95,007	87,364	2,008	89,372	80,111
Wisconsin	109,080	91,327	5,097	96,424	79,260
Minnesota	26,326	24,020	1,032	25,052	19,693
Iowa	79,521	76,242	67	76,309	68,630
Missouri	122,496	109,111		109,111	86,530
Kentucky	103,782	75,760	3,265	79,025	70,832
Kansas	12,931	20,149	2	20,151	18,706
Tennessee	1,560	31,092		31,092	26,394
Arkansas	780	8,289		8,289	7,836
North Carolina	1,560	3,156		3,156	3,156
California		15,725		15,725	15,725
Nevada		1,080		1,080	1,080
Oregon		1,810		1,810	1,673
Washington		964		964	964
Nebraska		3,157		3,157	2,175
Colorado		4,903		4,903	3,697
Dakota		206		206	206
New Mexico		6,561		6,561	4,432
Alabama		2,576		2,576	1,611
Florida		1,290		1,290	1,290
Louisiana		5,224		5,224	4,654
Mississippi		545		545	545
Texas		1,965		1,965	1,632
Indian Nation		3,530		3,530	3,350
Colored troops *a*		93,441		93,441	91,789
Total	2,763,670	2,772,408	86,724	2,859,132	2,320,272

a Colored troops organized at various stations in the States in rebellion, embracing all not specifically credited to States, and which can not be so assigned.

[Decision of the Second Comptroller.]

NOTE.—Claims of States for interest, etc.

The Second Comptroller of the Treasury in 1869 made the following decision: Interest can in no case be allowed by the accounting officer upon claims against the Government either in favor of a State or an individual. But in cases where the claimant has been compelled to pay interest for the benefit of the Government it then becomes a part of the principal of his claim, and as such is allowable. Such is the case of a State which has been obliged to raise money upon interest for the suppression of hostilities against which the United States should protect her. In such cases the amount of interest actually and necessarily paid will be allowed, without reference to the rate of it. (Section 997, Dec. 2 Comp., ed. 1869, p. 137.)

EXHIBIT No. 7.

[Supreme Court of the United States. Nos. 45 and 136. October term, 1895. The United States, appellant, v. The State of New York, No. 45. The State of New York, appellant, v. The United States, No. 136. Appeals from the Court of Claims. December 6, 1895.]

Mr. Justice HARLAN delivered the opinion of the court.

On the 3d day of January, 1889, the Secretary of the Treasury transmitted to the Court of Claims all the papers and vouchers relating to a claim of the State of New York against the United States then pending in the Treasury Department, for interest paid on money borrowed and expended in enrolling, subsisting, clothing, supplying, arming, and equipping troops for the suppression of the rebellion of 1861. That claim, the Secretary certified, involved controverted questions of law and exceeded $3,000 in amonnt. The communication accompanying the papers stated that the case was transmitted to the Court of Claims under and by authority of section 1063 of the Revised Statutes, to be there proceeded in according to law.

In further prosecution of this claim the State promptly filed its petition in the court below, and asked judgment against the United States for the sum of $131,188,02, with interest from the 1st day of July, 1862, together with such other relief as would be in conformity with law.

This claim was based on the act of Congress of July 27, 1861, c. 21, providing that "the Secretary of the Treasury be, and he is hereby, directed, out of any money in the Treasury not otherwise appropriated, to pay to the governor of any State, or to his duly authorized agents, the costs, charges, and expenses properly incurred by such State for enrolling, subsisting, clothing, supplying, arming, equipping, paying, and transporting its troops employed in aiding to suppress the present insurrection against the United States, to be settled upon proper vouchers to be filed and passed upon by the proper accounting officers of the Treasury." (12 Stat., 276.)

By a joint resolution of Congress, approved March 8, 1862, it was declared that the above act should be construed "to apply to expenses incurred as well after as before the date of the approval thereof." (12 Stat., 615.)

Before July 4, 1861, the State of New York, pursuant to a statute passed by its legislature April 15, 1861, c. 277, enlisted, enrolled, armed, equipped, and caused to be mustered into the military service of the United States for the period of two years or during the war thirty thousand troops, to be employed in suppressing the rebellion. That statute provided that all expenditures for arms, supplies, or equipments necessary for such forces should be made under the direction of the governor and other named officers, and that the moneys therefor should, on the certificate of the governor, be drawn from the treasury, on the warrant of the comptroller, in favor of such person or persons as from time to time were designated by the governor; and the sum of $3,000,000, or so much thereof as was necessary, was appropriated out of any moneys in the treasury not otherwise appropriated to defray the expenses authorized by that act, or any other expenses of mustering the militia of the State, or any part thereof, into the service of the United States. That act also imposed, for the fiscal year commencing on the 1st day of October, 1861, a State tax to meet the expenses authorized, not to exceed 2 mills on each dollar of the valuation of real and personal property in the State. (Laws of New York. eighty-fourth session, 1861, p. 634.)

There was no money in the treasury of the State in 1861 that had not been specifically appropriated for the expenses of the State government; none that could have been used to defray the expenses of enlisting, enrolling, arming, equipping, and mustering troops into the service of the United States.

Under the laws of the State the moneys authorized to be raised by the act of April 15, 1861, did not reach the State treasury and were not available for use until the months of April and May, 1862.

The total State tax rate fixed at the session of the legislature beginning on the first Tuesday in January, 1861, was 3½ mills, of which 1½ mills was the amount authorized by the above statute of 1861. The moneys realized from this tax were paid into the State treasury during the year 1862.

The State had no other means of raising the money required for the purpose of immediately defraying the expenses of enlisting, enrolling, arming, equipping, and mustering in such troops, except by borrowing money in anticipation of the collection of its taxes; and between June 3, 1861, and July 2, 1861, in order to provide for the public defense, it issued bonds in anticipation of such taxes to the amount of $1,250,000, payable on July 1, 1862, except that $100,000 was made payable June 1, 1862, at the rate of 7 per cent per annum, which at that time was the legal rate of interest under the laws of the State.

The issuing of these bonds was necessary for the purpose of providing the money required, and upon their sale the full amount of their face value was received and was used and applied by the State, together with other moneys, in raising troops. The entire sum so expended between the 23d day of April, 1861, and the 1st day of January, 1862, was $2,873,501.19, exclusive of interest upon the bonds or loans made by the State for that purpose.

In addition to the above sums, the State, during the years 1861 and 1862, paid, on account of interest that accrued on its bonds issued in anticipation of the tax for the public defense, the sum of $91,320.84.

By a statute of New York of April 12, 1862, the legislature specifically appropriated the sum of $1,250,000 for the redemption of comptroller's bonds, issued for loans in anticipation of the tax imposed by the act of April 15, 1861, and the additional sum of $91,320.84 for the payment of the accruing interest on those bonds. (Laws of N. Y., 1862, eighty-fifth session, c. 192, p. 364.)

Of the remainder of the above sum of $2,873,501.19 necessarily expended by the State of New York for the purpose stated, between April 23, 1861, and January 1, 1862, after deducting the amount of $1,250,000 raised by issuing bonds, $1,623,501.19

was taken from the canal fund of the State. That fund, under the constitution of the State, was a sinking fund for the ultimate payment of what is known as the canal debt. (Const. N. Y., 1846, art. 7, sec. 1.)

Under the tax rate of 1860 there had been levied and collected and paid into the treasury of the State the sum of $2,039,663.06 for the benefit of and to the credit of the canal fund. That sum reached the State treasury in April and May 1861, subject to be invested by the State officers pursuant to the requirements of law and the constitution of the State, in securities for the benefit of the canal fund. On May 21, 1861, the lieutenant-governor, comptroller, treasurer, and the attorney-general, constituting the commissioners of the canal fund, authorized the comptroller to use $2,000,000 of the canal fund moneys for military purposes until the 1st of October next, and $1,000,000 until the 1st day of January, 1862, at 5 per cent; and of this amount the sum of $1,623,501.19 was used by the comptroller for the purpose of defraying the expenses of raising and equipping such troops. The following was the order:

"STATE OF NEW YORK, CANAL DEPARTMENT,
"*Albany, May 21, 1861.*

"The comptroller is to be permitted to use $2,000,000 of the canal fund moneys for military purposes until the 1st day of October next, when the commissioners of the canal fund will invest $1,000,000 of the canal sinking fund under section 1, article 7, in the tax levied for military purposes until the 1st of July, 1862, at 5 per cent, and the comptroller may use $1,000,000 of the tax levied to pay interest on the $12,000,000 debt until the 1st of January, 1862, when the commissioners will, if they have the means, replace that or as large an amount as they may have the means to do it with from the toll of the next fiscal year, so as that the whole advance from the canal fund on account of the tax be $2,000,000. It is understood the comptroller will retain the taxes now in process of collection for canal purposes until the above investments are made, paying the funds 5 per cent interest therefor."

This order was signed by the commissioners of the canal fund.

On December 28, 29, and 31, 1861, the United States repaid to the State, on account of moneys so expended by the latter, the sum of $1,113,000, which sum with interest was placed in the canal fund on April 4, 1862. This left $510,501.19 unpaid of the moneys used from the canal fund.

The amount of interest at 5 per cent per annum on the moneys of the canal fund during the time it was used by the State in raising troops was $48,187.13. But during the same time the State had received interest on portions of those moneys, while it was lying in bank unused, to the amount of $8,319.95, and the net deficiency of the State on account of interest on such moneys during the period when they were so used was $39,867.18, which sum was paid into the canal fund from the State treasury.

The total amount paid by the State for interest upon its bonds issued in anticipation of the tax for the public defense, and upon the moneys of the canal fund used for the purpose of defraying the expenses of raising and equipping troops, was $131,188.02. No part of that sum has been paid by the United States.

The moneys above specified as actually expended by the State of New York were necessarily expended for the purpose of enlisting, enrolling, subsisting, clothing, supplying, arming, equipping, paying, and transporting such troops and causing them to be mustered into the military service of the United States, and were so paid and expended at the request of the civil and military authorities of the United States.

Prior to January 3, 1889, the State had presented, from time to time, various claims and accounts to the Treasury Department of the United States for charges and expenses incurred by it in enlisting, enrolling, arming, equipping, and mustering troops into the military service of the United States. Those claims amounted in the aggregate to $2,950,479.46, and included charges for all the moneys paid and placed as hereinbefore specified. The Department, from time to time, allowed thereon various sums, aggregating $2,775,915.24, leaving a balance of $174,564.22 not allowed, and the claims for which were pending in the Department unadjusted when this case was transmitted to the Court of Claims on the 3d day of January, 1889. Of that sum of $174,564.22 the sums hereinbefore specified, amounting to $131,188.02, constituted a part.

The claim of the State for expenditures in furnishing troops with clothing and munitions of war was filed in the Treasury Department in May, 1862, and included the above items of interest. The claim for interest has from that time been suspended in the Department, and was so suspended at the time it was transmitted to the Court of Claims.

The court, after finding the facts substantially as above stated, gave judgment in favor of the State for $91,320.84, on account of interest paid upon its bonds issued in anticipation of taxes imposed for the public defense. From that judgment the United States appealed. The State also appealed, and claims that it was entitled to judgment for the additional sum of $39,867.13 paid into what is called the canal fund, as interest upon the moneys it had borrowed from that fund to be repaid with interest.

The Government has moved to dismiss the State's appeal, its contention being that the judgment brought here by the State for review is not obligatory in character and appealable, but only ancillary and advisory. This motion assumes that the court below was without jurisdiction under existing legislative enactments to render a final judgment, reviewable by this court, upon any claim, whatever its amount, made against an Executive Department and transmitted to the Court of Claims to be there proceeded in according to law.

We recognize the importance of the question thus presented, and have bestowed upon it the most careful consideration. Its solution can be satisfactorily reached only by an examination of the various statutes regulating the jurisdiction of the Court of Claims, including those known as the Bowman Act of March 3, 1883 (c. 116, 22 Stat., 485), and the Tucker Act of March 3, 1887 (c. 359, 24 Stat., 505).

By the act of Congress of July 27, 1861 (c. 21), the Secretary of the Treasury was directed, out of any money in the Treasury not otherwise appropriated, and upon vouchers to be passed upon by the accounting officers of that Department, to pay the costs, charges, and expenses properly incurred by any State in enrolling, subsisting, clothing, supplying, arming, equipping, paying, and transporting its troops to be employed in suppressing the rebellion of 1861. (12 Stat., 276.)

The claim of New York was founded on the above act of Congress of July 27, 1861, if not on contract with the United States. It was transmitted by the Secretary of the Treasury to the Court of Claims under section 1063 of the Revised Statutes as one involving controverted questions of law.

By the act of June 25, 1868 (c. 71, sec. 7), the jurisdiction of the Court of Claims was enlarged so as to embrace several classes of claims that might be transmitted to it by the head of an Executive Department for adjudication. (15 Stat., 75, 76.)

The provisions of that act were preserved in section 1063 of the Revised Statutes, which is as follows:

"SEC. 1063. Whenever any claim is made against any Executive Department, involving disputed facts or controverted questions of law, where the amount in controversy exceeds three thousand dollars, or where the decision will affect a class of cases, or furnish a precedent for the future action of any Executive Department in the adjustment of a class of cases, without regard to the amount involved in the particular case, or where any authority, right, privilege, or exemption is claimed or denied under the Constitution of the United States, the head of such Department may cause such claim, with all the vouchers, papers, proofs, and documents pertaining thereto, to be transmitted to the Court of Claims, and the same shall be there proceeded in as if originally commenced by the voluntary action of the claimant; and the Secretary of the Treasury may, upon the certificate of any Auditor or Comptroller of the Treasury, direct any account, matter, or claim, of the character, amount, or class described in this section, to be transmitted, with all the vouchers, papers, documents, and proofs pertaining thereto, to the said court, for trial and adjudication: Provided, That no case shall be referred by any head of a Department unless it belongs to one of the several classes of cases which, by reason of the subject-matter and character, the said court might, under existing laws, take jurisdiction of on such voluntary action of the claimant."

It is clear that under this section no claim against an Executive Department, not otherwise described than as one "involving disputed facts or controverted questions of law," could be transmitted to the Court of Claims for adjudication unless the amount in controversy exceeded $3,000. It is equally clear that that section did not make the amount jurisdictional where a claim of that class is transmitted as one the decision of which would affect a class of cases, or furnish a precedent for the action of the Executive Department in adjusting a class of cases, nor where any authority, right, privilege, or exemption was claimed or denied under the Constitution of the United States. But, as bearing on the inquiry to be presently made whether that section was superseded by subsequent enactments, it should be here noted that there might be claims in the hands of an Auditor or of the Comptroller of the Treasury for examination, which in the first instance were to be passed on by some other Department than that of the Treasury.

Claims of that special class could not be transmitted by the Secretary of the Treasury to the Court of Claims, under section 1063 of the Revised Statutes, for adjudication, except "upon the certificate of the Auditor or Comptroller of the Treasury," having it under examination. This is indicated not only by the words of that section, but by sections 1064 and 1065, the first of which sections provides that "all cases transmitted by the head of any Department, or upon the certificate of any Auditor or Comptroller, according to the provisions of the preceding section, shall be proceeded in as other cases pending in the Court of Claims, and shall, in all respects, be subject to the same rules and regulations;" and the latter, that "the amount of any final judgment or decree rendered in favor of the claimant, in any case transmitted to the Court of Claims under the two preceding sections, shall be paid out of any specific appropriation applicable to the case, if any such there be;

and where no such appropriation exists, the judgment or decree shall be paid in the same manner as other judgments of the said court."

We come now to what is known as the Bowman Act, of March 3, 1883 (c. 116), entitled "An act to afford assistance and relief to Congress and the Executive Departments in the investigation of claims and demands against the Government." (22 Stat., 485.)

By the first section of that act it is provided:

"SECTION 1. Whenever a claim or matter is pending before any committee of the Senate or House of Representatives, or before either House of Congress, which involves the investigation and determination of facts, the committee or House may cause the same, with the vouchers, papers, proofs, and documents pertaining thereto, to be transmitted to the Court of Claims of the United States, and the same shall there be proceeded in under such rules as the court may adopt. When the facts shall have been found, the court shall not enter judgment thereon, but shall report the same to the committee or to the House by which the case was transmitted for its consideration."

The second section is in these words:

"SEC. 2. When a claim or matter is pending in any of the Executive Departments which may involve controverted questions of fact or law, the head of such Department may transmit the same, with the vouchers, papers, proofs, and documents pertaining thereto, to said court, and the same shall be there proceeded in under such rules as the court may adopt. When the facts and conclusions of law shall have been found, the court shall not enter judgment thereon, but shall report its findings and opinions to the Department by which it was transmitted for its guidance and action."

As the Bowman Act contains no words of express repeal, the question arises whether, by necessary implication, its second section superseded section 1063 of the Revised Statutes, in respect of claims transmitted by an Executive Department to the Court of Claims.

The Court of Claims was required by section 1063 of the Revised Statutes to adjudicate any claim properly transmitted from an Executive Department by a final judgment, while the Bowman Act prohibited any judgment being entered for or against a claim transmitted under that act; the duty of the court in cases involving controverted questions of fact or law transmitted to and heard by it under the Bowman Act being only to report its findings of fact and conclusions of law to the proper Department for "its guidance and action."

It is, nevertheless, suggested that the Bowman Act, although without words of repeal, covers the entire subject of claims involving controverted questions of fact or law that may be transmitted to the Court of Claims from an Executive Department, and it is argued that we must apply the rule that a prior statute is to be regarded as repealed or modified where "the last statute is so broad in its terms and so clear and explicit in its words as to show that it was intended to cover the whole subject, and, therefore, to displace the prior statute." (Frost v. Wenie, 157 U. S., 46, 58.)

If that act be held to have displaced the whole of section 1063 of the Revised Statutes (except the clause relating to claims transmitted by the Secretary of the Treasury upon the certificate of an Auditor or of the Comptroller of the Treasury), the result would be that after its passage the Court of Claims was wholly without jurisdiction to render judgment on any claim for money transmitted from an Executive Department, whatever its nature or amount. Such a construction would exclude from judicial cognizance by that court not only claims exceeding $3,000 in amount, and specifically designated as claims involving controverted questions of law and fact, but even claims the determination of which would affect a class of cases, or furnish a precedent for the future action of an Executive Department, and claims that involved an authority, right, privilege, or exemption asserted or denied under the Constitution of the United States. Congress, when it passed the Bowman Act, must have had in view the provisions of section 1063 of the Revised Statutes under which the Court of Claims had so long exercised jurisdiction of claims for money made against an Executive Department and transmitted to that court for final adjudication.

As the Bowman Act makes no reference to that section, and contains no words of repeal, we can not suppose that Congress intended to take from the Court of Claims jurisdiction to render judgment in cases coming before it under the Revised Statutes. The object of that act is expressed in its title, and was to afford assistance and relief to Congress and the Executive Departments in the *investigation* of claims and demands against the Government. To that end, and in respect of claims and demands involving controverted questions of fact or law and pending in the Executive Departments, authority was given to the heads of such Departments upon their own motion, and whether the claimant desired it or not, to obtain, for their "guidance and action," findings of fact and conclusions of law, without regard to the amount involved. (Billings v. United States, 23 Ct. Cl., 166, 174.) Neither expressly nor by necessary implication did that act take from an Executive Department the right to send to the Court of Claims, for *final adjudication*, any claim made against it that was embraced by section 1063 of the Revised Statutes. So far as the Bowman Act related to claims for money pending in an Executive Department, it only authorized the head of the Department to send them to that court for a report of facts and conclusions that would not have the force of a judgment reviewable by this court. In this view there is no conflict between the Bowman Act and the Revised Statutes. As there are no words of repeal in the Bowman Act, we have given it such construction as will make it consistent with previous legislation, and thus avoid the abrogation of existing statutes which Congress had not repealed either expressly or by necessary implication. The second section of the Bowman Act should be construed as if it were a proviso to section 1063 of the Revised Statutes. Thus construed the later statute is not in conflict with the earlier one. •

We turn now to the act of March 3, 1887 (c. 359), known as the Tucker Act, entitled "An act to provide for the bringing of suits against the Government of the United States." (24 Stat., 505.)

The first section of that act gives the Court of Claims original jurisdiction to hear and determine all claims founded upon the Constitution of the United States or any law of Congress, except for pensions, or upon any regulation of an Executive Department, or upon any contract, expressed or implied, with the Government of the United States, or for damages, liquidated or unliquidated, in cases not sounding in tort, in respect of which claims the party would be entitled to redress against the United States either in a court of law, equity, or admiralty if the United States were suable; nothing, however, in that section to be construed as giving to any of the courts mentioned in the act jurisdiction to hear and determine claims growing out of the late civil war and commonly known as "war claims," nor other claims theretofore rejected or reported on adversely by any court, Department, or commission authorized to hear and determine the same. Jurisdiction was also given of all set-offs, counterclaims, claims for damages, whether liquidated or unliquidated, or other demands whatsoever on the part of the Government of the United States against any claimant. It also provided that no suit against the Government of the United States should be allowed under that act unless the same was brought within six years after the right accrued for which the claim is made.

Other sections of that act are as follows:

"SEC. 12. That when any claim or matter may be pending in any of the Executive Departments which involves controverted questions of fact or law, the head of such Department, *with the consent of the claimant*, may transmit the same, with the vouchers, papers, proofs, and documents pertaining thereto, to said Court of Claims, and the same shall be there proceeded in under such rules as the court may adopt. When the facts and conclusions of law shall have been found, the court shall report its findings to the Department by which it was transmitted.

"SEC. 13. That in every case which shall come before the Court of Claims, or is now pending therein, under the provisions of an act entitled 'An act to afford assistance and relief to Congress and the Executive Departments in the investigation of claims and demands against the Government,' approved March third eighteen hundred and eighty-three [the Bowman Act], if it shall appear to the satisfaction of the court, upon the facts established, that it has jurisdiction to render judgment or decree thereon under existing laws or under the provisions of this act, it shall proceed to do so, giving to either party such further opportunity for hearing as in its judgment justice shall require, and report its proceedings therein to either House of Congress or to the Department by which the same was referred to said court." By its sixteenth section all laws and parts of laws inconsistent with that act were repealed.

What is the scope of the twelfth section of the Tucker Act? Did that section supersede section 1063 of the Revised Statutes, or section 2 of the Bowman Act?

It is difficult to tell what was intended by the words "with the consent of the claimant," in the twelfth section of the Tucker Act. If Congress intended that no claim, large or small in amount, involving controverted questions of fact or law, and pending in an Executive Department, should be transmitted to the Court of Claims, except with the consent of claimant, that intention would have been expressed in words that could not have been misunderstood; for that court had long exercised jurisdiction in cases of that kind. But in view of the words used, no such purpose can be imputed to Congress. The Tucker Act can not be held to have taken the place of section 2 of the Bowman Act; for section 13 of the Tucker Act distinctly provides for *judgment in every case* then pending in or which might come before the Court of Claims *under the Bowman Act*, of which that court could have taken judicial cognizance if the case had been commenced originally by suit instituted in that court by the claimant.

That Congress did not intend to supersede the Bowman Act is made still more apparent by the fourteenth section of the Tucker Act, declaring "that whenever any bill, except for a pension, shall be pending in either House of Congress providing for the payment of a claim against the United States, legal or equitable, or for a grant, gift, or bounty to any person, the House in which such bill is pending may refer the same to the Court of Claims, who shall proceed with the same in *accordance with the provisions of the act* approved March third, eighteen hundred and eighty-three, entitled 'An act to afford assistance and relief to Congress and the Executive Departments in the investigation of claims and demands against the Government,' [the Bowman Act] and report to such House the facts in the case and the amount, where the same can be liquidated, etc." It thus appears that any bill, except for a pension, in either House of Congress, providing for the payment of a claim against the United States, legal or equitable, or for a grant, gift, or bounty to any person, may be transmitted to the Court of Claims, to be proceeded in, not, let it be observed, under the Tucker Act, but under the Bowman Act of March 3. 1883, and to report the facts, etc., to such House. It is impossible therefore to hold that the Tucker Act displaced or repealed the second section of the Bowman Act.

In our opinion the twelfth section of the Tucker Act should be construed as not referring to claims which an Executive Department is entitled, under section 1063 of the Revised Statutes, to have finally adjudicated by the Court of Claims, nor to claims described in that section, in respect of which the Department, upon its own motion, and whether the claimant consents or not, desires from that court a report, under the Bowman Act, of facts and law for its guidance and action. It refers only to claims which the head of an Executive Department, with the expressed consent of the claimant, may send to the Court of Claims in order to obtain a report of facts and law which the Department may regard as only advisory. It no doubt often happened that the head of a Department did not desire action by the Court of Claims in relation to a particular claim, but, in order to meet the wishes of the claimant, was willing to have a finding by that court which was not followed by a judgment, nor by any report for the guidance and action of the Department. So that section 1063 of the Revised Statutes, the second section of the Bowman Act, and the twelfth section of the Tucker Act may be regarded as parts of one general system, covering different states of case, and standing together without conflict in any essential particular.

The claim of New York, being for money and founded on an act of Congress, was within the general jurisdiction of the Court of Claims. If not barred by limitation it could, in the discretion of the Secretary of the Treasury, have been transmitted or certified to the Court of Claims under the Bowman Act after its passage for a finding of facts or law, and that court, when the Tucker Act came into operation, could, under its thirteenth section, have rendered a final judgment, sending, however, to the Treasury Department a report of its proceedings; but the Secretary of the Treasury, in the exercise of an authority given him by statute and never withdrawn, chose to certify or transmit this claim to the Court of Claims under section 1063 of the Revised Statutes for final adjudication.

Touching the suggestion that the twelfth section of the Tucker Act entirely superseded the second section of the Bowman Act, it may be further observed that the Tucker Act repeals only such previous statutes as were inconsistent with its provisions. There is no inconsistency between the sections just named; one, as we have said, the second section of the Bowman Act, relating to claims involving controverted questions of fact or law, which an Executive Department may transmit to the Court of Claims without consulting the wishes of the claimant, in order to obtain a report of facts and law for its guidance and action; the other, the twelfth section of the Tucker Act, relating to claims of the same class transmitted to that court with the expressed consent of the claimant in order to obtain a report of facts and law that would be only advisory in its character.

The object of the thirteenth section of the Tucker Act is quite apparent. A case transmitted under the Bowman Act is, we have seen, one in which the findings of fact and law are made for the guidance and action of the Executive Department from which it came, and therefore a rendition of judgment in such a case, if it be one of which the court could at the outset have taken cognizance at the voluntary suit of the claimant, would be a saving of time for all concerned. If the cases embraced by the twelfth section of the Tucker Act were only those provided for by the second section of the Bowman Act, the thirteenth section of the Tucker Act, authorizing a final judgment or decree where the claim was one of which the court could originally have taken jurisdiction for purposes of final adjudication, would not have made special reference to cases coming before the Court of Claims under the Bowman Act.

Our conclusion, then, as to the several statutes under examination, so far as they relate to claims pending in an Executive Department, are—

First. Any claim made against an Executive Department, "involving disputed facts or controverted questions of law, where the amount in controversy exceeds $3,000, or where the decision will affect a class of cases, or furnish a precedent for the future action of any Executive Department in the adjustment of a class of cases, without regard to the amount involved in the particular case, or where any authority, right, privilege, or exemption is claimed or denied under the Constitution of the United States," may be transmitted to the Court of Claims by the head of such Department under section 1063 of the Revised Statutes for final adjudication; provided such claim be not barred by limitation, and be one of which, by reason of its subject-matter and character, that court could take judicial cognizance at the voluntary suit of the claimant.

Second. Any claim embraced by section 1063 of the Revised Statutes, without regard to its amount, and whether the claimant consents or not, may be transmitted under the Bowman Act to the Court of Claims by the head of the Executive Department in which it is pending, for a report to such Department of facts and conclusions of law for "its guidance and action."

Third. Any claim embraced by that section may, in the discretion of the Executive Department in which it is pending, and with the expressed consent of the plaintiff, be transmitted to the Court of Claims, under the Tucker Act, without regard to the amount involved, for a report, merely advisory in its character, of facts or conclusions of law.

Fourth. In every case involving a claim of money, transmitted by the head of an Executive Department to the Court of Claims under the Bowman Act, a final judgment or decree may be rendered when it appears to the satisfaction of the court, upon the facts established, that the case is one of which the court, at the time such claim was filed in the Department, could have taken jurisdiction, at the voluntary suit of the claimant, for purposes of final adjudication.

Whether the words "or matter" in the second section of the Bowman Act embrace any matters except those involving the payment of money, and of which the Court of Claims under the statutes regulating its jurisdiction could, at the voluntary suit of the claimant, take cognizance for purposes of final judgment or decree, need not be now considered.

It results that as the claim of New York exceeded three thousand dollars, and was certified under section 1063 of the Revised Statutes as one involving controverted questions of law, the court below had jurisdiction to proceed to a final judgment, unless, as suggested by the Assistant Attorney-General, the claim when transmitted to the Court of Claims by the Secretary of the Treasury was barred by limitation.

At the time the claim of New York was filed in the Treasury Department there was no statute of limitations in force expressly applicable to cases in the Court of Claims. But by the act of March 2, 1863 (c. 92, sec. 10), it was provided that (within certain exceptions that have no application to this case) every claim against the United States, cognizable by the Court of Claims, should be barred unless the petition setting forth a statement of it was filed in or transmitted to that court within six years after the claim first accrued; claims that had accrued before the passage of that act not to be barred, if filed or transmitted as above stated, within three years after the passage of the act. (12 Stat. 765, 767.) This limitation of six years was preserved in the Revised Statutes and in the Tucker Act. (R. S. sec. 1069; 24 Stat., 505.)

Was the claim of New York barred because more than six years passed after it accrued before it was transmitted to the Court of Claims? In Finn v. United States (123 U. S., 227, 232) this court said: "The general rule that limitation does not operate by its own force as a bar, but is a defense, and that the party making such a defense must plead the statute if he wishes the benefit of its provisions, has no application to suits in the Court of Claims against the United States. An individual may waive such a defense, either expressly or by failing to plead the statute; but the Government has not expressly or by implication conferred authority upon any of its officers to waive the limitation imposed by statute upon suits against the United States in the Court of Claims. Since the Government is not liable to be sued, as of right, by any claimant, and since it has assented to a judgment being rendered against it only in certain classes of cases, brought within a prescribed period after the cause of action accrued, a judgment in the Court of Claims for the amount of a claim which the record or evidence shows to be barred by the statute, would be erroneous." To the same effect was De Arnaud v. United States (151 U. S., 483, 495),

But, in United States v. Lippitt (100 U. S. 663, 668, 669), where the question was whether a claim that accrued in 1864, and which was presented to the War Department in 1865, and in 1878 was transmitted to the Court of Claims as one involving controverted questions of law, the decision whereof would affect a class of cases, the court said: " Limitation is not pleadable in the Court of Claims against a claim cognizable therein, and which has been referred by the head of an Executive Department for its judicial determination, provided such claim was presented for settlement at the proper Department within six years after it first accrued; that is, within six years after suit could be commenced thereon against the Government. Where the claim is of such a character that it may be allowed and settled by an Executive Department, or may, in the discretion of the head of such Department, be referred to the Court of Claims for final determination, the filing of the petition should relate back to the date when it was first presented at the Department for allowance and settlement. In such cases the statement of the facts upon which the claim rests, in the form of a petition, is only another mode of asserting the same demand which had previously and in due time been presented at the proper Department for settlement.

"These views find support in the fact that the act of 1868 describes claims presented at an Executive Department for settlement, and which belong to the classes specified in its seventh section *as cases* which may be transmitted to the Court of Claims. 'And all the cases mentioned in this section, which shall be transmitted by the head of an Executive Department, or upon the certificate of any Auditor or Comptroller, shall be *proceeded in* as other cases pending in said court, and shall, in all respects, be subject to the same rules and regulations,' with right of appeal. The cases thus transmitted for judicial determination are, in the sense of the act, commenced against the Government when the claim is originally presented at the Department for examination and settlement. Upon their transfer to the Court of Claims they are to be 'proceeded in as other cases in said court.'"

The same principle was recognized in Finn *v.* United States (123 U. S. 227, 232), in which case the court, referring to the act of 1863, limiting the time for bringing suits in the Court of Claims, also said: "The duty of the court, under such circumstances, whether limitation was pleaded or not, was to dismiss the petition; for the statute, in our opinion, makes it a condition or qualification of the right to a judgment against the United States that—except where the claimant labors under some of the disabilities specified in the statutes—the claim must be put in suit by the voluntary action of the claimant, or be presented to the proper Department for settlement, within six years after suit could be commenced thereon against the Government."

Upon the authority of those cases we adjudge that as the claim of New York was presented to the Treasury Department before it was barred by limitation, its transmission by the Secretary of the Treasury to the Court of Claims for adjudication was only a continuation of the original proceedings commenced in that Department in 1862. The delay by the Department in disposing of the matter before the expiration of six years after the cause of action accrued could not impair the rights of the State. Of course, if the claim had not been presented to the Treasury Department before the expiration of that period the Court of Claims could not have entertained jurisdiction of it.

For the reasons we have stated the motion of the United States to dismiss the appeal of the State is denied, and we proceed to the examination of the case upon its merits.

The entire sum for which the State asked judgment was $131,188.02, of which $91,320.84 represented the amount paid as interest on moneys borrowed for the purpose of raising troops for the national defense, and for the repayment of which, with interest at seven per cent, the State executed its short-time bonds. The balance, $39,867.18, represented the amount paid as interest on moneys received by way of loan from the canal fund and applied by the State for the same purpose.

On behalf of the Government it is contended that payment by the United States of the above sum of $91,320.84 is prohibited both by the statute (act of March 3, 1863, 12 Stat., c. 765; R. S., 1091) providing that interest shall not be allowed on any claim up to the time of the rendition of judgment thereon by the Court of Claims, unless upon a contract expressly stipulating for the payment of interest, and by the general rule based on grounds of public convenience, that interest "is not to be awarded against a sovereign government, unless its consent to pay interest has been manifested by an act of its legislature, or by a lawful contract of its executive officers." (United States *v.* North Carolina, 136 U. S., 211, 216; Angarica *v.* Bayard, 127 U. S., 251, 260.)

The allowance of the $91,320.84 would not contravene either the statute or the general rule to which we have adverted. The duty of suppressing armed rebellion, having for its object the overthrow of the National Government, was primarily upon that Government and not upon the several States composing the Union. New York came promptly to the assistance of the National Government by enrolling, subsisting, clothing, supplying, arming, equipping, paying, and transporting troops to be employed in putting down the rebellion. Immediately after Fort Sumter was fired upon its legislature passed an act appropriating $3,000,000, or so much thereof as was necessary, out of any moneys in its treasury not otherwise appropriated, to defray any expenses incurred for arms, supplies, or equipments for such forces as were raised in that State and mustered into the service of the United States. In order to meet the burdens imposed by this appropriation, the real and personal property of the people of New York were subjected to taxation. When New York had succeeded in raising thirty thousand soldiers to be employed in suppressing the rebellion, the United States, well knowing that the national existence was imperiled, and that the earnest cooperation and continued support of the States were required in order to maintain the Union, solemnly declared by the act of 1861 that "the costs,

S. Rep. 1——34

charges, and expenses properly incurred" by any State in raising troops to protect the authority of the nation would be met by the General Government. And to remove any possible doubt as to what expenditures of a State would be so met, the act of 1862 declared that the act of 1861 should embrace expenses incurred before as well as after its approval. It would be a reflection upon the patriotic motives of Congress if we did not place a liberal interpretation upon those acts, and give effect to what, we are not permitted to doubt, was intended by their passage.

Before the act of July 27, 1861, was passed the Secretary of State of the United States telegraphed to the governor of New York, acknowledging that that State had then furnished fifty thousand troops for service in the war of the rebellion, and thanking the governor for his efforts in that direction. And on July 25, 1861, Secretary Seward telegraphed: "Buy arms and equipments as fast as you can. We pay all." And on July 27, 1861, that "Treasury notes for part advances will be furnished on your call for them." On August 16, 1861, the Secretary of War telegraphed to the governor of New York: "Adopt such measures as may be necessary to fill up your regiments as rapidly as possible. We need the men. Let me know the best the Empire State can do to aid the country in the present emergency." And on February 11, 1862, he telegraphed: "The Government will refund the State for the advances for troops as speedily as the Treasurer can obtain funds for that purpose." Liberally interpreted, it is clear that the acts of July 27, 1861, and March 8, 1862, created, on the part of the United States, an obligation to indemnify the States for *any* costs, charges, and expenses *properly incurred* for the purposes expressed in the act of 1861, the title of which shows that its object was "to indemnify the States for expenses incurred by them in defense of the United States."

So that the only inquiry is whether, within the fair meaning of the latter act, the words "costs, charges, and expenses properly incurred" included interest paid by the State of New York on moneys borrowed for the purpose of raising, subsisting, and supplying troops to be employed in suppressing the rebellion. We have no hesitation in answering this question in the affirmative. If that State was to give effective aid to the General Government in its struggle with the organized forces of rebellion, it could only do so by borrowing money sufficient to meet the emergency; for it had no money in its treasury that had not been specifically appropriated for the expenses of its own government. It could not have borrowed money any more than the General Government could have borrowed money without stipulating to pay such interest as was customary in the commercial world. Congress did not expect that any State would decline to borrow and await the collection of money raised by taxation before it moved to the support of the nation. It expected that each loyal State would, as old New York, respond at once in furtherance of the avowed purpose of Congress, by whatever force necessary, to maintain the rightful authority and existence of the National Government.

We can not doubt that the interest paid by the State on its bonds issued to raise money for the purposes expressed by Congress constituted a part of the costs, charges, and expenses properly incurred by it for those objects. Such interest, when paid, became a principal sum, as between the State and the United States, that is, became a part of the aggregate sum properly paid by the State for the United States. The principal and interest so paid constitutes a debt from the United States to the State. It is as if the United States had itself borrowed the money through the agency of the State. We therefore hold that the court below did not err in adjudging that the $91,320.84, paid by the State for interest upon its bonds issued in 1861 to defray the expenses to be incurred in raising troops for the national defense was a principal sum which the United States agreed to pay, and not interest within the meaning of the rule prohibiting the allowance of interest accruing upon claims against the United States prior to the rendition of judgment thereon.

The Court of Claims disallowed so much of the State's demand as represented interest paid by it on money borrowed from the canal fund. The installment of interest paid into that fund by the State was $48,187.13. But as the State itself earned interest to the amount of $8,319.95 on a part of the money obtained by it from the commissioners of the canal fund, it only claimed $39,867.18 on account of interest paid to that fund.

The canal fund was made by the constitution of the State a sinking fund for the ultimate liquidation of what is known as the canal debt of New York. In April and May, 1861, $2,039,663.06 from the taxes of 1860 reached the treasury of the State, and under the constitution and laws of New York that amount should have been invested in securities for the benefit of the canal fund, and the interest derived from those securities paid into the fund. The State was permitted to use a part of the above sum under an agreement by its officers that interest thereon at the rate of 5 per cent should be paid. It recognized and fulfilled that agreement, and now claims that the interest it so paid to the canal fund constituted a charge or expense properly incurred in raising, subsisting, and supplying troops to suppress the rebellion.

We are of opinion that, so far as the question of the liability of the United States is concerned, there is, on principle, no difference between the claim for $91,320.84

and the claim for $39,867.18. We do not stop to inquire whether the action of the canal commissioners, in allowing the State to use a part of the moneys collected for the benefit of the canal fund, was strictly in accordance with law. Suffice it to say, that the canal fund was entitled to any interest earned upon moneys belonging to it, and fidelity to the constitution and laws of New York required the State to recognize that right in the only way it could at the time have been done, namely, by paying the interest that ought to have been realized by the commissioners of the canal fund, if they had invested in interest-paying securities the moneys they permitted the State to use for military purposes. If the canal-fund money, used by the State comptroller to defray the expenses of raising and equipping troops, had been borrowed upon the bonds of the State sold in open market, the interest paid on such bonds would, for the reasons we have stated, be a just charge against the United States on account of expenses properly incurred by the State for the purposes expressed by Congress. And such would have been the result if the moneys of the canal fund had been invested by the commissioners directly in bonds of the State, bearing the same rate of interest that was paid to the commissioners of that fund.

The substance of the transaction was that the State, for moneys that could not be legally appropriated for the ordinary expenses of its own government, and which the law required to be so invested as to earn interest for the canal fund, used those moneys for military purposes, under an agreement by its officers, subsequently ratified by the State, to pay interest thereon. It was, in its essence, a loan to the State by the commissioners of. the canal fund of money to be repaid with interest. The obligation of the United States to indemnify the State, on account of such payment, is quite as great as it would be if the transaction had occurred between the State and some corporation from which it borrowed the money. It is not the case of the State taking money out of one pocket to supply a deficiency in another over which it had full power; for, although the moneys brought into its treasury by the collection of taxes was under its control, the State was without power to manage and control taxes collected for the canal fund, except as provided in its constitution and laws. It could not legally have become a party to any arrangement or agreement involving the use, without interest, of the moneys of the canal fund that had been set apart for the ultimate payment of the canal debt.

We are of opinion that the claim of the State for money paid on account of interest to the commissioners of the canal fund is not one against the United States for interest as such, but is a claim for costs, charges, and expenses properly incurred and paid by the State in aid of the General Government, and is embraced by the act of Congress declaring that the States would be indemnified by the General Government for moneys so expended.

As the State was entitled to a larger sum than $91,320.84, the judgment is reversed, and the cause is remanded with directions for further proceedings not inconsistent with this opinion.

Reversed.

S. Rep. 145——6

CLAIM OF THE STATE OF NEVADA.

MAY 16, 1900.—Ordered to be printed.

Mr. STEWART, from the Committee on Claims, submitted the following

REPORT.

[To accompany Mr. STEWART's amendment to H. R. 11537.]

The Committee on Claims, to whom was referred the amendment by Mr. Stewart to the bill (H. R. 11537) making appropriations to supply deficiencies in the appropriations for the fiscal year ending June 30, 1900, and for prior years, and for other purposes, report as follows: This amendment is as follows:

To pay the State of Nevada the sum of four hundred and sixty-two thousand four hundred and forty-one dollars and ninety-seven cents for moneys advanced in aid of the suppression of the rebellion in the civil war, as found and reported to Congress on January twenty-second, nineteen hundred, by the Secretary of the Treasury, as provided in the act entitled "An act for the allowance of certain claims for stores and supplies reported by the Court of Claims under the provisions of the act approved March third, eighteen hundred and eighty-three, and commonly known as the Bowman Act, and for other purposes," approved March third, eighteen hundred and ninety-nine. (Thirtieth United States Statutes, page twelve hundred and six.)

The Secretary of the Treasury, on January 19, 1900 (in House Doc. 322, Fifty-sixth Congress, first session), reported that the amount of money advanced by the State of Nevada in aid of the suppression of the rebellion in the civil war was the exact amount as named in this amendment, and which report the Secretary of the Treasury was authorized to make under the provisions of the act of March 3, 1899 (30 U. S. Stats., p. 1206), and a copy of which report is attached hereto and made a part hereof.

The circumstances under which this claim arose are fully recited in Senate Report No. 544, part 2, Fifty-fifth Congress, second session, copy of which report is hereto attached and made a part of this report. Wherefore your committee recommend that said amendment do pass and that the same be duly referred to the Committee on Appropriations.

[House Document No. 322, Fifty-sixth Congress, first session.]

TREASURY DEPARTMENT, OFFICE OF THE SECRETARY,
Washington, D. C., January 19, 1900.

SIR: Referring to the act of March 3, 1899 (30 Stat., p. 1206), upon the subject of the claim of the State of Nevada for moneys advanced in aid of the suppression of the rebel-

2

CLAIM OF THE STATE OF NEVADA.

lion in the civil war, and calling for report to Congress by the Secretary of the Treasury thereon, I have the honor to transmit herewith copy of statement of the case made by the Auditor for the War Department January 18, 1900.

Respectfully,

L. J. GAGE, *Secretary.*

The SPEAKER OF THE HOUSE OF REPRESENTATIVES.

TREASURY DEPARTMENT,
OFFICE OF AUDITOR FOR THE WAR DEPARTMENT,
Washington, January 18, 1900.

SIR: In reply to your communication of March 11, 1899, requesting a report under provisions of act of March 3, 1899, paragraph "State claims" (Public, 190), upon the claim of the State of Nevada for moneys advanced in aid of the suppression of the rebellion in the civil war, I have the honor to state the following:

On December 24, 1889, the Secretary of War, acting in accordance with a resolution of the Senate of February 27, 1889, transmitted a full and complete statement showing the amount expended by the State of Nevada, with such interest on the same as the State had paid between February 10, 1865, and June 30, 1889, amounting in all to the sum of $412,600.31. This report is found in Executive Document No. 10, first session Fifty-first Congress.

From a certified statement of Samuel P. Davis, State comptroller of Nevada, made on December 19, 1899, it appears that since the time covered by the report of the Secretary of War, i. e., from June 30, 1889, to December 31, 1899, the State of Nevada has paid the sum of $58,401.27 as interest upon money paid by the State in aiding in suppressing the rebellion in the civil war. Accordingly, assuming this statement to be correct, the total amount expended by the State of Nevada, or by the Territory of Nevada and assumed by said State, with such interest on the same as the said State has actually paid, amounts to $471,001.58.

Upon reports of an examination of this claim, made by the State war claims examiners, the Third Auditor, and the Second Comptroller of the Treasury, under act of June 27, 1882, the sum of $7,559.61 was allowed and paid to the State of Nevada on April 10, 1888. This amount, deducted from the total amount paid by the State of Nevada, leaves the sum of $462,441.97 for which the State has not been reimbursed. The following is a tabulated statement of this claim:

Amount of claim of the State of Nevada, including interest up to June 30, 1889, as shown in the report of the Secretary of War (see page 10, Senate Doc. No. 10, Fifty-first Congress)	$412,600.31
Amount of interest paid by Nevada from June 30, 1889, to December 31, 1899	58,401.27
Total claim	471,001.58
Amount which the State was reimbursed on April 10, 1888, under act of June 27, 1882	8,559.61
Total paid by the State for which no reimbursement has been made	462,441.97

Respectfully,

F. H. MORRIS, *Auditor.*

Senate Report 544, Part 2, Fifty-fifth Congress, second session.

Mr. STEWART, from the Committee on Claims, submitted the following

ADDITIONAL REPORT.

[To accompany S. 3545.]

On December 12, 1881, Senator Grover, of Oregon, introduced Senate joint resolution No. 10, to authorize the Secretary of War to duly examine, adjust, and report to Congress the State rebellion war claims of the State of Oregon.

On December 13, 1881, Senator Fair, of Nevada, introduced Senate joint resolution No. 13, of a similar character, for a similar purpose, in relation to the similar State war claims of Nevada.

Both of said resolutions were referred to the Senate Committee on Military Affairs, from which committee Senator Grover, on May 12, 1882, reported a bill, to wit, S. 1673, as a substitute for said two resolutions (and also for Senate bill No. 1144), and accompanied the same with Senate Report 575 (see p. 31, et seq., Senate Report 145, Fifty-fourth Congress, first session), recommending the examination, adjustment, and report to Congress of the rebellion war claims of Oregon and Nevada.

On June 8, 1882, said Senate bill 1673 being under consideration in the Senate, Senator Miller, of California, submitted an amendment thereto, which the Senate adopted, so as to include in said bill the similar State war claims of the State of California, and said bill, being otherwise amended in the Senate and subsequently amended in the House, finally became the act of June 27, 1882 (22 U. S. Stats., 111).

The rebellion war claims of California, Oregon, and Nevada provided for in said act of Congress of June 27, 1882, are the identical State war claims of said three States recited in and provided for in Senate bill 3545, and reported in Senate Report No. 544, Fifty-fifth Congress, second session.

The Secretary of War, Hon. Robert T. Lincoln, declined to do anything under said act of June 27, 1882, as to these claims of these three States until Congress should first give his Department the aid which he twice officially declared to be necessary in order to enable him to duly examine and officially state the war claims of the several States named in said act. (See top of p. 29, Senate Report 145, Fifty-fourth Congress, first session.)

On August 4, 1886, in compliance with his repeated recommendation therefor, Congress gave the Secretary of War authority to appoint a board of three army officers to assist him in duly examining, adjusting, and stating an account between the United States and these three States in reference to these State claims, and this authority so given by Congress consisted in amending said act of June 27, 1882.

The army board provided for in said act so amended on August 4, 1886, was duly appointed on October 6, 1886, by the Secretary of War, Hon. W. C. Endicott, and the members thereof, before entering upon their duties, subscribed an oath, as provided for in said act, "to carefully examine all said claims, and to make a just and impartial statement of all thereof as required by said act of June 27, 1882." (See pp. 25 and 66, Senate Report 145, Fifty-fourth Congress, first session.)

Thereafter abstracts, vouchers, and voluminous evidence in support of all of said claims were duly filed by said three States in the Treasury Department for examination and adjustment under said two acts of Congress of June 27, 1882, and August 4, 1886, and the Treasury Department, after officially stamping all said papers, transmitted the same to the Secretary of War, through the then Third Auditor, so that the Secretary of War, aided by said army board, should duly examine and pass upon the "necessity for and reasonableness of" all the expenses so incurred by said three States, and to duly settle and audit the same, etc., as contemplated by said two acts. (See pp. 27, 28, 58, 59, Senate Report 145, Fifty-fourth Congress, first session.)

The Secretary of War, Hon. Robert T. Lincoln, in reply to a request for information in regard thereto, officially reported to Senator Maxey that said act of June 27, 1882, was deemed sufficiently broad to embrace all proper State claims of Nevada (those of California and Oregon were identical with those of Nevada), and, in consequence thereof, Senator Maxey, from the Senate Committee on Military Affairs, which then had the same under consideration, reported to the Senate that no additional legislation by Congress was needed in the matter of the State war claims of said State. (Pp. 25–28, Senate Report 145, Fifty-fourth Congress, first session.)

The Secretary of War, Hon. W. C. Endicott, on January 27, 1886, also officially reported to Senator Maxey (then also representing the Senate Committee on Military Affairs, having due charge of the subject-matter, in a letter printed in full on pages 28 and 29 of Senate Report 145, Fifty-fourth Congress, first session), in reference to the said act of June 27, 1882, as follows, to wit:

That while the title of the act and the wording of the first section thereof would seem to convey the impression that the claims were to be adjusted by the Secretary of the Treasury, "with the aid and assistance of the Secretary of War," the whole duty of examining and auditing the claims was, by section 2, imposed upon the Secretary of War, leaving the Treasury Department the simple duty of verifying the computations of the Secretary of War.

The full letter from which this extract is taken is as follows, to wit:

[Senate Mis. Doc. No. 54, Forty-ninth Congress, first session.]

Letter from the Secretary of War to Hon. S. B. Maxey, in relation to the claim of the State of Texas presented under the act of June 27, 1882.

JANUARY 29, 1886.—Referred to the Committee on Appropriations and ordered to be printed.

WAR DEPARTMENT,
Washington City, January 27, 1886.

SIR: Referring to our recent conversation in regard to the claim of the State of Texas presented under the act of June 27, 1882 (22 Stats., 111, 112), I have the honor to inform you that the first installment of the claim (amount, $671,400.29) came before the Department from the Third Auditor of the Treasury July 9, 1884, and the action then taken in the matter appears in the letter from this Department to Mr. Dorn, dated July 16, 1884, copy herewith. The papers herein mentioned were returned to the agent of the State July 25, 1884. November 2, 1885, the Third Auditor of the Treasury wrote to the Department, transmitting through Mr. W. H. Pope, agent of the State, the papers in the claim, which papers were received here November 17, 1885, and they are now being stamped and marked.

In regard to the subject of the State claims mentioned in said act, I beg to inform you that the great difficulty experienced in disposing of the claim of the State of Kansas, the first one presented thereunder, has caused the Department to delay taking up the other claims pending. While the title of the act and the wording of the first section thereof would seem to convey the impression that the claims were to be adjusted by the Secretary of the Treasury, "with the aid and assistance of the Secretary of War," the whole duty of examining and auditing the claims was, by section 2, imposed upon the Secretary of War, leaving the Treasury Department the simple duty of verifying the computations of the Secretary of War.

The policy thus indicated differed widely from that prescribed in section 236 of the Revised Statutes, that "all claims and demands whatever by the United States, or against them, and all accounts whatever in which the United States are concerned, either as debtors or as creditors, shall be settled and adjusted in the Department of the Treasury," and differs also from the provisions for the adjudication of State claims under the act of July 27, 1861 (12 Stat., p. 276), which were "to be settled upon proper vouchers, to be filed and passed upon by the proper accounting officers of the Treasury."

The claims arising under the act are said to amount to $10,000.000 (that of Texas is now stated at $1,842,443.78), and the vast labor of examining the papers, pointing out the evidence required to perfect the vouchers and show the necessity of calling out the militia, whose services are charged for, fixing the rate to be allowed on each voucher and tabulating the same, many thousands in number, must be performed by the Secretary of War, and no provision has been provided by Congress for this laborious work.

Two years were consumed in disposing of the claim of the State of Kansas, and if the same course is to be pursued with the other claims arising under the act it will be some time before the claim of Texas is reached, that of Nevada being next in order of receipt.

The subject of the claims was brought to the attention of Congress at the last session (see report of Secretary of War for 1884, pp. 4, 5, and estimates for 1886 on p. 206 of House Ex. Doc. No. 5, Forty-eighth Congress, second session), and it has again been presented in the Secretary's report for 1885 (pp. 35 and 36). An estimate to defray the cost of examining the claims will be found on p. 225 of House Ex. Doc. No. 5, Forty-ninth Congress, first session.

I inclose draft of a bill which, if enacted, will enable the Department to dispose of the matter.

Copies of the above-mentioned reports are inclosed.

Very respectfully,

WM. C. ENDICOTT,
Secretary of War.

Hon. S. B. MAXEY,
United States Senate.

In the performance of their duties under the authority of said two acts of June 27, 1882, and August 4, 1886, said army board was continuously engaged for over three years in aiding the Secretary of War in carefully examining, auditing, and making just and impartial statements of accounts between the United States and these three States as to and of these war claims of these three States, and when said statements were duly completed and signed the Secretary of War (then Hon. Redfield Proctor, now United States Senator), under the resolution of the Senate of February 27, 1889, transmitted all thereof, on December 14 and 19, 1889, to the Senate in three separate reports, which the Senate ordered to be printed in three separate documents, to wit, Senate Docs. Nos. 10, 11, 17, Fifty-first Congress, first session.

The sums of money recited by said Secretary of War in his said three statements of allowances to said three States, respectively, to have been duly paid in cash by these three States, under due authority of their respective legislatures therefor, on account of "the costs, charges, and expenses" incurred by them, on account of the 18,715 volunteers actually called by the United States into its military service, are the iden-

6

CLAIM OF THE STATE OF NEVADA.

tical sums of money named in Senate bill 3545, recommended February 3, 1898, by the Senate Committee on Claims to be paid to them, as recited in Senate Report No. 544, Fifty-fifth Congress, second session, pages 27 and 28.

These three States not having the cash on hand during the rebellion were compelled, under the authority of their respective legislatures, to borrow most of said cash so by them expended to aid "the common defense," which they did by selling their State interest-bearing bonds, all of which bonds said States have heretofore fully redeemed and paid.

While so submitting a statement of allowances of said sums of money in favor of said three States, said Secretary did, at the same time, also submit a statement of disallowances against said States, which, in the case of the State of California, aggregated the sum of $468,976.54, and in the case of the State of Oregon aggregated the sum of $21,118.73, which two sums are not included in this bill, although said two States did, however, fully pay the same in cash as a part of their State war expenses necessarily incurred during the war of the rebellion.

Said Secretary aided by said army board prior to so stating an account between the United States and the States of California, Oregon, and Nevada, did also under said two acts of June 27, 1882, and August 4, 1886, state an account between the United States and the State of Texas as provided for in said acts, and in their said statement of account and allowance did allow the State of Texas the sum of $1,075,793.37, of which sum $927,177.40 was paid to the State of Texas under the act of Congress of March 30, 1888 (25 U. S Stats., 71), and $148,615.97 thereof was subsequently paid to said State under the act of Congress of September 30, 1890 (26 U. S. Stats., 539; see also pp. 26, 27, 29, Senate Report 145, Fifty-fourth Congress, first session).

Part of the action had in Congress during the sixteen years last past, in support of these State rebellion war claims of California, Oregon, and Nevada, and the recommendations of the proper committees in both Senate and House for their payment, are recited in Senate Report No. 145, Fifty-fourth Congress, first session. The value of this report consists in part that it contains the full decision of the United States Supreme Court in the cases of The State of New York v. The United States, and of The United States v. The State of New York, recited on pages 71 to 81 thereof, declaring among other things the full and true meaning and intention of Congress in its act of July 27, 1861 (12 U. S. Stats., 276), to be that where a State had paid interest on money borrowed and paid out and expended for the "common defense," that the amount of such interest should like the principal be fully reimbursed such State.

The latest recommendation in reference to the State rebellion war claims of these three States is recited in Senate Report No. 544, Fifty-fifth Congress, second session, pages 27 and 28, made February 3, 1898, by Senator Teller, to accompany Senate bill 3545, "for the adjustment and payment of certain claims against the Government of the United States," an extract of which report is as follows, to wit:

STATE CLAIMS.

CALIFORNIA, OREGON, AND NEVADA.

That the Secretary of the Treasury be, and he hereby is, authorized and directed to pay, out of any money in the Treasury not otherwise appropriated, to the following-named States the sums mentioned in connection with each to reimburse said States for moneys expended by them, respectively, in the suppression of the war of the rebellion, to wit, the amounts when paid to be accepted in full satisfaction for each claim:

California	$3,951,915.42
Oregon	335,152.88
Nevada	404,040.70
Total	4,691,109.00

Favorable reports on the three above claims combined.—Senate: Nos. 1286 and 2014, Fiftieth Congress; No. 614, Fifty-first Congress; No. 158, Fifty-second Congress; No. 287, Fifty-third Congress; No. 145, Fifty-fourth Congress. House: No. 3396, Fiftieth Congress; No. 2553, Fifty-first Congress; No. 254, Fifty-second Congress; No. 258, Fifty-third Congress; No. 1648, Fifty-fourth Congress.

Passed the Senate in the Fiftieth, Fifty-first, and Fifty-third Congresses.

The claims of these three Pacific coast States have come to be regarded as inseparable because all are of the same character and arose out of similar conditions. They are for the reimbursement to these States of the money by them actually expended in defraying the "costs, charges, and expenses" incurred in placing at the disposal of the United States 18,715 volunteer troops, under calls and requisitions officially made upon them therefor, by the proper civil and military authorities of the United States during the rebellion, between 1861 and 1865. These claims are founded upon the act of Congress of July 27, 1861 (12 Stat. L., 276), "An act to indemnify the States for expenses incurred by them in defense of the United States;" the resolution of Congress of March 8, 1862 (12 Stat. L., 615), "declaratory of the intent and meaning of said act of July 27, 1861;" the resolution of Congress of March 19, 1862 (12 Stat. L., 616), "to authorize the Secretary of War to accept money appropriated by any State for the payment of its volunteers, and to apply the same as directed by such State," and also under other acts.

The troops provided by the three States individually were in numbers as follows: California, 15,725; Nevada, 1,180, and Oregon, 1,810. These claims, if allowed, would give California $3,951,915.42, Nevada $404,040.70, and Oregon $335,152.88. These sums are the same as those recited in three reports made by the Secretary of War to the Senate, which were printed during the Fifty-first Congress, and are known as Senate Executive Documents Nos. 10, 11, and 17 of the first session of that Congress. The raising of these troops was made necessary by the withdrawal of the regular troops stationed on the California coast at the beginning of the civil war. It is claimed that if the same number of troops had been sent to that coast from the Eastern States the transportation alone would have cost $5,483,385.

The indemnification for the "costs, charges, and expenses" properly incurred by these States for enrolling, subsisting, clothing, supplying, arming, equipping, paying, transporting, and furnishing these volunteer troops, employed by the United States to aid them to maintain the "common defense," was guaranteed by the acts already cited, and the United States Supreme Court, in the case of "The State of New York v. The United States," during the October term of 1895, held that in certain contingencies, very similar to those existing in these three Pacific coast States, the States were entitled to collect interest. These war expenses were met by each of these States borrowing money on bonds, and the interest paid on these bonds is included in the allowance herein made. The total allowance for these three States is $4,691,109.

An extract from said decision of the United States Supreme Court in said case is as follows, to wit:

The duty of suppressing armed rebellion, having for its object the overthrow of the National Government, was primarily upon that Government and not upon the several States composing the Union. New York came promptly to the assistance of the National Government by enrolling, subsisting, clothing, supplying, arming, equipping, paying, and transporting troops to be employed in putting down the rebellion. Immediately after Fort Sumter was fired upon its legislature passed an act appropriating $3,000,000, or so much thereof as was necessary, out of any moneys in its treasury not otherwise appropriated, to defray any expenses incurred for arms, supplies, or equipments for such forces as were raised in that State and mustered into the service of the United States. In order to meet the burdens imposed by this appropriation, the real and personal property of the people of New York were subjected to taxation. When New York had succeeded in raising thirty thousand soldiers to be employed in suppressing the rebellion, the United States, well knowing that the national existence was imperiled, and that the earnest cooperation and continued support of the States were required in order to maintain the Union, solemnly declared by the act of 1861 that "the costs, charges, and expenses properly incurred" by any State in raising troops to protect the authority of the nation would be met by the General Government. And to remove any possible doubt as to

8   CLAIM OF THE STATE OF NEVADA.

what expenditures of a State act would be so met, the act of 1862 declared that the of 1861 should embrace expenses incurred before as well as after its approval. It would be a reflection upon the patriotic motives of Congress if we did not place a liberal interpretation upon those acts, and give effect to what, we are not permitted to doubt, was intended by their passage.

Before the act of July 27, 1861, was passed the Secretary of State of the United States telegraphed to the Governor of New York, acknowledging that that State had then furnished fifty thousand troops for service in the war of the rebellion, and thanking the governor for his efforts in that direction. And on July 25, 1861, Secretary Seward telegraphed: "Buy arms and equipments as fast as you can. We pay all." And on July 27, 1861, that "Treasury notes for part advances will be furnished on your call for them." On August 16, 1861, the Secretary of War telegraphed to the governor of New York: "Adopt such measures as may be necessary to fill up your regiments as rapidly as possible. We need the men. Let me know the best the Empire State can do to aid the country in the present emergency." And on February 11, 1862, he telegraphed: "The Government will refund the State for the advances for troops as speedily as the Treasurer can obtain funds for that purpose." Liberally interpreted, it is clear that the acts of July 27, 1861, and March 8, 1862, created on the part of the United States an obligation to indemnify the States for *any* costs, charges, and expenses *properly incurred* for the purposes expressed in the act of 1861, the title of which shows that its object was "to *indemnify* the States for expenses incurred by them in defense of the United States."

So that the only inquiry is whether, within the fair meaning of the latter act, the words "costs, charges, and expenses properly incurred" included interest paid by the State of New York on moneys borrowed for the purpose of raising, subsisting, and supplying troops to be employed in suppressing the rebellion. We have no hesitation in answering this question in the affirmative. If that State was to give effective aid to the General Government in its struggle with the organized forces of rebellion it could only do so by borrowing money sufficient to meet the emergency; for it had no money in its treasury that had not been specifically appropriated for the expenses of its own government. It could not have borrowed money any more than the General Government could have borrowed money without stipulating to pay such interest as was customary in the commercial world. Congress did not expect that any State would decline to borrow and await the collection of money raised by taxation before it moved to the support of the nation. It expected that each loyal State would, as did New York, respond at once in furtherance of the avowed purpose of Congress, by whatever force necessary, to maintain the rightful authority and existence of the National Government.

We can not doubt that the interest paid by the State on its bonds issued to raise money for the purposes expressed by Congress constituted a part of the costs, charges, and expenses properly incurred by it for those objects. Such interest, when paid, became a principal sum as between the State and the United States; that is, became a part of the aggregate sum properly paid by the State for the United States. The principal and interest so paid constitutes a debt from the United States to the State. It is as if the United States had itself borrowed the money through the agency of the State. We therefore hold that the court below did not err in adjudging that the $91,320.84 paid by the State for interest upon its bonds issued in 1861 to defray the expenses to be incurred in raising troops for the national defense was a principal sum which the United States agreed to pay, and not interest within the meaning of the rule prohibiting the allowance of interest accruing upon claims against the United States prior to the rendition of judgment thereon.

Some of the conditions which existed in California, Oregon, and Nevada during the war of the rebellion which rendered it necessary, in the opinion of the legislature of these three States, for them to make special pecuniary provision for their volunteers respectively in the military service of the United States, may be recited as follows, to wit:

The only currency in these three States in which the troops of the United States had ever been paid up to February 9, 1863, was coin—gold and silver. But on February 9, 1863, the Secretary of the Treasury advised the Assistant Treasurer of the United States at San Francisco that after *that* date all checks of disbursing officers must be paid in United States notes only (see pp. 13, 14, Senate Report 145, Fifty-fourth Congress, first session), and which notes on February 13, 1863, were worth only 61 cents on the dollar in San Francisco and in the interior of Oregon were worth not more than 50 to 55 cents on the dollar.

The condition of public affairs existing in these Pacific coast States in the early part of 1863 is recited on pages 25 and 26 of House Report No. 254, Fifty-second Congress, first session, in words as follows, to wit:

In the early part of April, 1863, the overland mail and emigrant route was attacked by Indians and communication was closed between the Atlantic States and the Pacific coast. This route extended from the Missouri River to California via the Platte River, Salt Lake City, through Nevada to Sacramento, in California, and was the only means at that date of direct overland communication between the Missouri River and California. At this time the gold discoveries in California continued to invite a large immigration, the interest in which was more or less intensified by the continued extensive silver discoveries in Nevada Territory, and principally on the Comstock lode, in the western part of the Territory. The routes via Cape Horn, and especially that via the Isthmus of Panama, were rendered extremely doubtful, dangerous, and expensive on account of Confederate privateer cruisers hovering around the West India Islands and along both these sea routes, and in anticipation of other Confederate cruisers infesting the waters of the Pacific (which soon thereafter became the theater of the operations and extensive depredations of the Confederate privateer *Shenandoah*), the overland route, therefore, although in itself both dangerous and difficult, was yet considered the better and preferable route by which to reach the Pacific.

On account of a general uprising of the Indians along the entire overland route, and especially that portion between Salt Lake City, in the Territory of Utah, and the Sierra Nevada Mountains, and because of the doubts as to the loyalty of the Mormons to the Government of the United States, the maintenance and protection of the mail and emigrant route through that section of the country and along the aforesaid line was regarded by the Government as a military necessity. Apparently in anticipation of no immediate danger of attack on the Pacific Coast, nearly all the troops of the Regular Army at this time had been withdrawn from service throughout this entire region of country and transferred East to other fields of military operations. This left the entire country between Salt Lake City and the Sierra Nevada Mountains without adequate and efficient military protection. The Government thus having but few troops of its Regular Army in that region, was therefore compelled to call upon the inhabitants of Nevada Territory to raise and organize volunteer military companies to suppress Indian disturbances which threatened the entire suspension of all mail facilities and emigration from the East, as will be hereafter shown.

At the time of the calls upon Nevada for troops the prices of labor and supplies of all descriptions in Nevada were extremely high. There were then no railroads, and the snow on the Sierra Nevada Mountains formed an almost impassable barrier against teams from about the 1st of December until about June. The average cost of freight from San Francisco, the main source of supply for western Nevada, was about $80 a ton, and it was necessary to lay in supplies during the summer and fall for the remainder of the year. A great mining excitement prevailed at this time, occasioned by the marvelous development of the great Comstock lode, and wages were from $4 to $10 a day, in gold. The people who had emigrated to the new gold and silver fields went there for the purpose of mining and prospecting for mines, and were generally reluctant to enter the irregular military service of guarding the overland mail and emigrant route. Besides, on account of the extraordinary high price of supplies of every description, and also of wages and service of every kind, it was impossible for them to maintain themselves and families without involving much more expense than any compensation which could be paid them as volunteer troops under the laws of the United States, and, as will be seen by the letters of General Wright, hereafter quoted, they were expected, as volunteer troops, to furnish themselves with horses and equipments, in addition to what could be furnished by the Government.

The military authorities of the United States well knew at that time the exact condition of the country and of the roads across the mountains leading thereto, and of the cost of transportation and of the prices of labor and of supplies and of their own inability to furnish either horses or equipments for a military service that required mounted troops.

It was amid circumstances like these that the honorable Secretary of the Treasury, by telegraphic instructions to the assistant treasurer of the United States at San Francisco, Cal., under date of February 9, 1863 (on which date there was on deposit in the subtreasury at San Francisco, to the credit of the United States, a large amount of gold and silver coin), directed the paymasters of the Army to pay said volunteers in United States notes, commonly called greenbacks. An exemplification of the effect of such instructions is reported by the Secretary of War on pages 40 and 41, Senate Ex. Doc. No. 11, Fifty-first Congress, first session, in words as follows, to wit:

EXHIBIT No. 10.

DEPUTY PAYMASTER-GENERAL'S OFFICE,
San Francisco, February 13, 1863.

SIR: Yesterday payment of my checks was refused by the assistant treasurer in San Francisco. In reply to a note which I addressed to him I received the following:

"OFFICE OF THE ASSISTANT TREASURER UNITED STATES,
"San Francisco, February 2, 1863.

"SIR: Your communication of this date relative to the check of $80,000 presented but a few minutes since by Major Eddy and payment declined by me, etc., is just received.

"Under instructions from the honorable Secretary of the Treasury United States of February 9, 1863, I am advised that 'checks of disbursing officers must be paid in United States notes.' Not having notes on hand sufficient to meet the check presented and referred to you has compelled me to decline payment of the same for the time being.

"Respectfully, your obedient servant,

"D. W. CHEESEMAN,
"Assistant Treasurer United States.

"GEORGE H. RINGGOLD,
"*Deputy Paymaster-General, U. S. Army.*"

The effect of these instructions is abruptly to stop payment of the troops. I had drawn out a sufficiency, principally in coin, to pay the posts in Oregon and a portion of the troops in this immediate vicinity; the delay will, I fear, cause great dissatisfaction to those remaining unpaid, as there was a confident expectation that they would now be paid off, and in coin.

In connection with the above statement, I deem proper to forward herewith a copy of a letter recently received from Major Drew, of the Oregon cavalry, which so clearly sets forth the condition of things as regards legal tenders on this coast as to make comment on my part superfluous, except simply to add that gold is the only currency here, and that U. S. Treasury notes are worth only what they will bring on the street. They are quoted at 61 to-day.

I have the honor to remain, very respectfully, your obedient servant,

GEO. H. RINGGOLD,
Deputy Paymaster-General.

Lieut. Col. T. P. ANDREWS,
Acting Paymaster-General U. S. Army.

Respectfully referred to Treasurer of the United States with the request that the funds may be sent to assistant treasurer at San Francisco to meet the drafts in favor of paymasters, and to return these papers for such other action as may be necessary.

T. P. ANDREWS, *Paymaster-General.*

PAYMASTER-GENERAL'S OFFICE, *March 18, 1863.*

If the Treasurer will be kind enough to furnish us with any suggestions from the Treasury that would tend to do away with the causes of complaint in this, to us, difficult case, we should feel indebted.

T. P. ANDREWS, *Paymaster-General.*

PAYMASTER-GENERAL'S OFFICE, *March 18, 1863.*

TREASURER'S OFFICE, *March 19, 1863.*

Respectfully referred to the Secretary of the Treasury.

F. E. SPINNER, *Treasurer United States.*

On September 3, 1861, by command of Lieutenant-General Scott, there were issued from the Headquarters of the Army, General Orders, No. 16, as follows, to wit:

[General Orders, No. 16.]

HEADQUARTERS OF THE ARMY,
Washington, September 3, 1861.

The General in Chief is happy to announce that the Treasury Department, to meet future payments to the troops, is about to supply, besides coin, as heretofore, Treasury not ϵ in fives, tens, and twenties, *as good as gold* at all banks and Government offices throughout the United States, and most convenient for transmission by mail from officers and men to their families at home. Good husbands, fathers, sons, and brothers serving under the Stars and Stripes, will thus soon have the ready and safe means of relieving an immense amount of suffering which could not be reached with coin.

In making up such packages every officer may be relied upon, no doubt, for such assistance as may be needed by his men.

By command of Lieutenant-General Scott:

E. D. TOWNSEND,
Assistant Adjutant-General.

The financial conditions which existed continuously from September 3, 1861, to February 9, 1863, were such as made coin only the currency of the Government of the United States on the Pacific coast. The citizens of California volunteered to enter the military service of the United States under said conditions, and also under the promise expressed in said order of the War Department of September 3, 1861, that future payment for their military services was to be made in coin or in Treasury notes, "*as good as gold* at all banks and Government offices throughout the United States."

But this promise on the part of the War Department was not kept toward the volunteers from California, Oregon, and Nevada in the military service of the United States, in many cases detachments of which troops were not only not paid in coin, but were not paid even in Treasury notes, sometimes for periods covering a year or more; in consequence of which great demoralization existed in the Volunteer Army on the Pacific coast. (See pp. 14, 15, 16, Senate Report No. 145, Fifty-fourth Congress, first session.)

Not only this, but from June 17, 1850, and continuously thence until August 3, 1861, the practice of the War Department under the laws of Congress was to pay each soldier enlisted, recruited, or reenlisted in the States of California, Oregon, and Nevada a sum of money which, while Congress termed it a "bounty," yet it in fact and effect was, and was intended to be, merely extra or additional pay in the form of a constructive mileage equivalent to the cost of transporting a soldier from New York City to the place of such enlistment or reenlistment; said sum was to be paid to each Pacific coast soldier in installments, in the amounts, at the times, and in the manner as recited in the act of Congress therefor, approved June 17, 1850, the third section of which reads as follows:

SEC. 3. *And be it further enacted,* That whenever enlistments are made at or in the vicinity of the said military posts, and remote and distant stations, a bounty equal in amount to the cost of transporting and subsisting a soldier from the principal recruiting depot in the harbor of New York to the place of such enlistment be, and the same is hereby, allowed to each recruit so enlisted, to be paid in unequal installments at the end of each year's service, so that the several amounts shall annually increase, and the largest be paid at the expiration of each enlistment. (U. S. Stat., vol. 9, p. 439).

Congress, during the rebellion, not only changed the manner of maintaining a military force in these three Pacific coast States by relying to a very large degree, if not almost exclusively, upon volunteers to be enlisted and raised therein, but on August 3, 1861, repealed said law. (12 U. S. Stats., sec. 9, p. 289.)

Not only this, but in consequence of the high cost of living in California and Oregon, Congress, on September 28, 1850, passed an act paying to every commissioned officer serving in those States an extra $2 per day, and to all the enlisted men serving in the United States Army in those

States double the pay then being paid to the troops of the Regular Army. This law is as follows, to wit:

For extra pay to the commissioned officers and enlisted men of the Army of the United States, serving in Oregon or California, three hundred and twenty-five thousand eight hundred and fifty-four dollars, on the following basis, to wit: That there shall be allowed to each commissioned officer as aforesaid, while serving as aforesaid, a per diem, in addition to their regular pay and allowances, of two dollars each, and to each enlisted man as aforesaid, while serving as aforesaid, a per diem, in addition to their present pay and allowances, equal to the pay proper of each as established by existing laws, said extra pay of the enlisted men to be retained until honorably discharged. This additional pay to continue until the first of March eighteen hundred and fifty-two, or until otherwise provided. (U. S. Stat., vol. 9, p. 504.)

It will be here noticed that under these two acts of Congress, the one of the 17th of June, 1850, and the other of the 28th of September, 1850, the so-called "extra pay" and the so-called "bounty" or constructive mileage, were both paid during one and the same period of time by the United States to its own troops serving in the *Regular* United States Army stationed in these States.

If the necessity for this character of legislation for the *Regular* Army of the United States recited in these two acts existed *in a time of profound peace*—and no one doubts but that a necessity therefor did exist—then how much greater the necessity for similar legislation *in a period of actual war*, when the land carriage for supplies over a distance of 2,000 miles, from the Missouri River to these Pacific Coast States, was simply impossible, or at least impracticable, there not being then any overland railroad, and the two sea routes via Cape Horn and the Isthmus of Panama, as recited in the said reports of the Secretary of War, being both hazardous and expensive?

It was in view of these conditions and amid circumstances like these that the States of California, Oregon, and Nevada felt compelled to come to the financial relief of their own volunteers then serving in the Federal Army in these three States, and passed acts through their respective legislatures, under and by which each volunteer in each of said three States was to be paid the sum of $5 per month in coin, over and above the regular pay by them received from the United States during the existence of the rebellion.

In order to raise the money with which to pay this extra pay, each of said three States, under an appropriate act of its legislature, issued and sold its State coin bonds, all of which they have heretofore fully redeemed and paid, with legal interest.

SECOND.

There is, however, one fact in reference to the California Volunteers which did *not* obtain in the cases of the Oregon and Nevada Volunteers. This was as follows, to wit:

The California Volunteers were largely serving in the Territories of Arizona and New Mexico, though some were serving elsewhere, but all on the Pacific coast. In 1864 the period of the three years' enlistment of the California volunteers who had been mustered in 1861 into the military service of the United States was approaching termination.

The war in the East was still flagrant, and no one could then foretell the end thereof. General Lee had just invaded Pennsylvania with a large army, and though defeated at Gettysburg, yet extensive and devastating raids were made into the State of Pensylvania by the Confederate forces as late as July, 1864, by Generals Early, Johnson, and McCausland, the effects of which are represented to have been even more disastrous to the people of that State than those arising from the raids made therein in 1862 by Gen. Zeb. Stewart, of the Confederate cavalry. Chambersburg, Pa., was burned on July 30, 1864, the Confederates destroying extensive properties in the counties of Adams, Bedford, Cumberland, Franklin, Fulton, Perry, Somerset, and York, lying along the southern border of Pennsylvania and adjoining the northern Maryland line, the value of which property so destroyed is reported to have aggregated a very large sum.

The general commanding the Military Department of New Mexico at Santa Fe, Gen. Charles H. Carleton, was very anxious that the California volunteers then serving in New Mexico should there reenlist either for three years or during the war. Most of them desired to reenlist in New Mexico, but the Second Comptroller of the Treasury, Hon. John M. Brodhead, in September, 1863 (Second Comptroller's Decisions, September 8, 9, 1863, vol. 25, pp. 422 and 425, printed as section 2192, p. 283, of Digest of the Second Comptroller's Decisions, vol. 1, 1861 to 1868), decided that no volunteer who should reenlist should receive any mileage from the place of his discharge to the place of his original enlistment, *but only those should receive mileage who did not reenlist.*

This decision, in effect, was to pay a bounty, by way of mileage, to those volunteers who did *not* reenlist in the United States Army *and to refuse it to those who did reenlist.*

However valid these decisions may have been as declaratory of the supposed intentions of the law as then viewed by the Treasury Department, yet the practical effect thereof was to discourage reenlistments in the case of these volunteers from California, about to be discharged in New Mexico, where they were serving at the dates of said decisions, many hundreds of miles from the places of their original enrollment. Under these decisions the United States in fact decided, as aforesaid, to pay, and did pay, a bounty or mileage to those volunteers *who did not reenlist in the United States Army,* but refused to pay it to those who did so reenlist.

The serious, in fact, alarming, effect of these decisions of the honorable Second Comptroller upon the military condition of affairs in Arizona and New Mexico, where several regiments of these California volunteers were then serving, is shown by the great anxiety and serious concern of Brig. Gen. James H. Carleton, of the Regular Army of the United States, commanding the Department of New Mexico, so much so that he made it the subject of a special report to the Adjutant General of the Army, at Washington, D. C., recited on pages 60 and 61, Report of Secretary of War, Senate Ex. Doc. No. 11, Fifty-first Congress, first sessions, in words as follows, to wit:

EXHIBIT No. 22.

HEADQUARTERS DEPARTMENT OF NEW MEXICO,
Santa Fe, N. Mex., November 29, 1863.

GENERAL: Until Mr. Brodhead's decision was made, that volunteers who should be discharged by enlistment in veteran volunteers should not receive their mileage from the place of said discharge to the place of original enrollment, I entertained hopes that many, if not most, of the First and Fifth Regiments of Infantry, of the First Cavalry California Volunteers, and First Cavalry New Mexican Volunteers, would reenlist in the veteran volunteers. But since that decision was made it is very doubtful if the California volunteers will reenlist. Their present term of office will expire next August and September. Before that time other troops will have to be sent here to take their places, unless these can be induced to reenlist. The troops in this department should be made an exception to the general rule. In my opinion an order should be made giving all volunteers who reenlist in this department the $100 due on first enlistment and an increased bounty on the second over and above the bounty paid to soldiers in the East, which would be equal to the cost of getting soldiers from the East to New Mexico. The Government in this way would lose nothing, but would rather gain, because these well-disciplined men would then remain, doubtless, and they have now become familiar with the country, and can do better service for that reason than any newcomers. These men should receive their mileage on their first enlistment. In my opinion the law clearly allows it to soldiers honorably discharged. If the Government do not deny their traveling allowances and will give the bounty named, I believe the most of these regiments can be got to remain If the Government will not do this, I beg to give timely notice of the necessities which will exist to have troops sent to take their places in time to be in position before the term of service of these men expires.

The California troops do not wish to be sent as regiments back to California; they would rather be discharged here in case they do not reenlist. Some desire to go to the States, some to the gold fields of Arizona, some settle in New Mexico, and some go to California by whatever route they please. The true economy of the question would be promoted by making the bounties so liberal as to induce them to reenter the service for three years or during the war.

I am, General, very truly and respectfully, your obedient servant,

CHARLES H. CARLETON,
Brigadier-General, Commanding.

Brig. Gen. LORENZO THOMAS,
Adjutant-General, U. S. Army, Washington, D. C.

DEPARTMENT NEW MEXICO,
Santa Fe, N. Mex., July 12, 1865.

Official:

BEN. C. CUTLER,
Assistant Adjutant-General.

California, in consequence of the foregoing decision of the Second Comptroller of the Treasury, and to successfully retain veteran soldiers in the military service of the United States, determined, on April 4. 1864, for her own volunteers, who might enlist or reenlist in the United States Army, then serving on the Pacific coast, to revive substantially the aforesaid provision of the act of Congress of June 17, 1850, which had been in existence for the benefit of the Regular Army serving on the Pacific coast continuously from June 17, 1850, to August 3, 1861.

Under the provisions of said California State act of April 4, 1864, each California volunteer soldier so enlisting or reenlisting in the United States Army after April 4, 1864 (the date of the California act for this specific purpose), was to be paid in installments, at the time and in the manner substantially as recited in said Congressional act of June 17, 1850, a sum of money assumed to be equal to the cost of transporting a soldier from New York City to the place of reenlistment or the enlistment of such volunteer soldiers. In view of the scattered military stations of said California volunteers—extending, as they did, from Arizona on the south to Puget Sound on the north, and from San Francisco on the west to Salt Lake City on the east—this sum was fixed at $160 per each volunteer soldier, which sum at that time substantially represented about the average cost which the United States would have had to pay to transport a soldier from New York City to the places of such enlistment or reenlistment of said volunteers.

In reviving, on April 4, 1864, said act of Congress of June 17, 1850, in the manner and for the purposes therein recited. California used substantially the language which Congress had used in said act by calling said sum of money a "bounty," when, as aforesaid, it was, and was only intended to be, a *constructive mileage*, and which was paid by said State out of her State treasury for the use and benefit of the United States in aid of the "common defense" during the war of the rebellion, but not beginning until after April 4, 1864, and expected to be reimbursed as contemplated by said act of Congress of July 27, 1861 (12 U. S. Stats., 276), and joint resolution of March 8, 1862 (12 U. S. Stats., 615), and of March 19, 1862 (12 U. S. Stats., 616). In reference to this matter the Secretary of War, in Senate Ex. Doc. No. 11, pp. 22 and 23, Fifty-first Congress, first session, reported to the Senate as follows, to wit:

With respect to the circumstances and exigencies under which this expenditure was incurred by the State, it appears to be plain that it was the earnest desire of the legislature that such troops as the State had been or might thereafter be called upon to furnish the General Government should be promptly supplied. The time was approaching when the terms of most of the volunteer regiments raised in California in the early part of the war would expire. These regiments were occupying important stations in the State and in Territories of Utah, Arizona, and New Mexico, and it was obvious that it would become necessary either to continue them in service by filling them up with new recruits or reënlisted veterans, or, in the event of their disbandment, to replace them by new organizations. Volunteering under the calls of the previous year had progressed tardily, while lucrative employment in the State was abundant and the material inducements for men to enter the Army were small. It was probable that unless these latter were considerably increased recruiting would come to a standstill, and a draft, as in the Eastern States, have to be resorted to. That a draft in California was considered possible, and even probable, is shown by an official letter, written January 8, 1864, to the Adjutant-General of the Army by General Wright, commanding Department of the Pacific, in which he expressed the hope "of procuring quite a number of men who would prefer volunteering to running the chance of being drafted." (P. 205, Senate Ex. Doc. 70, Fiftieth Congress, second session.) The expectation that the mere fear of a draft would sufficiently stimulate volunteering had not, some months later, been realized; and under all circumstances, and prompted by the desire above mentioned, the legislature doubtless deemed it wise to enact the bounty law of April 4, 1864.

Attention is called in "Statement for Senate Committee on Military Affairs" (p. 27) to the third section of an act of Congress (9 U. S. Stats., 439) granting to persons enlisting on the Western frontier and at remote and distant stations a bounty equal in amount to the cost of transporting and subsisting soldiers from the principal recruiting depot in the harbor of New York to the place of enlistment, and it is argued that if it was just, proper, and expedient to grant such a bounty to men enlisting in the Regular Army in such localities in time of peace the allowance by California of a bounty to its volunteers when they were in the actual and active service of the United States in time of war, and "while the exigencies exceeded in degree those under which the United States have heretofore paid a much larger sum to its own Regular Army serving in said States (of California, Oregon, and Nevada) in a time of peace, may be deemed to have been in harmony with the policy so long and so frequently executed by the United States."

These "costs, charges, and expenses" so incurred by these three States therefore were:

(1) Military expenditures for recruiting 18,715 volunteers.
(2) Military expenditures in organizing and paying 18,715 volunteers.
(3) Military expenditures in and for Adjutant-General's Office.
(4) Military expenditures in paying volunteer commissioned officers between date of service and date of muster in by the proper mustering officers of the United States.
(5) Military expenditures of a general and miscellaneous character.

All "costs, charges, and expenses" for the military services of the *militia* in all these States were *suspended* and not allowed by the Secretary of War and are excluded from the present claims in accordance with recommendations heretofore made by the Committee on Military Affairs and Committee on Claims in the Senate and by the Committee on War Claims in the House.

Attention is specially called to two important resolutions of Congress adopted, the one on the 8th and the other on the 19th of March, 1862, the object of the first of which was to explain the act of Congress of July 27, 1861, and the object of the second was to encourage and invite appropriations of money to be made by the several States as they might deem to be appropriate in the interests of the United States and

wherein the obligation existed that the United States should indemnify by fully reimbursing the several States, out of any money in
the Federal Treasury not otherwise appropriated, the sums of money
which such States should appropriate and expend for the uses
and purposes recited in the acts of the legislature of each State
so appropriating the same. (12 U. S. Stats., 615, 616.) These two
resolutions are in words as follows, to wit:

A RESOLUTION declaratory of the intent and meaning of a certain act therein named.

Whereas doubts have arisen as to the true intent and meaning of act numbered
eighteen, entitled "An act to *indemnify* the States for expenses incurred by them in
'Defense of the United States,'" approved July twenty-seven, eighteen hundred and
sixty-one (12 U. S. Stats., 276):
*Be it resolved by the Senate and House of Representatives of the United States of Amer-
ica in Congress assembled,* That the said act shall be construed to apply to expenses
incurred as well after as before the date of the approval thereof.
Approved, March 8, 1862 (12 U. S. Stats., 615).

A RESOLUTION to authorize the Secretary of War to accept moneys appropriated by any State
for the payment of its volunteers and to apply the same as directed by such State.

*Resolved by the Senate and House of Representatives of the United States of America in
Congress assembled,* That if any State during the present rebellion shall make any
appropriation to pay the volunteers of that State, the Secretary of War is hereby
authorized to accept the same and cause it to be applied by the Paymaster-General
to the payments designated by the legislative act making the appropriation, in the
same manner as if appropriated by act of Congress; and also to make any regulations they may be necessary for the disbursement and proper application of such
funds to the specific purpose for which they may be appropriated by the several
States.
Approved, March 19, 1862 (12 U. S. Stats., 616).

In other words, the legislation enacted by Congress in its said act
and in resolutions, taken in connection with subsequent similar legislation duly enacted by these three States, constituted, in effect and intendment, statutory contracts binding upon the United States. It is evident that Congress, in advance of all legislative acts by these three
States making appropriations of money for their said volunteers, duly
declared that all moneys appropriated by their respective legislatures
and paid out of their respective State treasuries, intended for the exclusive use and benefit of their said volunteers, theretofore, then, or thereafter serving in the military service of the United States, should be
accepted by the United States, through the Secretary of War, and paid
to the State volunteers of the States so appropriating said moneys, for
the specific uses and purposes for which said States had so appropriated the same, and in the same manner, for the same purposes, and to
the same extent as if said moneys had been actually paid directly out
of the Federal Treasury under acts of Congress appropriating the
same. In other words, Congress approved, ratified, and confirmed *in
advance* all these appropriations of money so made by the legislatures
of these three States, and in fact, intendment, and effect Congress made
these State appropriation acts its own acts, the provisions of which
should be duly administered by its own proper officers for the objects
and purposes as recited in said State acts. These three Pacific coast
States substantially conformed to this legislation of Congress, and
strictly followed the same in all particulars where not inhibited by the
State constitutions or by the State laws of said States.

A copy of this resolution of Congress, adopted March 19, 1862, was,
on July 5, 1863, duly transmitted by Gen. George Wright, commanding the military department of the Pacific, to the governor of California, Hon. Leland Stanford, late Senator from California. The correspondence relating thereto is reported by the Secretary of War on page

183, Senate Ex. Doc. No. 11, Fifty-first Congress, first session, and is as follows, to wit:

HEADQUARTERS DEPARTMENT OF THE PACIFIC,
San Francisco, Cal., July 5, 1863.

His Excellency LELAND STANFORD,
Governor State of California, Sacramento City, Cal.

SIR: Inclosed herewith I have the honor to lay before your excellency a resolution to authorize the Secretary of War to accept moneys appropriated by any State for the payment of its volunteers, and to apply the same as directed by such State, approved March 19, 1862.

Under the provisions of this resolution Lieut. Col. George H. Ringgold, deputy paymaster-general at my headquarters, will accept any moneys which have been or which may be appropriated for the purpose set forth, and cause it to be applied to the payments designated by the legislative acts.

With great respect, I have the honor to be, your excellency's obedient servant,

G. WRIGHT,
Brigadier-General, Commanding.

STATE OF CALIFORNIA, EXECUTIVE DEPARTMENT,
Sacramento, July 16, 1863.

Gen. GEORGE WRIGHT,
Commanding Department of the Pacific.

SIR: Your favor of the 5th instant, with resolution relative to appropriations for the relief of volunteers in the several States, is at hand.

By reference to sections 3 and 4 of the act of the legislature approved April 27, 1863 (Statutes of 1863, folio 662), you will observe that the requirements of the law are such as to preclude our State officers from departing from its provisions, and would therefore be impossible to pay out the appropriations *in the manner* indicated by the resolution of Congress.

I am, General, very respectfully, your obedient servant,

LELAND STANFORD,
Governor of California.

In other words, while the State officers of California could *not*, under the laws of that State, legally pay over to any deputy paymaster-general of the United States Army any moneys appropriated by the legislature of that State for the exclusive benefit of its own volunteers then serving in the United States Army on the Pacific coast, yet all of said moneys were in fact duly paid over by the said officers of that State to all of its said volunteers, respectively, serving on the Pacific coast, and for all of which the United States received the full benefit over a third of a century ago.

It is respectfully submitted that these three States confidently expected that these appropriations of money so borrowed by them on their own credit and so made and advanced through their own legislatures to the United States and paid to their said volunteers then serving in the Army of the United States as a part of the military establishment on the Pacific coast during the war of the rebellion, should be fully reimbursed to them. In addition to the foregoing, these three States had been urged to make these very appropriations of money by General George Wright, commanding the Department of the Pacific, and by General Irwin McDowell, commanding the Division or Department of California and Nevada, and by General Benjamin Alvord, commanding the Department of Oregon, for the reimbursement of all of which appropriations said three States relied, not only upon the public exigencies which demanded such appropriations of money on their part, but wherein they rested their action upon the good faith as well as upon the legal and equitable obligations of the United States in all these premises to fully reimburse the same.

Wherefore it fully appears that these State rebellion war claims of these three States have all been carefully examined, legally audited,

S. Rep. 1351——2

and exactly stated by a competent tribunal created for such purposes under due authority from Congress, to which nine years ago they were reported by the honorable Secretary of War, since which they have been frequently recommended for payment by the proper committees in both Houses of Congress in numerous and exhaustive reports, as herein specifically named by number, date, Congress, and session.

These expenditures were all made in good faith by these three States to aid the United States to maintain the "common defense," and justice and the good faith of the United States alike demand that these three States should be now fully reimbursed by Congress for all these expenditures by them so then made.

o

The SPEAKER. The gentleman from Illinois asks the previous question on the adoption of the report.

The question was taken; and the previous question was ordered.

The question was taken on agreeing to the conference report; and the conference report was agreed to.

Mr. CANNON. Now I move that the House further insist on its disagreement to the Senate amendment indicated, known as the Nevada claim amendment.

The SPEAKER. The gentleman from Illinois moves that the House further insist on the disagreement to the amendment known as the Nevada claim amendment.

Mr. NEWLANDS. Mr. Speaker, I move that the House recede and concur.

The SPEAKER. The gentleman from Illinois moves that the House insist on its disagreement, and the gentleman from Nevada moves that the House recede and concur. The latter motion takes precedence.

Mr. CANNON. Now, Mr. Speaker, I desire to reserve my time, and will yield later such time of my hour as we shall agree just and equitable to the gentleman from Nevada. My colleague on the conference, the gentleman from Massachusetts [Mr. MOODY], desires to be heard upon this amendment.

The SPEAKER. The gentleman from Illinois reserves his time, with the assurance that he will yield to the gentleman from Nevada such time as he may require.

Mr. CANNON. Such time as is equitable.

The SPEAKER (continuing). And the gentleman from Massachusetts, one of the conferees, is recognized in his own right.

Mr. MOODY of Massachusetts. Mr. Speaker, I ask that the Clerk read the amendment for the information of the House.

The Clerk read as follows:

To pay the State of Nevada the sum of $462,441.97 for moneys advanced in aid of the suppression of the rebellion in the civil war, as found and reported to Congress on January 22, 1900, by the Secretary of the Treasury, as provided in the act of Congress approved March 3, 1899.

Mr. MOODY of Massachusetts. Mr. Speaker, I trust that the members of the House may ascertain exactly what this claim is and what kind of a precedent it will set, because if the claim is agreed to by the House all of you who represent any States that did not secede will be called upon to prosecute claims of like nature from your own State. The committee of conference without action of the House did not feel justified in agreeing to this item, for two reasons. First, because it was a recognition of a kind of State claim that has never been recognized by Congress before. There has never been a dollar paid from the Treasury of the United States in settlement of claims of the kind represented in this item. And, second, because if this claim is paid, a claim of $4,000,000 and over of the State of California must be paid, and a claim of $400,000 of the State of Oregon must be paid, because in every possible respect the claims of California and Oregon are on all fours with the claim of the State of Nevada.

I will, as briefly as I can, state exactly the facts out of which State claims which have been paid hitherto have arisen and out of which this claim, which is before us now, has arisen. At the beginning of the civil war the Treasury of the United States was empty. The Government of the United States called for aid in raising and equipping troops from all the loyal States, and those States responded. Congress passed a law which directed the Treasury to indemnify the States for the "cost, charges, and expenses properly incurred by any State" for enrolling, subsisting, clothing, paying, etc., troops which entered the service of the United States. Now, every claim under that statute has been paid; every dollar which the United States owes under that statute has been paid, except some claims for interest which are due and outstanding.

Mr. MONDELL. Did the State of Nevada have any claim under that statute?

Mr. MOODY of Massachusetts. The State of Nevada had a small claim, which I will refer to later on, which has been paid, now, there was a peculiar exigency on the Pacific coast. The war vessels of the Confederacy had destroyed water communication between the Atlantic and the Pacific coasts. The only route open was the overland route. The regular troops of the United States had been withdrawn from the Pacific coast. It became necessary to appeal to the States and Territories on the Pacific coast to raise troops for the benefit of the Government. They responded loyally; they did their work well. They performed as important a function in suppressing the rebellion as the troops of other States who crossed the Potomac, because it was just as necessary to keep open the overland route, protect that communication from an Indian rising, as it was to defend the capital of the United States.

At that time the cost of living on the Pacific slope was very great. The wages of labor were very high. It was difficult to raise troops for the service of the United States. These two conditions prevailed in all the States, but prevailed in none of them

to the same degree that it prevailed on the Pacific coast, according to the testimony before us. Accordingly the States of California and Oregon and the Territory of Nevada voted to pay their troops who entered into the service of the United States a certain sum in addition to the amount they received from the United States. They based their action somewhat on the policy the United States had adopted for the payment of the regular troops, because they had allowed those who served on the Pacific coast an extra allowance or compensation. But that policy had been abandoned by the United States and the statute prescribing it repealed at the beginning of the civil war, I suppose upon the ground that it was thought that the conditions that made the extra payments necessary had passed away.

Up to this point claims of the Pacific Coast States for the refunding of extra pay stand on the same footing with the claims of all other States. But there is one difference that ought not to be disregarded by the House. The Pacific slope was upon a gold basis. The troops were paid in greenbacks. That is all the difference, except in degree, between the States of Pennsylvania, New York, or Massachusetts and the States of California, Oregon, and Nevada.

The State of Massachusetts paid, for instance, in the civil war, as it did in the war with Spain, so much a month extra for troops that entered into the service of the United States on account of its quota. But the States of Massachusetts and Pennsylvania or Illinois, or any of the States, have never been paid anything by the United States on account of the bounties or extra monthly payment which they paid their troops. No State has ever yet been paid anything on account of the extra payments to their troops for which the State of Nevada now presents this claim.

Now, what next happened? The State of Nevada had no claim under the act of 1861. No State had a valid claim under that act for payments like those made by Nevada, for which the claim is now made. But Nevada and some other States, desirous of receiving back what they had paid out by way of bounty and by way of extra pay, caused the act of 1882 to be passed, and that is the next step in this proceeding.

Now, let me have the attention of the House one moment while I state the effect of that act. It was approved June 27, 1882, and it provided for an examination and investigation of the claims of Texas, Colorado, Oregon, Nebraska, California, Kansas, Nevada, Washington, and Idaho for moneys expended and indebtedness assumed in organizing, arming, equipping, supplying clothing, subsistence, transporting, and paying volunteer and military forces of said States that entered the service of the United States.

Section 4 of the act provides that the Secretary of the Treasury shall report to Congress for final action the results of such an examination and investigation.

Now, remember, Mr. Speaker, Nevada had no claim under the act of 1861. This provision was passed in 1882. Under it the Secretary of the Treasury, acting in combination with the Secretary of War, made a report. I hold in my hand the report upon the Nevada claim—366 pages of fine print. I want to take this occasion here and now to protest against an inquiry of this kind in the closing hours of Congress being thrown upon the committee in charge of a great money bill. How can we properly do our duty there? It ought to be before the Committee on Claims, investigated by the Committee on Claims, reported by the Committee on Claims, and considered by the House in a manner in which it is now impossible to consider it.

Mr. NEWLANDS. Will the gentleman please state in that connection that this bill has been favorably reported in this House four times——

Mr. MOODY of Massachusetts. I am not speaking of reports.

Mr. NEWLANDS. And has passed the Senate twice.

Mr. MOODY of Massachusetts. I never heard about this claim until the gentleman from Illinois came to me on the first day of the conference and handed me that report about three-quarters of an hour before our duties began, saying to me, "I wish you would look into that matter." I have been compelled to look into it in odd moments from that day to this; but I believe I have the substance of the controversy clearly in my mind.

Under the act of 1882 claims of California, Oregon, and Nevada were reported; and they were rejected, except $8,500, which was paid to the State of Nevada.

So we have taken two steps: First, the State of Nevada has no claim under the law under which the claims of these other States arose; second, a special act referring the claim of that State, together with others, to the Secretary of the Treasury who acted upon by that official and the claim rejected, as the claim of California was rejected, as the claim of Oregon was rejected. The claim of Texas was allowed and paid; the claim of Kansas was allowed and paid.

The representatives of the State of Nevada, having in mind the equities of which I have spoken, and which I do not intend to minimize at all, were not satisfied with that action of the Department.

certainty, but we have every reason to believe that that must be the case. Now we submit this to the candid judgment of the House.

I reserve the remainder of my time.

Mr. CANNON. I yield to the gentleman from Nevada [Mr. NEWLANDS] thirty minutes.

Mr. NEWLANDS. Mr. Speaker, I wish to say by way of preliminary, in reply to the charge of the gentleman from Massachusetts [Mr. MOODY] that this bill is thrust upon the House prematurely and without sufficient consideration, that this very claim was reported favorably in the Fiftieth Congress by the Senate Committee on Military Affairs and passed the Senate; that it was also in that Congress favorably reported from the Committee on War Claims of the House; that in the Fifty-first Congress it was reported by the Committee on Military Affairs and passed the Senate in a general deficiency bill, being stricken out in conference; that in that Congress also a favorable report was made by the Committee on War Claims of the House; that in the Fifty-second Congress a favorable report was made by Mr. DAVIS of Minnesota, from the Committee on Military Affairs, and a favorable report was also made in the House; that in the Fifty-third Congress the bill was again favorably reported by Mr. DAVIS of Minnesota, chairman of the Senate Committee on Military Affairs, and again in the House favorably reported by the Committee on War Claims; that in the Fifty-fourth Congress the bill was favorably reported to the Senate and also to the House, and that in the Fifty-fifth Congress the bill was reported favorably both in the Senate and in the House, and in the Senate was added to the omnibus claims bill aggregating a million dollars, which passed the House and went to the Senate, where about $8,000,000 of claims were added—claims which were collected together under a resolution of the Senate requesting the Committee on Claims to get together those claims of unquestioned equity and justice which had been repeatedly recognized by the Senate, and to put them into one bill in order to avoid the practice of forcing them upon general appropriation bills.

You will all remember that the conferees of the House went into that conference with their hands tied. They had succeeded in obtaining consideration in the House for the bill allowing $1,000,000 of claims under the Bowman Act, by giving the assurance that in conference they would allow nothing to be added to the bill. In the Senate, after a long conference, almost all the Senate amendments were stricken out; but with reference to the Nevada claim a provision was inserted referring the entire claim to the Secretary of the Treasury for a statement as to the amount due and the deductions to be made, and a report has been presented to Congress in accordance with the provisions of the omnibus bill, stating the account, making the amount due $460,000.

After this long delay the Senate, by unanimous vote, have put this bill upon the sundry civil bill, and the objection is now raised that it has not had sufficient consideration. I wish to say also, by way of explanation, that during almost the entire period of my service in the House of Representatives, with the exception of the last year or two, the condition of the Treasury has been that of a deficit, and it was impossible for me, during that period of depression and deficit, to obtain consideration for this bill before the House.

Now, I address myself to the justice and the equity of the claim itself, and that involves some consideration of the condition which existed when the payments were made upon which this claim is based.

We were engaged in the civil war. That war had been protracted for three years. All the energies of the Republic had been summoned for a final struggle. The United States had throughout that entire intermountain and Pacific coast region 18,000 regular troops engaged in keeping open the overland mail route, in protecting the immigrant routes, and in maintaining a sufficient show of force to prevent the Indian uprisings which had been so frequent prior to that time, and which were so serious subsequent to the war.

Those troops were needed at the front. Pursuing the ordinary course, it would have been necessary for the Government to have enlisted troops in the East and sent them to the West. That would have involved an expenditure of $200 and probably $300 for every man of the 1,100 troops furnished by the State of Nevada. The transportation and subsistence alone upon the road would have amounted pretty nearly to the entire amount of this claim.

An appeal to the patriotism of the people of that region was made. Nevada was a struggling Territory sparsely peopled. A requisition was made upon her for 1,100 men. It was a period of time when the gold excitement had broken out and the Comstock was aflame. Men were obtaining the high rates of wages that prevailed recently in the Klondike—from $5 to $10 a day. There were conditions of exceptional difficulty. This report to which the gentleman has alluded, and which sifts every item in this claim, contains the correspondence of the time and shows that serious difficulties were confronting the Government.

As showing how grave the apprehensions of the commanding officers were and how anxious they were to secure the full cooperation of the people of those States in the national defense, one of the officers reported that owing to the high wages it was almost impossible to obtain enlistments, and that from one company, I believe, there had been 50 desertions of men who wished to go to the mines. In Oregon, in a single company, if my recollection is right, there were 50 desertions. Then what was the condition in reference to the Federal currency in which the pay of the soldiers was made? It was at a discount of from 40 to 50 per cent.

That region was entirely upon a coin basis—gold and silver; so that the soldiers' pay, being $13 a month, which he had to exchange into gold, yielded him only $8 a month; and a dollar of gold had not the purchasing power of a dollar in greenbacks in the East, owing to the high cost of everything that entered into consumption. The rate of transportation for goods from San Francisco to Nevada was from 2 to 6 cents a pound. The rate of living was high; the expenses of living were great.

Now, had the Federal Government recognized that condition of things in the past? Yes. Uniformly from the time of the gold excitement in California up to the early years of the civil war it had been the custom to pay the Federal troops on that coast double pay, and to pay each officer $60 per month in addition. The condition which demanded that continued to exist, but for some reason, or through inadvertence, the law authorizing it was repealed in the early years of the war, so that the troops had to receive $13 in currency, worth $8 in gold, and it was necessary to change the currency into gold in order to make any use of it.

Mr. LIVINGSTON. Will the gentleman permit me to ask him a question?

Mr. NEWLANDS. Certainly.

Mr. LIVINGSTON. What was the number of troops engaged?

Mr. NEWLANDS. From Nevada, 1,100.

Mr. LIVINGSTON. That amount would be about how much per soldier?

Mr. NEWLANDS. About $400 per soldier; and the cost of transportation from New York would be nearly that amount.

Mr. LIVINGSTON. How much per capita would it be to that State for her soldiers? Have you estimated it?

Mr. MOODY of Massachusetts. It is a little over $4,000.

Mr. NEWLANDS. A little over $400.

Mr. LIVINGSTON. A little over $4,000.

Mr. NEWLANDS. Four hundred and sixty-two thousand dollars. Divide that by 1,100 makes about $400 per man, and not $4,000 a man.

Mr. PAYNE. Four times 11 makes 44. [Laughter.]

Mr. STEELE. And the transportation would have cost at that time nearly $1,000 for the soldiers to march from New York, as they would have had to march.

Mr. NEWLANDS. And the gentleman from Indiana says that the cost of transportation to the West would have been $1,000.

Mr. STEELE. Nearly $1,000.

Mr. NEWLANDS. Now, you will find in this voluminous correspondence here that the general commanding the United States forces called upon Nevada to make some addition to the pay so as to equalize it with Eastern pay, not in the way of bounty, not in the way of inducement to enlist, but simply as a just equalization of the pay of the soldiers of the East and soldiers of the West, so that each should secure approximately the same amount of pay.

And what did Nevada do? This little Territory of Nevada, without funds in its treasury, borrowed $100,000, and later other sums, passed a law giving its men $5 extra per month in gold, which made their total pay $13 a month in gold, hardly equal to the $13 in greenbacks paid in the East. The Territory incurred that debt, and Nevada, the subsequently organized State, upon which the burdens of statehood were forced by the Federal Government, a State which was invited into the Union by Congress for the purpose of aiding in passing the thirteenth and fourteenth amendments and in the great work of reconstruction, assumed that debt in the expectation that the Federal Government would reimburse it. This claim is for the moneys actually paid and the interest actually paid during that period.

I may say here that the present debt of Nevada is $300,000. It has labored under the burden of that debt, every dollar of it, or nearly every dollar of it, having its source in this requisition upon the Territory for troops and in its patriotic response.

The State of Nevada, unequal at the start to the burdens of statehood, suffering now under the most severe depression resulting from the prostration of its great mining industries, for it is the greatest silver-mining region in the world, is to-day finding it difficult to raise sufficient money by taxation to pay the expenses of the government, and has been compelled to borrow from its school funds for that purpose. And yet over $400,000 is in honor, justice, and equity due to it from the Federal Government, the power that persuaded it into statehood and to assume these extraordinary burdens.

of the same and warranting its place in the general appropriation bill.

The SPEAKER. The time of the gentleman has expired.

Mr. CANNON. I will yield to the gentleman five minutes more if he so desires.

Mr. NEWLANDS. I would be very glad to have a little extension of time.

Mr. LITTLEFIELD. I would like to ask the gentleman from Nevada a question before he proceeds.

Mr. NEWLANDS. Certainly.

Mr. LITTLEFIELD. My inquiry is as to whether or not this is a claim of new impressions, or whether it has precedent and stands on all fours with preceding claims of like character? Do I make it clear?

Mr. NEWLANDS. Certainly; I understand the gentleman. It has precedent, and is in the direct line of the action of the Federal Government for over twenty years in giving troops on the Pacific coast double pay.

Mr. LITTLEFIELD. But is it a new impression, so far as Congress is concerned, in reimbursing a State or Territory for expenses of this character?

Mr. NEWLANDS. I will say in response to the gentleman that numerous States have already received settlement of their claims arising from the war of the rebellion in sums ranging from four hundred thousand to two millions of dollars.

Mr. LITTLEFIELD. Well, I mean of this particular character?

Mr. NEWLANDS. Not to my knowledge of this exact, particular kind of claim, because the conditions are peculiar and different on the Pacific coast from those which prevailed East. The conditions there required this equalization of pay, and that condition had been recognized by the Federal Government for years prior to the civil war, a condition which did not confine the soldiers to the ordinary $13 a month paid generally, but allowed them $26 a month, or just double that sum.

Mr. WILSON of Idaho. And the gentleman from Nevada might also suggest that the Federal Government has paid its civil officers there double salaries, such as marshals, deputy marshals, and officers of that kind, who were engaged in the business of the Federal Government in that region.

Mr. NEWLANDS. That is entirely correct. The Federal officials received double pay.

Mr. WILSON of Idaho. And also received double mileage.

Mr. NEWLANDS. And also received double mileage. I thank my friend for the suggestion.

Now, Mr. Speaker, I trust that gentlemen on the floor of the House, and especially the members of the Committee on Appropriations, will not take advantage of a mere technicality and throw out a claim which has such merit as this. I ask, as a matter of justice, as a matter of right, and as a matter of equity, that gentlemen will not interpose this technical objection to the claim, but will consider the case upon its merits and allow this claim, which will relieve Nevada, depressed and prostrate as she is, from the burden of a debt incurred in equipping and maintaining the Federal troops and in maintaining the national defense. Nevada needs this aid in her advance toward a condition of material and deserved prosperity. [Applause.]

[Here the hammer fell.]

Mr. RICHARDSON. I hope the gentleman from Illinois will yield to me for a few minutes.

Mr. CANNON. I will yield to the gentleman from Tennessee five minutes, if that will be sufficient.

Mr. RICHARDSON. Mr. Speaker, I became familiar with this claim during the last Congress because of the fact that I was placed on the conference committee on what is called the omnibus war claims bill, upon which the Senate had placed the claim after the bill passed the House and went to that body. As one of the conferees of the House it was my duty to consider and investigate the claim with much care. I became thoroughly satisfied that the claim of the State of Nevada was just and honest and that it should be paid.

It was stricken from that omnibus war-claim bill not because the conferees believed it was unjust and that it should not be paid, but because it was not of the class of claims provided for in that bill.

Mr. LOUD. Might I ask the gentleman what were the character of claims that were provided for in that omnibus bill? If it did not take in everything under God's heavens, I should like to know what character of claims were left out?

Mr. RICHARDSON. It took in, in the first place, the claims which had been favorably found by the Court of Claims under the Bowman and Tucker acts. Next, the Senate placed upon it the French spoliation claims, and the bill, as it became a law, carried appropriations mainly for those two classes of claims. Now, the Senator from Nevada was one of the conferees of the Senate. I shall not divulge conference secrets. The Senator from Colorado [Mr. TELLER] was another member of the conference committee, and the Senator from Florida, Mr. Pasco, was another.

Mr. Speaker, this claim was placed upon that bill and was in conference. The House conferees were maintaining that nothing should go upon that bill except the war claims and the French spoliation claims, and in a patriotic spirit the conferees on the part of the Senate yielded this claim. I say it was patriotic in them to do so, because one of the conferees was the distinguished Senator from Nevada [Mr. STEWART], who believed the claim was just and that it should be paid.

Mr. LOUD. Will the gentleman yield?

Mr. RICHARDSON. I have only five minutes, and the gentleman can get time in his own right.

Mr. LOUD. The gentleman says there was nothing on the omnibus bill but war claims——

Mr. RICHARDSON. I did not say that. I said it was made up mainly of war claims and French spoliation claims. I am not going into that. That is true, and the gentleman knows it.

Now, while we struck this claim from that bill, we again referred it to the Secretary of the Treasury, and his report is here, and it shows that there is due the State of Nevada the sum appropriated for in this act, $462,000.

Mr. Speaker, the gentleman from Massachusetts [Mr. MOODY] says this claim ought not to be paid hurriedly, here in the closing hours of this Congress, but that it should be investigated. It has been investigated, as the gentleman from Nevada has stated. It has passed the Senate four or five times. It has been knocking at the door of Congress, like many other just claims, for thirty or forty years. The Senate has passed it four or five times. The House committees have reported it four or five times, and each time when it gets into conference it is dropped. On one time it was on the general deficiency bill instead of the sundry civil, as it is now.

The gentleman from Texas, Mr. Sayers, whom we all love and delight to honor, was a member of that conference committee. The Nevada claim was dropped in that conference, while the Texas claim was paid, and I have no doubt justly and properly paid. But there are a number of these claims, Mr. Speaker, and they are all about alike, so far as their justice is concerned. This claim arose when Nevada was a Territory. When Nevada was admitted into the Union the State assumed it. I am rather of the opinion that the Government of the United States should have paid it at that time. But the Government did not do it, and the State assumed it and it has been pending ever since. The gentleman says we must not consider and pay it hurriedly. There is no danger of that. It has been pressing for payment for many years. There are two reports from the Treasury Department, one making a voluminous record, as was shown you by the gentleman from Massachusetts [Mr. MOODY] and the gentleman from Nevada [Mr. NEWLANDS], each item being passed on.

In conclusion, Mr. Speaker, I shall not go over the merits of the claim. They have been presented carefully by the gentleman from Nevada. It has been reported upon twice by the Treasury Department. It has passed the Senate as we have stated, it has been found favorably by the committees of the House, and it does seem to me that, inasmuch as nearly all of the claims have been paid except this one, we ought to get clear of it.

The gentleman from Massachusetts [Mr. MOODY] says the California claim and the Oregon claim will each demand payment if this claim is paid. Then we have got them down to three claims, it seems. The others have all passed off the stage; and it seems to me now that if we get rid of this one, we will be in a condition probably in the next Congress to get rid of one more, and possibly all of them.

I think it is no argument against the justice and merits of this claim to say that California has a claim. California has a claim, and I have no doubt it will be energetically pressed at the proper time. Oregon, I have no doubt, will be found in the same category. But it certainly ought not to be insisted against the payment of this claim that there is one due California and another due the State of Oregon. The gentleman says they are not exactly like this. I venture to say if they are as meritorious as this one, they will be paid some day, and ought to be paid.

[Here the hammer fell.]

Mr. SHAFROTH. Will the gentleman from Massachusetts yield to me two minutes?

Mr. MOODY of Massachusetts. Is the gentleman in opposition to the claim?

Mr. SHAFROTH. I am in favor of it.

Mr. MOODY of Massachusetts. Then the gentleman should get his time from the gentleman from Illinois [Mr. CANNON].

Mr. CANNON. I am anxious for a vote, but I will yield to the gentleman two minutes.

Mr. SHAFROTH. Mr. Speaker, as I understand this bill, it provides for the reimbursement of the State of Nevada for moneys which it expended in the cause of the Union in 1865. Mr. Speaker, the amount which was saved to the National Government by reason of these expenditures upon the part of Nevada more than doubled the amount now claimed upon the part of Nevada. As the success in your efforts to raise them. I hope the legislature may assist you by some such means as have been adopted by California and Oregon."

But the fact remains that the declared purpose of the monthly allowance was to give a compensation to the Nevada volunteers (see section 1 of the act last referred to), and that when measured by the current prices of the country in which they were serving their compensation from all sources did not exceed, if, indeed, it was equal to, the value of the money received as pay by the troops stationed elsewhere, i. e., outside of the Department of the Pacific.

Mr. CANNON. Mr. Speaker, if the House will give me its attention two minutes, I will ask for a vote. This matter has been very fully discussed by the gentleman from Massachusetts [Mr. MOODY] and the gentleman from Nevada. If the House has paid attention, as I hope it has, it is in possession of the facts touching this amendment.

I have been compelled, not willingly, but I have been compelled to pay some attention to this matter. The Committee on Appropriations, of course, had no jurisdiction of it. The Committee on Claims, if it has any standing at all, has jurisdiction; but it is on this bill, which carries $65,000,000 for the whole public service, in pursuance of law. It is on this bill, and this bill can not pass until it goes off the bill or until the House concurs. Either the House must recede and adopt this, or, if the House refuses, then the Senate must recede from its amendments before the bill can pass; and the bill must pass.

Now, then, I am speaking of the sundry civil bill. I think, however, that if the House insists on its disagreement there is nothing left for the Senate except to recede from its amendment, because, under the usages between the two bodies, that body which proposes something in the shape of legislation, or something which is not authorized by law, always recedes if the other body refuses to accept it. So I can dismiss the parliamentary situation without further discussion.

Now, then, upon the right of this measure. If I determined it according to my sympathy, I would say, yes—a little State of 40,000 inhabitants, with its one Representative and its two Senators—it undoubtedly made this expenditure. At the same time, California, larger at that time and much larger now, made her expenditure of $4,000,000. Little Oregon made her expenditure of half a million dollars. Larger Massachusetts made her expenditure, of how much I do not know, and she paid her soldiers from her State treasury, partially, if not quite as much as they received during the civil war from the United States Treasury. Nevada has not been paid, nor has California, nor has Massachusetts, nor has Illinois, nor any other State. My sympathies with this small State—small as to number of population—are such that perhaps if I could segregate this claim and then pass over all the similar claims to arise from every other State, amounting (I speak conservatively) to one thousand million dollars, I think I might vote for this half a million.

Mr. NEWLANDS. I ask the gentleman not to raise specters and hobgoblins to arouse the apprehensions of the House.

Mr. CANNON. I am not "raising specters."

Mr. NEWLANDS. You said "a thousand millions!" That simply shows the power of your imagination.

Mr. CANNON. Not at all. Let us see. The gentleman says, "Don't raise specters." It is my duty, if I can, to plant my feet as a legislator, proceeding with care, guided by truth and by wisdom, because I act here not only for Nevada, but for every other State and its inhabitants. I said a thousand millions of dollars of claims similar in principle; and now I want the gentleman's attention. This was an extra allowance—call it pay; call it bounty; call it relief; call it what you please—that was paid by Nevada. Now let us take Massachusetts; let us take Illinois. Massachusetts paid the same extra pay and called it pay. Many of the States paid bounties and called them bounties. Many of the States gave relief in many different ways—calling it this, that, and the other—all upon the same foundation in principle.

Now, I say you may add the bounties, you may add the extra pay, you may add the relief that these various States of the North contributed; you may count the interest on those expenditures as it is counted upon this claim; and I say again, speaking conservatively, that the amount would be over rather than under one thousand million dollars. Therefore, without raising specters, I want to tell the truth; and I want to say that if we owed this money—if we had ever made similar payments to any State or to anybody—if there were a legal obligation—then we ought to pay it, whether the amount be half a million or two thousand millions. But if we do not owe it, if every State in the Union has been paid under the law every cent that it is entitled to, as it has been, then I do not see that we ought to make a precedent which will bring trooping here not only California and Oregon, but New York, and Illinois, and Massachusetts, and every other State, along the line of this precedent, knocking at the doors of the Treasury.

Mr. NEWLANDS. Can the gentleman refer to a single other State that allowed extra pay under similar conditions?

Mr. CANNON. Yes, sir; Massachusetts, as verified by the statement of the gentleman from Massachusetts [Mr. MOODY].

Mr. NEWLANDS. Can the gentleman refer me to any other State?

Mr. CANNON. California.

Mr. MOODY of Massachusetts. And Indiana.

Mr. NEWLANDS. Can the gentleman refer to another?

Mr. THROPP. Pennsylvania.

Mr. CANNON. Yes; Pennsylvania.

Mr. GARDNER of New Jersey. And New Jersey.

Mr. NEWLANDS. Those were bounties.

Mr. CANNON. Oh, no; extra pay. But it does not make any difference whether it was bounty or extra pay, or any other kind of relief—the principle, I say, is the same.

Now, as we can not dispose of this measure except by a vote of the House—as it can not be voted into a law except by a vote of the House—all I want is for the House to take an account of stock and see whether or not, with our eyes open, we can afford to make this precedent.

Mr. Speaker, I now ask for a vote.

The SPEAKER. The Chair will state the situation of this bill. All the disagreements upon amendments to this sundry civil bill have been settled except on amendment numbered 81, upon which the gentleman from Illinois [Mr. CANNON] moves that the House insist on its disagreement. The gentleman from Nevada [Mr. NEWLANDS] makes the motion of higher privilege that the House recede from its disagreement and concur in the amendment of the Senate. The vote will first be taken on the motion of the gentleman from Nevada.

The question having been put,

The SPEAKER said: The noes appear to have it.

Mr. NEWLANDS. I ask for the yeas and nays.

The question being taken, there were, in favor of ordering the yeas and nays, 32.

The SPEAKER. There has been no recent vote, and it will be necessary to count the other side. Those who are opposed to ordering the yeas and nays will rise and stand until counted.

Mr. NEWLANDS. I withdraw the call for the yeas and nays and ask for a division.

The question being again taken, there were—ayes 45, noes 97.

So the motion of Mr. NEWLANDS was rejected.

Mr. CANNON. I move that the House further insist on its disagreement to amendment numbered 81.

The motion was agreed to.

The SPEAKER. Does the gentleman ask for a further conference?

Mr. CANNON. No, sir.

MESSAGE FROM THE SENATE.

A message from the Senate, by Mr. GILFREY, one of its clerks, announced that the Senate had passed without amendment joint resolution 269, making appropriation for payment of the salaries of certain officers in the district of Alaska for the fiscal year ending June 30, 1901, and for other purposes.

A further message from the Senate, by Mr. PLATT, one of its clerks, announced that the Senate had passed bills of the following titles; in which the concurrence of the House was requested:

S. 4869. An act providing for the retirement of certain officers of the Army;

S. 4607. An act to provide for the settlement of accounts between the United States and the State of South Carolina;

S. 4144. An act to provide for the purchase of a site and the erection of a public building thereon at Huntington, in the State of West Virginia;

S. 4044. An act to provide for the appointment of dental surgeons for service in the United States Army; and

S. 3565. An act to establish a quartermaster's depot at Omaha, Nebr., and for other purposes.

The message also announced that the Senate had passed without amendment bills of the following titles:

H. R. 1871. An act for the relief of E. B. Crozier, executrix of the last will of Dr. C. W. Crozier, of Tennessee; and

H. R. 7066. An act granting an increase of pension to Hiram Childress.

The message also announced that the Senate had agreed to the report of the committee of conference on the disagreeing votes of the two Houses on the amendments of the Senate to the bill (H. R. 10308) to extend to certain publications the privileges of second-class mail matter as to admission to the mails.

POSTAGE ON SECOND-CLASS PUBLICATIONS, ETC.

Mr. GRIGGS. Mr. Speaker, I desire to submit at this time conference report for immediate consideration.

The SPEAKER. If there be no objection, the statement of the House conferees will be read instead of the report.

There was no objection.

The SPEAKER. The gentleman from Illinois asks the previous question on the adoption of the report.

The question was taken; and the previous question was ordered.

The question was taken on agreeing to the conference report; and the conference report was agreed to.

Mr. CANNON. Now I move that the House further insist on its disagreement to the Senate amendment indicated, known as the Nevada claim amendment.

The SPEAKER. The gentleman from Illinois moves that the House further insist on the disagreement to the amendment known as the Nevada claim amendment.

Mr. NEWLANDS. Mr. Speaker, I move that the House recede and concur.

The SPEAKER. The gentleman from Illinois moves that the House insist on its disagreement, and the gentleman from Nevada moves that the House recede and concur. The latter motion takes precedence.

Mr. CANNON. Now, Mr. Speaker, I desire to reserve my time, and will yield later such time of my hour as we shall agree just and equitable to the gentleman from Nevada. My colleague on the conference, the gentleman from Massachusetts [Mr. MOODY], desires to be heard upon this amendment.

The SPEAKER. The gentleman from Illinois reserves his time, with the assurance that he will yield to the gentleman from Nevada such time as he may require.

Mr. CANNON. Such time as is equitable.

The SPEAKER (continuing). And the gentleman from Massachusetts, one of the conferees, is recognized in his own right.

Mr. MOODY of Massachusetts. Mr. Speaker, I ask that the Clerk read the amendment for the information of the House.

The Clerk read the amendment as follows:

To pay the State of Nevada the sum of $462,441.97 for moneys advanced in aid of the suppression of the rebellion in the civil war, as found and reported to Congress on January 22, 1900, by the Secretary of the Treasury, as provided in the act of Congress approved March 3, 1899.

Mr. MOODY of Massachusetts. Mr. Speaker, I trust that the members of the House may ascertain exactly what this claim is and what kind of a precedent it will set, because if the claim is agreed to by the House all of you who represent any States that did not secede will be called upon to prosecute claims of like nature from your own State. The committee of conference without action of the House did not feel justified in agreeing to this item, for two reasons. First, because it was a recognition of a kind of State claim that has never been recognized by Congress before. There has never been a dollar paid from the Treasury of the United States in settlement of claims of the kind represented in this item. And, second, because if this claim is paid, a claim of $4,000,000 and over of the State of California must be paid, and a claim of $400,000 of the State of Oregon must be paid, because in every possible respect the claims of California and Oregon are on all fours with the claim of the State of Nevada.

I will, as briefly as I can, state exactly the facts out of which State claims which have been paid hitherto have arisen and out of which this claim, which is before us now, has arisen. At the beginning of the civil war the Treasury of the United States was empty. The Government of the United States called for aid in paying and equipping troops from all the loyal States, and those States responded. Congress passed a law which directed the Treasury to indemnify the States for the "cost, charges, and expenses properly incurred by any State" for enrolling, subsisting, clothing, paying, etc., troops which entered the service of the United States. Now, every claim under that statute has been paid; every dollar which the United States owes under that statute has been paid, except some claims for interest which are due and outstanding.

Mr. MONDELL. Did the State of Nevada have any claim under that statute?

Mr. MOODY of Massachusetts. The State of Nevada had a small claim, which I will refer to later on, which has been paid. Now, there was a peculiar exigency on the Pacific coast. The war vessels of the Confederacy had destroyed water communication between the Atlantic and the Pacific coasts. The only route open was the overland route. The regular troops of the United States had been withdrawn from the Pacific coast. It became necessary to appeal to the States and Territories on the Pacific coast to raise troops for the benefit of the Government. They responded loyally; they did their work well. They performed as important a function in suppressing the rebellion as the troops of other States who crossed the Potomac, because it was just as necessary to keep open the overland route, protect that communication from an Indian rising, as it was to defend the capital of the United States.

At that time the cost of living on the Pacific slope was very great. The wages of labor were very high. It was difficult to raise troops for the service of the United States. These two conditions prevailed in all the States, but prevailed in none of them

to the same degree that it prevailed on the Pacific coast, according to the testimony before us. Accordingly the States of California and Oregon and the Territory of Nevada voted to pay their troops who entered into the service of the United States a certain sum in addition to the amount they received from the United States. They based their action somewhat on the policy the United States had adopted for the payment of the regular troops, because they had allowed those who served on the Pacific coast an extra allowance or compensation. But that policy had been abandoned by the United States and the statute prescribing it repealed at the beginning of the civil war, I suppose upon the ground that it was thought that the conditions that made the extra payments necessary had passed away.

Up to this point claims of the Pacific Coast States for the refunding of extra pay stand on the same footing with the claims of all other States. But there is one difference that ought not to be disregarded by the House. The Pacific slope was upon a gold basis. The troops were paid in greenbacks. That is all the difference, except in degree, between the States of Pennsylvania, New York, or Massachusetts and the States of California, Oregon, and Nevada.

The State of Massachusetts paid, for instance, in the civil war, as it did in the war with Spain, so much a month extra for troops that entered into the service of the United States on account of its quota. But the States of Massachusetts and Pennsylvania or Illinois, or any of the States, have never been paid anything by the United States on account of the bounties or extra monthly payment which they paid their troops. No State has ever yet been paid anything on account of the extra payments to their troops for which the State of Nevada now presents this claim.

Now, what next happened? The State of Nevada had no claim under the act of 1861. No State had a valid claim under that act for payments like those made by Nevada, for which the claim is now made. But Nevada and some other States, desirous of receiving back what they had paid out by way of bounty and by way of extra pay, caused the act of 1882 to be passed, and that is the next step in this proceeding.

Now, let me have the attention of the House one moment while I state the effect of that act. It was approved June 27, 1882, and it provided for an examination and investigation of the claims of Texas, Colorado, Oregon, Nebraska, California, Kansas, Nevada, Washington, and Idaho for moneys expended and indebtedness assumed in organizing, arming, equipping, supplying clothing, subsistence, transporting, and paying volunteer and military forces of said States that entered the service of the United States.

Section 4 of the act provides that the Secretary of the Treasury shall report to Congress for final action the result of such an examination and investigation.

Now, remember, Mr. Speaker, Nevada had no claim under the act of 1861. This provision was passed in 1882. Under it the Secretary of the Treasury, acting in combination with the Secretary of War, made a report. I hold in my hand the report upon the Nevada claim—366 pages of fine print. I want to take this occasion here and now to protest against an inquiry of this kind in the closing hours of Congress being thrown upon the committee in charge of a great money bill. How can we properly do our duty there? It ought to be before the Committee on Claims, investigated by the Committee on Claims, reported by the Committee on Claims, and considered by the House in a manner in which it is now impossible to consider it.

Mr. NEWLANDS. Will the gentleman please state in that connection that this bill has been favorably reported in this House four times——

Mr. MOODY of Massachusetts. I am not speaking of reports.

Mr. NEWLANDS. And has passed the Senate twice.

Mr. MOODY of Massachusetts. I never heard about this claim until the gentleman from Illinois came to me on the first day of the conference and handed me that report about three-quarters of an hour before our duties began, saying to me, "I wish you would look into that matter." I have been compelled to look into it in odd moments from that day to this; but I believe I have the substance of the controversy clearly in my mind.

Under the act of 1882 claims of California, Oregon, and Nevada were reported; and they were rejected, except $3,500, which was paid to the State of Nevada.

So we have taken two steps: First, the State of Nevada has no claim under the law under which the claims of these other States arose; second, a special act referring the claim of that State, together with others, to the Secretary of the Treasury was acted upon by that official and the claim rejected, as the claim of California was rejected, as the claim of Oregon was rejected. The claim of Texas was allowed and paid; the claim of Kansas was allowed and paid.

The representatives of the State of Nevada, having in mind the equities of which I have spoken, and which I do not intend to minimize at all, were not satisfied with that action of the Department.

certainty, but we have every reason to believe that that must be the case. Now we submit this to the candid judgment of the House.

I reserve the remainder of my time.

Mr. CANNON. I yield to the gentleman from Nevada [Mr. NEWLANDS] thirty minutes.

Mr. NEWLANDS. Mr. Speaker, I wish to say by way of preliminary, in reply to the charge of the gentleman from Massachusetts [Mr. MOODY] that this bill is thrust upon the House prematurely and without sufficient consideration, that this very claim was reported favorably in the Fiftieth Congress by the Senate Committee on Military Affairs and passed the Senate; that it was also in that Congress favorably reported from the Committee on War Claims of the House; that in the Fifty-first Congress it was reported by the Committee on Military Affairs and passed the Senate in a general deficiency bill, being stricken out in conference; that in that Congress also a favorable report was made by the Committee on War Claims of the House; that in the Fifty-second Congress a favorable report was made by Mr. DAVIS of Minnesota, from the Committee on Military Affairs, and a favorable report was also made in the House; that in the Fifty-third Congress the bill was again favorably reported by Mr. DAVIS of Minnesota, chairman of the Senate Committee on Military Affairs, and again in the House favorably reported by the Committee on War Claims; that in the Fifty-fourth Congress the bill was favorably reported to the Senate and also to the House, and that in the Fifty-fifth Congress the bill was reported favorably both in the Senate and in the House, and in the Senate was added to the omnibus claims bill aggregating a million dollars, which passed the House and went to the Senate, where about $8,000,000 of claims were added—claims which were collected together under a resolution of the Senate requesting the Committee on War Claims to get together those claims of unquestioned equity and justice which had been repeatedly recognized by the Senate, and to put them into one bill in order to avoid the practice of forcing them upon general appropriation bills.

You will all remember that the conferees of the House went into that conference with their hands tied. They had succeeded in obtaining consideration in the House for the bill allowing $1,000,000 of claims under the Bowman Act, by giving the assurance that in conference they would allow nothing to be added to the bill. In the Senate, after a long conference, almost all the Senate amendments were stricken out; but with reference to the Nevada claim a provision was inserted referring the entire claim to the Secretary of the Treasury for a statement as to the amount due and the deductions to be made, and a report has been presented to Congress in accordance with the provisions of the omnibus bill, stating the account, making the amount due $460,000.

After this long delay the Senate, by unanimous vote, have put this bill upon the sundry civil bill, and the objection is now raised that it has not had sufficient consideration. I wish to say also, by way of explanation, that during almost the entire period of my service in the House of Representatives, with the exception of the last year or two, the condition of the Treasury has been that of a deficit, and it was impossible for me, during that period of depression and deficit, to obtain consideration for this bill before the House.

Now, I address myself to the justice and the equity of the claim itself, and that involves some consideration of the condition which existed when the payments were made upon which this claim is based.

We were engaged in the civil war. That war had been protracted for three years. All the energies of the Republic had been summoned for a final struggle. The United States had throughout that entire intermountain and Pacific coast region 18,000 regular troops engaged in keeping open the overland mail route, in protecting the immigrant routes, and in maintaining a sufficient show of force to prevent the Indian uprisings which had been so frequent prior to that time, and which were so serious subsequent to the war.

Those troops were needed at the front. Pursuing the ordinary course, it would have been necessary for the Government to have enlisted troops in the East and sent them to the West. That would have involved an expenditure of $200 and probably $300 for every man of the 1,100 troops furnished by the State of Nevada. The transportation and subsistence alone upon the road would have amounted pretty nearly to the entire amount of this claim.

An appeal to the patriotism of the people of that region was made. Nevada was a struggling Territory sparsely peopled. A requisition was made upon her for 1,100 men. It was a period of time when the gold excitement had broken out and the Comstock was aflame. Men were obtaining the high rates of wages that prevailed recently in the Klondike—from $5 to $10 a day. There were conditions of exceptional difficulty. This report to which the gentleman has alluded, and which sifts every item in this claim, contains the correspondence of the time and shows that serious difficulties were confronting the Government.

As showing how grave the apprehensions of the commanding officers were and how anxious they were to secure the full cooperation of the people of those States in the national defense, one of the officers reported that owing to the high wages it was almost impossible to obtain enlistments, and that from one company, I believe, there had been 50 desertions of men who wished to go to the mines. In Oregon, in a single company, if my recollection is right, there were 50 desertions. Then what was the condition in reference to the Federal currency in which the pay of the soldiers was made? It was at a discount of from 40 to 50 per cent.

That region was entirely upon a coin basis—gold and silver; so that the soldiers' pay, being $13 a month, which he had to exchange into gold, yielded him only $8 a month; and a dollar of gold had not the purchasing power of a dollar in greenbacks in the East, owing to the high cost of everything that entered into consumption. The rate of transportation for goods from San Francisco to Nevada was from 2 to 6 cents a pound. The rate of living was high; the expenses of living were great.

Now, had the Federal Government recognized that condition of things in the past? Yes. Uniformly from the time of the gold excitement in California up to the early years of the civil war it had been the custom to pay the Federal troops on that coast double pay, and to pay each officer $60 per month in addition. The condition which demanded that continued to exist, but for some reason, or through inadvertence, the law authorizing it was repealed in the early years of the war, so that the troops had to receive $13 in currency, worth $8 in gold, and it was necessary to change the currency into gold in order to make any use of it.

Mr. LIVINGSTON. Will the gentleman permit me to ask him a question?

Mr. NEWLANDS. Certainly.

Mr. LIVINGSTON. What was the number of troops engaged?

Mr. NEWLANDS. From Nevada, 1,100.

Mr. LIVINGSTON. That amount would be about how much per soldier?

Mr. NEWLANDS. About $400 per soldier; and the cost of transportation from New York would be nearly that amount.

Mr. LIVINGSTON. How much per capita would it be to that State for her soldiers? Have you estimated it?

Mr. MOODY of Massachusetts. It is a little over $4,000.

Mr. LIVINGSTON. A little over $400.

Mr. NEWLANDS. A little over $4,000.

Mr. NEWLANDS. Four hundred and sixty-two thousand dollars. Divide that by 1,100 makes about $400 per man, and not $4,000 a man.

Mr. PAYNE. Four times 11 makes 44. [Laughter.]

Mr. STEELE. And the transportation would have cost at that time nearly $1,000 for the soldiers to march from New York, as they would have had to march.

Mr. NEWLANDS. And the gentleman from Indiana says that the cost of transportation to the West would have been $1,000.

Mr. STEELE. Nearly $1,000.

Mr. NEWLANDS. Now, you will find in this voluminous correspondence here that the general commanding the United States forces called upon Nevada to make some addition to the pay so as to equalize it with Eastern pay, not in the way of bounty, not in the way of inducement to enlist, but simply as a just equalization of the pay of the soldiers of the East and soldiers of the West, so that each should secure approximately the same amount of pay.

And what did Nevada do? This little Territory of Nevada, without funds in its treasury, borrowed $100,000, and later other sums, passed a law giving its men $5 extra per month in gold, which made their total pay $13 a month in gold, hardly equal to the $13 in greenbacks paid in the East. The Territory incurred that debt, and Nevada, the subsequently organized State, upon which the burdens of statehood were forced by the Federal Government, a State which was invited into the Union by Congress for the purpose of aiding in passing the thirteenth and fourteenth amendments and in the great work of reconstruction, assumed that debt in the expectation that the Federal Government would reimburse it. This claim is for the moneys actually paid and the interest actually paid during that period.

I may say here that the present debt of Nevada is $300,000. It has labored under the burden of that debt, every dollar of it, or nearly every dollar of it, having its source in this requisition upon the Territory for troops and in its patriotic response.

The State of Nevada, unequal at the start to the burdens of statehood, suffering now under the most severe depression resulting from the prostration of its great mining industries, for it is the greatest silver-mining region in the world, is to-day finding it difficult to raise sufficient money by taxation to pay the expenses of the government, and has been compelled to borrow from its school funds for that purpose. And yet over $400,000 is in honor, justice, and equity due to it from the Federal Government, the power that persuaded it into statehood and to assume these extraordinary burdens.

of the same and warranting its place in the general appropriation bill.

The SPEAKER. The time of the gentleman has expired.

Mr. CANNON. I will yield to the gentleman five minutes more if he so desires.

Mr. NEWLANDS. I would be very glad to have a little extension of time.

Mr. LITTLEFIELD. I would like to ask the gentleman from Nevada a question before he proceeds.

Mr. NEWLANDS. Certainly.

Mr. LITTLEFIELD. My inquiry is as to whether or not this is a claim of new impressions, or whether it has precedent and stands on all fours with preceding claims of like character? Do I make it clear?

Mr. NEWLANDS. Certainly; I understand the gentleman. It has precedent, and is in the direct line of the action of the Federal Government for over twenty years in giving troops on the Pacific coast double pay.

Mr. LITTLEFIELD. But is it a new impression, so far as Congress is concerned, in reimbursing a State or Territory for expenses of this character?

Mr. NEWLANDS. I will say in response to the gentleman that numerous States have already received settlement of their claims arising from the war of the rebellion in sums ranging from four hundred thousand to two millions of dollars.

Mr. LITTLEFIELD. Well, I mean of this particular character?

Mr. NEWLANDS. Not to my knowledge of this exact, particular kind of claim, because the conditions are peculiar and different on the Pacific coast from those which prevailed East. The conditions there required this equalization of pay, and that condition had been recognized by the Federal Government for years prior to the civil war, a condition which did not confine the soldiers to the ordinary $13 a month paid generally, but allowed them $26 a month, or just double that sum.

Mr. WILSON of Idaho. And the gentleman from Nevada might also suggest that the Federal Government has paid its civil officers their double salaries, such as marshals, deputy marshals, and officers of that kind, who were engaged in the business of the Federal Government in that region.

Mr. NEWLANDS. That is entirely correct. The Federal officials received double pay.

Mr. WILSON of Idaho. And also received double mileage.

Mr. NEWLANDS. And also received double mileage. I thank my friend for the suggestion.

Now, Mr. Speaker, I trust that gentlemen on the floor of the House, and especially the members of the Committee on Appropriations, will not take advantage of a mere technicality and throw out a claim which has such merit as this. I ask, as a matter of justice, as a matter of right, and as a matter of equity, that gentlemen will not interpose this technical objection to the claim, but will consider the case upon its merits and allow this claim, which will relieve Nevada, depressed and prostrate as she is, from the burden of a debt incurred in equipping and maintaining the Federal troops and in maintaining the national defense. Nevada needs this aid in her advance toward a condition of material and deserved prosperity. [Applause.]

[Here the hammer fell.]

Mr. RICHARDSON. I hope the gentleman from Illinois will yield to me for a few minutes.

Mr. CANNON. I will yield to the gentleman from Tennessee five minutes, if that will be sufficient.

Mr. RICHARDSON. Mr. Speaker, I became familiar with this claim during the last Congress because of the fact that I was placed on the conference committee on what is called the omnibus war claims bill, upon which the Senate had placed the claim after the bill passed the House and went to that body. As one of the conferees of the House it was my duty to consider and investigate the claim with much care. I became thoroughly satisfied that the claim of the State of Nevada was just and honest and that it should be paid.

It was stricken from that omnibus war-claim bill not because the conferees believed it was unjust and that it should not be paid, but because it was not of the class of claims provided for in that bill.

Mr. LOUD. Might I ask the gentleman what were the character of claims that were provided for in that omnibus bill? If it did not take in everything under God's heavens, I should like to know what character of claims were left out?

Mr. RICHARDSON. It took in, in the first place, the claims which had been favorably found by the Court of Claims under the Bowman and Tucker acts. Next, the Senate placed upon it the French spoliation claims, and the bill, as it became a law, carried appropriations mainly for those two classes of claims. Now, the Senator from Nevada was one of the conferees of the Senate. I shall not divulge conference secrets. The Senator from Colorado [Mr. TELLER] was another member of the conference committee, and the Senator from Florida, Mr. Pasco, was another.

Mr. Speaker, this claim was placed upon that bill and was in conference. The House conferees were maintaining that nothing should go upon that bill except the war claims and the French spoliation claims, and in a patriotic spirit the conferees on the part of the Senate yielded this claim. I say it was patriotic in them to do so, because one of the conferees was the distinguished Senator from Nevada [Mr. STEWART], who believed the claim was just and that it should be paid.

Mr. LOUD. Will the gentleman yield?

Mr. RICHARDSON. I have only five minutes, and the gentleman can get time in his own right.

Mr. LOUD. The gentleman says there was nothing on the omnibus bill but war claims——

Mr. RICHARDSON. I did not say that. I said it was made up mainly of war claims and French spoliation claims. I am not going into that. That is true, and the gentleman knows it.

Now, while we struck this claim from that bill, we again referred it to the Secretary of the Treasury, and his report is here, and it shows that there is due the State of Nevada the sum appropriated for in this act, $462,000.

Mr. Speaker, the gentleman from Massachusetts [Mr. MOODY] says this claim ought not to be paid hurriedly, here in the closing hours of this Congress, but that it should be investigated. It has been investigated, as the gentleman from Nevada has stated. It has passed the Senate four or five times. It has been knocking at the door of Congress, like many other just claims, for thirty or forty years. The Senate has passed it four or five times. The House committees have reported it four or five times, and each time when it gets into conference it is dropped. At one time it was on the general deficiency bill instead of the sundry civil, as it is now.

The gentleman from Texas, Mr. Sayers, whom we all love and delight to honor, was a member of that conference committee. The Nevada claim was dropped in that conference, while the Texas claim was paid, and I have no doubt justly and properly paid. But there are a number of these claims, Mr. Speaker, and they are all about alike, so far as their justice is concerned. This claim arose when Nevada was a Territory. When Nevada was admitted into the Union the State assumed it. I am rather of the opinion that the Government of the United States should have paid it at that time. But the Government did not do it, and the State assumed it and it has been pending ever since. The gentleman says we must not consider and pay it hurriedly. There is no danger of that. It has been pressing for payment for many years. There are two reports from the Treasury Department, one making a voluminous record, as was shown you by the gentleman from Massachusetts [Mr. MOODY] and the gentleman from Nevada [Mr. NEWLANDS], each item being passed on.

In conclusion, Mr. Speaker, I shall not go over the merits of the claim. They have been presented carefully by the gentleman from Nevada. It has been reported upon twice by the Treasury Department. It has passed the Senate as we have stated, it has been found favorably by the committees of the House, and it does seem to me that, inasmuch as nearly all of the claims have been paid except this one, we ought to get clear of it.

The gentleman from Massachusetts [Mr. MOODY] says the California claim and the Oregon claim will each demand payment if this claim is paid. Then we have got them down to three claims, it seems. The others have all passed off the stage; and it seems to me now that if we get rid of this one, we will be in a condition probably in the next Congress to get rid of one more, and possibly all of them.

I think it is no argument against the justice and merits of this claim to say that California has a claim. California has a claim, and I have no doubt it will be energetically pressed at the proper time. Oregon, I have no doubt, will be found in the same category. But it certainly ought not to be insisted against the payment of this claim that there is one due California and another due the State of Oregon. The gentleman says they are not exactly like this. I venture to say if they are as meritorious as this one, they will be paid some day, and ought to be paid.

[Here the hammer fell.]

Mr. SHAFROTH. Will the gentleman from Massachusetts yield to me two minutes?

Mr. MOODY of Massachusetts. Is the gentleman in opposition to the claim?

Mr. SHAFROTH. I am in favor of it.

Mr. MOODY of Massachusetts. Then the gentleman should get his time from the gentleman from Illinois [Mr. CANNON].

Mr. CANNON. I am anxious for a vote, but I will yield to the gentleman two minutes.

Mr. SHAFROTH. Mr. Speaker, as I understand this bill, it provides for the reimbursement of the State of Nevada for moneys which it expended in the cause of the Union in 1865. Mr. Speaker, the amount which was saved to the National Government by reason of these expenditures upon the part of Nevada more than doubled the amount now claimed upon the part of Nevada. As the